Cognition

Cognition
THE THINKING ANIMAL

THIRD EDITION

Daniel T. Willingham

University of Virginia

PEARSON

Prentice
Hall

Pearson Education International

VP/Editorial Director: Leah Jewell
Executive Editor: Jessica Mosher
Editorial Assistant: William Grieco
Director of Marketing: Brandy Dawson
Senior Marketing Manager: Jeanette Moyer
Marketing Assistant: Alexandra Trum
**AVP/Director of Production and
   Manufacturing:** Barbara Kittle
Managing Editor: Joanne Riker
**Assistant Managing Editor
   (Production):** Maureen Richardson

Production Liaison: Maureen Richardson
Manufacturing Buyer: Sherry Lewis
Interior Design: TechBooks
Cover Design: Karen Salzbach
Cover Illustration/Photo: ANCIENT ART &
   ARCHITECTURE/Danita Delimont.com
**Composition/Full-Service Project
   Management:** TechBooks
Printer/Binder: Hamilton Printing

Credits and acknowledgments borrowed from other sources and reproduced, with permission, in this textbook appear on pages 559–560.

If you purchased this book within the United States or Canada you should be aware that it has been wrongfully imported without the approval of the Publisher or Author.

This work is protected by United States copyright laws and is provided solely for the use of instructors in teaching their courses and assessing student learning. Dissemination or sale of any part of this work (including on the World Wide Web) will destroy the integrity of the work and is not permitted. The work and materials from it should never be made available to students except by instructors using the accompanying text in their classes. All recipients of this work are expected to abide by these restrictions and to honor the intended pedagogical purposes and the needs of other instructors who rely on these materials.

10 9 8 7 6 5 4
ISBN 0-13-178928-7

*This book is dedicated
to my parents*

Contents

Preface

A long-standing goal of human enquiry is to understand ourselves. How can we characterize the human species? Here are some of the better-known proposals:

Man is by nature a political animal—Aristotle

Man is a noble animal—Sir Thomas Browne

Man is a tool-using animal—Thomas Carlyle

Man is a reasoning animal—Seneca

Man is a social animal—Benedict Spinoza

Man is a rational animal who always loses his temper when he is called upon to act in accordance with the dictates of reason—Oscar Wilde.

I suggest that all of these proposals are, in a sense, correct, but they are all rooted in another characteristic. We are able to act politically, to use tools effectively, to understand nobility, etc., because of our ability to think. The heart of the matter is that we are thinking animals, and it is thinking that affords these other abilities or, at least, affords our having these abilities in the manner that we do. The book you are reading is a study of cognition—of how humans think.

Most instructors believe that cognitive psychology does not have the intrinsic interest of some other areas of the field. To be honest, I've never cared much for the way that other textbooks have sought to keep students interested. The usual strategy is to include "real world" examples and lots of demonstrations, usually found in little boxes that appear every few pages. This strategy seems to confirm the reader's growing suspicion that they are bored by sending the implicit message, "Yes, yes, I know this stuff is boring, but hang in there, and every few pages I'll toss in one of those boxes with a demonstration or real-world application to keep you going."

I've done three things in this book to try to arouse the reader's interest in the material:

- I have explicitly stated the questions that motivate cognitive psychologists explicit. The questions we ask are of general interest, but we don't always do the best job of explaining the questions in any detail. We plunge right into the answers, which seem arcane. Each chapter in this book is organized around two or three straightforward questions that are easy to appreciate, and the importance of which are explained in detail.

- To the extent possible, I have used a narrative structure. By that I mean that there are causal links within and across chapter sections, so that it is clear why you are reading something. Nothing is more boring than a list of unconnected facts.

- I have tried to write in a non-stilted, not-especially-academic style.

Despite the light tone, this book is not light in content. An easy way to check the coverage is by examining the "key terms" section at the end of each chapter.

Pedagogy

Readability is fine, but the goal of a textbook is, after all, that students learn the material. Different students like and use different pedagogical features, so I've included a few different ones to help them learn.

- Brief previews of each section pose the broad questions and provide the broad answers contained in the section.

- Key terms are identified by bold-face type, and are defined immediately thereafter. They are also collected in a glossary.

- Each section closes with a series of questions. The "stand-on-one-foot" questions ask the student to summarize what they have learned in the section they have just read. The name comes from the Talmudic story of the heretic who went to great sages, asking each to summarize all of the Torah in the time that he could stand on one foot. (He finally found a willing sage in Hillel who quoted from Leviticus, "What is hateful to you, do not to others.") Thus, the idea is simply to get the reader to pause for a moment and make sure they understood the major points by summarizing what they have just read.

- The end of each section also includes questions that require considerably more thought; the student will need to apply what he or she has just learned to new situations, or to go beyond the material in some way. I call these "questions that require two feet." Answers to all questions are provided at the back of the book.

- There is a companion web site http://www.prenhall.com/willingham to accompany the text. The web site includes an online study guide for students (lots of self-test questions in different formats), a recap and summary of each chapter, links to relevant sites on the internet, and more.

I've also included an appendix containing background information and explanations of several concepts, such as statistical significance, that will be familiar to students who have taken other psychology courses but that beginning students may not know.

I hope that I have written a textbook that will make students enthusiastic about this field, and will make them want to know more than they can find in this book. Hillel's answer to the impatient heretic is not always quoted in full; after providing the summary of the Torah, Hillel added, "Now go and study," acknowledging that a one-sentence summary was bound to be lacking, and that the heretic should learn more. I have not succeeded in summarizing cognitive psychology in a sentence, but I can add the entreaty; I hope that this book will serve as a starting point from which students will want to learn still more about the field.

Supplement Program

Web site – www.prenhall.com/willingham

Includes an online study guide for students, chapter objectives, web links, flashcards of key terms, and much more!

PowerPoint slides

Prepared by Sameer Bawa, University of Virginia includes selected art from the text available in a chapter-by-chapter lecture format. These slides can be accessed on the text web site: www.prenhall.com/willingham and can be customized to fit your lecture style.

Instructor's Manual with Tests

Prepared by John Philbeck, George Washington University includes chapter outlines, suggestions for demonstrations, classroom activities, research and discussion questions, and more. The testing portion of the manual has approximately 65 questions per chapter.

TestGen Software

Computerized version of the test questions, which operates on both PC and MAC systems, includes 65 questions per chapter.

Research Navigator

Research Navigator is an online resource that features three exclusive databases full of source material, including:

• EBSCO's *ContentSelect Academic Journal Database,* organized by subject. Each subject contains 50 to 100 of the leading academic journals by keyword, topic, or multiple topics. Articles include abstract and citation information and can be cut, pasted, emailed, or saved for later use.

- *The New York Times Search-by-Subject One Year Archive,* organized by subject and searchable by keyword or multiple keywords. Instructors and students can view the full text of the article.
- *Link Library,* organized by subject, offers editorially selected best of the Web sites. Link Libraries are continually scanned and kept up to date, providing the most relevant and accurate links for research assignments.

Changes to This Edition

Much has happened in the field during the last three years, and I find that I have made modifications to nearly every section of every chapter. In addition to this updating, I have rewritten a number of sections for clarity, based on feedback from instructors and from students. In two instances, the literature developed to the point that it was appropriate to devote a new section to a topic. Hence, in chapter 7 ("Memory Retrieval") I've added a section on false memory and in chapter 8 ("Memory Storage") I've added a section on multiple systems theories of categorization.

I have also made three significant structural changes.

- I have added a chapter on methods of cognitive psychology. This addition came in response to a comment by Chandan Vaidya at Georgetown University. She mentioned that her students found it difficult to understand the idea of studying the mind; it seemed difficult or impossible, and it was difficult to distinguish from philosophy and from neuroscience. I realized that my students also struggled to understand exactly how cognitive psychologists could make progress in studying ephemeral mental processes. Chapter 2 explains how we do it. The first half covers behavioral methods, and the latter half covers neuroscientific methods, emphasizing how they contribute to cognitive theory. It replaces the "Brain Interlude" from the second edition.
- In response to requests from many instructors, I have integrated the cognitive neuroscientific material into the main text of the book, and I have eliminated the "brain boxes" that appeared in earlier editions. Cognitive neuroscience has become too central to the field to be relegated to side notes, and all chapters now include relevant neuroscientific material.
- I have split the material covering language into two chapters. Chapter 13 ("Language Structure") covers the definition of language and grammar. The other half of the chapter considers whether language is "special." This section covers animal language and linguistic relativity, and also features a new section on language development. Chapter 14 ("Language Processing") deals with the actual decoding and interpretation of written and spoken communication.

I would greatly appreciate feedback and suggestions regarding this text. It is easiest to reach me via electronic mail: willingham@virginia.edu

Acknowledgments

I am grateful to the team of people at Prentice Hall who worked so hard to bring this book to professors and students. Kristin Lynch was a careful and thoughtful copyeditor, Rachel Lucas was tireless in ensuring that the figures were accurate and useful, and Penny Walker did an excellent job as Production Editor in coordinating everyone's efforts, along with Jan Schwartz. I also thank my editor, Jessica Mosher, for her help throughout this process.

I also offer sincere thanks to my colleagues who reviewed the first and second editions: James Juola, University of Kansas; David Vago, University of Utah; Lenna Ojure, Virginia Military Institute; Kristy Nielson, Marquette University; Robert Crutcher, University of Dayton; John Philbeck, George Washington University; Patty O'Neil, University of Mississippi; Erik Altmann, Michigan State University; Ruth Spinks, University of Iowa; Kenneth Milles, Edinboro University; and Stan Klein, University of California, Santa Barbara. Their suggestions were invaluable in this revision. I also thank my colleagues who made an extra effort to help me obtain figures: Ian Davies, Ovidiu Lungu, Denny Proffitt, Mike Schutz, Ann Senghas, and Saul Sternberg.

I have had the remarkable good fortune to learn from and work with some great cognitive psychologists, all of whom are also gentle, warm-hearted people. As undergraduate I was privileged to take Ruth Day's remarkable Cognition course, which kindled my interest in the field. My thanks to my graduate school advisors—Bill Estes, Steve Kosslyn, and Mary Jo Nissen—who were so generous with their time and wisdom. John Gabrieli has also been an enduring influence as a colleague and friend. I'm also grateful to my cognitive colleagues at the University of Virginia—Chad Dodson, Michael Kubovy, Denny Proffitt, Tim Salthouse, Jackie Shin, and Bobbie Spellman—for their helpfulness with particular questions, for their encouragement in all matters, and for making it fun to come to work.

My thanks to my children, Rebecca, Esprit, and Sarah for their love and inspiration.

My thanks to my wife Trisha, for her unfailing love and support in this project and in all other projects that we undertake together or separately.

Finally, my special thanks to my parents, who have been patient and supportive guides throughout my life. I dedicate this book to them, for the advices.

Daniel T. Willingham
University of Virginia

Cognitive Psychologists' Approach to Research

1

Why Make Assumptions?

How Did Philosophers and Early Psychologists Study the Mind?

- Philosophical Underpinnings
- The Beginnings of Modern Psychology
- The Response: Behaviorism
- Behaviorism's Success

How Do Cognitive Psychologists Study the Mind?

- What Behaviorism Couldn't Do
- Failures of Behaviorism to Account for Human Behavior
- The Computer Metaphor and Information Processing
- The Behaviorist Response
- Abstract Constructs in Other Fields
- So What, Finally, Is the Cognitive Perspective?

Have you ever wondered how we see or how we remember things? Have you ever contemplated the strange nature of attention?

I didn't think so.

Most of the people I know do contemplate how the mind works, but only when their mind lets them down. They contemplate memory ("Why can't I find my keys?"), attention ("I *want* to find my keys, so why can't I concentrate?"), and vision ("How could I not see my keys when they were right in front of me the whole time?"). Questions such as "How does vision work?" seem somewhat interesting, but no more interesting than thousands of other questions. It's like someone asking you whether you want to know about the history of guitar making. "I don't know; maybe. Is it interesting?"

Truthfully, "How does vision work?" is a bad question because it's too general. In cognitive psychology, as in most fields, the devil is in the details, but that's where the fun is, too. Vision, attention, and memory become interesting only when you pose more specific questions about them.

This book poses questions about the mind and describes the answers cognitive psychologists have uncovered. The first thing we have to decide, then, is which questions to ask—how to get more specific than "How do we see?" You'll find that the questions we ask are deeply influenced by assumptions we make about the mind and, indeed, assumptions about what it is to be human. It seems obvious that it would be better not to make assumptions when we are just starting to study the mind. Therefore, the first question to take up is **Why make assumptions?** As we'll see, the answer is that it is difficult or impossible to avoid making assumptions. If that's true, we should at least be clear about the assumptions cognitive psychologists make. If you know the assumptions, it will be clearer to you why cognitive psychologists ask the questions they do, and if you understand why they ask a particular question, it will be much easier to understand the answer.

But the approach of cognitive psychologists developed in part as a response to other approaches that people had tried but that seemed to have flaws. Thus, our second question is **How did philosophers and early psychologists study the mind?** As we'll see, a number of different approaches have been tried in the last 2,000 years, but it was only about 125 years ago that a serious, systematic effort began to apply the scientific method to human thought. That date is some 200 years or more after the scientific method had been used in other domains of knowledge. Furthermore, cognitive psychology was not the first scientific approach to studying the mind; it arose in response to the flaws in other methods.

Finally, our third question is **How do cognitive psychologists study the mind?** As we'll see, the cognitive approach is informed largely by an analogy of the mind to a computer; like a computer, the brain takes in information, manipulates it, and then produces responses. The truth is more complicated than that, of course, and we elaborate on this metaphor later.

Why Make Assumptions?

Preview

People make two types of assumptions when they study the mind. The first assumption concerns which are the important questions. We can't study everything at once, so we must pick some aspect of the mind as a starting point for study. What we perceive to be the starting point is biased by our assumptions about the mind. The second type of assumption concerns beliefs about the mind (even very general, vague beliefs) that affect how everyone thinks about vision, attention, or memory before really knowing anything about them. In this section, we look at examples of these assumptions in the study of vision.

Psychologists typically make two types of assumptions in studying the mind. First, we make assumptions about what aspects of the mind are important enough to explain. We can't say, for example, "This study will explain everything about vision." Of course, we want to do that eventually, but we have to start somewhere. So what aspect of vision will we tackle first?

The second type of assumption is more obviously an assumption in that it is something we believe (maybe for good reason, maybe not) that affects our ideas about vision before we even start trying to learn about it.

Here's an example of each type of assumption. To begin with, we make an assumption about what it is that needs to be explained. For most of the last 2,000 years, people interested in vision have wanted to explain the conscious experience of visual perception, asking, "How do we consciously perceive the qualities of an object—its shape, size, and distance?" Unconscious processes involved in vision were not considered. Cognitive psychologists also seek to explain conscious visual perception, but they are more interested in the unconscious processes that eventually lead to conscious perception. In some ways, visual information in consciousness is the endpoint of vision; we need to explain the many steps that lead to this endpoint. Indeed, it has recently become obvious that some types of vision never become conscious. For example, some parts of the visual system help you move your body, but you are never aware of any aspect of this type of vision; I explain how this is possible in chapter 3.

The second type of assumption involves the beliefs that influence the questions we pose when we study something. For example, one dilemma about vision was this: The lens of the eye inverts the image of the world so that the image is projected onto the back of the eye upside down. We obviously don't see the world upside down, so how does the image get turned right side up? (See Figure 1.1.)

This question was posed in 1604 after Johanes Kepler speculated that the crystalline body of the eye functions as a lens does and therefore inverts the

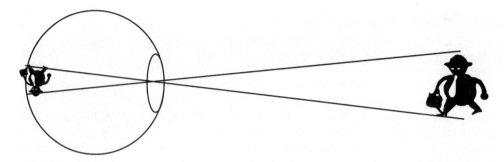

Figure 1.1. Light falling on the eye is inverted by the lens. Therefore, the image on the retina is upside down compared with objects in the real world.

image. (René Descartes put the idea to the test some 20 years thereafter, conducting an experiment with the eye of a bull.) This question bothered philosophers until the early 19th century, even though William Molyneux, writing in 1692, gave the correct answer to this problem: It's not really a problem. It doesn't matter that the top of the world is represented on the bottom of the retina (the light-sensitive cells at the back of the eye).

Why was the inversion of the retinal image so disturbing? Because of a background assumption about vision everyone was making. It seemed reasonable to assume that the conscious perception of the visual world was not in the retina but in some part of the brain. The assumption was that the retina presents an image to the part of the brain that handles conscious perception. You might think of the back of the eye as a screen on which another part of the brain watches the world go by—upside down. So the natural question to ask is, "How does the mind perceive the world right side up?" But this assumption is wrongheaded because the conscious visual part of the brain is not a little person watching the retina.

Mueller proposed instead that everything the mind perceives is a function of the state of the nerves coming into the brain. (He called it the "theory of specific nerve energies.") The pattern of neural activity *is* perception; perception is not the product of someone watching the pattern of neural activity. Therefore, it doesn't matter whether the top of the world is represented in the top or the bottom of the retina as long as there is a consistent relationship between what is in the world and the pattern of neural activity to which it leads. If the top of the world could be represented anywhere in the retina, that would be a problem, but with the top of the world consistently in the bottom of the retina, we understand what we are seeing.

Here's another way to think about it. As you might know, a computer graphic file is stored as a series of 1s and 0s. When they are interpreted by the software in your computer, they form an image of . . . let's say a cat. You would not expect that if you printed out the 1s and 0s on a piece of paper, they would form the image of a cat; the 1s and 0s are a different representation

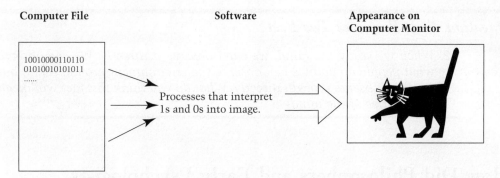

| Computer File | Software | Appearance on Computer Monitor |

Figure 1.2. A computer can represent the image of a cat in a format that looks nothing like a cat. The representation is interpreted by software in the computer and displayed as an image on the screen that is recognizable as a cat.

of the image of the cat (see Figure 1.2). In the same way, the pattern of neural activity on the retina doesn't have to look like the thing it's representing. Once you drop the belief that the pattern of neural activity on the retina must look like what is out in the world, you realize the inverted image is not a problem.

If making assumptions gets you in trouble, it seems obvious enough that we should avoid making assumptions. But it's much harder than you might think not to assume anything. Many of our assumptions are hard to spot because we take them for granted. Had I lived in the 17th century, I don't think I would have been smarter than everyone else. I would have been scratching my head with the rest of them.

Now we need to ask what assumptions cognitive psychologists make. How do they view the mind? What questions seem natural to ask if you're a cognitive psychologist? We get to that later in the chapter. In fact, we're not going to start our discussion with cognitive psychology. The field of cognitive psychology is only about 50 years old, yet people have been thinking about how the mind works for more than 2,400 years. It is misleading to wrench cognitive psychology out of that historical context. Many of the ideas in cognitive psychology grew out of older ideas, or in some cases, in direct opposition to older ideas. So we start with the older ideas, which set the stage for cognitive psychology.

Stand-on-One-Foot Question

> *1. What two types of assumptions are usually made when we study the mind?*

Question That Requires Two Feet

2. *When we study the mind, we can't observe it directly. We can observe what people do and we can observe the environment around them, but we can't observe thought directly. What do you think this fact will mean for theories of the mind?*

How Did Philosophers and Early Psychologists Study the Mind?

Preview

We can identify three waves in the history of the study of the mind before the advent of cognitive psychology. In the first wave, philosophers considered the workings of the mind. They were interested primarily in the acquisition of knowledge in all its forms. The second wave occurred in the late 19th century, when researchers applied the scientific method (which stresses observation, not reason alone) to the study of the mind. Although the scientific method had been developed during the Renaissance and applied to other issues, it had not been applied to the mind, mostly because of assumptions people held about how the mind was likely to work. Initially, psychology was largely the study of conscious experience, but it took a radical turn between 1910 and the 1920s, when consciousness was expunged and psychology became the science of overt behavior. This movement, called behaviorism, was the third wave. Behaviorism was ascendant until the late 1950s, when mental life reasserted itself as an important part of any explanation of human behavior.

In this section, we cover three basic trends in the history of the study of the mind before the development of cognitive psychology. The first trend concerns the philosophical background of the study of the mind. We discuss only Western philosophy because that is the philosophical tradition that influenced early psychologists and, eventually, cognitive psychologists. The second concerns the application of the scientific method to the study of the mind. The third concerns the abandonment of the study of the mind in favor of the study of behavior.

Philosophical Underpinnings

ANCIENT GREECE.   Approximately 2,400 years ago, the philosophers of ancient Greece left the first written record displaying consistent curiosity about and speculations on the workings of the mind (although there are bits and pieces scattered through earlier documents).

Philosophy is the pursuit of knowledge in all its forms, although over time many philosophical questions have been co-opted by the sciences. Because knowledge is central to philosophy, philosophers have been especially interested in how knowledge is acquired. There are three ways of asking how knowledge is acquired, and these three questions were later asked by cognitive psychologists:

- **Perception**. How do we gain access to knowledge about the world immediately around us?
- **Memory**. How do we retain knowledge about the world for later use?
- **Nature and nurture**. What is the origin of knowledge? Is knowledge gained through experience, or is it largely innate, with experience serving to release or activate knowledge we are born with?

The Greek philosophers posed questions about the mind that were relevant to their broader interests about knowledge. How accurate were their answers? They weren't even close. In fact, the Greeks were usually incorrect both in outlook and in detail. For example, Plato proposed that visual perception occurs when the eye emits some sort of beam, which combines with an essence of the object and then projects back to the eye. Incidentally, many adults today hold similar erroneous views. Studies show that, depending on exactly how you phrase the questions, as many as 86% of adults believe that vision involves some type of emission from the eye (Winer, Cottrell, Gregg, Fournier, & Bica, 2002).

We can see that the answers that Greek philosophers came up with were not accurate. But were their questions at least good ones? Many books will tell you that the Greeks' lasting contribution lies in the questions they raised, which set the agenda for future philosophers and eventually for cognitive psychology. I don't think that's quite accurate, though. Their real contribution lay not in their specific questions but in three assumptions they made that allowed them to pose those questions:

- The world can be understood and predicted because it works in systematic ways. If events occurred randomly or at the whim of capricious gods, trying to predict events would be hopeless.
- Humans are part of the physical world, and as is true for other entities in the world, we can potentially understand and predict how they will operate. If humans were completely different from physical objects and animals, we could never hope to predict what people might do or think.
- Explanations of events in this world should rely on other events within this world instead of invoking magical or mystical happenings. For example, Hippocrates proposed that epilepsy was a disease of the body (as other diseases were understood to be), thereby rejecting earlier views that it resulted from direct intervention of a god.

These beliefs seem so natural to us today that it is hard to remember that they are assumptions. Indeed, these three assumptions are critical to all the sciences. Experience tells us that these assumptions are helpful in trying to explain things around us; at the time the Greeks first made them, however, they were quite bold. Once you assume that the world is predictable, that you can understand it, and that humans have no special place in this world (meaning that human behavior can be explained just like anything else), it is natural to take the next step and ask a few questions about how the human mind works, such as how it perceives and remembers things. Again, it's the assumptions of the ancient Greeks that are most impressive rather than the questions or the answers they posed.

THE DARK AGES AND THE MIDDLE AGES.   Few contributions were added to the philosophy of mind between the time of Aristotle, who died in 322 B.C., and the birth of Descartes at the end of the 16th century. How is this possible?

Several factors contributed to the lack of progress. By 146 B.C., Greece was dominated by the Romans, who had a more practical mind-set than the Greeks. Pursuit of knowledge for its own sake was not especially esteemed, so no one was asking where knowledge comes from, as the Greeks had. After the fall of the Roman Empire in 476 A.D., Europe was dominated by various Germanic peoples, usually called barbarians. Although *barbarian* has unpleasant connotations that perhaps aren't fairly applied to these folks, it's doubtful that they were sitting around contemplating the workings of the mind. In addition, feudalism and the decline of urbanism did little to help intellectual life. Nor did the ascendance of the Christian church around the year 400 make for a favorable climate for philosophy of mind. The church was interested in the soul, not in scholarly pursuits unrelated to theology.

You shouldn't have the impression that intellectualism was dead during this age, but it was definitely channeled in certain directions, and those directions were not toward study of the human mind.

THE RENAISSANCE THROUGH THE 19TH CENTURY.   *The Advent of the Scientific Method.* The Renaissance refers to a time in Europe (the 13th through 17th centuries, very broadly) marked by the rise of humanism, a subsequent flowering of literature and the arts, and the beginnings of modern science. Humanism emphasizes secular concerns and the individual (as opposed to religious concerns and the religious community). From the viewpoint of a cognitive psychologist, a critical feature of the Renaissance was the return of one of the assumptions characteristic of ancient Greece: that the world can be understood and predicted, and even more, that trying to understand the world is a worthwhile pursuit. Thus, the literal meaning of *Renaissance* ("rebirth") is appropriate. The Renaissance also saw a birth: the birth of modern science.

What makes something scientific? We often think of science as being associated with white coats and antiseptic laboratory equipment. In fact, science is not characterized by the people who do it or by subject matter. Science is simply a *method* of finding out new things. The scientific method is well

Figure 1.3.   The two main methods of inquiry: reasoning and observation.

suited to some questions ("What does the heart do?") and poorly suited to other questions ("What makes a novel great?").

What made the scientific method new in the Renaissance was its emphasis on observation as a route to knowledge. How do you know something is true? There are two possible roads to the truth: You can sit in your armchair and reason about what you think must be true, or you can go out and observe what happens in the world. For example, you might reason that planetary orbits must be circles because a circle is a perfect shape, and it would make sense for the universe to be organized in terms of perfect shapes (see Figure 1.3). Or you might get a telescope and make observations of the planets and try to determine what orbital shape is consistent with your observations. Before the Renaissance, people did some observation, but contemplation and logic were more often considered the best route to knowledge.

There are two things to bear in mind. First, scientists have always used both methods. After you've made your observations, you still go back to your armchair to try to make sense of them, using reason. But the key is that then you go back out into the world again, armed with new predictions (the product of your armchair reasoning), which you will test with new observations. The second thing to bear in mind is that the fact that you're observing doesn't mean that you won't make (occasionally colossal) mistakes. Aristotle concluded that the mind must be located in the heart, not the brain, on the basis of the observation that people sometimes survived severe injury to the brain, but they never survived serious injury to the heart.

Renaissance scientists made mistakes of interpretation (like Aristotle and like scientists today), but they were sound in their emphasis on observation. The attempt to understand nature through observation had a number of dramatic successes during the Renaissance. Copernicus asserted that the earth revolves around the sun and not vice versa; Galileo formulated the law relating distance, time, and the speed of free-falling bodies; Isaac Newton discovered that gravity rules both heavenly bodies and the humble apple; and William

Harvey learned that blood circulates and that the heart functions as a pump. All these advances were triumphs of the observational method as a path to knowledge.

Why Didn't Psychology Start Until 1879?   The pace of science picked up in the 17th century as advances were made in astronomy, physics, chemistry, and biology. So why did it take another 200 years for scientists to apply the scientific method to the study of the mind? You might imagine that it was an equipment problem—scientists needed computers, sophisticated timing devices, and so forth. Forget it. Revealing experiments on the workings of the mind can be done with a deck of playing cards (invented in about the 10th century).

No, the problem was still one of assumptions. The Renaissance brought back two of the assumptions the Greek philosophers made: that the world can be understood and predicted and that explanations should be of this world (i.e., we can't invoke ghosts or gods in our explanations). But the third assumption—that humans have no special status—was difficult to resurrect.

Suppose we assume that humans have no special status in the world, so our behavior is as predictable as the behavior of physical bodies (e.g., a falling apple). Humans are more complex, obviously, but they are still predictable. What does being predictable imply? It implies that the mind follows a set of rules. When you're in Situation A, your mind follows Rule 1; when you're in Situation B, it follows Rule 2; and so on. In saying that behavior is predictable, we are essentially saying, "It is possible to have a complete understanding of human behavior such that I can know what a person will do before he or she does it." This view is called **deterministic**.

The alternative is a **nondeterministic** view. This view says, "No, there is something else that guides our thoughts and determines our actions. Call it a soul, if you like. It's the working of this other agent that gives us free will. We are free to act as we please, so you will never be able to predict another person's behavior accurately."

Under the nondeterministic view—accepting the belief that people have free will—studying the mind seems futile. Psychology tries to understand why people act as they do. But if they act as they do because of the vagaries of free will, which is by definition not bound by rules, how will psychologists ever understand human behavior? They won't.

During the Renaissance, most people probably assumed that free will existed. They would have recognized that the scientific method could analyze the behavior of inanimate bodies such as planets and falling rocks, but they would have believed that humans are wholly different. The idea of applying the scientific method to studying the mind probably would have seemed as ridiculous to them as it would seem to you if I suggested that we apply the scientific method to evaluating literature.

The foregoing discussion does not mean that scientists believe that there is no such thing as a soul or that there is no such thing as free will. Whether there is a soul is a question that science is not well suited to answer. Many scientists believe that humans have a soul and have free will. Yet, we cannot use these concepts in scientific theories and explanations of human behavior. Even if they exist, they are not understood in a scientific sense, so they don't mesh well with other scientific concepts.

The great philosopher Immanuel Kant raised a different objection to a science of the mind. He concluded that mental processes take place in time, but they don't take up any space and therefore can't be measured. Thus, the scientific method could not be applied to mental processes. Many people were persuaded by this argument and concluded that there was no point in trying to use the scientific method to understand mental processes.

During the Renaissance, then, there was no science of the mind because of a background assumption that the scientific method would not work on the mind because the mind was inherently unpredictable. But smart people were still contemplating the workings of the human mind. In the 300 years or so between Descartes and the beginnings of scientific psychology, many topics were debated that were rooted in one question: Where does knowledge come from? Like the Greeks, Renaissance philosophers were interested in memory and perception, but these interests often developed from the question of the origin of knowledge.

On the Origin of Knowledge.   Descartes, shown in Figure 1.4, is usually credited with the first modern extended treatment of philosophy of mind, written in the early 17th century. He set forth a fairly moderate view on the origin of knowledge, saying that there are ideas that come from experience as well as innate ideas that everyone is born with. The position that ideas are innate came to be known as **nativist** because ideas were seen as native to every human. Another group of philosophers (Thomas Hobbes, John Locke, George Berkeley) who came to be known as **empiricists** argued that all our knowledge comes from experience impinging on an impressionable mind. Later empiricists (David Hume, James Mill, John Stuart Mill) argued that the mind is more active in learning from experience, whereas the earlier empiricists had painted a picture of a rather passive mind being shaped by experience.

Gottfried Leibniz, in a direct response to Locke (but published much later), wrote that innate ideas are very important. He believed that experience serves only to liberate ideas that were in the mind already, presumably because one is born with such knowledge.

Immanuel Kant offered a compromise between nativist and empiricist views that was similar in spirit to Descartes's view, arguing that experience is the teacher, but *how* people experience things depends on native categories. For example, your perception of time and space does not depend on experience. You are born with the ability to perceive them; you don't need to be exposed to time and space the way you *do* need to be exposed to a language in order to learn it. Furthermore, how you perceive time and space does not depend on your experience. All humans experience time and space the same way because they are human.

Figure 1.4. René Descartes.

Nativist and empiricist views had been set forth by the Greeks, most force-fully by Plato and Epicurus, respectively, but philosophers in the Renaissance and beyond furthered these views, considered new arguments, and formulated compromise positions.

Perception. Descartes discussed perception for the same reason as the Greeks—to understand where knowledge comes from. Other philosophers, no-tably George Berkeley, discussed perception as part of the empiricist versus na-tivist argument. Berkeley was an extreme empiricist. In *An Essay Towards a New Theory of Vision*, he set out to show that even basic perceptual experi-ence is learned (Berkeley, 1709/1948–1957). Berkeley argued that even some-thing that feels as natural as the perception of distance actually requires experience. He discussed some cues to the perception of distance that are still recognized as important, but he discussed them to emphasize that there are no native, inborn ideas and that everything must be learned.

Memory.   The empiricists were also associationists. **Associationism** holds that knowledge originates from simple information from the senses and that this sensory information can be combined into more complex ideas. You know what an apple looks like because you have seen an apple before. But some complex ideas, such as the concept of democracy, clearly are not sensations. So where does this sort of knowledge come from? A complex idea such as democracy is the product of a number of simpler ideas that are joined together (associated). Things become associated if they occur at the same time.

Aristotle described the process of association, proposing several principles or rules by which associations are formed: Ideas would be associated if they were similar, or if they were very dissimilar, or if they happened in the same place or at the same time. All empiricists (Hobbes, Locke, Berkeley, Hume, James Mill, and John Stuart Mill, to name the best known) agreed that an association in time or place was important. If a clown appears every time you go to a particular shopping mall, you'll come to expect to see the clown when you enter the mall. Experimental work in the 20th century showed that the empiricists were correct in stressing time as a critical factor in associations. Locke and Hobbes were also correct when they stressed that repeating an association would make it easier to learn, and Locke added the (mostly correct) idea that learning associations also depends on whether they lead to pleasure or pain.

Summary.   This discussion has merely introduced the ideas of Renaissance and post-Renaissance philosophers. What's important to know is what they were trying to do. For the most part, they were arguing about the origin of knowledge. Renaissance philosophers also made observation part of their method, although they rarely conducted experiments as such. We might infer that they began to include more observation in their arguments about cognition because of the success of the scientific method in other fields. Many Renaissance philosophers borrowed metaphors from other sciences in discussing the mind. Locke talked about consciousness as a chemical compound, perhaps because he had been at Oxford University, where Robert Boyle had demonstrated that chemical compounds are composed of elements. John Stuart Mill also used the chemistry analogy. Hobbes was influenced by Galileo's movement studies and believed that thought was motion of the nervous system. Hume also discussed Newton and the possibility of finding basic laws of thought that would correspond to the laws of motion. Thus, in their use of scientific metaphors and their increasing use of observation in the world to support their ideas, we can see the creeping influence of the scientific method on Renaissance philosophers.

The Beginnings of Modern Psychology

In the last section, we saw that the intellectual apparatus was in place to start a science of the human mind as early as the 17th or 18th century, but background assumptions about the nature of thought led people to conclude that it

Figure 1.5. Wilhelm Wundt.

would not be worthwhile to apply the scientific method to this field. The first investigators who made the attempt would launch a new science.

Wilhelm Wundt, shown in Figure 1.5, usually gets credit for founding modern psychology in 1879, although he was not the first to publish a scientific psychological work. Gustav Fechner and Ernst Weber had performed landmark experiments years earlier. Why, then, aren't Fechner and Weber called the first psychologists? The reason you usually hear is that Wundt was the first to establish a laboratory devoted to psychology. It's not actually true. Wundt started his lab in 1879 at the University of Leipzig. William James started a lab in 1875 at Harvard. But James apparently used it only for demonstrations in teaching, so that lab is deemed not to count. Actually, the year doesn't matter so much. Wundt founded the discipline of psychology not because he started a lab but because he did what was necessary to get the science going.

Imagine for a moment that you have invented a new scientific field. Y[...] note that there is little agreement about what is ethical and what isn't, an[d] you think that the scientific method could be used to discover the one true set of ethical principles that all humans should use to guide their concepts of right and wrong. How will you launch your new science of ethicology? Here are some things you might do:

- Start journals devoted to ethicology to show that the field is making progress.
- Train students who can go out and teach ethicology.
- Write a textbook of ethicology to make it easier to teach others.
- Organize symposia on ethicology to gain publicity.
- Encourage universities to organize departments of ethicology.
- Spend a fair amount of time persuading people that the whole enterprise is possible because initially they'll think it's a crock.

Wundt did all these things for psychology. The idea of studying the mind using the scientific method seemed as improbable to a lot of people in the late 19th century as studying ethics using the scientific method does right now.

Another important thing you must do if you are starting a science is define its domain. What does the science seek to explain? There were two slightly different answers to this question around the turn of the 20th century. Wundt was inspired by the success of chemistry. The periodic table had just been worked out, and Wundt believed it was a realistic and worthwhile goal to try to work out a periodic table of the mind. What are the basic elements of consciousness, out of which more complex thoughts are constructed? Although Wundt later denied the chemistry analogy, his writings are suffused with the idea. This viewpoint came to be known as **structuralism** because the goal was to describe the structures that comprise thought. (We can recognize the associationism of Locke and others in this approach of combining simple concepts.)

Meanwhile, William James, the guy who started the laboratory that didn't count, was inspired by developments in evolutionary theory. A guiding principle for James was that mental processes must have a purpose; they must be *for* something. This viewpoint came to be known as **functionalism** because the emphasis was not on mental structures but on the function of mental processes.

The emphasis on what was to be explained differed between Wundt and James, but there was a common thread. Both sought to explain how thought worked, and for them, thought was nearly synonymous with consciousness. Structuralism and functionalism had different ways of framing this question, however, and they had different methods of gathering evidence. Wundt championed **introspectionism**, a method of study in which people tried to follow their own thought processes, usually as they performed some simple task such as listening to a metronome. Such introspection was said to require training. A person couldn't just listen to the metronome; someone more experienced had to teach the "right" way to listen, telling the trainee what he or she should be experiencing. If that sounds odd to you, it should. This method turned out to be a big problem. Because people were trained to report what they were thinking about, the trainer played a big role in shaping what people said they experienced. Five people may have had five different experiences when they looked at an apple, but after they had been trained they would all report the same experience, which was pretty much whatever the trainer believed they should say. I'm making the problem a bit extreme to illustrate the point, but that is the heart of it.

James also used introspection but of a different sort. He followed his own mental processes as a way of learning about them, but he was much less dogmatic about how introspection should be done. He frowned on dogma in psychology, and he had a healthy respect for objective experiments, which do not rely on introspection, although he disliked doing them himself. Perhaps because James later lost interest in psychology or because his distaste for dogma was not conducive to starting a movement in the field, functionalism never became a prominent school of psychology. Still, James had a more lasting impact on experimental psychology than any other 19th-century figure. His *Principles of Psychology* (1890) is still a source of ideas for cognitive psychologists.

Wundt's legacy is quite different. Although he worked out a detailed theory of psychology and published prolifically, little of his thinking remains influential. Still, he is duly credited with starting the field, and because he trained so many students, many of today's psychologists can trace their academic lineage to Wundt (including me; I was a student of W. K. Estes, who was a student of B. F. Skinner, who was a student of E. G. Boring, who was a student of E. Titchener, who was a student of Wundt).

The Response: Behaviorism

There was one big problem with Wundt's introspectionism: It didn't work. There was the problem of training people to introspect—a problem of the method they used—and there were other methodological problems. A more basic problem was that the introspectionists didn't come up with any interesting results. In the end, you can make all the arguments you want for why your method is the best, but if you don't learn something using the method, the whole enterprise begins to look silly. Between 1879 and 1913, the introspectionists had few results to which they could point.

In 1913, John Watson published a paper titled "Psychology as the Behaviorist Views It." In the first paragraph of that paper, Watson made it clear he sought to overturn psychology:

> Psychology as the behaviorist views it is a purely objective experimental branch of natural science. Its theoretical goal is the prediction and control of behavior. Introspection forms no essential part of its methods, nor is the scientific value of its data dependent upon the readiness with which they lend themselves to interpretation in terms of consciousness. (p. 158)

Watson was throwing down the gauntlet, calling for a complete shift in psychology. By 1913, psychology was considered a full-fledged science. Wundt had trained many students, and they in turn had founded psychology departments in academic institutions around the world. Most of them remained introspectionists of one sort or another. They were the establishment of psychology in 1913, and Watson challenged their assumptions with his four basic principles of **behaviorism**:

- Psychologists should focus only on that which is observable. Watson emphasized that objective measurement is crucial, and introspection obviously can't be measured objectively. If you were introspecting in front of a metronome, you could say that you're thinking about anything and nobody could prove you wrong.
- Psychologists should explain behavior, not thought or consciousness. Because objective measurement was so important, Watson maintained that consciousness was not a suitable subject for psychology. In other words, Watson was saying that the subject matter of the science should change.
- Theories should be as simple as possible. Everyone agreed on this basic principle of the scientific method; Watson raised the issue because the psychological theories of the time were becoming convoluted.
- The overarching goal of psychology is to break down behavior into irreducible constructs. Structuralists had been trying to find the basic building blocks of consciousness. Watson suggested instead that the search be for the basic building blocks of *behavior*. (His candidate for the basic building block was the conditioned reflex, which I describe shortly.)

Backtrack just a second. We said that Renaissance philosophers were concerned primarily with the origin of knowledge, and they addressed questions of memory and perception as part of that issue. The introspectionists were not really concerned with the origin of knowledge but instead were trying to explain the workings of the mind. What did they mean by *mind*? They meant *conscious thought*. Recall that Wundt was trying to do mental chemistry, to figure out the basic elements that compose consciousness.

Now Watson was saying, "Throw the mind out the window." Remember Kant's position that mental processes could not be measured, so applying scientific methods to them is impossible? Watson agreed with him! He was saying that introspectionism hadn't made progress because trying to deal with mental processes was hopeless. Instead, psychology should be redefined. It was not a science of mental processes but a science of behavior. The impasse psychologists faced was this: How can we explain the workings of mental processes, which are so complicated and elusive? Watson cut the Gordian knot by declaring that mental processes were irrelevant, and instead behavior should be the subject matter of psychology. This point of view was indeed tempting. Many of the problems that stumped researchers of the mind for centuries would simply disappear if instead of thought we studied behavior.

And psychologists went for behaviorism. It's fair to say that behaviorism was the dominant point of view in the United States from the 1920s through the 1950s (Gardner, 1985). It wasn't just a matter of expedience. Behaviorism worked—researchers using these methods obtained interesting experimental results. In the end, however, behaviorism was found lacking and was replaced by cognitive psychology. Before I explain what went wrong with behaviorism, let me tell you why it looked good for a while.

Behaviorism's Success

The philosophy underlying behaviorism was appealing because it was so straightforward. Psychologists could feel they were being scientific when they emphasized behavior because it is observable. Everyone can agree on what a person does, but it is much more difficult to say anything about a person's mental processes (see Figure 1.6). Everyone can agree that Joe hit Bill, but it's much harder to agree on what Joe's thoughts were when he hit Bill: Was Joe angry or frustrated, or was he just having a bad day?

Behaviorism also seemed to offer a promising start on the framework of a grand theory of behavior. Behaviorism, like almost every other science, sought to simplify complex subject matter by finding basic, irreducible units. Chemistry has the element, biology has the cell, physics has the atom, and psychology has . . . what? Behaviorists proposed that the basic unit of behavior is the **reflex**, an automatic action by the body that occurs when a particular stimulus is perceived in the environment.

Figure 1.6.   It is difficult to agree on what a rat is doing if you try to guess the rat's internal states; it's much easier to agree on the rat's behavior. The same is true of humans.

Before training	Training	After training
Bell → no response	Bell, followed by food	Bell → salivation
Food → salivation		

Figure 1.7.   Pavlov's classical conditioning procedure.

You are born with many reflexes. If you touch something hot, you will pull your hand away. You don't need to learn that reflex; you're born with it. Other reflexes are learned. For example, if every day I ring a bell and then give you a sour ball, in time the sound of the bell will elicit the responses usually elicited by the sour ball (e.g., salivation).

Does that example make you think of Pavlov's dogs? Watson proposed that the basic unit of behavior might be the conditioned reflex, as described by Pavlov. You are born with some innate reflexes (e.g., withdrawing your hand from pain), and others are the product of experience (e.g., salivating when you hear a bell). These learned reflexes are called **conditioned reflexes**. The training procedure (and the resultant learning) that produces conditioned reflexes is called **classical conditioning** (see Figure 1.7).

Classical conditioning begins with an **unconditioned stimulus**, which elicits an **unconditioned response**. *Unconditioned* means that the animal comes to the experiment with the predisposition to respond in a particular way. Food is an unconditioned stimulus leading to the unconditioned response of salivation because before the experiment is conducted, the unconditioned stimulus (food) leads to the unconditioned response (salivation). A **conditioned stimulus** evokes little or no response. If you ring a bell, a dog might turn toward the sound; if you ring the bell several times, the dog stops turning its head.

If you pair the conditioned stimulus (bell) with the unconditioned stimulus (food) enough times, the conditioned stimulus (bell) comes to elicit a **conditioned response**. The conditioned response is similar to (but not always identical to) the unconditioned response. In this case, the conditioned response would be salivation, but the animal might not salivate as much.

The idea that the conditioned reflex might be the building block of all thought and behavior sounds reminiscent of the empiricist philosophers: Simple associations build up to produce more complex thoughts. Indeed, the basic idea was very old. Aristotle noted that if two things happen at the same time often enough, they become associated.

So why is Pavlov famous? The difference between Pavlov's work and previous observations is that Pavlov was specific about how the learning takes place and therefore could speculate about the mechanism. Pavlov performed a simple operation to relocate one of the dog's salivary glands on the outside of its cheek so the number of drops of saliva it secreted could be measured accurately. Thus, he could get a precise measure of how much the dog salivated, which in this case is essentially a measure of the dog's expectation of being fed. Having this good experimental setup allowed Pavlov to ask other questions: How many times must the bell and food be paired for the animal to learn? What happens if I ring a different bell? What happens if sometimes I ring the bell and don't provide food? What happens if I ring the bell and give the dog a different type of food? Being able to ask (and answer) such specific questions allowed behaviorists to start thinking about a general theory of behavior, with the conditioned reflex at its center. (For a more recent review of classical conditioning, see Domjan, 2005.)

It wasn't long before people noticed that the conditioned reflex can't account for all behavior. In the conditioned reflex, two stimuli are presented to the animal, and the animal responds to stimuli, but animals can also actively do things that have important consequences. For example, suppose you try a new Chinese restaurant in town, and the food is awful. You figure that the cook may have had a bad night or you ordered something that happened to be bad, so you try again. Again, it's awful. So you don't go back. This experience obviously entails learning, but it is not classical conditioning. You actively made a choice (you went to the restaurant), and your choice had consequences (you got a lousy meal). The consequences of your choice influence the likelihood that you will make the same choice again. This type of learning is called **operant conditioning**. It occurs when the animal actively makes a response (the operant) and the probability of making that response in the future changes depending on the consequences the animal encounters. Operant conditioning was seen to be different from classical conditioning. In classical conditioning, a neutral stimulus (e.g., a bell) comes to have meaning. In operant conditioning, an initially neutral response (e.g., selecting a particular restaurant) comes to have meaning.

Edward Thorndike (1911) did some work in this vein in the early 20th century. He put a cat in a slatted box that had a door operated by a lever inside. Thorndike timed how long it took the cat to make its escape over a number of trials and discovered a systematic learning curve. On the basis of this and other experiments, Thorndike proposed the law of effect, which basically said that if you do something and good consequences follow, you're more likely to do it again, whereas if bad consequences follow, you're less likely to do it again. Still, it wasn't until the 1930s that the importance of this type of learning was fully appreciated, largely through the work of B. F. Skinner (1938).

Instead of following the story of behaviorism, I want to push ahead to cognitive psychology. (For a review of more recent work in operant conditioning, see Staddon & Cerutti, 2003.) Suffice it to say that from the 1920s to the early 1960s, virtually all experimental psychologists in the United States were behaviorists. Behaviorism dominated American psychology because, to a large extent, it worked. Behaviorists could make many good predictions about behavior. Most of their experiments were with animals, but there was a good reason for that choice. From the behaviorist perspective, behavior was mostly the product of what had happened to you, meaning what sorts of conditioned reflexes you had acquired through the environment and what sorts of behaviors had been rewarded or punished over the course of your lifetime. It was therefore difficult to conduct experiments on humans because the experimenter had no way of knowing what their history was and therefore what they already knew coming into the experiment. Investigators could raise an animal from birth and know exactly what its history was, so they used animals. But were animals really like people? Behaviorists figured that humans were much more complex, but the basic laws of learning probably were the same. They also noted that every science starts with simple situations. When Galileo wanted to investigate how objects move, he started with spheres rolling down planes, not leaves blowing in a high wind. Once you understand the simple situation, you can move on to more complex situations.

In the late 1950s, behaviorism began to crumble. There were a number of reasons, but they fall into two categories: (a) People started to doubt that behaviorism could do what it had promised, and (b) it became obvious that eliminating any discussion of mental processes from psychology was hurting more than it was helping. The replacement for behaviorism was cognitive psychology, and so our story begins.

Stand-on-One-Foot Questions

3. Why was the scientific method not applied to the human mind before the 19th century?
4. What psychological questions did philosophers address during the Renaissance?
5. What change did scientific psychology undergo in terms of what it sought to explain?

Questions That Require Two Feet

6. One of the assumptions that the Greeks made was that explanations for events in the world should be "of this world." In other words, there is not much point in proposing explanations of observable events in terms of unobservable forces. To what extent do you think people you know hold this assumption?
7. Behaviorism swept away the introspective method but should people's introspections be of any interest to psychology?

How Do Cognitive Psychologists Study the Mind?

Preview

The impetus for a new way to study the mind came from several sources. Among psychologists there was increasing dissatisfaction with the behaviorist position because it seemed unable to account for some important human behaviors, such as language. Scientists in other fields (including artificial intelligence and neuroscience) made great use of abstract constructs—hypothetical representations and processes—in accounting for intelligent behavior, although these were anathema to behaviorists. In moving away from behaviorism, cognitive psychologists needed to move toward something, and artificial intelligence offered a ready model. One could conceive of the human mind as similar in some respects to a computer. Both manipulated information as a way of generating intelligent behavior. This computer metaphor has remained influential, although it can be taken too literally. In the last part of this section, I show how a cognitive psychologist would analyze one very simple bit of behavior—answering the question "What is your hometown?"

What Behaviorism Couldn't Do

Serious problems for behaviorism were raised in the 1950s. Behaviorism was perceived by psychologists as proposing that the experiences of an animal during its lifetime completely determined its behavior—in other words, that the animal's genetic inheritance counted for nothing and that what the animal did was a function of what it had been rewarded and punished for doing.

Strictly speaking, that is not what behaviorism proposed, and indeed, such a proposal could only be called silly. Obviously, it is easy to train a pigeon to peck something and very difficult to train a rat to peck something; the predisposition to peck or not to peck is a product of the animal's genetic inheritance. But it is true that behaviorists did not emphasize the possibility of important genetic contributions to behavior. Almost everything they studied was the learning that took place during the lifetime of the animal, and so it seemed as though they were saying that when an animal is born it is a clean slate, a blank tablet, waiting to be written on by the environment.

In the 1950s, a number of important papers were published in ethology showing that the clean slate idea could not be true. Ethologists do not study animals in laboratory settings; they go into the wild and study animals in their natural habitat. Ethologists described **fixed-action patterns**, complex behaviors in which animals engage even though they have little opportunity for practice or reward. For example, the male stickleback fish performs a series of stereotyped mating behaviors, including establishing a territory, building a nest, luring a female into the nest with seductive wagging motions, and inducing the female to lay eggs in the nest by prodding her tail (Tinbergen, 1952). Behaviorist accounts do not offer a ready explanation for such stereotyped, complex behaviors. According to behaviorist principles,

Photo 1.1 Konrad Lorenz with goslings.

these actions should require more practice, and their performance should require reward.

Another dramatic finding from ethology was that of a **critical period**, a window of time during which an organism is primed to learn some particular information. If the organism doesn't learn the information within the critical period, later it may be unable to acquire the information. For example, there is a critical period during which chicks learn who their mother is (Hess, 1958). The first large object a chick sees during this time period is taken to be its mother, and the chick follows the object around thereafter. If a few days pass before chicks see a large object, the learning is more difficult to obtain. If the first object that chicks see is a large ethologist—for example, Konrad Lorenz—then the ethologist is taken to be Mom (see Photo 1.1). (For a review of this work, see Bolhuis & Honey, 1998; see also Berardi, Pizzorusso, & Maffei, 2000.)

As with fixed-action patterns, the results supporting critical periods indicate that the nervous system is not a learning machine that responds only to reward or punishment following an action. Rather, organisms seem to come into the world with a nervous system that is primed to learn particular things; it is part of their genetic heritage. This explanation sounds obvious, but it did not fit into the behaviorist theory in any obvious way.

The first problem with behaviorism, then, was that it could not account for some elements of animal behavior. The second problem was that people became uneasy about whether behaviorism could account for human behavior in all cases.

Failures of Behaviorism to Account for Human Behavior

The study of language was a dark cloud looming on the behaviorist horizon almost from the beginning. Keep in mind that behaviorists conducted almost all their experiments on animals. They were essentially offering a promise: "Don't worry, all our work with animals will apply to humans." Some people did worry, and their chief worry was that behaviorist principles derived from experiments with animals would not be able to account for human language. B. F. Skinner (1984) recounts in his autobiography that as a newly minted Ph.D. in the mid-1930s, he had such a discussion with the great philosopher Alfred North Whitehead:

> Here was an opportunity which I could not overlook to strike a blow for the cause, and I began to set forth the principal arguments of behaviorism with enthusiasm. Professor Whitehead was equally in earnest—not in defending his own position, but in trying to understand what I was saying and (I suppose) to discover how I could possibly bring myself to say it. Eventually we took the following stand. He agreed that science might be successful in accounting for human behavior provided one made an exception of *verbal* behavior. Here, he insisted, something else must be at work. He brought the discussion to a close with a friendly challenge: "Let me see you," he said "account for my behavior as I sit here saying, 'No black scorpion is falling upon this table.'"
>
> The next morning I drew up the outline of a book on verbal behavior. (pp. 149–150)

Skinner may have outlined the book the next morning, but it was not until 1957 that he published *Verbal Behavior*. His analysis of language was straightforward behaviorism. How does a child learn language? Through reward in the environment. That is, the infant learns that saying "Da" elicits excitement from the parents, which is very rewarding. But the parents get used to the child saying "Da," and soon the child must produce a more complex utterance, such as "Dad," to be rewarded. Through reward, the child learns ever more complex utterances. The analysis was more sophisticated than that, but it did not stray far from the behaviorist line.

Two years after Skinner's book was published, a review appeared that soon attracted more attention than the book, although the review was not published in a major journal. It was written by a young linguist named Noam Chomsky (1959) and can be summarized this way: "Not only is Skinner's account wrong, but a behaviorist explanation cannot, in principle, ever account for language". Chomsky argued that Skinner had grossly underestimated the complexity of language. First, he attacked Skinner's account of the "scorpion on the table" problem. To account for why a person utters a remark at any given time, Skinner could only say that the behavior was under stimulus control, meaning that some subtle property of the stimulus (combined with the individual's history) had elicited this verbal response. Chomsky pointed out that this explanation is really not an explanation. If you see a painting and say "Dutch," it is presumably due to some subtle property of the painting. But you might just as well have said "Stinks," "Nice," or "Too much red." In each case, Skinner could only say that, because of the comment you made, he must infer that that particular aspect of the stimulus (stinkiness, niceness, redness) was controlling your behavior. That is no explanation.

A second important point Chomsky made was that language is **generative**, meaning that people can create novel sentences. Behaviorism can explain why you might repeat a behavior (you were rewarded last time), but it's not nearly as good at describing why you do something novel, such as utter a sentence you've never said before. After all, the ability to generate novel utterances is the heart of language. We seldom say the same thing twice in just the same way.

Indeed, how is it that you can say or comprehend a series of words you've never said or heard before, such as "Banana peels have nothing to do with success as a cab driver"? How do you get the grammar right? It's tempting to say, "There are *rules* for what makes a sentence grammatical. It's like the formula for a line: $y = mx + b$. You put in values for m, which is the slope, and for b, which is where the line runs into the y axis, and you have described a line. In the same way, there might be abstract formulas you use to construct a sentence. You plug in the ideas for the things you want to say, and the formulas turn your ideas into a grammatical sentence." This idea was a big blow to behaviorism. Starting in the 1950s and 1960s, psychologists of language proposed such sets of rules (called grammars) and left behaviorist accounts behind.

Convinced that the results of animal experiments did *not* extend to human linguistic abilities, many psychologists, not just those who studied language, were shaken by Chomsky's argument. If behaviorism can't account for language, who knows how else it will fail?

The impression that behaviorist principles couldn't give a complete account of human behavior was reinforced by studies of memory. Here's an example from a study by Weston Bousfield (1953). Suppose I give you this list of words to remember:

lion, onion, Bill, firefighter, carrot, zebra, John, clerk, Tim, nurse, cow

Ten minutes later, I ask you to recall the words. Most people do not recall the words in the order they heard them. They recall one category, such as animals, then another category, and so on. How can this result be explained? When participants are asked what they are doing in such studies, they say they are using a retrieval strategy. They know that one animal will make them think of other animals, so it's easiest to remember all the animals at once. A behaviorist would shrink from the term *strategy* because a strategy is not observable. But people clearly reorder the words, and they say they are doing so to help them remember better. Can we ignore what the people say they are doing? We can't ignore the fact that people reorganize the word order—that's observable behavior—so how can we account for it? Behaviorism dictated that psychologists shouldn't consider a person's plans, goals, or strategies in accounting for what they do. But the idea of strategy seemed to be a major component of what people did in memory studies such as this one.

Behaviorism did not provide a framework in which to use constructs such as grammars or strategies. But if behaviorism were abandoned, what would take its place? A replacement was found through analogy of the human mind to a computer.

The Computer Metaphor and Information Processing

Metaphors are very important in the study of the mind (Daugman, 1990). No one knows what the mind is or how it works, so people often say, "I think the mind is like . . .". For example, Descartes was impressed by animated statues in the gardens at the chateau of Saint-Germain-en-Laye, outside Paris. As a visitor strolled through the gardens, he or she stepped on hidden plates that set the statues in motion. In one, Perseus descended from the ceiling of a grotto and slew a dragon that rose from the water. The system animating the statues was based on hydraulics—water moving through hidden pipes—and Descartes proposed a hydraulic system of nerve function (1664/1972).

In the 19th century, many researchers likened the brain to a telephone switchboard (Photo 1.2); the criss-crossing pattern of connectivity of neurons is reminiscent of an enormous switching station (von Helmholtz, 1910/1962). Donald Hebb (1949) proposed a model of neural functioning in the late 1940s that invoked solenoids and capacitors.

In the 1950s, a new metaphor became available. Artificial intelligence researchers realized that early computers solved number-crunching problems with symbols. The number 6 was not physically realized with six pieces of something in the computer, the way an abacus represents 6 with six beads. The computer uses a binary code in which the sequence 0-1-1-0 might mean "6," but 0-1-1-0 is just a symbol, one that could just as easily represent "bird" or "twiddling thumbs." So artificial intelligence researchers began speculating on what a computer might be capable of if the symbols it used represented something other than numbers.

Naturally, when 0-1-1-0 means "6" and the goal is to get a computer to manipulate numbers, we have certain expectations. We want to be able to add numbers, subtract them, and so forth, and we expect that the basic laws of addition will be built into the computer. For example, the order in which numbers are added by the computer shouldn't matter: $6 + 3 = 9$ is equivalent to $3 + 6 = 9$. Thus, a computer uses representations (e.g., 0-1-1-0) and processes that do

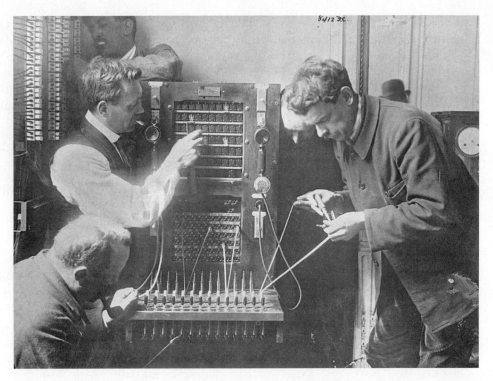

Photo 1.2.   There is a tendency to compare the brain to the most complicated device known. In the late 19th century, the telephone switchboard was a popular metaphor for the brain.

things to the representations (e.g., addition and subtraction). A **representation** is a symbol (0-1-1-0) for an entity in the real world ("6"). A **process** manipulates representations in some way.

That's clear enough for computers. What if we can approach human thought that way? Suppose that humans, like computers, use representations and processes. If we think of humans as processors of information, we can set up new questions for the study of the mind. What we want to know about humans is (a) what kind of symbols or representations humans use and (b) what processes humans use to manipulate those representations.

Here's another way to use the computer metaphor. Computers have hardware and software. The hardware is the actual physical piece of machinery (the central processing unit, the hard drive, the memory chips, and so on). The software is the set of instructions that tells the hardware what to do. Why not think of humans that way? This approach has been fruitful for neuroanatomists studying the hardware and cognitive psychologists studying the software of the brain. You could say that behaviorists wanted to talk only about what was observable—what was seen on the screen of the computer and what was typed on the keyboard—and therefore were missing most of the interesting information.

This metaphor proved very powerful and became known as the **information processing** model. This approach to studying the human mind is characterized by three assumptions.

- Humans are processors of information, just as computers are processors of information. The processing of information supports human thought and behavior.
- Representations (of objects and events) and processes that operate on these representations underlie information processing.
- Information processing typically occurs within largely isolated modules, which are organized in stages of processing. Thus, one module receives information from another module, performs an operation on the information, and passes the information on to another module.

I provide an example of this information processing perspective toward the end of this chapter. For now, keep in mind that humans take in information from the environment (e.g., through sight and hearing), transform that information (e.g., by interpreting it in light of memory), and then emit more information (e.g., through speech).

The Behaviorist Response

The idea that psychologists could propose hypothetical representations used by the mind is powerful. We've already mentioned the case of language, in which sentence grammar seemed necessary to account for the ability to generate novel sentences. Memory is another domain of behavior in which hypothetical processes and representations are potentially useful.

It is easy to keep a small amount of information in mind for a short time (about 30 s). You might look up a telephone number and cross the room to the phone, repeating the number to yourself. You dial the number, and then it is gone from your memory. If you are interrupted as you cross the room so that you stop repeating the number, you'll have to look it up again. Clearly, you usually remember things for longer than 30 s. Why do you remember the phone number only for that long?

Here's an account you might give. You might say that there are two types of memory: long-term memory, which can keep memories for years, and primary memory, which is used to maintain information for 30 s or so. Primary memory is useful because it is hard to get material into long-term memory, and you don't always need to remember things for years.

Primary memory could be said to contain representations. Just as a computer has a representation (0-1-1-0) for the concept "6," your mind has a way to represent "6." Furthermore, primary memory uses processes that manipulate representations. For example, if you wanted to remember "6" for several minutes, a process would continually refresh the concept "6" so it remains accessible.

A behaviorist would object, "Where, exactly, is this mystical representation of '6'? I don't see it." The response is that primary memory is an **abstract construct**, a theoretical set of processes (e.g., refresh) and representations (e.g., 6) that are useful in explaining some data. Any abstract construct you propose is therefore a minitheory. It is a proposal about the way the mind operates.

A behaviorist would argue that proposing the abstract construct of primary memory is wrong for these reasons:

- The construct is circular. The behavior that people easily recall information for 30 s is explained simply by stating that it occurs because we have a memory system designed to remember things for 30 s.
- The concept diverts attention from the important issues. Remember, psychology is a science of behavior, not of thought.
- The proposition is impossible to verify because it is not observable. There is no way to confirm whether primary memory exists because it can't be seen, touched, or measured in any way.

It was difficult for psychologists to abandon the idea that if they talked about representations and processes, then they were not being scientific. They needed support for the idea that abstract constructs could be scientifically useful. Such support came from two fields: computer science and neuroscience.

Abstract Constructs in Other Fields

It looked as if the information processing perspective might be useful in accounting for human thought, but there was still the issue of whether investigators were being scientific if they used abstract constructs. In both computer science and neuroscience, however, researchers were using abstract constructs freely with no apparent loss of rigor.

ARTIFICIAL INTELLIGENCE.   Artificial intelligence is the pursuit of intelligent behavior by a computer. The idea is to get a computer to produce output that would be considered intelligent if a person produced it. Most researchers think that a program that gets a computer to complete a task can be considered a theory of how the human mind completes the task. These theories rely completely on abstract constructs. These researchers propose that certain information is contained in memory—that this information can be combined or used in specific ways, according to a set of rules, and that these rules and the information in memory drive behavior.

Here's an example. In the mid-1950s, Allen Newell and Herb Simon (1956) developed a program that proved theorems in formal logic. It ran on a computer called JOHNNIAC, which used vacuum tubes (see Photo 1.3). The program worked by starting with a list of axioms—statements that it could

Photo 1.3. JOHNNIAC, a vacuum tube-based computer, on which the Logic Theorist program ran.

take as true—and a list of rules for how the axioms could be combined. The program also remembered proofs that it had already discovered so they could be used as needed. The program had a number of strategies it used to discover proofs; for example, sometimes it tried working backward by starting with the conclusion and trying to get back to the initial premises.

Three things are critical about this program and what it represents. First, the behavior the program produced was quite impressive. Until that time, behaviorists could more easily ignore artificial intelligence because the artificial intelligence programs didn't do anything sophisticated. Behaviorists could say, "Computers are nothing but fancy adding machines. What they are capable of is not really behavior." But here was a program constructing logical proofs; this certainly sounds like sophisticated behavior.

Second, Newell and Simon were not simply saying, "Look, we can get a computer to do something that looks like thought. Cool, huh?" To this, a behaviorist might reply, "So what? You programmed the computer to solve proofs, and it solves proofs. *You* are the intelligent agent because you programmed the computer." But Newell and Simon were saying that the method the computer used to solve the problem was like the method humans used. They provided evidence for this by asking people to prove the theorems and to describe what they were doing as they did it. People reported strategies similar to those the program used (e.g., working backward).

The third important thing about the program is that it used abstract constructs. You can't see or touch the strategies that the program used. The usual response of behaviorists to a theory that entailed strategies was, "That's not scientific. You can't observe strategies." But there was nothing unscientific or mystical about the program. The artificial intelligence researcher could say, "I'm being quite specific about what I mean by 'strategy.' Look, there's the strategy right there in the program, and here are the rules describing when the strategy is invoked."

NEUROSCIENCE.   Another way to be specific about an abstract construct is to tie it to a brain structure. It's one thing to propose the existence of a primary memory system. It's something else again to find a primary memory system located in the dorsolateral frontal cortex of the brain.

The links between brain structure and function have been pursued since the 19th century. One way to do this is by examining people with brain damage caused by stroke, tumor, or disease. Some of these people have quite specific cognitive problems. For example, suppose you find a patient with brain damage whose cognitive functioning appears completely normal in every other respect but who has no primary memory—he can't keep a phone number in mind for 30 s. If you know the location of the brain damage, you might infer that you know the location of primary memory. If this patient has damage to brain area X and no longer has primary memory, then brain area X must support primary memory.

This inference is correct up to a point. The problem is, how do we know which part of the brain is damaged? In the 1950s, the main way to know where brain damage had occurred was as a consequence of surgery. If a surgeon must go in and remove some tissue (e.g., to remove a tumor), we know the exact location of the brain damage because the surgeon caused it. In the late 1950s and early 1960s, there were a few cases in which dramatic and important things were learned about cognition from such patients.

Perhaps the most famous patient of this sort is H.M. (Corkin, 2002), who is known by his initials to protect his privacy. H.M. had epilepsy that was unresponsive to even very high dosages of medication. His seizures were frequent, severe, and so debilitating that he could not continue in school. Seizures usually have a focus, meaning that they start in one part of the brain

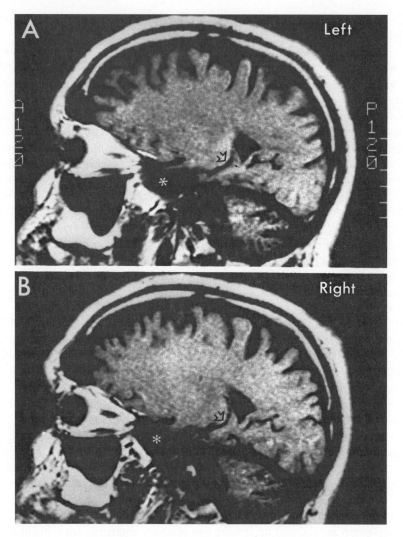

Figure 1.8. Brain image from H.M., taken in 2002. The asterisk shows where structures were removed.

and then spread. If a surgeon can take out the part of the brain that is the focus, the seizures may stop.

H.M. underwent surgery in 1957, in which a number of structures near the center of his brain were removed. A brain image of H.M. taken with magnetic resonance imaging (see chapter 2) is shown in Figure 1.8. At that time, the best knowledge about the function of these structures was that they were important to the sense of smell, so it was thought that H.M. probably would lose his sense of smell. That seemed a small price to pay to eliminate the seizures.

Unfortunately, however, H.M. lost his ability to form new memories. His primary memory is normal. He can remember a phone number for 30 s just as you or I can. His long-term memory is fine, too, if you ask him about events that happened before the surgery. He can remember his friends in high school, what was happening in the world in the early 1950s, and so on. What he can't do is form new long-term memories. Thus, H.M. has learned almost nothing new since 1957. He does not know who the president is now or what year it is. He wouldn't know that we went to war in Iraq or that the Berlin Wall has fallen. If you spent an hour in pleasant conversation with H.M. and then left the room for a few minutes, upon your return he would not remember having met you.

The point here is that data from H.M. provided dramatic evidence in favor of using an abstract construct such as primary memory in a theory of how memory works. We know that the hippocampus and other structures that H.M. lost are important for transferring information from primary memory into long-term memory. But we know that those structures don't support primary or long-term memory themselves because these types of memory work fine in H.M. So we need to find which parts of the brain support those other functions.

Suppose now that you're not a neurologist but an experimental psychologist interested in learning and memory. On the one hand, the behaviorists are saying, "You can't use terms such as *primary memory*. They are not rigorous because they refer to things that cannot be observed." On the other hand, findings such as those from H.M. strongly suggest that the concept of primary memory would be useful. What would you do?

So What, Finally, Is the Cognitive Perspective?

We have discussed some of the developments that have influenced cognitive psychology:

- Behaviorism could not account for all the experimental data, especially in studies of language and memory.
- It looked as if abstract constructs would help account for the data.
- Neuroscientists and artificial intelligence researchers provided examples of how abstract constructs could be used effectively in a scientific way.
- The interaction of representations and the processes that manipulate them can be likened to the workings of a computer.

This brief overview also makes the assumptions of the cognitive perspective seem obvious. The chief assumption is that there are representations as well as processes that operate on them. Another assumption is that we can discover these processes and representations. There is currently no way to observe these processes directly. We infer the existence of these processes based on people's behavior. For the moment, let's just say that the assumptions of the cognitive perspective appear reasonable, but we should never forget that they are assumptions. (For a perspective on the use of representations in cognitive theory, see Markman & Dietrich, 2000.)

So that's the approach and the assumptions behind it. How is it applied? Here's the way a cognitive psychologist would think about a problem. Suppose you and I meet at a party and we make the usual small talk:

> YOU: So, how's it going, or something?
> ME: All right. Where are you from?
> YOU: Pittsburgh. How's your research going?
> ME: Uhh . . . you don't really care, do you?
> YOU: No, that was me being polite. I'm going to go to the bar now.

Take one little part of that interchange. I ask where you're from. You answer. It takes you perhaps half a second, but consider all that had to happen during that half a second. My question "Where are you from?" comes to you as a series of sounds. First, these sounds must be interpreted as speech. Speech interpretation, it turns out, is not trivial. Take just one component of speech interpretation: figuring out the boundaries of words. You'd think that there should be pauses between words—little breaks where there is no sound—but that's not the case. There are little breaks when people talk, but they don't correspond to the boundaries of words. So the first thing that must be done is to figure out the words of the sentence.

Then you have to assemble the words into something with meaning. Why is this a complex process? The question "Where are you from?" in this context is easy to interpret, but the same utterance could mean something very different in another context. For example, if I said, "Where are *you* from?" right after you spilled your drink all over yourself, it would probably be taken as an expression of scorn, not a polite pleasantry.

Once you know what I'm asking, you have to find the answer in memory. Your memory is loaded with information: what Rene Zellweger looks like, what oatmeal is, the lyrics of many songs you hate but can't forget, where Brazil is located, and so on. Among the mountains of information in your memory, how can you almost instantly pluck out exactly the right piece of information and ignore everything else?

Once you have the right piece of information ("Pittsburgh"), you have to decide what to do with it. I've asked you where you're from and you've retrieved the answer, but are you going to answer my question? Not necessarily. If you believed I might have something against Pittsburgh, you might be reluctant to tell me you're from there. If you knew that I love Pittsburgh, you might think you'll set off a long soliloquy on the poetic beauty of the three rivers, and you might prefer to avoid that. All of us are constantly making social and practical decisions about what to say and what not to say.

Suppose you decide to go ahead and say "Pittsburgh." You still have to decide *how* to say it. You could say "Pittsburgh," or "I'm from Pittsburgh," or "Pittsburgh, Pennsylvania," or "I hail from Pittsburgh," or "Pittsburgh—what's

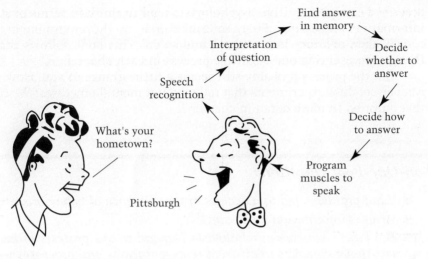

Figure 1.9.   The processes that might be involved in answering the simple question "What's your hometown?"

it to you?"[1] Every time you say something, there is more than one way to phrase it, and you have to select which way you are going to use.

Now suppose you know you're just going to say "Pittsburgh." You have to send the proper commands to the muscles of the lips, tongue, and so on to form the word.

Here's the point. I ask you what your hometown is, and in less than a second, you say "Pittsburgh." But an amazing amount of cognition (unconscious, of course) had to happen in that brief second (see Figure 1.9). You perceived what I said, looked up the answer in memory, and so on. Each of these processes looks pretty amazing just on its own.

This example outlines how cognitive psychologists think about problems. They look at cognitive tasks and try to figure out which processes are absolutely necessary to getting the task accomplished. Cognitive psychologists tend to think of mental work as being performed in stages (in our example, speech perception, memory, decision making, motor control), and a psychologist usually studies just one of these stages. Each stage is so complex that it's enough of a challenge to understand just one. In trying to characterize these stages, cognitive psychologists devise theories in terms of abstract constructs: hypothetical representations and processes that operate on those representations.

That's the overview of the cognitive perspective. I've tried to give a sense of how cognitive psychologists think about problems. The remainder of the book describes the answers cognitive psychologists have proposed. As

[1]My wife won't let me forget the time I tried to pretend I was Canadian and said, "I'm from Toronto, Canada," whereas a Canadian would say, "I'm from Toronto, Ontario." If you're an American and don't see why this is funny, consider someone saying, "I'm from Philadelphia, USA."

described earlier, cognitive psychologists tend to think in terms of stages of information processing. First, information from the environment is perceived, then memory is contacted, and so on. This book follows that stage theory in presenting one cognitive process in each chapter.

But the process probably still seems a little strange to you. How exactly can one conduct experiments that tell us about mental processes? We consider that question in more detail in chapter 2.

Stand-on-One-Foot Questions

8. *What problems led to a decline in the influence of behaviorism?*
9. *What is information processing?*
10. *How did cognitive psychologists respond to the protests of behaviorists that references to abstract representations and processes were not scientific?*

Questions That Require Two Feet

11. *Do you think some of the things humans learn might be subject to critical periods?*
12. *At the start of this chapter, I mentioned that most of the people I know tend to notice the workings of their mind only when it fails. How often do you think that your mind fails, relative to the number of times it succeeds in carrying out a cognitive process?*
13. *The "What's your hometown?" example emphasized that many cognitive processes are involved in performing what seems to be a simple cognitive task. The basic approach was to figure out processes that had to occur to make the behavior happen. Would that approach apply equally well to the subcomponents we identified, such as identifying words in the sentence and finding the answer in memory?*

KEY TERMS

abstract construct	deterministic	nondeterministic
associationism	empiricist	operant conditioning
behaviorism	fixed-action patterns	process
classical conditioning	functionalism	reflex
conditioned reflex	generative	representation
conditioned response	information processing	structuralism
conditioned stimulus	introspectionism	unconditioned response
critical period	nativist	unconditioned stimulus

Methods of Cognitive Psychology

2

Can We Use Behavioral Data to Test Cognitive Theories?

- Testing Cognitive Theories
- Descriptive Research
- Relational Research
- Experimental Research

Can We Use Neuroscientific Data to Test Cognitive Theories?

- Where Is the Damage?
- Where Is the Activation?
- The Behavioral Side of the Equation
- Problems and Limitations of Localization Studies
- Do We Really Need Cognitive Psychology?

The Five-Minute Brain Anatomy Lesson

- Cerebral Cortex
- The Rest of the Brain

In chapter 1, we discussed in some detail the objections the behaviorists raised to the cognitive program. One of their principle concerns was the use of nonobservables in theory, for example, creating a theory of how memory works that includes processes such as primary memory and long-term memory. No one can actually *see* or otherwise directly observe short-term memory, so how can we use it to explain human behavior? Cognitivists replied that they were going to use human behavior to test their models. But if so, it seems inevitable that their reasoning would end up being circular. They want to explain how humans behave, yet they plan to test whether the model is right using that same behavior. **Can we use behavioral data to test cognitive theories?** As we'll see, this strategy can be effective. The secret is to create theories that are detailed enough to make specific predictions about what the pattern of data should look like if the theory is correct, and what the data will look like if it is not correct.

You may be wondering "Well, what about the brain? Why do you keep saying that things like primary memory are unobservable? Can't we look for them in the brain?" **Can we use neuroscientific data to test cognitive theories?** Doing so turns out to be more complicated than we would initially guess. For example, you have likely heard or read about brain imaging techniques whereby scientists can locate the part of the brain that is active when a particular cognitive activity takes place. Suppose we determine that the caudate nucleus (near the center of the brain) is active when people redirect attention. Now what? How are we better off than if we found out that it was the hippocampus that was active? This sort of information—the apparent brain location of cognitive activity—*can* be useful, but the simple existence of the information is not proof that we understand cognitive function. In this chapter, we discuss in more detail what you need to know for neuroscientific data to be useful to cognitive theory and how cognitive psychologists have used such data.

Can We Use Behavioral Data to Test Cognitive Theories?

Preview

Although testing theories that use abstract constructs seems daunting, it can be done. The critical job is to specify how these constructs, which are unobservable, will change behavior, which is observable. There are three broad classes of behavioral research that contribute to this goal. Descriptive research simply describes the world. Relational research describes how different factors change together (e.g., as income increases, level of education increases). Cognitive psychologists most often use experimental research, in which the researcher changes one factor and observes the other (e.g., changing the ink color of printed words to see if that affects memory for the words).

To better understand why behaviorists thought that psychology had to be rooted in observable behavior, consider the definition of science. We said in chapter 1 that science is not defined by its subject matter but by its method. Definitions of this method vary, but they usually include three properties: empiricism, public verifiability, and solvable problems. Empiricism in this sense is different than the 17th-century philosophical movement mentioned in chapter 1. In science, **empiricism** means that we are dedicated to learning about the world by trying things out: We develop a hypothesis about the world, and then we test it. This method could be contrasted with learning about the world through logic and reason without experimentation, or with learning about the world by studying sacred texts such as the Bible. **Public verifiability** means that we must make our hypotheses and our experiments available to everyone to examine and to critique. Imagine your reaction if I said that I had scientific proof that ingestion of chocolate led to small but consistent increases in intelligence, but when you asked to see this proof I refused to show it to you. You wouldn't think that my claim was worth the time of day, and you'd be right. A final characteristic of science is that it deals with **solvable problems**. This principle recognizes that science is well suited to studying some problems (how do planets move?) and ill suited to studying other problems (is it moral for a starving man to steal food?).

Behaviorists argued that the cognitive approach was unscientific because it was not empirical; one couldn't conduct studies to confirm or disconfirm cognitive theories. For that reason, they also believed the cognitive program failed the "solvable problems" criterion; one couldn't use scientific method to explain thought, they argued, any more than one could use scientific method to explain morality.

Behaviorists had a point. Unobservable mental processes are very powerful as theoretical devices because there is no limit to what they can do; the theorist is free to invent any process or representation he or she chooses with any desired properties. Let's make this concrete. Suppose I am at a large party with my wife, Trisha, making small talk with friends. I go over to the drink table and I note that they have Coke, Sprite, beer, wine, iced tea, and ginger ale. I keep the offerings in mind so I can tell Trisha what her choices are. When I return, Trisha asks "Do they have beer?" and I immediately reply "Yes."

I kept the six types of drinks available in memory so I could tell Trisha what was available. When she asked about beer, I had to search the contents of primary memory[1] and determine that beer was among the choices. How did this search take place? Three relatively simple alternatives come to mind, although we could likely list more. First, I might have searched through the list in primary memory, one item at a time, halting the search when I came to "beer" because I had found the item she asked about. Second, I might have searched through all items in the list, not continuing the search even if I found the item. It may seem odd to continue searching once I have found the target

---

[1]For the moment, think of the term "primary memory" to be the same as "short-term memory." As you'll learn in chapter 5, they are not exactly the same.

(beer) in primary memory, but doing so makes the search simple in another way; I always search the same way (i.e., the entire list) each time I do the task. A third possibility is that I don't search through the list one item at a time but rather am able to compare the target Trisha asks about—beer—to all items in the list simultaneously, effectively searching through the entire list at once.

So which of these three possibilities is correct? We can't directly observe primary memory to find out. We could ask the **participant**—a participant is anyone who provides data for psychological research—"How did you search primary memory?" But I don't have a lot of confidence in my ability to introspect about this process, and even if I did, my introspection would have all the problems we discussed in chapter 1. So how do you make this theory testable?

Testing Cognitive Theories

Cognitive psychologists solved this problem by articulating not only their theories of mental processes, but also how the mental processes that are unobservable interact with the observable world. Thus, they didn't create theories of behavior, but they specified the behavior that could be expected if their cognitive theory was right. We can derive predictions of overt behavior that differentiate the three theories of primary memory if we make the simple assumption that the search process takes time. The first theory says that you stop the search when you find the target. Therefore, it predicts that the search will be faster when the target is present than when it is not. "Beer" was third on the list so I would stop the search after the third item. We'd predict that if Trisha had asked about cranberry juice, the search would have taken longer because I would have had to search through the whole list to determine it wasn't there. The second theory, however, says that you always search through all items in primary memory. Therefore, it predicts that these two searches (target present, target absent) will take the same amount of time. The last model, in which all drinks in primary memory are evaluated simultaneously, makes a different type of prediction. According to the first two theories, the search takes longer, on average, as items are added to the list. According to the third theory, the number of items in primary memory does *not* affect how long the search should take. Because they are all searched simultaneously, I can search through two items as quickly as I search through six items. It's easiest to appreciate these different predictions graphically, as shown in Figure 2.1.

We're obviously not going to set up a party to test this theory (more's the pity). A more efficient experimental setup would be to have the participant sit in front of a computer. On each trial, some letters (instead of the drinks) appear on the screen to be held in primary memory and, after a brief pause, a new letter appears. The participant presses one button if the new letter was in the first set and another button if it was not. The experiment

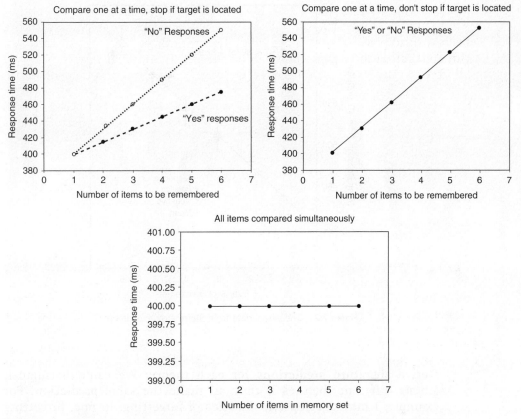

Figure 2.1.   Different predictions of the data outcome for three theories of searching short-term memory.

I've just described is similar to one conducted by Saul Sternberg (1966). The results of Sternberg's experiment were quite clear cut. As shown in Figure 2.2, the data were consistent with the second theory but not with the other two; you scan primary memory one item at a time, and you don't stop if you find that target.

Thus, it is possible to experimentally test cognitive theories, even though they use unobservable abstract constructs. We can summarize the necessary steps in the following way:

Develop alternative theories: Our understanding is much deeper if we have at least two possibilities in mind and try to choose among them, rather than having one model which we try to confirm or disconfirm. For example, suppose that I developed the hypothesis that memory scanning was parallel. I conduct my experiment and I find that the data don't support the theory, but I don't know what theory the data *do* support.

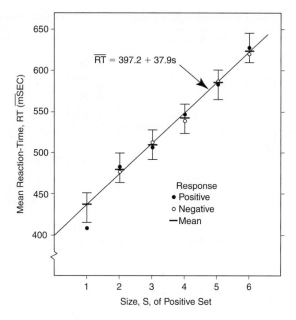

Figure 2.2.   The actual data from Sternberg's experiment.

Derive signature predictions for each theory: We can't distinguish among different theories if they all make the same prediction. For example, I may develop two theories of forgetting. In one, forgetting occurs because memories decay over time. In the other, new learning interferes with old learning. My planned experiment is to read a list of words to participants in the morning and then test their memory in the afternoon. But both theories make the same prediction—forgetting will have occurred—either due to decay (Theory 1) or interference (Theory 2).

This step—deriving predictions—entails solving the key problem with which we started. The problem was that the theories to be compared used unobservable abstract constructs (different methods of searching primary memory). In developing predictions for each theory, we specify how these search processes interact with the observable environment. We specified observable things that the experimenter can change (number of items to be remembered, presence or absence of the searched item in the list), and we specified observable behaviors that would result from the workings of the unobservable search process (changes in time to respond). Thus, a key part of our theory is that it makes contact with the objective, observable world.

Obtain data to compare the theories: The need for this step is self-evident. The real concern is to ensure the experiment is designed and conducted properly. That is the subject matter of a course in experimental methods, but we review here some of the basic approaches to research.

Descriptive Research

In **descriptive research**, one simply describes some behavior as one finds it in the world. Three commonly used methods are descriptive: naturalistic observation, case studies, and self-report. These methods never provide decisive data for cognitive psychologists—that is, they do not tell us which candidate theory is correct—but they can provide inspiration for other types of work, or highlight behavioral phenomena that had been ignored. Also, it's sometimes useful to have a systematic description of some aspect of the world, even if it's not directly applicable to a theory. The U.S. census is one such description, and it's an example of descriptive research. A political poll is another.

Naturalistic observation refers to observing behavior in its natural setting. For example, if you wanted to know how good people are at mental calculation, you could sit in a restaurant for several hours, and surreptitiously record how people calculated the amount to tip: mentally, with paper and pencil, or with a calculator (see Photo 2.1). We encountered an example of naturalistic observation in chapter 1—ethologists who observe animals in the wild and carefully record their behavior.

Naturalistic observation usually involves observation of more than one participant. In a **case study**, the researcher observes an individual on a number of occasions. Case studies are seldom naturalistic. The researcher usually interacts with the participant of the study, sometimes asking him or her to perform tasks of interest. Case studies are often used when a group of similar participants is unavailable so intense study of an individual is the only method one can use. For example, neurological patients with rare brain disorders are often the subject of case studies. One of the best known case studies is "Victor," a boy found living on his own in the forest in Southern France in the late 18th century. What would the cognitive abilities be of a human who grew up only in the presence of animals, without observing other people? This question was addressed in the case study *The Wild Boy of Aveyron* (Itard, 1962).

Cognitive psychologists usually consider descriptive research a starting point, a source of ideas, rather than definitive data. For example, the psychologist David Rosenbaum once observed a waiter transferring glasses from a tray, where they were stacked upside down, to a table. Rosenbaum noticed that the waiter twisted his arm and wrist into an uncomfortable position every time he picked up the glass, and then untwisted to a comfortable position (which rotated the glass so it was right side up) as he set it on the table; the waiter never picked up the glass comfortably, and then twisted his arm so the glass would be right side up. Rosenbaum believed this behavior was consistent with a particular theory of motor control, but he was not satisfied with this

Photo 2.1.   Naturalistic observation entails merely watching people in the real world and recording behavior that interests you. Restaurants provide an excellent locale.

naturalistic observation. He went on to conduct a number of experiments in his laboratory on similar problems to test the theory (Rosenbaum, Vaughan, Barnes, & Jorgensen, 1992). Rosenbaum wasn't satisfied with the observations alone because there could be many reasons that the waiter picked up the glasses as he did. He might have had an injury that made it less painful to do it that way, or there might have been something particular to the glasses or the height of the tray that made that motion more comfortable, and so on. To ensure those factors weren't important (and that he was really observing something consistent about the human motor system), Rosenbaum would need to vary the conditions of the movement and to have several people try the task—in short, he'd have to conduct an experiment.

Relational Research

Descriptive research seeks to describe some aspect of the world. **Relational research** examines two or more aspects of the world with an eye to seeing whether they are related. For example, I might measure people's memory ability and measure their age, and then determine whether one is related to the other. Many studies have shown that, as we age, our memory abilities decline (Zacks, Hasher, & Li, 2000). Or I might measure students' self-esteem and their success in school to see whether they are related. It turns out that people with high self-esteem tend to have high grade point averages (GPAs), and those with low self-esteem tend to have low GPAs (Baumeister, Campbell, Krueger, & Vohs, 2003). Note that in relational research one takes two measures from each individual: a measure of self-esteem, and a measure of success in school, for example.

Relational research sounds like it is closer to the type of work that will be more useful to cognitive psychologists than descriptive research, and indeed, that's true. In the last section, I said that the key to evaluating cognitive theories is to test predictions that they make about behavior. Those predictions often describe associations of factors such as self-esteem and success in school, or in the prior example, the number of items to be held in primary memory and the time to scan primary memory.

Relational research is still not decisive, however. The problem is that knowing that factors are associated doesn't tell us why they are associated, and the *why* is usually critical to evaluating theories. Take the self-esteem and GPA example. My theory of cognition might predict that all cognitive processes operate more smoothly when a person has high self-esteem. I discover that self-esteem and GPA are associated as my theory predicts, and I conclude that my theory is right. But my theory predicts that high self-esteem *causes* high GPA. The data don't necessarily tell me that's true, they just tell me that they are associated. It could be that having a high GPA causes one to feel better about oneself. That's certainly plausible. It's also plausible that some third factor causes changes in both. For example, maybe a supportive home environment causes students to have high self-esteem *and* causes high GPAs, whereas a difficult, chaotic home has the opposite effect. Indeed, it appears that the beneficial effects of self-esteem have been oversold in many arenas of human affairs (Baumeister et al., 2003).

Relational research tells you that changes in Factor A (e.g., self-esteem) tend to go with changes in Factor B (e.g., GPA), but it doesn't tell you whether changes in A cause changes in B, or whether changes in B cause changes in A, or whether Factor C (e.g., home environment) causes changes in A and in B.

Experimental Research

Relational research tells us that two things go together, but it doesn't tell us whether changes in one cause changes in the other, which is usually important for evaluating theories. How can we gain information about causality? We need to eliminate the problem described previously—third factors (C) that are associated with the factors that interest us (A and B). The problem was that we were taking people as they came to us—the kids with high self-esteem might also have more supportive home environments, they might have more friends, their teachers might like them more, who knows? But suppose we take 50 random kids and *make* their self-esteem high. All those kids now have high self-esteem, but there is no reason to think that they share any other quality such as supportive home environments because we selected them randomly. Now we can measure their academic performance and see whether the self-esteem boost gave them an academic boost.

That is the core of experimental research. Just like relational research, we measure whether two things are related, but in **experimental research** we change one factor and observe the effect of the change on the other. Thus, we might manipulate people's self-esteem by administering a phony personality test and giving participants false feedback, telling half of them that they are charismatic and the other half that they are not, and then administering some cognitive task for them to perform[2]. In an experiment, the **independent variable** is the one that the researcher manipulates—here, it's self-esteem. The **dependent variable** is the other factor the researcher measures—it's the one that he or she thinks will vary, depending on how the independent variable is manipulated. Usually, the independent variable is something that the researcher believes will influence cognition, such as how many items must be scanned in a primary memory experiment or the brightness of an object in a perception experiment. The dependent variable is often some measure of cognitive performance (e.g., how accurately the participant responds, how quickly the participant responds). Note that there is not an independent or a dependent variable in relational research because the researcher doesn't manipulate anything.

The great advantage of an experiment is that we can be much more confident that we understand the relationship between two factors when they have been evaluated in an experiment, rather than in a case study or in relational research. Still, a single experiment does not decisively settle an issue. Suppose, for example, that telling people that they are charismatic not only raises self-esteem, but also makes them happy, and it was the happiness that affected their cognitive performance. We would need to conduct another experiment to ensure that this alternative account was not correct. In general, clear answers to complex questions emerge only after systematic work, sometimes taking years.

Such work is, however, essential to avoiding mistakes, some of which might be costly. For example, it may seem self-evident that success in school may cause high self-esteem, rather than the other way around. However, this possibility appears to have been overlooked in California in the late 1980s. The state instituted a program designed to make students feel good about themselves, with the intention of raising academic performance. The program was a failure. There is a modest relationship between self-esteem and academic performance, but the causality goes in the other direction: Make kids good students, and they will feel good about themselves, but making kids feel good about themselves doesn't make them good students. That California officials did not have this possibility firmly in mind when they instituted this self-esteem program highlights the importance of the proper interpretation of relational and experimental research.

---

[2]Sometimes there are potential ethical problems in conducting research. For example, the experimenter would later tell the participants that the personality test was phony, but might not the participants feel foolish or be upset afterward? Research that might cause harm to participants is not undertaken lightly. It must be approved by an ethics committee set up to protect the rights of participants.

Students often raise two objections to cognitive experiments. The first is that the vast majority of them are conducted on college students, who tend to be young, wealthy, and of European descent. Can researchers draw conclusions about "the human mind" when they have in fact tested just a small, nonrepresentative segment of humanity? This issue is sometimes called the **college sophomore problem**. It's a fair question. Until the 1990s, cognitive psychologists weren't all that worried about it. They reasoned that the basic architecture of the cognitive system probably *was* the same in Europeans, Asians, Africans, and so on. Although culture would shape social interactions, the basic cognitive system is part of our genetic inheritance and is unlikely to vary much. More recently, researchers have begun to appreciate that culture can shape some cognitive processes (Nisbett & Norenzayan, 2002), although it appears that these differences are not central to thought. They are ornaments on the basic framework, you might say. Another answer (although less satisfying) is that psychologists test participants who are readily available (college sophomores) and whatever peculiarities there are in this population will be worked out later, when other groups are tested.

The second common objection to experimental work in cognitive psychology is that the experiments don't seem very much like real life. That is, they are low in **ecological validity**. A participant sits alone in a dim room trying to remember nonwords such as "lum" and "wik." What can such an exercise tell us about how the mind works? (See Photo 2.2.) Again, this criticism makes some sense. Psychologists must be mindful of the relationship between

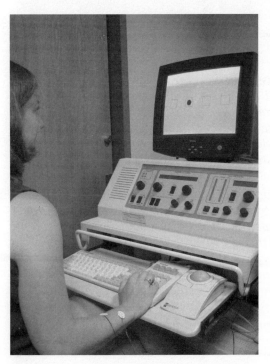

Photo 2.2. An experiment in my laboratory that appears to be low in ecological validity. Note that the participant has electrodes on her arm. Like many experiments, the odd equipment is important. The experiment concerns the effect of motor imagery on movement, and the electrodes can detect minute muscle activity, to ensure that she only imagines making movements and doesn't actually make subtle movements.

what happens in the laboratory and the world that the laboratory is meant to model. But experience has shown that scientific experiments might create strange little worlds and still be informative. Biologists use Petri dishes and physicists use cyclotrons because they provide controlled environments that make it possible to examine parts of our world that are too complex to investigate in their natural state. Similarly, psychologists attempt to strip down the complex world into its essential components.

In summary, cognitive psychologists can use behavioral data to test cognitive theories. To do so, they must specify how the unobservable abstract constructs in the theory are influenced by observable manipulations and have some expression in observable behavior. Psychologists use experiments to evaluate whether the predicted relationships between these variables hold true.

Stand-on-One-Foot Questions

1. What are the three characteristics of the scientific method?
2. What are the three steps in doing behavioral research?
3. What are the three broad classes of behavioral research, and how do they differ?

Questions That Require Two Feet

4. Scientific journals use a process called peer review whereby two or more experts in the discipline read and critique an article before it is published in the journal to ensure the science is sound. On occasion, you will hear one scientist criticize another for publicizing a scientific result (e.g., in a press conference) before the article has undergone the peer review process. Why the criticism? Isn't the scientist living up to the public verifiability ideal?

5. You may have heard that Freud's psychoanalytic theories were not very scientific (although they did contain many ideas that proved useful). A key criticism of his theory was that it could account for everything. If someone with a very strict father grew up to be shy, the theory had an explanation, but if someone with a very strict father grew up to be outgoing, the theory could account for that as well. It would seem that success in accounting for data would be considered a strength. What's the problem? (Think of the three steps of behavioral research.)

6. Is it possible to conduct experiments examining the differences between men and women?

Can We Use Neuroscientific Data to Test Cognitive Theories?

Preview

The neuroscientific technique that cognitive psychologists use most often is localization, which refers to finding the location in the brain that supports a cognitive function. Localization requires tools to identify locations in the brain. These are of three types: Some tools record the activity of small groups of brain cells, some localize where brain damage has occurred, and some record the activity of brain systems that include millions of cells. As noted in chapter 1, even a simple bit of behavior (answering the question "What is your hometown?") entails many cognitive processes. This section also discusses how those processes can be isolated to make localization possible.

It would seem self-evident that if you're interested in the mind, you ought to be interested in the brain. After all, it is the brain that gives rise to the mind. Until the mid-1980s, however, most cognitive psychology textbooks contained little information about the brain, and that choice accurately reflected the research strategy of the field. Cognitive psychologists used the behavioral measures described in the first part of this chapter.

Today, cognitive psychology is greatly informed by neuroscience. This change has its roots in the mid-1970s, when better tools to examine the human brain became available. The information about the brain that has proved most useful to cognitive psychologists is **localization**, which means finding a location in the brain that supports a particular cognitive process or function. For example, if we propose that people use visual images to solve certain problems, we should be able to find a location in the brain that stores images or part of the brain that supports a process to manipulate them, perhaps by rotating them or making them larger or smaller.

How can we find evidence of localization? Two families of methods have been used:

- If brain area X supports cognitive function Y, then damage to area X will lead to an impairment in tasks that require function Y. For example, if the temporal cortex of the brain supports the storage of mental images, then damage to the temporal cortex should lead to impairment in the use of mental images.
- If brain area X supports cognitive function Y, then area X will be active when function Y is engaged. For example, if the temporal cortex of the brain supports the storage of mental images, then the temporal cortex should be active when people use visual images.

These principles seem straightforward enough, and the principles dictate the tools we need. For the first method, we need some method of knowing where the brain is damaged. For the second method, we need some way of measuring brain activity. We examine each in turn.

Where Is the Damage?

Damage to the brain can result from many causes, such as a stroke, an infection, an operation to relieve epilepsy or remove a tumor, or a degenerative disease such as Alzheimer's disease, to name a few. Examining patients who have some damage to the brain and using that information to infer the function of different parts of the brain has a long history of success. In the early 1860s, Paul Broca reported the case of a patient who had damage to the left frontal lobe and had a problem producing speech. The patient could understand language, as long as the grammar was simple, but could produce speech only poorly. A few years later, Carl Wernike reported the case of a patient who had damage to a different part of the brain; this patient could not understand speech, and although he could speak fluently, what he said did not make sense. These observations caused a sensation because they clearly indicated that different functions could be assigned to different parts of the brain. People inferred that these areas handled production and perception of speech, respectively. Note that the inference takes this form:

> If the patient cannot understand language, and the patient has damage to ventral lateral frontal cortex, then the ventral lateral frontal cortex supports language.

To make that conclusion, psychologists needed to know the location of the damage, but there were few ways to determine this in the late 19th century. One method was to wait until the patient died and then physically inspect the brain to see the location of the damage, but it might be decades until the patient died. (Broca's patient died young because of an infection.) Another method was to focus on the small population of cases in which the location of the damage was known because it was the result of brain surgery, but most brain damage is the consequence of stroke, not surgery, so the investigator won't get to examine many people.

Much better would be a method by which one could see the brain damage without opening the patient's skull. Why not take an X-ray picture of the brain? X-ray images show internal structure, but they compress the three-dimensional brain into a two-dimensional image. The resulting image not only loses volumetric information, but it's also a big blur.

A better solution is **computed tomography** (commonly called a **CT scan**) using X-ray technology to show three-dimensional structure. The patient lies on a gurney with his or her head in the center of a large doughnut-shaped structure. Around the perimeter of the doughnut are X-ray sources and X-ray detectors. As the X-rays are directed through the patient's head, some are absorbed by various structures (the skull, blood, the brain itself), and some pass all the way through the head to the X-ray detector on the other side. The denser a structure, the more X-ray energy it absorbs.

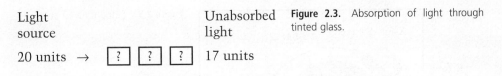

Figure 2.3. Absorption of light through tinted glass.

The detector on the other side of the X-ray source can tell you how much of the X-ray has gotten through the head, but what absorbed some of the X-rays along the way, and where was it? You are left with the average density of the brain. Figure 2.3 shows a simple model for how this is done, using visible light and tinted glass. The square represents a cube of tinted glass. If we shine a light through the cube with an intensity of 20 (in arbitrary units), a clear cube absorbs 0 units and a black one absorbs 20 units. If we shine a light through three cubes and measure 17 units coming out the other side, how can we determine the tint of each cube?

Figure 2.4 shows an array of nine tinted glass cubes. We know the intensity of light going into each row and column (20 units) and the remaining intensity after the light shines through each row and column, shown at left. Can we derive the value of each individual cube?

If we look at the top row, we know that the three cubes combined to absorb 3 units of light, but we don't know which cube absorbed how much. But if we look at all the rows and columns simultaneously, the possible values each cube can take are constrained. As shown in the diagram on the right, we can derive the value for each cube.

That is what a CT scan does. It uses multiple X-ray values, as shown in Figure 2.5. Each detector gives the density of the tissue in a single line, but if we combine the densities along intersecting lines, we can derive the density for a single point.

We can tinker with the numbers and determine the values for each cube in our simple example. A CT scan deals with thousands of values, so the calculations are performed by a computer. The resulting values represent the average density of a cube of tissue; if there are density differences within that tissue, you won't see them. A CT scan provides a three-dimensional map of values, a sculpture of density values, usually presented in two-dimensional slices.

Light source

		20	20	20			20	20	20	
		↓	↓	↓						
20	→	□	□	□	17	20 →	1	2	0	17
20	→	□	□	□	8	20 →	4	3	5	8
20	→	□	□	□	17	20 →	1	2	0	17
		14	13	15			14	13	15	

Unabsorbed light

Figure 2.4. Determining absorption values in an array.

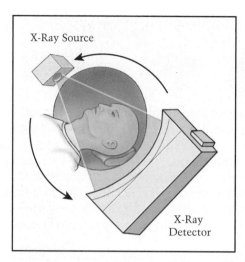

Figure 2.5. Setup for a CT scan.

X-Ray Source

X-Ray
Detector

How do we use these density values? The tissues of interest vary in density. Bone is very dense, blood is not dense at all, and brain cells (the part we care about) are of intermediate density. This technique allows us to see tumors, which differ from surrounding healthy tissue in density, and to see the result of stroke. So, we can localize some types of damage to the brain without opening the patient's head.

A second method using similar logic, **magnetic resonance imaging (MRI)**, provides much better resolution. MRI also yields a tissue density map, but the principle is not X-ray detection. Instead, MRI exploits the magnetic properties of hydrogen atoms, which are plentiful in organic matter. In their normal state, hydrogen atoms spin around an axis, and these axes are oriented randomly. The MRI machine generates a strong magnetic field that causes hydrogen atoms to orient their axes in parallel. A second magnetic wave is then applied to make only certain atoms spin, or resonate (just as sound waves of the correct frequency make a tuning fork resonate). The concentration of the hydrogen can be read from the intensity of the resonance. (Localizing these intensity values actually requires a third signal, but you get the idea.) An example of an MRI image can be seen in Photo 2.3.

These methods are of interest because we want to localize function in the brain. One way to do that is to apply the principle that if brain area X is damaged and cognitive function Y is lost, we can infer that area X supports function Y. These methods allow us to make confident statements about which part of the brain is damaged.

Where Is the Activation?

A different approach to localization measures ongoing activity in the brain while an organism engages in a behavior. If brain area X supports function Y, then activity should be observed in area X when function Y is engaged.

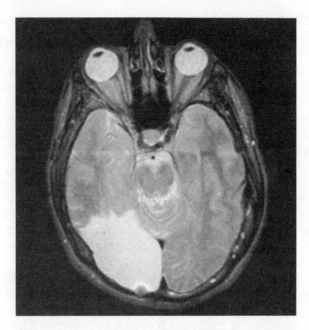

Photo 2.3. An example of an MRI scan. This is a horizontal view, as if the top of the head has been cut off and you're looking down on the brain. The eyes are plainly visible at the top of the figure. The bright section at the back (left occipital lobe) is where a large section of the patient's brain was removed (to treat epilepsy) and the space has been filled with cerebrospinal fluid.

How do we know when part of the brain is active? To understand the most commonly used measures of brain activity, you need to know a bit about the basics of brain activity.

As you may know, the cells in the brain that support cognition are called **neurons**. There are approximately 10^{12} neurons in the brain (that's one thousand billion). Neurons are interconnected, and one neuron can "tell" another neuron that it is firing. If enough of a neuron's neighbors are active, that indicates to an individual neuron that it too should be active, and it will, in turn, communicate this activity to its neighbors.

Neural communication is both chemical and electrical. Neurons release chemicals that influence their neighbors. The effect of the chemicals is to change the neighboring neuron's membrane so electrically charged ions can pass through it. Under normal circumstances, there are more negative ions inside the neuron's membrane than in the fluid surrounding the neural membrane; the charge across the membrane—its membrane potential—is about -70 mV. When a neuron fires, the membrane allows positively charged ions to rush into the neuron, changing the membrane potential to 140 mV. Thus, the chemical influence of neighboring neurons causes a chemical change in the neural membrane, which results in an electrical change in the neuron.

The firing of a neuron is an all-or-none event. The neuron fires if the influence of its neighbors reaches some threshold. Although the response seems to be "on" or "off," the neuron can communicate a degree of activity by the frequency of firing (in other words, how many of these firings occur per second). Because neural firing is an electrical event, if we can measure electrical activity in the brain, we can measure the activity of neurons.

Neuroscientists have two chief ways to eavesdrop on the electrical conversations of neurons. **Single-cell recording** is a technique that records the number of times per second that an individual neuron fires. Single-cell recording studies are almost always performed on nonhuman animals. The animal undergoes surgery in which a small hole is drilled in the skull and a plastic anchoring device is attached. An electrode probe can be placed through the anchoring device and directly into the desired part of the brain. The brain does not have pain receptors, so the probe does not hurt the animal. The probe is insulated, except for the tip, so the probe's tip can record electrical activity, specifically, neural firings.

The basic technique in single-cell recording is to have the animal engage in some behavior while the researcher records electrical activity from a brain area of interest. For example, the investigator might record from a cortical area while a monkey is making a reaching movement. The result might be that a particular neuron fires when the monkey reaches in a particular direction but does not fire when the monkey reaches in another direction. By having the monkey engage in many different behaviors, the researcher can investigate the precise conditions under which the neuron fires. By finding an association between a neuron's activity and the behavior, scientists can begin to understand what the neuron contributes to behavior.

The second method, most often used with humans, is an **electroencephalogram (EEG)**. During an EEG, electrodes are placed over the participant's scalp. Each electrode reads the electrical activity of the neurons below it. The ability of an EEG to localize activity is not as good as that of other methods. The electrical activity is very weak, of course, so the signal must be greatly amplified. Usually 12 to 64 electrodes are used, so each electrode records the summed activity of millions of neurons. Furthermore, the skull and protective tissue covering the brain are fairly good insulators that diffuse the electrical signal. One advantage of EEG, however, is that it can provide precise information about when neural activity takes place (temporal information). In fact, EEG can tell when a neuron fires to an accuracy of a thousandth of a second, or 1 ms.

If you simply put electrodes on a person's head, what you would see is not a flat line (representing no electrical activity) and then some activity once he or she does some task. Instead, you would see a wavy line all the time, representing continuous brain activity. Neurons have resting potentials, which means that they are always firing at a rather slow pace (just how quickly or slowly depends on the type of neuron). Thus, each electrode summarizes millions of neurons, each of which is always slightly active. To get around this problem, researchers measure **event-related potentials (ERPs)**. In

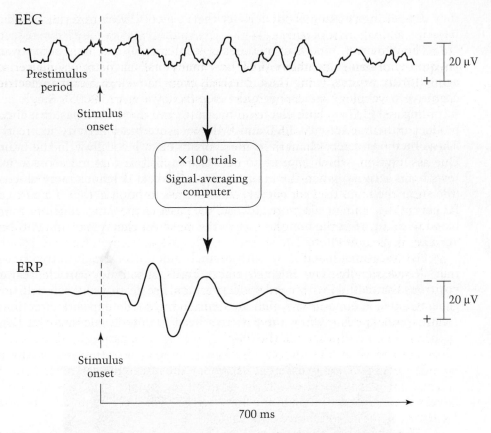

Figure 2.6.   Comparison of electroencephalogram (EEG) and event-related potential (ERP) waves.

this technique, the researcher administers tens or hundreds of trials that are similar to one another, then averages all squiggly EEG waves from these trials (see Figure 2.6).

The resulting average wave is smooth. Researchers often compare two types of ERPs that are similar but vary on one dimension. For example, a researcher studying memory might compare ERPs when the participant successfully recalled a word with ERPs when the participant couldn't recall a word (recall vs. no recall) at each of the 64 electrodes. There probably will be no difference in the ERPs of these two types of trials at most of the electrodes, but any electrode sites that do show a difference will help the researcher localize successful recall in the brain.

Again, EEG is not a very good technique for spatial localization, but it is good for temporal resolution. EEG may tell you only that a difference in successful and unsuccessful retrieval appears in the ERP of the right frontal lobe, which is pretty vague, but the technique could tell you very precisely at what time you start to see a difference in successful and unsuccessful recall. Researchers are starting to use EEG in combination with other techniques so they can get information about activity that is precise both in terms of when it occurs and where it occurs.

The two most important methods of localizing human brain activity are **positron emission tomography (PET)** and **functional magnetic resonance imaging (fMRI)**. Studies using these methods have had a significant impact on cognitive psychology since the mid-1990s (Fellows et al., 2005). Single-cell recording and EEG are both electrical measures and therefore measure a direct product of neural activity. PET and fMRI measure brain activity indirectly. These methods detect changes in metabolism or in blood flow in the brain. One assumption, which appears to be well founded, is that metabolism follows brain activity; when the brain is more active, it demands more glucose (the sugar the brain uses for energy). Another assumption is that if a particular part of the brain needs more glucose, the vascular system will shunt more blood to that part of the brain to satisfy the need. An example of an fMRI image may be seen in Photo 2.4.

PET measures blood flow with a small amount of a radioactive tracer that decays rapidly. The injected tracer emits subatomic particles called positrons that collide with nearby electrons and are destroyed. Each collision generates two gamma rays, which are emitted in exactly opposite directions. All this is happening while the patient's head is in (you guessed it) a large

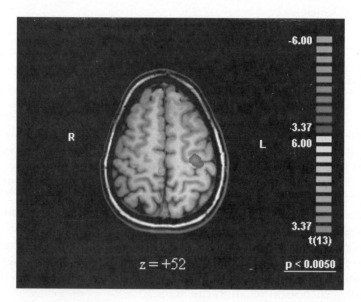

Photo 2.4. An example of an fMRI image. This is a horizontal slice through the brain—it's as though the top of the head were cut off and you were looking down. The $z = +52$ tells you where the slice was made. (In this case, it's pretty close to the top of the head.) Activation is color coded; redder colors mean more active, and blues and greens signify inhibition. R and L signify right and left of the head. Radiological images often reverse right and left.

doughnut-shaped device that determines where the gamma rays originated. More gamma rays means more positrons, which means more radioactive isotope, which means more blood, which means more neural activity. Although this pattern of inference might seem tortuous, the science behind it is well founded.

The technique of fMRI works much like the type of MRI we've already discussed (which is sometimes called structural MRI to emphasize that it reveals neural structure but not activity). fMRI takes advantage of the magnetic properties of blood hemoglobin, the protein that carries oxygen to all cells of the body. Blood from which the oxygen has been absorbed is deoxygenated. Oxygenated blood has magnetic properties, but deoxygenated blood does not. fMRI techniques calculate the ratio of oxygenated to deoxygenated blood in a local area. You would think that an active area would have mostly deoxygenated blood because the brain has absorbed all the oxygen. Actually, the opposite is true; the vascular system floods the active part of the brain with oxygenated blood.

The Behavioral Side of the Equation

Recall that there are two inferences we want to make that will help us localize cognitive function in the brain:

- If brain area X supports cognitive function Y, then damage to area X will lead to an impairment in tasks that require function Y.
- If brain area X supports cognitive function Y, then area X will be active when function Y is engaged.

We have discussed ways of figuring out whether area X is damaged (for lesion studies) and whether area X is active, but we have not yet discussed how to isolate cognitive function Y. We discussed this problem earlier in the chapter; we said that telling someone a personality test indicated he or she is charismatic might actually make the person happy instead of or in addition to raising his or her self-esteem. A similar problem arises in neuroscientific studies. For example, in chapter 1 we mentioned patient H.M., who cannot learn new information. Suppose you read a list of words aloud to him and asked him a few minutes later to recall the list, but he was unable to remember any of the words. You are tempted to conclude that H.M.'s memory is impaired. But how do you know it's his memory that is causing the problem? What if he has an attention problem and ignored the words you read? What if his memory is fine, but he didn't understand the words? To test these possibilities, you could ask H.M. to immediately repeat the words so you know he's paying attention, and you could test his language ability in other ways to make sure he can understand the words in the memory task. Basically, that's what you do in all lesion experiments. Usually, there are many potential reasons someone could be impaired on a task, so you have to administer other tasks to determine the cause.

PET and fMRI studies measure brain activity, but the problem is that much of the brain is active much of the time. If you wanted to know which part of the brain is involved in reading a word, for example, you couldn't simply put people in a scanner and have them read aloud. Instead, you must administer at least two similar tasks that differ in the particular function you want to study. For example, you might conduct a study like this one.

Condition	Description	Hypothetical Processes Involved
1	See fixation point	Attention
2	See random letter strings	Attention + vision
3	Read words	Attention + vision + reading
4	Say related word	Attention + vision + reading + memory

For each task, we have a set of cognitive processes that we think are needed to accomplish the task. We can take a PET scan showing the brain areas that are active for Condition 2 and subtract the activation from Condition 1, and that should subtract out the activations caused by attention, leaving us with just the activations caused by the visual processes engaged when the participant looks at letters. We can do similar subtractions to isolate other cognitive processes because each successive condition adds one cognitive process. Other techniques in fMRI do not use subtractions per se, but they still make use of task comparisons like this one.

Problems and Limitations of Localization Studies

Let's summarize what we've said so far. Our ultimate goal is to gain support for hypothetical cognitive processes and representations. One way to do that is to localize these processes or representations in the brain. We do that by two inferences:

- If brain area X is damaged and cognitive function Y is impaired, then X supports Y.
- If brain area X is active while cognitive function Y is performed, then X supports Y.

So far, we have discussed how we know when brain area X is damaged (localizing the lesion) and how we know when X is active (using single-cell recordings and imaging techniques). We've also discussed how to isolate function Y. Unfortunately, these inferences are not as straightforward as we would like.

Lesion studies may fail to show cognitive impairment; the brain may have found a new way to support the behavior, or the patient may consciously adopt new strategies for these tasks to minimize his or her reliance on the missing cognitive process. Area X may support function Y, there can be damage to area X, and yet you don't observe any deficit.

Another possible source of error in lesion studies is that we may incorrectly assign a cognitive function to a particular brain area that has been lesioned if it is not the brain area itself that supported the function. Fibers connecting two brain areas may have passed through the area that was lesioned, and the loss of this connection might have caused the observed loss of function.

Another problem lies at the very heart of the logic of interpreting lesion studies. Consider this metaphor. Suppose you remove a spark plug from a car, with the result that the engine coughs. You cannot conclude that the spark plug was a cough suppressor. Damage to area X leading to loss of function Y does not allow the conclusion that X supports Y. Just as the interactions among the components of a car are complex and loss does not provide a clear window to function, we can expect the interactions of the components of the brain to be complex.

Functional imaging studies have different problems of interpretation. One potential problem is that of correlated activity. Functional scans show all the brain activity associated with a particular cognitive function. Some of that activity may be reliably associated with the function—every time you perform the function, you get the activity—even if the brain area showing the activity is not crucial to getting the function done. For example, frontal cortical areas reliably show robust activation in memory studies, but if that cortex is damaged or missing, patients do not show a devastating loss of memory.

Another problem in interpreting imaging studies lies in the task analysis. Recall that each participant would perform several tasks, each task adding one cognitive process. If the tasks are not analyzed correctly, the whole enterprise falls apart.

What do we do about all these problems? The answer is that we cannot rely on any one method; we must try to use all methods simultaneously. If they all point to the same answer, we can have more confidence that we have successfully localized a cognitive process. Notice that the methods have different drawbacks. For example, patients with a lesion might find another way to perform a task, and functional imaging might indicate activity in a brain area that is not crucial for a cognitive process. These drawbacks are mirror images of one another; lesion studies might tell you which brain areas are essential for a cognitive process but might miss areas typically associated with a process, whereas imaging studies show you all areas associated with a cognitive process but not which areas are crucial for getting the job done. The strengths and weaknesses of different techniques complement one another. The strategy of employing multiple techniques to address the same question is usually called using **converging operations**. If different methods converge on one answer, our confidence that the answer is correct greatly increases.

Do We Really Need Cognitive Psychology?

In this chapter, we've gone over the approach that cognitive psychologists use to study the mind. Part of that approach has been to use the physical structure of the mind—that is, the brain—to help us determine how the mind works. We might ask, therefore, whether we might not be better off studying the brain. If we believe that the workings of the mind depend on what happens in the brain, why not study the brain to start with?

We should recognize that there are often different, but equally valid, ways of describing the same thing. It is sometimes useful to think of *levels* of description. A common example is the relationship of chemistry and physics. Both physicists and chemists agree that most or all of chemistry is reducible to physics. That doesn't mean that chemistry is pointless, or that chemists are merely biding their time until the physicists come along and finish the job. In the same way, we might say that cognitive events are, of course, reducible to brain events, but that doesn't devalue the cognitive level of description.

These different levels of description are particularly important when we're talking about the brain. The reason is that even a simple behavior—for example, seeing and recognizing a friend—calls on many different brain regions. So if we study brain region X, we might understand what it does, but to understand how we recognize a friend, we need to know about brain regions X, B, R, O, and C, and in addition, we need to learn how they communicate and interact. Studying the brain alone will not lead us to examine the interaction of brain areas X, B, R, O, and C. Actually, it is quite the opposite—it is studying the cognitive level of description that will reveal the importance of a function such as recognizing a friend, and that in turn will motivate us to study complex brain interaction.

Finally, there are important practical results of studying a cognitive level of description of what the brain does. For example, consider cochlear implants (Rauschecker & Shannon, 2002). These are microelectrode arrays implanted in the inner ear to directly stimulate the auditory nerve of the brain. Early versions of cochlear implants attempted to directly replace the input that the cochlea would usually provide. Newer versions take advantage of a psychological principle: As long as a sound contains enough high-frequency harmonics, the fundamental frequency will be "reconstructed" by the mind, even if it is not present in the signal. Designers can omit low sound frequencies from a cochlear implant—simplifying the job the implant must perform—at no cost to the perception of important sounds such as speech. Thus, if we are trying to develop electronic devices to replace faulty brain parts, we need to know more than the anatomy and physiology of the brain. It is also useful to have a cognitive description of how the brain works because that can suggest more efficient designs for such devices.

In sum, although neuroscience informs cognitive psychology, and indeed, cognitive psychology informs neuroscience, one is not a replacement for the other.

Stand-on-One-Foot Questions

7. *What information must be known for localization to be helpful, and why do we need this information?*

8. *Why is it important to use converging operations in localization?*

Questions That Require Two Feet

9. *It seems that brain imaging has a huge impact on the public, especially on their view of a phenomenon as scientific. Why do you suppose that's true?*

10. *Studies of human patients with lesions are not true experiments because we cannot induce lesions for the sake of an experiment. If we wanted to conduct a true experiment that investigates the consequence of a brain lesion, what might we do?*

The Five-Minute Brain Anatomy Lesson

In describing brain structures, we often talk about the position of one relative to another. Brain structures are large enough that one might want to refer to only part of it; it's tiresome to refer to "the part of the cerebellum that's closer to the top of the head and toward the back of the head." As shown Figure 2.7, toward the top of the head is called **dorsal**; toward the bottom is **ventral**; toward the front is **anterior** or **rostral**; toward the back is **posterior** or **caudal**; toward the middle is **medial**; and toward the side is **lateral**. Thus we could replace the cumbersome phrase "the part of the cerebellum that's closer to the top of the head and toward the back of the head" with "dorsal posterior cerebellum."

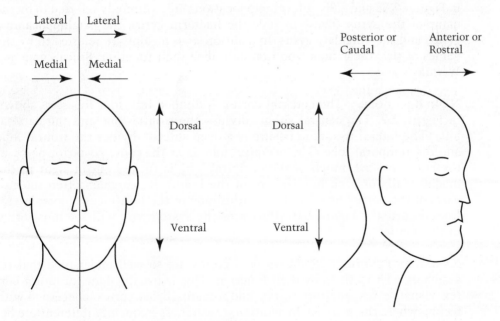

Figure 2.7.   Directional descriptors of brain anatomy.

Cerebral Cortex

The cerebral cortex is the layer of cells that covers the outside of the brain. When you see a picture of the brain, you're typically looking at cerebral cortex. This cell layer is quite thin (about 3 mm), but unfolded the sheet of cells would cover about 2.5 ft². That large sheet is crumpled to fit into the skull, hence the wrinkled appearance of the brain. The valleys are called **sulci** (singular **sulcus**) and the hills are called **gyri** (singular **gyrus**). The brain is separated into two hemispheres—left and right—and the cortex folds down into the space between them.

The cortex is not uniform. There are different types of cells in different areas, and most important for our purposes, different parts of the cortex serve different cognitive functions. Researchers refer to different areas of cortex in several ways. We use three naming systems: naming by lobe, naming by function, and naming by landmark. It may seem confusing (or better, stupid) to use three different systems to name the same thing. For example, the primary motor cortex (function) could also be called the precentral gyrus (landmark) or posterior frontal cortex (lobe). (It's also called Brodman's area 4 and M1.) Why not pick one name? I could have translated everything into one system, but doing so would be a disservice to readers because certain structures are very commonly referred to by the name in a particular system. If you referred to the lateral temporal cortex and everyone else is calling it the fusiform gyrus, the other kids would make fun of you.

NAMING BY LANDMARK.   Each gyrus and sulcus in the brain is named, as shown in Figures 2.8a and 2.8b. A few brain locations are commonly referred to by the name of the gyrus: These include the **fusiform gyrus**, the **parahippocampal gyrus**, and the **cingulate gyrus**. In addition, two regions are referred to by the names of the researchers who first described their function: **Broca's area** and **Wernike's area**.

NAMING BY LOBE.   The cerebral cortex is divided into four lobes, as shown in Figure 2.9. The central sulcus divides the frontal lobe and the parietal lobe. The lateral fissure (a fissure is a deep sulcus) divides the frontal lobe and the temporal lobe. The occipital lobe is at the most posterior point in the brain (indeed, much of the occipital lobe is tucked out of sight in the medial walls of each hemisphere of the brain). Researchers often refer to parts of the cortex by a location within one of the four lobes ("dorsolateral frontal cortex"). Figure 2.10 illustrates the system you will see most often in this book.

NAMING BY FUNCTION.   Some areas of cortex are so well understood that researchers refer to them by their function. This is usually done for motor cortex, visual cortex, auditory cortex, and somatosensory cortex (concerned with feeling where the body is). In addition, researchers frequently differentiate between structures such as primary and secondary visual cortex. *Primary* usually

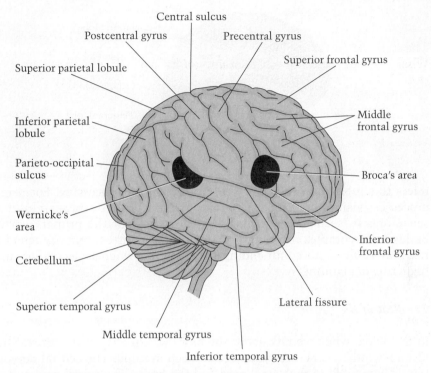

Central sulcus

Postcentral gyrus   Precentral gyrus

Superior parietal lobule   Superior frontal gyrus

Inferior parietal lobule   Middle frontal gyrus

Parieto-occipital sulcus

Wernicke's area   Broca's area

Cerebellum   Inferior frontal gyrus

Superior temporal gyrus   Lateral fissure

Middle temporal gyrus

Inferior temporal gyrus

Figure 2.8a.   A lateral view of the brain, showing the names of gyri and sulci, Broca's area, and Wernicke's area.

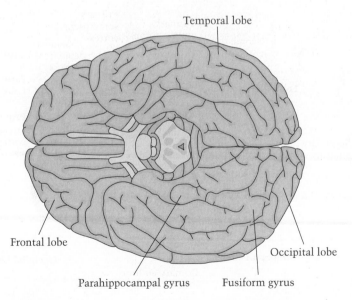

Temporal lobe

Frontal lobe

Occipital lobe

Parahippocampal gyrus   Fusiform gyrus

Figure 2.8b.   A ventral view of the brain (i.e., from the bottom).

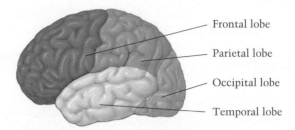

Figure 2.9. The four lobes of the cerebral cortex.

refers to simpler and *secondary* to more complex processing. For perceptual processes (vision, audition, somatosensation), *primary* means closer to the sense organs; secondary cortex takes the output of the primary cortex and builds more complex meaning from it. In motor cortex, *primary* refers to cortex that is closer to commanding the muscles, whereas *secondary* involves higher-level planning.

The Rest of the Brain

In this book, when we talk about the brain we usually mean cortex. There are just a few other structures you need to keep in mind. The central nervous system is composed of the spinal cord and the brain. The **spinal cord** collects somatosensory information about pressure, temperature, pain, and so on, and sends motor information to the muscles. Perched on top of the spinal cord is the

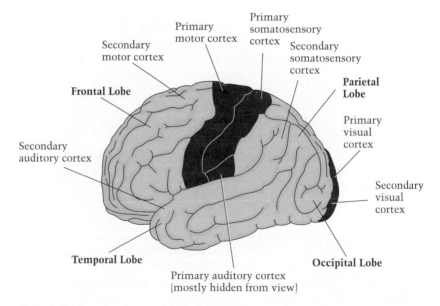

Figure 2.10. Functional areas of the brain.

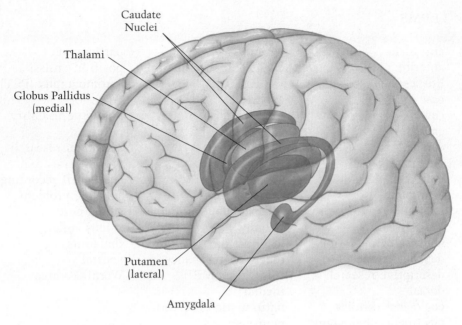

Caudate
Nuclei

Thalami

Globus Pallidus
(medial)

Putamen
(lateral)

Amygdala

Figure 2.11.   The basal ganglia.

brain. The cortex is the outer portion of the brain. Below the cortex are a number of subcortical (below the cortex) structures (see Figure 2.11). Here is a list of the subcortical structures we talk about and what they are believed to do:

Thalamus A relay station for sensory and motor information. For all senses except smell, the receptors first send information to the thalamus, which passes it on to the cortex.

Amygdala Believed to be important in the processing of emotion (especially fear) and probably information about social functions.

Caudate and **putamen** Separate but related structures important in movement and some poorly understood cognitive functions.

Hippocampus Important in memory.

Cerebellum Important in motor control and probably in some higher-level cognitive functions, but just what it does is not clear.

In these first two chapters, we discussed the background to cognitive psychology—that is, why cognitive psychologists think about the mind in the way that they do—and how one can make progress in studying the mind. We are ready to begin exploring some of the findings of the last 50 years regarding how your mind works. We begin with visual perception, which is, in a sense, the beginning of cognition because it's one of the first and most important ways that you gather information about the world.

KEY TERMS

amygdala
anterior
Broca's area
case study
caudal
caudate
cerebellum
cingulate gyrus
college sophomore
  problem
computed tomography
  (CT) scan
converging operations
dependent variable
descriptive research
dorsal
ecological validity
electroencephalogram
  (EEG)

empiricism
event-related potentials
  (ERPs)
experimental research
functional magnetic
  resonance imaging
  (fMRI)
fusiform gyrus
gyrus (gyri)
hippocampus
independent variable
lateral
localization
magnetic resonance
  imaging (MRI)
medial
naturalistic observation
neurons
parahippocampal gyrus

participant
positron emission
  tomography (PET)
posterior
public verifiability
putamen
relational research
rostral
single-cell recording
solvable problems
spinal cord
sulcus (sulci)
thalamus
ventral
Wernike's area

CURRENT DIRECTIONS IN COGNITIVE SCIENCE

Recommended reading

Miller, G. A., & Keller, J. (2000). *"Psychology and neuroscience: Making peace." (pp. 153–161) In this chapter, I argued that neuroscience should not be thought of as a replacement for a cognitive level of analysis, but I didn't say much about how progress in neurobiology and psychology should be brought together. These authors offer a perspective on how this might happen.

Visual Perception

What Makes Visual Perception Hard?

How Are Visual Ambiguities Resolved?

- Shape
- Brightness
- Distance and Size
- Top-Down Influences in Vision
- An Alternative: The Ecological Approach

What Is Visual Perception For?

- Identifying Objects
- Navigation

Of all the cognitive functions your brain performs, vision is both the most remarkable and the most difficult to appreciate. It is difficult to appreciate vision precisely because it is so marvelous; vision works so efficiently, so effortlessly, that you have no clue what it is doing or how difficult its task. Consider this: For $5, you can buy a calculator that can perform long division far more quickly and accurately than any human. For $15, you can buy a computer program that can beat 99% of the population in chess. Yet there is no computer that can drive a truck. Why not? It's clear that a robot could turn a steering wheel and press an accelerator; the problem is that there is no computer that can rapidly perceive the road, other cars, pedestrians, and so on.

This example should tell you one thing: Vision is hard. The first question we'll take up is **What makes visual perception hard?** We can't simply ask, "How do humans see?" That question is not specific enough. We need to know why it's hard to see—what specific problems must be solved for vision to work—before we can start to think about how the human visual system might solve those problems. As we'll see, vision is hard because the pattern of light that falls on your eye is consistent with many different scenes out in the world; the problem is figuring out which scene is actually out in the world. For example, what is the object depicted in Figure 3.1?

You probably said that this object is a square, but it could be a cube, the bottom of a pyramid, or a number of other solids. Thus, even this simple picture is consistent with more than one object in the world, and knowing the object's identity for certain is impossible. You may well be protesting, "Dan, we're all very impressed by your square, but the fact is that we do see, and we usually see accurately." That's true, and vision happens quickly and its product (your conscious visual perception) is consistent. When you walk into a room, you immediately perceive the objects that are in the room, their relative positions, their colors, their textures, whether they are moving, and so on. Indeed, everyone would agree on these properties, just as everyone agrees that Figure 3.1 depicts a square.

Why does everyone agree if knowing the identity of the object is impossible? The fact that we all see a square in Figure 3.1 tells us that the perceptual system somehow resolves the ambiguities inherent in a two-dimensional representation. The second question we will take up is **How does the visual system resolve ambiguities?** The answer is that the perceptual system makes assumptions about the way objects in the world usually look so we can resolve the

Figure 3.1.   This object appears to be a square, but it could be a cube or any other three-dimensional object with one square face that happens to be oriented toward you.

ambiguity of figures such as the square. For example, one assumption the visual system makes is that objects are unlikely to be oriented at improbable angles. There are many ways in which a cube could be oriented in space, but very few of those orientations of the cube leave just one face of the cube visible to the observer. It would be like seeing a coin that just happens to be edge-on so it looks like a line. Such orientations are so rare that your visual system assumes that they don't happen. Figure 3.1 is much more likely to be a square than a just-happens-to-be-oriented-that-way cube, so the visual system gambles that it's a square.

Okay, we can see. But why? **What is vision for?** Broadly speaking, vision serves two goals. First, it allows us to know the qualities of an object at a distance (how big is it, is it moving, and does it have large pointy teeth?). This knowledge helps us behave in appropriate ways (attack small edible-looking things, flee from large aggressive-looking things). The "at a distance" feature is helpful because we can evaluate what something is without having to walk up and touch it. The second function of vision is that it serves action, meaning that we know where things are so we can move around effectively (pounce with accuracy on the small edible-looking thing, skirt immovable objects as you're fleeing from the aggressive-looking thing). So, briefly put, the function of visual perception is to (a) identify objects and (b) help us navigate in the world. How do we identify objects, and how does vision help us navigate? As we'll see, these two functions are actually handled by separate parts of the brain.

What Makes Visual Perception Hard?

Preview

As we've just discussed, visual perception is complicated, but it's not easy to appreciate that fact because our cognitive systems are so good at analyzing visual stimuli. In this section, we examine more closely what makes visual perception difficult. The crucial point is that the image falling on the retina does not fully determine what is in the world. For example, size and distance are indeterminate; if the image of something is small, the object in the world might be either small or far away. Other indeterminisms we'll discuss include shape and orientation (if you see what looks like an ellipse, what's in the world might really be an ellipse, or it might be a circle that is turned slightly to the side), as well as light source, reflectance, and shadow.

The chief problem the visual system faces is the **inverse projection problem**, which relates to the way that light from the world falls on the **retina** (the layer of light-sensitive cells on the back of the eye). How do we recover the three-dimensional shape of a real world object from a two-dimensional projection on the retina? An infinite number of three-dimensional objects could give rise to a two-dimensional projection. We cannot know what is out in the world solely on the basis of the information source available to us—neural impulses from

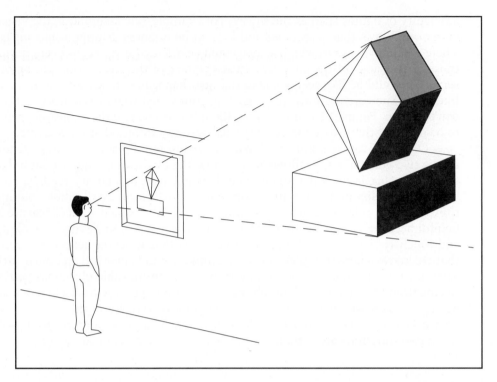

Figure 3.2. A three-dimensional object seen from a single perspective creates a unique two-dimensional projection. However, this two-dimensional projection is consistent with an infinite number of three-dimensional objects. In this figure, the observer sees the sculpture so it looks like a kite on a rectangle rather than a diamond on a box.

the retina of the eye—because the world is three dimensional, and the image projected on the retina is two dimensional.

To get a feel for what this means, suppose you are a painter and I am a sculptor, and you want to paint a picture of my groovy sculpture. How will you go about this? You could put a pane of glass in front of my sculpture and simply trace the form (and background) that you see through the glass, as shown in Figure 3.2. That would work marvelously as long as you didn't move your head. If you moved your head—for example, if you leaned to the right—the location of the sculpture would move relative to the glass, so the painting would be ruined. But if you stick with one point of view you can reliably turn a three-dimensional scene into a two-dimensional scene. There is a single mapping of the three-dimensional scene into two dimensions, even if you bring in a different painter, as long as the positions of the sculpture, the glass, and the painter stay the same.

But if you show someone else the two-dimensional painting on the pane of glass, could that person know what the sculpture looks like? In other words, could he or she reconstruct the three-dimensional scene? No, because an infinite number of possible scenes are consistent with any two-dimensional picture. That's the inverse projection problem your visual system constantly faces. In the case of the visual system, the two-dimensional representation is the pattern of light on the retina. Your retina is two dimensional, and recovering three-dimensional information about objects in the world poses the same problems as described in the sculpture painting example. So, the visual system must deal with **shape and orientation indeterminacy**.

A second thing we want to know about an object is its surface features: what color it is, how dark or light it is, and so on. Shape can distinguish a cherry from an apple, but it is color, not shape, that will tell us whether the cherry is ripe.

We run into a problem in trying to determine an object's color and brightness because the only source of information we have about surface features is the light that enters the eye. The technical term for the amount of light the eye receives is **luminance**. Three factors contribute to luminance: the amount of illumination (a 100-W light bulb, a 25-W light bulb, the sun), the reflectance of the object (white, black, gray), and whether the object is in shadow. A piece of coal viewed in bright sunlight actually has higher luminance than a snowball viewed in candlelight. Nevertheless, the coal looks black and the snowball looks white. How does the visual system unravel the three factors that contribute to luminance so it gets the reflectance of objects right?

For an example, look at the Mach card stimulus in Figure 3.3. What does it look like to you? This figure could depict an arrow-shaped object that is white on top and gray on the bottom. Or the object could be an open book, face-down, illuminated from the top, so the bottom is in shadow. Thus, this is called **light source, reflectance, and shadow indeterminancy**.

Object size and distance also are indeterminate from a two-dimensional representation. Bear in mind that everything you know about objects in the world comes from the image that the object projects onto the retina. In general, larger objects do project larger images onto the retina, but the size of the retinal projection also depends on the distance between the object and the observer. If you see a square that appears small, is it truly a small square, or is it actually a large square that is far away? Thus, this is called **size and distance indeterminancy**.

One real world example of the relationship between object size and distance involves the sun and the moon. Although the moon is much smaller than the sun, it is also much closer. It so happens that these two factors balance out nearly perfectly; the sun and moon project same-size images on the retina and thus appear to be the same size when viewed from the earth. That's why the moon just covers the sun during a total eclipse. The moon

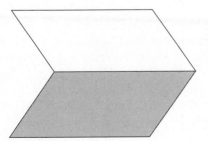

Figure 3.3. A Mach card. The gray part of the figure could be gray because the surface of the object depicted is gray, or it could be gray because the surface is white but it is in shadow.

would not appear to be the same size as the sun from a vantage point nearer or farther than the earth.

The main things you would want to know about an object—its shape, the color and brightness of its surface, its size, its distance—are indeterminate from the information that is available to the retina, so that's why vision is hard. How then are we able to see?

Stand-on-One-Foot Question

1. *Name the three indeterminacies that make visual perception difficult.*

Questions That Require Two Feet

2. *Size and distance are indeterminate, so if you see a car that appears small, you can't know whether it is a big car far away or a small car close by. Yet, you seem to have no problem figuring that out. Why?*

3. *The apparent size of the tip of your thumb when held at arm's length is about the same size as the moon, viewed from the earth, as Tom Hanks showed us in the movie* Apollo 13. *Would it work the same way if you stood on the moon and looked at the earth? That is, would the tip of your thumb appear about the same size as the earth?*

How Are Visual Ambiguities Resolved?

Preview

How does our cognitive system resolve the ambiguities inherent in visual perception so we can accurately interpret what we see? The answer is that we make unconscious assumptions that resolve the ambiguities. Shape and orientation are resolved by assuming that objects are not in unusual orientations. Shape perception is also influenced by the frame of reference in which the object is viewed. Light source, reflectance, and shadow are resolved by making assumptions about the color of objects and typical ambient lighting. Size and distance are usually resolved by using cues to distance in the environment (e.g., an object that partially covers another must be closer to the observer).

Ecological psychologists propose that all these problems and ambiguities may be more in the minds of psychologists than in the visual fields of observers. They propose that the environment actually provides a variety of cues that make the job of vision much simpler than it first appears. We examine the sorts of cues they claim that people use.

The short answer to the question of how visual ambiguities are resolved is that these insoluble problems become solvable if you are willing to make assumptions. Your visual system makes assumptions about the nature of objects in the world and how they are illuminated. You should note that these assumptions are not made by some executive part of the visual system. Rather, they are built into the way the visual system itself is engineered, the same way many cameras are designed with the assumption that pictures will be shot in daylight.

Yet the assumptions built into the visual system do not guarantee a correct solution. Indeed, if you know these assumptions, you can create two-dimensional paintings that look compellingly three dimensional, or you can induce the visual system to make errors as visual illusions do. The main point is that vision is not a representation of exactly what is in the world; it is a representation of what is probably in the world. It's a construction based on wise gambles. We'll go through the key visual properties of objects—shape, brightness, size, and distance—one by one.

Shape

Let's start with the square shown in Figure 3.1. Why do you call the figure a square and not a cube? Your visual system is sensitive to what sorts of objects are likely to have projected a particular image onto your retina. Yes, the object could be a cube, but think of all the different angles at which a cube could be positioned. Only a few views of a cube look like a square, so your visual system assumes that what you're seeing is actually a square. Hermann von Helmholtz (1910/1962), one of the first giants of vision research, called this the **likelihood principle**. This principle has been important in many modern theories of vision, although as some researchers have pointed out, it's hard to distinguish whether the visual system interprets stimuli using likelihood or simplicity as the guide (Chater, 1996; Pomerantz & Kubovy, 1986; van der Helm, 2000).

We can state generally that the likelihood principle implies that a two-dimensional straight line will be interpreted as being straight in three dimensions, and lines that appear parallel in two dimensions will be interpreted as parallel in three dimensions. From most vantage points, lines that are truly parallel (or nearly so) in three-dimensional space will appear that way in a two-dimensional representation, whatever the viewing angle. (This principle works only for short lines, such as those that define the edges of objects.) To see that this is true, take out your wallet, a pen, or another object with parallel sides. Watch the opposing, nearly parallel edges of the object as you rotate it, and you'll see that the edges remain parallel even as the angle of viewing changes.

But there is another way in which our square is ambiguous. Couldn't it be a diamond that has been rotated? This question illustrates the importance of **frame of reference** in the perception of shape: The position or orientation or motion of an object is always defined relative to something else. For example, using the earth as a frame of reference, the sun moves around the earth. Using

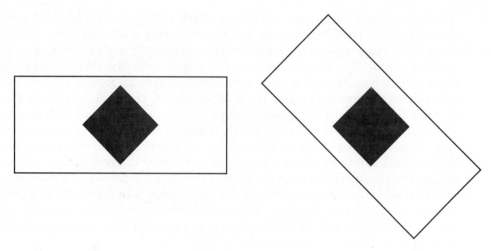

Figure 3.4. Visual and gravitational frames of reference.

the sun as a frame of reference, the earth moves around the sun. The same relationship is true at smaller scales; if you and I face each other and there is a pencil on the floor to my right, the pencil is to your left. When we locate the pencil relative to a spatial frame of reference centered on me, you don't share that frame of reference. Using the room as the frame of reference, however, we would both think of the pencil as being in the same location.

Much of the time, the perceptual system uses gravity to establish a frame of reference that is independent of the viewer's position. Look at the square in Figure 3.1 again, this time tilting your head 45 degrees. It still looks like a square, right? That's because your frame of reference is still based on the surrounding environment, defined by gravity.

Figure 3.4 shows two versions of the same shape, which looks different in the two panels. At left it looks like a diamond, and at right it looks like a rotated square (Kopferman, 1930). Steve Palmer and his associates (Palmer, Simone, & Kube, 1988; see also Lipshits & McIntyre, 1999) demonstrated that the gravity-based orientation of a diamond or square can be overridden by a purely visual frame of reference, in this case a rectangle. Participants were to report whether they saw a square or diamond (relative to gravity). On some trials, there was no reference frame except gravity. On other trials, the square or diamond was surrounded by a rectangle that was either upright or tilted at 45 degrees. Thus, there were two possible frames of reference, visual and gravitational, that could either agree (as in the left panel of Figure 3.4) or disagree (as in the right panel). Participants were faster to make their decision when the two reference frames agreed than when they disagreed.

It is clear that in addition to assumptions based on likelihood, such as whether we are viewing an object head-on given particular visual information, frames of reference play a critical role in shape disambiguation and perception of orientation.

Figure 3.5.   The three factors that contribute to luminance—light source, shading, and shadow.

Brightness

A change in luminance (the amount of light hitting the retina) can result from a number of factors. For example, the cylinder in Figure 3.5 appears to be uniformly colored, and there is a light shining on it from the right. However, it is possible that the cylinder is illuminated evenly but is colored lighter gray on the right and darker on the left. The visual system makes several simple assumptions to choose between these alternatives.

First, the visual system assumes that surfaces are uniformly colored. That's why shading makes such a difference in the three-dimensional quality of a painting. Changes in shading are assumed by the visual system to reflect shadows caused by hills and valleys in the surface of an object, not variations in the brightness of the object itself. The full moon looks so flat because it is uniformly bright. When the light of the sun strikes the many craters and hills of the moon, it reflects at many angles. Thus, the brightness is even across the entire full moon, making it appear to be a disk and not a sphere.

The second assumption is that gradual changes in brightness could be caused by shadows. Shadows have fuzzy edges, but changes in the reflectance of a surface typically do not (Casati, 2004). Hence, it is easy to distinguish the change in brightness caused by the cylinder's shadow from the change in brightness caused by the light and dark square of the checkerboard; the shadow has fuzzy borders. Another important cue to shadows comes from movement. If an object moves, its shadow moves in association with the object.

Nevertheless, there is still ambiguity in decoding information that comes from shape. Look again at the Mach card in Figure 3.3. It could be a

Photo 3.1. Light sources are assumed to come from above, so this object appears to be an indentation or crater. See what happens to the figure if you turn the book upside-down.

book that is open with its spine toward you, with a light source from above, or it could be a book that is open and facing you, with a light source from below. In interpreting shading information, the visual system assumes that light comes from above an object—a sensible assumption because vision evolved in a world where light almost always comes from the sun. The assumption that light comes from above is what makes the crater in Photo 3.1 look concave; turn this book upside-down and see what happens when the pattern of shading changes. Even when we can clearly see that the light source is not from above, we cannot adjust our visual system to the violation of this assumption, so common objects such as faces look strange, as shown in Photo 3.2.

Now let's consider the checkerboard pattern in Figure 3.5. Believe it or not, the white squares that are in shadow are the same shade of gray as the dark squares that are not in shadow. (Cover the surrounding areas, and compare the two squares to see that this is true.) The visual system uses **local contrast** to evaluate the likely shade of each square; the perceived surface lightness depends on the light-to-dark ratios of areas that are next to one another in the same plane. Squares surrounded by darker squares (in shadow or not) are considered to be light. The sharp boundaries of the squares also help the visual system determine that the boundaries are likely to be created by paint, not shadows, because shadows usually have fuzzy edges. Thus, the checkerboard is easy to interpret as being a field with light and dark squares. Hence, the light squares look light even when they are in shadow.

Photo 3.2.   Another example of the impact of the assumption that light sources come from above. We know that facial features are convex, but light coming from below makes them appear concave, yielding an eerie effect.

The fact that you don't perceive the similarity of brightness between the light squares that are in shadow and the dark squares seen in full light may seem like a failing of the visual system. But as Edward Adelson (1998), who designed this illusion, points out, it does not reflect a failing of the visual system but rather a success. Your visual system does not need to assess the absolute brightness of regions of space. It needs to analyze complex scenes to find simple, meaningful components, such as "checkerboard with dark and light patches, partly in shadow."

Distance and Size

Size and distance trade off: When an object is far away it appears small, and when it is near it seems large. How can we determine the true size and distance of the object? There are two classes of answers to this question. One group of strategies is rooted in the visual system, whereas the other is information derived from the environment.

CUES IN THE VISUAL SYSTEM.   There are three cues to depth that are based on properties of the visual system. The first is **accommodation**. The lens of the eye changes shape in order to focus an image on the retina. The shape change of the lens varies, depending on how much the muscles that change the shape are flexed. This cue is important only at relatively close ranges (less than 1 m or so), where the muscles must work quite hard.

Another cue to depth is **convergence**. As an object gets closer, your eyes "cross" increasingly more to gaze at it. You point your eyes at an object so the light reflecting from it falls on the center of the retina, which is called the **fovea**. This part of the retina is the most accurate at seeing small details. Because your eyes are some distance apart, when objects are fairly close to you, your eyes start to cross to keep the image on the fovea of each eye. However, convergence is useful as a cue to distance only when objects are fairly close. For objects that are moderately far away (say, more than 20 feet), the eyes are nearly parallel, so convergence is not helpful.

Stereopsis is a more important cue to distance. Because the eyes are in different places, they get slightly different views of an object. Hold one finger in front of your face, and rapidly open and close your left and right eyes, alternately. Does your finger seem to change positions? This difference in view of the left and right eye is called **retinal disparity**.

Now look at the left part of Figure 3.6. When both eyes are rotated so points *A* and *B* fall on the fovea, they receive different views. The points seem closer together to the left eye than to the right eye; compare the size of the angles created at the fovea by *A* and *B* in each eye. In the right side of the figure, the difference between the views of the two eyes is not as extreme, so the angles are closer to being the same. Thus, the disparity between the views of the left and right eyes is larger for nearby objects. The visual system uses the difference between the left and right eye to figure out how far away an object must be. If a tree appears in roughly the same place on the left and right retinas, it is quite distant. If its position is very different in each eye, the visual system would know the tree is nearby.

The cues that we've been discussing—accommodation, convergence, and stereopsis—are all based on properties of our eyes. We now turn to other cues to distance or size that are inherent in the environment.

CUES IN THE ENVIRONMENT.   Experience is one thing that tells us the size of objects; this cue is called **familiar size**. When we see a car, we assume it is the size of a normal car, even if it is far away and therefore appears small. Similarly, people should be people-sized, houses house-sized, and so forth. We don't often see an object that we've never encountered before, which would give us no clue as to its likely size.

Bill Epstein (1965; see also Marotta & Goodale, 2001) showed the importance (and the limits) of familiar size as a cue to distance. He took photographs of a dime, a quarter, and a half-dollar, and then printed each coin as the size of a quarter. Epstein mounted the photographs on black rods and placed them an equal distance from the observer. The room was darkened, and the photographs

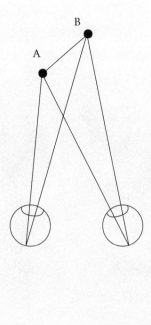

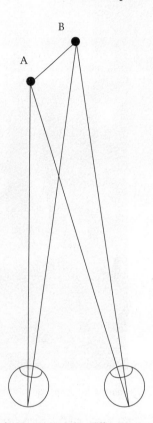

Figure 3.6. The left and right eye get different views of objects, and this difference is greater when the observer is closer to the object. In the left-hand figure, the distance between *A* and *B* seems larger to the right eye than to the left eye. The greater distance is apparent from the greater angle of the two lines going to the right eye. The difference between the left eye and the right eye is not as great in the figure on the right, where the distance between observer and object is greater.

were illuminated with a spotlight. The participants had to view them monocularly (i.e., with one eye only). The participants believed the photographs were real coins, and because they appeared to be the same size, participants judged them to be different distances away (e.g., a real dime would have to be closer than the half-dollar for the coins to look the same size).

Thus, familiar size can influence the perception of size and distance. But Epstein's results changed completely when people viewed the stimuli binocularly (i.e., using both eyes), seeing the coin photos as they actually were—equidistant and of equal size. Binocular viewing made a difference because participants could use stereopsis, and pitted against familiar size, stereopsis was the clear winner.

Familiar size solves the size–distance trade-off by providing information about size. Other cues in the environment concern distance and are often called **pictorial cues**. Many of these cues are used in a well-known painting

Photo 3.3.   Jean-François Millet's painting *The Gleaners* uses many pictorial depth cues.

by Jean-François Millet, *The Gleaners*, shown in Photo 3.3. One such cue is
occlusion. An object that is in front of another will partly overlap it. In the
painting, the image of the central figure overlaps the figure on the left. That is
possible only if she is in front of the figure on the left.

The Gleaners provides another cue to distance called **texture gradient**. In
the foreground, individual stalks of cut wheat are visible, but higher in the
picture plane, they are not. In the real world, we can make out more detail
when things are nearby, so objects in the lower part of the picture that are
more detailed look closer. It is possible, of course, that the background is not
farther away, and there happen to be no individual stalks of wheat in those regions; but again, the visual system assumes that surfaces (in this case, the surface of the field) are uniform, so the lack of detail higher in the picture plane
is interpreted as indicating distance.

This picture also gives some sense of **linear perspective**. Lines that are
parallel in three-dimensional space converge in two-dimensional space if you
extend them far enough. (Recall we said before that they still look parallel if
they are short.) The farther the distance, the closer they are to converging. For
example, the sides of a road appear to get closer together in the distance, as
shown at the left in Figure 3.7. This is less obvious from our everyday experience but equally true of parallel lines in three dimensions, as shown at the
right in Figure 3.7.

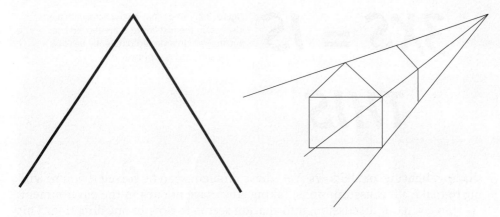

Figure 3.7.   Linear perspective. At left, two parallel lines in a plane (the sides of a road) converge in the far distance. At right, the three parallel sides of a house converge in the distance.

There is subtle linear perspective in *The Gleaners* as well. You can see some lines or shadows on the field to the left of the leftmost figure and to the right of the rightmost figure. As in Figure 3.7, these lines converge toward a vanishing point on the horizon.

The **relative height** of objects also is a cue to distance. The rightmost figure in the painting appears closer than the others not because she occludes anyone but because she is lower in the visual field. To her right is a figure on horseback. This figure is very high in the visual field, indicating great distance, which is reinforced by the very small size. This is not a microscopic horse hovering over her shoulder.

The final distance cue used in the painting is **atmospheric perspective**. Objects in the distance look indistinct and often have a hazy, bluish appearance. The air is full of dust and water particles that scatter light, so if you view a distant object, more of the light reflected from the object is scattered by the time it hits your eye. The image of these distant objects is blurred because much of the light has been scattered.

Why are there so many cues to distance? The reason is that they are useful for objects at different distances. It's true that size and distance trade off, but distance is usually discernible from one of these cues, and knowing distance helps us decide on size.

Top-Down Influences in Vision

We've seen that visual processing is complicated because the two-dimensional image on the retina underspecifies what the three-dimensional world looks like. You can't tell what the shape of an object is from the retinal projection because shape and orientation trade off; you can't tell the size or distance of an object because these two factors trade off; and you can't tell whether an object is white, gray, or black because differences in luminance could result from

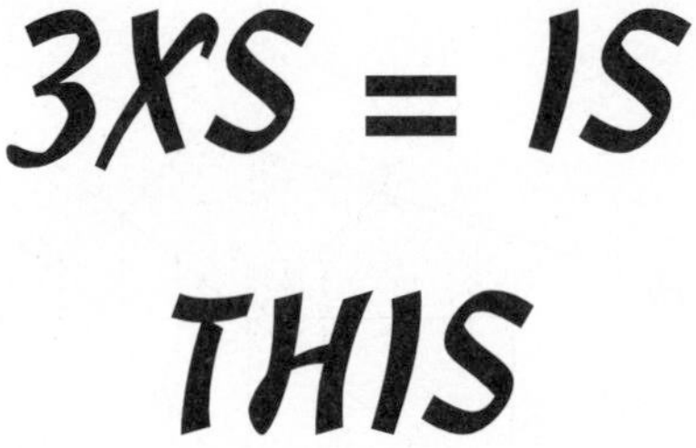

3XS = IS
THIS

Figure 3.8. The final two characters are identical in the first line and the second line, but they are interpreted differently because of the surrounding context.

shading, lighting, or shadows. Yet, these problems can be solved if you're willing to make a few assumptions, taking advantage of cues in the environment.

So far in our discussion, information seems to flow in one direction. This **bottom-up processing** begins with raw, unprocessed sensory information and builds toward more conceptual representations. But bottom-up processing can't handle all vision alone (Kayser, Körding, & König, 2004).

For example, how can the mind arrive at different interpretations of the last two characters in each line of Figure 3.8? This demonstration seems to argue for **top-down processing** in which conceptual knowledge influences the processing or interpretation of lower-level perceptual processes. If you're reading the second line in the figure, the conceptual knowledge that you are reading letters leads you to interpret the ambiguous characters as the letters that complete the word "THIS." People do use conceptual information when they see, up to a point.

In a classic experiment showing the effects of conceptual information on vision, Stephen Palmer (1975) presented participants with complex scenes. Participants were given 2 s to look at the scene—plenty of time to figure out that it was a kitchen, for example. Next, one of three objects was flashed within the scene very briefly: either a contextually appropriate object (bread), a similarly shaped contextually inappropriate object (a mailbox), or an object that didn't fit the context and wasn't shaped like the target object. The objects were flashed for just 65 ms. Participants correctly identified the contextually appropriate object 80% of the time but were right only 40% of the time for the other objects. Similar effects have been demonstrated by Irving Biederman (1981).

Of course, you would recognize the mailbox eventually, even when it is out of context. However, there are some instances in which you can't identify an object without the context. For example, the third shape from the right at the bottom of Figure 3.9 could be the letter *C*, a hook, or a sideways hill. There's really no telling. Once it is seen in context, as at the top of the figure, it is perfectly recognizable, but in isolation none of the parts is identifiable.

We've been assuming that processing is mostly bottom-up. In that case, you would look at Figure 3.9 and identify the nose, the ear, the eye, and so on, and finally put all the pieces together and figure out that it's a face. But we've just said that you can't figure out that an item is a nose (or an ear, or whatever) until you know that it's part of a face. Palmer called this situation

Figure 3.9.   This figure is easy to recognize when the parts are seen together (in a sensible spatial arrangement), even though it is composed of parts that are difficult to recognize alone.

the **parsing paradox.** Parsing means figuring out the pieces of a larger whole. Thus, the parsing paradox is the apparent impossibility of identifying the face in Figure 3.9 until you know it has a nose, a mouth, and so on. But you can't identify the nose, mouth, and so on, until you know it's a face.

Palmer suggested that the resolution to the parsing paradox is that we do both top-down and bottom-up processing simultaneously and each type of processing helps the other, as shown in Figure 3.10.

There is obviously a role for top-down processes in visual perception; vision operates more quickly when contextually consistent information is perceived and ambiguous stimuli are perceived in a way that is consistent with context. But top-down processes must take a back seat to bottom-up processes. When something truly unusual appears in the environment (say, a chimp typing at a computer), you may be slower to perceive it because it is out of context, but you do perceive it.

An Alternative: The Ecological Approach

A second point of view on the whole problem of vision contends that the model posed at the beginning of the chapter is flat-out wrong. (I heard you sigh.) Up until now, we have been discussing what is often called the **computational approach,** which assumes that the information in the environment is impoverished—all the retina has to work with is a series of lines—and

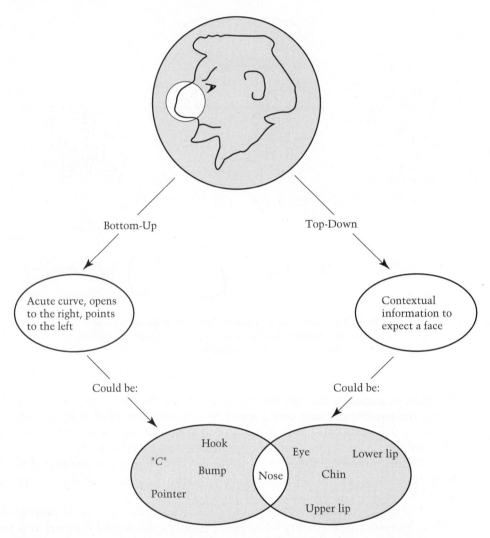

Figure 3.10.   We can use top-down and bottom-up processing simultaneously to identify objects.

therefore the visual system must do a great deal of computing to recover the three-dimensional shapes and movements of the environment.

    J. J. Gibson (1979) is considered to be the founder of the **ecological approach** to visual perception. Gibson believed vision looks so hard because psychologists have done a terrible job of describing the environment. According to Gibson, the environment contains a variety of cues that specify what is out in the world, but psychologists act as though the environment were composed of nothing but lines. If the retina had no information besides lines, it would be extremely challenging to get an accurate representation of what's in the world. Gibson believed that there is much more information in the world of which

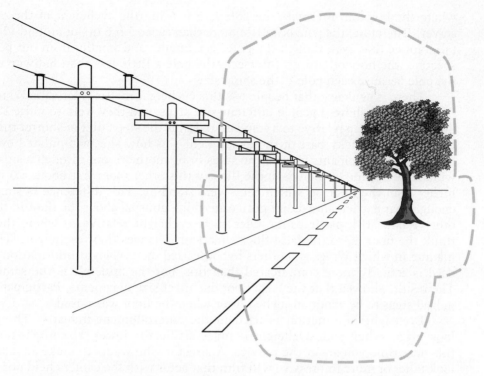

Figure 3.11. An example of how eyeheight provides information about object size. Objects meet the horizon at the eyeheight of the observer (outlined in gray). If the observer's eyeheight is 5 ft from the ground, the horizon intersects the telephone pole at 5 ft. The horizon intersects a little less than halfway up the pole, so the pole is somewhat more than 10 ft tall. Adapted from *The Ecological Approach to Visual Perception,* by J. J. Gibson et al., 1979, Boston: Houghton Mifflin, Fig. 9.6, p. 165.

we can take advantage. The visual system need not perform elaborate computations because the information in the visual environment is quite rich. Let's go through two examples of these sorts of information sources.

OBJECT SIZE.   If I see an unfamiliar object (or a familiar object that can take many different sizes, such as a tree), how can I determine its size?

The approach we've been using until now would say that because it's an unfamiliar object I'd have to first figure out about how far away it is. I could do that from stereopsis. Then, I'd note how big the retinal image is (i.e., how big it looks) and work back to how big the actual object is, based on its distance.

Other researchers pointed out that better size information was already in the environment (Mark, 1987; Rogers, 1996; Warren, 1984). The horizon line intersects with an object at the **eyeheight** of the observer (at the height of the observer's eyes). Figure 3.11 shows the gray outline of an observer's head—let's say mine. I'm about 6 ft tall, so my eyeheight is around 5 ft 6 in. Therefore, the horizon intersects with the object at 5 ft 6 in. Notice that the horizon intersects with the telephone poles a little below the middle of the pole; the spot where the horizon intersects the pole is 5 ft 6 in. (the eyeheight of the observer). Therefore, the pole is a little more than twice 5 ft 6 in., or around 12 ft tall. Notice that even though the poles get smaller and smaller from our perspective, the horizon always intersects the pole a little less than halfway up the pole because each pole is the same size.

There is evidence that people use this eyeheight metric. Maryjane Wraga (1999a, 1999b) showed people different-size steps, and they were to judge the height of each step relative to a standard rod (was the step taller or shorter than the rod?). The tricky part of the experiment was how she manipulated eyeheight. The participants viewed the steps from another room through a small window. On some of the trials, the floor of this other room was about 6.5 in. higher than the floor on which they were standing. This difference is small enough that participants didn't notice anything unusual about the floor in the other room. Still, participants judge their eyeheight relative to where they think the floor is, so the false floor effectively changes their eyeheight. (The manner in which Wraga and others hypothesized the eyeheight information is used is actually more complicated than this, but the principle is the same.) The results showed that the false floor did affect size judgments: Participants judged steps to be about an inch shorter when the floor was raised.

Eyeheight information is used in the entertainment industry. Things look bigger when your eyeheight is made artificially lower. You might note this next time you are at the movies. A director who wants to make an actor look taller or more impressive will film that actor with the camera held not at eye level, but at perhaps waist level, effectively lowering the eyeheight of the moviegoer and thereby making the participant seem taller (see Photo 3.4).

DISTANCE FOR NAVIGATION.   Suppose you're playing left field in a baseball game and someone hits a ball your way. How do you get to the right position to catch it? Well, maybe you calculate the trajectory of the ball, judge where it is going to land, and run to that spot. That would take a fair amount of calculation. But it turns out that a simple cue in the environment can be used instead.

Michael McBeath, Dennis Shaffer, and Mary Kaiser (1995) provided evidence that people actually catch a fly ball by running so the trajectory of the ball looks like a straight line. Imagine a two-dimensional picture in which the baseball goes upward and to the left. If you run in a direction that makes the ball appear to travel in a straight line, you will go directly to the spot where the ball will land. The details of the geometry are complex, but the basic point is quite simple. There is even evidence that Frisbee-catching dogs use this principle (Shaffer, Krauchunas, Eddy, & McBeath, 2004). It's a beautiful example of the ecological approach.

The ecological approach holds that most vision researchers make the problem of visual perception more difficult than it actually is. Once we have fully described all the rich sources of information available in the environment, they argue, many of the problems of visual perception disappear. Are they right?

Photo 3.4. *The Terminator* is shot with the camera low to the ground. We assume that the camera is at our eyeheight, so the Terminator appears taller and more intimidating.

To a point, I think the answer must be yes. Ecological psychologists have made this point in the experiments described previously and in others. Still, it is not difficult to find common ground between the two perspectives; even the most determined ecological researchers admit that the perceptual system must do some processing on the information in the environment, and even the most determined computational researchers admit that the environment may contain subtle sources of information that the visual system can use. Thus, the difference between the perspectives may best be thought of as one of emphasis.

Stand-on-One-Foot Questions

4. *What assumptions does the visual system make about luminance?*
5. *What's the difference between top-down and bottom-up processing?*
6. *Summarize the differences between the computational and the ecological points of view.*

Questions That Require Two Feet

7. *Can you use your book and the writing on the cover to demonstrate a frame-of-reference effect in the same way we showed one with the diamond and the rectangle around it?*

8. *I once stood on a hill overlooking San Francisco on a brilliantly clear day, and the city looked like a small model seen at about 30 ft rather than a full-size city seen at a distance. Why?*

9. *Can you think of a way to use what you know about perceived size and eyeheight to improve your relationship with a young child?*

What Is Visual Perception For?

Preview

Vision helps you know what objects are in the world and helps you navigate (move around). For objects to be recognized, there must be some representation in memory of what they look like. But an object such as a car looks very different from the front, back, and side. Does that mean you need three mental representations to be sure you can recognize it from each perspective? One group of theories holds that you have a single mental representation of an object that is suitable from any angle. Another group of theories proposes that you keep several representations of each object in memory. We discuss the merits of each of these ideas. We also discuss navigation and focus on the difference between conscious visual perception and visual perception that supports navigation. One set of visual processes supports our conscious perception of where things are and what objects are out in the world. Another set of processes, privileged to the motor system, helps you move, but you can't get conscious access to their contents.

Attributes of objects, such as size, shape, and distance, are not the end of perceptual processing because only occasionally do we want information about a single attribute. More often, we combine attributes in the visual field to achieve one of two goals: We want to know the identity of objects around us, and we want to know their locations. Knowing an object's identity helps us know what to do to it. If it's an apple, eat it; if it's a stapler, squeeze it; if it's a book of "Family Circus" comic strips, ignore it. Knowing an object's location is helpful so you will know where it is relative to you, where the best place to grasp it is, whether there are obstacles in the way if you decide to grasp it, and so on.

One part of the perceptual system is responsible for figuring out what an object is. Another is responsible for figuring out properties of the object (size, orientation, and so on) that are important for interacting with it. Object identity has been much more thoroughly studied, so we can say more about how that might work. Only recently was it concluded that the visual action system is separate from the object identity system; most of our discussion focuses on how researchers drew that conclusion.

Identifying Objects

We have discussed how the visual system determines the attributes of objects (their distance, size, and brightness). But how does it identify what those objects are? Shape is the most obvious characteristic we use to identify objects—for example, a banana is easy to recognize because of its shape—but other properties can be helpful, too. For example, you can identify the handle on a chest of drawers by its location, even if it has a very unusual shape. A piece of cheese and a brick may have similar shapes, but they are distinguishable based on their color and texture. Thus, the first thing we should realize is that many cues contribute to visual object recognition. Most researchers have focused on shape, however, probably because it is the most reliable cue to object identity.

The core question of object identification is this: What does the memory representation that supports object identification look like? Suppose you recognize that an animal is a cat. Some information in memory must enable you to identify that animal. You have to have some information stored about what cats look like. What kind of information is it?

There are two families of answers to this question. First, the representation in memory could be specific to your viewpoint; you store how the object looks to you, not its actual structure. This is called a **viewer-centered representation** because the representation of the object depends on how the viewer sees it. The second family of theories claims that you store how the object looks independent of any particular viewpoint. In **object-centered representation**, the locations of the object's parts are defined relative to the object itself, not relative to the viewer. A viewer-centered representation of an airplane might contain the information that its nose is to the left of its tail. That representation won't work, however, if the plane is turned around or if the viewer is looking at the plane from the front. The object-centered representation locates an object's parts relative to its other parts; thus, it would contain the information that the plane's nose is attached to the fuselage.

For both families of theories, a key problem is dealing with rotated objects. You never know in what orientation you'll see a cat; it might be running, climbing a tree, or curled up by a fire. Think of what an odd profile a cat has when it is curled up by a fire. According to object-centered theories, the representation in memory can't be specific to one viewpoint because an object can appear in different orientations. This claim seems self-evident, yet the viewer-centered theories have a response, as we'll see.

OLDER THEORIES.   An early viewer-centered theory of object recognition was the **template** theory, which proposed that we recognize an object by comparing its retinal image to a representation of the object in memory. Basically,

Figure 3.12. In the top figure, the observer recognizes the armadillo because it matches his armadillo template. If the same armadillo is turned 180 degrees, the observer cannot identify it because it no longer matches the template.

this theory held that we store pictures of what objects are supposed to look like, with labels attached, and then compare images with these templates. If a template matches what we see, we have identified the object. There are many problems with this model. The easiest one to appreciate is depicted in Figure 3.12.

As Figure 3.12 shows, if the armadillo turned a bit, it wouldn't match the template, so you'd need another template to match that view of the armadillo. Such a system would require an enormous number of templates. The truth is that no one ever took the template-matching idea very seriously, but it remains popular as a whipping boy, especially in cognitive psychology textbooks.

Template matching does have some practical uses, however. Vending machines use template matching to evaluate paper money. A bill must be inserted in the machine at a particular orientation so the machine can identify it.

Feature-matching theories (e.g., Selfridge & Neisser, 1960) put forward in response to the problems of template-matching theories still used a viewer-centered representation, but they avoided many of the problems of template theories by proposing **critical features** of stimuli. For example, the letter *T*

	Vertical lines	Horizontal lines	Oblique lines	Right angles	Acute angles	Continuous curves	Discontinuous curves
A		1	2		3		
B	1	3		4			2
C							1
D	1	2		2			1
E	1	3		4			
F	1	2		3			
G	1	1		1			1
H	2	1		4			
I	1	2		4			
J	1						1
K	1		2	1	2		
L	1	1		1			
M	2		2		3		
N	2		1		2		
O						1	
P	1	2		3			1
Q		1			2	1	
R	1	2	1	3			1
S							2
T	1	1		2			
U	2						1
V			2		1		
W			4		3		
X			2		2		
Y	1		2		1		
Z		2	1		2		

Figure 3.13. The top row labels the features of letters in the alphabet. Each letter can be described according to the number of each feature it contains. From *Human Information Process: An Introduction to Psychology,* by P. H. Lindsay and D. A. Norman, 1977, New York: Academic Pres, Table 7.1, p. 264.

could be defined as having two features: a horizontal line and a vertical line. Changing the size or color of the letter won't change its critical features. You can think of a set of critical features as being a set of lines and curves out of which you could create letters, as shown in Figure 3.13.

Feature-matching theories have several important advantages over template theories. First, in our example, letters can still be recognized even after different transformations. For example, all uppercase As share the same set of critical features. Although they may vary in size, and some have extra, noncritical features such as serifs, most capital As have two diagonal lines and one horizontal line. Feature theories also appear to be consistent with known neurophysiology. David Hubel and Torsten Wiesel won a Nobel prize for their groundbreaking work showing that brain cells in visual cortex seemed to respond to lines at different orientations. These cells seemed to be acting as feature detectors, bolstering the feature theory (see Hubel & Wiesel, 1979, for a review).

There are problems with feature matching, however. For example, a sideways letter *R* is not hard for people to identify, although it has none of the critical features of an upright *R*. Furthermore, it is hard to see how feature theories can account for the perception of natural objects. Researchers built feature theories that could recognize letters of the alphabet. It's fairly obvious what the features of a letter are, but what are the features of a dog? Can you develop a theory of how a dog could be "broken down" into features?[1]

OBJECT-CENTERED THEORIES.   Feature-matching theories failed because they could not recognize rotated letters (and presumably other rotated objects) and because there was no obvious way in which they could be extended to natural objects. The solutions to these problems were to make the representations object-centered rather than viewer-centered and to show that natural objects can be broken down into features.

The object-centered answer to recognizing an *R* that is rotated relative to the viewer starts by noting that the parts of the *R* are not rotated relative to one another. If your frame of reference is the object, then all parts are where they are supposed to be relative to one another. Thus, when you are looking at a natural object like a dog, you shouldn't look for a head at the top and feet at the bottom. You should look for a head connected to a neck, feet connected to legs, a tail connected to the back, and so on (Biederman & Gerhardson, 1993). The relationships between the parts do not change, depending on whether the dog is facing left or right, running, or curled up.

But using this representation of parts relative to each other relies on your being able to recognize the parts themselves. How do you do that? How do you "decompose" a dog into parts?

Several feature theories that use geometric solids, instead of simple lines and curves, have been offered. An influential one was proposed by Irving Biederman (1987), who argued that object recognition is supported by a set of 36 shapes he called geons (simple shapes that look like bricks, cylinders, and so on) that operate like letters of the alphabet. Complex objects can be built from them, as shown in the left column of Figure 3.14, and in Photo 3.5.

A strength of Biederman's theory is that geons are easy to distinguish from one another. For example, from most viewing angles, the geon called a brick has three parallel edges and intersections that look like arrows, and a

---

[1]You may wonder why researchers based their theories on letters of the alphabet. There were good reasons for doing this. First, people wanted to make their theories comparable to one another. If my theory recognizes letters and yours recognizes faces, how can we compare the theories to see which one works better? Letters gave everyone a standard stimulus set with which to work. Second, letter recognition was an important applied problem. There are obvious uses to devising a machine that can recognize letters of different fonts and sizes.

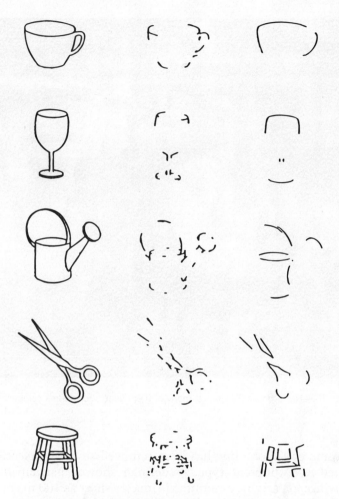

Figure 3.14. Examples of common objects that can be constructed with the geons proposed in Biederman's theory. The center and right columns show two ways of decomposing the figures: by either retaining line vertices (center) or omitting them (right). In accordance with Biederman's theory, it is easier to identify objects when the vertices are still present. From *"Recognition-by-Components: A Theory of Human Image Understanding,"* by I. Biederman, 1987, *Psychological Review, 94(2)*, Fig. 16, p. 135.

cylinder has two parallel edges, two curved edges, and two line intersections that look like a *Y*.

Biederman showed participants pictures of objects constructed from geons, similar to those in Figure 3.14. The pictures were degraded in one of two ways. In each case, he deleted the same total length of line segments. In the center column, the intersections have been left intact, and in the right column, many of the intersections have been removed or changed—for example,

Photo 3.5. The artist used simple shapes, many of them geons, to create a compelling sculpture.

in some cases, one line has been removed so an intersection could be interpreted as a different type. Biederman showed participants the incomplete drawings for varying amounts of time (as short as 100 ms or as long as 5 s) and asked them to name the objects depicted. If the vertices were present, people were pretty good at this task. They named 90% of the pictures they could see for 750 ms. With the vertices removed, however, participants only got 30% correct, even if they saw the pictures for 5 s. These data support Biederman's contention that line intersections are crucial for correctly interpreting geometric solids, and other data indicate that geons may be important in visual memory (Cleary, Langley, & Seiler, 2004). These geometric solids, according to Biederman, are the building blocks of visual object identification.

Although the Biederman model is appealing, not all evidence supports it. Some common objects such as shoes have parts, but the parts don't look like any of the geons. The theory cannot readily account for the recognition of such objects.

VIEWER-CENTERED THEORIES. It seems that object-centered theories would almost have to be right. If the representation of an object is based on your location, you would need a different representation each time you or the object

Photo 3.6. Seen from different angles, the author's car ('93 Ford Probe GT—sweet ride!) looks quite different.

moved. Seen from different angles, common objects can look radically different, as shown in Photo 3.6.

Alternatively, you could mentally rotate the image of an object to fit your mental representation. Thus, a sideways *R* rotated to its normal orientation would match your viewer-centered memory representation of an *R*. The problem with this approach is that it assumes you know how to transform the object so it matches the representation in memory. Should you rotate it clockwise or counterclockwise? Should you twirl it toward or away from you? Don't you need to know what you are looking for before you know how to transform it? But if you know what you're looking for, you've already identified it and there is no need to rotate it. There are technical solutions to these problems (Ullman & Basri, 1991), but they are beyond the scope of this book.

Another, better solution appears to be a compromise: We store multiple viewer-centered representations of objects (perhaps about 40) and then apply some transformations. There is evidence supporting this multiple-view theory. If you have seen an object from only one point of view, you will have only one representation of that object. So, what do you do if you see it from a different point of view? As we said, you rotate your image of the object until it matches the representation. That process of rotating the object takes time. Therefore, if you present the letter *R* rotated 90 degrees from its typical orientation, it should take longer to recognize than if you present *R* in its typical orientation. Note that according to the viewer-independent theory, the orientation of the object shouldn't matter.

Michael Tarr (1995) conducted an experiment to test this hypothesis. He showed participants slides of objects made out of cubes; the objects could look quite different from one viewpoint or another, as shown in Figure 3.15. Tarr trained participants to recognize different objects that were always presented from the same point of view. Later he presented the objects from a novel point of view to see whether participants could recognize them. They could, but the more an object was rotated from the view in which they had seen it during training, the longer participants took to recognize it. It was as if participants' memory of what the object looked like was rather two dimensional—they knew what the object looked like from one point of view—and identifying the

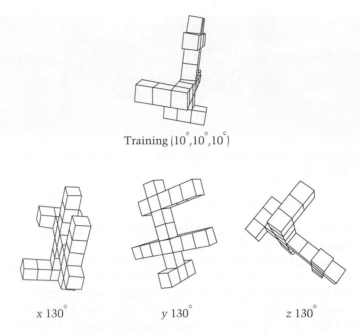

Training $(10^\circ, 10^\circ, 10^c)$

$x\ 130^\circ$ $y\ 130^\circ$ $z\ 130^\circ$

Figure 3.15. Stimuli of the sort used in Tarr's (1995) experiment. The top figure shows a stimulus participants might see at training; the bottom figures show three rotations of this figure in three different planes.

object from another point of view required mentally rotating the stimulus. In another experiment, Tarr presented objects from several points of view during training. In that case, the time it took people to recognize the object was consistent with their imagining the object rotating to the nearest position they had seen during training.

Does this mean that the multiple-view researchers are returning to a template theory in which a nearly infinite number of templates is needed to recognize objects as they rotate through minute angles? Clearly not. Multiple-view theories acknowledge that some process must be available to regularize the image of the object, but that problem becomes much easier to deal with if several views of a complex object may be stored; its appearance will never be too far from one of the stored images.

So which type of theory is correct—decomposition in parts (object centered) or viewer centered? Researchers have tried to collect definitive neuroscientific evidence and have discovered that the brain appears to use both types of representation. Single-cell recording studies in nonhuman primates show that some neurons code objects from a specific viewpoint (e.g., Epstein, Graham, & Downing, 2003; Logothetis, Pauls, & Poggio, 1995), whereas others do not (e.g., Booth & Rolls, 1998). Brain imaging data from humans also show evidence for both types of representation. These clever studies examined adaptation—the brain activation caused by seeing an object drops if you see the same object

Photo 3.7.   See if you can identify these three objects when they are upside down.

repeatedly. But what happens if you see the same object from different views? The viewer-centered theory predicts that the brain activation will drop, whereas the object-centered theory predicts that it will not. Data from different studies support both theories (Burgund & Marsolek, 2000; Fang & He, 2005; Grill-Spector & Malach, 2001; Kourtzi, Erb, Grodd, & Bulthoff, 2003).

These data support earlier theoretical suggestions that the mind may use two methods of recognition, one from each basic approach that serve different functions (Cooper, Schachter, Ballesteros, & Moore, 1992; Farah, 1990; Jolicoeur, 1990; Tarr & Pinker, 1990). The decomposition-into-parts approach may work well to distinguish between a car and a truck, for example, but it can't make finer-grained distinctions between a Ford and a Chrysler. The decomposition-into-parts idea seems to work well for objects that have some telltale geons that make it easy to identify the object regardless of the orientation. The multiple-view approach seems to retain more information about details and thus may be effective for recognizing objects that don't have telltale parts and for distinguishing between closely related objects such as different varieties of cars. Still other theories suggest that both types of representations might work together for object identification (Foster & Gilson, 2002).

ARE SOME OBJECTS SPECIAL?   Look at the objects in Photo 3.7. Could you recognize them without turning the book upside down? Martin Yin (1969) was the first to report that people are greatly impaired in recognizing upside-down faces, but the cost to perceiving other objects did not seem as great. Perhaps you've had this experience when a friend is looking through your photo album. If you're seated across from your friend and are viewing the photos upside down, it's difficult to recognize the faces of people in the photos—even of yourself! The impairment indicates that faces might be perceptually special in some sense. Some data support that interpretation, but as we'll see, this conclusion is controversial.

The "specialness" of face processing is supported by a neuropsychological deficit called **prosopagnosia**, which is a selective deficit in recognizing faces. A patient with prosopagnosia can recognize objects—a radio, a glove, a car—but cannot visually recognize faces, even that of a spouse. However, the patient can recognize people by the sound of their voice or by other nonvisual information, so the deficit appears to be specific to the visual processing of faces (Hécaen & Angelergues, 1962). Because face processing can be damaged selectively, this might be taken to imply that there is a face-processing module that is separate from other types of visual processing.

Brain imaging data appear to be consistent with that hypothesis. Face recognition is strongly associated with activation in the fusiform gyrus of the brain, which is located on the ventral part of the temporal lobe (Kanwisher, McDermott, & Chun, 1997). This area seems so specific for face processing that some have called it the fusiform face area. For example, Galit Yovel and Nancy Kanwisher (2004) showed people houses and faces (either upright or inverted), and asked them to do one of two tasks. One task required focusing on the specific shape of the parts (e.g., the windows or the eyes), and the other task asked them to focus on the distance between the parts. They found that the fusiform face area was always active for the faces and never the houses, and the task performed on the stimuli didn't matter much. The importance of processing faces seems plausible in light of evolution. Because we evolved as a social species, recognizing other individuals is important.

Another explanation of these data is possible. Note that the task of identifying a face is different than identifying an object because you are to say which specific face you see. For an object, you just need to know it's a radio, not which radio. That's hard because all faces share a lot of features in common: two eyes, a nose, a mouth, and so on. It's the distance between the parts that seems to be very important for identifying individual faces. (Of course, some faces have a single identifiable feature—e.g., Hitler's mustache—but not many.) Thus, perhaps the fusiform face area is really specialized to identify individuals, and that requires different processing than identifying a broad object category (Tarr & Gauthier, 2000). In this sense, the fusiform face area supports perceptual expertise (Gauthier, Curran, Curby, & Collins, 2003; Tarr & Cheng, 2003). The same area might support the car enthusiast's ability to distinguish a 1972 Ford Mustang from the 1973 model. It might appear to researchers that the fusiform face area supports face processing only because all of us are face-processing experts—we must differentiate faces all the time.

Jim Haxby and his colleagues (Chao, Martin, & Haxby, 1999; Haxby, Gobbini, Furey, Ishai, Schouten, & Pietrini, 2001; Haxby, Gobbini, & Montgomery, 2004; O'Toole, Jiang, Abdi, & Haxby, 2005) offered a third account of these data. They acknowledge that perceiving faces leads to activation in the fusiform gyrus but point out that brain imaging techniques emphasize the areas of greatest activation. A lot of other areas also show lower levels of activation, but researchers tend to ignore those areas. The peaks of activation for faces may be localized, but large, overlapping areas of the temporal lobe may actually be contributing to the recognition of faces and other objects. In one important demonstration of this idea, Haxby et al. (2001) measured brain activation in fMRI as participants viewed faces, cats, bottles, scissors, shoes, houses, and chairs. The researchers showed that even a brain area that responded maximally to just one type of stimulus still showed identifiable patterns of response to the other categories of objects. Thus, they argue, an area might respond maximally to faces, but it's not just a face area because it still responds to other types of stimuli and seems to be helping to identify them.

A great deal of research has been conducted since the year 2000 to address these three possibilities: localized representation, depending on object type (e.g., faces in one part of the brain); localized processing (e.g., visual expertise in one part of the brain); or distributed representation (e.g., localized peaks of activation for faces, but contribution from large areas of cortex). The topic is so actively researched because it's so important. Researchers are really trying to figure out the principle by which perceptual representations are organized in the brain. Are representations clustered together in the brain so faces are all in the same place? Or are processes clustered together in the brain so all perceptual expertise is in the same place? Or, perhaps nothing is clustered together, and both processes and representations are distributed.

Researchers have tried to pit one theory against the other. For example, would someone who developed prosopagnosia also lose his or her expertise with other stimuli? In a well-known case, a sheep farmer who became prosopagnosic after a stroke was still able to identify individual sheep from photographs of their faces, even though he could not recognize people (McNeil & Warrington, 1993). Other experiments have examined brain activations when butterfly experts or car experts look at butterflies or cars, and activations when these same experts look at faces. Some studies report that activation is in the fusiform face area for faces but in a separate area for these visually expert perceptions (Grill-Spector, Knouf, & Kanwisher, 2004; Rhodes, Byatt, Michie, & Puce, 2004). Other studies, however, report that the brain activation for faces and for expertise is largely overlapping (Gauthier, Skudlarski, Gore, & Anderson, 2000).

In the end, definitive data to choose among these three theories are not yet available. Given the importance of the question and the potential complexity of the answer, it is not surprising that the issue has not yet been settled.

Navigation

The second function of vision is to help us move around in the world. When you reach out to grab a coffee cup, how do you know the location of the cup? If you're like me, your intuition is that you are conscious of the cup's location, and you guide your hand to that location. Strangely enough, the evidence indicates that your conscious awareness of the cup's location is not important in guiding your hand. There is another visual system of which you are unconscious that operates in parallel with the conscious one and that drives movements.

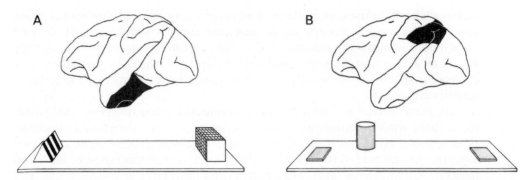

Figure 3.16.   Representation of the tasks used by Ungerleider and Mishkin (1982), as well as the brain areas that support them. Part A shows nonmatching to sample—the monkey would have just seen one of the two objects and must pick the novel one. A lesion to the ventral pathway (shaded on the figure) compromises performance in this task. Part B shows the landmark task—the monkey simply chooses the trap door closer to the cylinder. Damage to the dorsal pathway impairs performance of this task. From Mishkin, M; Ungerleider, L. G; & Macko, K. A. (1983). Object vision and spatial vision: Two cortical pathways. Trends in Neurosciences, 6(10) Oct 1983, 414–417. Figure 2 is on p. 415. Trends in Neurosciences is published by Elsevier.

A key finding came from visual researchers examining the primate brain. Leslie Ungerleider and Mortimer Mishkin (1982; see also Ungerleider & Haxby, 1994) proposed that there are two visual pathways in the brain. One pathway identifies objects, and the other determines the location of objects. They proposed this hypothesis after studying brain anatomy and then tested it in monkeys. They had two tests: one for object identity and one for object location, depicted in Figure 3.16. The object identity test is called nonmatching to sample. Here's what happens. A sliding door rises, and the monkey sees an object. The monkey knocks the object aside to find a reward such as a peanut. The door then goes down and comes back up, and the monkey sees two objects: the one it just saw and a new object. If the monkey knocks aside the new object, it will find another peanut reward. If it knocks aside the object it just saw, it gets nothing. That's how the task got its name; the first object is the sample, and the monkey is supposed to pick the nonmatching object. Note that the monkey doesn't need to know anything about object location to perform the task well; all it needs to do is recognize the object it just saw.

The object location task is called the landmark task. In this task, the monkey sees two trapdoors. Under each trapdoor is a well containing either a peanut reward or nothing. A landmark (usually a cylinder) lies closer to one trapdoor than the other, and the monkey should simply choose the trapdoor closer to the cylinder. Thus, for this task object identity is irrelevant; the monkey merely needs to know the location of the trapdoors and the cylinder.

Ungerleider and Mishkin (1982) trained some monkeys until they were very good at each task. Next, the researchers lesioned part of the monkeys' brains. One group of monkeys had part of the temporal lobe removed, and the other group had part of the parietal lobe removed. The results were dramatic. The group with the temporal lobe lesion performed well on the landmark task but could no longer succeed at nonmatching to sample. The group with the parietal lesion showed just the opposite pattern of results. Ungerleider and Mishkin interpreted their results as showing that there are two streams of processing in the visual system: a "what" stream that identifies objects and a "where" stream that determines where objects are located. This model can be called the **what/where hypothesis** (see also Ungerleider & Haxby, 1994). There are also data indicating separation of "what" and "where" processing in other senses such as touch (Reed, Klatzky, & Halgren, 2005) and audition (Clarke, Adriani, & Tardif, 2005).

This result was very influential in vision research, but there have always been one or two oddities in this interpretation. For example, how can the spatial information be separate from the processes that identify objects? Don't you need to know where an object's parts are to identify it?

Ungerleider and Mishkin's findings have been reinterpreted in an interesting and convincing way. Melvyn Goodale and David Milner (1992, 2004; Goodale & Westwood, 2004) suggested that it is better to think of them as "what" and "how" streams (which we'll call the **what/how hypothesis**). They argue that spatial information is present in both streams, but its function differs. The "what" stream in the temporal lobe identifies objects and is associated with consciousness. The end product of this processing stream is the conscious perception of where objects are, what they are, their colors, and so on. The "how" stream handles information that helps us move. Thus, the "how" stream knows the shape and location of objects so we can grasp them effectively and reach to the right spot.

There are convincing data for the separation of two streams of visual processing in the human brain. For example, either stream can be selectively damaged, leaving the other intact. Patients with **visual agnosia** typically suffer damage to the border of the temporal and occipital lobes, and have difficulty recognizing objects using vision but can do so using other senses. Some of these patients, however, are able to accurately direct movements using vision. One of the more dramatic examples is patient D.F. described by Milner and Goodale (1995). She had a great deal of difficulty visually recognizing objects, so much so that even recognizing *properties* of objects was tough— when shown a cylinder with a slot cut into it, D.F. could not describe the orientation of the slot. Yet, when handed a card and instructed to put the card in the slot, she was able to do so effortlessly. The interpretation is that the dorsal system (which supports perception for movement) can perceive the slot, but the ventral system (which supports object recognition and conscious perception) cannot perceive the slot. The opposite pattern of results has also been observed. Patients with **optic ataxia** usually suffer damage to the superior parietal cortex (dorsal system), and they are impaired in using visual guidance for movement (Perenin & Vighetto, 1988; see also Himmelbach & Karnath, 2005).

Figure 3.17.   A view of a virtual reality town, similar to the one used by Aguirre and D'Esposito (1997).

When reaching for an object, they grope about unsurely, like a person seeking a light switch in the dark, but they can identify objects by sight without problem.

Brain imaging evidence also supports the separation of the dorsal and ventral visual streams. For example, Geoff Aguirre and Mark D'Esposito (1997) had their participants spend several sessions exploring a small town in virtual reality, similar to the one shown in Figure 3.17. Then, the researchers administered a test of their knowledge. Participants saw a landmark (e.g., a building) and were asked to make one of two judgments—whether the landmark looked accurate (or had been changed slightly)—or to make a judgment about the relative position of another landmark. When participants judged what landmarks looked like, the ventral system was active. When they judged the location of landmarks, the dorsal system was active (see also Faillenot, Toni, Decety, Caregorie, & Jeannerod, 1997; Kohler, Kapur, Moscovitch, Winocur, & Houle, 1995).

Most of the time, there would be no way of knowing that there are two such visual streams because they are in agreement. However, Dennis Proffitt and his associates have shown that under some circumstances we can observe the separate operations of the two systems. Here's a way to appreciate their

Photo 3.8. Hills look steeper than they actually are. This hill is only 7 degrees.

separate operation. What was the steepest hill you've ever walked on? How steep was it, in terms of degrees? (A flat road is 0 degrees, and a vertical cliff would be 90 degrees.) Most people guess that the steepest hill they've ever seen might be 45 or 50 degrees. In fact, the steepest street in San Francisco, a city renowned for its steep hills, is only 18.5 degrees; in my home state of Virginia, no public street can have a hill steeper than 9 degrees, by law. People overestimate steepness—not just in their memories but even when they are right in front of the hill. Furthermore, if you hand someone a pair of calipers to be set at the angle of the hill, the person will create an angle very similar to the angle given as a verbal estimate (Proffitt, Bhalla, Gossweiler, & Midgett, 1995).

If you misperceive a slope to be much steeper than it really is, why don't you fall down when you try to walk on it? The conscious "what" system generates the perception that results in the overestimation of the steepness of the hill, but the "how" system generates the spatial information used for stepping. Denny Proffitt and his colleagues (1995) tested this hypothesis by having 300 people make judgments about the steepness of nine different hills on the campus of the University of Virginia, one of which is shown in Photo 3.8. Participants gave two estimates of the hills' steepness. They judged the steepness of each hill verbally and by adjusting a little picture to make it as steep as the hill in front of them. By both of these measures, participants overestimated the steepness of the hills, as shown in Figure 3.18. They also made a judgment via the unconscious "how" system by placing their palms flat on a small board mounted on a tripod and adjusting it (without looking at it) so it was parallel to the hill in front of them. The researchers found that

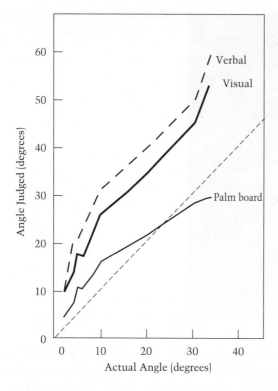

Figure 3.18. Graph showing judgment of the steepness of nine hills compared with the actual steepness. Perfectly accurate judgments would fall on the dotted lines. When participants used the palm board to estimate the hills' steepness they were much more accurate than when they gave verbal estimates or adjusted a picture of a hill visually.

participants' estimates of the hill by the palm board measure were quite accurate and interpreted this result as showing that the "how" system can judge the actual angle of the hill.

In this chapter, we've discussed the basics of visual perception. Yet, we've discussed it as though the mere presence of a visual stimulus were enough for it to be processed. That is inaccurate. It is quite possible not to see a large object that that is right in front of you . . . if you're not paying attention to it (Mack, 2003). Attention is vital for all kinds of cognitive processing, not just vision, and we will discuss attention in chapter 4.

Stand-on-One-Foot Questions

10. *What are the two basic ideas about how objects are represented?*

11. *What are the three ideas of how object representations are organized in the brain?*

12. *Name two types of evidence indicating that "what" and "how" are represented separately by the visual system.*

Questions That Require Two Feet

13. *Why do you suppose hills look so much steeper than they are? Hint: Consider how much harder it is to climb an 8-degree hill than a 4-degree hill.*

14. *Are there some objects that you almost always see in the same orientation? Do you think that your mental representation of those objects might reflect that select experience?*

15. *If you've seen the movie* Shallow Hal, *can you think of a way that the what/how theory is applicable?*

KEY TERMS

accommodation
atmospheric
    perspective
bottom-up processing
computational
    approach
convergence
critical features
ecological approach
eyeheight
familiar size
feature-matching
    theories
fovea
frame of reference
inverse projection
    problem

light source,
    reflectance, and
    shadow
    indeterminacy
likelihood principle
linear perspective
local contrast
luminance
object-centered
    representation
occlusion
optic ataxia
parsing paradox
pictorial cues
prosopagnosia
relative height
retina

retinal disparity
shape and orientation
    indeterminacy
size and distance
    indeterminacy
stereopsis
template
texture gradient
top-down processing
viewer-centered
    representation
visual agnosia
what/how hypothesis
what/where hypothesis

CURRENT DIRECTIONS IN COGNITIVE SCIENCE

Recommended readings

Mack, A. (2003). "Inattentional blindness: Looking without seeing." (pp. 3–10) As noted at the end of this chapter, I treated perception with the assumption that the viewer was paying attention. Mack reviews fascinating work that indicates there is no perception in the absence of attention, which may be the solution to one of the questions set forth in chapter 1: "How could I not see my keys when they were right in front of me?"

Martino, G., & Marks, L. E. (2001). "Synesthesia: Strong and weak." (pp. 19–26) Martino and Marks describe different types of synesthesia, a phenomenon of cross-talk among different sense modalities. In the strong form, experience in one modality (seeing red) leads to a vivid experience in another modality (hearing a particular tone). In a weaker form of synesthesia, the experience is one of associations of meaning, rather than of direct perceptual experience. Martino and Marks' analysis of synesthesia makes for an interesting follow-up to our discussion of vision because it helps us think about what happens next in visual processing.

Attention

4

In What Way Is Attention Limited?

- Parallel Performance
- Consistent Attention Requirements
- Allocation of Attention
- Reduction in Attention Demands With Practice: Automaticity

What Is The Fate of Sensory Stimuli That Are Not Selected to Receive Attention?

- Early Filter Theories
- Late Filter Theories
- The Movable Filter Model
- What Is Selected?
- How Does Selection Operate?

Why Does Selection Fail?

- Properties of Attention That Cause Selection Failures
- Interaction of Attention With Other Components of Cognition

Suppose I ask you to walk the length of a balance beam. You, game stranger that you are, do so. Then I ask you to walk it again but this time to simultaneously sing "Yankee Doodle." You walk and sing. Then I tell you that this is a special balance beam, sections of which can be heated or cooled, and as you walk its length (barefoot) I'd like you to say whether the section you've just stepped on is hot or cold. You'll still be singing, so just interrupt the song when necessary. You perform that task. Then I ask you to do it again, but as you walk along, I'll squirt different scents at you with an atomizer, and as you're walking, singing, and distinguishing hot from cold you should also remember the scents I squirt because you'll have to recite them after you've finished walking the beam.

Clearly, you can walk, sing, feel temperature, or sniff without trouble, but doing them simultaneously is difficult. You're going to perform more slowly as I add tasks, and you're going to start making errors. Why? The short and obvious answer is that you can't pay attention to all tasks at the same time. But what is attention? In an often-quoted passage, William James commented, "Everyone knows what attention is." More than 100 years later, a leading attention researcher replied, "No one knows what attention is" (Pashler, 1998, p. 1). Of course, James meant that everyone has an intuitive sense of what is meant by attention; Pashler meant that we don't have a complete scientific understanding of attention.

Attention can be understood to mean the mechanism for continued cognitive processing. This definition presumes that some preliminary cognitive processing takes place, with or without attention, and that attention affords further processing. For example, suppose that you're alone in a museum gallery, contemplating a Corot, and two women enter, talking to one another. Even though your attention is directed to the painting, we might guess that your cognitive system would process the fact that you were no longer alone, that you had two companions, and perhaps that they were women. Attention (and the continued cognitive processing it brings about) would be necessary to identify what they were talking about. This definition is applicable not only to perception, but also to action; we speak of paying attention to tasks such as driving, building a model airplane, or walking on a balance beam.

This definition brings to the fore two properties of attention. First, we might guess that attention is **limited**; continued cognitive processing cannot occur for all available stimuli simultaneously. This point brings up the question **In what way is attention limited?** Our definition makes attention seem like mental fuel; you only have so much fuel to expend, so if you expend it on one cognitive process, there is necessarily less for other processes. This metaphor is intuitively appealing, but the predictions it suggests are difficult to prove. Nevertheless, it is clear that attention is limited in some way.

Second, we know from everyday experience that attention is **selective**; you can expend your mental fuel on one or another cognitive process as you see fit. The very fact that attention is limited means that it must be selective.

What happens to the cognitive processes to which you give little or no attention? The perceptual apparatus is always working, but you are not always aware of all the information it processes. For example, you are probably seated as you read this, but you probably aren't aware of pressure from your chair. The sensation is always present but you are not aware of it because of the limited nature of attention—you can't focus on both the pressure sensation and reading this text, and you select the text as the focus of attention. (At least you were until I mentioned your chair.) But what happens to the unattended sensation of pressure? **What is the fate of sensory stimuli that are not selected to receive attention?** That depends on just how you choose to direct attention. You may direct some attention to other stimuli, such as when you're reading a book but still listening to a television to determine the outcome of a vital episode of *Green Acres*. Or you may try to shut out all distractions, as when you're attempting to read your cognitive psychology textbook and ignore your roommate's annoying baby-talk phone conversation with his girlfriend. As we'll see, you have some control over how tight the selection of attention is, but even when you're doing your best to focus on one thing, other material is still processed to some extent.

The final question we pose concerns selection. Although people can try to select the focus of their attention, they are not always successful. **Why does selection fail?**

In What Way Is Attention Limited?

Preview

It appears that we have a limited amount of attention to expend on cognitive processing. Psychologists have made predictions about the limits of attention.

- Attention can be distributed between tasks as the person sees fit.
- Tasks require less attention with practice.

There is evidence that supports these two statements. Two other predictions are not supported: That attention can be distributed to more than one task at a time may be correct, but it's difficult to collect persuasive evidence on this point. The fourth prediction—that performing multiple tasks does not change how each task is performed—appears not to be correct.

Psychologists have likened attention to mental fuel that makes continued cognitive processing possible. This definition is close to the way researchers thought about attention when they first started considering its limited nature (Bryan & Harter, 1897) and has been central to more recent formulations as well (Kahneman, 1973; Moray, 1967). What can we say about the particular way in which attention is limited? We can make a list of predictions consistent with a limited capacity for attention and with our own experience:

- Attention can be distributed to more than one task at a time; that is, it is possible to perform multiple tasks in parallel.
- The performance of a particular task requires a particular amount of attention that is consistent across situations and does not change when other tasks are being performed.
- When tasks compete, the person can allocate attention to each task in the proportions that he or she desires.
- With sufficient practice, a task will come to demand fewer attentional resources.

These four assumptions sound reasonable and fit with our everyday experience, but we cannot be sure the first two are true. However, there is evidence that the final two are true. Let's look at these assumptions in more detail.

Parallel Performance

It seems obvious that it is possible to perform more than one task in parallel. After all, you frequently do two things at once: talk to a friend while you drive, listen to music while you read, or walk and chew gum. A good way to learn about the limited nature of attention is to give the cognitive system too much to do and then observe the consequences. To investigate attention in the laboratory, researchers use a **dual task paradigm** in which the participant must perform two tasks at once.

Here's the key question about parallel performance: How do you know that you're really doing these tasks in parallel and not switching attention rapidly between the two tasks? Couldn't I take a step on the balance beam, then sing a phrase of the song, then take another step, and so on, so smoothly and seamlessly that it seems as if I'm doing the two tasks at the same time?

Researchers have tried to get around this problem by using continuous tasks rather than discrete tasks. A **discrete task** has an identifiable beginning and ending, and there is usually a pause between the end of one trial and the beginning of the next. For example, in a simple response time task a stimulus is presented (a light appears on a computer monitor or a tone sounds), and the participant responds by pressing a button as quickly as possible when the stimulus occurs. Figure 4.1 shows a **response to stimulus interval**, which is the period of time after the participant has responded but before the next stimulus appears. During this period, the participant waits for the next stimulus to appear and could easily switch attention to some other task. Even if the researcher makes the next stimulus appear immediately after a response, the

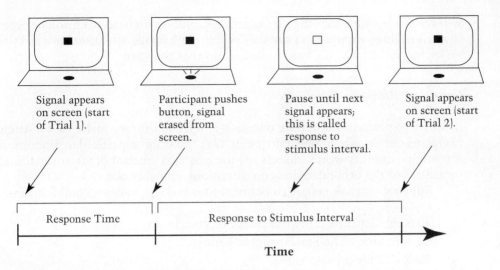

| Signal appears on screen (start of Trial 1). | Participant pushes button, signal erased from screen. | Pause until next signal appears; this is called response to stimulus interval. | Signal appears on screen (start of Trial 2). |

Response Time

Response to Stimulus Interval

Time

Figure 4.1. Simple response time task with a visual signal and a button-press response.

participant can simply switch attention to the other task at this point, effectively taking a break from this task.

A **continuous task**, in contrast, uses a continuous stream of stimuli and often demands a continuous stream of responses. For example, in a pursuit tracking task, a target moves on a computer screen, and the participant must chase the target with a cursor controlled by a joystick. Performance is measured as the distance between the cursor and target. The target is always moving, so it would seem that even a momentary lapse of attention would make performance suffer. Another continuous task is touch typing. In one experiment, a skilled typist could recite nursery rhymes aloud while typing with only a 10% loss of typing speed (Shaffer, 1975). This study was meant to show that typing required little attention for a highly skilled typist.

The problem with such evidence is that it is probably possible to switch attention between two tasks, even if one of them is a continuous task, because the participant need not treat it as if it were continuous (Broadbent, 1982; Welford, 1980). For example, experienced typists often report that once they've seen a word, they don't really need to think about the word as they type it, and a number of studies indicate that that is true (Salthouse, 1984). Just because the hands are typing at a steady rate doesn't mean that attentional resources are needed at a steady rate. In the case of typing, it seems likely that attention is needed in bursts; a burst of attention might be needed to read a word and then very little attention would be needed to type the word.

Thus, using dual task paradigms does not seem to guarantee evidence that people can share attentional resources between tasks. No matter how much it looks as if the participant is dividing attention between two tasks, it will remain possible that the participant is rapidly switching attention between the tasks. Thus, we wouldn't say that people *can't* divide attention between two tasks, but rather that it's hard to be certain that they can.

Consistent Attention Requirements

If we try to perform more than one task at a time, the two tasks vie for attentional resources. Does one particular task take up a particular amount of attention—in other words, does it require a certain amount of attentional fuel, regardless of the other demands on attention? Probably not.

Suppose you ask people to perform four tasks in various combinations:

Task A: Generate a mental image of your room.
Task B: Sing "The Star-Spangled Banner."
Task C: Play a video game.
Task D: Remember a list of six words.

You find that participants can generate a mental image of their bedroom (Task A) and simultaneously sing "The Star-Spangled Banner" (Task B) with little apparent cost to the imaging. However, if they are imaging and then start playing the video game (Task C), there is a cost to the imagery task. Therefore, the attentional cost of playing the video game seems to be greater than that of the singing (C > B).

But if you ask participants to remember the list of six words (Task D), you find that adding the video game (Task C) causes little cost to remembering the words, whereas singing (Task B) incurs a high cost. Now it appears that the attentional cost of singing is greater than that of playing the video game (B > C). In short, you can't evaluate the attentional demands of a task by pairing it with a secondary task; the attentional demands of a task look different, depending on the task with which you pair it. We cannot say that a task demands a particular amount of attention independent of other tasks.

MULTIPLE RESOURCE THEORIES.   You can't make a mental image of your room and play a video game simultaneously because you don't have enough attention. So, why can you play the game and sing at the same time? One answer would be that there are different types of attention. This is called a **multiple resources** approach to attention (Navon & Gopher, 1979; Norman & Bobrow, 1975). Just as the name implies, the idea is that you have several independent pools of attention, not one general pool. Each works just as we described for the more general attention resource idea, but there are believed to be several types of attention, each specific to particular types of task.

What characterizes these separate attentional pools? In other words, how do they differ? In one of the early articles taking the multiple resources approach, David Navon and Daniel Gopher (1979) cited research indicating a separation based on sensory modality (vision, hearing). They cited an article by Lee Brooks (1968) showing that when participants were trying to recall a sentence, a simultaneous vocal task was much more disruptive than a simultaneous spatial task, but when they were trying to recall the shape of a line diagram, a simultaneous vocal task was less disruptive than a spatial task. Thus, there could be separate attentional pools for visuospatial processing and for auditory processing or, more simply put, for vision and for hearing.   *NO*

Later research, however, did not support that idea. Jon Driver and Charles Spence (1994) showed that there are links between attention in vision and attention in hearing. Participants in their experiment had speakers to their left and right. On each trial a different three-word triplet came out of the left and right speakers, and participants were told to repeat the triplet from one speaker. They were told before each trial to which speaker they should attend. On some trials, they also had visual information, with a person speaking the words they were to repeat. The tricky part was that the visual information was presented on a screen either on the same side as the speaker that had the auditory information they were supposed to repeat or on a screen by the other speaker; thus, the visual information could be either consistent or inconsistent with the information coming over the auditory channel on the same side (see Figure 4.2).

Driver and Spence's (1994) experiment indicated that auditory and visual information are not completely separate. When the visual information was presented on the side consistent with the auditory information, people got about 68% of the words correct; when it was not, they got about 52% correct. Thus, auditory and visual attention do seem to be tied together; participants could not allocate visual and auditory attention to different locations in space without cost. Nevertheless, it is true that an auditory task will tend to interfere with another auditory task more than with a visual task. The final word seems to be that there is some division along modality lines but not completely separate pools of attention.

Chris Wickens (1984, 1992) suggested a different way of splitting up attention in a multiple resource theory with three dimensions of tasks relevant to attention. He asked first, which stage of processing does the task emphasize? For perception the hard part is perceiving the stimulus, whereas for response the hard part is selecting the right reaction. Second, does the task use a verbal or spatial code of processing? Third, what are the modalities of input and output? The input might be visual or auditory; the output might be spoken or manual. Wickens argued that there might be separate attentional resource pools for each combination of these dimensions. In other words, searching for a visual target would be a perceptual task with visual input, and that would call on a particular pool of attentional resources. Different tasks have different properties, so the three task dimensions would require eight separate pools of attention.

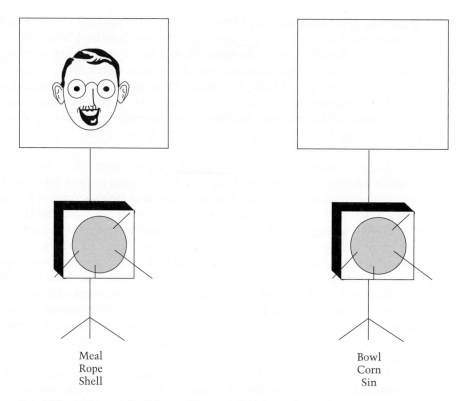

Figure 4.2. Basic setup for Driver and Spence's (1994) experiment. Participants heard different groups of three words coming from speakers on their left and right and had to repeat the words from one speaker. A person on the screen mouthed the target words on either the same side as or the opposite side from the auditory information.

The idea seems intuitively appealing. Unfortunately, it is difficult to specify how different tasks would call on these different hypothetical pools. For a theory to be useful, it must be predictive; in other words, we must be able to analyze two tasks and judge how similar they are in terms of the demands they would place on the different attentional pools. One of the chief criticisms of the multiple resources theory is that it's not clear how many of these attentional pools are supposed to exist or how they are related to tasks (see Allport, 1989; Luck & Vecera, 2002, for a discussion of some of these issues).

Most researchers believe that it is useful to think of attention as limited, but it has proved frustratingly difficult to be specific about how this happens. It seems that the simple idea of an undifferentiated pool of attentional resources cannot be right, but a satisfactory alternative has not been outlined. Two other properties of attention have been studied in detail, however, and we have a better understanding of them. First, we can allocate attention to different tasks as we see fit, and second, attentional demands appear to shrink as we practice a task.

Allocation of Attention

Psychologists have assumed that when tasks compete for attentional resources, people can allocate more or less attention to a particular task according to their goals. For example, suppose you are driving and simultaneously talking to a friend when it suddenly begins to rain hard, making it difficult to see. You would probably allocate more attention to driving the car and less to the conversation.

The assumption that you can allocate attention in this manner is supported by controlled laboratory studies. George Sperling and Melvin Melchner (1978) showed participants arrays of letters. An inner set of 4 letters was surrounded by an outer set of 16 letters. The arrays flashed by, one at a time, on a computer screen. Each appeared for just 240 ms, and the number of arrays that flashed by on each trial varied. Participants knew that 2 digits would appear in the arrays sometime during the trial, and they were to report the identity and location of the digits. On some trials, they were told to allocate 90% of their attention to the inner set of 4 letters; on others, they were to allocate 90% of their attention to the outer set of letters; and on others, they were to attend to the inner and outer arrays equally. Figure 4.3 shows the probability of correctly detecting a target. The graph shows the data for just one participant,

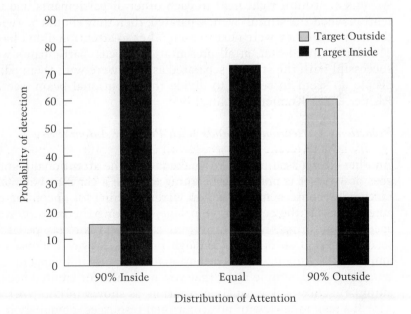

Figure 4.3. Graph from Sperling and Melchner (1978) showing the probability that a single participant detected the target. The x axis represents the instructions: to direct 90% of attention to the outside or inside stimuli, or to maintain equal attention to both. The black bars show performance when the stimuli actually appeared on the outside, the white when they appeared on the inside. The data show that participants can direct their attention as they are instructed, and that doing so affects performance.

but these data are typical. The important point is that when participants are told to attend mostly to one location, they get most of the targets appearing in that location. Participants can indeed allocate attention as they see fit, and that allocation is reflected in task performance (see also Gopher, Brickner, & Navon, 1982).

For a long time, cognitive psychologists believed that attention could only be allocated to one place at a time. Attention was likened to a flashlight beam (Posner, Snyder, & Davidson, 1980) that could not be split. More recently, researchers have shown that the beam can be split and that people can attend to two locations at once. In one experiment, Stephanie McMains and David Somers (2004) asked participants to keep their eyes fixated at a central location and to attend to two other locations—one to the left of fixation, and one to the right. At each location, a series of digits and letters rapidly flashed. The participant's job was to signal when the digits at the left and right locations matched. A series of digits also flashed at the fixation point, but participants were to ignore these. Participants were able to perform this matching task, but how can we know that they weren't just switching attention between the two locations? McMains and Somers tested participant's success rate on this task, varying the presentation speed of the stimuli. Predictably, if the stimuli were presented more slowly, participants were better at the task. More interestingly, the experimenters tested participants with the two streams of stimuli right next to each other. If participants had to switch attention when the stimuli were separated, then they should be twice as good at the task when they were next to each other so attention didn't have to switch. The data showed that, at all presentation speeds, participants were about as successful with the stimuli separated as they were with them adjacent. Thus, people do seem to be able to divide the attentional beam (see also Awh & Pashler, 2000; Kramer & Hahn, 1995).

Reduction in Attention Demands With Practice: Automaticity

Another strong assumption we make is that the attentional demand of a task goes down as it is practiced. Learning to drive a car may have taxed your attentional resources at first as you were watching for oncoming cars, making sure to stay in the center of your lane, checking the mirrors, watching your speed, monitoring the pressure you applied to the gas pedal, reading the road signs, and so on. With enough practice, however, these tasks became **automatic**, taking few or no attentional resources and happening without intention. Indeed, simple tasks that you now take for granted because they are automatic once took great concentration, as shown in Photo 4.1.

If a task takes few or no attentional resources, obviously it makes little demand on attention, so you should be able to perform several automatic tasks at once. Indeed, an experienced driver thinks nothing of driving while eating, talking on a cell phone, and listening to the radio—an accomplished task, if not attractive to watch. In addition, an automatic process that happens

Photo 4.1. This girl recently learned to tie her shoes, and it still requires some attentional resources. With daily practice, it will soon become automatic.

without intention occurs regardless of whether you want it to: if certain conditions are present in the environment, the automatic process occurs. For example, on occasion a passenger in my car will slam his or her foot against the floorboard in a vain effort to stop my car, due to some trifling matter such as an oncoming truck. I always inform such passengers that their foot motion is perfectly understandable; the proper stimulus was present in the environment (danger) to bring about an action (braking) even though the action is futile.

How do we know that automaticity has these two characteristics (it requires little or no attention, and it happens without intention)? First, let's consider whether automatic processes really don't require attention.

AUTOMATICITY AND ATTENTION. In a classic experiment on the training of automaticity, Richard Shiffrin and Walter Schneider (1977) used a visual search task to show the reduced attentional demand of automatic processes. On each trial, participants were given a memory set (e.g., the letters *G* and *M*) and were told to search upcoming stimuli for those characters. Participants then saw a series of cards with letters on them, and they had to report whether

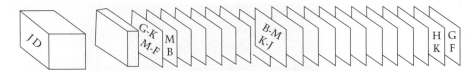

Figure 4.4. Sample trial from Schneider and Shiffrin's (1977) task, showing cards that flashed in front of participants. The block at the far left represents that memory set.

a member of the memory set had appeared on one of the cards. The memory set items are called **targets**, and the nontarget items on the cards are called **distractors**. On each trial, a new memory set and new cards were used (see Figure 4.4).

We can use this task to examine automaticity because if the visual search is automatic (takes no attention), the participant ought to be able to carry out the visual search on many stimuli simultaneously. Therefore, the number of stimuli on each card shouldn't matter; if there are four stimuli on each card, you'll still be able to do the visual search as effectively as if there is one stimulus on each card.

Each participant did two versions of the task. Sometimes the memory set was selected from among the same group of letters on each trial. For example, the memory set might be selected from the letters (*GMFP*) and the distractors from (*CNHD*). This was the categorical condition. For the mixed condition, both the memory set and the distractors could be selected from the same pool of letters (e.g., *RVJZBWTX*). Each participant alternated blocks of trials using the categorical and mixed stimuli.

After a great deal of practice (9,216 trials!), searching for the target became automatic, but *only* if the target set was selected from the same set of letters on each trial (i.e., in the categorical condition). If a letter could be a target on one trial and then a distractor on the next trial, automaticity never developed (see Figure 4.5).

Thus, there appears to be good evidence that with practice tasks become less demanding of attention. The exact mechanism by which this happens is still under debate. Some researchers have suggested that some of the intermediate steps in a complex series of processes are eventually eliminated (Anderson, 1993; Newell & Rosenbloom, 1981), whereas others suggest that a second process that does not demand attention develops more slowly and finally takes over the task (Willingham, 1998b).

Gordon Logan (1988, 2002) suggested a different account of automaticity: Increasing facility with well-practiced tasks may reflect an increasing role of memory. For example, if I asked you how many letters are in the word *quotidian*, you would have to spell it to yourself and count the letters. If I asked you the same question a few minutes later, you wouldn't go through the same process; you'd remember what you had said earlier and say it again. Logan suggested that memory may play just such a role in automaticity. In every task, memory competes with slower processes that calculate an answer

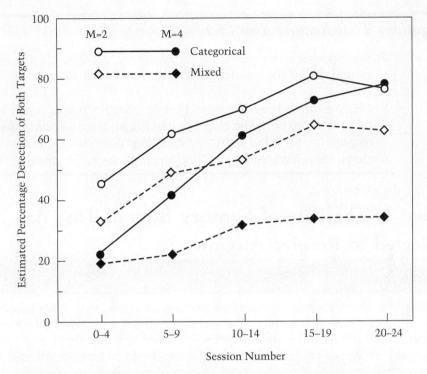

Figure 4.5. Results from Shiffrin and Schneider's (1977) study. Note that in the early sessions, participants were always more likely to succeed when there were two targets (*M = 2*) than when there were four (*M = 4*), and that was equally true in the categorical and mixed conditions. By the end of the training, participants were equally good when *M = 2* and *M = 4*, but only for the categorical condition. In the mixed condition, participants were much better at detecting the target when there were fewer stimuli on each card.

to the task at hand. As you practice, you have more answers in memory, making it increasingly likely that on any given trial you can use an answer from memory and not need to do the calculation.

Stand-on-One-Foot Questions

1. *Can people divide attention between more than one task? How is this known?*
2. *What is the key condition for automaticity to develop?*
3. *Describe and briefly evaluate the theory that there are multiple pools of attention.*

Questions That Require Two Feet

4. Some people can read while instrumental music is playing in the background, but if the music has words, they find it distracting. Why might that be?

5. I once heard a comic remark that he thought it was funny that people turn the radio off when they are looking for a house number in a strange neighborhood. What theory of attention does this comedian favor?

6. Do you think it's safe to talk on a cell phone while driving?

What Is The Fate of Sensory Stimuli That Are Not Selected to Receive Attention?

Preview

We attend to only a subset of the stimuli that are out in the world. What happens to the other stimuli? They must be processed and identified at least to some extent; otherwise, how else would you know when to redirect attention to these other stimuli? In this section, we discuss just how much processing is performed on these unattended stimuli. It seems that the physical characteristics of unattended stimuli are identified (color and shape of visual stimuli, loudness and pitch of auditory stimuli), but little information about their meaning is processed. We also look at how selection operates. Does attention focus on objects or regions of space? The answer is that it seems to select objects, not space.

You can't attend to everything simultaneously because of the limited nature of attention. Attention must also be selective, and if you select some things to attend to, you will necessarily not be selecting others. What happens to the sensory stimuli that are not selected?

That question may initially strike you as odd—why should anything happen to unattended stimuli? Don't I just fail to perceive them? It is true that attention is required for conscious perception. In fact, you may not perceive something that is *right in front of you* if you are not attending to it. In a dramatic study of this phenomenon, Daniel Simons and Chris Chabris (1999) asked people to watch a video of six people playing a ball-catching game. Three wore black shirts, and three wore white. Participants were to count the passes between the white team. The players moved constantly so the task was quite attention demanding. In the middle of the video, a person in a gorilla suit walked right in the middle of the six people, thumped his chest, and sauntered off. As long as participants were engaged in the task that required close attention to the players, they do not perceive the gorilla, even though it appeared right before their eyes. It appears that without attention there is no perception (for a brief review of such phenomena, see Mack, 2003).

Photo 4.2. Even when your attention is focused on a task such as reading, you are simultaneously monitoring sensory input to see if your attention should be redirected.

But that can't be quite right. What if you're attending to one stimulus and another stimulus in the environment requires your notice? For example, what if you were sitting in the library reading *Anna Karenina* and someone shouted, "Is that a fire?" Even though you were attending to the book, you would perceive the shout. Indeed, if there were absolutely no processing of stimuli that you were ignoring, you would have to periodically make a conscious decision to monitor your environment to see if anything important was happening: "Let's see, is anyone shouting 'fire'? Is someone tapping me on the shoulder? Is water dripping on my head?" (see Photo 4.2).

Indeed, you know that attention can be diverted in this way, so there must be some processing of material that you are ignoring. That's why the definition of attention is that it's the mechanism for continued cognitive processing; everything is processed to some extent, and attention affords continued processing. In this section, we are asking how much processing occurs in the absence of attention. Most of the work on this topic has concerned the amount of perceptual processing that occurs on stimuli that are not attended.

We have to start our discussion of this problem by outlining an assumption. It's probably a justifiable assumption, but we should be explicit about it anyway. The assumption is that perception follows a processing course like

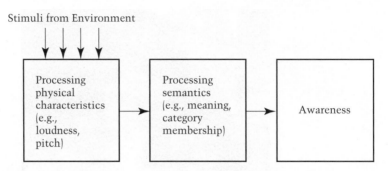

Stimuli from Environment

| Processing physical characteristics (e.g., loudness, pitch) | Processing semantics (e.g., meaning, category membership) | Awareness |

Figure 4.6. Simple diagram showing the assumed order in which sensory stimuli are processed.

that in Figure 4.6. It is assumed that the physical characteristics of a stimulus are processed first. For visual information, these would be shape, color, spatial location, and so on. For auditory information, they would be loudness, pitch, spatial location, and so on. After we know the physical characteristics of the stimulus, more processing is necessary to determine what the object is and therefore its meaning: That shiny red globe is an apple, which means that it is edible, it has seeds, it is a member of the category *fruit*, and so on.

A great deal of sensory information (sights, sounds, smells) bombards us at any given moment, but at the other end of the processing stream only a fraction of that information enters awareness. One hypothesis holds that attention acts as a filter, stopping most of the information before it reaches awareness. The attentional filter stops the processing of most sensory information, allowing continued processing (and eventual entry to awareness) of only the sensory information to which we are attending. We are constantly evaluating information not currently in awareness to decide whether other stimuli are worthy of attention.

Theories about how attention acts as a filter fall into two categories: early filter theories and late filter theories. These terms refer to where the filter operates in the processing stream depicted in Figure 4.6. An **early filter** is located early in the processing stream, usually right after the sensory characteristics are processed; thus, according to early filter theories, all stimuli are processed so their sensory characteristics are determined, and then they hit the filter. Most stimuli are not processed past that point, but the filter allows through whichever stimuli are being attended to.

A **late filter** appears later in the processing stream. All stimuli are processed to determine their physical and semantic characteristics, and only then do the stimuli hit the filter; only the stimuli that are attended to go on to enter awareness. You can see that the key difference between these theories is the location of the filter.

Early Filter Theories

What is the evidence for the early filter theories? One of the first studies relevant to this question was performed by Colin Cherry (1953) using the **dichotic**

Figure 4.7.   The dichotic listening procedure.

listening task, depicted in Figure 4.7. In this task, participants listened to material on headphones. Each earpiece played a different message, and participants were asked to pay attention to just one of the messages. To ensure participants were attending as instructed, they had to **shadow** the message, meaning that they had to repeat the message aloud. Thus, as they were shadowing what they heard over the right earpiece, another message was playing in the left earpiece. Later, participants were asked to report what they knew about the message from the unattended ear. Participants were terrible at reporting the unattended message. In fact, Cherry found that participants didn't even notice if the unattended message switched into another language or if the message was played backward. Participants did notice if the unattended speech turned into a pure tone or if the gender of the speaker changed.

Cherry concluded that unattended speech is not analyzed to a semantic level; that is, it is not analyzed for meaning. Instead, it is analyzed for physical characteristics such as pitch and loudness. Thus, if you're focusing attention on the message in the left ear, you don't know anything about the meaning of what's coming in the right ear. But you know its physical characteristics, so you can tell when it becomes grossly different from speech (like a pure tone) or when the pitch changes (because the gender of the speaker has changed). A dramatic example of the extent to which people don't know the meaning of unattended speech was provided by Moray (1959), who played the same word list for participants in the unattended ear 35 times. On a later test, participants didn't recognize any of them.

Donald Broadbent (1958) was one of the first to propose a theory incorporating an early attentional filter. Broadbent suggested that information comes into a very brief sensory store (discussed in chapter 5) in which its physical characteristics are ascertained. The filter occurs just after this sensory store, and only a small portion of this information makes it to the next stage, which is primary memory. Primary memory is associated with awareness, and it is where meaning is assigned to stimuli (primary memory is also discussed in chapter 5).

Photo 4.3. Why is it so hard to ignore people who talk on cell phones? People need to talk loudly to be heard on cell phones. The loudness is an unusual stimulus characteristic, so (according to the early filter theory) your attention is consistently drawn to the voice because of this physical characteristic.

Let's focus on the idea that all stimuli are analyzed for their physical characteristics, but only a limited number (those to which you attend) are also analyzed for their semantic content. Recall that unattended stimuli must be processed in case something important requires your attention. If you are in a crowd and someone shouts "Fire!", the loudness of the unattended message will make you shift your attention to the source of the sound (see Photo 4.3). But presumably if someone merely said "Fire," you wouldn't hear it because the word doesn't stand out from any other stimuli.

Late Filter Theories

Late filter theories, in contrast to early filter theories, suggest that all stimuli are evaluated not just for their physical characteristics, but for their meaning (Deutsch & Deutsch, 1963; Norman, 1968). If the meaning is important, the stimulus might break into ongoing processing and demand attention. It turns out that this theory is not correct. But if it's wrong, why if you're talking to a friend and a second friend says your name does your name attract your attention? Isn't it the meaning of what your second friend said that attracted your attention?

This effect has been tested in the laboratory using the dichotic listening task (Moray, 1959; Wood & Cowan, 1995). While the participant shadowed a message in one ear, the other earpiece played something in the unattended ear and then added a message with the participant's name. Participants sometimes (but not always) noticed their own name on the unattended channel; about 33% showed the effect. Another way to interpret this result is that about one third of the participants don't follow the instructions, instead switching their attention to the unattended channel every now and then. This possibility seems likely because when Wood and Cowan told people that they should be ready for new instructions during the task, 80% detected their name. It seems likely that the increase resulted from more participants sampling the channel they were not supposed to attend to because they were listening for the new instructions. A more recent experiment in which the task was a search through visual stimuli showed that one's name (and other emotional targets) didn't seem effective in grabbing attention (Harris, Pashler, & Coburn, 2004).

This problem—participants not fully following instructions—plagued another type of experiment that initially seemed to support late filter theories. In this clever experiment (Corteen & Wood, 1972), the experimenters used an indirect measure of semantic processing. Instead of asking participants directly about what they heard on the unattended channel, the experimenters measured **galvanic skin response (GSR)**, which detects nervousness. Your palms are always somewhat moist, but the sweat evaporates quickly; when you're nervous, there is more sweat. GSR accurately measures how sweaty your palm is.

In Corteen and Wood's (1972) study, participants were first exposed to a training session in which they heard some words and occasionally received a mild electric shock. The shock was administered every time one of three city names was mentioned. Soon, participants got nervous in anticipation of the shock, and that nervousness was apparent on the GSR measure. In the second phase of the experiment, participants performed a dichotic listening task, shadowing an irrelevant message coming into their right ear. In the left ear, they heard lists of words that included the city names that had been paired with shock and some new city names. No shocks were administered during this part of the experiment. Although participants could not report which words had been presented to the unattended channel, they showed the GSR response 38% of the time to the old city names, 23% of the time to new city names, and just 10% of the time to irrelevant nouns. Thus, even if people were unaware of the words on the unattended channel, it seemed that they were unconsciously analyzing these words for meaning.

But this influential study was later shown to have the same problem as the Moray (1959) study; it appeared that the effect is due to participants shifting attention to the unattended channel. Michael Dawson and Anne Schell (1982) tried much harder than previous experimenters to measure when participants shifted attention to the channel they were supposed to be ignoring.

For example, the experimenters assumed that participants attended to the wrong channel when they made a mistake in shadowing or when they reported having become aware of a word on that channel. When the researchers eliminated all trials on which participants might have switched attention to the wrong channel, the main effect of interest—heightened GSR to the city names on the unattended channel—was greatly reduced. It didn't disappear completely, but the effect was not as robust as it had appeared previously.

Other studies have taken very careful measures to ensure that participants don't switch attention (e.g., Lachter, Forster, & Ruthruff, 2004) and reported no indication of semantic processing of unattended information. Still other studies (e.g., Dupoux, Kouider, & Mehler, 2003; Franconeri, Hollingworth, & Simons, 2005) have indicated that effects of the unattended channel are observed when that information is especially salient due to its physical characteristics, which causes participants to switch attention to the unattended channel.

The Movable Filter Model

We have seen that all information is probably not analyzed in terms of its semantic content every time—that is, the late filter theory is wrong. We could account for all the data with an early filter model, such as that proposed by Broadbent, allowing that sometimes the focus of attention will lapse and participants will attend to material that they are supposed to be ignoring. In fact, we could even propose that the attentional system is biased to do exactly that. It is prudent to constantly monitor the environment around us, so the attentional system might be biased not to maintain attention to one location as dichotic listening tasks demand.

One possibility is that you can control the filter to be either early or late, depending on your needs, a point made forcefully by Michael Posner and Charles Snyder (1975). You can choose to allocate attention completely to some material or to allocate attention mostly to the material, while periodically switching attention to other material. Unattended stimuli would always be analyzed for physical characteristics and would not be analyzed for meaning.

Some data are consistent with that suggestion. William Johnston and Steven Heinz (1978) had participants listen to two word lists spoken simultaneously over headphones. Both lists were presented to both ears. Participants were told to shadow, but some participants were instructed to shadow based on the physical characteristic of the words; they were to shadow the words spoken by a man, so the participant could attend to the pitch of the word to select which one to shadow. Other participants were asked to shadow based on the semantic content of the words; they were to shadow the word that described an occupation, such as *teacher*. While they were doing the shadowing task, all participants also performed a secondary task. They watched a computer screen and pressed a button as quickly as possible when a light appeared on the screen. This secondary task provides an indirect measure of the amount of attention the shadowing task demands. The more attention the shadowing task took, the less attention would be available to watch for the light.

Response times to the light were longer when participants had to shadow based on the semantic content of the words rather than their physical characteristics (482 vs. 433 ms). Furthermore, participants made more errors when they shadowed based on semantic content rather than physical characteristic (20.5% errors vs. 5.3% errors). This experiment indicates that participants are capable of processing words at a semantic level as they perform a secondary task, but there is a higher attentional cost to doing so relative to processing only at a physical level; both shadowing performance and performance on the secondary task are worse.

The available behavioral evidence seems to indicate that all stimuli are analyzed at a physical level, but further processing demands some attentional resources. The decision to expend these resources depends on the circumstances. The likelihood that an unattended sound enters awareness depends on allocation of attentional resources, which varies with the situation. It seems that there is a fixed filter—and it seems to be early—but we can allocate our attentional resources so it's more like having a late filter by frequently sampling other perceptual channels.

Neural evidence indicates that attention may change even early sensory processing. Marty Woldorff and Steven Hillyard (1991) had participants perform a dichotic listening task. Both the attended and unattended sides presented sequences of brief tones, and participants were to make a difficult perceptual discrimination on the attended stimuli. Participants performed enough trials that the same stimulus would be attended on some trials and ignored on others. EEG was simultaneously recorded, and the EEG data showed that processing of the stimuli in primary and secondary auditory cortex was different, depending on attention. This difference began as early as 20 ms after the stimulus occurred. If the attentional filter is movable, this experiment may be an example of the limit to which the filter may be early—attention modulated the processing of the auditory stimulus almost immediately. Other data indicate that attention modulates visual processing in the thalamus, which is the structure that receives input from the retina *before* the cortex (O'Connor, Fukui, Pinsk, & Kastner, 2002).

What effect does attention have on sensory cortical processing? The processing increases, either due to a boost from attention or because attention inhibits cortical processing of other stimuli that might compete. The increase in processing has been verified in functional brain imaging experiments. For example, in one experiment (Yantis et al., 2002) participants watched a box at the center of a screen while letters rapidly appeared to the left and right. Without moving their eyes, participants were to attend to one of the letter streams, monitoring it for a target. When the target appeared, participants were to switch attention to the other letter stream. Secondary visual cortical areas showed greater activity (as measured by fMRI) associated with attention to the visual stimuli.

The caveat on this reasonable conclusion is that the amount of processing may well be open to training. Stefan Koelsch, Erich Schröger, and Mari Tervaniemi (1999) examined whether processing outside attention differs in professional musicians compared with nonmusicians if the stimuli are musical. The researchers capitalized on an effect called mismatch negativity, an effect of the brain's electrical activity as measured by event-related potentials (see chapter 2 for more details). If the investigator plays a repetitive auditory stimulus and occasionally throws in an "oddball," a negative potential in the brain's frontal lobe is observed. The researchers had professional musicians and nonmusicians listen to a repetitive major chord (composed of three pure tones). Participants were to ignore all stimuli and read a book they had brought. On 14% of the trials, one of the three tones was marginally diminished in frequency. The professional musicians showed mismatch negativity to the "oddball" chords, even though they were ignoring the stimuli. Indeed, half of them did not notice that the deviant chords had appeared, but they still showed the effect; the nonmusicians did not. Thus, training and experience can affect what is processed outside attention.

What Is Selected?

When we talk about attention being selective, we should pause to ask exactly what is selected. Until the early 1980s, many researchers believed that attention was like a spotlight (Norman, 1968; Posner, Snyder, & Davidson, 1980) and that objects falling within it were subject to more perceptual processing. Thus, attention was believed to select spatial locations. Today, it is believed that attention selects objects, not spatial locations.

We've already discussed evidence that it's possible to "split the beam." But that doesn't mean that attention isn't directed to locations—it might just mean that people can attend to two locations at once. But two other predictions of the beam metaphor do not seem to be true. First, if attention worked like a beam, then the amount of time required to shift attention from one location to another should be proportional to the distance attention must travel. Second, experiments were conducted that directly compared whether attention was directed to spatial locations or to objects, and objects won. Here's how these two points were made.

If the beam idea were right, it should take a longer time to move the attentional beam a greater distance, but that appears not to be true. Ho-Wan Kwak, Dale Dagenbach, and Howard Egeth (1991; see also Sagi & Julesz, 1985) tested this prediction by asking participants to judge whether two simple stimuli (*T* or *L*) were the same or different. The letters flashed briefly on the screen, and the experimenters varied the distance between them. Figure 4.8 shows that the time it took to make the judgment did not vary as the distance between the letters changed. From these data, it seems that attention moves ballistically from one location to another and does not sweep along in space as a beam would.

Other results directly support the idea that attention selects objects, not space. For example, participants can selectively attend to just one of two objects that overlap in a single spatial location. Ulric Neisser and Robert Becklen (1975) had participants watch a monitor with two different video images superimposed. One video showed two people playing a hand-slapping game, and

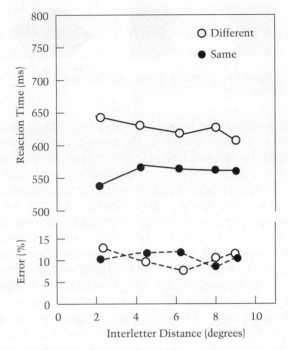

Figure 4.8.   Figure from Kwak et al. (1991) showing that the distance between two stimuli does not affect performance in terms of response times or errors. "Different" and "same" refer to whether the stimuli were the same or different.

the other showed three people playing a ball-catching game. Participants were to attend to one video or the other, and they had to indicate when certain key events, such as the ball being thrown, happened in the video they were watching. Thus, the task was a bit like a visual version of dichotic listening with shadowing. Neisser and Becklen found that participants knew very little about the unattended video, a result similar to those from dichotic listening studies. Participants find it easy to attend to just one object of two, even if they are in overlapping spatial locations. If attention were directed by spatial location, that should not be possible (or at least it should not be so easy).

Here's another prediction of the object-based account. If attention were directed to space, we would expect that the farther an object is from the location where attention is directed, the less attention it gets. If two object parts are equidistant from the location, they should get equal amounts of attention. For example, if your attention is focused on Judy's face, each of her hands would get the same amount of attention if they are equidistant from her face. Now, suppose that Judy has one hand behind her back, Sherry is standing next to her, and Sherry's left hand is the same distance from Judy's face as Judy's right hand. The spatial theory of attention would predict that Sherry's hand and Judy's hand will get equal amounts of attention because they are equidistant from Judy's face, the focus of attention. The object view of attention would predict that Judy's hand

Figure 4.9. Stimuli of the sort used in Baylis and Driver's (1993) experiment.

will get more attention. By looking at Judy's face, you select an object (Judy) for attention, and all parts of the object therefore get more attention.

Gordon Baylis and Jon Driver (1993) tested this prediction. They showed that it is harder to judge the relative distance of two corners when the corners were parts of different objects than when they were parts of the same object. On each trial, participants saw a picture similar to Figure 4.9. They were asked which angle was higher, the one on the left or the one on the right. Some participants were told to examine the white parts of the figure to make these judgments. For these participants, the figure on the left would require comparing parts (the angles) of a single object, but the figure on the right would require comparing parts of two separate objects. Other participants were told to compare the angles of the black parts of the figure; for these participants, the figure on the left required comparing parts of two objects, the figure on the right just one. Thus, Baylis and Driver were able to use the same stimulus for each condition; they got participants to interpret the figure as depicting one or two objects by using different instructions. The results showed that participants were reliably slower in making the judgment (by about 30 ms) when the instruction led them to compare the angles of two objects rather than one object. Again, this result is consistent with the idea of attention being focused on objects, not regions of space.

Kathleen O'Craven, Paul Downing, and Nancy Kanwisher (1999) collected evidence with fMRI indicating that attention selects objects for processing, not a location in space. The researchers had participants view stimuli of a semitransparent face superimposed on a house, with one stimulus moving and the other not. The parts of the brain that respond to each stimulus are well established: faces in the fusiform face area (on the ventral aspect of the temporal lobe; see chapter 3), places in the parahippocampal place area (also on the ventral aspect of the temporal lobe, but not the same as the fusiform face area), and motion in area MT (in the middle of the temporal lobe).

Participants were to compare successive faces or houses to say whether they were the same or different. The cortical activation depended on attention; thus, the fusiform face area was active only when the participant attended to the faces, even though the faces were always present—likewise, the parahippocampal place area. In addition, area MT was active only when the attended stimulus was moving, not the ignored stimulus, even though the motion was always present and was irrelevant for the task. This finding provides further evidence that when a stimulus is attended, all its attributes are attended, regardless of whether they are relevant.

This study provides compelling neural evidence supporting the behavioral evidence that attention selects objects, not areas in space, for processing. But how exactly does selection operate?

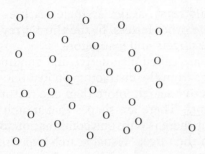

Figure 4.10. Stimulus arrays of the sort used by Treisman and Gelade (1980). In each array, the target is a small Q. In the top and center arrays, the target is easy to find because a single dimension differentiates the targets from distractors. In the bottom array, more than one dimension is necessary to distinguish the target from distractors. The top and center arrays yield automatic searches and pop out; the bottom array does not.

How Does Selection Operate?

The process by which attention selects some objects for further processing has been studied most thoroughly in visual search paradigms in which the participant looks through a large array for one particular character. To get a feel for this type of task, look for the small letter *Q* in the three arrays in Figure 4.10.

You probably found it easy to locate the large *Q* in the first two arrays and more difficult in the third. In the first array, a single feature of the *Q*—the diagonal line that differentiates a *Q* from an *O*—differentiates it from the other letters present. In the second array, again, a single feature—its size—makes the target different from the other letters. In the third array, however, no single feature differentiates the targets and distractors.

These two types of searches are called disjunctive and conjunctive. In a **disjunctive search**, the target differs from the distractors on just one feature, as in the two top arrays. In a **conjunctive search**, more than one feature differentiates the target from the distractors. There are shapes that match the target and sizes that match the target, but there is only one combination (or conjunction) of shape and size that match the target. Visual search experiments have been done with many different features, such as different shapes, sizes, colors, textures, and spatial orientations (see Quinlan, 2003, for a review).

When you do this sort of search task, it certainly feels as though some are easier, and laboratory experiments confirm this feeling. The major finding is that disjunctive searches are parallel, whereas conjunctive searches are serial. A **parallel search** is one in which all elements in the array are processed simultaneously. A **serial search** is one in which the elements of the array are evaluated one at a time.

The critical finding from laboratory experiments is this: Increasing the number of elements in the array does not affect the reaction time to find the target in the disjunctive search, but it increases the search time in the conjunctive search. The disjunctive search is parallel—all elements are evaluated simultaneously—so increasing the number of items to be evaluated does not raise the total search time. The conjunctive search is serial—elements are checked one by one—so increasing the number of items raises the search time. The participant will locate the target, on average, after checking half the items in the array. (Note that this key measure of the effect of adding distractors is the same as that used in the Shiffrin and Schneider studies of automaticity.)

The importance of the difference between disjunctive and conjunctive searches was emphasized by Anne Treisman and Garry Gelade (1980). They proposed that individual features (e.g., color and shape) are loaded **preattentively**; that is, attention is not needed to know if one of these features is present in the environment, and a search for a single feature can be conducted in parallel. A conjunctive search, however, requires knowing that more than one feature *belongs to an individual object*. That requires attention, according to Treisman and Gelade, because attention binds features together to assign them to an object. Thus, it does not require attention to know that there is something red in the environment, or something large, but it does require attention to know that there is an individual object that is both red and large.

Stand-on-One-Foot Questions

7. *In the final analysis, is the attentional filter early or late?*

8. *What does selective visual attention select?*

9. *Summarize when a visual search is easy and when it's hard.*

Questions That Require Two Feet

10. *In many horror movies, the heroine calmly takes a shower and doesn't notice the scuffling sounds made by the clodhopper shoes of the zombie carrying the axe. How can this be explained as a problem of attention?*

11. *After reading this discussion, can you think of a situation from your own experience indicating that attention is directed to objects, not spatial locations?*

Why Does Selection Fail?

Preview

It seems to happen that we want to attend to something but cannot do so; selection fails. In this section, we discuss two varieties of selection failure. One type is due to particular features of attention itself. For example, the attentional system appears biased not to return to an object that it recently investigated. The other type of failure is due to the way that attention interacts with other systems. For example, it is impossible to select responses very rapidly, a phenomenon called the psychological refractory period, which has the appearance of a limitation of attention.

In the last section, we made it sound as though the selective aspect of attention is wholly under our conscious control and that if selection fails, it is due to a lack of attentional resources. A moment's reflection will tell you that is not so. It would be marvelous if attentional selection were so simple; you would say to yourself, "I'm going to attend to this book chapter for the next hour," and you would do so, instead of finding yourself at the bottom of a page in a reverie about the marvelous spareribs you had last summer when you spilled sauce down your bathing suit. Yes, you can select what you want to attend to, but the selection does not last as long as you'd like. Attention wanders. Furthermore, there are times that you actually can't select what you would like for attention. There are two classes of reasons for such failures. Some are due to properties of attention itself, others to the way attention interacts with other components of cognition.

Properties of Attention That Cause Selection Failures

INHIBITION OF RETURN.   Your attention system appears to have a bias not to go back to something that it has recently examined. This effect was first described by Mike Posner (1978; Posner & Cohen, 1984). The task was quite simple. Two boxes appeared on a computer screen, aligned horizontally, with a crosshair between them. Participants were told to focus on the crosshair while keeping their index fingers poised above two response buttons. When an *X* appeared in one of the boxes, the participant was to push the corresponding response button as quickly as possible. (We'll call the X a GO signal because participants were to respond to it.) On some trials, however, one of the boxes would flicker before the X appeared; participants were told that the flickering in no way predicted where the X would appear and that they should therefore ignore it. (We'll call the flicker the warning signal.)

The interesting finding concerned the effect of the warning signal (if it was present) when it appeared in the same location as the GO signals. If the delay between the warning and GO was 300 ms or less, participants were faster to respond compared with trials without a warning. If the delay was longer than 300 ms, participants were slower to respond.

Posner and Cohen interpreted this result as follows. Although participants want to ignore the warning, they cannot. It captures attention automatically. At about 300 ms, however, attention disengages and cannot immediately reengage at the box that flickered. Thus, if the GO signal appears in the box less than 300 ms after the warning, there is a response time benefit because attention is already localized in the right spot. If the GO signal appears more than 300 ms after the flicker, there is a cost to response time because attention cannot return to the box. That is **inhibition of return**. Further work showed that the effect can be quite long-lasting, perhaps as long as several seconds (Tassinari & Berlucchi, 1995).

Why would the attention system have inhibition of return built into it? Possibly to make search more efficient; if you are investigating a field of objects one by one, it makes sense that there be a bias not to return to an object that has already been inspected (Posner & Cohen, 1984). It may be that as an object becomes the focus of attention, it is "tagged" so it will not be the focus of attention for some brief time thereafter (Klein, 1988). Indeed, if an object is signaled (warning), then moves, and then is signaled again (GO signal), you still get inhibition of return, which indicates that the effect shows a bias in the system not to inspect the same object again, not the same location of space again (see Klein, 2004, for a review).

IRONIC PROCESS OF MENTAL CONTROL.   Inhibition of return describes a situation in which it is hard to select something that you want to select. There are also times when you cannot help but attend to something that you don't want to attend to. In his memoirs, Tolstoy recalls that his brother used to claim that he had learned the secret of how all men could be happy and live without conflict, and he had written the secret on a green stick, which he had buried. When Tolstoy begged to see the stick, his brother said that he'd show it to him once he had done three things, one of which was to stand in a corner and not think of a white bear (Biriukov, 1906/1996) (see Photo 4.4).

Dan Wegner and his colleagues (Wegner, Schneider, Carter, & White, 1987) performed something close to this procedure in the laboratory. They simply asked participants to "think aloud" for 5 min. If they were warned not to think about a white bear, white bear thoughts intruded approximately seven times during the 5-min period.

Photo 4.4.   Don't think of this.

Wegner (1994) proposed that there are two processes by which you seek to control the contents of your mental events. The **operating process** seeks mental contents consistent with what you want to think about; for example, if you set as your goal not to think about a white bear, the operating process will search for distractions from that thought. The **monitoring process** searches for mental contents that are inconsistent with what you want to think about. For example, if you're trying not to think about white bears, it searches for mental contents about white bears and related matters. This monitoring process serves as a warning system that you are about to fail in your desired mental control.

A key assumption of the theory is that the operating process demands attentional resources, but the monitoring process does not. Thus, if attentional resources are scarce, perhaps because you're thinking of something else or you're under stress, the operating process can't do its job of searching for the appropriate mental contents. The monitoring process can do its job, however, because it doesn't require attention. Because the operating process isn't generating appropriate thoughts, the monitoring process often finds inappropriate thoughts and brings them to awareness to alert the system that these inappropriate thoughts are present. That process, in effect, generates the unwanted thoughts. Keep in mind that these ironic effects occur only under mental load—for example, if you're tired or distracted. Under normal circumstances, mental control works pretty well.

Maintaining Attention: Vigilance.   **Vigilance** is simply the ability to maintain attention, usually in a search task to detect a target or small set of targets, which might be visual, auditory, and so on. Vigilance is important in many military applications and manufacturing jobs. In a typical vigilance task, there are stretches of time in which nothing happens. Driving, for example, is not a vigilance task because the driver is continually making adjustments of speed and direction. Quality control inspection, however, is a vigilance task; the inspector checks items that are nearly identical but must maintain attention to spot the occasional item that was not produced correctly.

It isn't as easy as you might think to measure performance on a vigilance task. For example, how could you tell whether a sonar operator is doing a good job? Presumably, he or she should not miss reporting a ship when a ship is really out there. But suppose the operator simply called out, "There's a ship!" all the time. He or she wouldn't miss any ships but would constantly cause false alarms. Another person might be very conservative in calling something a ship, so that if he or she said, "There's a ship," you could be sure that there was, but this person would often fail to identify a ship when there really was one out there. Thus, different people have different criteria in a task like this.

In fact, the same person could adopt different strategies. I might say to you, "Whatever you do, don't let a ship get by; if anything looks like it could be a ship, call it a ship." Or I might say, "Whatever you do, don't say you see a ship if it's not really a ship." Your absolute sensitivity in detecting ships doesn't change, obviously, but the type of mistakes you make may change, depending on your strategy. It turns out that there is a way to analyze these two factors separately. We can separate **sensitivity**, which is your absolute ability to detect ships, from **bias**, which is a measure of whether you are liberal or conservative in saying that you see a ship. The method of separating sensitivity from bias is called **signal detection theory**. It is described in the Appendix; for now, you need to know that vigilance is measured in terms of sensitivity, not bias. People's sensitivity in a vigilance task drops after the first half hour or so.

Why does sensitivity decrease? The first thing you would think is, "Well, people get bored," but there are many other possibilities. Alertness might drop when a person does the same thing for a while. Motivation could decline. It could be a process of habituation; if you are exposed to the same stimulus repeatedly, it loses its force. Think about eating a really spicy dish; the first mouthful tastes like fire, but mouthfuls toward the bottom of the bowl don't have the same power.

Much of the research investigating vigilance has examined the characteristics of tasks that seem prone to sensitivity declines (e.g., Koelega, Brinkman, Hendriks, & Verbaten, 1989; Parasuraman & Davies, 1977; See, Howe, & Warm, 1995; Smit, Eling, & Coenen, 2004). Researchers have explored whether the speed of the task is important, whether it is a perceptual or more cognitive task, among other characteristics. A straightforward explanation of vigilance has not yet emerged, and we still can't predict with confidence whether a new vigilance task will show a sensitivity drop.

As more and more tasks are automated, more and more vigilance tasks are created—a human must oversee the task to ensure that it is operating correctly. Fortunately, the automation is also getting more sophisticated so now some systems can provide a warning cue to the human operator that he or she should pay close attention because a dangerous situation is developing. Such warning systems already exist in some power plants and aviation applications. A study by Edward Hitchcock and his colleagues (Hitchcock et al., 2003) showed that such warnings are very effective in helping operators maintain attention, as long as the warnings are reliable.

One of the more important practical implications of vigilance tasks was recently highlighted by Jeremy Wolfe and his colleagues (Wolfe, Horowitz, & Kenner, 2005). They pointed out that many of the most important visual scanning tasks are ones in which a target is rarely observed: looking for a weapon in a luggage X-ray, for example. The visual search tasks that psychologists use usually contain targets 50% of the time. How do people do on visual scanning tasks in which targets are rare? In their task, semitransparent targets (which sometimes overlapped) appeared against a noisy background—not unlike baggage X-ray screening. The stimuli remained visible on the screen until the participant responded. If targets were present 50% of the time, participants only missed 7% of them. But if they appeared only 1% of the time, errors more than tripled to 30%. The data showed that when targets were rare, participants spent less time searching than when they were frequent—because they see the target so rarely, they simply give up searching too quickly.

Interaction of Attention With Other Components of Cognition

We have discussed three ways in which the design of the attention system causes problems in selection: There is a bias not to return to a recently attended object. Attention will perversely select an undesired object when resources are scarce, and the ability to select the same type of stimuli repeatedly seems to dissipate after about half an hour. In this section, we describe a different class of attentional failures that occur not because of how attention operates but because of how it interacts with other parts of the cognitive system.

You'll recall that many of the experiments purporting to show capacity limitations used a dual task methodology; that is, participants were asked to do two things at once. We concluded that there aren't enough attentional resources to fuel both tasks, but it is also possible that performance suffers because of other cognitive processes that contribute to the tasks.

Suppose that a structure in the brain is necessary to perform visual tasks, a sort of screen where the conscious experience of vision happens. You can have only one thing on this screen at a time, so you can't do two visual tasks at the same time (e.g., play a video game and generate a mental image of your room). This is a **structural explanation** because it posits that interference between two tasks is caused by competition for mental structures, not for attentional resources.

We can make an educated guess as to which structures would be involved in performance limitations. If two tasks require the same perceptual modality—for example, if both are visual tasks—there will be more interference than if they use different modalities. Similarly, if they require the same output modality (e.g., arm movements), there will be more interference than if they call for different responses (one arm movement and one vocal response). Other work shows that structural limits can be more subtle, however. We review two effects here.

PSYCHOLOGICAL REFRACTORY PERIOD.   Alan Welford (1952) and, more recently, Hal Pashler (1998; Ruthruff, Pashler, & Hazeltine, 2003) pointed out a less obvious structural explanation for performance limitations. They suggested that there may be a response selection bottleneck. They proposed that three basic processes are necessary for performing any task, even a very simple task such as pushing a button when a light comes on. The three processes are perception (seeing the light), **response selection** (choosing the response of pushing the button), and response production (generating the muscle commands that move your finger). Welford (1952) and Pashler (1998) suggested that a person can select only one action at a time; you might be able to perceive two stimuli simultaneously and generate two movements simultaneously, but you can't select two actions simultaneously.

As evidence for the performance bottleneck, Pashler (1998) points to the **psychological refractory period**—a period of time after one response is selected during which a second response cannot be selected. For example, suppose that when a light appears on the left side of a computer screen, you are to push a button with your left hand, and when a tone sounds, you are to depress a pedal with your foot. Suppose it takes you about 500 ms to press the foot pedal when you hear the tone. What happens if I flash the light and then sound the tone a mere 50 ms after the light comes on? You will be slower to depress the pedal in this case. The reason is shown schematically in Figure 4.11. Stimulus 1 is presented and then Stimulus 2 is presented while the first stimulus is still being perceived. Once Stimulus 1 is perceived, response selection for Stimulus 1 is initiated. But when perception of Stimulus 2 is complete, the response for Stimulus 2 is not initiated; it cannot be started until response selection for Stimulus 1 is complete. That is the selection bottleneck.

The effect of the bottleneck is sizable; response time to the tone might be 700 ms instead of 500 ms. According to Figure 4.11, if response selection for Stimulus 1 were completed by the time Stimulus 2 was presented (in other words, Stimulus 2 is moved to the right in the figure), there should be no bottleneck. That prediction is true; as the interval between the first and second stimulus increases, the response time to the second stimulus gets shorter.

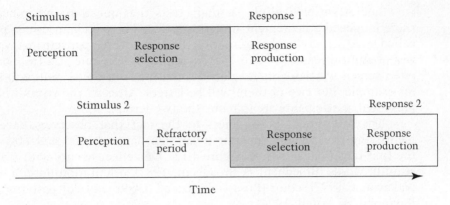

Figure 4.11. Graphic representation of the refractory period. Time moves from left to right. The response selection for Stimulus 2 cannot begin until the response selection for Stimulus 1 is completed, that is the source of the refractory effect.

The psychological refractory effect is obtained with many different types of stimuli and responses, even if the second response is an eye movement (Pashler, Carrier, & Hoffman, 1993) or a foot movement (Osman & Moore, 1993; see Pashler, 1998, for a review, and Schumacher et al., 2001, for an exception). This result is important because it demonstrates interference even from extremely simple tasks, not just from tasks that demand a lot of attention, and from tasks that do not share obvious structural demands (not just tasks that are both visual, for example). If the tasks were more complex—say, riding a bicycle and working math problems—you would interpret interference between them in terms of attention. Naturally, you're slower to work math problems if you're simultaneously riding a bicycle: Both tasks demand attention. But in the example just described, we are talking about very simple tasks that should take very little attention.

If there is an output bottleneck, you might think, "Heck, maybe we don't need this idea of attentional capacity in the first place. Maybe the problems we see when people try to do two tasks at once are due to output bottleneck problems. The problem is not capacity sharing—it's the crowding of outputs." But that can't be the whole story because capacity seems to be limited even when no output is required; for example, people can't attend to many different types of sensory input at once. Nevertheless, the evidence for an output bottleneck raises the possibility that what we believed were effects of limited attention may actually have nothing to do with attention.

ATTENTIONAL BLINK. The psychological refractory period demonstrates that performance may be poor in a dual task paradigm for reasons other than capacity limitations, in this case, because successive responses cannot be selected rapidly. What if successive tasks did not demand responses? Would there still be a decrement in performance?

The **attentional blink** paradigm tests that question and indicates that there is indeed a decrement in performance. The paradigm uses a procedure called rapid serial visual presentation (RSVP) in which participants watch a series of stimuli (usually 10 to 15) that appear briefly one at a time on a computer screen. Participants may be told that most of the stimuli will be digits, for example, but two of them will be letters. After all the stimuli have been presented, participants are to name the two letters.

The attentional blink refers to the fact that observers have trouble identifying the second target if it appears between 100 and 600 ms after the first target, as shown in Figure 4.12. This effect occurs with a variety of stimuli: words (Broadbent & Broadbent, 1987), orientation (Joseph, Chun, & Nakayama, 1997), color (Ross & Jolicoeur, 1999), and dot patterns (Shapiro, Raymond, & Arnell, 1994).

What causes the attentional blink? It cannot be a response selection effect because participants need not hurry their responses; the dependent measure is accuracy, not time. It might seem that the effect is more likely perceptual—perhaps the first stimulus masks the second, for example. But there are data

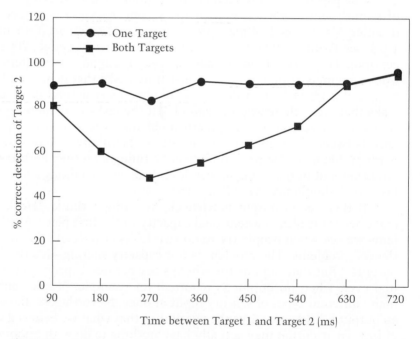

Figure 4.12. Typical results of the attentional blink experiment. In the one target condition, participants are told to report only the second of two targets, and the time between the first and second targets does not affect performance. In both targets' conditions, participants are to report both targets, and performance is poor when the second target appears approximately 100 to 600 ms after the first target. Data based on "Temporary Suppression of Visual Processing in an RSVP Task: An attentional Blink!" by J. E. Raymond K. L. Shapiro, and K. M. Arnell, 1992, *Journal of Experimental Psychology: Human Perception & Performance*, 18, pp. 849–860.

showing that the attentional blink is still robust when the first target is visual and the second target auditory or vice versa (Arnell & Jolicoeur, 1999). Another experiment argues against a perceptual account of the attentional blink. Rene Marois, Do-Joon Yi, and Marvin Chun (2004) conducted an attentional blink study using pictures of faces and scenes as stimuli while participants were scanned with fMRI. Recall from chapter 3 that there are brain areas that are known to be active when faces or scenes are perceived. The researchers asked the question "Will those areas be active when the stimulus is not perceived because of the attentional blink?" The data showed that the relevant cortical area *was* active, even when the participant was not aware of the stimulus, although the activation was still higher when the participant perceived it. Parts of the lateral frontal cortex, however, were active only when the stimulus was consciously perceived.

These data argue for a two-stage model of visual attention, in which early visual processing categorizes the stimulus, but attention is necessary for the stimulus to be registered into a more durable state that makes it accessible to consciousness and subsequent verbal report. The attentional blink seems to represent a bottleneck of attention that affects this second stage (Arnell & Duncan, 2002; Chun & Potter, 1995; Jolicoeur, 1999; but see Awh, Serences, Laurey, Dhaliwal, van der Jagt, & Dassonville, 2004).

Our discussion of attention has led us to consider what happens after we perceive an object. The attentional blink indicates that after perception there is a stage of processing that transforms the stimulus into a more durable representation, and that new representation enables us to verbally report it and is associated with awareness of having perceived it. That next stage of processing is the subject of chapter 5.

Stand-on-One-Foot Questions

12. *What properties of attention can cause selection failures?*
13. *Name some sources of apparent attention limitations that are more likely due to other components of the cognitive system.*

Questions That Require Two Feet

14. *Suppose your friend had an ugly breakup with his girlfriend, and he finds he can't stop thinking about her. Try as he might not to think about her, he just can't stop. What would you advise him to do?*
15. *Apply the terminology from signal detection theory to car alarms and comment on their effectiveness.*
16. *What would you do to make the people who screen carry-on baggage at airports more accurate?*

KEY TERMS

attention
attentional blink
automatic
bias
conjunctive search
continuous task
dichotic listening
discrete task
disjunctive search
distractor
dual task paradigm
early filter

galvanic skin
   response (GSR)
inhibition of return
late filter
limited
monitoring process
multiple resources
operating process
parallel search
preattentively
psychological refractory
   period

response selection
response to stimulus
   interval
selective
sensitivity
serial search
shadow
signal detection theory
structural explanation
target
vigilance

Sensory Memory and Primary Memory

5

What Is Sensory Memory?

- Early Span of Apprehension Studies
- Sperling's Partial Report Procedure
- Characteristics of Iconic Memory
- Echoic Memory

What Are the Characteristics of Primary Memory?

- Impetus to Study Primary Memory
- How Forgetting Occurs
- Representation
- Capacity

How Does Primary Memory Work?

- Models of Primary Memory
- Working Memory
- Neural Basis of Working Memory
- Working Memory as a Workspace

It is natural to think of memory as a storehouse or repository for facts, rather like a library. In chapter 1, we said that cognitive psychologists conceive of the mind as using representations and processes that manipulate those representations. Thus, psychologists interested in memory want to know what these representations look like, how they enter the storehouse in the first place, and how they are retrieved from the storehouse.

In this chapter, we consider what happens to memories before they enter the storehouse of **secondary memory**. This repository is available to the cognitive system, but its information is not readily available for use by cognitive processes. First, the information must go from secondary to **primary memory**, a hypothetical buffer in which information can be briefly held and manipulated. We have said that processes operate on representations to make cognition happen; primary memory is where processes operate on representations from memory.

For example, if I ask you, "What color is a polar bear?", the answer "White" is in your secondary memory, but this fact is not available to cognitive processes (e.g., the processes that would enable you to answer my question) until it is retrieved from secondary memory and put into primary memory. Only then is the information available to the processes that construct the sentence to answer my question. Thus, primary memory serves as a staging ground for thought. In addition, primary memory serves as a temporary buffer for information. If you and I were in the grocery store and I asked you to get chocolate, bread, and margarine while I shopped for other things, you would maintain these three items in primary memory. You need to retain this information only briefly while you look for the items, so you probably don't enter the details in secondary memory. Thus, primary memory both retrieves information from secondary memory and takes in information from the environment, either for temporary maintenance or possibly for entry into secondary memory.

If this description is accurate, we might first want to know how material gets from the environment into primary memory. The process turns out to be complicated. Material perceived in the environment goes through another buffer called **sensory memory** before it ever gets to primary memory. Our first question, therefore, must be **What is sensory memory?** As we'll see, sensory memory has an enormous capacity. A great deal of information can rush into sensory memory simultaneously, but such memory is very short lived, lasting no more than a second.

Once we have some understanding of sensory memory, we'll be in a better position to consider primary memory. A key question that we want to be answered is **What are the characteristics of primary memory?** Researchers became interested in primary memory because it appeared to be fundamentally different from secondary memory. These differences should be reflected in characteristics of primary memory, including how forgetting occurs, how memories are represented, and how much information can be stored at once. Primary memory initially seemed easy to characterize on these dimensions, but it turned out to be more complex than researchers had first appreciated.

Finally, we consider the question **How does primary memory work?** We discuss two conceptions of primary memory: the short-term memory model and the working memory model. The short-term memory model eventually was shown to be incorrect, but it continues to be so important to cognitive psychology that some familiarity with it is necessary. The working memory model has been quite successful in accounting for a great deal of data. We close this chapter with some examples of how working memory contributes to cognitive processing.

What Is Sensory Memory?

Preview

The seeds of the study of sensory memory were planted by the introspectionists. Recall that they were interested in the contents of consciousness, and they were therefore interested in the amount of information that could rush into consciousness simultaneously. They determined that people could perceive four or five complex stimuli (e.g., letters) in a very brief exposure. Participants in their experiments often reported that they felt as though they had perceived more letters but forgot some of them even as they were reporting the others. It was not until 1960 that psychologist George Sperling showed conclusively that many more stimuli are actually perceived, but only four or five are reported because the remainder are forgotten. Sperling proposed the existence of a memory system that can hold a large number of items, but only for a second or so. In this section, we consider the characteristics of sensory memory: how much information it can hold, the type of information it holds, how forgetting occurs, and so on.

How much information can you take in simultaneously? In other words, how much can you perceive in an instant? This question has been of interest since psychology's earliest days, and if you think back to chapter 1 and recall the program of the introspectionists, you'll realize it makes sense that they would be interested in this topic. Remember that they were interested almost exclusively in conscious processes. Thus, it was important to them to know how much information could get into consciousness at once. They called this measure the **span of apprehension**. Studies of the span of apprehension paved the way for the study of sensory memory because even though researchers were trying to study a purely perceptual process—how much information could be perceived in a very brief exposure—it seemed that memory processes nevertheless were involved in the tasks they used. We begin by briefly reviewing the span of apprehension studies, which will help you understand why the first sensory memory studies were conducted.

Early Span of Apprehension Studies

An early study of the span of apprehension was conducted by Stanley Jevons (1871), a logician. Jevons took a small cup, dipped it into a bowl of black beans,

Jevons's Estimate	Actual Numbers												
	3	4	5	6	7	8	9	10	11	12	13	14	15
3	23												
4		65											
5			102	7									
6			4	120	17								
7			1	20	113	30	2						
8					25	76	24	6	1				
9						28	76	37	11	1			
10						1	18	46	19	4			
11							2	16	26	17	7	2	
12								2	12	19	11	3	2
13										3	6	3	2
14										1	1	4	6
15											1	2	2
Totals	23	65	107	147	156	135	122	107	69	45	26	14	11

Figure 5.1.   Results of Jevons's (1871) experiment.

and then tossed the beans onto a black tray, on which there was a small white box. Some of the black beans fell into the white box and some on the black tray. Jevons did this while looking elsewhere, so he had no idea how many beans would fall into the white box. He glanced in the box and immediately estimated how many beans were in the box. Then, he counted them to see how close he was. He did this 1,027 times, and he found that if there were 3 or 4 beans, his instant estimate was always correct. With 5 beans, he was still very good but not perfect (about 95%). His accuracy dropped as the number of beans increased, so if there were 15 beans, he was correct a little less than 20% of the time (see Figure 5.1).

So what is Jevons's span of apprehension? You can see that it depends on how you want to define *span*. If you think that his span is the maximum number of beans he could perceive reliably without error, his span is 4 because he began to make mistakes when there were 5 beans or more. That estimate seems a bit conservative, considering he was 95% correct when there were 5. However, you wouldn't want to say his span is 15 because he was right less than one fifth of the time when there were that many beans. The usual strategy in these situations is to take the 50% mark, where the participant was right half the time and wrong half the time. In Jevons's case, that put the span of apprehension at 9.

Naturally, Jevons's laboratory conditions could not be everything one would desire for such an experiment. The chief problem was that he had to rely on "a momentary glance" as his exposure to the stimuli, and it's possible that the duration of his momentary glance varied. Perhaps without meaning to, he glanced a little longer when there were a lot of beans in the box, for example. More sophisticated equipment became available by the 1920s that allowed precise timing of the exposure of visual stimuli. One such device is a tachistoscope, which uses a shutter like that of a camera to allow the participant to see the stimulus for a precise amount of time. Today, such experiments are conducted on computers. A number of experimenters conducted span of apprehension experiments with better-controlled exposure durations (and substituting black dots on a white card for the beans). Their estimates of the span of apprehension were close to Jevons's; they averaged around 8.4 (Fernberger, 1921; Glanville & Dallenbach, 1929; Oberly, 1924).

These experimenters controlled the duration of stimulus presentation, but there was another problem they could not solve. They were not measuring the span of apprehension directly; instead, they were measuring the span of what participants could apprehend *and report*. For example, Douglas Glanville and Karl Dallenbach (1929) reported that some of their participants said that as they were reporting some stimuli, they were forgetting the others. One participant said, "Do not think that the judgment is often made during the exposure except when figures are few in number, or patterns are familiar. Otherwise I have meaning of pattern left from exposure and from that I figure out the number of forms on the card" (p. 220). A popular textbook of the time (Woodworth, 1938) concluded that the span of apprehension must be somewhat higher than measurements showed because participants might forget as they report, but how much higher was not known.

Sperling's Partial Report Procedure

It wasn't until 1960 that a better method of testing the span of apprehension was devised. George Sperling (1960) came up with the **partial report procedure** for the experiments in his Ph.D. dissertation. Sperling used arrays of numbers and letters like those in Figure 5.2. Participants saw a display of 4 to 12 items for 50 ms and then had to report as much of it as they could. In a full report, participants reported about 4 items, or 33%, of a 12-item array (top row, Figure 5.2). As in earlier experiments, Sperling's participants said that they could see more items but forgot them quickly.

In a partial report, participants saw the display for 50 ms, as before. Then they heard a tone at one of three pitches: high, medium, or low. The pitch of the tone was a cue for which row of the display the participant was to report; participants didn't have to report the whole array, only the cued row. When the partial report procedure was used, participants got, on average, 3 items from the desired row correct (middle row, Figure 5.2). This result doesn't seem so exciting, but keep in mind that participants did not know which row they would have to report because the tone was random each time. Sperling (1960) reasoned that participants must have been equally prepared to report any of the three rows because they couldn't know which row they would have

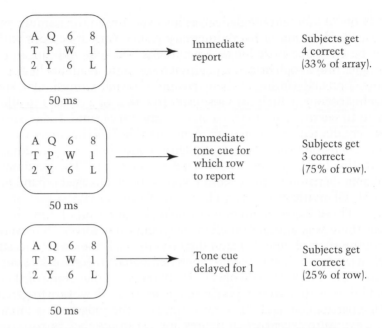

Figure 5.2. The design and representative results of Sperling's (1960) experiment. Note that the partial report procedure (center) indicates that much of the array is perceived, but if the cue in the partial report procedure is delayed 1 s (bottom), much of the information from the array is lost.

to report. The same logic is used in classroom testing: A professor can't test students on all the material they are supposed to know, so the exam contains a subset of the material, and the professor assumes that students' performance on this subset of the material is a reasonable estimate of their knowledge of all the material. Sperling reasoned that the percentage of the row participants got correct was a good estimate of their knowledge of the entire array. Participants reported an average of 3 items correctly (75% of the row) when the partial report procedure was used, so Sperling inferred that they knew 75% of the full array, or 9 items. Thus, the full report indicates that the span of apprehension is 4 items, but the partial report procedure indicates that it is 9 items.

If that were true, it would mean that participants perceive much of the array (about 75%), but they lose that information very quickly, either because it decays almost immediately or because interference results from reporting the other items. Sperling (1960) tried another experiment in which he showed participants the array and then waited 1 s before presenting the tone that told participants which row to report. Now, the partial report advantage was gone: Participants averaged only 1 item (25%) from the desired row, indicating that they could report about 4 items from the array, as in a full report (bottom row, Figure 5.2). Thus, it looked as if the material was lost through decay, not interference from report.

Sperling (1960) argued that when the array of stimuli is presented, it enters a large-capacity **iconic memory** from which the contents decay rapidly. The participant therefore rushes to report the contents of iconic memory, but by the time he or she has reported 4 letters, the contents have faded. (Sperling actually used the term *sensory memory*, which later came to refer to any of a number of short-term sensory buffers, including a visual buffer, an auditory buffer, and possibly others. The term *iconic memory* came to refer to the visual buffer, and we follow that terminology here.)

Characteristics of Iconic Memory

LARGE CAPACITY.   It's possible that iconic memory maintains most of what the perceptual system encounters. Under some conditions, the capacity of iconic memory can be quite large. For example, Emanuel Averbach and George Sperling (1961) presented their participants with arrays of 18 characters, with either a dark field or a light field before and after the letters. The results of this simple manipulation were dramatic. When the prefields and postfields are dark, iconic memory has a bigger capacity and also lasts much longer. The icon—that is, the contents of iconic memory—is still available after a 2-s delay, whereas the icon is gone after 0.5 s with bright prefields and postfields. The bottom line is that the capacity of iconic memory can be large—it holds 17 letters at the briefest delay with the dark fields—but the size and duration depend heavily on the details of experimental situation.

SPONTANEOUS DECAY AND POTENTIAL TO BE ERASED.   We have described the loss of information from iconic memory as being caused by spontaneous decay. Even if the participant does nothing but look at a simple white (or black) field, the contents of iconic memory will degrade. That finding is clear enough from Sperling's original experiments. In the early 1980s, researchers realized that although iconic memory does spontaneously decay, the decay begins not when the stimulus disappears but when it first appears.

Vincent Di Lollo (1980) demonstrated this effect in a compelling way. In this experiment, participants knew that the basic stimulus was an array of 25 dots. They first saw 12 dots on a field for 10 to 200 ms. After a brief delay (10 ms), they saw another stimulus with 12 dots for 10 ms; thus, they saw a total of 24 dots from the 25-dot array, and their task was to say which dot was missing. Because they didn't see all 24 dots at the same time, iconic memory had to serve as a bridge between the first 12 and the second 12. This task is normally quite easy because the time to be bridged is just 10 ms, well within the duration of iconic memory. All that varied in the experiment was the duration of the first array. Surprisingly, errors increased when the first stimulus was presented for a longer time, as shown in Figure 5.3.

Researchers had been thinking that iconic memory was some effect of stimulation persisting in the visual system; thus, iconic memory would begin to decay when the stimulus disappeared from the environment. Di Lollo's

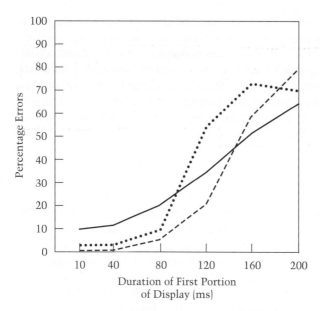

Figure 5.3. Results from Di Lollo's (1980) experiment showing that iconic memory starts to decay at stimulus onset, not when the stimulus disappears. In this paradigm, iconic memory was needed to bridge between two stimuli; the graph shows that if the first stimulus was present for a longer time before the second appeared, performance was worse. Each line represents data from one participant.

experiment indicated that iconic memory began to fade when the stimulus first appeared, not when it was extinguished.

In addition to spontaneous decay, there is a second way in which information can be lost from iconic memory. The experimenter can also erase the icon; the technical term is to **mask the icon**, which means to present some random visual stimuli that replace the material currently in iconic memory. In the early 1960s, a number of studies showed that the partial report advantage disappears if the stimulus array is followed by a mask, consistent with the idea that the mask erases the contents of iconic memory (see Breitmeyer & Ganz, 1976, and Turvey, 1973, for reviews).

BRIEF DURATION. As has been emphasized in our description of these experiments, iconic memory can hold a lot of information, but the memory is short lived, perhaps as short as 500 ms and typically no longer than 1 s, depending on the experimental situation. But even under optimal circumstances, iconic memory lasts only a few seconds, a far cry from other types of memory, which can last your entire lifetime.

REPRESENTATION. Iconic memory initially was believed to be a rather literal representation of the physical characteristics of the stimuli. In other words, if the stimulus *A* is in iconic memory, there is no information about whether *A* is a number or a letter; iconic memory stores the physical shape of the stimulus but nothing about what it means. Researchers drew this conclusion because only physical characteristics were effective partial report cues. For example, Sperling's initial experiments used the physical location of the stimulus (top, middle, or bottom row) as the cueing characteristic, which yielded a partial report effect. Other physical characteristics also seemed to yield cueing effects, such as the size of stimuli when participants were directed to report either large or small stimuli (Von Wright, 1968). But when information about stimulus category was used ("Report only the letters, not the digits"), a partial report effect was not found (e.g., see Sperling, 1960). Researchers concluded that iconic memory must not include categorical information, but that view was later challenged because some experiments showed a partial cueing effect from semantic information. The mixture of results may reflect the fact that semantic information is partly available in iconic memory.

We do not currently know what iconic memory does for the cognitive system. Nevertheless, the effects provide important clues about how the visual system and primary memory interact; researchers use the idea of iconic memory in accounting for other phenomena (Becker, Pashler, & Anstis, 2000; Kerzel & Ziegler, 2005).

Echoic Memory

Echoic memory is the auditory version of iconic memory. Again, *sensory memory* is a more general term. Iconic and echoic memory are both forms of sensory memory.

There is good evidence for some storage of sound in the very short term. One source of evidence comes from masking experiments conceptually similar to those we discussed for vision. For example, Dominic Massaro (1970) had participants listen to a tone and identify it as high or low in pitch. The task was made difficult by the presence of a masking tone of random pitch that followed the target tone. If the delay between the target and mask was rather long (350 ms), participants averaged about 90% correct, but if the mask followed the target without delay, participants averaged just 60% correct.

Presumably, the negative effect of the mask decreases with delay because the auditory system has had more time to get the stimulus into a more stable state (perhaps to transfer it to primary memory). Once the delay between the stimulus and the tone reaches 250 ms, the mask doesn't matter, presumably because 250 ms is how long it takes to get the target safely out of echoic memory and into primary memory. We can tentatively place the duration of echoic memory at 250 ms (Cowan, 1987; see Kaernbach, 2004, for a review of echoic memory).

Stand-on-One-Foot Questions

1. *What is the point of the partial report procedure?*
2. *What are the characteristics of sensory memory?*

Questions That Require Two Feet

3. *Sensory memory is certainly a real phenomenon, but it doesn't seem that we would use it very often. Ralph Haber commented that it would be useful only for reading, at night, during a lightning storm. Can you think of a time when you use iconic memory, however briefly? Hint: Think of the movies.*

4. *Most people have noticed that if they stare at something for 30 s or more and then look at something blank (a wall or sheet of paper), they see an afterimage of what they stared at. Is that a demonstration of iconic memory?*

What Are the Characteristics of Primary Memory?

Preview

It has long been noted that it is possible to hold some information in mind for a brief period of time. For example, if a friend mentions five things he or she needs from the grocery store, you can repeat them back immediately. In the late 1950s, researchers began to think that such brief memories might be supported by a separate memory system. We discuss three characteristics of primary memory: forgetting (caused by both interference and decay); the format in which the information is coded (in terms of sound, visual appearance, and meaning); and the amount of information that can be held, or capacity (which depends on the type of information).

Impetus to Study Primary Memory

In this section, we characterize primary memory on three dimensions: how material is lost from primary memory, how the system codes material, and how much material it can hold. This work began in the late 1950s when three classic articles were published, energizing psychologists to study primary memory. The concept of a primary memory separate from secondary memory had been around since the late 19th century, but little research had been done on the topic. These articles triggered an avalanche of activity during the 1960s, and primary memory remains a vibrant research topic today.

First, Donald Broadbent (1958) published a work that likened the human mind to an information processing system, starting with a large-capacity sensory memory, then going through a filter that deletes most of the information, and finally entering primary memory. Information can enter primary memory not only from sensory memory, but also from secondary memory. Broadbent's particular formulation was less important than the fact that at the heart of his information processing model he made a distinction between primary and secondary memory.

A second influential article by George Miller (1956) emphasized that, across a number of tasks, the number 7 kept popping up as a limit on human performance. The article was really about this limit to information processing, but it is almost always cited for its inclusion of the primary memory limit of seven items, plus or minus two.

These publications by Broadbent and Miller convinced researchers that primary memory was important. The third (actually a pair of papers) gave researchers a method by which to study primary memory. Similar findings were published almost at the same time by two different laboratories: John Brown's (1958) in England and Lloyd Peterson and Margaret Jean Peterson's (1959) in the United States. Brown and the Petersons showed that participants forget even a very small amount of information over a very short delay if they are distracted. The task they used is somewhat similar, so it is called the Brown–Peterson task. The task worked like this. The participant heard a trigram of three consonants such as *TPW* and then a three-digit number like *529*. The participant's task was to immediately start counting backward by threes, beginning with the three-digit number (529, 526, 523, and so on). After some delay (between 0 and 18 s), the experimenter stopped the participant's counting and asked him or her to report what the three consonants were. The point of the backward counting was to prevent the participant from rehearsing the letters.

Three letters are well within the primary memory capacity of most participants, so when the delay was 0 s, participants were nearly 100% correct. But if the participant counted backward for 18 s, recall dropped to around 10% (see Figure 5.4).

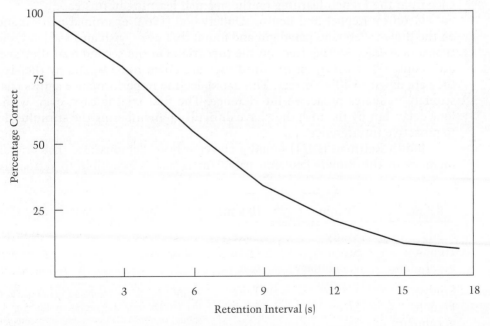

Figure 5.4.   Results from Peterson and Peterson's (1959) study showing forgetting of very little information (three letters) after a brief delay (18 s) if participants are distracted.

8 a.m.	9 a.m.	10 a.m.
Study Spanish vocabulary	Study French vocabulary	Take French test
Sleep	Study French vocabulary	Take French test

Figure 5.5. If we compared performance on the French test, the people in the top row would show proactive interference compared with the people in the bottom row.

How Forgetting Occurs

Much (but not all) of the forgetting from primary memory occurs due to interference. **Proactive interference** occurs when older learning interferes with new learning. For example, suppose that you're trying to learn some French vocabulary words. Look at the two schedules in Figure 5.5. In both cases, you study French vocabulary for an hour and then take a test, but in one case you've just finished studying Spanish. You are likely to remember less French if you've just finished studying Spanish. That is proactive interference: Earlier learning interferes with new learning.

In **retroactive interference**, later learning interferes with earlier learning, as shown in Figure 5.6. In this case, studying Spanish comes after the learning we are concerned with (French), so we would say that there is retroactive interference from learning Spanish. (Naturally, there is also proactive interference from the French learning on the Spanish learning in this case.)

Geoffrey Keppel and Benton Underwood (1962) examined performance on the Brown–Peterson paradigm and found that even with an 18-s delay, participants average 95% correct on the first trial. On the second trial they average about 70% correct, on the third they are down to 55%, and by the sixth they are down to 40% correct. This rapid decline in performance across trials strongly indicates proactive interference. The first trial is easy, even with a long delay, but by the fifth they have difficulty remembering the stimulus due to proactive interference.

Judith Reitman (1971) found a clever way to demonstrate that primary memory in the Brown–Peterson paradigm is also susceptible to retroactive

8 a.m.	9 a.m.	10 a.m.
Study French vocabulary	Study Spanish vocabulary	Take French test
Study French vocabulary	Sleep	Take French test

Figure 5.6. If we compared performance on the French test, the people in the top row should show retroactive interference compared with the people in the bottom row.

interference. She reasoned that retroactive interference increases as the new material becomes more similar to the old material. For example, there would be considerable retroactive interference if you first studied baseball statistics and then studied football statistics, but there would be much less if you first studied baseball statistics and then studied dance steps. Reitman varied what people did during the delay period of the Brown–Peterson paradigm: Either they listened to a humming sound, or they listened to syllables, searching for a target. Because the target material was nouns, if primary memory is susceptible to interference, the second task should interfere more because it's verbal. That's exactly what Reitman found.

Forgetting in primary memory occurs not only due to interference, but also due to **decay,** a spontaneous decomposition of the representation over time. Some researchers have suggested that decay may be necessary because without it interference would overwhelm the system. Here's an example suggested by Erik Altmann and Wayne Gray (2002). Suppose you are driving on a highway and every few seconds you pass a sign posting a new speed limit. After the 100th sign, how could you remember the current speed limit and not confuse it with the previous 99? There should be massive proactive interference. A decay process would mitigate interference because items 1 to 99 would have been decaying by the time you hit the 100th. From this functional view of decay, Altmann and Gray predicted that the longer something is in primary memory, the more it will decay, and the harder it will be to remember.

In Altmann and Gray's (2002) task, a digit appeared on the computer screen, and participants categorized it using one of two rules: high/low or even/odd. Only one rule applied on each trial, and the current rule was updated every few trials by a message that appeared briefly on the screen (each message was a speed limit sign, so to say). The important point is that participants had to remember the current rule in order to categorize digits correctly. The experimenters predicted that as time passed since a rule update, task performance would get worse because it would be harder to remember the current rule (due to decay). Figure 5.7 shows percentage error as a function of how many trials have passed since the rule was updated. Performance indeed gets worse (errors increase) the longer the rule has been in primary memory. Thus, the final word on forgetting in primary memory is that interference (proactive and retroactive) and decay contribute to forgetting.

Representation

It appears that material can be coded in primary memory in at least three ways: visuospatially, acoustically (in terms of sound), and semantically (in terms of meaning). There is also evidence for a primary memory component that can store tactile memories—that is, how things feel on the skin—but not much research has been directed toward that representation (Harris, Miniussi, Harris, & Diamond, 2002; Romo & Salinas, 2003).

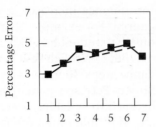

Percentage Error

Trials Since Rule Changed

Figure 5.7.   Data from Altmann and Gray's (2002) study of decay in working memory. The data show the percentage of errors participants make in categorizing digits as a function of how many trials have elapsed since the rule changed. The longer the rule has been in working memory, the more errors participants make, indicating decay of the rule from working memory. The dashed line represents the general trend of the data. Data from *"Forgetting to Remember: The Functional Relationship of Decay and Interference,"* by E. M. Altmann and W. D. Gray, 2002, *Psychological Science, 13.* Fig. 4, p. 31.

The earliest research indicated that everything in primary memory was coded acoustically, and the type of coding was pointed to as a difference between primary and secondary memory: Primary memory seemed to use an acoustic code, whereas secondary memory used a semantic code. As we'll see, that conclusion that these codes were unique to each memory system was premature, but the early work did establish that primary memory used an acoustic code at least some of the time. Alan Baddeley (1966) conducted a convincing experiment on this point. To get a feel for how it worked, read the following list aloud, look away from the page, and see whether you can recall the words:

mad, man, mat, cap, cad, can, cat, cap

That probably seemed pretty difficult. Now try to do the same thing with a second set of words:

big, long, broad, great, high, tall, large, wide

Finally, try it with a third list of words:

cow, day, bar, few, hot, pen, sup, pit

As you probably noticed, the first list contained words that sounded the same. Baddeley asked participants to remember five words drawn from the lists shown here; 24 five-word lists were compiled from each master list. When the words all sounded the same, participants could produce only 9.6% of the sequences perfectly. When the words were semantically related, as in the second list, they could produce an average of 71.0% of the lists perfectly. When the words were neither acoustically nor semantically related, as in the third list, participants could produce 82.1% of the lists perfectly. Thus, there is a huge cost to performance when the words sound the same, as well as a smaller cost when the words are semantically related. Baddeley concluded from this result that the words had been coded acoustically in primary memory (see also Mueller, Seymour, Kieras, & Meyer, 2003).

The conclusion that an acoustic code was important in primary memory was strengthened by findings showing that if the experimenter presented words visually as written words, participants would recode them into an acoustic code. Conrad (1964) showed this in an ingenious experiment. He presented a series of letters on a screen at a rate of 1 per 0.75 s. After six letters appeared, participants were to write them down on an answer sheet, guessing if necessary. One twist was that only a subset of the letters of the alphabet were used: *B, C, P, T, V, F, M, N, S,* and *X.* Conrad was interested in what sorts of errors people made. If they didn't remember *B,* for example, would they just randomly put in one of the other nine letters? No. Participants made systematic errors, based on the sound of the letters. Making such errors is called the **acoustic confusion effect**.

For example, when *M* was presented in the stimulus, if people made an error they were very likely to recall the letter as *N,* which sounds like *M,* rather than recalling *X* or *V,* which look a bit like *M* but don't sound like it.

Nevertheless, we do not rely only on an acoustic code in primary memory. What do we do with spatial information, for example? Suppose I said to you, "I'd like you to imagine a 4 × 4 matrix of squares because that might help you in this next task. Suppose the upper right-hand cell is the starting square, and in that square, I'd like you to put a 1. In the next square down, put a 2. In the next square to the left, put a 3. In the next square to the left, put a 4." Then, I ask you to reproduce my instructions to you. Almost everyone reports attempting this primary memory task using a spatial code.

One source of evidence that people code this type of information spatially comes from interference experiments. What would happen if you asked a participant to perform a spatial task at the same time as the matrix task? Alan Baddeley and his colleagues (Baddeley, Grant, Wight, & Thomson, 1975) asked participants to do this primary memory matrix task while performing a pursuit tracking task in which they had to follow a little spot of light with a handheld stylus. As you might expect, having to do this spatial tracking task played havoc with their primary memory in the matrix task. Performance went from an average of a little over two errors without the tracking task to about nine errors with the tracking task. But how do we know that it was the *spatial* nature of each task that interfered and not just that it's hard to do two tasks at once? The experimenters administered a second version of the matrix task that was not spatial. They replaced the words *left, right, up,* and *down* with *good, bad, slow,* and *quick.* The sentences became a little odd ("In the next square to the *quick,* put a 2"), but that didn't matter because the participants' job was to report back the sentences, regardless of whether they were sensible. In this version of the task, participants didn't code the sentences spatially, and the tracking task had no effect on their performance. Again, the point of these experiments is to show that there is a spatial medium in which to maintain information for short periods of time.

We use a third type of code in primary memory—a semantic code that can maintain information about what things mean. A particular task paradigm that has been used frequently to investigate semantic codes in primary memory is called **release from proactive interference**. We noted that proactive interference occurs when information learned earlier interferes with the learning of new information; it is observed in the Brown–Peterson task when performance in remembering the letter trigrams decreases over trials. Release from proactive interference refers to the fact that the proactive interference dissipates if the stimulus materials are changed. For example, Delos Wickens and his associates (Wickens, Dalezman, Eggemeier, & Thomas, 1976) used the standard Brown–Peterson paradigm, but instead of consonant trigrams, participants were to remember the names of fruits, such as *apple, pear*, and *orange*. After three trials, different groups of participants heard different stimuli. One group (the control group) heard the names of fruits again; another group heard the names of vegetables, another flowers, another meats, and a final group the names of professions. As shown in Figure 5.8, there was considerable difference in the performance on this fourth trial.

Notice that the group that continued to hear the names of fruits performed the worst; they continued on the downward trend caused by proactive

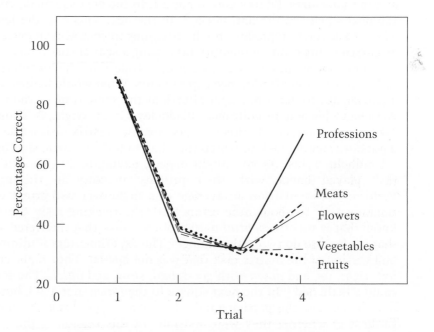

Figure 5.8. Results from Wickens et al. (1976). All five groups used the Brown–Peterson paradigm for the first three trials with fruits as stimuli. Notice how performance declined because of proactive interference. On the fourth trial, the stimuli changed for four of the groups. Notice that performance increased when the meaning of the stimuli changed. The reduction in proactive interference with the change in stimuli is called release from proactive interference.

interference. The other groups showed varying amounts of release from proactive interference; the most dramatic improvement came from participants whose stimuli were professions, which are arguably the most different from fruits. This experiment constitutes evidence that <u>primary memory codes semantics or meaning;</u> if it did not, the change in semantic content on the fourth trial would make no difference in performance.

Capacity

How much information can primary memory hold? You may have heard the number 7 mentioned as the capacity of primary memory, and indeed, this was the figure cited by George Miller (1956) in his well-known paper mentioned earlier. Around the turn of the 20th century, researchers began to use the **digit span task** to measure the capacity of primary memory. In this task, the experimenter reads aloud a series of digits at a rate of one digit per second. The participant must repeat back the digits in the correct order. The experimenter increases the number of digits until the participant cannot repeat them back without error. Most adults can reproduce about seven digits. Average digit span is often described as "seven plus or minus two" to reflect the fact that people's performance varies, but most of us can recall between five and nine digits. Thus, an early view was that the capacity of primary memory was about seven. But we've just finished saying that primary memory can hold different codes. Might it not be the case that the capacity depends on the code? That does appear to be true.

The capacity of the acoustic code is actually best described not in terms of the number of items but in terms of time; the capacity is basically as much material as you can say to yourself in about 2 s. For the semantic code, the capacity is best described in terms of chunks, and the capacity of the visuospatial code is about four objects.

An important clue to the capacity of the acoustic code comes from the **word length effect**. Participants can remember more short words than long ones in a primary memory task. This effect was demonstrated by Alan Baddeley, Neil Thomson, and Mary Buchanan (1975). They gave participants a simple short-term memory task—listen to country names and repeat them back—and found that participants averaged 83% correct if the names were short (Chad, Cuba) but only 56% if the names were long (Somaliland, Australia).

What is the capacity of primary memory when a semantic code is used? Herb Simon (1974) published an article on the capacity of primary memory. Simon tested his own primary memory using stimulus materials of different lengths. Simon found that he could remember about 7 one- or two-syllable words but only 6 three-syllable words. He then tested his primary memory capacity using brief phrases with which he was familiar, such as "Milky Way" and "Lincoln's Gettysburg Address." Simon found he could remember about 4 of these phrases on average. Finally, he tried some long phrases, such

Size of Item	Syllables	Words	Chunks	Syllables per Chunk
1 syllable	7	7	7	1.0
2 syllables	14	7	7	2.0
3 syllables	18	6	6	3.0
2 words	22	9	4	5.5
8 words	26	22	3	8.7

Figure 5.9. Results from Simon (1974). Simon tested just one participant (himself), but the results are representative. There are two important points to note. First, the capacity of primary memory when measured in syllables or words varies quite a lot, but it varies much less when measured in chunks, indicating that chunks are the right way to measure memory. Second, the amount of information per chunk makes a difference in capacity; as the number of syllables per chunk increases, the number of chunks recalled decreases.

as "Four score and seven years ago" or "To be or not to be, that is the question" and found he could remember 3 long phrases. These data are summarized in Figure 5.9.

What do these results tell us about the capacity of primary memory? Simon could recall fewer three-syllable words than one-syllable words. This result is in line with the word length effect reported by Baddeley et al. (1975). But when words were knit into familiar phrases, Simon could maintain 22 words in primary memory. That seems too many words to keep on his 2-s tape loop, so these phrases must have been represented in terms of their semantic content.

Simon emphasized the importance of chunking in the capacity of primary memory: A **chunk** is a unit of knowledge that is decomposable into smaller units. Chunking is finding a way to combine several units, such as treating the letters B, L, U, and E not as four separate letters but as one word. Simon noted that he could maintain more syllables in primary memory if they were organized into chunks of greater size and held together through the semantic relationships between their parts. This is easy to appreciate in the stimuli that Simon used. The two-word idioms and the eight-word phrases have coherence as chunks because of the semantic relationship of the words, recalled from secondary memory. Simon was able to treat "Four score and seven years ago" as an effective chunk because he was familiar with that phrase; it was already in secondary memory. "Arise with strength! For we have raised our flag" (the first line of the Djibouti national anthem, in English) would not work as well. Thus, the capacity of primary memory when using a semantic code depends on the stimuli, specifically, how easily they can be chunked, which depends in part on what is already in secondary memory.

What is the capacity of primary memory when a visuospatial code is used? The answer may well depend on the units in which information is represented. Does primary memory represent visual information in terms of object features (lines, colors, and so on) or in terms of unified objects? For

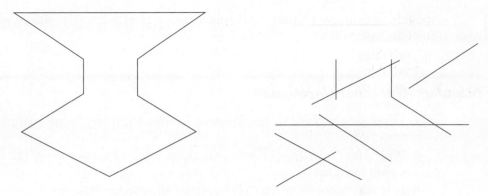

Figure 5.10. Two figures containing the same nine-line segments. Clearly, the figure on the left would be easier to remember because the lines can be chunked on the basis of their spatial relationships.

example, the two shapes in Figure 5.10 show the same nine lines, but those on the left form an object.

Steven Luck and Edward Vogel (1997; see also Lee & Chun, 2001; Vogel, Woodman, & Luck, 2001) showed people two arrays, one after the other, with either colored squares, black lines at different orientations, or colored lines at different orientations. The type of stimulus was always the same in the first and second arrays. The task was to compare them and say "same" or "different." When the arrays differed, it was only by one feature—that is, one color or one orientation. The important finding was that all three stimulus types—color, orientation, or color and orientation combined—showed the same result: Primary memory capacity was about four items. Notice that for the condition in which color and orientation were combined, participants were really keeping track of eight features, not four, because each object in the array had both a color and an orientation; adding an extra feature induced no cost to primary memory capacity. Two more recent reports, however, indicate that the complexity of the figures may play some role—that is, one can remember fewer complex stimuli such as shaded cubes compared with simple stimuli such as color patches (Alvarez & Cavanagh, 2004; Davis & Holmes, 2005). Thus, it is clear that the capacity of visual primary memory can be characterized in terms of the number of objects, but the features of those objects may play some role as well.

The capacity of primary memory varies, then, depending on which code is used. When an acoustic code is used, the capacity is limited by time (approximately 2 s). When the code is semantic, the capacity is flexible because meaningful units (chunks) can be used, but the larger the chunk, the smaller the capacity. When the code is visuospatial, the capacity is about four objects.

We have discussed three characteristics of primary memory: how forgetting occurs, the codes that are used, and the capacity. Now we can discuss models of primary memory and speculate on how primary memory is used in cognition.

Stand-on-One-Foot Questions

5. What are the three representations in which primary memory may code material?
6. Why does forgetting occur in primary memory? Define each of the mechanisms you list.
7. Is it accurate to say that the capacity of primary memory is seven plus or minus two items?

Questions That Require Two Feet

8. Some researchers have tried to examine primary memory without any possibility of proactive interference by administering only one trial to each participant. Can you argue that proactive interference may have been at work in such experiments nevertheless?
9. In this section, we discussed proactive and retroactive interference using the example of studying French or Spanish. Given that you must study more than one subject, it seems as though there is always going to be proactive or retroactive interference. What is the best way to minimize the effects of interference?
10. Languages use different sounds to represent numbers. Would you therefore expect that the digit spans of people who speak different languages would be different? How about the digit span of an individual who speaks two languages?

How Does Primary Memory Work?

Preview

In this section, we discuss two specific models of primary memory and discuss how primary memory contributes to cognition. The modal model of primary memory is an amalgam of many closely related models proposed in the 1960s. Although it is now known to be incorrect in its details, it has been influential in psychology. A second model, the working memory model, is currently believed to be an accurate description of primary memory. We also discuss its brain basis, which has been extensively studied. Researchers have investigated how primary memory contributes to cognition by studying its relationship to general intelligence and to reading.

Models of Primary Memory

Baddeley's **working memory** model (Baddeley, 1986, 2003; Baddeley & Hitch, 1974) accounts well for the data we've discussed in this chapter; indeed, these data were collected to test the model. Another model, the short-term memory model, was so important in the late 1960s and early 1970s that every cognitive psychologist must be familiar with it. For that matter, the model was so important that the designations *short-term memory* and *long-term memory* seeped into popular culture. Thus, although some aspects of the short-term memory model are now known to be incorrect, we take a quick look at it.

SHORT-TERM MEMORY AND THE MODAL MODEL.   From the mid-1960s through the early 1970s, psychologists proposed a number of models of human memory that used the sensory, short-term, and long-term systems. The models had so many features in common that Bennet Murdock (1974) pointed out that one could construct a **modal model** of memory simply by listing the properties that these models shared (see Figure 5.11). He named it after a statistical measure, the mode, which is the number that occurs most often in a group of numbers. This was not a criticism of memory theory at the time; Murdock was pointing out that there was general agreement among many researchers on the basic architecture of memory. Some other important models in this vein were proposed by Waugh and Norman (1965) and Atkinson and Shiffrin (1968).

The modal model emphasizes the flow of information through the cognitive system. Information enters from the senses to sensory memory. There may be sensory memory for each sense, such as smell and taste, but we know that iconic and echoic memory exist. Some of the information is lost from sensory memory, and some is passed on to short-term memory. Whatever you pay attention to in iconic memory is passed on to sensory memory.

Information in short-term memory decays after approximately 30 s unless it is rehearsed. To **rehearse** means to practice material in an effort to

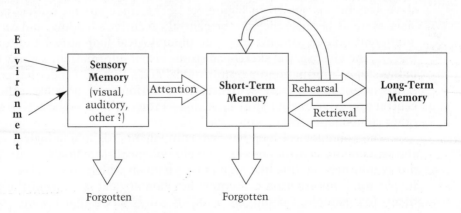

Figure 5.11.   The modal model, showing sensory, short-term, and long-term memories and their interactions. This model has been superseded by newer research.

remember it. If it is rehearsed, it can be maintained indefinitely. The amount of processing in **short-term memory** determines the likelihood that information will enter long-term memory; information that is processed longer in short-term memory is more likely to be encoded (passed on) to long-term memory. Individual models varied in terms of exactly what sort of processing in short-term memory was likely to lead to entry into long-term memory.

Information can also enter short-term memory from long-term memory. Because short-term memory is the site of consciousness, this makes sense. The fact that you like maple syrup on pancakes but prefer lingonberry jam on toast is in long-term memory but not short-term memory. When I ask, "What do you like on pancakes?", you retrieve the answer from long-term memory and enter it into short-term memory.

Finally, note that Figure 5.11 shows no arrow that indicates forgetting from long-term memory. That's because forgetting from long-term memory was believed to occur via interference, not decay.

The modal model was shown to be incomplete or inaccurate in several respects (see Nairne, 2002, for a discussion). For example, the description of rehearsal (the process by which material is transferred from short-term to long-term memory) was incomplete because it proposed that short-term memory used only an acoustic code and long-term memory only a semantic code. The model also proposed that forgetting in short-term memory occurred primarily through decay.

Despite these inaccuracies and deficiencies, the very broad architecture of the modal model—sensory memory feeding into primary memory, which feeds into secondary memory—remains influential today.

Working Memory

The basic architecture of working memory is fairly simple (Baddeley, 2000, 2001, 2003; Baddeley & Hitch, 1974). It includes a central executive and three slave systems, as shown in Figure 5.12. The three storage buffers are called slave systems because they do the central executive's bidding, and each stores a different type of information. The **phonological loop** stores auditory information, the **visuospatial sketchpad** stores visual information, and the **episodic buffer** stores information in a multimodal code; that is, a code that can represent visual, auditory, or semantic information, and possibly others. The **central executive** doesn't store anything—rather, it directs the activities of the other components. We examine each in turn.

The phonological loop has two components: the **phonological store** and the **articulatory control process**. The phonological store holds about 2 s of auditory information. It is like a short tape loop on which you can copy auditory information. Information can enter the phonological store from the environment; for example, I could say a list of words aloud that I want you to remember. Information can also enter via the articulatory control process, which literally means talking to yourself (articulation). You might use the

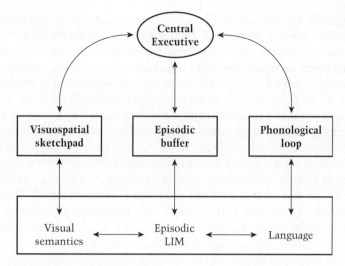

Figure 5.12. The basic components of working memory. The central executive communicates with the other components, which do not communicate with one another. The central executive controls the activity of the other components.

articulatory control process by repeating a grocery list to yourself. The articulatory control process can also be used to refresh information that is already in the phonological store to keep it from fading.

Evidence for the nature of the phonological loop comes from **articulatory suppression** studies. The articulatory control process that writes material to the phonological loop is supposed to be very similar to speech. Therefore, you shouldn't be able to use it while you're speaking. If you're talking out loud, you can't put anything on your tape loop because the articulatory process is already busy. So, suppose an experimenter asked a participant to talk while he or she performed a standard primary memory task. The experimenter wouldn't want the participant to have to think of what to say because that would require attention, so the participant might just say "blahblahblah" aloud while viewing words on a screen to be remembered. How would the participant approach this memory task if the words can't be coded acoustically because the articulatory control process is busy? He or she would have to find some other way to code the words.

If the participant is not coding the words in terms of sound, the acoustic confusion effect should disappear. You'll recall that it's hard to remember a list of words that sound alike (*mad, man, mat*). That effect does indeed disappear if participants say "blahblahblah" while they hear the words: Participants remember words that sound alike (*man, mad, mat*) as well as they remember words that don't (*pit, sup, bar*). That's because speaking aloud occupies the articulatory control process, forcing them to code the words in some way other than acoustically, so they are not susceptible to the acoustic confusion effect (Baddeley, Lewis, & Vallar, 1984). You might wonder whether the effect is caused by the attentional requirements of saying "blahblahblah," even though it might seem that saying such a simple syllable repetitively would not demand much attention. The experimenters compared articulatory suppression with finger tapping, another simple task that did not require articulation. With that secondary task, the acoustic confusion effect was still present.

Even though articulation will get material into the phonological store, simply listening to something, even if you are not trying to remember it, guarantees that it will get into the phonological store through **obligatory access**. For example, Herbert Colle and Alan Welsh (1976) looked at participants' memories for strings of letters presented visually with a short delay, tested either in silence or while listening to a tape of a foreign language they did not know. (It was a passage from *A Hunger Artist* by Franz Kafka, in the original German.) Colle and Welsh found that there was significant interference from the speech; errors increased an average of 12%. The interpretation is that speech sounds gain obligatory access to the phonological store, even if you're trying to ignore them, and interfere with memory for target consonant strings. (Some of us discover obligatory access on our own; many 9-year-old children love to shout random numbers at a friend who is trying to remember a telephone number, then watch the friend sigh and return to the phone book to look up the number again.)

The visuospatial sketchpad is conceived of as a visual analog to the phonological loop. It is a medium in which to keep visual or spatial information active. Earlier in this chapter, we discussed evidence that people maintain spatial information in primary memory. (Remember the matrix task with sentences such as "In the next square to the left put a 3.")

Baddeley proposed that spatial information (where things are) and visual information (what they look like) are separable in the visuospatial sketchpad. We noted in chapter 3 that visual and spatial information might be handled separately in perception; it might well be that they are also separate in the visuospatial sketchpad.

Many studies have examined whether visual and spatial aspects of stimuli are remembered separately in working memory (e.g., Baddeley & Lieberman, 1980; Logie & Marchetti, 1991; Quinn & McConnell, 1996). The most thorough study was a series by Karl Klauer and Zengmei Zhao (2004), who used an interference procedure. Participants had to either remember the location of a dot on a computer screen (spatial task) or a Chinese ideograph (visual task). There was a 10-s retention interval, and then participants selected from among eight possible stimuli (locations or ideographs). During the 10-s interval, participants performed one of two interference tasks. (In a control condition, there was no intervening task.) In the spatial interference task, participants saw 12 asterisks on the screen, 11 of which were moving in random directions. The goal was to locate the stationary asterisk. In the visual interference task, participants saw a series of 14 color patches, one at a time, and for each had to categorize it as red or blue. The idea of the experiment is this: If visual and spatial working memory storage are really separate, then the visual interfering task (color discrimination) should disrupt memory for the visual stimuli (ideographs) but have less impact on memory for the spatial stimuli (dot location). The spatial interference task should have the opposite effect.

The results supported the prediction. Compared with the control condition (no interference task), the spatial interference task had no impact on visual memory, but it made spatial memory about 6% worse. The visual interference task had the opposite effect: It made spatial memory a little bit worse (about 3%) but had a bigger impact on visual memory. These behavioral data are consistent with neuroscientific data that indicate separate brain locations for visual and spatial memory, both from brain-damaged patients (e.g., Carlesimo, Perri, Turriziani, Tomaiulo, & Caltagirone, 2001; Postle, Jonides, Smith, Corkin, & Growdon, 1997) and from neuroimaging studies (e.g., Courtney, Ungerleider, Keil, & Haxby, 1996; Owen, Stern, Look, Tracey, Rosen, & Petrides, 1998).

The phonological loop and visuospatial sketchpad were part of the original working memory model proposed in 1974, and a good deal of evidence indicates that these components exist. Baddeley added the episodic buffer just a few years ago, and there are therefore fewer relevant data. He proposed the episodic buffer as a way of solving a few problems in the original model. One significant problem was that there was no way for auditory and visual information to interact, and there is evidence from verbal span tasks that they do interact (Chincotta, Underwood, Ghani, Papadopoulou, & Wresinski, 1999). The epidsodic buffer is proposed to be multimodal—that is, many modalities can be represented there, including auditory, visual, and semantic information. The episodic buffer is the workspace of working memory. It's where different types of information can come together to be manipulated to solve problems.

A second problem with the original model was that it didn't provide a way for the components of working memory to interact with long-term memory. We have seen evidence that chunking is very important for working memory capacity; "Four score and seven years ago" can be treated as a single chunk, or unit, in working memory because the phrase exists in long-term memory. So there must be a way for working memory and long-term memory to interact. But this is not so straightforward because the articulatory loop stores sounds and long-term memory stores meaning. How can those connect? The multimodal episodic buffer offers a mechanism.

Less work has been directed toward elucidating the central executive that plays the role of cognitive supervisor, especially in doing the vital work of focusing, dividing, and switching attention. Researchers initially focused on understanding the phonological loop and visuospatial sketchpad exactly because they believed that they would be easier to understand. Baddeley (1996) commented that in some ways his research strategy could be compared with undertaking an analysis of *Hamlet* by focusing on Polonius and ignoring Hamlet. By this he meant that the central executive is the most interesting part of working memory because its responsibilities are so great. The last few years have seen an increase in research directed at processes of mental control, but much of this work is both too advanced and too speculative for a beginning text.

Neural Basis of Working Memory

In addition to behavioral evidence, neuroscientific evidence has proven important to the working memory theory. A general idea that appears to work pretty well is this: Storage of material in working memory occurs in the same location where perception occurs. That is, you store auditory and visual material in the same parts of the brain that perceive auditory and visual material.

Most researchers agree that portions of the back of the brain support the brief storage of material: The parietal lobe of the left hemisphere stores visuospatial information, and the parietal lobe of the right hemisphere stores verbal information. Eraldo Paulesu and his colleagues (Paulesu, Rith, & Frackowiak, 1993) conducted a brain imaging study that came to the same conclusion. Participants either saw letters and tried to memorize them, or they saw letters and judged whether their names rhymed (e.g., "C" and "P"). Participants are likely to say the letters to themselves in the rhyming task, but they needn't store them, whereas both processes would be part of the memory task. As predicted, comparison of the two tasks showed activation in the ventrolateral parietal cortex, and patient data support that interpretation (Vallar & Baddeley, 1984; Vallar & Papagno, 2002).

The visuospatial sketchpad seems to have two separate storage locations, respecting the dorsal/ventral division of the visual system. Brain imaging studies show that tasks requiring memory of object locations activate dorsal parietal cortex, whereas tasks requiring memory for the visual appearance of objects activate the ventral temporal cortex (Ranganath & D'Esposito, 2005; Wager & Smith, 2003). Examples of these two types of memory tasks appear in Figure 5.13.

The foregoing discussion has only concerned storage. What about processes that put things into the storage areas? Connecting neuroscientific data to psychological data has not been as straightforward for this problem. Everyone agrees that prefrontal cortex—that portion of the frontal lobes in front of the motor strip—is important, but it has proven difficult to be certain just what it does and how it is organized. Some have argued that the prefrontal cortex is indeed responsible for rehearsing—that it maintains the activity in the storage areas in the back of the brain (e.g., Cohen et al., 1997; Jonides, Lacey, & Nee, 2005; Ranganath & D'Esposito, 2005). There is debate as to whether different parts of prefrontal cortex are specialized by material (e.g., rehearsing objects vs. rehearsing locations; Baddeley, 2003; Sala, Rama, & Courtney, 2003) or whether different parts are devoted to rehearsal and others to manipulation of the material (D'Esposito, Postle, Ballard, & Lease, 1999). Even more unsettling, a large-scale analysis of data from patients with brain damage seemed to conflict with all brain imaging data. Although brain imaging studies consistently show a lot of prefrontal activation during working memory tasks, patients with prefrontal damage are not reliably impaired on the tasks (D'Esposito & Postle, 1999). This pattern of data has led some researchers to suggest that the prefrontal cortex serves some other function that happens to be part of most working memory tasks (and so prefrontal cortex is

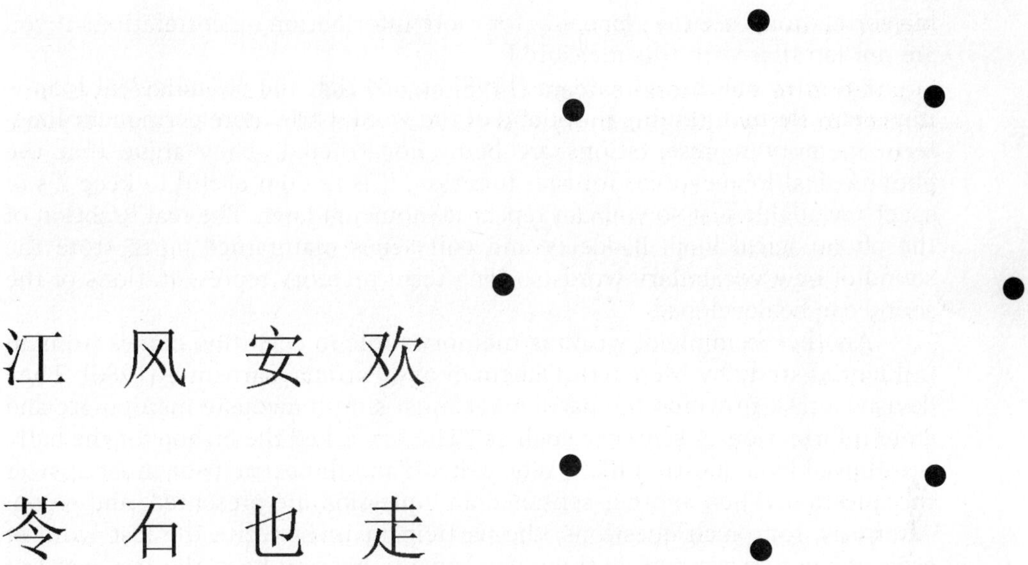

Figure 5.13. Stimuli used in a typical experiment comparing visual and spatial working memory (Klauer & Zhang, 2004). For the visual task, one of the eight Chinese ideographs was briefly presented. For the spatial task, one of the eight dot positions was presented. In either task, there was a 10-s delay and then all eight stimuli (ideographs or dots) were presented, and the participant selected the target with a cursor.

active in imaging studies) but is not crucial to getting the working memory task done (and so damage doesn't affect the task). In summary, we know that the prefrontal cortex is somehow related to regulating mental activity, but we are not yet sure what the processes are that go into that regulation (see Thompson-Schill, Bedny, & Goldberg, 2005, for a review).

Working Memory as a Workspace

A key feature of the working memory theory (as opposed to the modal model) is its emphasis that working memory is used for other cognitive functions, and not just for the brief storage of information. We review several examples of how working memory is used.

The phonological loop appears to be important in acquiring new vocabulary terms. In a number of studies, researchers have looked at the relationship between the size of the phonological loop and the number of words in the vocabulary of children in the early and middle childhood years (for a review, see Baddeley, Gathercole, & Papagno, 1998). The size of the phonological loop is measured by digit span and by asking the children to repeat nonwords, such as *loddernaypish*, which presumably can be repeated only if the child successfully maintains in the phonological loop the sounds that the experimenter utters. Vocabulary size correlates with digit span and correlates even better with nonword repetition: The correlations are on the order of .35 to .60. (That's a big correlation—see the Appendix for more information on correlations if you are not familiar with this measure.)

Baddeley and his colleagues (1998) argued that the phonological loop is important for maintaining the sound of the word while more permanent long-term memory representations are being constructed. They argue that the phonological loop evolved for that function. It is seldom useful to keep 2 s of speech available just so you can repeat it moments later. The real function of the phonological loop, Baddeley and colleagues maintained, is to store the sound of new vocabulary words so long-term memory representations of the sound can be developed.

Another example of working memory's role in cognition comes from an influential study by Meredyth Daneman and Patricia Carpenter (1980). They devised a task in which the participant must simultaneously manipulate and store information: A sentence such as "The boy asked the bishop for the ball" is followed by a question like "Who asked?," and the participant must answer the question. Then another sentence and question are presented, and so on. After, say, four such questions, the participant must recite the last word of each of the four sentences; thus, participants have to keep the last word of each sentence in mind while trying to listen to the new sentences and answer questions about them. The experimenter varies the number of sentences, and the final measure of working memory span is the greatest number of sentences in which the participant can answer all the questions and recite the last word of each sentence correctly. This measure of working memory span is an extremely good predictor (correlation = .72) of reading comprehension in college students.

The interpretation of this high correlation is that working memory is often important in comprehending sentences during reading. This fact is especially apparent in sentences such as "The package dropped from the airplane reached the ground safely" (Fodor, 1995). In sentences like this, the grammatical structure can fool the reader, who might think that *dropped* is the main verb of the sentence (as it would be in "The package dropped from the airplane safely"). In fact, *dropped* must be interpreted as part of an adjectival phrase; "dropped from the airplane" tells you which package is being discussed. In sentences like this, the grammatical role of some of the words can be misinterpreted. But if this material is still in working memory, the reader can reinterpret the early part of the sentence. If it's not in working memory, it must be reread. Thus, a good working memory span might help reading comprehension. (This type of sentence is discussed further in chapter 14.)

In this chapter, we've considered how you maintain information for a brief period of time, and how you work with it while you're maintaining it. But that only covers a fraction of the memory capabilities we need; we usually need to use memories that are older than 30 s. Somehow, memories must be retained for long periods of time. In the next three chapters, we discuss how those memories are put into the memory vault, how they are retrieved, and the format of the representation used to store them.

Stand-on-One-Foot Questions

11. Explain the difference between the concepts of primary memory, short-term memory, and working memory.
12. Describe the components of the phonological loop and how they operate.

Questions That Require Two Feet

13. Service people often thank me after they have done me a favor. For example, I will walk into a department store and ask someone at the perfume counter where the men's shoe department is, and the clerk will answer: "Go to the back of the store, past lingerie. Take the elevator to the fifth floor, walk straight ahead, and turn right at the overcoats; it's right there. Have a nice day, and thank you for shopping with us." What's wrong with adding this last sentence?
14. Suppose that a person with brain damage has almost no articulatory loop; the digit span is one or two items instead of the usual seven. How good would you expect the person's long-term memory to be?

KEY TERMS

acoustic confusion
  effect
articulatory control
  process
articulatory
  suppression
central executive
chunk
decay
digit span task
echoic memory
episodic buffer
iconic memory
mask

modal model
obligatory access
partial report
  procedure
phonological loop
phonological store
primary memory
proactive
  interference
rehearse
release from
  proactive
  interference

retroactive
  interference
secondary memory
sensory memory
short-term memory
span of
  apprehension
visuospatial
  sketchpad
word length effect
working memory

6

Memory Encoding

What Determines What We Encode in Memory?

- Factors That Help Memory: Depth and Emotion
- Factors That Don't Help Memory: Intention to Learn and Repetition
- Match Between Encoding and Retrieval: Transfer Appropriate Processing

Why Do We Encode Information As We Do?

- Prior Knowledge Reduces What We Must Remember
- Prior Knowledge Guides the Interpretation of Details
- Prior Knowledge Makes Unusual Things Stand Out

In many ways, life would be simpler if memory were dictated by the intention to remember—in other words, if you remembered the things you wanted to remember and forgot the things you wanted to forget. For example, I want to remember people's names, so why can't I do it? When I'm introduced to someone new, I think to myself, "That's Lisa; got to remember her name." But 5 min later when we're joined by someone else, the name is gone and I'm left to rely on the lame "Do you two know each other?" (Then I'm so focused on having forgotten the name that when she introduces herself I'm not even listening.)

Similarly, we all have things we'd like to forget. I could live the rest of my life quite happily without the memory of certain moments at junior high dances, but those memories seem branded in my brain, and they pop into consciousness, unbidden, usually at moments when I would pay cash money for them to lie dormant.

In chapter 5, we considered primary memory as a gateway to the storehouse of memory. It's always possible that I wasn't really paying attention when Lisa first said her name—I was thinking that my shirt was wrinkled, or I was wondering whether I had something stuck in my teeth—and I never really had "Lisa" in primary memory. But let's assume for the moment that I did. Why didn't the name get into secondary memory, even though I wanted it to? Apparently, information is not guaranteed to go into secondary memory just because you want it to. This fact brings up the question **What determines what we encode in memory?** Researchers have examined a number of different factors, such as whether the material engenders emotion or how often the material is repeated. It turns out that whether something is stored depends on what you do with it; basically, if you think hard about something and use it, the mind figures that you may need to use this material again, and so it is stored. A precise definition of what it means to "think hard about something" turns out to be tricky; we discuss some of the possibilities in this chapter.

This answer leads naturally to a second question: **Why do we encode information as we do?** If whether you remember something depends on how you think about it, what determines how you think about it? The answer is that how you think about something depends, in large measure, on what you already know about it (your prior knowledge). To take an extreme example, suppose you overhear someone in a restaurant say, "Zut! Qu'est-ce que cet petit singe a laissé dans ma chaussure?"[1] If you don't speak French, you might think, "Oh, someone over there is speaking a foreign language," and you'd probably forget the incident. If you did speak French, you would probably be curious to know what was happening at that other table and would think about the incident a lot. Prior knowledge is crucial to how you process new experiences and therefore to the likelihood that you will remember them later.

---

[1]"Hey! What did that little monkey leave in my shoe?"

What Determines What We Encode in Memory?

Preview

Researchers have examined four factors as possible influences on encoding. Whether the material brings an emotional response and whether you relate the material to other things you already know are two factors that have a significant impact on later memory. How much you may want to remember something and simple repetition do not help memory much, if at all.

The extent to which you relate new material to things you already know is the most important factor in encoding, but getting a clear definition of this factor has been difficult. The relationship between what you think about at encoding and what you think about at retrieval is also important to memory.

Factors That Help Memory: Depth and Emotion

If you tried to think of factors that might influence memory, you might speculate that something will get into secondary memory if it is important to you. "Important to you" might mean emotionally significant. As we'll see in this section, emotion has some influence on memory, but the effect is not huge. More important to memory is the extent to which you think about the events meaning, a factor cognitive psychologists call "depth."

DEPTH OF PROCESSING. In the late 1960s, the question "What determines what we encode in secondary memory?" was framed in terms of primary memory. In other words, most researchers believed that what mattered most was what happened in primary memory; if material were processed a certain way or for a certain length of time in primary memory, then it was encoded to secondary memory.

Fergus Craik and Robert Lockhart (1972) proposed an alternative called the **levels of processing framework** (for a variety of perspectives, see Conway, 2002). They suggested that the most important factor determining whether something will be remembered is the **depth of processing**. According to Craik and Lockhart (1972), in a task such as remembering a word, **deep processing** refers to greater degrees of semantic involvement—that is, thinking about what the word means and how its meaning relates to other words. For example, if you answered the question "What sorts of things come to mind when I say the word *rose*?", you would be engaged in deep processing of the word. My question would prompt you to think about what the word means and what is associated with the concept *rose* in your memory. You might think that a rose is a flower of romance, that roses are fairly expensive, that they are found in formal gardens, that they have thorns, that they have a nice scent, and so on. **Shallow processing** refers to thinking about surface characteristics of the stimulus. For example, if you answered the question "How many syllables are in the word

Table 6.1. *Four Levels of Processing Words*

Level of Processing	Question the Participant Must Answer	Sample Stimulus for Which Participant Answers "Yes"	Sample Stimulus for Which Participant Answers "No"
Structural	Is the word in capital letters?	TABLE	table
Phonemic	Does the word rhyme with *weight?*	Crate	Market
Category	Is the word a type of fish?	Shark	Heaven
Sentence	"He met a _____ in the street."	Friend	Cloud

rose?" you would be engaged in shallow processing. This question encourages you to think about the physical properties of the word itself. Other questions that would encourage shallow processing would be "How many vowels are there in the word *rose?"* or "Is the word *rose* printed in uppercase or lowercase letters?" We don't categorize processing simply as deep or shallow; there can also be degrees of depth of processing. At least this is supposed to be true in theory. As we'll see in a moment, specifying slightly deeper or shallower processing has proved difficult, and that's a weakness of the framework.

In an experiment, depth of processing can be manipulated by having the participant answer a question about a word. Table 6.1 lists four levels of processing that are progressively deeper. This table comes from a series of experiments by Craik and Endel Tulving (1975), who sought to gather evidence for the levels of processing framework. As you can see, participants answered questions that led them to think about different properties of the stimulus word, such as what the printed version looks like or what it sounds like.

Depth of processing has a huge effect on people's ability to remember under most testing conditions (but not all, as we'll see later). Craik and Tulving (1975) showed just how strong the effect is, using the levels of processing shown in Table 6.1. Participants were told that the experiment tested perceptual processing, not memory. On each trial of the experiment, participants heard a question such as "Does the word rhyme with *cake?"* Participants saw a word flashed on a tachistoscope for 200 ms and then had to answer the question as quickly as possible by pressing one of two buttons to indicate "yes" or "no." They performed 40 such trials, and after a brief rest, were presented with a surprise recognition test. The experimenters didn't want participants to actively try to remember the words because then participants would bring their own strategies to the task. Participants' performance on the recognition test is shown in Figure 6.1.

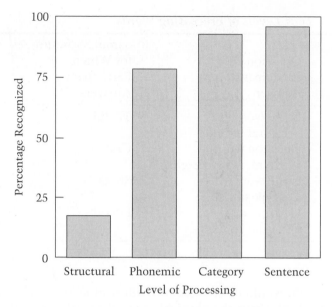

Figure 6.1.   The basic levels of processing effect, showing that words that are processed more deeply are better remembered than words that are processed more shallowly.

The levels of processing framework holds that deeper processing leads to better memory. At first, it might seem that doing the deep processing is just more difficult. Maybe your memory is better simply because you put more work into it in the first place. But Craik and Tulving (1975) tested that possibility by conducting an experiment in which the shallow processing condition was very difficult. Before each word was presented, the participants saw something like *CVCCVC* (where *C* meant consonant and *V* meant vowel). Then they saw a word like *WITCH* and had to say whether it had the pattern of vowels and consonants specified by the first stimulus. It took participants much longer to perform this shallow processing task than to perform the deep processing sentence task. Nevertheless, shallow-processed words were recognized 57% of the time on a later test, and deep-processed words were recognized 82% of the time. So, deeper-processed words are not better remembered simply because deep processing takes more effort.

LABORATORY STUDIES OF EMOTION AND MEMORY.   I'm not alone in finding an emotional event (e.g., embarrassment at dances) particularly memorable. David Rubin and Marc Kozin (1984) asked people to report their clearest memories from childhood. Participants tended to describe birthdays, car accidents, early romantic experiences, and the like, which seems to indicate an important role for emotion in memory (see Photo 6.1). Other studies have shown that there is a positive correlation between how vivid a memory seems and how emotional it is (Pillemer, Goldsmith, Panter, & White, 1988; Walker,

Photo 6.1. Most events that people report remembering well have an emotional component.

Vogl, & Thompson, 1997). It appears that it's the intensity of the emotion that is important, and whether it's positive or negative doesn't matter (Talarico, LaBar, & Rubin, 2004).

Nevertheless, this sort of evidence is not airtight. Suppose that because my junior high dance was an emotional experience, people talked about it a lot; thus, it's a memory that was emotional *and* was discussed a lot. That's the core problem with relational (not experimental) research (see Chapter 2). The heart of the problem is that we have no control over what people do in this situation. If they want to talk about the dance humiliation, they will.

It's hard to conduct true experiments that examine the effect of emotion on memory using emotional and nonemotional materials. Everything should be the same except the emotion so any difference in the memorability of the stimuli can be attributed to the emotion, not some other characteristics of the stimuli. But how can the same set of materials be emotional for one group of participants and nonemotional for the other?

This problem is very difficult, but Larry Cahill and Jim McGaugh (1995) found a clever technique. All their participants saw the same slide show of a boy visiting his father at work in a hospital; in the middle of the slide show, participants saw graphic surgery slides, which most participants would find upsetting. Participants heard different stories to go with the slides, however. For the emotional condition, participants were led to believe that the graphic surgery slides were real. For the nonemotional condition, the narration said that the boy visited his father just as the hospital personnel were practicing

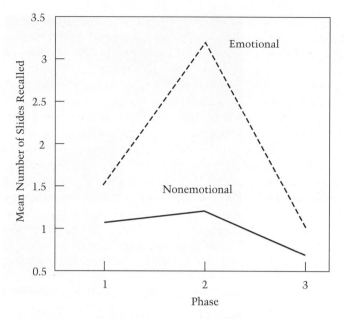

Figure 6.2. Data from Cahill and McGaugh's (1995) experiment. The slide show that participants saw was divided into three phases. All participants saw the same set of slides, but some heard a story about the slides that made the slides during Phase 2 much more emotional. These participants remembered the Phase 2 slides better on a later test.

emergency procedures, so the people who appeared to be undergoing surgical procedures were just actors made up to look injured.

Two weeks later the participants returned, expecting to see another set of slides, but instead they took a test of their memory of the first set of slides. (Participants were first asked whether they had expected a memory test, even though they had not been told about it, to ensure they hadn't been rehearsing the material. All participants said that they hadn't expected the test.) In the first test, participants were asked to recall as much of the story as they could, both the general story line and specific details. Their responses were tape-recorded so they could be scored later. The scorers judged that a specific slide was remembered if the participant mentioned a piece of information that could be known only from having seen the slide and not from hearing the story or from seeing one of the other slides.

Figure 6.2 shows the results. The first and third phases depicted the arrival and departure from the hospital, respectively. The second phase showed the graphic surgery slides. As the graph shows, memory is equivalent in the two groups during the first and third phases, which were unemotional for both groups. Memory of the slides is the same during these phases, but it is much better for the emotional group only during the second phase. It looks as if memory is slightly better for the emotional group in the first and third phases as well. Although the average recall is a bit higher, the difference is not statistically significant; it could have occurred by chance and therefore should not be taken to represent an important difference. (The concept of statistical significance is very important in interpreting results from experiments. If you're not familiar with it, see the explanation in the Appendix.)

This study does an excellent job of isolating the effect of emotion from other possible characteristics of stimuli, and it shows quite convincingly that emotion does make things more memorable.

But is emotion really helping memory or is emotion just focusing attention, which in turn helps memory? There is some reason to think that arousal causes a narrowing of attention (Easterbrook, 1959) so whatever is the focus of attention will be well remembered, but whatever is not the focus of attention will actually be remembered worse than if there were no emotion. Some studies seem to show that pattern (Burke, Heuer, & Reisberg, 1992; Wessel & Merckelbach, 1997). Participants remembered the basic idea or gist of the to-be-remembered material very well, but they were actually worse in remembering the peripheral details.

But these studies all engendered emotion with rather shocking visual stimuli (e.g., graphic surgery slides). Cara Laney and her colleagues (Laney, Campbell, Heuer, & Reisberg, 2004) noted that such stimuli may naturally be attention magnets due to their gruesome nature and due to the fact that their appearance is often a surprise. But emotion can arise not only from shocking stimuli, but also thematically. In fact, most of the emotional memories from our personal lives are thematic—a birthday, the death of a loved one—not a shocking accident or the like (Laney, Heuer, & Reisberg, 2003). Laney and her colleagues investigated the effect of thematically induced emotion on memory by having participants watch identical slide shows about a day in the life of a college student while they heard one of two accompanying narrations. In the neutral condition, the student described details of her life as though chatting with a friend, characterizing it as busy but happy, and the show culminated with people gathering in her room to celebrate her birthday. In the emotional condition, she described her life as miserable with everything going wrong, and the show culminated with friends gathering in her room to talk her out of committing suicide.

Two days later, participants took a surprise memory test with questions about the gist of the story and about visual details that were central or peripheral to the story. The data showed that memory in the emotional condition was superior to the neutral condition for all types of stimuli. Thus, this experiment shows that shocking material may be an attention magnet, so that there is a cost to other, peripheral material, but there is an effect of emotion over and above that attention effect. When emotion is engendered by a theme, rather than a shocking stimulus, there is a memory boost for the entire event.

Another experiment using quite a different methodology provides further evidence that it's emotion that provides the memory boost, and not attention. Kristy Nielson and her colleagues (Nielson, Yee, & Erickson, 2005) had participants listen to a list of 35 words, whereupon their memory for the words was immediately tested. Then participants watched one of two videotapes, either an arousing one (oral surgery) or a nonarousing one (demonstration of proper tooth brushing). Participants watching the arousing videotape showed better memory for the words, after both a 30-min and a 24-hr delay. The effect of the emotional videotape could not be due to "attention magnet" effects because the videotapes were viewed *after* participants encoded the words. But that raises another question: How does emotion that occurs after encoding influence memory for an event?

A full explanation would take us rather far afield, but here's a brief summary. A memory is encoded as we are thinking about an experience. But even after we stop thinking about it, the neural changes that correspond to that memory are not complete. The biological processes that create the memory continue after our conscious minds have moved on to something else. This process is called consolidation, and it occurs in two stages, one lasting minutes to hours and the other lasting weeks or perhaps even years (for a review, see Dudai, 2004).

Emotion may well have its affect on memory through hormones that are released during stress (e.g., epinephrine) and by several types of neurotransmitters (e.g., adrenergic and glucocorticoid receptors) that may be modulated during arousal (see McGaugh, 2004, for a review). An emotional event may have an impact on memory not only for the event itself, but also for recent events that are undergoing consolidation.

The amygdala, a structure near the center of the brain, appears to be crucial for identifying that something emotional is happening and then coordinating modulation of neurotransmitters and hormones, which in turn have the effect of recruiting neural systems to respond, including the memory system (Richardson, Strange, & Dolan, 2004; see Phelps, 2004, for a review). Neuroscientific studies support this crucial role for the amygdala in emotional memory. Patients with damage to the amygdala have been shown the slide show about the boy visiting his surgeon-father at the hospital. Although patients report that they find the surgery slides very upsetting, they do not show especially good memory for them, as normal controls do (Cahill, Babinsky, Markowitsch, & McGaugh, 1995). Furthermore, brain imaging studies show that the amygdala is especially active when people view emotional slides (positive or negative) but is not active when participants view slides that are interesting, but not emotional (e.g., surrealist paintings) (Hamann, Ely, Grafton, & Kilts, 1999).

We might wonder, however, about the strength of the emotion in this experiment or indeed in any experiment. Seeing slides of surgery is upsetting, to be sure, but events that touch us as individuals are likely to be more upsetting (Eich & Macaulay, 2000). Would the effect of emotion on memory be stronger if we were examining events that affected the participants more than a slide show? We know it's difficult to study memory for events such as birthdays and first dates, but perhaps we're missing something important by ignoring them.

In fact, there is a rich literature on people's memories of highly emotional events that happen outside the laboratory. This literature initially led to the conclusion that this level of emotion had a profound impact on people's memories—so profound that a special memory process might be engaged during moments of great emotion. Later experiments indicated that proposal probably was not true; nevertheless, the impact of these studies was great, so they are worth reviewing.

FLASHBULB MEMORIES. If you want to study highly emotional events, you can't do so in the laboratory. It's simply not ethical to make people feel extremes of emotion by telling them that they are the lucky millionth participant to be tested in the laboratory and that at the end of the experiment they will be presented with a Ferrari. It would be ethical if you gave them the Ferrari, I suppose, but the billionaire eccentric enough to support this experiment has not yet stepped forward. Thus, if you want to study the effect of high levels of emotion, you must study events that occur naturally in people's lives, and ideally, an event that is similar in the lives of a large group of people; after all, your birthday and mine might be very different in terms of how memorable they are.

Roger Brown and James Kulik (1977) were the first to conduct such a study. They asked participants to remember where they were when they heard that President John Kennedy had been assassinated. Participants reported surprisingly detailed memories and were confident that they could remember details such as what they were wearing, exactly where they were, who told them the news, the words that were used, and so on. Brown and Kulik used the term **flashbulb memories** for richly detailed memories encoded when something emotionally intense happens. Flashbulb memories have three special characteristics, according to Brown and Kulik: They are very complete, they are accurate, and they are immune to forgetting. Brown and Kulik suggested that a special memory process is responsible for flashbulb memories. Only in times of great emotional duress, a "NOW PRINT" process can take a memorial "snapshot" of whatever is happening at that moment.

The problem is that it is very difficult to assess whether people's flashbulb memories are accurate. Perhaps people want to think that they remember highly emotional situations, so they set a low criterion for how confident they have to be before they claim to have a memory. Ideally, psychologists want to compare people's memory of how they heard about Kennedy's assassination right after they heard the news with their memory a year or so later. That way, we could test whether flashbulb memories are accurate and immune to forgetting.

Beginning in the 1980s, a number of researchers performed this test. When an event occurred that they believed would trigger flashbulb memories, they administered surveys to people asking about the circumstances under which they heard the news, and then they contacted people later, asked them the same questions, and compared their memories. Such experiments were conducted for events like the attempted assassination of President Ronald Reagan (Pillemer, 1984), the explosion of the space shuttle *Challenger* (McCloskey, Wible, & Cohen, 1988), the assassination of Swedish Prime Minister Olof Palme (Christianson, 1989), the death of King Baudouin of Belgium (Finkenauer, Luminet, Gisle, El-Ahmadi, Van der Linden, & Philippot,

1998), and the announcement of the O. J. Simpson verdict (Schmolck, Buffalo, & Squire, 2000). These experiments have generally shown that people are very confident that they remember these emotional events, but the accuracy of their memory for the events is not especially good.

Jennifer Talarico and David Rubin (2003) conducted a careful study of Duke students' memories for the terrorist attacks on September 11, 2001. Fifty-four students were contacted on September 12 and were asked to provide details about hearing the news (where they were, who they were with, and so forth). They were also asked to provide similar details about the most memorable event that had happened to them from the previous weekend. (Typical events included attending a party, a sporting event, and so forth.) Students were contacted again, either 1, 6, or 32 weeks later, and were asked to recall both events—the terrorist attack and the everyday event—and to provide the same details they had recalled on September 12 (where they were, who they were with, and so forth). Participants also rated their confidence that the memory was accurate, as well as their feeling that, when they remembered the event, they were "reliving" it.

The results are shown in Figure 6.3. As you can see from the top panel of the figure, the flashbulb memory is subject to forgetting, just like the everyday memory. The number of recalled details that are consistent with the September 12 version decreases over time, and the number of inconsistent details increases. So flashbulb memories are no more accurate than everyday memories. But the second panel shows that participants think about flashbulb memories differently. Participants' beliefs that the memory is accurate does *not* decrease over time, nor does the extent to which they feel they are reliving the event. That is not true of the everyday memories. (You may be surprised that the memory for 9-11 was not better than the everyday memory—shouldn't there have been an effect of emotion? But the researchers

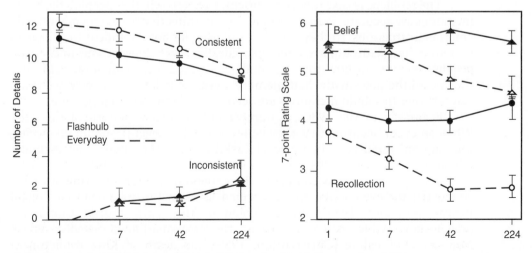

Figure 6.3.   Results from Talarico and Rubin's (2003) study of flashbulb memories of 9/11.

Photo 6.2. Is hearing the news about 9/11 a flashbulb memory for you?

asked for "the most memorable event" from the previous weekend, and many of them were fairly emotion laden.)

In a rather well-publicized error, President Bush showed some inconsistencies in his recollection of how he heard the news of the terrorist attacks. On two different occasions, he mentioned having watched a videotape of the first plane crashing into the tower, although such videotapes were not broadcast on the morning of September 11. On another occasion, he recalled hearing the news from Advisor Karl Rove, although he actually heard it from Chief of Staff Andy Card. Although President Bush was criticized in some quarters for possibly being dishonest about his memory, it's explainable as a typical memory error (Greenberg, 2004).

So what's the upshot on emotion and memory? There is good evidence that the emotionality of an event does affect how memorable it is, but there is not good evidence that a special mechanism takes over for flashbulb memories.

Factors That Don't Help Memory: Intention to Learn and Repetition

Intention to learn and repetition seem so plausible as memory influences that it is worth going over how we know that they don't influence memory.

INTENTION TO LEARN.   The levels of processing framework proposes that intention to learn—that is, whether or not you're trying to learn—has no impact on memory. Can we really dismiss effort? Certainly, some teachers believe that effort to remember is important; why else would they exhort students, "Remember this!" We need to examine research that has looked directly at the effect of effort to learn on memory.

Research on levels of processing was crucial in showing that memory is not affected by effort to learn. Most of these studies used **incidental memory tests** on words, in which the participants are not expressly told that their memory will be tested; rather, they are just told to do something to the words (e.g., answer a question about them). Then later they get a surprise memory test. In an **intentional memory test**, participants are told that their memory will be tested; the researcher assumes that participants will engage in some processing they believe will be effective for memory.

In depth of processing experiments, researchers used incidental memory tests to evaluate the effect of different types of processing on the words (deep vs. shallow). The experimenters wanted control over the participants' processing and did not mention the upcoming test.

Suppose we wanted to test the effect of the participants' expectation of a later memory test. We could simply tell half the participants that they will later be tested and not tell the other half. Thomas Hyde and James Jenkins (1973) conducted exactly that study. Participants saw a list of 24 words, one at a time, for 3 s each and were to perform one of two tasks for each word: either determine whether the word contained the letter *a* or *q* (shallow task) or rate the "pleasantness" of the word (deep task). If the word invoked pleasant thoughts ("daisy") participants gave it a high rating, and if it invoked unpleasant things ("grave") they gave it a low rating. For both the deep and shallow processing conditions, half the participants were additionally told that their memory of the words would be tested (intentional condition); the remaining participants were not told about the upcoming memory test (incidental condition). Whether the test was incidental made no difference in participants' performance on the memory test, as shown in Figure 6.4. Wanting to remember something doesn't help your memory. All that matters to your memory is whether you do the deep or the shallow processing.

At the beginning of the chapter, we said that intention to learn is not a guarantee that you'll remember something. That might be true, yet it could still be possible that wanting to remember would have some effect. The Hyde and Jenkins (1973) study shows that intention to learn has no effect at all.

Further reflection may make this conclusion more believable. After all, if effort had much impact on memory, studying would be much easier. Your memory (like mine) is probably cluttered with things you didn't intend to put

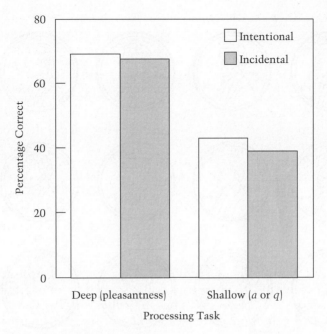

Figure 6.4. Results from Hyde and Jenkins's (1973) study showing that intention to learn had no impact on learning. The experiment also showed the typical depth of processing effect.

in there—advertising jingles, for example. But the presence of a jingle in my memory raises another question. I don't think I processed it very deeply. Nor was viewing the commercial a particularly emotional experience for me, and we said emotion was the other factor that might influence memory. So, if that memory didn't have emotion or depth of processing going for it, what's it doing in my memory? The ready answer is that I know it because I've heard it hundreds of times. Does repetition affect memory?

REPETITION.   Suppose that the likelihood that something makes it into secondary memory depends on how often you see it. Stimuli in the environment that are often repeated should be remembered. But consider this: You think you know what a penny looks like, right? Can you say, with confidence, right now, which way Lincoln faces? Try it. Where is the date written on a penny? Does the phrase "In God We Trust" appear on the front of a penny?

Raymond Nickerson and Marilyn Adams (1979) showed 36 college students the 15 versions of a penny in Figure 6.5. Participants were asked to select which penny was most likely the right one and then to rate the other drawings as (a) "Could easily be right, if my choice proves wrong"; (b) "Might possibly be right, if my choice proves wrong"; or (c) "Definitely not correct." Less than half the participants (15 of the 36) correctly picked A. Twelve thought it could easily be right, 4 thought it might be, and 5 were sure it was wrong. Pennies E, G, and J were popular choices.

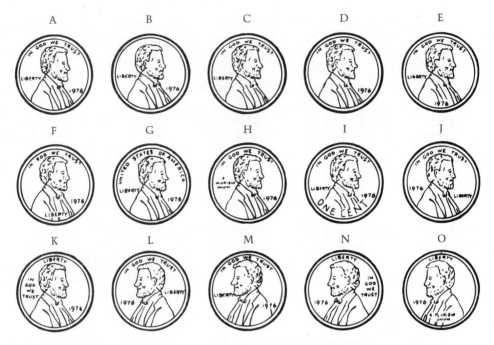

Figure 6.5. Fifteen penny drawings used in Nickerson and Adams's (1979) recognition memory test.

Why was this task so prone to error? Obviously, the participants had seen thousands of pennies in their lifetimes. We seldom, if ever, really notice (i.e., process deeply) which way Lincoln is facing, what's written on a coin, or any of the other details. When you are looking through your handful of coins in search of a penny, what you're thinking is, "I need the brown one." Pennies are distinguished from other coins by color, not by the way Lincoln is facing. Dimes are the small ones, not the coins with Roosevelt on them; quarters are the big ones; and nickels are the thick ones with smooth edges. You have had thousands of exposures to pennies, but each exposure amounted to little more than "Good, I've got a brown one, so I won't get four brown ones in change." In fact, if you give people just 15 s to study an unfamiliar coin (a mercury dime, used from 1916 until 1945), they remember it quite well and know it better a week later than they know the penny (Marmie & Healy, 2004).

Nickerson and Adams's (1979) experiment gives us an important clue to memory. Sheer repetition of a stimulus in the environment won't necessarily lead to its being encoded in memory because presenting the stimulus does not guarantee that the participant will think about (or even notice) all aspects of the stimulus; participants note the color and size of pennies and little else, so that's the information about pennies that ends up in secondary memory, just as the levels of processing framework predicts. Thus, when we speculate that "repetition" is important for memory, it may be that repeated *thought* about the object is crucial to encoding the object into memory, not repeated *exposure* to the object (Craik & Watkins, 1973).

But that doesn't explain why I can remember an advertising jingle. One possibility is that with more repetitions, it becomes more likely that at least one of the repetitions will be processed deeply. Even if I ignore the advertisement 99 times, perhaps the next time will be the one in which I encode the music deeply and start humming along. (There may also be other effects of repetition that we're not concerned with here, for example, greater liking of the product; see Janiszewski & Meyvis, 2001.)

Match Between Encoding and Retrieval: Transfer Appropriate Processing

Does deeper processing during encoding always lead to better memory? From our discussion so far, it seems as if depth makes it more likely that information gets into secondary memory or makes its representation stronger in some way, so you might think the answer is "Yes." Yet, this way of discussing memory focuses only on what happens when you first encounter the material and ignores what might be happening when you later try to remember it, that is, at retrieval.

The mental processes at retrieval must be considered when we're thinking about encoding effects. Donald Morris, John Bransford, and Jeffrey Franks (1977) performed a simple but ingenious experiment in which they varied not only encoding processes (as in a typical depth experiment), but also processes at retrieval (see Figure 6.6). In their experiment, participants heard words and were asked to do one of two tasks. Some participants answered a rhyming question, as described earlier ("_____ rhymes with eagle; legal"). The other participants answered a sentence frame question in which they needed to think about what the word meant to determine whether it would fit the sentence frame ("I met a _____ in the street; cloud"). The rhyme condition was a standard shallow task, and the sentence frame was a deep task.

Each participant took one of two memory tests. One was a standard recognition test in which participants heard a list of words and had to say

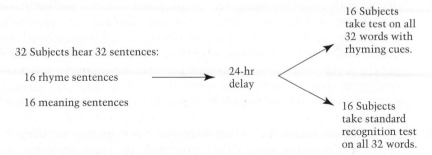

Figure 6.6.   Design of Morris et al.'s (1977) study.

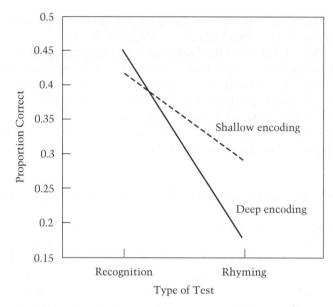

Figure 6.7.   Results of Morris et al.'s (1977) experiment showing that it's not just the depth of processing at encoding that's important; the match between the encoding task and the retrieval test is also important.

which ones they had heard before. As shown in Figure 6.7, Morris and his colleagues (1977) got the usual depth of processing effect when participants took this test. Other participants were not given a recognition test but took a cued recall test in which they had to try to remember the words, given a list of cues. A cue is something in the environment (or something you come up with yourself) that serves as a starting point for memory retrieval. In this context, the cue amounts to a hint. Some of these cues rhymed with a word on the original list. For example, if one of the words was *legal*, the word *regal* might have been on the list of cues. These rhyming cues were different from the ones participants heard the first time they saw the words.

As shown in Figure 6.7, when memory was tested with rhyming cues, the usual depth effect reversed: The participants who did the supposedly shallow rhyme task remembered more than those who did the supposedly deep sentence frame task. This result seems obvious once someone tells you about it, but it wasn't at all obvious at the time. Who would have thought you could get the levels of processing effect to reverse by changing the test? Most psychologists were thinking that depth of encoding made the memory representation stronger in some way, which would mean that memory would be better for any type of test.

These researchers had an interesting explanation for the reversal of the depth of processing effect. They proposed that memory depends not on the depth of encoding but rather on the extent to which there is a match between the processes engaged at encoding and at retrieval. To illustrate this, suppose you are participating in a memory experiment and you are presented with a word like *bone*. You are going to think about the concept *bone* in some way, and there must be particular processes in the mind that enable you to do that thinking. For example, if you are asked what *bone* makes you think of, there are processes that search your memory to find associated concepts, and perhaps you think of a skeleton. Morris et al. (1977) emphasized the importance of the memory search processes that help you come up with the associated concept *skeleton*. They argued that if those same processes were used at retrieval, you would be very likely to remember the original word *bone*. If other processes were engaged when you were trying to retrieve the word, you would be less likely to remember it. For example, if at retrieval you were encouraged to think of words that sound like *phone*, you would be less likely to remember the word *bone* because you had used different processes at encoding (you used processes that helped you think of the associated concept *skeleton*).

The general hypothesis is that when the same processes are used to think about words at encoding and retrieval, memory will be successful; when different processes are used at encoding and retrieval, memory will not be successful. This hypothesis is known as **transfer appropriate processing**. According to this hypothesis, one type of encoding, such as deep processing, is not inherently better than another.

Can studying the brain help us to better understand the process of encoding? Any sort of encoding into secondary memory (whether deep or shallow) depends on the hippocampus and related structures in the medial temporal lobe. Patients with damage to the medial temporal lobe—amnesic patients like H.M.—are unable to get anything into secondary memory, and experiments with rats and monkeys support the importance of the medial temporal lobe to encoding (Corkin, 2002; Squire, Stark, & Clark, 2004).

For this reason, we might have guessed that the effect of the level of processing will be in the hippocampus, but the real action is observed in the prefrontal cortex. This area shows robust activation in brain imaging experiments during deep processing but little during shallow processing (Buckner & Koutstaal, 1998; Demb, Desmond, Wagner, Vaidya, Glover, & Gabrieli, 1995). In fact, if you observe the level of activity in prefrontal cortex for a particular stimulus at encoding, that can actually tell you the probability that the stimulus will be remembered later (Brewer, Zhao, Desmond, Glover, & Gabrieli, 1998; Wagner et al., 1998). However, if the prefrontal cortex is lesioned, memory is impaired, but it is not wiped out the way it is when the medial temporal lobe is damaged (e.g., Shimamura, Janowsky, & Squire, 1991). The exact role that the prefrontal cortex plays at encoding is still not clear, but many researchers believe that the prefrontal cortex is important for determining what the hippocampus processes. Thus, when you process deeply, prefrontal cortex selects the semantic (meaning-based) aspects of the word for the hippocampus to put into secondary memory. When you process shallowly, a different area of the prefrontal cortex selects the sound of the word (for example), the hippocampus processes *that*, and it ends up in secondary memory. At this point, no one is sure and the question is being actively pursued (e.g., Simons & Spiers, 2003; Wagner, 2002), but this scenario is consistent with transfer appropriate processing.

Transfer appropriate processing seems to explain the general pattern of results we have discussed, but it has the same problem as the levels of processing idea—circularity. Memory should be better when the same processes are engaged at encoding and at retrieval, but how do we know whether the processes are the same or different? Keep in mind that there is no way to directly observe cognitive processes. We can observe tasks and then make educated guesses about what sorts of cognitive processes would be engaged to perform those tasks. Thus, the only way to make a judgment about the similarity of cognitive processes during encoding and retrieval is to make the reasonable guess that similar tasks will employ similar cognitive processes at encoding and retrieval. But there is no way to objectively measure the similarity of tasks.

In some cases, it seems a safe bet that two tasks must require fairly different processes; for example, different cognitive processes may be involved in thinking of a word that rhymes with *bone* and thinking of a word related to *bone*. But we don't have an objective way to measure similarity for processes. Still a third task would be judging how many syllables are in the word *bone*. Is that task more similar to thinking about a word that rhymes with *bone* or a word related to *bone*? There is no way to tell.

So, does transfer appropriate processing replace the idea of depth? Only in a sense: The transfer appropriate processing idea forces us to realize that there are interactions between encoding and retrieval. The depth of processing framework was based on the idea that you could simply make a better memory in the storehouse, one that would be better no matter how it was retrieved. In that sense, transfer appropriate processing is more accurate.

Nevertheless, depth is important because deeper encoding does lead to better recall under most conditions in which memory is usually tested. That's important simply as a practical matter. It tells us that if you want to remember something, deep encoding is the way to go, even if the theory behind the principle isn't completely adequate.

SUMMARY. Psychologists do not yet understand what factors determine what people encode in memory, but we have made some progress. Emotion has some effect on memory. Depth of processing has an effect, but it cannot be viewed in isolation. Repetition and effort to learn have little if any effect on memory unless they are coupled with either emotion or depth. That is, repeated deep encoding is better than just a little deep encoding. We have to look at how memory is tested at retrieval and especially at the match between encoding and retrieval processes.

Stand-on-One-Foot Questions

1. What factors affect encoding?
2. Does repetition affect memory?
3. What are the problems with the levels of processing framework?

Questions That Require Two Feet

4. Suppose a friend knows that you're taking a cognitive psychology class and asks for your advice on how to study for exams. What would you say? Would your advice be any different to someone who wants to remember people's names at parties?
5. Many people say that emotional events are well remembered (as in flashbulb memories), but others say that they don't remember emotional events very well. (Some people, for example, say that their wedding day was "just a blur.") What explanation might you give for this disparity?
6. Why do you think you remember some advertisements well and others not so well?

Why Do We Encode Information As We Do?

Preview

We have seen that encoding is determined by how the participant processes the material—that is, what the participant thinks about. But what determines how the participant thinks about the material?

The answer to this question is that how participants process material depends largely on what they already know about it. Prior knowledge affects encoding in three ways: by reducing what we have to remember, guiding our interpretation of details, and making unusual things stand out.

Encoding alone does not determine memory—we also have to look at retrieval processes to predict whether something is going to be remembered—but memory does start with encoding. In the experiments described in the previous section, participants were usually told how to process the material at encoding. What do participants do with material when they are not told what to do? That depends on what they already know about it. In a classic demonstration,

John Bransford and Marcia Johnson (1972) read the following paragraph to participants:

> The procedure is actually quite simple. First you arrange items into different groups. Of course one pile may be sufficient depending on how much there is to do. If you have to go somewhere else due to lack of facilities that is the next step; otherwise, you are pretty well set. It is important not to overdo things. That is, it is better to do too few things at once than too many. In the short run this may not seem important but complications can easily arise. A mistake can be expensive as well. At first, the whole procedure will seem complicated. Soon, however, it will become just another facet of life. It is difficult to foresee any end to the necessity for this task in the immediate future, but then, one can never tell. After the procedure is completed one arranges the materials into different groups again. Then they can be put into their appropriate places. Eventually they will be used once more and the whole cycle will have to be repeated. However, that is part of life.

The paragraph doesn't make much sense, and not surprisingly, participants remembered very little of it. But some participants were given a title before the paragraph was read, and they performed much better. The title is "Washing Clothes." Read the paragraph again now that you know the title, and you'll see that it makes much more sense. If you are given the title after reading it, it doesn't help. You have to know the title in advance. Why is the story easier to remember if you know the title?

When you are reading something, things in your memory that are related to it can come into awareness more easily and shape how you think about what you're thinking about. Hence, when you know the title is "Washing Clothes" and you read "First you arrange items into different groups," it readily comes to mind that this vague sentence refers to sorting clothing by color. Your prior knowledge (about washing clothes) shapes ongoing processing (reading).

We can point to three ways in which previous knowledge affects encoding. Prior knowledge reduces what you have to remember, guides your interpretation of ambiguous details, and makes unusual things stand out.

Prior Knowledge Reduces What We Must Remember

We defined a chunk as a unit of knowledge with subcomponents that are related to one another, often semantically; because they often occur together, it is possible to think of these subcomponents as a single unit. The term *chunking* refers to the process of creating a chunk. Suppose I ask you to memorize some letters (Bower & Springston, 1970). I read them aloud to you, pausing for 1 s between groups.

FB ICB SNC AAP BS

You'd remember some of the letters, perhaps all, but it would take some effort. Think how much easier it would be if I gave you exactly the same list of letters but I paused in different places.

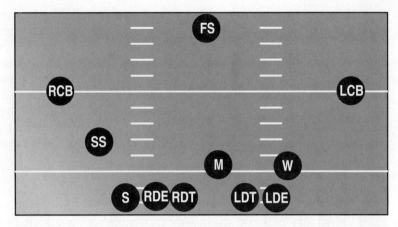

Figure 6.8. A person with a good background knowledge of football would easily chunk this pattern as a zone defense with three men deep, and would also know that S stands for strong outside linebacker, RDE stands for right defensive end, and so forth.

FBI CBS NCAA PBS

Both lists are organized into chunks by the pauses, but for the second list the chunks derive meaning from prior knowledge. You already know these letters as groups, so the second list essentially has four things in it to remember. Things that are presented as individual items might be encodable as a single, higher-order unit if you have the right background knowledge.

William Chase and Herb Simon (1973) conducted a series of experiments in the early 1970s pointing out the importance of background knowledge in chunking. They tested participants with background knowledge in chess, showing them a chessboard with pieces set up to represent the middle of an ongoing game. Participants viewed the board for just 5 s, and then the board was taken away. After some delay, participants were handed an empty chessboard and the pieces, and were asked to replace as many of the pieces as they could. Nonexperts got 8 or 10 of 32 pieces correct, but chess experts got nearly all of them right every time. Why? Chess experts have much more background knowledge. When they look at a chessboard, it looks to them like the second version of the letter task (FBI, CBS, NCAA, PBS). I look at the board and think, "The horsie is over there, and the pointy-headed guy is next to it" (see Figure6.8). The expert glances at the board and thinks, "Queen's gambit declined, 12 moves in, but white has castled early." Knowledge in memory allows the expert to chunk numerous piece positions, representing the whole board in three or four chunks. I, in contract, have to remember the board piece by piece because I can't condense multiple-piece positions into one chunk. When it's time to recall, the chess expert can unpack each chunk into its constituents to replace the pieces appropriately. These sorts of expert knowledge effects have been demonstrated for baseball (Hambrick & Engle, 2002), dance steps (Allard & Starkes, 1991), bridge hands (Engle & Bukstel, 1978), maps (Gilhooly, Wood, Kinnear, & Green, 1988), and music (Meinz & Salthouse, 1998).

How can we be certain that it's really the experts' background knowledge that makes the difference? Maybe the experts are just smarter than other people. Or perhaps they have superior memories, and that's what made them chess experts in the first place. To test this, the experimenters placed the pieces on the board randomly instead of in a way that would simulate an actual game; in this case, the chess experts' advantage disappeared. Their extensive experience with chess was rendered irrelevant when the pieces were placed randomly, so we know it was their prior experience that allowed them to create chunks. (For a review of chunking work, see Gobet et al., 2001.)

Prior Knowledge Guides the Interpretation of Details

Prior knowledge makes things easier to remember by reducing how much you must remember, and this happens through chunking. Prior knowledge also guides what details you are likely to pick out of a complex story or scene to think about. You are likely to notice the details relating to things you already know about. For example, I am interested in theater; I like going to plays and reading them. I went to see a play called *Voir Dire*, which is about a jury's deliberations, with a friend of mine who is an attorney. At the end of the play, there was a lot of overlap in what we remembered about it, but there were also some interesting differences. My friend remembered a lot of the legal details—mostly things the playwright had gotten wrong or things she was impressed to see he had gotten right—whereas I remembered moments in the play that I perceived to be turns in dramatic tension and resolution of tension. I'm not an attorney, so I have no background knowledge about legal matters and was oblivious to the happenings in the play that she noticed. Prior knowledge guides what details of an event you attend to and think about and therefore which details end up in secondary memory. How does this work?

Sometimes, the prior knowledge that is applied at encoding is an isolated fact; for example, knowing the abbreviation *FBI* allows you to treat the three letters as a single chunk. At other times, the prior knowledge is best thought of as a set of related facts; the facts come in a packet, so to speak. Such a packet of information is called a **schema**. There have been a number of different definitions of a schema since Sir Frederic Bartlett (1932) first introduced the idea, but the different definitions agree on certain points: A schema is a memory representation containing general information about an object or an event; a schema represents what is generally true of the situation or event; and it represents not a single event but a type of event. Furthermore, the facts within a single schema are related to one another. These two aspects of a schema are especially important: It is general, and it contains information about related facts.

For example, a schema for the concept *dog* would include the information that a dog typically has four legs, is friendly, is furry, and so on. These characteristics are generally true, but each one need not be true. For example, if you met a three-legged dog, you would still think of it as a dog. However, if

Photo 6.3.   A relatively good example fitting the schema for "car." A car can have two or four doors, be a convertible or hardtop, be various sizes, and so on. In the absence of other information, we assume default values: midsize, four-door, hardtop.

that piece of information is not specified, then you assume that the normal default value of the schema is true and the dog has four legs. A **default value** for a particular piece of information is the value that would normally be true, and thus that you assume is true, unless you are told otherwise. If I tell you I have a dog with three legs, you will change the value of "number of legs" to 3 for the representation of my particular dog. But the default value for "number of legs" in the dog schema would still be 4 (see Photo 6.3).

Because bits of information in a schema are related, as soon as you think about a dog all its characteristics become more available in your mind. For example, suppose that I tell you, "I just got a puppy, which probably wasn't a great idea because my landlord has put in new carpets." What does getting a puppy have to do with new carpets? As soon as I say "puppy," the knowledge becomes available that puppies aren't housebroken. When I say "landlord," information in the landlord schema becomes available, including the information that landlords typically are concerned that damage will be done to rented apartments. Understanding this sentence seems effortless, but it turns on having the right information in memory. I don't have to explicitly say, "I'm worried this puppy will pee on the carpet because that's what puppies do, which will ruin the carpets, which will make the landlord angry because the carpets belong to him." The background information stored in schemas allows the listener to make these inferences from the minimal information in the sentence.

Schemas not only help us make inferences, but also help us interpret ambiguous details. Returning to the "Washing Clothes" paragraph, we would say that the prior knowledge of the theme of the paragraph (as provided by the title) activates a schema for the steps in washing clothes. This background knowledge guides the interpretation of ambiguous sentences such as "First you arrange items into different groups" and "If you have to go somewhere else due to lack of facilities that is the next step." Without the schema, the sentences would carry little meaning.

Schemas can influence encoding even if none of the details are ambiguous by guiding attention. R. C. Anderson and James Pichert (1978) examined this idea. In their experiment, participants read a story about what two boys did when they stayed home from school. Just before reading it, participants were told to read the story either from the perspective of a criminal thinking about robbing the house or from the perspective of a prospective buyer; thus, experimenters activated either a "burglar" schema or a "homebuyer" schema. After a 12-min delay, participants were asked to remember everything they could about the story. As expected, the details that participants attended to and remembered were those consistent with the activated schema: They remembered 64% of the items that were consistent with the activated schema and 50% of the items that were consistent with the other schema. For example, participants who took on the perspective of a burglar were more likely to remember objects that were easy to remove from the house rather than things that would be important to a homebuyer, such as a large yard.

Prior Knowledge Makes Unusual Things Stand Out

Prior knowledge leads you to expect that what usually occurs in a given situation will reoccur. If something unexpected happens, then it stands out. For example, if you went to a restaurant and the server gave you a menu, that would not stand out. However, if the server didn't give you a menu but instead took you back to the kitchen so you could view all the dishes and pick out what appealed to you, that would violate your expectations of what happens in a restaurant (and it would be memorable). That happened to me in a restaurant about 20 years ago, and I still remember it well. (I requested a large fish I noticed in the corner of the kitchen, obviously just caught. The server told me it was inedible, and I didn't ask what it was doing there.)

There has been a lot of research on people's knowledge of what usually happens in common situations. Roger Schank and R. P. Abelson (1977), two computer scientists, proposed that knowledge about common situations such as visiting a restaurant is encoded in a knowledge structure called a **script**, which is a schema for a series of events. For example, you probably have scripts in memory for routine events such as visiting a doctor. If asked, you could quickly generate a list of what each of these events entails: You check in with the receptionist, you read an ancient magazine, a nurse takes you to an exam room, you undress, you sit for a while freezing until the doctor arrives, and so on.

There is fairly good agreement about the events that are part of such scripts, at least within the culture of American college students. Gordon Bower, John Black, and Terrence Turner (1979) asked 161 students to describe what happens in one of these scenarios. They found quite good agreement among the components that each student listed for these events, as shown in Table 6.2.

The researchers predicted that memory for the details of a particular event will depend, in part, on how well it fits the script. They predicted that things that are inconsistent with the script will be very well remembered. For example, a server asking you to select your food in the kitchen is inconsistent with the script (you're supposed to use a menu) and relevant to the goals of the script (getting food; see also Photo 6.4). Other information that is not in the script but is irrelevant (e.g., if the server wore green pants) would not be especially well remembered. The researchers confirmed their hypothesis: Participants had good memory for things that were inconsistent with the script that were relevant to the goals, remembering 53% of the script violations, 38% of the regular parts of the script, and 32% of the irrelevant information (Bower et al., 1979).

Photo 6.4. There is a script for riding an elevator. You get in, push the button for the floor you want, perhaps move to the back, face the door, and monitor the elevator's progress by watching the lighted numbers. This fellow is breaking the script by turning his back on the door, which would likely make you wonder what he was up to, if you were riding with him.

Table 6.2. Empirical Script Norms at Three Agreement Levels

Going to a Restaurant	Attending a Lecture	Getting Up	Grocery Shopping	Visiting a Doctor
Open door	ENTER ROOM	*Wake up*	ENTER STORE	*Enter office*
Enter	*Look for friends*	Turn off alarm	GET CART	CHECK IN WITH RECEPTIONIST
Give reservation name	FIND SEAT	Lie in bed	Take out list	SIT DOWN
Wait to be seated	SIT DOWN	Stretch	Look at list	Wait
Go to table	Settle belongings	GET UP	Go to first aisle	Look at other people
BE SEATED	TAKE OUT NOTEBOOK	Make bed	*Go up and down aisles*	READ MAGAZINE
Order drinks	*Look at other students*	Go to bathroom	PICK OUT ITEMS	*Name called*
Put napkins on lap	*Talk*	Use toilet	Compare prices	Follow nurse
LOOK AT MENU	Look at professor	*Take shower*	Put items in cart	*Enter exam room*
Discuss menu	LISTEN TO PROFESSOR	*Wash face*	Get meat	Undress
ORDER MEAL	TAKE NOTES	Shave	Look for items forgotten	*Sit on table*
Talk	CHECK TIME	DRESS	Talk to other shoppers	Talk to nurse
Drink water	Ask questions	Go to kitchen	Go to checkout counters	NURSE TESTS
Eat salad or soup	Change position in seat	Fix breakfast	*Find fastest line*	Wait
Meal arrives	Daydream	EAT BREAKFAST	WAIT IN LINE	Doctor enters
EAT FOOD	Look at other students	BRUSH TEETH	*Put food on belt*	Doctor greets
Finish meal	Take more notes	Read paper	Read magazines	Talk to doctor about problem
Order dessert	*Close notebook*	*Comb hair*	WATCH CASHIER	Doctor asks questions
			RING UP	DOCTOR EXAMINES
Eat dessert	*Gather belongings*	*Get books*	PAY CASHIER	
				Get dressed
Ask for bill	Stand up	Look in mirror	*Watch bagger*	Get medicine
Bill arrives	Talk	Get coat	Cart bags out	Make another appointment
PAY BILL	LEAVE	LEAVE HOUSE	Load bags into car	LEAVE OFFICE
Leave tip			LEAVE STORE	
Get coats				
LEAVE				

Items in all capital letters were mentioned by the most subjects, items in italics by fewer subjects, and items in lowercase letters by the fewest subjects.

This phenomenon has been best studied in the case of scripts, but it may well apply to other types of information as well. In fact, Jeffrey Zacks, Barbara Tversky, and Gowri Iyer (2001; Schwan & Garsoffky, 2004) suggested that script-like knowledge structures are used not only at retrieval, but also to interpret ongoing behavior as it happens. They had participants watch videotapes of routine activities such as making a bed and press a button when they thought the behavior reached the boundary of a "natural unit." For example, in making a bed, a unit might be "spreading the top sheet" or "putting the pillowcases on." Some participants were asked to find boundaries for the smallest unit that seemed natural, some for the largest. The data indicated that people are biased to perceive event boundaries in a hierarchical fashion and that the parts tend to correspond to functions. The researchers argued that these are characteristics of scripts, indicating that the knowledge structures that participate in memory retrieval also guide the ongoing perception of events.

In this chapter, we've discussed how material is encoded into long-term memory. How is this material retrieved from long-term memory? We've already had a hint that the match between encoding and retrieval is important. That factor will be a theme in the next chapter, where we consider retrieval in more detail.

Stand-on-One-Foot Question

7. How does prior knowledge affect encoding?

Questions That Require Two Feet

8. Think of an area in which you have expertise. Is your memory for material related to that area superior to that of your friends who do not have the same expertise?

9. What do you think the schema for the concept librarian might look like? How about the schema for the concept engineer? Does the fact that you can generate these schemas make you think you are prejudiced?

10. Can you think of a way to chunk the material in this section of the chapter?

11. Suppose you had a good deal of prior knowledge about a particular topic. Would that make deep processing easier or more difficult?

12. Do you remember the translation of the French sentence at the beginning of the chapter? Why might you be more likely to remember this sentence as opposed to the others in this chapter?

KEY TERMS

deep processing
default value
depth of processing
flashbulb memories
incidental memory
   test

intentional memory
   test
levels of processing
   framework
schema
script

shallow processing
transfer appropriate
   processing

Memory Retrieval

Why Is Memory Retrieval Unreliable?

- Measures of Memory
- Differences in Cues
- Encoding and Retrieval Redux
- Retrieval Cues and Memory Test Sensitivity
- Retrieval Cues and the Physical Environment
- Retrieval and Prior Knowledge
- False Memory

Why Do We Forget?

- Occlusion
- Unlearning
- Decay
- Changes to Target Memories
- Repression
- The Permanence of Memory

In chapter 6, we discussed why some material ends up in secondary memory and some doesn't. The storehouse metaphor leads naturally to several questions. First, is it guaranteed that we can get information from the storehouse? A moment's reflection will tell you that the answer is "No." We've all had the frustrating experience in which we know that we know something, but we can't retrieve it. ("You know, that singer who's kind of weird. She wore that swan dress one time. No, not Sinead O'Connor. Bjork, that's the one!") This difficulty brings up the question **Why is memory retrieval unreliable?** To put it another way, why can we sometimes retrieve a memory, whereas other times we can't retrieve the same memory? From what you learned in chapter 6, you won't be surprised that successful retrieval of a memory depends largely on the cues available at the time of retrieval.

But sometimes cues will not help; the memory is simply lost. You know that you once knew something, but you've forgotten it. Perhaps you've looked through old high school papers—a geometry homework set, for example—and thought, "I can't believe I ever knew this stuff." In cases like this, it doesn't feel to you that if you were given enough time or better cues you'd eventually be able to retrieve the memory. Rather, it feels as if the memory of how to do those geometry problems is simply gone. Why do some memories become irretrievable? That is, **Why do we forget?** The idea that memories simply fade away with time corresponds to our everyday experience, but it is difficult to prove. It is more certain that new things you learn can interfere with things that you already know, thereby causing forgetting.

Why Is Memory Retrieval Unreliable?

Preview

There are different ways of measuring memory. One measure may indicate that you don't remember something, even though another indicates that you do. It thus appears that some measures of memory are more sensitive than others, that is, better able to detect memories that are poorly represented in the storehouse. A crucial factor in sensitivity is the match between encoding and retrieval, but prior knowledge also has an effect, just as it does at encoding. In fact, prior knowledge can influence retrieval to such an extent that a completely false memory can be created.

It might seem that after information is stored into secondary memory, you should be able to retrieve it whenever you want. As you know, memory doesn't work this way. Sometimes you try to remember Bjork's name and it pops right out of the storehouse, so to speak. Other times, you can't quite get it, but when someone provides the name you immediately recognize it as correct (and you confidently reject Sinead O'Connor as incorrect). There are different ways to retrieve memories—or to measure whether a person remembers something—and the way memory is measured has a big impact on whether a piece of information appears to be in secondary memory.

Measures of Memory

Before we can talk about the details of retrieval, we need to be more precise about the different ways to measure memory. First, we need to define a **cue**, which is information in the environment that is used as a starting point for retrieval. If I simply say to you, "Remember," the command makes no sense. Are you supposed to be remembering something about pickles, your second-grade teacher, or the structure of barium? A cue for what is to be retrieved from secondary memory might be provided by the experimenter ("Try to remember what I told you an hour ago") or the environment (an advertisement for motor oil reminds you to get your oil changed), or you might provide it yourself (you mentally retrace your steps in an effort to remember where you might have left something).

Memory tests differ in the cues that the experimenter provides. A **free recall** test provides very few—the experimenter says little more than "Tell me what you remember." In a **cued recall** test, the experimenter adds some hints, or cues, about the material you're supposed to remember (e.g., "some of the words were fruits."). In a **recognition test**, the experimenter provides the targets along with **distractors** (also called **foils**, or **lures**), and the participant must pick out the targets from among the distractors (e.g., "did you see 'orange' or 'apple?'"). In a **savings in relearning** test, the experimenter asks the participant to learn some material (e.g., a word list) to a particular criterion (e.g., until he or she can recite the list perfectly two times in a row). The number of practice trials it takes to reach the criterion is recorded. At retrieval, the experimenter asks the participant to learn the same material to the same criterion a second time. If the participant can reach the criterion in fewer trials, that represents savings in relearning—the participant learns the material faster the second time—which presumably results from some residual memory of the earlier experience.

In general, free recall is the most difficult memory task, followed by cued recall, then recognition. (Savings in relearning is still easier but is used much less often.) In this case, "easy" or "difficult" refers to the likelihood that you will successfully retrieve the material you encoded. We can also refer to difficulty as the **sensitivity** of a test, that is, its ability to detect memories. A test seems easy because it is sensitive, and detects a memory, if one is present.

Although tests of memory generally vary in sensitivity as I've described, there is a problem to bear in mind. The apparent sensitivity (i.e., ease or difficulty) of a test depends on *which* cues the experimenter provides. For example, I may say, "Remember this word" and show you a slide with the word *Boat* written on it. Then, an hour later, I give you one of four recognition tests, each of which has the target (*Boat*) and one distractor, and you have to choose which stimulus you saw (*a* or *b*). Figure 7.1 lists four possible tests that vary in difficulty because the distractors vary. Similarly, a cued recall test will be

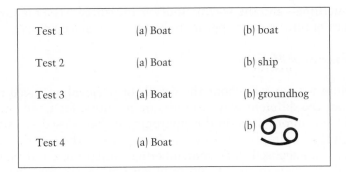

Figure 7.1. Four possible tests of your memory of the stimulus *Boat* in ascending order of difficulty.

harder or easier, depending on the quality of the hints. Still, it is generally true that recognition is easier than cued recall, which is easer than free recall (Hart, 1965, 1967; Tulving & Pearlstone, 1966), and this relationship is relevant to the question we are addressing in this section: Why is memory retrieval unreliable?

Differences in Cues

Why do different measures of memory lead to different performance? Psychologists have found it useful to think about measures of memory in terms of the cues that they provide.

In a free recall test, the instruction is typically "Try to recall the information I showed you earlier." It is understood that you are to recall information from the time and place at which the experimenter had you encode some material. This information about the time and place at which a memory was encoded is usually called the **context**, but in this example you don't have complete information about the context. The experimenter might have said, "Try to recall the information I showed you an hour ago, in this room." Of course, even if the experimenter didn't give you that specific information ("an hour ago, in this room") you might use that information to help you remember the required information. In so doing you are generating your own cues to memory.

In a cued recall test, the experimenter provides the context and adds some hints about the material. The hints might be some semantically related words ("One of the words referred to a card game") or a cue based on sound ("One of the words rhymed with *smoker*").

In a recognition test, the experimenter again provides a cue about the context but now also provides the target material along with some other material that was not presented at encoding. The participant's job, therefore, is to determine which stimuli go with the encoding context (see Table 7.1).

It seems that free recall, cued recall, and recognition differ in that they provide successively more complete cues. One idea holds that memories may

Table 7.1.   ***Types of Memory Tests***

Type of Test	Sample Instructions	Reference to Context?	Information About Target	What Must Participant Do?
Free recall	"Please remember the word list."	Yes	None	Generate the target material from the context information.
Cued recall	"Please remember the word list. One of the words was the name of a card game."	Yes	Usually semantic (i.e., related to meaning)	Generate the target from the context information using the cue.
Recognition	"Was the word *poker* on the list you saw before?"	Yes	Target itself	Determine whether the stimulus provided matches the context information.

differ along a simple dimension of how strong they are; the weaker the memory is, the more cues you need to retrieve the memory. The sensitivity of a test is determined by the quality and quantity of cues it provides. We can call this view the **strength view of memory**.

Later experiments showed that there are problems with a strength view of memory. For example, retrieval doesn't work the same way each time. If someone asks you to name the three Rice Krispies characters, you may draw an utter blank on one occasion, whereas another time you might immediately rattle off, "Snap, Crackle, Pop." If the memory is strong, you should retrieve it every time, and if it's weak, you should fail each time; after all, the retrieval cue ("Name the Rice Krispies characters") is the same each time.

Endel Tulving (1967) emphasized this point in a classic experiment. He had people encode a list of 36 common nouns once, then make three successive attempts to recall the list, then encode it again, make three more recall attempts, and so on. Not surprisingly, people recalled more words with each successive encoding. What was more interesting is what happened when they made several recall attempts of the list. Over all recall attempts, participants got an average of 14.21 items correct. On each successive attempt, participants remembered 3.97 words (on average) that they hadn't recalled on the previous attempt, but they also forgot 3.89 words (on average) that they had remembered on the previous attempt. In other words, a participant might report a word on the first test, then fail to recall it on Tests 2 and 3, then recall it again on Test 4, and so on. Tulving pointed out that this pattern of data argued against a simple strength theory of memory; there is no reason for the strength of a memory to wax and wane on successive tests.

Note that this doesn't mean that strength doesn't play some role in memory. The strength with which a cue ("Name the Rice Krispies characters") evokes a target may be one contributing factor. But the variability of memory performance shows that strength is not the whole story.

Encoding and Retrieval Redux

Chapter 6 emphasized that the match between encoding and retrieval is important for memory. What do we know regarding what people think about at encoding and at retrieval? For encoding, what you think about depends on what you already know about the target material. At retrieval, what you think about is greatly influenced by the cues you are given. A memory can be retrieved or not retrieved because the cues for retrieval differ on the two retrieval attempts.

Indeed, in chapter 6 we saw that changing retrieval cues can have a big impact on memory. Rhyming cues given at retrieval might be good or bad for memory, depending on whether you were thinking about the way the word sounded at encoding. But our discussion of retrieval in this chapter makes it sound as though this effect should be more fine grained: Retrieval cues should matter not only at a rough cut (the cues are "about meaning" or "about sound"), but also if all cues concern meaning.

What happens if we change the meaning of retrieval cues? Researchers find that changing the meaning of a word between encoding and retrieval has a sizable effect on memory. Leah Light and Linda Carter-Sobell (1970) had participants read sentences that contained a homophone in a way that biased the meaning toward one definition. For example, participants might have seen this sentence: "The harassed customer bought strawberry jam at the supermarket." At recall, participants saw an adjective–noun phrase and had to say whether the noun appeared in one of the sentences they saw earlier, ignoring the adjective. Participants saw words from the sentence ("strawberry jam"), a new adjective with a word from the sentence ("raspberry jam"), or a different adjective that changed the meaning of the accompanying noun from the sentence ("traffic jam"). As shown in Figure 7.2, changing the adjective hurts recognition, but changing the adjective so it changes the meaning of the noun hurts recognition even more.

This effect is not surprising. We would expect that people would have two separate concepts for *jam* in memory: one for the stuff you spread on toast, and one for traffic tie-ups. At encoding you think of one meaning, and at retrieval the cue biases you to think of the other, so you fail to recall the word. What would happen, though, if you didn't change the meaning of the word but emphasized different aspects or properties of the word?

To determine whether emphasizing a particular property of a concept influenced participants' subsequent memory for it, Richard Barclay and his associates (Barclay, Bransford; Franks, McCarrel, & Nitsch, 1974) gave 20 participants target words in the context of a sentence that encouraged them to think of a particular property of the word's referent. For example, a participant

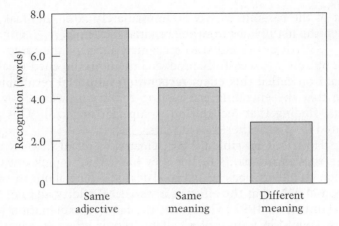

Figure 7.2. Light and Carter-Sobell's (1970) study showed that biasing the meaning of a noun at recall hurts recognition performance.

might hear "The man lifted the piano" or "The man tuned the piano." At recall, each participant received two nonconsecutive cues that were pertinent to the target words. For *piano*, the cues were "something heavy" and "something with a nice sound." Each participant only heard one sentence with *piano* in it, but each participant heard both cues at recall (on separate testing occasions), so one cue was appropriate and the other inappropriate. Out of 10 words, participants remembered an average of 4.6 that were cued according to the appropriate meaning and just 1.6 that were cued with the inappropriate meaning. Note that in this experiment, it was properties of an object that were changed, not the object itself (as in the *jam* experiment). Nevertheless, there is a sizable effect of changing the cue at retrieval.

Retrieval Cues and Memory Test Sensitivity

This preceding discussion gives us a hint about what is behind the variable sensitivity of different retrieval tests. It's not that more retrieval cues per se are better for retrieval, but having more cues makes it more likely that one of them will match what you thought about at encoding, leading to successful retrieval. In other words, a recognition test is more likely than a cued recall test to make you process the material the way you did at encoding. If a cued recall test was designed to make participants more likely to think about the material in the same way as they did at encoding, it should be more sensitive than a recognition test.

Endel Tulving and Donald Thomson (1973) set out to show that effect. In their experiment, participants were told that they would see word pairs, and they were to remember the words written in capital letters. An accompanying word written in lowercase letters might help them, but they would be tested on the words in capital letters. Participants saw a list of 24 word pairs such as *glue–CHAIR, ground–COLD,* and *fruit–FLOWER,* and then took a recognition test of the capitalized words. Immediately after this task, participants were given the list of cues from the original list: *glue* _____, *ground* _____, and *fruit* _____. Participants failed to recognize many of the target words on the first test but then successfully produced them on the cued recall test. Tulving and Thomson called this effect **recognition failure of recallable words** to emphasize that the encoding and testing conditions were designed to reverse the usual finding that recognition is superior to recall. This effect has been repeated in many other experiments.

How is it possible for participants to recall *CHAIR* given the cue *glue*, even though moments earlier they had failed to pick out *CHAIR* on a recognition test? There has been a good deal of debate about this phenomenon. (One proposal held that the effect is a statistical oddity and not of any importance; see Hintzman, 1992.) Currently, the favored explanation is that the cause of the recognition failure of recallable words effect lies in the lowercase cues, which are selected to be low associates of the target words. The words *chair* and *glue*, for example, are not completely unrelated. You can make a connection between the two words if you think about the joints of a chair, which are often glued. So, the presence of the word *glue*, which the experimenter says you are free to ignore, makes you think about the target in an unusual way. If on the recognition test you see *CHAIR* alone and you think about chair in the normal way—as something to sit on—that's not what you thought about at encoding. You thought about something with glued joints, so you say to yourself, "Nah, I didn't see the word *CHAIR* before. Gee, I don't know which of these three words was on the list; I'll just guess." You might guess wrong. Later on the recall test you see the cue *glue*, and there is some chance you'll say to yourself, "Oh yeah, I thought about glue at encoding—glued joints it was. On a chair. Right, *glue* went with *CHAIR*."

Tulving and Thomson's (1973) experiment shows that the match between encoding and retrieval is critical; if you think about the stimulus in different ways at encoding and retrieval, you may not recognize it. We can predict, then, that if participants never really connect the cue and stimulus words (*glue–CHAIR*) semantically, the recall failure effect should disappear, and that seems to be the case (Arlemalm, 1996; Bryant, 1991).

Retrieval Cues and the Physical Environment

We know that memory is better when the processes engaged in thinking about the material are the same at encoding and retrieval. Can we extend this idea to physical context? Is memory better if the physical context is the same at encoding and retrieval? If you learn some material while you're in a dormitory room, for example, will you remember it when you are tested in a lecture hall? In fact, researchers have demonstrated that there are **context effects** of the physical environment on memory, but they are generally weak.

Duncan Godden and Alan Baddeley (1975) had participants encode and retrieve information while they were either underwater or on dry land. Participants, who were members of a diving club, were outfitted with apparatus that enabled them to hear words read to them underwater and write them on special boards. Then, they heard and recalled word lists while underwater, on dry land, or switching between the two conditions at encoding and retrieval. (There was a 4-min delay between encoding and retrieval in all cases so participants who were switching would have time to make the change.) The results showed that memory was about 40% better in the same context. To be certain that it was the different context and not the disruptive effect of switching that affected memory, Godden and Baddeley conducted a second experiment in which participants encoded and retrieved words on dry land, but during the 4-min delay half of the participants had to jump in the water, swim, and dive down 20 feet before exiting the water and trying to recall the words. This extra, possibly disruptive activity had no effect on memory, indicating that in the first experiment it was the change in context that was affecting memory, not the disruption of switching contexts.

Does physical context affect memory under ordinary conditions as well as underwater? Steven Smith, Arthur Glenberg, and Robert Bjork (1978) had college students study lists of words presented on slides in a windowless room off campus by the experimenter neatly dressed in a tie and jacket. On a second day, the students studied another word list that was read aloud, this time in a room on campus with windows, and the experimenter was dressed sloppily. On a third day, they were asked to remember both lists in one or the other context. The experimenters reported that memory was somewhat better if the context matched between encoding and retrieval (59% correct) than if it didn't match (46% correct). All these changes in the environment (room, experimenter, words heard vs. seen) produced a modest effect (see Photo 7.1).

These studies showed that memory is somewhat better when the physical environment is the same during encoding and retrieval. Nevertheless, context effects are usually small or nonexistent; the effect is present for free recall, smaller for cued recall, and absent altogether for recognition (Smith, 1988). It may well be that the effect, when present, is due to the extent to which the participant integrates the target word and the environmental context (e.g., the word *powder* might be encoded differently underwater and on dry land). Seen that way, environmental context effects are rather like any other context effects in that they depend on the match between thoughts at encoding and at retrieval.

Retrieval and Prior Knowledge

In chapter 6, we saw that prior knowledge (as represented in a script or schema) influences how new material is processed and therefore how it is encoded. For example, if something is occurring that can be described by a script ("visiting a restaurant") and a relevant detail is inconsistent with the script (the server takes you to the kitchen to select your food), that inconsistent event will be well remembered. Does prior knowledge also influence retrieval? Yes, but at retrieval it influences memory of the typical events, not the atypical ones.

Photo 7.1. Studying in your home and then being tested in your classroom produces minute context effects, if any.

Suppose that you are trying to remember a story I told you last week about my daughter's birthday party. You have prior knowledge about children's birthday parties that can provide retrieval cues. For example, you probably know that cake and ice cream are usually served at kids' parties, so you might try to remember what sort of cake was served or whether something other than cake was served, such as an enormous chocolate chip cookie. Your expectation that cake was served may be so strong that you may think to yourself, "I really don't remember cake being served, but this was a child's birthday party, so there had to be cake; let me try one more time to remember what kind."

Sir Frederic Bartlett (1932), who first developed the idea of a schema, gave a classic example of its effects on retrieval. He read this Native American folk-tale called "The War of the Ghosts" to English schoolboys:

> One night two young men from Egulac went down to the river to hunt seals, and while they were there it became foggy and calm. Then they heard war-cries, and they thought: "Maybe this is a war-party." They escaped to the shore, and hid behind a log. Now canoes came up, and they heard the noise of paddles, and saw one canoe coming up to them. There were five men in the canoe, and they said:
>
> "What do you think? We wish to take you along. We are going up the river to make war on the people." One of the young men said: "I have no arrows." "Arrows are in the canoe," they said. "I will not go along. I might be killed. My relatives do not know where I have gone. But you," he said, turning to the other, "may go with them." So one of the young men went, but the other returned home.
>
> And the warriors went on up the river to a town on the other side of Kalama. The people came down to the water, and they began to fight, and many were killed. But presently the young man heard one of the warriors say: "Quick, let us go home: that Indian has been hit." Now he thought: "Oh, they are ghosts." He did not feel sick, but they said he had been shot.
>
> So the canoes went back to Egulac, and the young man went ashore to his house, and made a fire. And he told everybody and said: "Behold I accompanied the ghosts, and we went to fight. Many of our fellows were killed, and many of those who attacked us were killed. They said I was hit, and I did not feel sick." He told it all, and then he became quiet. When the sun rose he fell down. Something black came out of his mouth. His face became contorted. The people jumped up and cried. He was dead.

This story has elements that would have been unfamiliar to English schoolboys in the 1930s. It includes unfamiliar cultural elements such as canoes, and the story structure itself is different from English stories, which typically have logical links between one event and another; this story introduces new actions without making it clear how they relate to previous actions. Bartlett (1932) reported that when his participants tried to recall this story later, their recall was influenced by their schema of what a story is supposed to be like. They added details to put logical connections between events, omitted other details, and changed unfamiliar terms to ones they knew better. Bartlett called attention to one participant who substituted the word *boat* for *canoe* when he recalled the story, and another who reported *fishing* instead of *seal hunting*. The particular results Bartlett reported have not always replicated well (Roediger, Wheeler, & Rajaram, 1993), but the basic effects he reported are very well supported.

Bartlett argued that retrieval is largely a process of **reconstruction**, not simply a matter of pulling information out of the memory storehouse. Rather, Bartlett argued, retrieval is a process whereby we use information from the memory storehouse and information about the world (in the form of schemas) to reconstruct what probably occurred.

Table 7.2.   ***Sample Recognition Test***

Original Story	Recognition Test Sentences	Type of Sentence	Average Recognition Rating
Dan went to a restaurant. The hostess seated him. He scanned the menu. He selected what he wanted, and the server took his order. Dan waited for his food. The waitress brought his food.	Dan waited for his food.	Consistent with the script; in the story	5.46
	Dan paid the bill.	Consistent with the script; not in story	3.91
Dan ate his meal and left the restaurant.	The restaurant was cold.	Irrelevant to script; not in story	1.71

This idea is supported by data from the study by Gordon Bower and his colleagues (Bower, Black, & Turner, 1979). You'll recall that in chapter 6 we said that events that are inconsistent with the script but relevant to its goal are well remembered. The experimenters also reported what happens if participants are asked about information that is consistent with the script but was not presented in the original story. For example, participants read a story about going to a restaurant that did not mention the patron paying the bill. A recognition test asked participants to rate their confidence that they had seen seven sentences in the story. The participants not only gave high ratings to sentences from the script that were actually contained in the story (average = 5.46), but also to actions that were consistent with the script but never mentioned in the story (average = 3.9). These ratings were much higher than the ratings they assigned to events that were not in the story but were unrelated to the script (average = 1.71). (See Table 7.2 for sample sentences.)

Thus, it appears that prior knowledge in the form of scripts and schemas influences not only encoding (remember the "Washing Clothes" paragraph from chapter 6), but also retrieval.

But how can we be certain that these effects occur at retrieval? It seems plausible that these schema effects occur at encoding; the participant listening to the story changes it as it goes to make it fit his or her schema. At recall, the participant remembers the changed story, so reconstruction doesn't occur at all. James Dooling and Robert Christiaansen (1977) determined a clever way to show that reconstruction can occur at recall. They asked participants to read this paragraph:

Carol Harris was a problem child from birth. She was wild, stubborn, and violent. By the time Carol turned eight, she was still unmanageable. Her parents were very concerned about her mental health. There was no good institution for her problem in her state. Her parents finally decided to take some action. They hired a private teacher for Carol.

After a 1-week delay, a group of participants were given a recognition test for sentences and had to say whether each sentence was in the story. The critical sentence was "She was deaf, dumb, and blind." Very few participants believed that this sentence had been part of the story. A second group of participants underwent the same testing procedure, except that right before taking the recognition test they were told that Carol Harris was Helen Keller's real name. Many of these participants incorrectly "recognized" the critical sentence as having been in the story. This experiment shows clearly that reconstruction can occur at retrieval. There was no opportunity for the memory error to occur at encoding because participants didn't know that their background knowledge about Helen Keller would be relevant until retrieval.

False Memory

In the previous section, we saw that it's possible to remember an event that actually never happened—for example, your knowledge about what usually happens in a restaurant can make you falsely remember that a menu was offered to a customer when that never happened in the story. This type of error is an unfortunate by-product of a *good* feature of your memory. Your memory system will include as part of a memory information that is probably right—the server usually offers a menu, so even if you have no specific memory of that event, it's sensible to assume that it happened. Although the memory system is usually making a good gamble by including such information as part of the memory, on occasion it's wrong, and that's one type of **false memory**, usually defined as a memory of an event that never happened.

Cognitive psychologists have found that false memories of this sort can be quite easy to produce. For example, have a look at this list of words:

bed
rest
tired
dream
wake
snooze
blanket
doze
slumber
snore
nap
peace
yawn
drowsy

Participants who hear this list and are immediately asked to recall it remember the words in the middle of the list about 50% of the time. They also remember the word "sleep" from the list about 50% of the time (Deese, 1959; Roediger & McDermott, 1995). The odd thing is that "sleep" isn't on the list. This false memory effect is very robust. Participants report high confidence that "sleep" was on the list (Roediger & McDermott, 1995), and they report the word even when warned that they will be tempted to report items associated with the list items (Gallo, Roberts, & Seamon, 1997). Kathleen McDermott (1996) introduced a 2-day delay between study and test, and found that participants were actually more likely to recall the never-presented item than any of the presented items (see Figure 7.3).

Why does this false memory occur? One way to think about it is that it's rather like the restaurant schema. Even in a list-learning experiment, your memory system will use background knowledge if it seems applicable. In this case, it's obvious to the participants that the words are related, and the relationship revolves around the concept "sleep." That background knowledge— that "sleep" is related to the other words and is therefore very typical of the list—becomes folded into the memory for the list without the participant intending it to, just as the server offering a menu is typical of a restaurant visit and therefore gets folded into the memory of a particular visit to a restaurant.

A quite different explanation is also possible. Perhaps when participants hear the list of sleep-related words, they actually think of the word "sleep" during encoding. Then at recall, they remember thinking about "sleep" when

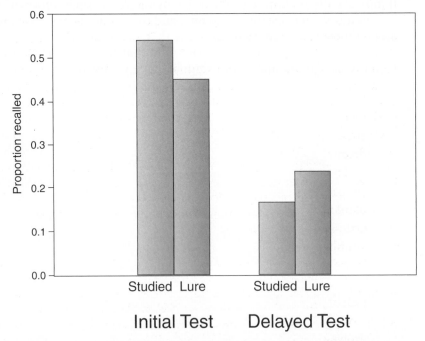

Figure 7.3. Results of McDermott (1996). Note that, with a delay, the rate of "remembering" the material is higher for the lure word that was not on the list them any of the words that were on the list.

they heard the list and don't realize that they are remembering their own thought, not what the experimenter said (Johnson & Raye, 1981; Roediger, Watson, McDermott, & Gallo, 2001). This example represents another type of false memory. You have the content of the memory right, but you're mistaken about the source. The **source** of a memory refers to where and when it was encoded, whether someone told you the information or you experienced it directly, or just thought about it. For example, I know that George Bush won the 2004 presidential election. But I have lost the source for that memory. I don't know whether I saw the result on television, or read it in the newspaper or on the web. I also cannot recall when I learned about the outcome—I either stayed up to see the returns, or I got up early the next day. The source of that memory is gone.

Knowing the source of a memory can be quite important to using it. For example, you may remember that someone said a movie was terrific. But was the source a trusted friend, or was it someone on an advertisement for the movie? Other times, you are confused about whether the source of a memory was something in the environment, or whether it was your own thought. For example, as you're pulling out of your driveway, you believe that you remember turning off the stove, but then you wonder whether you are remembering actually turning off the stove or *thinking* about turning off the stove. **Source confusion** occurs when one mistakes one's own thought for an event (or vice versa), or when you misremember where and when an event occurred (Johnson, Hashtroudi, & Lindsay, 1993; Johnson & Raye, 1981).

Creating source confusions and subsequent memory errors in the laboratory is not difficult. For example, Brian Gonsalves and his associates (Gonsalves, Reber, Gitelman, Parrish, Mesulam, & Paller, 2004) had participants view a series of 350 words, one at a time, on a screen. Each word was a concrete noun (e.g., "table"), and participants were to generate a mental image corresponding to the word after they saw it. For half the words, a photograph of the object was presented 2 s later. For the other words, a blank rectangle was presented. Twenty minutes later, participants heard all 350 words again, as well as 175 new distractors. Participants had to judge whether they had viewed a photograph of the word during study. Participants believed that they had seen a photograph of 27% of the items for which they had only created a mental image. Other studies (e.g., Garry, Manning, Loftus, & Sherman, 1996) have shown that the phenomenon occurs for entire events, not just confusable items such as words in a long list.

Gonsalves and his associates (2004) also measured participants' brain activation during this study. They found that the parts of the brain that support visual imagery—precuneus, right parietal cortex, and anterior cingulate—were more active during encoding for words that would later be falsely remembered as having been presented with a picture. This indicates that producing a vivid mental image might make the participant more likely to falsely remember that he or she actually *saw* a picture. This interpretation fits with the general idea that people judge whether they *saw* something or *thought about* something based on how much perceptual detail there is in the memory. If there is a lot of detail, people suspect that they are remembering something that they saw (Johnson et al., 1993).

There is an important real-life application of this research. Until the mid-1990s, many clinicians used a technique called guided imagery, in which clients were encouraged to imagine events from childhood. Guided imagery was supposed to help the client uncover early memories. Thus, a clinician who suspected that a client had been sexually abused as a child might ask the client to imagine typical scenarios, such as being approached by an adult when she was a child in bed, to determine whether the imagery brings any submerged memories to consciousness. Such guided imagery sessions might be lengthy and occur over multiple weeks. The danger of this technique is that source confusion might occur, and the images will begin to seem familiar to the client, not because they are submerged memories at last remembered, but because the images produced in prior therapy sessions are becoming familiar. Based on false memory research, various clinical groups (e.g., the Royal College of Psychiatrists) began warning about the dangers inherent in guided imagery in the mid-1990s.

In the previous examples, participants confused their own thoughts with something from the environment. Another type of source confusion occurs when two perceptual sources are confused. In an experiment demonstrating this phenomenon, Elizabeth Loftus and her colleagues (Loftus, Miller, & Burns, 1978) showed their participants a slide show depicting an auto accident. After seeing the slide show, the participants completed a questionnaire about the events in the show. For half the participants, the questionnaire mentioned, in passing, information that did not match the slides. For example, one question was "Did another car pass the red Datsun when it stopped at the yield sign?" when the slide actually showed a stop sign, not a yield sign. Participants later had to select which sign they had seen, and those who were misled by the questionnaire were about half as likely to get it right as those who were not. A likely interpretation of these data is that participants who were misled are experiencing a source confusion: They remember something about a yield sign, but they forget that it was in the questionnaire, not in the slides (Lindsay & Johnson, 1989).

The practical implications of this effect may be profound. The memory of an eyewitness to a crime may be open to modification, depending on the questions that are asked. Indeed, Loftus and John Palmer (1974) conducted a study that seems very similar to exactly that effect. They asked participants who had just seen a short film of an auto accident to estimate the speed of the cars by asking "How fast were the cars going when they hit each other?", but they varied the verb, replacing "hit" with "smashed," "collided," "bumped," or "contacted." Participants estimated higher speeds when the verb used was more violent. More surprising, this simple alteration changed participants' memory for the accident. When they returned to the lab a week later, they again answered questions about the accident, including the question "Did you see any broken glass?" In fact, there was none, but 34% of participants who heard the verb "smashed" remembered that there was, compared with just 14% of participants who heard the verb "hit" (see Photo 7.2).

Photo 7.2. The questions that eyewitnesses are asked after an accident or crime can be a source of false memories.

Providing misleading information will frequently lead to false memories, and participants can be quite confident about their accuracy (Zaragoza & Mitchell, 1996). The effect is usually stronger with a longer delay (Higham, 1998), and more often works with peripheral details of an event, rather than the central features (e.g., Heath & Erickson, 1998).

In summary, there are two broad classes of false memory. One type occurs because the memory system (without the individual's intention or awareness) includes prior knowledge in a memory so one "remembers" something that never happened. The second type occurs because the participant misremembers the source of a memory. For a readable introduction to this field, see Schacter (2001), and for a review of the neuroscientific approach, see Schacter and Slotnick (2004). In the remainder of this chapter, we cover another type of memory error—forgetting.

Stand-on-One-Foot Questions

1. *What four measures of memory are commonly used, and what does it mean to say that they differ in sensitivity?*
2. *Why do different measures of memory differ in sensitivity?*
3. *Which is more important to effective retrieval: the format of the test (recognition, cued recall) or the cues the test provides?*

4. *How does prior knowledge affect retrieval?*

5. *What are the two main ways that false memories may be created?*

Questions That Require Two Feet

6. *Suppose you asked a friend to tell you what he or she was doing exactly 19 months ago. How much do you think he or she could tell you, and why?*

7. *You probably have had the experience of walking past a friend without recognizing him or her in a place where you don't typically see that person (as when you see a college friend in your hometown during spring break). How can the ideas discussed here explain that phenomenon?*

Why Do We Forget?

Preview

Forgetting can occur because (a) you don't have the right cue for retrieval, (b) the association between the cue and the target memory is compromised in some way, or (c) the target memory itself is lost. There is some evidence supporting each mechanism. We briefly consider the possibility that some memories are never lost. The popular notion that all memories are recorded somewhere in the brain is almost certainly wrong, but it does appear that with sufficient practice, a subset of memories will never be lost.

In trying to explain why something that *can* be retrieved sometimes is not retrieved, we emphasize cues, and indeed, changes in cues can make an easily accessible memory seem to be forgotten. Something might happen to make you interpret the cues differently, as in recognition failure of recallable words, or a change in environmental context might do the same. Sometimes, however, a memory seems to be lost not temporarily but permanently: It cannot be retrieved. What happens when information is forgotten?

Figure 7.4 depicts the components of a memory situation. Any instance of memory can be thought of as composed of a cue or cues (either from the environment or generated by the person) and the target material. The cue and the target are linked or associated, and this link may be strong or weak. For example, the cue may be the question "What is your phone number?", which is associated with the target information—the number. Again, cues can be a source of forgetting. Changes to cues (cue bias) might lead to what amounts to a temporary failure to retrieve; if you had the right cues, you could retrieve the memory. But it's also possible that changes in cues could lead to permanent forgetting. For example, you might encode a memory when you are 12 years

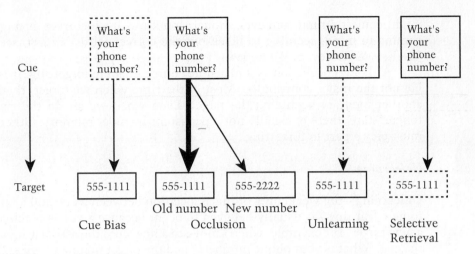

Figure 7.4. This simple model illustrates different theories of how forgetting could occur. The thick arrow represents a more robust association; dotted lines indicate some degradation.

old and then try to retrieve it at age 40. The cues that would have been effective at age 12 may not work at 40 because the way you interpret them has changed. Indeed, the cues may be thoughts and feelings that are virtually impossible for you to have now. Without those cues, the memory cannot be recovered. Thus, in some situations the cues associated with a memory cannot be recovered, and so the memory cannot be retrieved.

Three theories of forgetting incorporate changes to the links between cues and associated target memories. In occlusion, there is a stronger link from the cue to some undesired memory than to the target, and the cue therefore always calls up the undesired memory. In unlearning, a link is believed to weaken when the cue is practiced with another target memory. In decay, the link is believed to spontaneously weaken over time.

Occlusion

Occlusion makes it seem as if the memory is hidden or covered by another memory. The cue may be associated with the target just as strongly as it ever was, but it may also be associated with other memories more strongly, and every time the cue is presented, another memory intrudes. For example, if you move to a new city, whenever you are asked what your phone number is, your old phone number may consistently intrude, making it difficult to remember the new number.

An easily appreciated example of occlusion is the **tip-of-the-tongue phenomenon** (Brown & McNeill, 1966). This aptly named effect occurs when you are certain you know a concept but cannot think of the proper term for it. For example, someone might ask you the term for "a nautical device using the angle of the sun and horizon to find your position." An incorrect term, *compass*, might come to mind, and even though you know it's incorrect, it might keep coming to mind, seeming to block out the correct term, *sextant* (see Burke, MacKay, Worthley, & Wade, 1991).

Although occlusion is a plausible source of some forgetting, it is probably not the major contributor. Most of the time when we forget, there is not another memory occluding the target. Even when we are in the tip-of-the-tongue state, there is usually not a persistent intruder memory. Other factors must play a part in forgetting.

Unlearning

Unlearning—the weakening of the association between a cue and a target due to new learning—is usually believed to occur because a cue is practiced with a new target. For example, when I move to a new city, the association between the cue "What is your phone number?" and the target memory "555-2222" not only gets stronger, but also the association between that cue and my old number "555-1111" gets weaker. Notice that a theory of forgetting would not *have* to posit that it gets weaker. We could say that this old association just stays the same, but eventually the association to the new phone number is strong enough to "drown out" the old association.

Arthur Melton and Jean Irwin (1940) first proposed unlearning. In their experiment, participants learned a list of 18 nonsense syllables such as *vez*. Participants practiced the list five times. On each practice run, they saw a word presented for 2 s and were asked to spell the word that they believed would appear next.

Thirty minutes later, participants were retested on the list. Melton and Irwin (1940) varied what different participants did during the 30-min wait; some read magazines, whereas others had to learn a second list of nonsense syllables. The experimenters varied how much participants studied the second list (either 5, 10, 20, or 40 repetitions). The critical measure came when everyone was retested on the first list. The experimenters were interested in whether **intrusions** occurred when people were retested on the first list. That happened when a response from the second list was produced instead of one from the first list. (More generally, an intrusion produces an answer that would be correct in another context.) If the old targets were still in memory, participants would show intrusions, and the more they studied the second list, the more intrusions there would be. This is true up to a point, but as shown in Figure 7.5, as the second list is studied more, the number of intrusions begins to drop. Melton and Irwin proposed that studying the second list caused unlearning of the first list.

Unlearning may well account for some types of forgetting, but it is not clear that it is a significant contributor to forgetting most of the time. If the chief problem in forgetting were the degradation of the associative bond between the cue and response, then *any* task that relies on that bond should be impaired. The paradigms that arguably lead to unlearning—including the one used by Melton and Irwin—lead to poor recall performance, but recognition

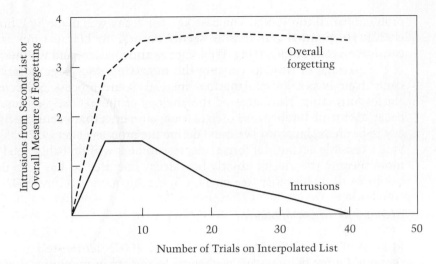

Figure 7.5.   Graph from Melton and Irwin's (1940) experiment showing that more practice on a second list does not produce more intrusions from the second list, when you later try to recall the first list. Initially there is a rise, but then the number of intrusions falls. Nevertheless, forgetting increases. The measure of intrusions and forgetting is a complex percentage estimate designed to make these two measures comparable on one graph.

performance is relatively unaffected. Yet, recognition should rely on the associative bond between cue and target just as much as recall does.

Decay

The **decay** theory of forgetting proposes that the link between a cue and a target memory spontaneously decays over time. If you rehearse the memory again it will be "refreshed," but all links are breaking down, so refreshing the association doesn't prevent decay: It simply revives the link. Most people would find this idea reasonable because the passage of time seems to be a culprit in forgetting.

A simple version of decay theory was proposed by Edward Thorndike (1911), the great turn-of-the-twentieth-century learning theorist. His law of disuse proposed that if a memory is not used, it decays. This idea, however, predicts that older memories should always be more decayed than newer memories and therefore more difficult to retrieve. Yet we know that some older memories remain strong, whereas newer memories are lost. I can't recall what I had for breakfast a few days ago, but I still remember the name of my first-grade teacher.

We could combine decay theory with some version of a strength theory and say that all memories decay at a constant rate, but some start out with more strength than others. Older memories that began with more strength, such as my first-grade teacher's name, could be easier to retrieve than recent memories that have less strength. Until the 1930s, most psychologists believed that something like this was the reason behind forgetting. In the last section, we went over problems with a strength theory, but people didn't spot these problems until the 1960s. The case against decay was made by John McGeogh (1932). He pointed out that it seems natural to blame time as the great causative agent in forgetting. We forget as time passes, and we therefore think of the passage of time as causing the forgetting. McGeogh pointed out that time itself is not an explanation; instead, some process *occurring in time* causes forgetting. He suggested the analogy of metal rusting. Metal rusts not because of time but because of oxidation, a process that occurs in time. For decay to be an explanation, we must define the process of decay. For decay to provide a testable account of forgetting, researchers will probably need to propose more specific theories of exactly how decay operates, as has been done for decay in working memory (see chapter 5; see Altmann & Gray, 2002).

Changes to Target Memories

Mike Anderson (2003; Anderson & Levy, 2002) demonstrated convincingly that one source of forgetting is changes to the target memories themselves. At first this fact seems surprising, even counterproductive. If a memory must be forgotten, wouldn't it be better if the links were lost rather than the target memory itself? What if you need the target memory in some other context? Anderson points out, however, that dampening the target memory makes sense in some situations. We discuss two situations in which it has been shown that memory representations are dampened.

INHIBITION.   Cues are usually associated not with just one target memory but with many memories, most of which you don't want to retrieve along with a specific target. If one memory completely dominates retrieval, we say that occlusion has occurred. Most of the time, however, occlusion does not occur; you successfully retrieve the target, even though other memories are also associated with the available cues. **Inhibition** could suppress the unwanted, competing memories to keep them from being retrieved instead of the target memory. Any given cue might lead to the activation of several candidate memories, so inhibition dampens the undesired memories and allows the desired memory to be retrieved.

If this process of inhibition occurs, it should make suppressed memories more difficult to retrieve. In other words, retrieving a memory will actually dampen related memories that the cue also activates but that are not retrieved. This phenomenon of **retrieval-induced forgetting** was demonstrated by Mike Anderson and his colleagues (Anderson, Bjork, & Bjork, 1994). Participants studied word pairs that were a category and an instance of the category (*fruit–banana, fruit–orange*). After the study phase, they practiced retrieving half of the items in cued recall (*fruit–or_____*) and didn't practice the other half. Some categories (*drink*) were not practiced at all, and these items served as a baseline of comparison. The final phase was a cued recall test for all items. Sample results for the final test are shown in panel A of Figure 7.6.

When participants had practiced retrieving a pair such as *fruit–orange*, they improved on that pair compared with unpracticed items such as

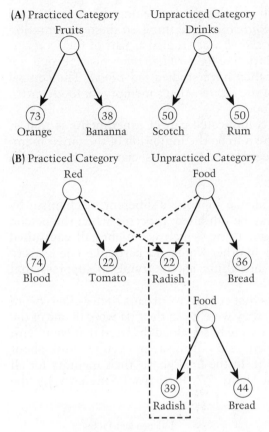

(A) Practiced Category
Fruits

Unpracticed Category
Drinks

(73) Orange   (38) Banana

(50) Scotch   (50) Rum

(B) Practiced Category
Red

Unpracticed Category
Food

(74) Blood   (22) Tomato   (22) Radish   (36) Bread

Food

(39) Radish   (44) Bread

Figure 7.6. The numbers indicate the percentage of participants recalling the stimulus. Panel A shows that practicing *fruits–orange* leads to poorer performance on an unpracticed item (*fruits–banana*) compared with items from a category that wasn't practiced (*drink–scotch*). Panel B shows that this poorer performance is due to inhibition of the item, not the link to it. Practicing *red–blood* inhibits *radish* (another *red* thing), even if memory for *radish* is probed using the cue *food*. Because a different cue to *radish* still leads to poor performance, we know the inhibition is not in the association of the cue *red* to *radish*. The inhibition is observed even when a different cue (*food*) is used; hence, the inhibition must be in *radish* itself. The bottom part of the figure shows the control condition—performance on *food–radish* when *red–blood* is not practiced. From *"Inhibitory Processes and the Control of Memory Retrieval,"* by B. J. Levy and M. C. Anderson, 2002. *Trends in Cognitive Sciences*, 6, p. 300.

drink–Scotch. That's no surprise—practice improves memory. More important, an unpracticed item such as *fruit–banana* was *worse* at final recall by virtue of being in the same category as the practiced item (*fruit–orange*). That's retrieval-induced forgetting.

But various theories could explain this effect. For example, retrieving *fruit–orange* could make the *fruit–banana* link weaker; this unlearning account seems consistent with this experiment. The selective retrieval account can make a unique prediction, however. Because it is supposed to be the target memory (*banana*) that is inhibited, the particular cue should not matter. In other words, practicing *fruit–orange* should inhibit *banana* regardless of whether *banana* is cued by *fruit* or by something else.

Anderson and Bobbie Spellman (1995) tested that prediction. They used a paradigm similar to that of Anderson and colleagues (1994) but with the added twist that some of the instances fit more than one category. As shown in panel B of Figure 7.6, *tomato* and *radish* fit two of the studied categories: *red* and *food*. Practicing retrieval of *red–blood* will impair an unstudied pair in the same category, like *red–tomato*. According to the inhibition hypothesis, practicing retrieval of *red–blood* should also impair the unstudied pair *food–radish*. Why? Bear in mind what practicing retrieval of *red–blood* does:

It inhibits the representation of all red things, dampening the incorrect red things to help you retrieve *blood*. *Radish* is a red thing, so the representation of *radish* is inhibited, even though *radish* was studied as part of the *food* category. As shown in Figure 7.6, inhibition of *food–radish* takes place: People are less likely to recall *food–radish* if they have studied *red–blood*. The control condition is shown at the bottom of the figure—that's memory for *food–radish* when people didn't practice *red–blood*.

The key point in this rather complicated pair of experiments is that at least one source of forgetting is shown to be the inhibition of the target memory representation itself, not the degradation of the associative links between the cue and the target memory.

CONTROLLED RETRIEVAL. Other evidence supports a different mechanism by which a memory representation may be inhibited: It occurs when the person actively tries not to think about something, which we might call **controlled retrieval** (Anderson & Green, 2001). In other words, if a particular cue leads to a memory that you would rather not think about, trying to suppress that memory can actually work.

In this experiment, participants first studied word pairs such as *flag–sword* and *ordeal–roach*. In the next phase, they were given the first word of one of the pairs, and for most of these cues, they were to say aloud the word that went with it. For some cues, however, they were told *not* to say or even to think about the associate but to try to suppress it. In the final phase, their memory for all the words was tested, as shown in Figure 7.7. Participants' memory for the

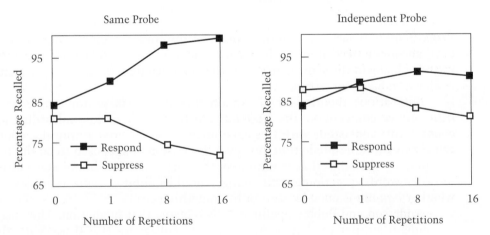

Figure 7.7. Anderson and Green (2001) showed the effects of controlled retrieval, or trying to forget. If participants try not to think about a memory when given a cue, they find it more difficult to later retrieve that memory when given the cue. The more times the memory is suppressed, the harder it is to later retrieve (left panel). The right panel shows that it's hard to access the memory even if the cue is different from the one used during the suppression trials. This cue independence indicates that the memory itself is inhibited, not the association between the cue and the memory. From *"Suppressing Unwanted Memories by Executive Control,"* by M. C. Anderson and C. Green, 2001, *Nature, 410,* Fig. 1, p. 366.

suppressed words was impaired, and the more times they suppressed a word, the worse their memory for it was. Furthermore, their memory was impaired regardless of whether they were tested with the original cue (*ordeal*) or a new cue (*insect–r____*). The fact that the memory for *roach* is impaired even with a different cue indicates that what is inhibited is not the association between a cue and the target memory but the target memory itself.

SUMMARY.   We've talked about three ways in which memory can be forgotten. (a) Cues may be ineffective because they are interpreted differently than they were at encoding. (b) The associative links between memories may be lost due to decay or unlearning, or a link may be ineffective because the cue also leads to another memory via a stronger associative link. (c) The representation of the memory itself may be dampened, either by the process of inhibition or by the person actively stopping retrieval.

Which of these is the most important factor in forgetting? In a practical sense, cues are clearly the most important. If you don't have the right cues, there is no chance that you'll retrieve a memory. Also, most memories have multiple cues associated with them, so if you lose an associative link, or if the memory is somewhat inhibited, more and better cues might still enable you to retrieve the memory. There is a great deal of evidence regarding the importance of cues. There is also evidence that inhibition of memory representations contributes to forgetting. There is less evidence that the loss of associative links makes a significant contribution to forgetting.

Repression

Repression is the active forgetting of an episode for the sake of self-protection: Remembering it would be too painful. The term implies some active form of dampening the memory, but this dampening process happens outside awareness. It is not simply that you try not to think about the memory.

We're treating repression separately from other types of forgetting because the focus in this area of research has not been on how forgetting and remembering work, but rather on whether repression occurs at all. It is difficult to gather scientific evidence about repression, and the study of repression is itself charged with emotion.

To be certain that repression can occur, we need to verify that (a) the event the person remembers actually happened; (b) the event now remembered was, at some point, forgotten; and (c) the forgetting was due to repression and not another process.

Gathering evidence has been extraordinarily difficult. Repression has most often been associated with childhood sexual abuse, a crime that is usually without witnesses and that is difficult to corroborate. Regarding the second question—was the event forgotten?—it is surprising to learn that people can forget that they have remembered. Jonathan Schooler, Miriam Bendiksen, and Zara Ambadar (1997) described the case of W.B., a 40-year-old woman who recounted recovering a memory of having been raped at knifepoint when she was 16. W.B. described the memory recovery as having been triggered by an encounter with a male coworker at a party. She commented on his advances toward a young woman, and he defended himself by saying, "She isn't exactly a virgin" (p. 268). W.B. was so upset that she left the party. That night she had nightmares and awoke knowing that she had been raped. It certainly sounds as though that memory had been repressed. However, her ex-husband reported that several times during their marriage, W.B. had mentioned that she had been raped, but her statements had always been completely without emotion. W.B. had no recollection of having told her ex-husband. This case study, then, shows that even if a person says that he or she has completely forgotten an event for some period of time, we cannot simply take that belief at face value. The third criterion to verify that repression has occurred is that the forgetting must not be due to some other process. In this chapter, we've been discussing many sources of retrieval failure. Isn't it possible that the memory was not actively repressed, but rather that the appropriate cues were not in the environment until the time of memory recovery?

Given these three stringent criteria, is there evidence for a process of repression? There are several case studies indicating that repression does occur. For example, Jonathan Schooler (2001) reported seven cases, each of which had been carefully researched to comply with the criteria listed previously. Nevertheless, repression appears to be quite rare; most studies show that memory for traumatic events is vivid in both children and adults (Leopold & Dillon, 1963; Peace & Porter, 2004; Pynoos & Nader, 1989), although memories may not be wholly accurate.

Like other memory researchers (e.g., Schacter, 1996), as well as a panel of experts appointed by the American Psychological Association to study the issue (Alpert, Brown, Ceci, Courtois, Loftus, & Ornstein, 1996), I believe repression occurs, although it is always difficult to draw broad conclusions based on case studies of individuals.

The Permanence of Memory

From the previous sections, you might conclude that forgetting is caused mostly by a lack of good cues. Perhaps everything is recorded in your mind, like a library of videotapes, and if you can't remember something it's not because the tape is lost but because you can't find it due to poor cues. This idea is written up in newspaper and magazine articles from time to time, usually reported as though it is fact. Most memory researchers, however, would disagree.

This idea is impossible to disprove, however, because the basic proposition is that all memories are retrievable if you can get the right cues. If you can't remember something, you can always say, "Well, I just don't have the right cues yet." Even after testing with a million different cues, you can maintain that the next cue might be the right one, and you will remember. Although I can't state flatly that this proposal must be wrong, I think it's unlikely to be true.

The reasons were laid out in an article by Geoff Loftus and Elizabeth Loftus (1980), pointing out that three factors support the idea that all memories lie somewhere in the memory vault: spontaneous recovery, memory under hypnosis, and an interesting study by neurologist Wilder Penfield. As we'll see, there are problems with each of these sources of evidence.

SPONTANEOUS RECOVERY. **Spontaneous recovery** is the sudden uncovering of a long-lost memory. Often, there is an identifiable cue that clearly leads to recovery of the memory. For example, people who revisit a house they lived in during childhood may report that the sight of a room brings back vivid memories. It's as though the cue (seeing the house again) is one end of a very fine chain, and if you pull it gently, you find there are charms (memories) attached to the chain (see Stone, Hunkin, & Hornby, 2001, for an experimental example).

Even if we accept the fact that the recovered memories are accurate, the fact that some memories can be spontaneously recovered does not mean that all memories are recorded. It means that some memories that you haven't retrieved in a long time can be retrieved again if you are given the right cues.

MEMORY AND HYPNOSIS. We sometimes hear or read about amazing feats of memory performed under hypnosis (bricklayers accurately reporting descriptions of bricks they laid in walkways years ago, and so on). In a word, bunk.

It is easy enough to test whether hypnosis helps memory. In one study, David Dinges and his colleagues (Dinges, Whitehouse, Orne, Powell, Orne, & Erdelyi, 1992) showed participants 40 drawings of common objects. Participants immediately tried to remember as many as they could. One week later, they attempted to recall the drawings, with half the participants under hypnosis and half not. The experimenters asked the participants to recall the whole list five times; they wanted to give an effect of hypnosis every opportunity to become manifest. They also examined participants who were very susceptible to hypnosis and participants who were not to see whether that factor made a difference. Hypnosis did nothing to improve the accuracy of memory. Many such experiments have been conducted (Lytle & Lundy, 1988; Register & Kihlstrom, 1987; for a review, see Erdelyi, 1994).

PENFIELD'S EXPERIMENTS. As part of the preparation for brain surgery, Wilder Penfield (1959) directly stimulated patients' brains. A local anesthetic was administered in the scalp, and part of the skull was removed (see Photo 7.3). Penfield then used a stylus that generated a very mild electrical current to stimulate different places in the patient's brain. The patient was awake during this procedure but felt no pain. (The brain has no pain receptors.)

When Penfield (1959) stimulated some parts of the brain, a patient might say that a memory had been triggered. For example, one patient said, "Oh, a familiar memory—in an office somewhere. I could see the desks. I was there and someone was calling to me—a man leaning on a desk with a

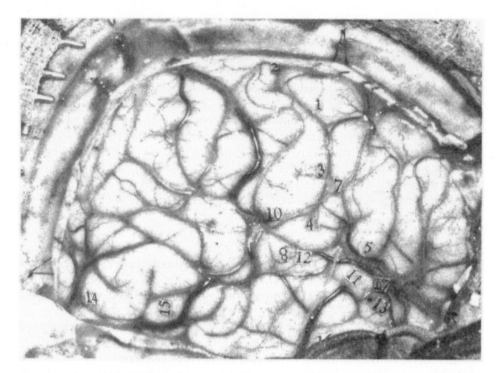

Photo 7.3.   One of Penfield's patients during an operation. The numbers help the surgeon keep track of where he has stimulated the brain.

pencil in his hand" (p. 45). Another patient reported hearing her small son playing in the yard outside her kitchen window, as well as the typical neighborhood sounds. If these are indeed memories, the fact that they can be produced via direct stimulation of the brain certainly fits the idea that everything is recorded in the brain but often cannot be accessed. Perhaps the normal route to recalling memory has been bypassed—Penfield with his stylus reached in and physically jiggled loose a memory that otherwise would have been unrecoverable.

Such results sound compelling, but there are a lot of problems in interpreting them. First, these results occurred in only a small fraction (fewer than 10%) of Penfield's patients, even among those who were stimulated in the part of the brain in which memories are believed to be stored (the temporal lobe). Second, those who did report it often said that the experience was not especially like a memory. For example, the woman who heard her son playing in the yard was asked 10 days later whether this experience was a memory. She said, "Oh, no. It seemed more real than that" (Penfield, 1959, p. 51). Thus it's possible that Penfield's stimulation created pictures in the person's consciousness based on things in their memories but did not evoke an actual memory. In much the same way, dreams are constructed out of things that occurred to you, but they are not exact replays of events. It seems likely that the

---

Vocabulary Recognition
1. romper
    a. to roam   b. to break   c. to look   d. to roar   e. to search
2. mandar
    a. to make   b. to mend   c. to yell   d. to command   e. to arrange

Grammar Recall: Write the correct form of the verb given in the blank provided.
1. El _____ (estudiar). He studies Spanish
2. Yo _____ la menor (ser). I am the youngest.

Idiom recall: Write the English meaning of the Spanish idiom.
1. hace mal tiempo _____
2. en vez de _____

Figure 7.8. Sample questions from Bahrick (1984).

memories of Penfield's patients were **constructions**: experiences that feel like bona fide memories to the person experiencing them but are actually combinations of a real memory and other information, such as what the person believes probably happened.

PERMASTORE. Is forgetting inevitable? We all have certain bits of information that we know so well, it is difficult to believe we could ever forget it. In J. D. Salinger's book, *The Catcher in the Rye*, Holden Caufield helps a little girl adjust her skate and gets a rush of nostalgia from the feel of the skate key. He comments, "You could put a skate key in my hand in about fifty years in pitch black, and I'd still know what it is."

Some evidence shows that Holden was right. Enough practice makes memory immune to forgetting. Harry Bahrick did a series of studies on the permanence of memory (see Bahrick, 2000, for a review). In one study, Bahrick (1984) rounded up 733 people who had studied Spanish in high school between 1 and 50 years earlier and gave them vocabulary tests, comprehension tests, and so on (see Figure 7.8). Bahrick looked at how much Spanish the participants had retained, estimating how much they had initially learned by how many courses they had taken, their grades, and so on. He also measured how much practice these people had had with Spanish since they last took a Spanish class (whether they had visited a Spanish-speaking country, how often they estimated they were exposed to Spanish in the media, whether they had studied another Romance language, and so on).

As you can appreciate, this was a stupendously complex study to conduct, but it paid off with a very interesting result. First, as you would expect, people forget their Spanish. The forgetting is rapid for the first 3 to 6 years, but then it more or less plateaus, and there is little additional forgetting until about 30 years have passed. Then, there is a second, more gradual drop-off until about 50 years (the last time point measured). This pattern, shown in Figure 7.9, was observed for almost all the measures of Spanish that Bahrick used.

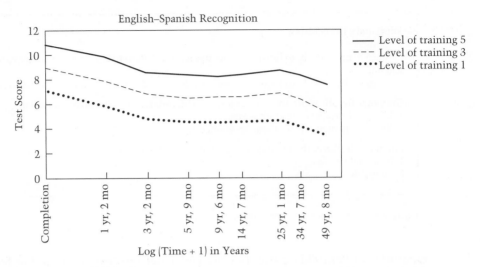

Figure 7.9.   The effect of training level on the retention of recognition vocabulary from Bahrick (1984).

There are two results to note here. First, for some of these participants, this knowledge of Spanish was retrievable 50 years after it was last encoded or rehearsed, even if it had not been practiced at all during the intervening time. For all practical purposes, we might say that this information was not going to be forgotten. Bahrick referred to such memories as being in **permastore**, a hypothetical state of memory from which information is not lost.

Knowledge of Spanish did not end up in permastore for everyone; what seemed to make the difference was extended practice. The longer participants had studied Spanish, the more Spanish they had in permastore. Studying Spanish for at least several years seemed to ensure that some of it would end up in permastore.

Whether permastore is really a form of memory, separate from secondary memory, is not known. Bahrick argues that it is separate because he notes that most memories have a life span of 3 to 6 years—after that they are forgotten—and others have a life span of 50 years or more, but no memories have a life span of 10 years or 20 years. There is no forgetting between 6 and 50 years, which indicates a transition to a different state of memory. Other researchers, such as Ulric Neisser (1984), think that "permastore" is just a description of secondary memories that are so well represented that they will not be forgotten. There has been little work on permastore compared with other types of memory, probably because it is so difficult to conduct studies of the sort Bahrick has done.

We've discussed encoding and retrieval together because the match between those processes is so important. But in so doing, we've skipped a stage—storage. We said in chapter 1 that the ultimate goal of cognitive psychologists is to describe the representations used by the mind, and the processes that operate on those representations. In chapter 8, we consider the format of memory representations.

Stand-on-One-Foot Questions

8. Describe in general terms the three ways that information may be forgotten.
9. Is all learning permanent, with failures of retrieval caused only by interference?
10. Can memory of traumatic events in childhood be repressed?

Questions That Require Two Feet

11. Given what you know about forgetting, how would you advise someone to schedule his or her time studying in school?
12. In chapter 4, we discussed ironic processes of control, and the theme was that it is very difficult *not* to think about something (e.g., white bear). In this chapter, Anderson's work on controlled retrieval indicates that not thinking about a memory can make you forget it. What's going on?

KEY TERMS

construction
context
context effects
controlled retrieval
cue
cued recall
decay
distractors, foils, lures
false memory
free recall
inhibition

intrusions
occlusion
permastore
recognition failure of
   recallable words
recognition test
reconstruction
repression
retrieval-induced
   forgetting
savings in relearning

sensitivity
source
source confusion
spontaneous recovery
strength view of
   memory
tip-of-the-tongue
   phenomenon
unlearning

CURRENT DIRECTIONS IN COGNITIVE SCIENCE

Recommended readings

Garry, M., & Polaschek, D. L. L. (2000). "Imagination and memory." (pp. 29–35) In this chapter, we discuss false memory relatively briefly. This topic has been the subject of a great deal of research since the mid-1990s, and the authors adroitly summarize many of the interesting findings, focusing on which mechanism is responsible for most false memories.

McNally, R. J. (2003). "Recovering memories of trauma: A view from the laboratory." (pp. 36–43) When we think of repression, we typically think that something extraordinary happened to an ordinary person that caused the repression. McNally reports on research following a different perspective—people who are capable of repressing memories not only have had extraordinary things occurring to them, but also the person him- or herself has a cognitive system that differs from other people's.

Wells, G. L., Olson, E. A., & Charman, S. D. (2002). "The confidence of eyewitnesses in their identifications from lineups." (pp. 44–50) I mentioned in passing that people can have a lot of confidence in false memories. In this article, Wells, Olson, and Charman review some of this literature as it applies to eyewitness testimony and consider what impact these findings ought to have on our legal system.

Memory Storage 8

What Is in the Storehouse?

- The Classical View of Categorization
- The Probabilistic View of Categorization
- The Multiple Systems View of Categorization

How Is Memory Organized?

- Addressing Systems
- Content-Addressable Storage
- Hierarchical Theory
- Spreading Activation Theories
- Spreading Activation Models: An Example
- Distributed Representation (Parallel Distributed Processing)

What Else Is In Memory?

- What Are Separate Memory Systems?
- Five Separate Memory Systems
- Cognitive Differences Among Memory Systems

In chapters 6 and 7, we addressed how memories get into the storehouse and how they are retrieved. This final chapter on memory discusses the storehouse itself. The first question we might consider is **What is in the storehouse?** Suppose I show you a coffee cup and ask you to name it. You say, "It's a cup." I ask you how you know that, and you say (after giving me a fishy look), "Well, it has a handle, it's the right size, and you could put coffee in it, so it's a cup." I then show you a tea bowl from a Chinese restaurant and ask you to name that. Again, you say, "It's a cup." This cup has no handle and is much smaller, yet it's still a cup. Similarly, if I showed you a cup with a small hole in it (so it couldn't hold liquid), it would still be a cup. Many different-looking objects are identified as cups. So, the provisional answer to the question "What is in the storehouse?" must be "The storehouse contains memory representations that allow us to identify objects with different properties as nevertheless belonging to the same class." As we'll see, this property of memory representations is very useful, but we still don't know exactly how these representations work.

Our second question concerns organization within the memory storehouse. In chapter 6, we skipped over a daunting aspect of retrieval—finding the right bit of information among the millions of things you know. If you had 10,000 comic books and you wanted to be able to find any one of them quickly, what would you do? You'd organize them, of course: chronologically, by main character (Superman, Green Lantern), or by plot (superhero loses powers, world is held hostage by nuclear threat). The organization of memory is crucial to solving such retrieval problems. You have a good organization system that allows you to access material quickly. Our next question, then, is **How is memory organized?** As we'll see, memory is organized around meaning.

Our last question is one that psychologists did not pose in a serious way until recently: **What else is in memory?** We normally think of memory of the sort that we've discussed to this point—childhood memories, knowledge that you gain in school, and so on. But there are many other ways that your mind and brain change based on experience (e.g., learning motor skills). Those changes also constitute memory. In the final section of this chapter, we discuss systems of memory other than the familiar one.

What Is in the Storehouse?

Preview

A key component of memory is the ability to generalize. Initially, researchers assumed that people assigned objects to categories by using a list of properties that an object must have to be a member of the category. However, some objects are more typical of a category than others; for example, an apple is a typical fruit, but a raisin is not. If categorization were achieved with a list of properties, we wouldn't get typicality effects. New models were proposed to account for these data—prototype and exemplar models—

(continued)

that were based on the idea that people categorize objects not with rules but by judging their similarity to other objects of the same category. More recently, researchers have suggested that a single type of category may not successfully account for all the data and thus have proposed models that use multiple systems of categorization.

When you see an apple, how do you know it has seeds inside? You've never seen this apple before, but you know about the seeds because you generalize from other apples to this apple; in other words, you put this object in the category *apple*. You can identify the class or category to which an object belongs, even if you've never seen that particular example of the object before. A **category** is a group of objects that have something in common (e.g., *dog* is a category). An **exemplar** is an instance of a category (a particular dog is an exemplar of the category *dog*). Your experience allows you to **generalize**, that is, to apply information gathered from one exemplar to a different exemplar of the same category. In other words, things you know from your experience with dogs (it eats, it breathes, it could bite you but probably won't, it smells when wet) can be applied to any dog.

The importance of the ability to generalize is hard to overestimate. The first sentence of Ed Smith and Doug Medin's (1981) book about categorization is "Without concepts, mental life would be chaotic." It would be chaotic because you would approach any object you had not interacted with as though it were completely novel. "Hey, look at this furry thing. Hmm. Four legs. Wagging tail. I wonder whether it has lungs? I wonder whether it can fly?" Concepts, then, are the mental representations that allow us to generalize.

The Classical View of Categorization

According to the **classical view of categorization**, first articulated by Aristotle, a **concept** is a list of necessary and sufficient conditions for membership in a category. In other words, a concept is the mental representation of *dog* or any other class of objects. A concept does not refer to one particular example of the object; it represents all objects that can be included in that category. Every object must have all attributes on the list, and having those attributes is sufficient to be an example of the concept. For example, the concept *grandmother* is composed of two conditions: female and parent of a parent. Those two conditions are necessary to be identified as a grandmother—you must have both of them to be a grandmother—and they are sufficient, meaning it does not matter what sort of other characteristics you have or do not have, you're still a grandmother if you have those two (see Photo 8.1).

In one classic study, Jerome Bruner and his colleagues (Bruner, Goodnow, & Austin, 1956) set out to show that participants learn categories by hypothesis testing, actively constructing hypotheses about what rule might describe category membership and testing the rule. Note that this study was conducted in the mid-1950s, when most psychologists would have been behaviorists and the idea of hypothesis testing would have been

Photo 8.1.   According to the classical view, Steven Tyler and George H. W. Bush are equally good representatives of the category "Grandfather."

somewhat radical. The experimenters used cards with four features: number of figures on the card, shape of the figures, color of the figures, and number of borders around the edge of the card. The experimenter might give a participant a card with three black circles and two borders, and the participant had to select another instance of the category from among all possible cards laid out on a table. The participant's job was to figure out what made a card an example of the category. The results showed that participants indeed generated hypotheses about what category structure might be and made card selections to test their hypotheses.

This experiment is an example of the classical view of categories because the experimenters assumed that category membership should be set up as a list of necessary and sufficient conditions where one or two features of the cards determined category membership, and everything else was irrelevant. It turns out, however, that many categories in the real world don't work that way, a fact revealed by typicality effects.

TYPICALITY EFFECTS.   **Typicality** refers to the fact that not all exemplars are equally good members of a category—that is, how do we decide whether something is a typical representative of its class? For example, not all birds are equally "birdy." Some birds are really good examples of a bird (a real bird's bird), whereas

***Table 8.1.   Some Results of Rosch's
(1973) Typicality Ratings***

Category	Member	Rating
Fruit	Apple	1.3
	Plum	2.3
	Pineapple	2.3
	Strawberry	2.3
	Fig	4.7
	Olive	6.2
Sport	Football	1.2
	Hockey	1.8
	Wrestling	3.0
	Archery	3.9
	Gymnastics	2.6
	Weight-lifting	4.7
Bird	Robin	1.1
	Eagle	1.2
	Wren	1.4
	Chicken	3.8
	Ostrich	3.3
	Bat	5.8
Vehicle	Car	1.0
	Boat	2.7
	Scooter	2.5
	Tricycle	3.5
	Horse	5.9
	Skis	5.7

others are pretty crummy birds. In the following list, how would you rate each bird from 1 (terrific example of a bird) to 7 (not a good example of a bird)?

wren

chicken

robin

ostrich

eagle

Eleanor Rosch (1973) gave participants lists such as this and asked them to rate the items as typical members of their category (see Table 8.1). The first thing you might note about this task is that it doesn't seem stupid. One response you could give when asked to perform this task is to say, "What are you talking about, 'birdy birds, nonbirdy birds?' They're all birds. Except the bat." The fact is, when Rosch said "birdy birds," "fruity fruits," or "furniturey furniture," people knew what she was talking about. Not only do people think some birds are birdier than others, but they also agree on which ones are the birdy ones, as shown in Table 8.1. This result means that we need to reexamine the way people categorize. If the classical view of categorization were true—if an object could be labeled on the basis of a list of necessary and sufficient conditions—there would be no gradations of membership in the concept; a penguin and a robin would be seen as equally good examples of the concept *bird*.

Ed Smith, Ed Shoben, and Lance Rips (1974) showed that people are more efficient in categorizing typical examples than atypical examples. On each trial, participants saw a word on a computer screen and had to decide as quickly as possible ("Yes" or "No") whether the word was an example of a category. Some were typical instances (*robin*), some were medium typicality (*cardinal*), and some were low typicality (*goose*). As expected, response times were faster for more typical examples.

This effect of typicality on categorization is also observed when participants are asked to freely generate examples of a category (Battig & Montague, 1969; Van Overschelde, Rawson, & Dunlosky, 2004). The central finding is that the most frequently generated exemplars are the ones that are rated as most typical of the category. This finding holds true not only for adults, but also for children as young as 5 (Nelson, 1974; Rosner & Hayes, 1977). Some examples appear in Table 8.2.

Typicality also makes a difference in how people use concepts in reasoning. Lance Rips (1975; see also Heit, 2000; Murphy & Ross, 2005) asked people to make some inferences using either typical or atypical examples of a category as a reference point. For example, they were told that one small group of species had a contagious disease, and then asked to estimate the probability that other animals had the disease. The results showed that if a more typical bird (the robin or sparrow) had the disease, it was judged that other birds probably had the disease. If an atypical species such as the ostrich was described as having the disease, it was judged less likely that other species did. Participants know that typical instances of a category share many properties with other members of the category. When confronted with a new feature (the disease) whose distribution is not known, participants assume that it is distributed in the same way as other features; if a typical instance has the feature, it's likely that the other instances of the category have the feature. (People with a lot of knowledge about the category—a bird expert, in this example—use other strategies that make use of their deeper knowledge; López, Atran, Coley, Medin, & Smith, 1997; Proffitt, Coley, & Medin, 2000.)

The Probabilistic View of Categorization

We have seen that typicality makes a difference when we use concepts: Typical examples of concepts are categorized more quickly, they are easily brought to mind as examples of the category, and we use them differently in

Table 8.2. Probabilities with Which Items Were Listed as Category Exemplars

Fruit		Beverage	
Response	Total (First)	Response	Total (First)
Apple	.95 (.58)	Water	.80 (.11)
Orange	.86 (.14)	Coke	.48 (.25)
Banana	.71 (.07)	Milk	.46 (.05)
Grape	.52 (.02)	Juice	.43 (.07)
Pear	.50 (.03)	Soda	.42 (.18)
Peach	.40 (.04)	Orange juice	.33 (.04)
Strawberry	.40 (.04)	Sprite	.31 (.03)
Kiwi	.30	Pepsi	.29 (.05)
Pineapple	.26 (.01)	Tea	.29 (.02)
Watermelon	.24 (.01)	Coffee	.24 (.01)
Tomato	.21 (.03)	Lemonade	.23 (.02)
Plum	.21	Apple juice	.20 (.02)
Grapefruit	.18	Dr. Pepper	.13 (.01)
Mango	.18 (.01)	Gatorade	.11
Cherry	.15 (.01)	Kool-Aid	.11 (.01)
Lemon	.15	Mountain Dew	.09
Blueberry	.14	Grape juice	.07
Cantaloupe	.14	Ice tea	.10
Raspberry	.12	Pop	.07 (.03)

Source: From Van Overschelde, et. al., 2004.

making inferences. These facts must be accounted for in a theory of categorization. Therefore, the classical view of categorization cannot be complete.

In the **probabilistic view of categorization**, category membership is proposed to be a matter of probability. The mind's representation of a concept is not set up to make a black-and-white judgment about category membership. Rather, an object is seen as more or less likely to be a member of a category. A central assumption of this view is that there is no feature or group of features that is essential for category membership. Rather, each member of the category will have some but not all the features. For example, a given bird might have the features "sings" and "eats insects" but not the feature "lives in trees." There are two versions of the probabilistic view: prototype theories and exemplar theories.

PROTOTYPES.   A crucial experiment in developing the prototype view was conducted by Mike Posner and Steve Keele (1968). Rather than using categories that

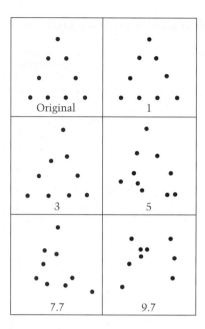

Figure 8.1. Random dot categories of the type used by Posner and Keele (1968). The numbers refer to the distance (in arbitrary units) that each dot was moved to change the original figure.

their participants already knew, such as birds or furniture, they created two categories from scratch. The categories were patterns of dots; each feature was one dot located in a particular position. Posner and Keele created the categories by taking random dot patterns and calling them "A," "B," and "C" (see Figure 8.1).

Those patterns were defined as the **prototypes** that had all the features characteristic of those categories. To create an example for Category A, the experimenters took the prototype for dot pattern A and moved each dot a bit in a random direction. To create another example for Category A, they used the same prototype and again moved the dots randomly to get a different pattern. They created four examples of each category, mixed the examples in random order, and then asked participants to categorize them. Participants just guessed initially, but they got feedback as they went regarding whether their categorization judgments were right or wrong, so after a while they learned to categorize correctly. They had to keep studying the list until they could categorize all 12 items correctly two times in row.

The interesting phase of the experiment came next. Participants were given a recognition test of three types of stimuli: old stimuli, which they had seen in the first phase of the experiment; new stimuli, which were novel examples of the category; and the prototypes from which the examples had been generated. They were to select the familiar member of the category from among four choices, so chance performance would be 25%. Participants got 86.0% of the old items correct and 67.4% of the new items correct; they remembered the items they had seen before quite well and could also recognize new members of the category. Most interesting, they got 85.1% correct on the prototypes. Participants selected the prototype, which they had never seen before, as accurately as the training items.

Most researchers interpreted these data as showing that the memory representation supporting categorization is an amalgamation of the examples of the category. As you see many examples of Category A, you abstract the critical features of Category A, and the memory representation you put in the storehouse has the characteristic features of the examples of Category A. It's as though you average all the examples of Category A that you see. Thus, during the training session, where you are given feedback about which stimuli are As, Bs, and Cs, what you end up storing is basically the prototype of A (and, of course, separate representations for the prototypes of B and C).

To say whether a new stimulus is an A, B, or C, you compare it with your stored representation of each prototype and judge which one it is more similar to. If the new stimulus is one of the prototypes, it will match what is in your memory; because you have been taking the average of all the different examples, which were derived through small random changes to the prototypes, the averages and the prototypes are identical. In a second experiment, Posner and Keele (1970) showed that the prototype is still very well recognized after a 1-week delay.

These data seem to demonstrate that people abstract the central features of examples and store the prototype. How else could we account for Posner and Keele's (1970) results and their participants' recognition of prototypes that they had never seen? But we should ask whether people store only the prototype. For example, I can categorize a new cat when I see it, but I also recognize specific cats, such as the orange one who has commandeered a corner of my yard for his restroom. Have I stored a representation of the prototypical cat, and alongside, representations of all the cats I can identify as individuals? It is possible that prototypes are not involved after all.

EXEMPLAR MODELS.   Doug Medin and Marguerite Schaffer (1978) showed that prototypes are not necessary to understand categorization or typicality effects. Posner and Keele's (1970) results indicate that abstraction takes place, and according to the prototype model in Figure 8.2, the abstraction takes place at encoding. But why would it have to take place at encoding? Suppose that you store every experience you have with an example of a category—for example, every experience you have with a dog—and then abstract a prototype only when you need it (see Figure 8.3). Thus, the same process of abstraction could take place, but at retrieval, and only if the prototype is needed.

Furthermore, typicality effects would work out perfectly in such a model. You would judge typicality by comparing the similarity of an object to all the exemplars in memory. If you see a sparrow sitting in a tree and compare it with all the birds in memory, the similarity is very high; therefore, you would think this sparrow is a very "birdy" bird. A flightless, 6-foot-tall ostrich is not very similar to birds in memory, so you wouldn't think it was such a good example of a bird. The **exemplar model** maintains that all exemplars are stored in memory, and categorization judgments are made by judging the similarity of the new exemplar to all the old exemplars of a category.

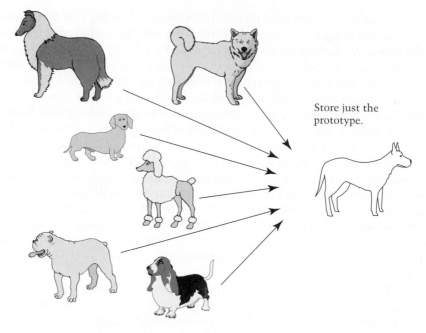

Store just the prototype.

Figure 8.2. Schematic of the prototype model. Although many exemplars are seen, only the prototype is stored. The prototype is updated continually to incorporate more experience with new exemplars.

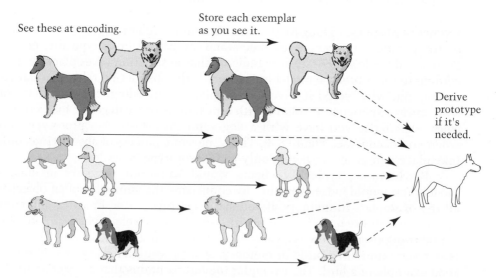

See these at encoding.

Store each exemplar as you see it.

Derive prototype if it's needed.

Figure 8.3. Schematic of the exemplar model. As each exemplar is seen, it is encoded into memory. A prototype is abstracted only when it is needed, for example, when a new exemplar must be categorized.

In both the exemplar and prototype models, similarity is the key factor in categorization. Yet, the models are very different in terms of what they propose is stored in memory. The exemplar model holds that multiple exemplars of a category are stored in memory, and the prototype model holds that only the prototype is stored.

As you can see, the exemplar and prototype models propose very different types of storage, but they are both similarity models, and thus both make very similar predictions about categorization performance. When comparing exemplar models to prototype models, researchers must specify the model of categorization in enough detail to run a computer simulation of human performance using the model. These models make specific predictions about how fast people learn categories, how fast they forget them, what transfer to new exemplars should look like, and so on. We can compare the success of exemplar and prototype models by comparing their predictions with actual human performance. If the prototype model predicts that participants will get 65% correct after 100 training trials and the exemplar model predicts it will be 72%, and humans get 71%, then obviously the exemplar model is doing a better job of predicting the data. Research that relies on comparing the performance of specific models with human data is called mathematical psychology. In these contests, exemplar models have usually come out ahead of prototype models, but there are exceptions (Estes, 1994; Minda & Smith, 2001; Nosofsky & Zaki, 2002; Smith, 2005; Smith & Minda, 2000), and some critics have suggested that both types of models are so flexible that they are very difficult to compare—the models can be tweaked to fit nearly any data pattern (Olsson, Wennerholm, & Lyxzen, 2004). Still other models of categorization suggest that similarity alone cannot account for human categorization abilities, and suggest that there must be different systems that support different types of categorization.

The Multiple Systems View of Categorization

In the late 1980s, new results came out indicating that researchers might have been a bit hasty in throwing out the classical view. In some cases, it looked like humans *did* use rules to categorize. In a seminal study on this topic, Lance Rips (1989) had participants make categorization judgments with very little information about the object (just one feature). He also restricted the choices to two categories; one of the categories was inflexible as to the described feature and the other was not. For example, one item was "The object is 3 inches in diameter. Is the object a pizza or a quarter?" Most participants (63%) said it was a pizza, even though a separate group of participants had more often (70%) judged that a quarter was more similar to a 3-inch object than is a pizza. Rips argued that people are sensitive to necessary, inflexible features. A quarter must be a particular size; this feature cannot change, so it's like a rule.

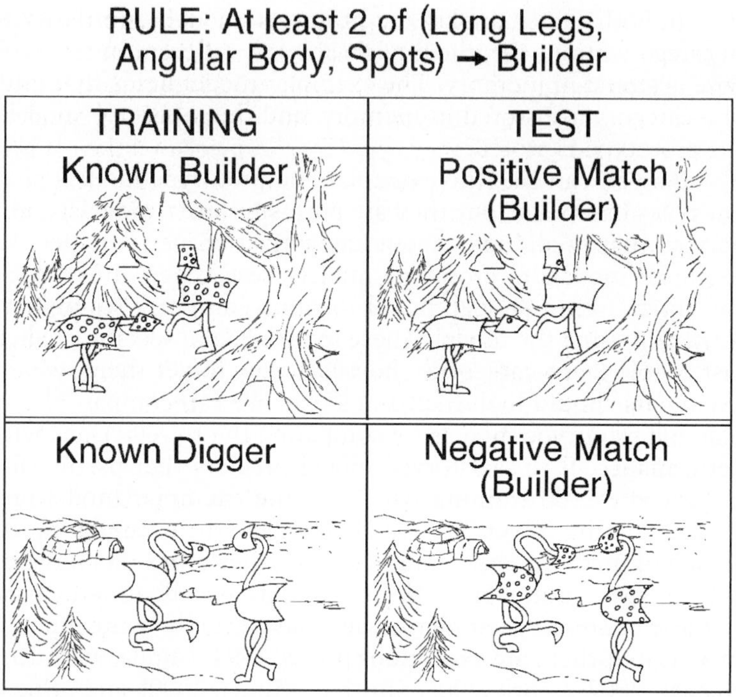

RULE: At least 2 of (Long Legs, Angular Body, Spots) → Builder

TRAINING	TEST
Known Builder	Positive Match (Builder)
Known Digger	Negative Match (Builder)

Figure 8.4. "Diggers" and "builders" from Allen and Brooks (1991)."Negative match" means that the rule yields one category, but the new exemplar looks very similar to an exemplar from training that was in the other category. "Positive match" means that the rule and the similarity to training exemplars yield the same answer. Figure 1 from Allen, S. W., & Brooks, L. R. (1991). Specializing the operation of an explicit rule. Journal of Experimental Psychology: General, 120, p. 4.

Scott Allen and Lee Brooks (1991) believed that people might be able to use *either* rules or similarity. In their experiment, participants saw new creatures and were asked to categorize them as "diggers" or "builders" (see Figure 8.4). During training, some participants were encouraged to learn the categories by memorizing exemplars and their category. Others were given a rule by which to categorize. Builders have two of the following three characteristics: long legs, an angular body, and spots. After the training phase came a test phase in which participants saw new exemplars. The experimenters showed participants new exemplars, some of which were actually builders, but they looked very much like diggers that participants had seen during training (in Figure 8.4 this is called a "negative match"). Participants in the memory group called them diggers 86% of the time, indicating that they were comparing the new items with remembered items from training. But those in the rule group called them diggers just 45% of the time, indicating that they were most often relying on the rule.

Researchers have developed models that use multiple systems of categorization. For example, Rob Nosofsky's RULEX model (Nosofsky & Palmeri, 1998; Nosofsky, Palmeri & McKinley, 1994) proposes that people initially try to use a simple categorization rule, and if that doesn't seem to work, they try a more complex rule. If they are still making errors, they supplement the rules by memorizing a few of the exemplars that don't fit that rule. Thus, the RULEX model uses both rules and exemplars. (For another model using rules and exemplars, see Erickson & Kruschke, 1998.)

Perhaps the best developed of these theories is that of Greg Ashby and his colleagues (Ashby, Alfonso-Reese, Turken, & Waldron, 1998; Ashby & Maddox, 2005; Ashby & O'Brien, 2005), who, in addition to developing a mathematical model of category learning, also tie learning to the brain. Ashby argues that there are four different systems in the brain that are responsible for learning different types of categories. Two of the types of categorization are ones that we haven't discussed.

Ashby's theory gains support primarily from neuropsychological data. For example, when categories can be described by a simple rule (as in the Bruner et al. [1956] experiment with the cards), categorization is really a problem-solving task that depends on working memory. As predicted, patients with working memory deficits are impaired on learning categories described by a simple rule (e.g., Brown & Marsden, 1988). Brain imaging experiments show that the prefrontal cortex and the caudate nucleus, which work together as a circuit to support working memory, are active during simple categorization tasks (e.g., Konishi, Karwazu, Uchida, Kikyo, Asakura, & Miyashita, 1999).

Ashby is not alone in trying to use neuroscientific data to argue that there are multiple systems of categorization (e.g., Folstein & Van Petten, 2004; Kéri, 2003; Patalano, Smith, Jonides, & Koeppe, 2001). Finding behavioral differences among these hypothetical categorization systems is more difficult, but researchers are beginning to explore this possibility (e.g., Maddox, Ashby, Ing, & Pickering, 2004; Rouder & Ratcliff, 2004). Still, some researchers are not persuaded that multiple system theories of categorization are correct (e.g., Zaki, 2004).

SUMMARY   The classical view of categorization was that categories were defined by a set of necessary and sufficient rules. In the 1970s, it became clear that category structure is not all or none, as the classical view would predict, but rather it is graded; some exemplars of a category are considered more typical, or better examples of the category, than others. This finding and others led to probability models in which categorization is viewed as a matter of probability, not all-or-none decisions. Two types of probability models were developed: prototype models (in which exemplars are abstracted into a prototype that is stored) and exemplar models (in which all the exemplars are stored). In the late 1980s, new results indicated that similarity could not account for all categorization. It seemed that rules are used to categorize at least some of the time. The latest theories include at least two separate mechanisms for category learning.

Stand-on-One-Foot Questions

1. *Describe the classical view of categorization. What data indicated that it could not provide a complete account of categorization?*
2. *What are the two main types of categorization theories that rely on similarity, and what is the key difference between them?*
3. *What is the final word on the difference between the rule-based view of categorization and the similarity view?*

Questions That Require Two Feet

4. *What is the logical problem with a model that proposes that each new exemplar is stored in memory and categorization decisions are made based on its similarity to groups of exemplars already in memory?*
5. *You may have noticed that newspapers (especially the more sensationalist tabloids) often run headlines that report on a grandma doing something atypical of grandmas: "Grandmother Swims English Channel," "Grandma Guns Down Intruder." Given what you have learned about categorization, comment on why newspapers do this.*

How Is Memory Organized?

Preview

Organization allows us to retrieve the right memory from the storehouse. Our memory system does not merely allow us to find the desired memory quickly. If what is desired is not in memory, the system provides something close in meaning, or it provides material that may help us guess about the desired information. One early theory of memory organization, the hierarchical model, suggested that concepts were placed in a taxonomic hierarchy (*animal* above *bird*, *bird* above *canary*). Later models used an idea called spreading activation, whereby thinking about one concept would bring semantically related concepts to mind (e.g., thinking about the concept *doctor* makes it a little more likely that you'll think of the related concept *patient*). A variant of the spreading activation model uses distributed representation, meaning that one concept is represented by many units of the model; in fact, many concepts are in those units simultaneously, and which concept is represented at any moment depends on the state of the entire model.

We each have an amazing amount of material stored in memory (although it doesn't always feel that way). Most college students have a reading vocabulary of perhaps 60,000 words. Add to that all your memories about what things are, how things work, memory for faces, voices (Mom), music ("who let the dogs out . . ."), and so on. The mind is faced with the formidable problem of finding useful information quickly among these riches, and our ability to find memories efficiently is truly amazing. For example, people can identify popular songs when presented with a snippet as short as 200 ms (Schellenberg, Iverson, & McKinnon, 1999). We are unsure about how categorization operates; yet, can we nonetheless say something about how memory is organized? We can, but let's start by explaining a bit about memory systems in general so you will have a better idea of what the human memory system might be doing. You will also understand why cognitive psychologists have posed the questions we consider.

Addressing Systems

Let's begin with an information storage system that we understand: a library. How do you find the right book in a library? Books are ordered according to the Library of Congress system so we can look for them according to their subject matter. To find a particular book, you need its unique number, which you find in the catalog—a master list with the specific numbers of all the library's volumes. The system used in a library is called an **addressing system** because each entity in the storehouse has a unique address, which is critical for finding what you want. If the number 798.30 is erased from the book or from the master list, or if the book is accidentally shelved as 898.30, no one will be able to retrieve it, or at least not quickly.

Your computer uses an addressing system to find information on its hard drive (the computer's storehouse). When you create a new computer file and store it on the hard drive, its location goes into a master list called a disk directory.

The human mind, however, does not use an addressing system; our memory behaves in ways inconsistent with such a system. If your mind used an addressing system, the kinds of memory errors you made would be unpredictable. For example, suppose someone asked you, "Is there a good coffee shop around here?" If your master memory list contained the name of a good coffee shop at memory address 78342, but your memory system made an error in one digit and looked up memory location 88342, anything could be at that address and you might answer the question by saying, "Ratatouille." Your memory system doesn't work that way, however. If you make a memory error, it tends to be a near miss: an answer that is wrong but is at least related to the right answer. Usually, such errors are related in terms of meaning. For example, I might ask you, "What was Buffalo Bill's last name?" You might answer "Hickok," which is wrong (it was Cody), but close because it was the last name of another well-known Bill from the Old West.

Content-Addressable Storage

In **content-addressable storage**, a system that seems to work more like human memory, the content of the memory is itself the storage address. You find a memory's location in the storehouse based on the actual content of the memory.

This system would produce near misses; if you search memory for the name of a well-known Bill from the Old West (Buffalo Bill) and you have a similar concept in memory (Wild Bill), Wild Bill Hickok pops out of memory. Content-addressable storage systems are very fast, and the time it takes to retrieve a memory from the storehouse does not increase as you add more information. Our memory systems also seem to work that way; as we learn more things, it doesn't take longer to retrieve facts about the old things.

Unfortunately, the feature of this system that makes the speed possible also poses a problem. The point of the system is that you access memories based on their content. But how does a memory "know" when it is being called on? Every memory must have the capability of knowing what you're asking for and evaluating whether its content is a good enough match. Making each memory "smart" in this way requires a big commitment in processing resources, whether the system is computer memory built on this principle or a speculative model of how the brain works.

The human memory system has a capability even beyond that of a simple content-addressable system, however, which is best illustrated by example. Suppose I ask you this question: "Does Tobey McGuire have a large intestine?"

You would answer "Yes" to this question, but why would you do so? It's likely that you've never encoded that fact, so it can't be in memory. On what basis do you give a confident "Yes"?

Your "Yes" is not based on a fact in memory about Tobey McGuire; it is based on an inference. When you try to retrieve information that has not been encoded directly, your memory system often pulls up related information that allows you to make an inference to answer the question, as follows:

FROM MEMORY: Humans have a large intestine.
FROM MEMORY: Tobey McGuire is a human.
INFERENCE: Therefore, Tobey McGuire has a large intestine.

The requested information is not in memory, but you do have in memory other information that can help you answer the question, and that information is retrieved. How does the memory system "know" the right information to produce when what is requested is not in the system?

I mentioned at the start of this section that the discussion of memory systems and their capabilities was relevant here because it was one such capability that motivated cognitive psychologists in their study of the organization of memory. This is the question that motivated the initial work on the organization of secondary memory: What is the organization that allows not just the simple retrieval of facts but also the retrieval of relevant facts that we would not expect to necessarily be explicitly stored?

Hierarchical Theory

The **hierarchical theory**, one of the first models to address this question, came from Allan Collins and Ross Quillian (1969, 1972). It proposed a clever solution.

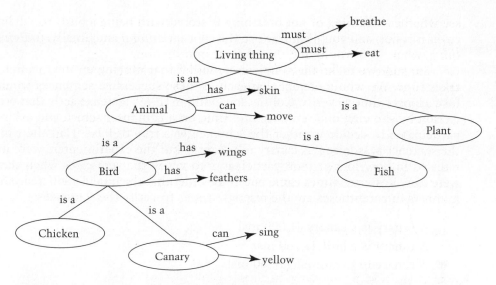

Figure 8.5.   An example of a hierarchical network described by Collins and Quillian (1969) representing *animal*, *canary*, and *chicken*, among other concepts. There are also links such as "is a" and "has."

In their model (and in many of the models that followed) memory is composed of two basic elements: nodes and links.

Nodes represent concepts such as *red, candy, bird, president,* and so on. Nodes have levels of **activation**, meaning that they have some level of energy or excitement. In practical terms, nodes become active when the concept they represent is present in the environment. Thus, the concept *bird* might become active through my seeing a picture of a bird, seeing a real bird, or hearing or reading the word *bird,* and so on.

Links represent relationships between concepts, such as "has this property" or "is an example of." As shown in Figure 8.5, links in a hierarchical memory structure connect nodes and can provide property descriptions of concepts. Thus, the idea that a living thing must breathe is represented in the model through a concept (*living thing*), a property (*breathe*), and a link (*must*).

An important characteristic of the model is **property inheritance**. Moving down the hierarchy from *animal* to *bird* to *chicken,* we see that concepts inherit properties from the concepts above them in the hierarchy. Hence, an animal is a type of living thing, so it inherits the properties of living things. For example, chickens inherit the properties *must breathe* and *must eat* from the concept *animal* (but see Sloman, 1998).

You'll remember that we asked earlier what happens when an inference is needed to answer a question. The inheritance of properties can be important in such situations. If I were to ask you, "Does a canary breathe?" the model predicts that you would first go to the node representing the concept *canary.* You would examine the properties associated with *canary* and discover that breathing or not breathing is not part of the representation of what a canary does, so you would move up one level in the hierarchy to the concept *bird* to see whether breathing or not breathing is stored with being a bird. You'd discover it is not, and you'd continue to the concept *animal* and, finally, to *living thing*, where you would find the relevant information.

Suppose we make the simple assumption that moving up the hierarchy takes time. We would predict that each of these successive sentences would take a longer time to verify. Collins and Quillian (1969) tested exactly that prediction by showing one sentence at a time on a computer screen and asking participants to decide whether the sentence was true or false. Half the time the sentence was false ("A canary is a plant"), but the experimenters were interested in how long it took participants to verify the sentences when they were true. Response times came out in the order that the model predicted. The numbers in parentheses are the response times to verify the sentences:

A canary is a canary. (1,000 ms)
A canary is a bird. (1,160 ms)
A canary is an animal. (1,240 ms)

The effect worked just as well for properties.

A canary can sing. (1,305 ms)
A canary has wings. (1,395 ms)
A canary has skin. (1,480 ms)

Thus, the findings seemed to support the model for the tricky ability we discussed in regard to McGuire's intestine. Unfortunately, it soon became apparent that the model didn't always make the right predictions. One problem was that the hierarchy sometimes didn't seem to hold. For example, people were faster to verify the sentence "A chicken is an animal" than to verify "A chicken is a bird."

Another problem of this model grows out of a property that initially seemed to be a strength. Looking at Figure 8.5, you'll notice that the property *has wings* is stored only once, with *bird*; it makes sense to store this property along with all the other common properties of birds. The principle of **cognitive economy** refers to designing a cognitive system in a way that conserves resources. Yet, this principle does not appear to be true in the brain, at least not the way Collins and Quillian (1969) implemented it. Carol Conrad (1972) gave participants a list of words and asked them to write down what each word made them think of. She found that participants often wrote information that was one or two levels higher in the hierarchy. For example, if you give people the word *robin, canary,* or *bluebird* they are very likely to write the verb *flies* as one of the properties, even though *flies* goes with the higher-level concept *bird*. The property *flies* also seems to be stored along with *robin, canary,* and *bluebird*.

Spreading Activation Theories

Allan Collins and Elizabeth Loftus (1975) proposed a **spreading activation model** to address the shortcomings of the earlier model. This is another network

Time

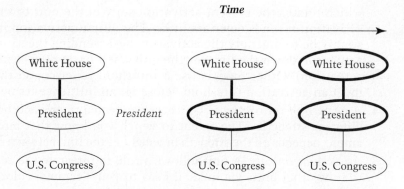

Figure 8.6.   When the word *President* is perceived in the environment (left), the corresponding concept becomes active in memory (center), and activation spreads to related concepts (right). The amount of activation depends on the weight of the link between concepts.

model, again consisting of nodes and links, but now the links represent associations between semantically related concepts. Memory is thus conceived as a vast web of linked concepts called a **semantic network**. Collins and Loftus used links that had properties such as *is a* and *has a*. Later models that built on their work did not (see McClelland, 1981), and our discussion is based on these. In a semantic network, as in a hierarchical network, nodes can become active, and you can think of this activity as the node having energy. Nodes become active through stimulation from the environment. Thus, the concept *President* might become active through my seeing a picture of the president or through hearing or reading the word *President*.

Figure 8.6 shows three nodes in a memory network. (I'm taking a break from canaries and chickens.) Time moves from left to right in the figure, so at left we see a node without activation; then, the word *President* comes in from the environment (because someone said it, for example), and at right we see the same node, now activated, with the activation represented by the thicker border on the node. Active nodes send some of their activity to other linked nodes, which can also become active. Activated nodes send a high proportion of their activation to closely related concepts. Hence, *President* might send a lot of activation to *White House* but less to *Congress*. This principle is shown in the right part of the figure.

A formal definition has been proposed for the six properties of a semantic network (Rumelhart, Hinton, & McClelland, 1986):

1. *A set of units.* Each unit represents a concept.
2. *A state of activation.* Each unit has its own state of activation, an amount of "energy" at a given moment.
3. *An output function.* Units pass activation to one another. The amount of activation a unit passes to its neighbors depends on its output function,

which relates the current activation state of the unit to the amount of activation it sends down its links. The output activation function may simply be to multiply the activation by 1 (sending the same amount of activation down the links as the unit itself has) or 0.5 (sending half the activation). Other models use a threshold function, so the unit must meet an activation threshold before it can influence its neighbors.

4. *A pattern of connectivity.* Units are connected to one another by links of different strengths. The extent to which you know that birds fly, for example, depends on the strength or weight of the link between *bird* and *flies*.

5. *An activation rule.* A unit follows a rule to integrate the activation sent to it by other units via links. If I say to you, "caramel color, carbonated, cold," these words are closely associated with the concept *cola*. Suppose that these three concepts (*caramel color, carbonated, cold*), which were activated when I said the words, send activation of 0.85, 0.48, and 0.15 to the concept *cola*. What will the activation of *cola* now be? Should we add the three, yielding 1.48? Should we find the mean, yielding 0.49? Should we allow only activations higher than 0.25 to enter our calculations and take the mean of those, yielding 0.67? The activation rule determines how the inputs should be combined.

6. *Learning rules to change weights.* A semantic network cannot be static. The knowledge of the network is in weights, so there must be a mechanism to change the weights if the model is to learn. Suppose you didn't know that horses love candy peppermints. The link between *horse* and *peppermint* would be 0. Now that you've read that fact one time, what should the weight of that link be? There must be a rule by which the weights change. (Horses do like peppermint, by the way.)

Spreading Activation Models: An Example

We've gone over the properties of spreading activation models. For a better sense of their strengths, let's have a look at one example developed in some detail (McClelland, 1981). Table 8.3 lists information about 27 men. All the information in this list can be represented in a semantic network. A subset of the list is shown in Figure 8.7; the units in the center of the network do not represent any concept, but they are important for passing activation between nodes.

This sort of model has a number of useful characteristics. First, it obviously allows for the retrieval of properties. If you say "Lance," that word is perceived and the *Lance* node becomes active. That node passes activity to other nodes, and it will lead to activity of the nodes *Jets, 20s, junior high, married*, and *burglar*.

Second, the model allows content-addressable storage. Recall that this is a system whereby memories are accessed not by an address but by their content. For example, if we activated the nodes *Jets* and *40s*, the activation would spread and *Art* and *Clyde* would become active. If we activated *Jets* and *30s*, then the four Jets in their 30s would become active: *Al, Mike, Doug,* and *Ralph.*

*Table 8.3.   **The Jets and the Sharks***

Name	Gang	Age	Education	Marital Status	Occupation
Art	Jets	40s	Junior high	Single	Pusher
Al	Jets	30s	Junior high	Married	Burglar
Sam	Jets	20s	College	Single	Bookie
Clyde	Jets	40s	Junior high	Single	Bookie
Mike	Jets	30s	Junior high	Single	Bookie
Jim	Jets	20s	Junior high	Divorced	Burglar
Greg	Jets	20s	High school	Married	Pusher
John	Jets	20s	Junior high	Married	Burglar
Doug	Jets	30s	High school	Single	Bookie
Lance	Jets	20s	Junior high	Married	Burglar
George	Jets	20s	Junior high	Divorced	Burglar
Pete	Jets	20s	High school	Single	Bookie
Fred	Jets	20s	High school	Single	Pusher
Gene	Jets	20s	College	Single	Pusher
Ralph	Jets	30s	Junior high	Single	Pusher
Phil	Sharks	30s	College	Married	Pusher
Ike	Sharks	30s	Junior high	Single	Bookie
Nick	Sharks	30s	High school	Single	Pusher
Don	Sharks	30s	College	Married	Burglar
Ned	Sharks	30s	College	Married	Bookie
Karl	Sharks	40s	High school	Married	Bookie
Ken	Sharks	20s	High school	Single	Burglar
Earl	Sharks	40s	High school	Married	Burglar
Rick	Sharks	30s	High school	Divorced	Burglar
Ol	Sharks	30s	College	Married	Pusher
Neal	Sharks	30s	High school	Single	Bookie
Dave	Sharks	30s	High school	Divorced	Pusher

Third, it is easy to see how typicality grows naturally out of the model. A concept such as *robin* will have strong links to many concepts that are in turn strongly linked to bird (*small, sits in trees, lays eggs*). An atypical bird such as an ostrich has many links to concepts that are weakly linked to bird (*large, runs fast, can't fly*). If I say "bird," all the nodes that have strong links to that concept will become active. Thus, it is easy for me to describe the typical bird. Similarly, in the model in Figure 8.7, if I say "Jet," the features of the prototypical Jet become active, even if no one Jet has all the typical qualities.

Fourth, the model naturally creates **default values** that a variable or an attribute takes in the absence of any other information. For example, how does a bird get around? In the absence of any other information, we can assume that it flies; this is the default state. Default values are assigned for concepts as a natural part of the spreading activation. If you have reason to think that the object you're dealing with is a bird, then the connection between *bird* and *flies*

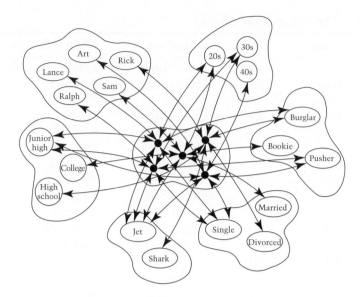

Figure 8.7. Some of the information from Table 8.3 presented in a network.

will lead to activation in the concept *flies* unless you are specifically told that this bird does not fly.

Fifth, spreading activation models are resistant to faulty input. Suppose I tell you, "I went to a pretty good restaurant last night. I can't remember the name, but it was a fast-food place, and they had something called a Big Mac, and the restaurant had green arches out front." You would say to me, "You mean McDonald's, but the arches are gold." Notice that you've retrieved the right memory even though I've given you faulty information. It's easy to imagine that you could check the memory system for a description of my restaurant and find nothing; indeed, you've never heard of a restaurant matching the description I gave. But your memory system is resistant to faulty input and can come up with the right memory. Spreading activation models have this property. The concepts *fast food* and *Big Mac* are so strongly linked to *McDonald's* that the node is activated, despite the fact that *green arches* might inhibit its activation a bit. Once *McDonald's* is activated, that in turn activates *golden arches*, which makes me surmise that you have made an error in your description.

There is evidence consistent with the idea that concepts in memory become active and that when the activity surpasses a threshold they enter awareness. Many paradigms demonstrate an effect called **repetition priming**. The participant reads a list of words and sometime later (perhaps an hour) performs a second task. Some of the words used in the second task are in the original list, but the participant is not told that. Table 8.4 lists the type of tasks that researchers have used to measure priming.

In each task described in Table 8.4, participants show some bias caused by the processing of the words on the original list. These repetition priming

Table 8.4.   **Tasks Used to Measure Priming**

Task	Description	Priming Measure	Reference
Fragment completion	Participants must complete word fragments to form words. Each fragment has just one possible completion.	Number of fragments successfully completed that were on the original list versus fragments completed that were not.	Tulving, Schacter, & Stark (1982)
Stem completion	Participants must complete word stems to form a word. Each fragment has at least 10 possible completions.	Number of stems completed to make a word on the original list versus stems completed to make words not on the list.	Warrington & Weiskrantz (1968)
Category exemplar generation	Participants must name category members.	Somewhat unusual category members appear on the original list. Priming is measured by how many of these unusual members are mentioned by participants.	Graf, Shimamura, & Squire (1985)
Lexical decision	Participants see a letter string appear and must respond with a button press as quickly as possible to indicate whether the letter string forms a word.	Priming is reflected by shorter response times to words that were on the list compared with words that were not.	Just & Carpenter (1980)

effects are often interpreted as showing that nodes representing concepts become active when participants first read the words on the list, and for the second task an hour later, they are still somewhat active, making these concepts easier to access. Repetition priming effects indicate that activation of nodes lasts an hour or more and that this activation is measurable.

Another effect, **semantic priming**, indicates that activation passes between nodes. Participants are shown two letter strings and must push one button if both are words and another button if one or both are nonwords (e.g., "marb"). When both letter strings are words, response times are faster when the words are semantically related (*doctor–nurse*) than when they are not (*radio–nurse*) (Meyer & Schvaneveldt, 1971). A straightforward interpretation is that when participants saw the word *doctor*, the node representing the concept

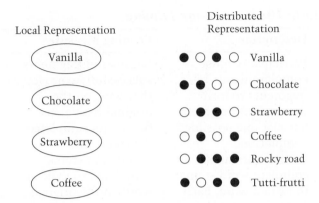

Figure 8.8. Examples of local representations (each node represents one concept) and distributed representations (each concept is represented across multiple nodes).

became active and immediately passed activation to all semantically related concepts, including *nurse*. When participants read the word *nurse*, the concept representing it was already somewhat active so it was easier for them to identify the word.

Distributed Representation (Parallel Distributed Processing)

In contrast to the spreading activation model, in which each node represents a single concept with **local representation**, another class of models uses **distributed representation**, meaning that a concept is represented across multiple nodes. Suppose, for example, that I have four nodes. In a local representation, each node represents a concept: *vanilla, chocolate, strawberry*, and *coffee*. If the *vanilla* node has an activation of 1, then I'm thinking about vanilla, and so on for the other nodes. That would be the one-node, one-concept scheme described earlier. In a distributed representation, you must look at all four nodes simultaneously, and meaning is based on what all four nodes are doing, as shown in Figure 8.8. You can't look at one node and know whether the concept *vanilla* is active. You have to look at all four nodes simultaneously. One advantage of a distributed representation is obvious: You can get more concepts into the same number of nodes with a distributed representation.

Many distributed network models, called **parallel distributed processing (PDP)** models, have a structure that looks something like Figure 8.9, with a series of input nodes, some number of "hidden" nodes, and a series of output nodes. In a simple taste network, for example, the input nodes would get their input from the senses of taste and smell. For example, vanilla ice cream might input the values +1 0 0 +1 −1 +1 0 0 into the eight input nodes. These inputs activate the hidden nodes, which in turn activate the output nodes. The output nodes represent the concepts *vanilla, chocolate, strawberry*, and so on.

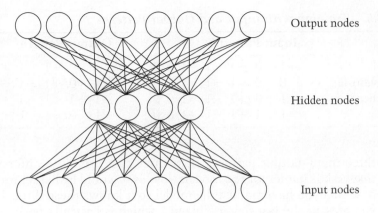

Output nodes

Hidden nodes

Input nodes

Figure 8.9. A parallel distributed processing network showing nodes and links.

This model has all the advantages of the model using local representations and some new ones. For one, the model exhibits another very useful property of memory called **graceful degradation**, which means that if part of the system is damaged or malfunctions, it doesn't shut down. Performance gets worse, but the system is still somewhat functional. For example, if one or two of the nodes were removed from the model in Figure 8.9, the rest of the model would still work—not perfectly, though, as the pattern of activation would be disrupted—because each node gets inputs from many other nodes. If just a few nodes are lost, each node still gets most of its usual input. Graceful degradation seems to be a property of the human memory system as well. The amount of damage to cognitive function is roughly proportional to the amount of damage to the part of the brain that supports it. Minimal damage causes minimal cognitive loss. This feature is very different from a computer's memory, where minimal damage can be catastrophic.

Another strength of these models is that they can actually learn. In many models using local representation, knowledge (e.g., that birds have wings) is put into the model by the experimenter. In contrast, distributed models know nothing at the beginning of training. It is assumed that the learner is given feedback about correctness as training progresses, and the models have methods to change the connection weights based on the feedback. The rule for how the weights are changed depends on the difference between the input and the output; that is, the larger the difference, the less correct the output and the larger the weight change. Thus, the strength of the model is that it seeks not only to show us how memories are represented after they are learned, but also how memories are acquired.

An important strength of this learning process is that it automatically finds both prototypes and exceptions to prototypes. Suppose we include training of three flavors: vanilla, French vanilla, and vanilla bean. As you can see from Table 8.5, the input patterns of these three flavors are quite similar, and so is the output pattern. It should be harder for the model to learn to distinguish these

Table 8.5.   Training with Input and Output Patterns

Flavor	Input Pattern	Output Pattern
Vanilla	+1 0 +1 −1 +1 0 0	+1 0 +1 −1 +1 0 0
French vanilla	0 0 +1 −1 +1 0 0	+1 0 +1 −1 +1 0 −1
Vanilla bean	−1 0 +1 −1 +1 0 0	+1 −1 +1 −1 +1 0 0
Bland	+1 −1 +1 −1 +1 0 0	+1 0 +1 −1 +1 −1 0

three input–output patterns than three that are quite different; and indeed, that task is harder for the models, just as it would be harder for you. Now suppose that you have trained the model so it knows these three flavors, and then you present the last flavor, "bland," which is basically ice cream with no flavoring at all. What should a memory model do with this novel flavor? You might think, "If you've never tasted it before, there is nothing in memory about this flavor, so you don't know what it is." But that wouldn't happen. You would say, "It's not vanilla, but it tastes more like vanilla than like chocolate." That is generalization, which I mentioned at the beginning of the chapter: You are responding to a new stimulus in the way you would respond to an old stimulus that is similar. Generalization is a key property of category memory, and it's a natural outgrowth of this sort of model.

The parallel distributed processing approach seems to have a lot of advantages. Nevertheless, it does have drawbacks. The most serious is that these models have not been used very effectively to explain why the mind works as it does. Mike McCloskey (1991) draws a distinction between a simulation and an explanation, and he gives an example like this one. Suppose I have a black box, and in this box is a device that verifies sentences. You type a sentence on a keyboard (e.g., "A canary is a bird") and 1,160 ms later the word "TRUE" appears on the screen. The box can verify a wide range of sentences, and its accuracy and the time it takes is similar to that of human data. Without looking in the box, would you say that I have an explanation of how this process works? No. You'd say that I have successfully *simulated* the process on a machine.

McCloskey (1991) suggested that this situation is analogous to that of parallel distributed processing models. They are black boxes, because when the model is through learning, it might be giving you the correct output, but it's hard to understand which features of the model led to that correct output. Everything is distributed in the model, so you can't just look at the weights of the links or the activations of the nodes and thereby understand the processing. As Michael Mozer and Paul Smolensky (1989) put it "One thing that connectionist networks have in common with brains is that if you open them up and peer inside, all you can see is a big pile of goo" (p. 3). Goo does not make for a very satisfying explanation of the sort that cognitive psychologists seek. But that is not to say that parallel distributed processing approaches are not valuable. These models can be used at a level that is relevant to cognitive theory, one can experiment on the effects of changing aspects of the model (e.g., producing "lesions" to it), and one can investigate the computational requirements of tasks in terms of the model.

But wait a minute. When we open the brain, we *don't* just see a big pile of goo. Can't we look at the brain and determine whether representation in the brain is local or distributed? A more recent study (Quiroga, Reddy, Kreiman, Koch, & Fried, 2005) provided some tantalizing data pertinent to this question. The researchers had a rare opportunity to conduct a single-cell recording study on humans. The participants were epileptic patients who had been implanted with electrodes in an effort to localize where their seizures began. During their stay in the hospital for this procedure, they also participated in some studies. The researchers found individual neurons that were active to very selective visual stimuli. For example, one neuron in the left posterior hippocampus of one patient responded to pictures of Jennifer Aniston. It responded well to all sorts of different pictures of her, but only when she was alone (presciently, it did not respond to pictures of her with Brad Pitt), and it did not respond to any other famous or nonfamous faces, buildings, landmarks, animals, or objects. A neuron in the right anterior hippocampus of a different patient, responded selectively to pictures of Halle Berry, including her dressed as Catwoman (but not to other actresses dressed as Catwoman), and even to the letter string "Halle Berry." Other neurons responded to famous places such as the Sydney Opera House, specific animals (e.g., seals) or objects (e.g., food items).

What do these results mean? They don't necessarily mean that you have a single Jennifer Aniston neuron. That would be a poor design indeed—if that neuron happened to die, you would suddenly not recognize her anymore. As the researchers point out, given their limited time, they could only test a fraction of the possible images that could have driven each neuron. Indeed, the fact that they found an image that selectively activated the neuron relatively quickly may be taken as evidence that there were lots of possible images that would activate it. But these results do argue against a highly distributed representation, at least in the brain regions from which they recorded, because that would predict that neurons would respond to many images. But this work should not be taken as definitively showing that the distributed representation can't be right. This is just one study, recording from a small group of patients in a few brain areas. More data are needed.

In summary, we've discussed three different types of memory representation. The hierarchical theory used a local representation with nodes and links organized in a hierarchy. Spreading activation theories add the idea of activation moving along the links and remove the hierarchical organization. Parallel distributed processing models use a distributed representation.

Stand-on-One-Foot Questions

6. *Name two formidable problems that any large memory storage device, including human memory, must solve.*

7. *Name some of the advantages of the spreading activation model that uses a local representation.*

8. *What is the difference between spreading activation models that use local representation and those that use distributed representation?*

Questions That Require Two Feet

9. *Can you see how the spreading activation model might be related to early associationist ideas discussed in chapter 1? If not, can you see how it might be applied to the flow of consciousness?*

10. *Given what you know about the brain, do you think a local representation or a distributed representation is more realistic?*

11. *One way of measuring what concepts are connected in a spreading activation model is simply to name a word and ask people to say the next word that comes to mind. For example, what do you think of when you hear* salt? *Presumably, when you hear the word, it passes its activation to linked concepts. You pick the most active word as your response. Try another one. What is the first word you think of when you hear* pepper? *For* salt, *the first word many people pick is* pepper, *but few people who hear* pepper *list* salt *as the first associate (although you may have because I had just reminded you of the association between them). Why should* salt *activate* pepper *but* pepper *not activate* salt? *What does this result imply for spreading activation models?*

What Else Is in Memory?

Preview

Most researchers believe that there are many forms of memory and that the type of memory we discussed in chapters 6 and 7 is just one form. That view is motivated primarily by the fact that these different memory systems are located in different parts of the brain. At least five memory systems have been identified that have distinct anatomic bases. The differences among them at a cognitive level of description are less well understood.

Have we covered everything that is in the storehouse? Until about 1980, the answer might have been a guarded "Yes." Memory research was conducted using mostly verbal materials in a laboratory setting and often tested memory for these materials over short intervals. Since then, several important distinctions have been proposed that broadened our definition of memory. A number of researchers have suggested that there are several types of memory—the storehouse contains fundamentally different types of representations.

What Are Separate Memory Systems?

Why is this question interesting or important? Recall that in chapter 1 we said that cognitive psychologists were interested in mental representations and the processes that operate on them. When researchers propose that there are separate memory systems, they are proposing that there is more than one type of memory representation. We can draw an analogy to your computer: A word processing program such as Microsoft's Word uses a particular format to store data. The Word program is a set of processes that can work with this representation to read and modify the data in the file. If you have Adobe Acrobat on your hard drive, it uses a different format for its files. The Acrobat program is a different set of processes, and it uses a different type of representation. Cognitive psychologists want to know how many different types of representations there are in the brain, and how many sets of processes that operate on them. As we'll see shortly, most cognitive psychologists believe that there are at least five memory systems, and probably more. Before I tell you about those, however, I want to say a bit more about the type of evidence one needs to conclude that memory systems are really separate.

An obvious prediction you would make is this: If there are separate memory systems in the brain, then sometimes we should see a person with brain damage that disables one memory system, but leaves the other system intact. This finding is called an **anatomic dissociation**, meaning that different tasks are supported by different parts of the brain. Those sorts of data have in fact been observed since the mid-1960s. You may recall patient H.M, the man who had much of his medial temporal lobe removed to relieve epilepsy, leaving him with profound anterograde amnesia—he couldn't store new memories. By 1965, his memory had been tested using just about every type of material you could think of: words, nonwords, rhythms, songs, faces, and so on (Corkin, 2002). It later turned out that H.M. could learn new motor skills (Corkin, 1968; Milner, 1966). For example, he was asked to trace the outline of a star when viewing his hand and the paper in a mirror (see Photo 8.2). It's very difficult—your hand seems to move in ways you don't expect—but improvement is rapid. H.M. improved with practice, showing that he learned the skill. Interestingly, when shown the testing apparatus the next day, H.M. had no memory of having used it before, but he still could perform the task quite rapidly, making it clear that he had learned it. The anatomic dissociation in this example is that the medial temporal lobe (which is damaged in H.M.) seems important for conscious recollection of the testing situation, but doesn't seem important for skilled performance of the motor task.

Now, one interpretation of these data is that we're seeing the workings of two memory systems: One memory system supports recall and recognition (and is damaged in H.M.), and another supports learning new motor skills, which is intact in H.M. That is in fact the conclusion that researchers have

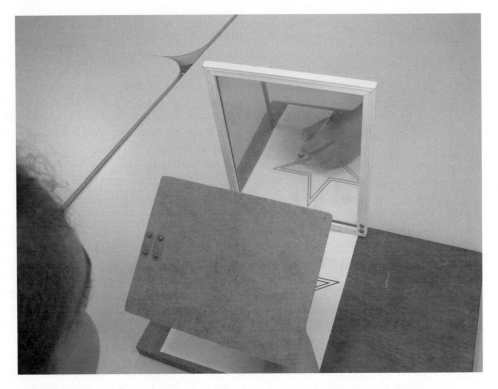

Photo 8.2. Mirror tracing apparatus.

settled on, but it's important to note that it was not the first interpretation they favored. Psychologists, like all scientists, want their theories to be as simple as possible. There is a simpler account of the experiment with H.M. (and similar experiments with other patients who have the same type of amnesia). Perhaps there is a single memory system, and one process within that system has been damaged in the amnesic patient. Most memory tasks require that damaged process, so the patient's memory usually looks terrible. But there are a few tasks, like mirror tracing, that don't require that process, so the patient learns them normally. Throughout the 1970s, psychologists tried different versions of this theory. Perhaps it was encoding that was faulty in amnesia (Cermak & Butters, 1972) or retrieval (Warrington & Weiskrantz, 1970).

Researchers tried to formulate some version of a theory that would account for the tasks that amnesic patients learn normally and those on which they are impaired, but it proved very difficult. For example, if retrieval is the problem in amnesia, why is it that amnesic patients can retrieve memories from childhood? By the early 1980s, most researchers concluded that this variety of theory—a single system with one damaged process—wouldn't work. There must be multiple systems of human memory (Cohen & Squire, 1980; O'Keefe & Nadel, 1978).

Table 8.6. **Memory Systems**

	Neural Substrate	**Reference or Review**	**System Function**
Declarative	Conscious remembers facts and events	Hippocampus and other structures	Squire (1992)
Priming	Briefly activates existing representation	Occipital, temporal, and frontal cortex	Schacter, Chiu, & Ochsner (1993)
Motor skill learning	Acquires new motor skills	Striatum, motor cortical areas	Willingham (1998a)
Classical conditioning	Learns relationships between perceptual stimuli and motor responses	Cerebellum	Thompson (2005)
Emotional conditioning	Learns relationships between perceptual stimuli and emotional responses	Amygdala	Fanselow & Poulos (2005)

Five Separate Memory Systems

The initial driving force behind the multiple systems theories were findings like those described previously. Patients with anterograde amnesia, who couldn't learn any new information as measured by the usual memory tests, were shown to be capable of new learning when tested in other ways. First, it was shown that they could learn motor skills, then that they could learn a classically conditioned response (Warrington & Weiskrantz, 1979), and then that they could learn perceptual skills such as reading mirror-reversed words (Cohen & Squire, 1980). Through the 1980s and 1990s, researchers tested a wider variety of patients and began using more advanced brain imaging techniques as they became available. By the late 1990s, most researchers would have agreed that there are at least five anatomically separate systems, listed in Table 8.6 (for a review, see Gabrieli, 1998; Willingham, 1997a) and depicted in Figure 8.10. We briefly discuss each of those five systems.

DECLARATIVE MEMORY. The **declarative memory** system supports conscious memory of facts, for example, knowing that America declared its independence in 1776, that no two snowflakes are alike, how to put a CD in your computer, and so on. The declarative memory system also stores personal events, for example, your memory of what you did after dinner last night, your memory of your last birthday, and so on. When people use the term "memory" in the everyday sense, they are referring to the declarative system, and indeed, up until now when we have used the term "secondary memory" we've been talking about declarative memory.

Declarative memory is often contrasted with **procedural memory**, a term that encompasses all the other memory systems described here. Learning in

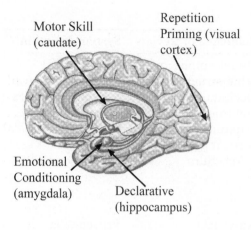

Motor Skill
(caudate)

Repetition
Priming (visual
cortex)

Emotional
Conditioning
(amygdala)

Declarative
(hippocampus)

Figure 8.10.   Some of the brain areas supporting memory. This is a sagittal view of the brain, meaning that you're looking at it from the side, but it's been sliced right down the middle. The front of the brain is on the left in this figure. A single figure showing all the areas that contribute to all types of memory would be too crowded—this figure just gives you a sense of the separation of four of the five memory systems.

procedural systems changes the way you respond to or do things (e.g., riding a bicycle). Procedural learning also occurs outside awareness—you don't have conscious access to the representation that supports the learning. For example, if you learn to ride a bicycle, you can't consciously contemplate that knowledge the way you can contemplate that you know the name of the first president of the United States. The representation that allows you to ride a bicycle can only be used for action, not for conscious thought.

The declarative memory system is supported by a network of subcortical structures, as well as parts of the cortex. The most important subcortical structures are the hippocampus and some nuclei of the thalamus (Squire, 1992). Many of the most important cortical areas are in the temporal lobe, and these appear to be important for storing memories (e.g., Martin & Chao, 2001). Other areas in frontal cortex appear to be important for the retrieval of declarative memories (Buckner, Petersen, Ojemann, Miezin, Squire, & Raichle, 1995; Thompson-Schill, Kurtz, & Gabrieli, 1998).

As noted previously, studies of amnesic patients have been very important in determining the brain basis of the declarative system. Brain imaging studies have also been informative. For example, studies have shown that it is possible to peek at the brain, observe its activity during encoding, and, on the basis of that activity, predict whether an item is likely to be remembered or forgotten. Anthony Wagner and his associates (Wagner et al., 1998) had participants lay in a scanner and make judgments about words. The researchers used event-related fMRI, which allows the measurement of brain activity in a narrow time window (as short as several seconds) so they could determine the amount of brain activity immediately after each stimulus was presented. Later, outside the scanner, participants took a recognition test for the material, and each participant's performance on each stimulus was categorized as being remembered well, remembered weakly, or forgotten. The researchers then examined whether the activity of any part of the brain at encoding predicted whether items would later be remembered or forgotten. The right dorsolateral prefrontal cortex (in the frontal lobe) and the left parahippocampal cortex (in the temporal lobe) showed more activity for items that would eventually be remembered than for items that would eventually be forgotten (see also Brewer, Zhao, Desmond, Glover, & Gabrieli, 1998).

REPETITION PRIMING.   Priming makes representations of concepts more available for use because they have been used recently (repetition priming; see Table 8.4). Thus, reading the word "cherry" makes you slightly faster in reading the word again a short time later, or makes it more likely that you will say "cherry" if someone asks you to name a fruit. There are several different ways of measuring repetition priming listed in Table 8.4. Although repetition priming is usually visual, auditory priming is also possible (e.g., Schacter & Church, 1992).

Repetition priming is supported by the cortical perceptual areas—visual priming by visual cortex, and auditory priming by auditory cortex. Damage to visual cortex, for example, disrupts priming (Gabrieli, Fleischman, Keane, Reminger, & Morrell, 1995). Brain imaging studies show that repetition priming is associated with a *decrease* in activity in cortical regions (Bergerbest, Ghahremani, & Gabrieli, 2004; Schacter & Buckner, 1998). This decrease in activity is usually interpreted as reflecting easier processing—because the stimulus has been identified recently, the brain area that supports its identification doesn't have to work as hard the second time around.

MOTOR SKILL LEARNING.   Motor skill can be defined as the improved accuracy of movements in space or time as a consequence of practice (Willingham, 1998a). This technical-sounding definition corresponds well to our everyday understanding of motor skills—it's how we learn to hit a golf ball or drive a car. But motor skill doesn't only support special talents; we rely on skilled movements through much of our day. You tie your shoelaces in the morning with great speed and accuracy compared with when you first learned the skill. Your efficiency in walking, in driving a car, in producing legible handwriting—all depend on motor skill, and these tasks would be slow and laborious indeed without it.

Motor skill is so pervasive in what we do and the term describes so many different activities that we should perhaps not be surprised to learn that many different parts of the brain contribute to motor skill learning. The most important of these are the basal ganglia, primary and secondary motor cortex, prefrontal cortex, the cerebellum, and parietal cortex (Ungerleider, Doyon, & Karni, 2002; Willingham, 1998a). Many of these brain areas also support motor planning and execution—motor skill learning happens via changes to that part of the brain that support movement in the first place.

Several researchers (Doyon et al., 2003; Willingham, 1998; Willingham & Koroshetz, 1993) have drawn a distinction between adaptation skills and sequencing skills. Adaptation skills are those where a new relationship between vision and movement is acquired. For example, an experimenter might ask a participant to wear prism spectacles, which make the world appear 30 degrees to the right of its actual location. Participants initially make very inaccurate movements when they wear the spectacles, but learn how to correct for them fairly rapidly. Patients with cerebellar damage, however, show poor learning of this task (e.g., Morton & Bastian, 2004), and brain imaging studies also implicate cerebellar involvement (Imamizu et al., 2000). Sequencing skills are those where a particular sequence of movements is learned. For example, the participant might repeat a series of button presses (rather like dialing a phone number) with the goal of improving speed. With practice, the participant will get faster at making that particular sequence of movements, compared with other sequences (Willingham et al., 1989). That skill depends on the striatum, secondary motor cortex, and probably some areas of prefrontal cortex (Willingham et al., 2002; see Poldrack & Willingham, 2006, for a review). We address motor skill learning in more detail in chapter 9.

CLASSICAL CONDITIONING.   We discussed classical conditioning in chapter 1 using food as the unconditioned stimulus. A different stimulus has often been used in experiments with humans. The unconditioned stimulus is a puff of air to the eye, which leads to an unconditioned response, blinking. The conditioned stimulus (a tone) is paired with the air puff until the conditioned stimulus elicits a conditioned response (blinking). Both patient studies and brain imaging studies implicate the cerebellum in this type of learning (Blaxton et al., 1996; Gerwig et al., 2005; Woodruff-Pak, Goldenberg, Downey-Lamb, Boyko, & Lemieux, 2000). The motivation for these studies came, in part, from very careful work in animals (primarily the rabbit) where the neural circuit was worked out in great detail, and the cerebellum was identified as the key site of learning (for a review, see Thompson, 2005).

EMOTIONAL CONDITIONING.   **Emotional conditioning** is a classical conditioning situation in which one of the unconditioned responses is an emotion. Fear is the emotion that has been studied most frequently. For example, a participant might be shown different color slides, and each time the slide depicts a snake, the participant is given a mild electric shock. In time, pictures of snakes will come to elicit fear. This type of learning depends on the amygdala. As with classical conditioning, the motivation for this work in humans came from very detailed knowledge of the neural circuit supporting emotional conditioning in other species (e.g., LeDoux, 2000), which corresponds well to human brain imaging studies (e.g., Knight, Nguyen, & Bandettini, 2005).

EPISODIC AND SEMANTIC MEMORY.   There is another distinction that is important to know about, although its status is not quite as clear as that of the systems described in Table 8.6. Endel Tulving (1972) proposed that there are two subsystems within declarative memory. **Episodic memory** is associated with a particular time and place (i.e., you know when and where you acquired the material). Episodic memories are also associated with a "this happened to me" feeling; there is a personal quality to the act of remembering. If I asked you, "When was the last time you bought a pair of shoes?", you would recall an episodic memory. Such memories can be contrasted with **semantic memory**.

Suppose I asked you, "Is a loafer a type of shoe?" You would answer, "Yes," but there is no time or place information associated with that memory, nor is there an "it happened to me" feeling. Semantic memory is sometimes called knowledge of the world. All your knowledge of what things are, what they look like, how they work, and so on is part of semantic memory.

Tulving (1972, 1983, 2002) argued that semantic and episodic memory differ in a number of important ways. Episodic memories are more prone to forgetting, are more likely to contain sensory information, are organized by time, and take longer to remember. Semantic memories are less prone to forgetting, they contain more conceptual than sensory information, they are organized by meaning rather than time, and they are recalled more quickly.

There is some evidence supporting the semantic versus episodic distinction. First, there have been reports of patients who have a selective loss of episodic but not semantic memory (Wheeler & McMillan, 2001). For example, Endel Tulving and his colleagues (Hayman, Macdonald, & Tulving, 1993; Rosenbaum et al., 2005; Tulving, Schacter, McLachlan, & Moscovitch, 1988) reported on a man, K.C., who suffered extensive damage to the left hemisphere and some damage to the right as a consequence of a motorcycle accident at age 30. K.C. shows intact intellectual functioning, and his semantic memory seems to be intact. His vocabulary appears to be normal, and he can remember technical terms associated with his job. What K.C. seems to have lost is his episodic memory. He does not remember events from his life that should be quite vivid, for example, the events surrounding a train derailment in which 240,000 people (including K.C.) had to evacuate their homes for a week, or any of the circumstances of the death of his brother by drowning.

What of neuroimaging? In the mid-1990s, it seemed that a fairly clear distinction could be drawn: Semantic retrieval was consistently associated with activity in the left frontal cortex, whereas episodic retrieval was more often associated with right frontal activity (see Buckner & Petersen, 1996). More recent data, however, have shown that that distinction is not as reliable as was first believed (Cabeza & Nyberg, 2000; Mayes & Montaldi, 2001; Rajah & McIntosh, 2005). Most direct comparisons of episodic and semantic memory have shown some differences of activation, but they are not consistent across studies.

A difficulty with the interpretation of these studies is that episodic and semantic memories are different in more ways than the distinction proposes. Episodic memories are typically encoded and rehearsed much less often than semantic memories. I might encode an episodic memory only once (the time I went to McDonald's and they let me try on one of the McDonald's caps) and then rehearse the memory over the course of a few years when I tell the story. But how many times have I rehearsed the semantic knowledge that a quarter is 25 cents? This difference in rehearsal makes it difficult to interpret neurologic studies as straightforward evidence supporting the episodic versus semantic distinction.

Because of conceptual problems such as these, some memory researchers (Glenberg, 1997; Johnson & Hasher, 1987; McKoon, Ratcliff, & Dell, 1986; Richardson-Klavehn & Bjork, 1988; Toth & Hunt, 1999; Weldon, 1999) have argued that episodic and semantic memory are not separate memory systems (but see also Schacter & Tulving, 1994). They interpret the different anatomic bases as reflecting a few different processes at work or perhaps the difference in the amount of practice the memories have received. They suggest that the distinction may be most useful for its heuristic value. In other words, the distinction helps our thinking about memory and may help us generate interesting experiments, regardless of whether it turns out to be psychologically important.

Cognitive Differences Among Memory Systems

The multiple memory systems hypothesis is rooted in anatomy on the assumption that these memory systems are different because they are localized in different parts of the brain. Basing memory systems on anatomy seems to make sense, but we want to see cognitive differences among memory systems as well. If declarative memory and motor skill learning are really different, this difference should be visible in behavior, not just anatomy. For example, perhaps the rate of learning is different, or perhaps one type of learning is more flexible than the other. However, differences in behavior between the putative memory systems have been difficult to observe.

How do the hypothetical memory systems differ? The most reliable difference has been in terms of awareness; this distinction separates declarative memory from all other memory systems. Declarative memory is always associated with awareness, meaning that you are always aware that you are learning something, and you are aware of what you are learning. If you learn that hydrogen has an atomic weight of 1, for example, you are aware of having learned something, and you are aware of what you have learned. Other types of learning are not necessarily associated with awareness. For example, in a priming task, you might see the word stem *sta* _____ and complete it to spell *stamp* in part because you saw that word an hour ago, but you need not be aware of this priming effect for it to influence your behavior.

Unfortunately, it has been difficult to find convincing evidence of other differences. Much of the focus has concerned potential differences between declarative memory and other memory systems. For example, it was suggested that declarative learning is fast and can even occur on a single trial, whereas other types of learning such as motor skills are slow and require multiple trials (Sherry & Schacter, 1987). Such a distinction is hard to evaluate, however, because it is not clear how to equate the two tasks. If we want to compare the speed of learning a word list to the speed of learning how to ride a bicycle, how long should the word list be to make it a task of equivalent difficulty? How much practice riding the bicycle is equivalent to, say, one reading of the word list? Such problems in comparing what may be inherently different types of memory make it difficult to evaluate claims about behavioral differences.

CURRENT STATUS OF MEMORY SYSTEMS. Research since the mid-1980s has shown that our previous definitions of memory were too narrow because they were restricted to conscious, declarative forms of memory. Most memory theorists believe that many cognitive systems are capable of learning. For example, your visual system learns with experience, and that learning can support performance on priming tasks. Similarly, the motor control system that allows you to move around in the world changes with experience, and those changes support motor skill learning. So you have a system that is devoted to memory—that's the declarative system with the storehouse—but you also have other systems that are dedicated primarily to another function such as vision or movement, and these systems also have the capability to learn. The motor system can learn motor skills, the visual system can learn perceptual skills, and so on. In these forms of memory, nothing is stored per se, but there are changes to the actual processes; the motor system or the visual system is changed. Declarative memory seems to fit the storehouse idea, with memory being supported by the creation and storage of new representations.

There is one other important distinction about memory that we need to make. There are occasions that we have rather vivid mental images associated with memory. For example, if I asked you "What does your best friend look like?" you would probably report that you picture his or her face as you answer this question. In one sense, we have already discussed memories associated with imagery because they are declarative. But these memories do have some properties that differ from memories that are not associated with images. We discuss this matter in chapter 9.

Stand-on-One-Foot Questions

12. *What key feature would make potential memory systems separate?*
13. *What is the origin of the multiple memory systems idea?*
14. *What is the current count of memory systems?*

Questions That Require Two Feet

15. *How likely does it seem to you that separate memory systems interact in some fashion?*
16. *When I was about nine I ran a low-grade fever for about 3 months. The doctors gave me a great many tests, trying to determine the cause. Many of these tests were painful. Until my mid-20, the smell of denatured alcohol (as you would smell in a hospital) made me uneasy. Which memory system supported that learning?*
17. *Can you think of a time when two of your memory systems may have conflicted?*

KEY TERMS

activation
addressing system
anatomic dissociation
category
classical view of
  categorization
cognitive economy
concept
content-addressable
  storage
declarative memory
default values
distributed
  representation

emotional conditioning
episodic memory
exemplar
exemplar model
generalize
graceful degradation
hierarchical theory
links
local representation
nodes
parallel distributed
  processing (PDP)
probabilistic view of
  categorization

procedural memory
property inheritance
prototypes
repetition priming
semantic memory
semantic network
semantic priming
spreading activation
  model
typicality

CURRENT DIRECTIONS IN COGNITIVE SCIENCE

Recommended readings

Brown, V. R., & Paulus, P. B. (2002). **"Making group brainstorming more effective: Recommendations from an associative memory perspective."** (pp. 51–58) When we've discussed memory in this book, we've always treated it as memory of an individual. But what happens when you remember collaboratively, such as when you and a friend try to piece together the details of a trip you both took? In this article, Brown and Paulus use a memory framework to discuss the collaborative nature of creativity when a group of people brainstorm.

Öehman, A., & Mineka, S. (2003). **"The malicious serpent: Snakes as a prototypical stimulus for an evolved module of fear."** (pp. 61–67) Throughout our discussion of memory, we've acted as though humans are a relatively blank slate—that is, that we learn based on our experiences alone, and our genetic heritage does not impact the ease or difficulty of learning particular material. Öehman and Mineka provide a fascinating review of work showing that that is not true. Humans show emotional conditioning (specifically fear conditioning) very easily to snakes.

Visual Imagery

What Purpose Does Visual Imagery Serve?

- Imagery in Early Psychology
- Imagery Reenters Psychology
- Imagery and Perception

Are Visual Images Supported by a Separate Representation System?

- Propositional Versus Analog Representation
- The Metaphor Is Misleading
- Demand Characteristics and Tacit Knowledge
- The Brain and the End of the Imagery Debate

How Does Visual Imagery Work?

- Image Generation
- Image Maintenance
- Image Inspection
- Image Transformation

If you want to, you can imagine Orlando Bloom walking on the moon. In fact, you can put a ponytail on Orlando and make him stand on his head and plow through the lunar surface like a motorboat, with his ponytail acting as a propeller. What use is a cognitive ability that allows such nonsense?

The first question we pose in the study of mental imagery is **What purpose does visual imagery serve?** This may seem like an odd place to start, but the function of a mental process is actually crucial to the way we study it. Once we know the function of a process, we know something about what the process must do; knowing its job helps us define the mechanisms the process might use. Our study of perception is informed by our belief that perception tells us about the physical features and locations of objects. The function of mental imagery has been the subject of some debate, as we discuss in this chapter. At this point, the fairly settled view is that imagery serves a memory function (making the visual properties of objects available under some conditions) and a problem-solving function (allowing us to try out changes in the positions of objects or our bodies by moving them in our mind's eye before we move them physically).

These two functions both imply that mental images are pictorial representations; images are a way of representing information in the mind that is different from verbal representations. If you want to tell me how to get from your house to the dry cleaners you can either write out directions in sentence form, or you can draw a map. We can propose that similar representations are used in the mind—representations that are verbal and representations that are pictorial—although as we'll see, we don't think either in words or in pictures, exactly.

The proposal that mental images are a different sort of representation from verbal representations upset some researchers. Bear in mind what cognitive psychology is all about: We're trying to discern the processes and representations that the mind uses to support thinking. If we all agree that there are verbal representations, and then someone proposes that there are also mental images, that rather significant addition requires not only a new set of representations (images), but also a whole new set of processes that can operate on those representations. There's no reason to think the processes that manipulate verbal representations can be applied to images, just as you wouldn't expect a computer's word processing program to be able to use files that represent images.

It might seem obvious that we do, in fact, use mental images, even if proving they exist is complicated. If we pose the following questions to participants, they almost always report using visual imagery to answer them:

What shape are a German shepherd's ears?
Which is a darker green, a Christmas tree or a frozen pea?
In which hand does the Statue of Liberty hold her torch?
How many windows are there in your house or apartment?

It's obvious that people believe that they use mental imagery, but it is not obvious that mental images actually serve a function. Remember, we first started thinking about a separate mental representation system because of the functions images serve. If we could get verbal representations to serve those same functions, would we still think that visual images might be necessary? **Are visual images supported by a separate mental representation system?** The answer is "Yes," but it was rather difficult to prove. In fact, the existence of such a system was not proved to the complete satisfaction of most psychologists until about 1980. We'll go over why it was so complicated to settle this question. Once that question was resolved, researchers started to take more seriously the next question: **How does visual imagery work?** What does the representation of a visual image look like, and how does it operate? We discuss how visual images are generated, inspected, and transformed.

What Purpose Does Visual Imagery Serve?

Preview

This section describes a bit of the history of visual imagery in experimental psychology to learn how and why people have studied imagery. Introspectionists believed that visual images were a direct window to thought. After behaviorism swept introspectionism aside in the 1920s, visual imagery went largely unstudied. In the 1960s, visual imagery reentered experimental psychology, mostly through Alan Paivio's ingenious demonstrations of the importance of visual imagery to memory. In the early 1970s, researchers began to examine ways in which mental images could be transformed (e.g., rotated or expanded). This work made salient two functions of imagery: It allows you to inspect visual properties of objects, and it allows us to try out changes mentally before going to the trouble of executing them in the real world.

Visual images have been of interest to researchers since the beginnings of experimental psychology in the late 19th century, and philosophers were intrigued for centuries before that, at least back to Plato. The same is true of memory, perception, and other cognitive processes, but there has been general agreement about the functions those other processes serve in cognition. Visual perception determines the locations and some characteristics of objects in the world. Memory makes available the properties of objects that are not currently present but that you have experienced before in the same or similar objects. So what is visual imagery for? If I say, "Image a cat," and you do so, what function could that serve? Perhaps because it is not immediately obvious, the answer to this question has changed over the history of experimental psychology. The history of visual imagery research has been contentious, partly because the view of imagery's function has changed. Our views of imagery's function developed, in part, as a reaction to the past, so to get to the bottom of this issue we must go back to the start of experimental psychology.

Imagery in Early Psychology

Recall from chapter 1 that experimental psychology began with an approach called introspectionism. To account for the contents of consciousness, the introspectionists sought to describe a small set of irreducible elements that could be combined to create more complex mental states, especially mental images. No sharp distinction was drawn between generating a mental image and seeing an object (Wundt, 1894). Imagery was considered tantamount to thought: Psychologists believed that they could understand thought by understanding images.

The advent of behaviorism in 1913 meant that imagery was largely ignored by psychologists in the United States for about 50 years, until the early 1960s. The main reason for that neglect was that it was deemed impossible to study imagery objectively. By definition, images are accessible only to the person doing the imagery, so the experimenter has no choice but to take the participant's word for whatever he or she claims to be seeing. That's no way to build a science. Woodworth and Schlossberg (1954) summed up the attitude toward the study of imagery in their very popular textbook:

> An outstanding characteristic of modern experimental psychology is its emphasis on objective experiments. As we have just seen, this reliance on objectivity misses some aspects of the act of recalling. One such aspect is the presence of images, but imagery is such a fluid thing that it is very difficult to study. (pp. 720–721)

In other words, imagery is interesting—what a pity we can't study it.

Imagery Reenters Psychology

Beginning in the 1960s, Alan Paivio discussed a role for imagery in a paired associate task. In this task, the experimenter presents a pair of words to the participant (*fork–tape*), and later the participant must produce the word *tape* if given the word *fork*. Most of Paivio's experiments used verbal materials and required verbal recall. How, then, could he show that imagery played a role in memory when he used only verbal materials? Paivio used two strategies: He varied the characteristics of the stimuli, and he varied the instructions to the participant.

The characteristic that Paivio usually varied was the concreteness or abstractness of the stimulus word. **Concrete words** such as *potato* refer to a physical object. **Abstract words** such as *intellect* do not refer to a physical object. Paivio (1963) reasoned that people could use imagery for concrete words but not for abstract ones. In a direct test of this hypothesis, Paivio (1965) administered a paired associate test, varying the concreteness or abstractness of the word pairs. There are four possible combinations of concrete and abstract words in a paired associate test: concrete–concrete, concrete–abstract, abstract–concrete, and abstract–abstract. Memory is best when both words are concrete and worst when both are abstract. Paivio interpreted this result as showing the effectiveness of imagery in memory.

To examine the reported use of imagery as a learning strategy, Paivio and Dennis Foth (1970) used a list of 30 word pairs. On each trial, the participant was instructed to rehearse a word pair either via an image (including drawing the image to ensure that the participant had created one) or via verbal mediation (including writing the phrase created to link the two words). Each participant performed some verbal rehearsal and some imagery rehearsal. Paivio and Foth also varied the types of word pairs: Some were abstract (*democracy–intellect*), and some were concrete (*tree–pencil*). Participants had better recall for abstract stimuli when they used verbal encoding, and they performed better with concrete stimuli when they used imagery.

To account for these data, Paivio proposed a **dual coding hypothesis** stating that there are two ways to represent concepts: through a mental image or through a verbal representation. Concrete concepts such as *fork* can be represented via a verbal representation that would be used in understanding and producing language and in certain types of thinking. Concrete concepts can also be represented as visual images. Abstract concepts, in contrast, have only one representation. For example, a concept such as *democracy* would have only a verbal representation, not a visual one (see Figure 9.1). What sort of image, after all, could represent *democracy*? Someone voting? Someone reading a noncensored newspaper? Those images are neither compelling nor specific. There might also be concepts for which there is a visual image but for which a verbal description is harder to generate. For example, someone who knows the odd shape of a crankshaft might have a hard time describing it, although he or she can image it.

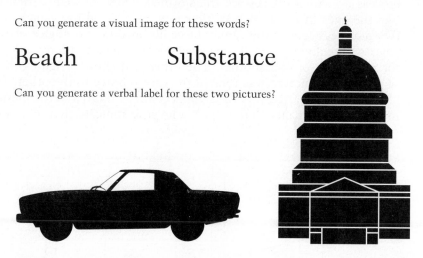

Can you generate a visual image for these words?

Beach   Substance

Can you generate a verbal label for these two pictures?

Figure 9.1. It's easy to generate an image of *beach*, a concrete word, but hard to generate an image of *substance*. Most people would agree that the picture on the left should be named *car*, but there would be less agreement about the picture on the right. It could be called *democracy*, or it could be *capitol* or *dome*. If the picture on the right is a bad representation of *democracy*, what would be a better one?

Verbal and imagery representations operate in parallel, and if both are working, it is more likely that memory will be successful; if one representation can't be retrieved when you try to recall the memory, you might be able to retrieve the other one. Concrete words are easier to remember than abstract words because they are more likely to activate a representation in the imagery system. Abstract words are likely to activate only a verbal representation. Thus, concrete words are better remembered because there are two representations, and if one fails, the other representation might still be available.

Paivio's theory describes in considerably more detail exactly how imagery and verbal representations relate and why memory is better when images are used, but that story would take us too far afield into memory (see Paivio, 1986, 1991, and Sadoski & Paivio, 2001, for reviews). The key point is that Paivio showed that imagery affects memory. He probably did more than any other person to bring visual imagery back within the purview of experimental psychology. This work does not address directly how imagery is believed to work or how images are generated or transformed; rather, it examines how imagery affects memory.

Imagery and Perception

Imagery seems to be most obviously related to perception. Although Paivio took note of this fact, his experiments did not directly address the possible relationship of imagery and perception. However, other researchers examined this relationship.

Roger Shepard and Jacqueline Metzler (1971) sought to examine the process by which images are transformed. They showed participants shapes like the ones in Figure 9.2. Participants were asked to evaluate whether the two pictures were of the same object but at different angles or whether the objects were different. Half the objects depicted were different; they were mirror reflections of one another. The other half showed figures that were the same, but one picture was rotated in space relative to the other. The amount of rotation was varied, and the figures could be rotated in the picture plane or in depth. Participants were to pull a lever to indicate their decision (same or

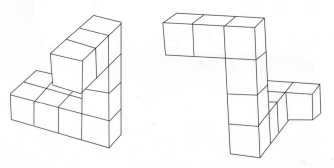

Figure 9.2. Figures similar to those used by Shepard and Metzler (1971).

different). Eight participants each performed 1,600 trials over the course of 8 to 10 hour-long sessions.

The interesting trials were those on which the objects were the same. Two findings stood out. First, the amount of time it took participants to make their decision was an orderly function of the degree of rotation between the two pictures, as shown in Figure 9.3. Second, response time was the same whether the rotation was in the picture plane or in depth.

Researchers got very excited about these results for three reasons. First, the experiment opened an entirely new area of research. Until that point, most researchers had treated images as static; if you imaged a tree, for example, the tree just sat there. When Shepard and Metzler (1971) studied how images are transformed, they highlighted an important function of mental imagery: It allows us to try something out mentally before we try it out physically. Will the sofa fit in the alcove? Can I reach the top shelf with this feather duster? Will this magazine hide the stain on the coffee table? These are questions we might try to answer using visual imagery.

A second reason psychologists were enthusiastic about Shepard and Metzler's (1971) results is that their data were so orderly. The graph shows a remarkably systematic relationship between the angle of rotation between the

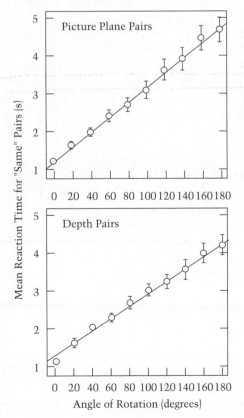

Figure 9.3. Results from Shepard and Metzler (1971). The graphs show the time it takes participants to respond "same." Note that the mean values form an almost perfect straight line. The lines above and below each circle are a measure of variability; the lines are very small, which means that most of the individual values are quite close to the mean. Also note that the slope of the line going through the points is the same for the picture plane pairs and the depth pairs. This indicates that the speed with which mental rotation can be performed is about the same in the picture plane and in depth.

two figures and the amount of time it took people to decide that the figures were the same. This orderliness hints that the task depends on a single process.

So what is the single process? That's the third thing that got researchers excited about the result. An obvious candidate is mental rotation of the image. All eight participants in this experiment reported performing this task by mentally rotating one of the objects to see whether it could be matched to the other object, implying that there is a representation to be rotated. A mental image is not a picture in the head; indeed, that wouldn't make any sense—who would be looking at such a picture? But an image has some similarity to a picture because the parts of each have the same functional relationship to one another (Shepard & Chipman, 1970).

These data and similar experiments by Shepard and his colleagues (see Shepard & Cooper, 1986, for a review) helped convince researchers that it is possible (and important) to study another aspect of imagery: The functions afforded by the transformation of images. Furthermore, this work made real the possibility that there may be a representation system (imagery) that is qualitatively different from the verbal representation system.

We began this section by raising the question "What is mental imagery for?" Let me summarize the progression of the answers. The introspectionists believed that imagery was a window into all thought processes and therefore put imagery at the center of their psychology. The behaviorists pointed out that imagery was unobservable because it was completely private to the observer, and they believed it was not relevant to the concerns of psychology because psychology was the science of behavior, not of thought. The field lay dormant for about 50 years until Paivio pointed out that mental imagery is indeed important because it affects memory and speculated that imagery may be supported by a separate representation system. Shepard and others offered a way of studying mental transformations in imagery (the unobservable events that behaviorists exorcised) and offered compelling (but not conclusive) circumstantial evidence that imagery might be supported by a separate representational system.

We return to the work of Shepard and his colleagues later in the chapter when we discuss imagery transformations. Shepard raised the possibility that images constituted a separate representation system, but he did not make it a priority to prove that this was the case. As it turns out, some scientists were far from convinced that this work demonstrated that visual images were important to human cognition. In the next section, we discuss a decade of research that did not address how imagery operates but rather was concerned with demonstrating that mental imagery is important to human cognition in the first place.

Stand-on-One-Foot Questions

1. *What was the key result from Paivio's work, and how did he account for it?*
2. *What were the two key results from Shepard and Metzler's (1971) study, and why were they so important?*

Questions That Require Two Feet

3. *We've discussed in detail the fact that imagery helps memory. Do you think it would help memory still more if the images were bizarre? What is your reason for your answer?*

4. *Given what we've discussed about the apparent overlap of perception and imagery, can you see any situations in which it might be downright dangerous to listen to a sporting event on the radio?*

Are Visual Images Supported by a Separate Representation System?

Preview

Some researchers argued that visual images did not have to be supported by a separate representation system and that the data from imagery experiments could be accounted for by verbal representations. They also argued that although the sensation of seeing visual images in the mind's eye might be real, this does not imply that there is a separate representation that helps cognition. In addition, they proposed that many of the results of imagery experiments could be explained by the participants' knowing what was expected of them and being willing or eager to produce the expected results. Imagery researchers met these criticisms and convinced cognitive psychologists that there is indeed a separate representation for visual images.

How could there be a question about whether visual imagery exists, when it seems so clear to most of us that we have and use visual images? This section summarizes a decade of active research (roughly 1972 to 1982) on exactly this point. The conclusion turned out the way you might have guessed, but it is instructive to go through the argument because it shows that firm conclusions about the mind are won only through systematic research.

Propositional Versus Analog Representation

Many of the arguments against the use of visual imagery in psychological theory were put forward by Zenon Pylyshyn (1973, 1981, 2002, 2003), who offered four key reasons psychologists should be cautious in proposing a new representational system.

THE PROBLEM.   A key argument against a separate set of images to represent visual imagery is that images simply aren't needed to account for human behavior; instead, verbal representations are sufficient to take care of everything. The verbal representation in question is the **proposition**, usually defined as the most basic unit of meaning that has a truth value (i.e., the proposition is either true or false). Propositions have a particular syntax: They take the form *relation(argument)*. A relational term can be a verb, an adjective, or a conjunction, and the arguments are nouns. For example, the proposition *red(car)* represents the idea that a particular car is red. The proposition *kicked(giraffe, lion)* represents the idea that the giraffe kicked the lion.

Images, however, often are defined as **analog**, meaning that they have some of the important qualities of pictures but are not themselves pictures. As noted earlier, Shepard and Chipman (1970) proposed that one of these qualities is that the parts of images have the same functional relation to one another as parts of pictures. Stephen Kosslyn (1980) outlined five key properties that differentiate propositions from images:

1. A proposition is relational. That is, it describes a relation between an object and a quality or between two objects. An image does not describe a particular relation. For example, look at Photo 9.1, which shows a woman and her dog. A mental image you generate based on this picture would not tell you how the woman and dog relate to one another. A proposition such as *pulls(dog, woman)* necessarily has a relation in it, however. It specifies how the dog and the woman relate to one another. In *pulls(dog, woman)*, the dog relates to the woman by pulling and the woman relates to the dog by being pulled. That sort of relational information is not inherent in an image.

Photo 9.1. A woman and her dog; actually, Dr. Bobbie Spellman (whose work is described in chapter 7) and her dog, Nikki. An image based on this photo would have very different properties than a proposition describing it.

2. Propositions conform to a syntax. There is a right way and a wrong way to form a proposition. An image has no syntax.

3. A proposition has a truth value. *pulls(dog, woman)* either truly reflects the state of the world or it doesn't. This is not so for an image. An image based on Photo 9.1 is equally consistent with *pulls(dog, woman)* and *pulls(woman, dog)* (Wittgenstein, 1953). The image does not make an unambiguous statement about the world.

4. A proposition is abstract. The proposition makes a statement about a woman and a dog, but says nothing about their relative sizes, their colors, and so on. An image is necessarily specific on these points.

5. An image occurs in a spatial medium. That means images preserve geometric qualities of real objects in space. A proposition, however, does not.

We can see that there are differences between images and propositions. Yet, some researchers said that a second type of representation is not needed—we can account for everything the mind does by using propositions.

Here's an example. One strategy to demonstrate that images are used by the mind is to show that people's behavior during imagery tasks reflects the spatial properties of images. For example, Stephen Kosslyn (1973) had participants memorize pictures of objects. (Sample drawings are shown in Figure 9.4.) In the second phase of the experiment, participants were asked to verify parts of the object: The experimenter would say, "Focus on the speedboat. Is there a propeller?", and the participant should respond "Yes." (On half the trials, a part would be named that was not part of the image—for example, "Is there a mast?".) Half the participants were asked to focus on the left or top of the image when they generated it, and half were asked to focus on the bottom or right. Participants focusing on the left were quick to verify parts on the left (the propeller), slower to verify parts near the center (a porthole), and still slower to verify objects near the right (an anchor). Kosslyn interpreted these results as

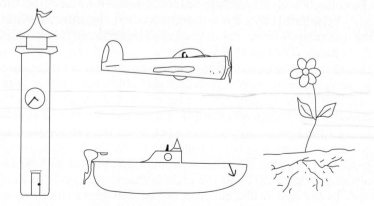

Figure 9.4. Sample pictures from Kosslyn's (1973) experiment. Participants were asked to memorize these pictures so they could image them later.

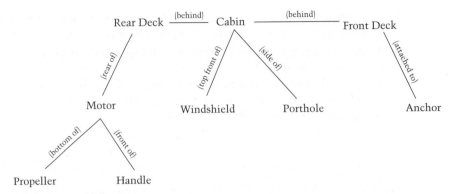

Figure 9.5. Hypothetical propositional representation of the motorboat in Kosslyn's (1973) experiment.

showing that participants had to scan across the image to locate the requested part and thereby verify it.

Kosslyn (1980) described a phone call he received from computer scientist Danny Bobrow shortly after this experiment was published. Bobrow pointed out that another, purely verbal representation would yield the same result that Kosslyn reported (see Figure 9.5). It consists of nodes that represent object parts (e.g., the propeller and porthole) and links that represent relations (*behind, attached to*). If it takes more time to traverse a greater number of links in the representation, the same pattern of results that Kosslyn reported in the imagery condition would still be seen. For example, starting with your attention focused on the propeller, you must traverse three links to get to the porthole but four links to get to the anchor. The point is that an experiment that appears to support the use of visual images may not *compel* an account involving images if we can account for the data using only propositions.

But wait a minute. Don't psychologists care that people *feel* like they are using visual images? How can you be using propositions to scan images when it so clearly feels like you're scanning something like a picture?

Pylyshyn (1973) did not argue against the internal sensation of generating and manipulating visual images. The argument is about what those sensations mean. The fact that you have a sensation of a visual image doesn't mean that there is a representation supporting the visual image. The sensations may be an **epiphenomenon**, a perfectly real phenomenon that is not related to the function of the system but is a by-product of the processes that are doing the actual work. Here's an example. I used to have an old Honda station wagon. Every time I went over 65 miles per hour, the car shook. If I slowed down to 60, there was no shaking. If I sped up to 70, the car started shaking. From this, it seems I can conclude that shaking made the car go fast. This conclusion is obviously ridiculous, but the logic is exactly the same as in the imagery case.

In the case of the car, you notice that every time you accomplish a particular type of task (going fast) you get a sensation (shaking), so you assume that the sensation causes the task to be accomplished (shaking makes the car go fast). In the case of imagery, you notice that every time you accomplish a particular type of task (mental rotation) you get a sensation (it feels as if you're seeing pictures in your head), so you assume that the sensation causes the task to be accomplished (pictures in the head are solving the imagery task). The sensation of the images could be an epiphenomenon. Like the shaking of the car, the sensation of mental imagery may be perfectly real, yet it might not be involved in the processes that are getting the work done.

The main barb to this criticism is that the burden of proof should be on those who want to claim that imagery is supported by a separate system of representations. That's because a theory with just one type of representation (propositions) is more **parsimonious** than a theory with two representations (propositions and images); it is the simplest theory possible that still accounts for all the data. The idea that parsimony is important in scientific theory, often called **Occam's razor,** was proposed by William of Occam, a 14th-century philosopher. He suggested that when two scientific theories account for the facts equally well, the simpler theory is preferred. A propositional theory was a simpler one because it used only one form of representation.

THE RESPONSE.   No one disputed that people use propositional (verbal) representations. The question was whether it was necessary to add to the cognitive system another set of representations, plus all the processes to manipulate those representations.

Imagery researchers did not try to prove that a propositional representation could not possibly account for the data. Instead, they collected data that made it increasingly difficult to make a propositional representation plausible. The results of this research program showed that certain tasks had properties that were very easy to account for with visual images but clumsy to account for using only propositions. I'll provide two examples (for more detail, see Kosslyn, 1980) involving scanning and screen detail.

Recall that in the scanning experiment with the motorboat there was an alternative explanation. It could be that the propositional representation was used and that it took more time to traverse a greater number of links in the representation. In a follow-up experiment, Kosslyn, Thomas Ball, and Brian Reiser (1978) used new stimulus materials to ensure that it was the distance between scanned objects that was important, not the number of parts or objects scanned. In other words, it should still take a long time to scan a long distance, even if the distance is filled with white space. Participants were asked to memorize a map depicting a fictional island, with landmarks such as a well and a hut.

After they memorized the map, participants were asked to image it and to scan between pairs of landmarks. Participants were to focus attention on the first location and press a button when they "arrived" at the second location. They were to press another button if the second location was not on the map. (On some occasions, the second location was not depicted on the map, although it was a plausible location, such as "beach.") The time it took for participants to "arrive" at the second location was again a linear function of distance scanned, even though there were no object parts intervening between the beginning and endpoints of the scan. These results confirmed that it is indeed distance that determines scanning time.

Another property of imagery concerns the amount of detail or "grain" participants report. If images are represented in a spatial medium, then physical features are not represented in an image if the image is made very small; if you image a tiny elephant, you may not be able to see its toenails in your mind's eye. Kosslyn (1975, 1976) tested this prediction. He asked participants to imagine a rabbit with a fly next to it (see Figure 9.6). Once they said they had the image in mind, he asked them a question about a rabbit: "Does a rabbit have a pink nose?" Another set of participants got exactly the same tasks, except that they were asked to imagine the rabbit next to an elephant.

Participants were faster to answer whether a rabbit has a pink nose when the rabbit was imaged next to a fly than when it was imaged next to an elephant. As you would expect, this task was performed with many different animals. In fact, to ensure that it was the size and not the particular animals that led to the results, Kosslyn had participants image enormous flies and tiny elephants. Participants' introspective reports were in line with the predictions. When asked to report a physical detail of an animal that they had imaged in a very small size, participants reported zooming in on the animal to increase its size so they could inspect the image for the desired detail.

The approach of imagery researchers was to turn the parsimony argument back against those who believed that propositions alone could account for all the data. Imagery theorists kept producing experimental findings that were easy to account for if images exist. To keep a single system of representations (just propositions) would have required an increasingly complex set of

≈ 2,250 ms to answer "Does a rabbit have a pink nose?"

≈ 2,050 ms to answer "Does a rabbit have a pink nose?"

Figure 9.6. Sample illustration of what participants were supposed to image in Kosslyn's (1975, 1976) experiments. In one case, they imaged a rabbit next to an elephant, and in another they imaged a rabbit next to a fly. Participants were slower to verify that a rabbit has a pink nose in the former than in the latter, presumably because they had to enlarge the image of the rabbit to see its nose.

processes to act on that simple set of representations. It was theoretically still possible to get along with nothing but propositions, but such a theory would have many many processes, some of which were obviously tossed in to account for the latest imagery results. Meanwhile, the imagery account was simple. Thus, by the early 1980s, it was the imagery theory that was more parsimonious than the propositional theory.

The Metaphor Is Misleading

THE PROBLEM.   Pylyshyn (1981) argued that the idea of mental imagery often was used as a metaphor ("looking at a picture in the mind's eye") and that this metaphor is dangerously misleading. Who exactly is looking at a mental image? If there are pictures in the head, there must be a viewer who can see the pictures. This approach conjures up images of a **homunculus**, a small person sitting at the center of the brain, pulling levers and spinning dials (and looking at visual image screens) to make thought happen. A homunculus is a fatal feature to have in a model because it simply moves the problem of cognition one step farther into the mind. We would still want to know how the mind of the homunculus worked. Pylyshyn claimed that arguing for images was the same as arguing for a homunculus to sit in the mind and appreciate the visual images.

THE RESPONSE.   Pylyshyn's (1981) criticisms forced imagery theorists to be more specific about what they believed imagery representations contained and how it worked. Most researchers held to some version of a **picture theory of imagery**, meaning not that there are literally pictures in the head but rather that seeing an object leads to a certain pattern of activation in the brain associated with the experience of seeing. A representation is stored in memory that is capable of restoring that pattern of activation, at least in part, and that is the experience of visual imagery (Bower, 1972; Hebb, 1968; Neisser, 1967, 1972).

Demand Characteristics and Tacit Knowledge

THE PROBLEM.   Pylyshyn (1981) pointed out that participants could hardly fail to guess what was supposed to happen in most imagery experiments. For example, rotating images a greater distance should take a longer time because rotating real objects a greater distance takes a longer time. **Tacit knowledge** is participants' knowledge of how objects in the real world behave. According to one argument, participants use tacit knowledge to simulate real-world movement and thereby produce results in imagery experiments that match real-world phenomena (e.g., scanning longer distances takes a longer time, and rotating images a greater distance takes a longer time). By another account, participants know what results the experimenter expects, and the participant tries to produce the expected data, in an effort either to be nice or to appear "normal" (i.e., like everyone else). **Demand characteristics** are signals to the participant about the desired, appropriate, or expected behavior in an experiment. Do experimenters subtly communicate to participants what they should do? Do participants have tacit knowledge of how imagery works?

THE RESPONSE.   Pierre Jolicoeur and Stephen Kosslyn (1985) told the people testing the participants that they should not expect a linear relation between time and distance scanned, but rather a *U*-shaped function. Despite these instructions to the experimenters, the participants produced data showing the linear relation between distance and scanning time. Thus, it doesn't seem that experimenters subtly communicate to participants what they should do. (Or if they do, participants ignore them.)

Other data indicated that participants don't know what the "expected" results are in an imagery experiment. Michel Denis and Mayvonne Carfantan (1985) administered a questionnaire about imagery to 148 undergraduates taking their first course in psychology. Each of the 15 questions described a basic paradigm in the study of visual imagery and asked the participant to select the correct outcome from among several alternatives. For example, one question read:

If it takes a given time to imagine a 60-degree rotation for one object . . .

   a. It takes longer to imagine a 120-degree rotation.
   b. It takes less time to imagine a 120-degree rotation.
   c. It takes the same time to imagine a 120-degree rotation.
   d. Can't answer.

Very few students could predict the basic result at issue in imagery experiments (that it takes a longer time to scan longer distances). Only about 15% correctly said that it takes longer to rotate the object 120 degrees. Most (41%) believed it takes the same amount of time. Thus, it appears that participants don't have much tacit knowledge to go on if they want to produce the "correct" results in imagery experiments.

The Brain and the End of the Imagery Debate

By the early 1980s, most cognitive psychologists had made up their minds that the evidence in favor of a representational system of mental images was compelling. In the late 1980s and early 1990s, a new tool became available that convinced any final holdouts. Imaging of the brain using PET and fMRI allows indirect measurement of how active different parts of the brain are. The predictions for imagery are quite clear. If imagery is a separate representation that has a lot in common with perception, then when participants perform imagery tasks, the part of the brain that usually handles visual tasks will be most active; that's an area toward the back of the brain called primary visual cortex. If, instead, propositions do the work behind these imagery tasks, then the language centers of the brain should be most active during imagery tasks because propositions are linguistic. The results of neuroimaging studies supported the imagery theorists' predictions.

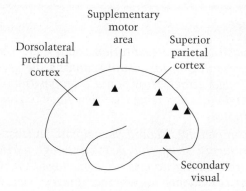

Figure 9.7. Areas of overlap in activation from a visual perceptual and a visual imagery task, as revealed by PET (Kosslyn et al., 1997).

In one particularly interesting study (Kosslyn, Thompson, & Alpert, 1997), the experimenters used a vision task and an imagery task that were quite different. The idea is that if these two different tasks showed common areas of activation, it would be compelling evidence that there is overlap in processes supporting perception and imagery. The perceptual task was naming common objects. In the imagery task, participants saw a lowercase letter, which was a cue to image the uppercase version of the letter. The activations for the imagery and perceptual tasks showed a good deal of overlap. A total of 21 areas were active: 14 were active in both conditions, 2 in perception but not imagery, and 5 in imagery but not perception. Key areas active in both are shown in Figure 9.7; note that they include secondary motor areas.

A number of other investigators reported activation of primary or secondary visual cortex during imagery tasks (Charlot, Tzourio, Zilbovicius, Mazoyer, & Denis, 1992; Chen, Kato, Zhu, Ogawa, Tank, & Ugurbil, 1998; Fletcher, Frith, Baker, Shallice, Frackowiak, & Dolan, 1995; Klein et al., 2004; Le Bihan, Turner, Zeffiro, Cuenod, Jezzard, & Bennerot, 1993; Mellet, Tzourio, Denis, & Mazoyer, 1995; for a review, see Kosslyn & Thompson, 2003). The same finding is observed with auditory imagery, which activates primary and secondary auditory cortex (e.g., Bunzeck, Wuestenberg, Lutz, Heinze, & Jancke, 2005). The important conclusion from the imaging work is that the activations observed are in the same brain areas known to support visual perception rather than areas known to support language (as the propositional theory of imagery would predict).

Stand-on-One-Foot Questions

5. *List the key criticisms of the idea that visual images are supported by a separate representation system.*

6. *What are the key differences between images and propositions?*

7. *How did imagery theorists respond to the criticisms of propositional theorists?*

Questions That Require Two Feet

8. *We discussed how a propositional representation could yield the same results as an imagery representation for visual scanning (i.e., scanning longer distances takes a longer time). How could a propositional representation account for participants reporting that they have to zoom in to see a small detail on an image?*

9. *Psychologists seemed to completely discount participants' introspections about how they perform imagery tasks; that is, even though participants are quite sure that they are creating images, their feelings that they are doing so seem to not count as evidence for whether images exist. Why do you think cognitive psychologists distrust participants' introspections?*

How Does Visual Imagery Work?

Preview

Images are generated sequentially from parts: First, one part is generated, then another part, and so on. Evidence from neuropsychology shows that there are separate processes for the visual and spatial aspects of imagery. The number of objects that can be actively maintained in imagery appears to be limited but can be increased via chunking. Images may be inspected, apparently through processes similar to inspection processes in perception. Images of transforming objects exhibit many properties that physical objects show when they move; for example, an image of a rotating object has inertia.

We began our discussion by trying to determine the function of imagery. Some researchers suggested that imagery has a memory function (Paivio, 1971) and helps us solve problems by imagining the outcome of moving things without actually moving them (Shepard & Cooper, 1986), whereas others suggested that imagery may have no function and may be an epiphenomenon (Pylyshyn, 1973, 1981). For a decade, work proceeded to show that imagery is not an epiphenomenon but is supported by a separate representation system.

Having established that imagery is not an epiphenomenon, we can return to the question "How does imagery work?" There are two components to this question. First, we might ask where images come from: How are they generated and maintained? Second, we might ask how they are used: How are images inspected and transformed (i.e., rotated or expanded)?

Image Generation

Images are generated one part at a time. This finding is a bit surprising because it does not match our introspection; it feels to us as though images pop into mind all at once.

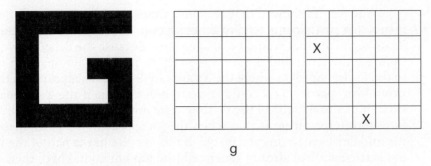

g

Figure 9.8. Sample block letter to be imaged (left) and the cue to image it (center) in Kosslyn et al.'s (1988) experiment. Participants were to verify whether the two Xs (right) would be covered by the block capital.

Kosslyn and his associates (Kosslyn, Cave, Provost, & von Gierke, 1988) examined the issue of image generation by parts using a modification of a task first described by Podgorny and Shepard (1978). They first showed participants block capital letters such as the one in Figure 9.8. Participants were to familiarize themselves with these letters so they could image them. Later, participants were shown the lowercase version of the letter and then a blank grid like the one in Figure 9.8, and they were told to image the uppercase block letter on the grid. After a brief delay, Xs appeared in two of the cells, and participants were to say whether the imaged letter would cover both Xs. An important aspect of the experiment's design is that the delay between the lowercase cue and appearance of the Xs was only 500 ms. Previous estimates of the time it takes to generate images were on the order of at least 1.5 s, so participants should still have been generating the image when the Xs appeared.

The results showed that images with more parts take longer to generate than images with fewer parts. In this case, multiple-part images are letters that take multiple strokes to write, such as *G*, and images with fewer parts are letters that take fewer strokes to write, such as *L*. The number of strokes necessary to complete the letter varied from two to five. The response time was about 900 ms for a two-stroke letter such as *L* and about 1,200 ms for a five-stroke letter such as *G*. This extra time must be used to generate the image because in a separate condition in which the block capital was present (and therefore imagery was unnecessary), the number of segments in the letter didn't affect judgment time.

A second feature of this experiment was that the experimenters systematically varied the locations of the Xs. On some trials, the Xs appeared in locations that they believed would be imaged first, and on other trials, the Xs appeared in locations that they believed would be imaged last. They assumed that participants image block capitals by strokes, in the same way that they write them. Thus, the block capital *G* would be imaged beginning with the topmost horizontal bar, then the vertical bar on the left, then the bottom horizontal bar, and so on. (The experimenters verified this order by watching a separate group of participants as they drew block capital letters.)

The results showed that response times were shorter for *X*s on line segments that participants tend to generate first, and response times increased for *X*s on segments that would be imaged later. Because the delay between the cue to image the letter and the *X*s was so short, participants' speed in responding to the *X*s depended on where the *X*s appeared. If the *X*s appeared in the top horizontal bar, participants could respond quickly, but if the *X*s appeared in the small horizontal "tail" of the *G*, they were not so quick to respond. A straightforward interpretation is that when the *X*s appeared, the participants were in the middle of generating the image. If the *X*s were in the part of the image that the participant had already generated (the top horizontal bar), then the participant could respond quickly (about 850 ms), but if the *X*s were in a part that the participant had yet to image, the participant had to continue generating the image to see whether the *X*s would be covered, so the time to respond was longer (about 1,400 ms).

VISUAL VERSUS SPATIAL ASPECTS OF IMAGE GENERATION.   Think back to our discussion of perception in chapter 3, and you can see that this result in imagery is broadly consistent with the idea that imagery and perception overlap a good deal. (Indeed, the overlap of imagery and perceptual processes has been a theme throughout the imagery literature; see Craver-Lemley & Reeves, 1992; Finke, 1980; Finke & Shepard, 1986; O'Craven & Kanwisher, 2000; Podgorny & Shepard, 1978.) It appears that images are generated in parts, which necessarily means that the parts must be put together in the correct spatial configuration; in other words, the parts of the object imaged might be separate from their spatial configuration. We discussed the neuroanatomic separation of object identity and spatial location in visual perception, referring to the "what" stream and the "where" stream (Ungerleider & Mishkin, 1982). Therefore, it seems possible that anatomically separate processes support the generation of image parts and the configuration of the parts into the correct spatial locations.

Supporting evidence can be gleaned from patients with brain damage. If a patient has selective brain damage to the "what" stream or the "where" stream, we would expect selective deficits in imagery, either in generating the parts or in manipulating the spatial aspect of an image. More generally, researchers have drawn a distinction between visual imagery and spatial imagery. It's a bit confusing because the term *visual imagery* is often used to describe any sort of imagery task in the visual modality. In this context, **visual imagery** refers to imagery tasks that emphasize what things look like, and **spatial imagery** tasks require knowledge of where objects or parts of objects are located in space. Table 9.1 lists some visual imagery and spatial imagery tasks, and data from patients with brain damage is largely consistent with the prediction: Patients with dorsal damage have trouble with spatial imagery tasks, and patients with more ventral damage have trouble with visual imagery tasks (Farah, 1984; Levine, Warach, & Farah, 1985; Riddoch & Humphreys, 1987)

Functional imaging results lead to the same conclusion—visual and spatial imagery are to some extent separated in the brain. For example, Sharlene Newman and her associates (Newman, Klatzky, Lederman, & Just, 2005)

Table 9.1. *Visual Imagery and Spatial Imagery*

Visual Imagery	Description	Spatial Imagery	Description
Animal tails	Judge whether an animal has a long tail proportional to its body size.	Letter rotation	Participant must say whether a rotated letter is mirror reversed.
Colors	Name the color of a common object that has a characteristic color (e.g., a football).	Mental scanning	Participant judges whether an arrow, if continued, would hit one of two distant dots.
Size comparison	Compare sizes of two objects that are close in size (e.g., a cigarette pack and a popsicle).	Letter corners	Classify corners of a block letter as to whether each is at the top, bottom, or middle of the letter.
State shapes	Participant hears three state names and must say which two states are the most similar in shape.	State locations	Participant hears three state names and must say which two states are the closest on the U.S. map.

asked their participants to answer questions involving the comparison of two objects either in terms of their geometry (size or shape, e.g., "which is bigger, a pumpkin or a cucumber?") or in terms of a material dimension (roughness, hardness, or temperature, e.g., "which is harder, a potato or a mushroom?"). Comparing geometric properties generated more activation in the dorsal pathway, whereas questions about material properties were associated with activation in the ventral pathway (see also Alivisatos & Petrides, 1997; Jordan, Heinze, Lutz, Kanowski, & Jancke, 2001; for a review, see Mazard, Tzourio-Mazoyer, Crivello, Mazoyer, & Mellet, 2004). Naturally, as tasks become more complex, both dorsal and ventral pathways would participate (Koshino, Carpenter, Keller, & Just, 2005).

You'll recall that in chapter 3 we reviewed many results indicating strong ventral temporal lobe activation associated with the perception of objects (although there is controversy about how to interpret it). Several studies show that the same areas are active when participants mentally imagine these stimuli, although the overlap between perception and imagery is not perfect (Ishai, Haxby, & Ungerledier, 2002; Ishai, Ungerleider, & Haxby, 2000; O'Craven & Kanwisher, 2000).

We have seen that there is good evidence that visual images are generated from memory representations used to identify objects. One way to think about this is that imagery is rather like perception running backward. Low-level perceptual processes can write to a screen of limited spatial extent; this screen is the location of visual experience (where we have the awareness of seeing something). What is written to the screen gets stored in memory in a secondary memory representation. This secondary memory representation is a visual image. We also have the ability to take this representation and write its contents back on the screen. That is visual imagery. Some researchers have applied complex modeling techniques to brain imaging data to argue that this simple model is correct (Mechelli, Price, Friston, & Ishai, 2004).

Image Maintenance

We've been talking about the processes involved in generating an image. Bear in mind that once an image is generated, it does not remain in memory unless it is actively maintained, and that requires attention. You can easily demonstrate this fact yourself. Look at Photo 9.2. Now try to image that photo and continue reading. The image disappears if you divert attention from it. An image fades very quickly and needs constant refreshing, perhaps because imagery shares processes with vision, and vision requires fast fading so our view of the world doesn't get confused as we move our eyes (Kosslyn, 1995).

Images are limited, then, because they must be refreshed continually. They are also limited in the amount of information they can contain. Again, you can appreciate this fact intuitively simply by imaging an object and adding objects to your image; you'll quickly find it difficult to keep all the objects in mind. Nancy Kerr (1987; see also Attneave & Curlee, 1983; Cornoldi, Cortesi, & Preti, 1991) studied the capacity limitations of visual imagery. She showed participants a matrix with one square designated as the start of a pathway. The

Photo 9.2. Create a mental image of Café Nasty in Amsterdam.

Table 9.2.   Results of Kerr's (1987) Imagery Capacity Experiment

Matrix Size	Number of Squares	% Correct
3×3	9	99
$2 \times 2 \times 2$	8	99
6×6	36	57
$3 \times 3 \times 4$	36	79

picture of the matrix was removed and the participant heard seven direction instructions (*left, right, up, down,* and so on) for the pathway. The matrix was shown again and the participant was to show the current location within it. The matrices varied in size, and some were two-dimensional and some three-dimensional. As shown in Table 9.2, dimensionality had a big impact on performance. Performance was much better on a $3 \times 3 \times 4$ matrix than a 6×6 matrix, even though the matrices had the same number of squares.

One interpretation of this result is that participants chunk spatial dimensions; it is easier to maintain an image of four 3×3 arrays than to maintain a single 6×6 array. Kerr (1987) tested this possibility in another experiment by presenting participants with an 8×8 array but instructing them to consider it as composed of four 4×4 arrays. To aid in this chunking, she added heavy lines to the 8×8 matrix so the 4×4 arrays were apparent. As shown in Table 9.3, performance was almost the same on this 8×8 array as it was on a $4 \times 4 \times 4$ array and better than it was on an 8×8 array without instructions to chunk.

Image Inspection

What does it mean to inspect a visual image? Again, it sounds like we're talking about a person (make it a very small person) who inspects a screen in the brain. I keep emphasizing that that's not what is meant because it is so easy to misunderstand the claim. Inspecting the image means interpreting the representation that is on the visual buffer. It requires a small person no more than perception does.

Several sources of evidence help us understand **image inspection**, which we can define as processes we engage to better know the visual characteristics of an image. We engage similar processes in visual perception. When you're

Table 9.3.   Effects of Chunking in Kerr's (1987) Experiment

Matrix Size	Number of Squares	% Correct
8×8 Without chunking	64	30
8×8 With chunking	64	53
$4 \times 4 \times 4$	64	59

looking at a painting, for example, you scan the painting, looking at different parts of it, and perhaps moving closer to an area to get a good look at it. It is believed that the inspection of images recruits some of the same processes that are used in inspecting the world in perception. Several sources of evidence indicate that this is true; visual perception and imagery interfere with each other if you attempt to inspect different objects, and the two processes complement each other when you inspect a single object.

Especially striking are demonstrations by Ronald Finke and his associates (see Finke, 1996, for a review) that participants can use imagery to combine simple parts and then see unexpected wholes on the visual image. For example, Finke, Steven Pinker, and Martha Farah (1989) showed that participants can manipulate mental images of simple figures and recognize the resulting patterns as something different from what they started with. Here are the instructions participants heard. The first item was for practice. (The answers appear at the end of the chapter.)

Practice

Imagine the letter Q. Put the letter O next to it on the left. Remove the diagonal line. Now rotate the figure 90 degrees to the left. The pattern is the number 8.

Test Items

1. Imagine the number 7. Make the diagonal line vertical. Move the horizontal line down to the middle of the vertical line. Now rotate the figure 90 degrees to the left. What is it?

2. Imagine the letter B. Rotate it 90 degrees to the left. Put a triangle directly below it having the same width and pointing down. Remove the horizontal line. What is it?

3. Imagine the letter Y. Put a small circle at the bottom of it. Add a horizontal line halfway up. Now rotate the figure 180 degrees. What is it?

4. Imagine the letter K. Place a square next to it on the left side. Put a circle inside the square. Now rotate the figure 90 degrees to the left. What is it?

5. Imagine a plus sign. Add a vertical line on the left side. Rotate the figure 90 degrees to the right. Now remove all lines to the left of the vertical line. What is it?

6. Imagine the letter D. Rotate it 90 degrees to the right. Put the number 4 above it. Now remove the horizontal segment of the 4 to the right of the vertical line. What is it?

The transformations were successfully carried out 58.1% of the time (so the final image looked the way the experimenters intended). When the transformations were executed correctly, participants could identify the object that the new resulting pattern depicted 59.7% of the time. Thus, this task is not trivially easy, but it is quite possible to mentally manipulate images, inspect the results, and in so doing discover a new emergent pattern.

Another aspect of image inspection is the ability to inspect different parts of an image in isolation from other parts. We have already discussed this ability earlier, when we talked about Kosslyn's (1975) results showing that participants can zoom in on parts of an image when necessary to inspect a specific subpart. For example, a participant might focus on a rabbit's nose to determine whether it is pink and even rescale the size of the image if necessary to make this determination (see also Bundesen & Larsen, 1975, for more on size rescaling).

It seems that we would need to shift attention to various locations of the visual image to inspect different parts of it. There is evidence that this attentional process has much in common with those that support visual perception. These data come from patients with brain damage. Edoardo Bisiach and Claudio Luzzatti (1978) tested patients with **hemispatial neglect** who ignore half the visual world (almost always the patient's left side). This is a deficit of attention, not perception. Visual perception is normal if attention can somehow be focused on the neglected side of the world, but under most circumstances it cannot. The patient behaves as if that side of the world does not exist. If you show the patient a painting and ask for a description, the left side will be ignored. If you ask the patient to split a candy bar down the middle, the cut will be made about three-fourths of the way to the right: The left half is ignored, so the patient divides the half that he or she sees.

Remarkably, this deficit of attention extends to visual imagery. Bisiach and Luzzatti (1978) asked the patients to imagine taking a walk around Milan, their hometown. At one point, patients were asked to "walk" into the Piazza del Duomo, a well-known square in Milan, and describe what they saw; they described landmarks on the right side of the piazza (see Figure 9.9). Patients were asked to continue their mental walk and again enter the Piazza del Duomo and describe what they saw, but this time from the opposite end of the square. Patients again described only objects on the right side, but because they entered from the other side, they were now describing the objects they had previously ignored. These patients can image the whole square, but because of their attention deficit, either they image just half of it at a time, or they image the whole thing but cannot direct attention to the left side of the image. In either case, the important point is that the perceptual deficit extends to imagery. The implication is that attention is directed to inspect both the parts of an image and perceptual scenes in the same way.

Image Transformation

We mentioned earlier that image transformation is used to examine the consequences of a physical action before we go to the trouble of taking the physical action. Will your car fit in that tight parking space? Is this brick the right size to prop up the sofa with the missing leg?

In the course of this chapter, we have described some of the ways in which images can be transformed. A list of these transformations (as well as

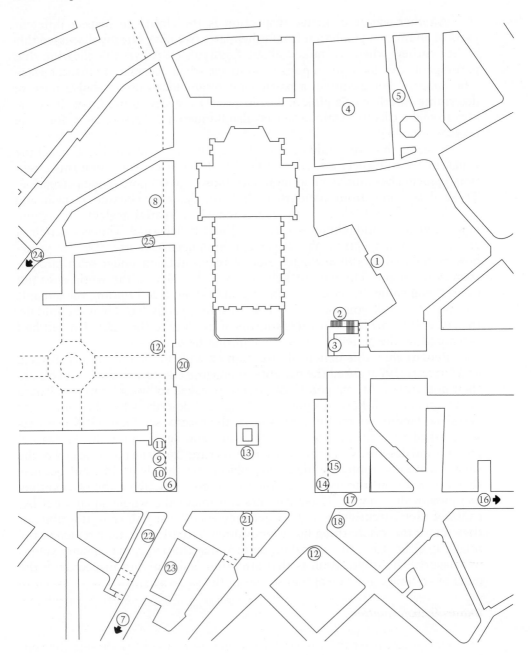

Figure 9.9. Map of the Piazza del Duomo in Milan. Patients first imagined the square as if looking at the front of the cathedral from the opposite side of the square (bottom of the figure). They described almost exclusively locations on their right: the Royal Palace (1), the stairs (2), and the Archiepiscopal palace (4). When the same patients later imagined themselves looking in the square from the reverse perspective, they failed to mention these sights (now on their left), instead mentioning places on the opposite side of the square: a jeweler's shop (9), a shirt shop (10), and the Galleria (20).

Table 9.4. Image Transformations

Transformation	Description	Citation
Rotation	Rotate the image about an axis.	Shepard & Metzler (1971)
Expansion and contraction	Expand (or shrink) an image in size.	Bundesen & Larsen (1975)
Sequenced transformation	Apply more than one spatial manipulation in a sequence.	Sekuler & Nash (1972)
Folding parts to make a whole	Move parts of an object that have limitations on how they can move to make a whole with a different shape (e.g., fold paper to make a box).	Shepard & Feng (1972)
Transforming color	Change the color of an object.	Watkins & Schiano (1982)

some that we haven't discussed) appears in Table 9.4. Most of the work examining the transformation of visual images has asked participants to rotate the images. An important result of this work is the conclusion that mental image transformation faithfully reflects the physical properties of objects. Mental images in motion obey the same laws of motion as real objects. How do we know that?

Objects in the world rotate all of a piece; that is, you don't see one part rotating, then the next part rotating, and so on. Thus, the complexity of the object (how many parts it has) doesn't affect the ease with which we can perceive the object rotating. The same should be true of imagery. Lynn Cooper (1975) tested this hypothesis, using made-up objects with different numbers of angles to represent different levels of object complexity. Figure 9.10 shows both a simple and a complex object used in this experiment. Participants first underwent training to learn which orientation was to be considered standard and which was mirror reversed. In later sessions, participants were asked to judge whether the standard or mirror-reversed figure was presented, but the figures were rotated either 0, 60, 120, or 180 degrees from the training orientation. The critical question was whether the time it took for participants to make the rotation varied with the complexity of the object, and the answer is that it did not. It's as easy to image a complex object rotating as a simple one, just as it's equally easy to perceive the rotation of a complex object or a simple object.

A second source of evidence that mental transformations mirror the real world is that imaging rotations takes longer if the rotation would be difficult in the real world. Parsons (1987) showed participants drawings of hands and asked

Form B

Form H

Figure 9.10.   A simple and a complex figure from Cooper's (1975) experiment.

them to judge whether each one was a right or a left hand (see Figure 9.11). The data showed that, as with other stimuli, greater rotation took a longer time. More interesting was that it took longer to make the judgment if the rotational movement would be uncomfortable to make because of a biomechanical constraint—that is, because of the way the joint is constructed. (Parsons had participants rate the comfort of different hand positions.)

Participants saw the right hand, palm down, as the "standard" hand, and the hand was rotated through various angles. Parsons recorded the time it took respondents to judge whether the hand shown was a right or a left hand. Participants were much slower to identify a hand with the thumb pointing down than one with the thumb pointing up, even though both positions were 90-degree rotations from the "standard" hand. This result indicates that participants performed this task by imagining their own hands making the required transformation and that when they would be slow to assume a particular position

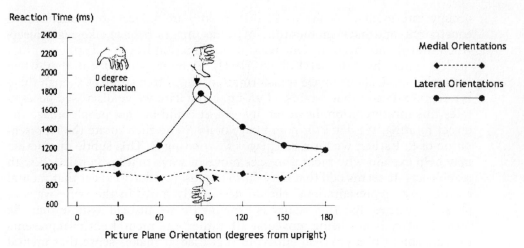

Figure 9.11. Stimuli from Parson's (1987) experiment. Figure 8 from Parsons, L. M. (1987). Imagined spatial transformations of one's hands and feet. Cognitive Psychology, 19, p. 196 Publisher is Academic press.

(as with the right thumb pointing down) they were slow to mentally image taking that position (see also Cooper & Shepard, 1975). Again, this result is consistent with the idea that mental imagery mirrors what occurs in perception.

More evidence that mental images mirror perception comes from experiments showing that rotating images have momentum. There is no reason an image of a rotating object shouldn't be able to stop on a dime, except that a real object doesn't do that. But how do we know that when participants imagine a rotating object, they actually imagine it rotating just a bit beyond the stopping place they might intend because of momentum? Jennifer Freyd and Ronald Finke (1984) tested this possibility by showing participants three pictures of a rectangle in successive positions of rotation, telling them to remember the third picture (the target). The experimenters then showed the participants a test picture, which they were to compare with the target picture. Presumably, they would compare the test picture (which was visible) with an image of the target. The experimenters reasoned that if rotating images have momentum, participants would likely remember the target picture as continuing the rotation slightly and should say that the test picture was the same as the target if the test actually continued the rotation slightly. That's exactly what the results showed. If the test stimulus continued the rotation, participants made errors about 45% of the time. If the test stimulus was rotated slightly the wrong way, they made errors only 5% of the time. Freyd and Finke interpreted these results as showing that the rotation continues to a small extent, so there is momentum in the rotation of a visual image, just as there is in the rotation of a real object (see also Freyd, 1987; Munger, Solberg, & Horrocks, 1999).

We have seen that mental images show many of the same properties of actual physical objects. Mental images, like real objects, rotate holistically, occupy intermediate positions as they rotate, are subject to biomechanical constraints, and have momentum. Why do images behave like real objects when they do not need to? One possible explanation lies in a distinction first made explicit by Michael Kubovy (1983). Kubovy pointed out that when researchers talk about image transformation, they often speak as though there is a representation that rotates. Nothing in the data we've discussed necessitates this interpretation, however. Instead, it could be that people image the object rotating. We don't form an image of an *R* and then rotate the representation of *R*. Rather, we form an image of a rotating *R*. This subtle distinction may help explain why mental images move in ways that are consistent with real objects. It seems odd that they do so because we don't expect that mental entities (e.g., representations) should necessarily move in the same ways as physical entities. But this oddity is explained if we instead assume that the mental entity is not being moved at all; rather, the mental entity represents the movement of a physical entity. In that case, it makes sense that mental images move as physical objects because they represent the physical world.

In this chapter, we focused on a function that can take place entirely inside the head; however, as we've seen, it is nevertheless affected by properties of the physical world. In chapter 10, this relationship is reversed. We discuss the topic in cognitive psychology that is the most grounded in physical reality—how we move—and we observe how this physical process is influenced by our mental make-up.

Stand-on-One-Foot Questions

10. *Name the key processes involved in using visual imagery.*
11. *Describe the difference between visual imagery and spatial imagery, and describe the anatomic locations of each.*
12. *How do we know that images are generated by parts, not all at once?*

Questions That Require Two Feet

13. *What evidence have we discussed in this chapter that is relevant to Baddeley's working memory theory?*
14. *Many of the functions of imagery described in this chapter are closely tied to imagery itself. We've talked about using transformations to imagine the outcome of moving physical objects, and we've talked about the memory function of imagery. Can you think of another cognitive process that imagery might help?*
15. *How good is your ability to generate images of smells? Relate your perceived ability to the potential function of this imagery ability.*

KEY TERMS

abstract words
analog
concrete words
demand characteristics
dual coding hypothesis
epiphenomenon
hemispatial neglect

homunculus
image inspection
Occam's razor
parsimonious
picture theory of
   imagery
proposition

spatial imagery
tacit knowledge
visual imagery

CURRENT DIRECTIONS IN COGNITIVE SCIENCE

Recommended reading

Behrmann, M. (2000). "The mind's eye mapped onto the brain's matter." (pp. 11–18) Behrman offers a more detailed view of the brain basis of mental imagery than we outlined here. She also discusses the laterality issue. It was once believed that mental imagery was a "right brain" function. We now know that characterization is simplistic, and Behrman provides a more realistic view of laterality and imagery.

Answers to imagery questions on p. 294

1. The letter *T*
2. A heart
3. A stick figure person
4. A television
5. The letter *F*
6. A sailboat

How Do We Select a Movement?

- Efficiency Theories
- Synergy Theories
- The Mass Spring Model

How Are Movements Sequenced?

- Motor Program Theories
- Hierarchical Control in Motor Programs
- Sequencing in the Brain

How Is Perceptual Information Integrated Into Ongoing Movements?

- Vision
- Proprioception

How Are Motor Skills Learned?

- Three Properties of Motor Skill Learning
- Two Approaches to Motor Skill Learning

The end product of thought is usually behavior, and behavior entails some movement: You shift your eyes to look at something, you reach to move a pawn in a chess game, you dance closer to an attractive stranger. **Motor control** refers to our ability to plan and execute movements. In this chapter when we speak of motor control, we're talking about the physical process of getting a movement accomplished, not *why* we want to make the movement. In other words, our topic concerns accomplishing a goal, not choosing one.

Among the various cognitive functions, motor control is rather like visual perception in that it is difficult to appreciate the difficulty and complexity of the function precisely because humans are so good at it. Attempts to get machines to make coordinated movements have been, in many instances, impressive, but they still have a distance to go until they equal biological systems.

A few years ago, researchers developed a "robot rat" (Talwar, Xu, Hawley, Weiss, Moxon, & Chapin, 2002). A human using a computer keyboard can get a living rat to move forward, and to turn right or left, via operant conditioning. How does it work? Electrodes implanted in the rat's brain can stimulate two centers: One electrode stimulates neurons that would be activated if something touched the rat's whiskers, and the other stimulates a reward center that makes the rat feel good. The whisker neurons provide cues for which direction the rat should move; if the rat then makes the correct movement, it is rewarded by stimulation of the reward center. The rat carries the electrodes and the other equipment on a little backpack so the rat is free moving, and the equipment can include a small camera so the researcher can see where the rat is going. The researchers suggested that the robot rat could be useful on rough terrain where robots have trouble moving (as in rubble left after an earthquake). This comparison of the robot rat and the mechanical robot is notable: Biological systems (humans or rats) can figure out ways of moving in environments that are difficult to negotiate and that they have never seen before. Why are biological systems better than robotic systems?

To answer that question, we have to understand some requirements for *all* moving things, whether animal or robot. For a movement system to be effective, it must have flexibility so any given movement can be made many different ways, even something simple such as flipping on a light switch. Flexibility is important because there are times when the environment will prevent you from using your usual strategy, for example, an obstacle in front of a switch might force an awkward reach instead of the more typical reach. There are also times that your body does the same, for example, if you're carrying groceries you might flip the switch with your elbow. The fact that we have more than one way we can execute a movement raises the question: Given that we're usually *not* limited, **How do we select a movement?** The obvious answer might be "Pick the simplest," but as we'll see, there are several ways to define simplicity. It may be that the motor system combines several different principles to select the appropriate movement.

The foregoing question makes it sound as though we select one movement at a time, although that is not the case. Rather, we must assemble sequences of multiple movements. One advantage that computers have over the rat (and us) is raw processing speed. It takes at least 100 ms for us to process visual feedback—somewhat less for proprioceptive feedback (the feeling of having moved). That means that we can't execute a single movement, observe its effect on the environment, make another movement, observe *its* effect, and so on. For even moderately fast movements, that would take too long, so we have to sequence movements in advance. **How are movements sequenced?** We review evidence that movements are sequenced in hierarchical programs.

When considering the robot rat (or any motor system) it is easy to focus on the motoric aspects of the rat's behavior and to forget about its reliance on perceptual information. But the ability to move through obstacle-filled terrain depends on knowing the location of the obstacles. Furthermore, it isn't enough to know where the obstacles are at the start of the movement; we want to update that perceptual information as the movement is ongoing. Imagine yourself at the end of a long, obstacle-free hallway. Assuming you are sighted, would you be comfortable walking its length blindfolded? Why not? People are used to sampling perceptual information as movements are ongoing, perhaps to update the movement plan in midstream. **How is perceptual information integrated into ongoing movements?**

A motor system also needs to incorporate learning. We usually think of motor skill learning in terms of identifiable skills that people practice, such as playing soccer or violin, but we all have a vast repertoire of motor skills that we take for granted. If your movements never improved in speed or accuracy regardless of how much you practiced, how long would it take you to tie your shoes? How safe would highways be if everyone drove as though it were their first time behind the wheel? Our final question in this chapter is **How are motor skills learned?** We discuss three basic principles of motor skill, as well as two theoretical approaches that researchers have employed.

How Do We Select a Movement?

Preview

Even the simplest reaching movement can be made in an infinite number of ways. How do we select one way to move from among these infinite choices? Three classes of theories address this problem. Efficiency theories propose that we select the most efficient movement. The problem then becomes to find the right definition of efficiency. Synergy theories suggest that the problem is minimized because many parts of the body are designed to work together in systematic ways, so there are not as many choices as it first appears. The mass spring theory proposes that the pathway of the movement does not need to be planned.

Because of its flexibility, the motor system can accomplish a given goal under different circumstances. For example, to pick up the coffee cup on my desk, I might have to reach around my computer speaker, grasp the cup handle at an awkward angle, and delicately pull the cup toward me in a curved trajectory to avoid hitting a swing-arm lamp. If my wrist were in a cast and I couldn't bend it (which I would normally do when making a reaching movement), the other parts of my arm would compensate for my wrist being immobile, and the reaching movement would still occur smoothly.

Flexibility like this is rooted in a basic property of the motor system: Any movement can be made in an infinite number of ways. Thus, when one way is made difficult or impossible by obstacles in the environment or bodily limitations, we can still find another way to make the movement. Yet, flexibility presents a problem to the psychologist interested in accounting for motor behavior. If there are an infinite number of options for performing even the simplest movement, how do we ever decide which way to make a move? This **degrees of freedom problem** can be appreciated through a simple demonstration. Grasp an object, preferably one that is immobile, but don't try to move it. Your hand is now in a new position; to get your hand to that new position, you had to move your arm. Keeping your hand immobile on the object, move your arm. You're able to move it, right? This fact shows that there was more than one way in which your arm could end up as you grasped the object; you can tell that's true because if there was only one single position in which your arm could end up, you would not have been able to move it. So why did your mind choose the final arm position it did instead of one of the other possible positions?

The endpoint of the movement is the position of your arm when your hand is at the goal position (grasping the cup). The path of movement that your hand takes on the way to the endpoint is called the **trajectory**, and it opens an infinite number of pathways to the object. An **effector** is a part of the body that you use to affect the environment, such as your hand or foot. What if you reach with your other hand, or try to grasp the cup in your teeth, or rake it toward you along the table with your forearm? These possibilities must be eliminated so a reaching movement using one endpoint, one trajectory, and one effector can be made.

Now that we have a feel for the degrees of freedom problem, we can move on to the three classes of theories that address its solutions: efficiency theories, which favor the most efficient movement possible; synergy theories, which minimize the degrees of freedom problem; and the mass spring model, which argues that trajectories are naturally "calculated" because of the way the body is designed.

Efficiency Theories

Efficiency theories claim that all possible movements toward a goal are evaluated for their efficiency, and the most efficient movement is executed. For example, moving your hand in a straight line to the cup is more efficient than moving it in a serpentine pattern. (For a review, see Todorov, 2004.)

The problem is that there are a number of measures of efficiency that sound quite reasonable. Take the idea of moving the effector the shortest distance possible. Do we mean the shortest distance in Cartesian space? But movements could instead be planned in terms of **joint space**, a representation for planning movements that uses joint angles. You can think of getting your hand to a desired location by setting your joints at particular angles. The most efficient movement might not be the one that makes your hand travel the shortest distance in Cartesian space, but the one that makes you move your joints the shortest distance. These definitions of efficiency lead to different movements.

When we consider how joint angles are derived, we realize that they are set by muscle contractions that create torques on the joints. Perhaps, therefore, efficiency should be defined as the movement that calls for the minimum joint torque (Nakano et al., 1999; Nozaki, Nakazawa, & Akai, 2005; Uno, Kawato, & Suzuki, 1989). One potential problem with this solution is that nothing in the nervous system is set up to detect torque change. Muscle torque should be directly related to the tension exerted on muscles, however, so another potential solution would be to minimize muscle stiffness (Hasan, 1986), or to minimize the energy that muscles use (e.g., Anderson & Pandy, 2001; Rasmusssen, Damsgaard, & Voigt, 2001).

Another definition of efficiency takes advantage not only of the spatial characteristics of movement, but also of the typical profile of movement speed. Your hand picks up speed slowly, reaches maximum speed in the middle of the movement, and then decreases speed slowly. If the hand increased or decreased speed very rapidly, we would say that the movement was jerky. We can define **jerk** (in a reaching movement) as the rate of acceleration of the wrist. Tamar Flash and Neville Hogan (1985; see also Smeets & Brenner, 1999) proposed that the degrees of freedom problem is solved by selecting the movement that minimizes jerk.

Which of these definitions of efficiency is the correct one to solve the degrees of freedom problem—distance traveled in Cartesian space, distance traveled in joint space, joint torque, joint stiffness, or effector jerk? The usual strategy to compare these hypotheses is to make precise measurements (e.g., the speed at different points during the reach, or the shape of the trajectory) and then compare models based on these different principles to see which one most accurately predicts how people move. Most of the models are fairly good at predicting the main features of movement; the tests are rather technical. (For examples of this sort of work, see Admiraal, Kusters, & Gielen, 2004; Gomi & Kawato, 1996; Todorov & Jordan, 1998.)

Synergy Theories

Some researchers have emphasized that although any movement can be performed in many different ways, some possibilities are eliminated because muscles are designed to work together; they do not need to be independently controlled all the time. There are more than 600 muscles in the human body. Each can take two states—contracted or relaxed—so in theory there are 2^{600} possible states for the system as a whole. We can immediately cut that number in half because there is a strong bias in the system for opposing muscles to

Start   Finish

Task 1

Task 2

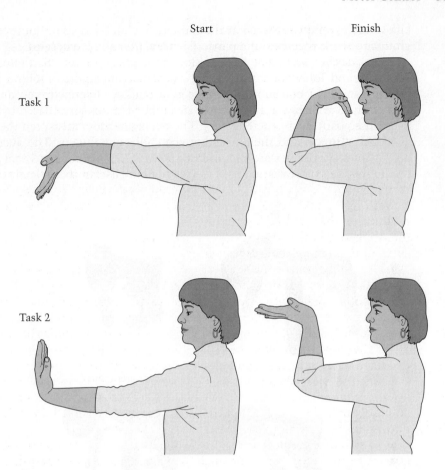

Figure 10.1.   Example of a synergy. In Task 1, start with both your elbow and your wrist extended (your knuckles are as close to your forearm as possible). Then, simultaneously flex your elbow and flex your wrist. In Task 2, start with your elbow extended but your wrist flexed. Now, flex your elbow, but extend your wrist. This movement is much harder, indicating that there is a synergy for your elbow and wrist to be flexed or extended together, not in opposition.

take opposite states. Muscles are organized in pairs on opposite sides of a joint; when one contracts, the opposite muscle relaxes to allow the bone to move at the joint. (Muscles can only pull—they can't push.)

But coordinated organization goes beyond pairs of muscles. Joints are also biased to work together. To see this, extend your elbow so your arm is straight, and extend your wrist so the back of your hand is as close to your forearm as you can get it, as shown in "Task 1, Start," in Figure 10.1. Now, flex your wrist and your elbow at the same time so you end up as shown in "Task 1, Finish." That should be fairly easy. Now, start again, with your elbow extended, but this time with your wrist already flexed, as shown in "Task 2, Start." This time *extend* your wrist while you flex your elbow, so you end up as shown in "Task 2, Finish." Task 2 should be much more difficult than Task 1. Typically, the wrist and elbow either flex or extend together, so it is difficult to flex your elbow and extend your wrist at the same time. Such biases for joints or muscle groups to work together in a particular way are called **synergies**.

To derive formal evidence for synergies, Marco Santello, Martha Flanders, and John Soechting (1998) asked participants to pretend that they were grasping 57 common objects (e.g., a bucket, a screwdriver, and a door-knob) while wearing a glove with 15 embedded sensors that provided data about the positions of their fingers. The experimenters measured the joint angles of the fingers and the angles between adjacent fingers. The average hand postures for six objects are shown in Figure 10.2. The data were analyzed with a complex set of statistical procedures called discriminant analysis, which

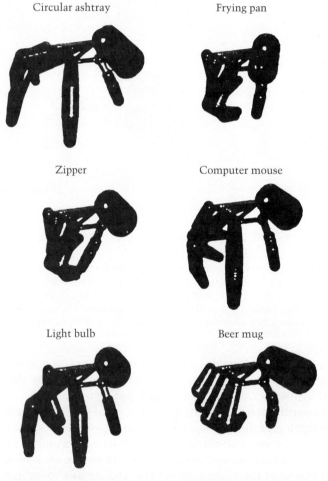

Circular ashtray

Frying pan

Zipper

Computer mouse

Light bulb

Beer mug

Figure 10.2. Reproduction of average hand postures produced by one subject for six different objects. To make it easier to compare postures, the hand has been rotated so the palm is always downward. From "Postural Hand Synergies for Tool Use," by M. Santello, M. Flanders, and J. F. Soechting, 1998, *Journal of Neuroscience, 18,* Fig. 2, p. 10107.

basically tells how different the hand postures are for various items. The analysis showed that certain joint angles were frequently correlated; for example, the angles of the second joint of the ring finger and the second joint of the pinky were usually very similar. Looking at the postures overall, the experimenters determined that two basic postures account for most of the difference among the grasps that participants made. The experimenters concluded that there may be just a few synergies that regulate the basic shape of the hand, along with a mechanism that makes finer adjustments for different objects. Researchers have also examined kicking, a natural defensive behavior in the frog. They showed that three basic synergies can be combined in different ways to allow the frog to kick in different directions (d'Avella, Saltiel, & Bizzi, 2004; see also d'Avella & Bizzi, 2005).

Evidence for synergies can be found not only in grasping, but also in reaching. Some movements could make you unsteady on your feet; for example, when you use an elevator, your center of gravity changes when you reach toward the controls because your arm has mass, and the pressure you exert pushing a floor button also pushes your body backward. Yet, reaching, pressing, or pulling something doesn't ordinarily make you unsteady because you make **anticipatory postural adjustments**, muscle contractions that correct for the change in your center of gravity. Such corrections are necessary when the surface you are standing on shifts, and also when you change your center of gravity by moving some other part of your body—for example, pushing an elevator button. The particular type of anticipatory postural adjustment—in the back, legs, abdomen, and so on—is designed to counteract whatever is making you unstable (Nashner, Woollacott, & Tuma, 1979). Although there are many ways that you might become unstable, it is believed that a relatively small number of synergies combine to achieve this task, and more recent evidence indicates that's true. Lena Ting and Jane Macpherson (2005) recorded data from hindlimb muscles in cats that stood on moving platforms. The resulting muscle activations were very complex, but a mathematical analysis revealed that they had a relatively simple underlying structure consistent with the synergy theory. The researchers argued that the muscle activity pattern is well explained by a model that uses four basic synergies, each of which can be scaled to have greater or less force (see also Krishnamoorthy, Latash, Scholz, & Zatsiorsky, 2003, for an example in humans).

The Mass Spring Model

The degrees of freedom problem is made more manageable if trajectories are not calculated. How is that possible? The **mass spring model** capitalizes on a biomechanical property of the way our muscles and limbs are designed: They can be likened to springs. As a simple analogy, consider a café door that swings in either direction. It is mounted on hinges with springs so when you push and release the door, the springs push it back toward the jamb, the door's inertia takes it past the jamb, the spring brings it back to the center, and it continues

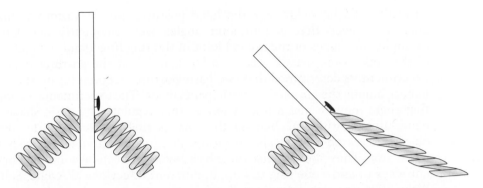

Figure 10.3. The café door analogy of muscles and joints. If a door can move freely in a door jamb and is set with springs on each side, the door will always return to the center of the jamb if the springs are of equal tension. If the springs are not of equal tension, as shown in the right side of the figure, then the door will not return to the center of the jamb.

to swing in smaller arcs until finally coming to rest in the center of the door jamb. Why does the door come to a rest in the middle of the door jamb? Obviously, it does so because the springs are of equal tension. You don't need to know the path the door is going to take to know where it will stop. If one spring were too tight, the door would end up not in the middle of the jamb but more to one side, as shown in Figure 10.3. Your muscles and joints can be likened to the café door. Joints move when muscles contract, pulling the bone. You can move the position of a joint by changing the tension of the muscles attached to it.

If you changed the tension of the springs on the door, you wouldn't need to know the path that the door would take to get to its endpoint. Similarly, perhaps if you change the tension of your muscles, you won't know the path your hand will take. All you really care about is its endpoint. You could just set the opposing muscle tensions so your hand will end up in the right stopping place; you don't need to plan the trajectory, so there is a huge reduction in the complexity of the degrees of freedom problem.

To test this hypothesis, Andres Polit and Emilio Bizzi (1978) had a monkey sit in a chair facing a line of lights, as shown in Figure 10.4. The monkey's forearm was strapped to a hinged rod so it could sweep in an arc parallel to the floor, and the monkey's view of its arm was blocked by a collar. The task was to swing the forearm to point at a light when it came on. When successful, the monkey was rewarded with a sip of fruit juice. A motor at the hinge allowed the rod to be moved by the experimenter, who would displace the rod to the right or left in midmovement. The monkey was very good at recovering from the displacement and pointing the rod at the light. This result is not all that surprising. The arm wasn't visible, but the monkey could feel that its arm had been displaced because special receptors in the joints, skin, and muscles detect the location of the parts of the body. This sensation of body location is called **proprioception**.

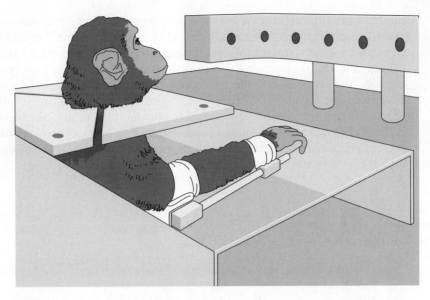

Figure 10.4.   A monkey in position to respond in Polit and Bizzi's (1978) experiment. From "Characteristics of Motor Programs Underlying Arm Movements in Monkeys," in A. Polit and E. Bizzi, 1979, *Journal of Neurophysiology, 42,* Fig. 1, p. 184.

Now comes the interesting result. Pollit and Bizzi cut the dorsal roots of the spinal cord, which meant that the monkey received no proprioceptive information from its arm to its brain; the arm felt completely numb. But the monkey still made accurate pointing movements, even when the experimenters disturbed the location of the arm in midmovement. How is that possible? The monkey could not see or feel its arm. Wouldn't the monkey have to know that its arm had been displaced so it could correct for the displacement?

This puzzling result is explained in terms of the mass spring theory. Just as a café door ends up in the middle of the door jamb even if you knock it out of place, the monkey's limb ends up pointing to the light even when it is knocked out of place. Just as the café door's final location is fixed by the tension of the springs and it doesn't need to "know" that it has been displaced to end up there, the final position of the monkey's arm is determined when the monkey sets the tension of opposing muscles, and it does not need to know that the arm has been displaced. (For another theory emphasizing the endpoints of movements but using a different approach, see Feldman, 1986; Flash & Gurevich, 1997.)

Some more recent evidence provides provocative neurophysiological evidence favoring the mass spring model. Michael Graziano and his colleagues (Graziano, Taylor, & Moore, 2002) electrically stimulated the primary and secondary motor cortices of monkeys while their arms were unconstrained. Stimulation studies done in the past had almost always used brief (50 ms) pulses of stimulation; this study stimulated for 500 ms. The researchers argued that this value is closer to the length of time accompanying normal reaching and grasping. They found that the stimulation evoked complex movements across many joints—for example, when one brain site was stimulated, the monkey opened its mouth, put its hand in a grip position, and brought the hand to the mouth. Most remarkable, this complex movement was executed *regardless of the starting position of the limbs.* In other words, the stimulation predicted the endpoints of the movement, not the particulars of how the movement would be executed. This result provides nice physiological support for the mass spring model and other models emphasizing the endpoints of movements.

Stand-on-One-Foot Questions

1. *What are the three main approaches to solving the degrees of freedom problem?*
2. *Which criteria of efficiency have been proposed for efficiency theories?*
3. *Is it possible to move against a synergy?*

Questions That Require Two Feet

4. *What is the heart of the degrees of freedom problem, and is it always a problem?*
5. *The mass spring theory proposes that trajectories aren't planned. Wouldn't that pose a problem when there is an obstacle between your hand and the thing you want to reach? How do you avoid bumping into the obstacle if you don't plan the trajectory?*

How Are Movements Sequenced?

Preview

An important theory of movement sequencing is the motor program idea, which argues for a representation of movement sequences that can be executed without perceptual feedback. The latest evidence supports the program idea, although in a form modified from the original proposal. Some evidence shows that programs have movements organized in hierarchies.

The previous section discussed simple movements such as reaching, but often our movements are more complex. You don't simply reach for a cup of coffee: You reach for it, grasp it, bring it to your mouth, tip the cup, swallow the coffee, replace the cup, and release the handle. These parts of the movement must be executed in the correct sequence or you'll end up with coffee in your lap. Movements are planned several components at a time. How are complex sequences of motor behavior generated?

Motor Program Theories

Steven Keele (1981; Keele & Posner, 1968) proposed that complex motor control may be directed by a **motor program**, which can be likened to a computer program in that it has a list of motor commands to be executed in order. The motor program has had slightly different definitions at different times, but the key concept has three features:

1. A program contains a full set of commands for movement.
2. These commands can be executed without the need for perceptual feedback.
3. The commands are abstract, meaning that they can be applied to more than one set of muscles.

The concept is general enough that a number of different theories could be described as motor program theories. Still, the three principles listed previously are specific enough to be tested, and the evidence generally supports these principles.

The idea that a motor program contains a list of commands is supported by data showing that the time it takes to initiate a series of movements depends on the number of movements in the series. Franklin Henry and Donald Rogers (1960) were the first to describe this effect. In some cases, they had participants hold down a telegraph key, and then release it. In other cases, participants were to release the telegraph key, and then grab a tennis ball. In other cases, a third movement was tacked on; participants knew in advance what the required movement sequence was, and a tone indicated when they should start the sequence. Henry and Rogers observed that the time to release the telegraph key increased with the complexity of the movement sequence. Similar effects have been observed in other motor tasks, such as typing (Sternberg, Monsell, Knoll, & Wright, 1978; Verwey, 1999) and speech (Klapp, Anderson, & Berrian, 1973). Why should the number of movement components to be made *later* affect how quickly a person makes the first movement? It appears that we don't plan a movement, execute it, plan the next movement, execute it, and so on. Rather, we plan a sequence of movements all at once.

The second feature of the motor program is that perceptual feedback is not needed for its execution. As described previously, experiments by Taub and his colleagues showed convincingly that monkeys can still produce a number of actions (walking, climbing, reaching) even if they lack proprioception (Taub & Berman, 1968). Studies of humans show that they are less accurate than monkeys when deprived of proprioception, but they are nevertheless able to make movements (e.g., Rothwell, Traub, Day, Obeso, Thomas, & Marsden, 1982). Although the gross features of motor programs are probably executable without perceptual feedback, feedback seems to be quite important for ongoing movements. In a later section of this chapter, we discuss how perceptual feedback is used, but for the moment, suffice it to say that it's probably true that motor programs can be executed without feedback. It's also true that programs seem to use feedback to fine-tune the movements.

The third feature of the motor program is that it can be applied to different muscle groups. Suppose that I asked you to write a phrase with your dominant hand, and then to write the same phrase with your nondominant hand or with a pen attached to your foot. Your writing would be sloppier when you wrote in these unfamiliar ways, but the handwriting would still look like yours, not someone else's. Figure 10.5 gives a demonstration of this phenomenon, first shown by Bernstein (1947, reprinted in Keele, Cohen, & Ivry, 1990; see also Castiello & Stelmach, 1993; Wing, 2000). Two things are clear from the figure. The overall shape of the writing is roughly similar, but the writing does differ in legibility. Indeed, more detailed analysis shows that there are important differences in the timing and fluency of the strokes (Wright, 1990). These differences are understandable, given the likely differences in the coordination of the limbs, which are used for quite different tasks. The phenomenon is also observed with tasks other than handwriting (e.g., Keele, Jennings, Jones, Caulton, & Cohen, 1995).

We have discussed three sources of data consistent with an abstract motor program. Programs contain sets of commands for motor movements; these commands can be executed without perceptual feedback; and these commands can be applied to different effectors. The data we have reviewed tell us that the program idea seems to be at least partly right; programs can be executed without perceptual feedback and can be applied to different effectors, although the resulting movements are not as skilled under these circumstances.

Hierarchical Control in Motor Programs

There is compelling evidence that motor sequences are organized hierarchically. A hierarchy is simply a tree diagram (see Figure 10.6). The circles in the diagram are called nodes, and the lines connecting the nodes are called links, just as in the network memory models described in chapter 8.

In most hierarchical sequencing schemes, **movement nodes** are proposed to control the muscles that make movement possible. The nodes above them in the tree are **control nodes** that tell the movement nodes what to do. Thus, in Figure 10.6, node 4 would make the right finger, and then the left index finger, flex.

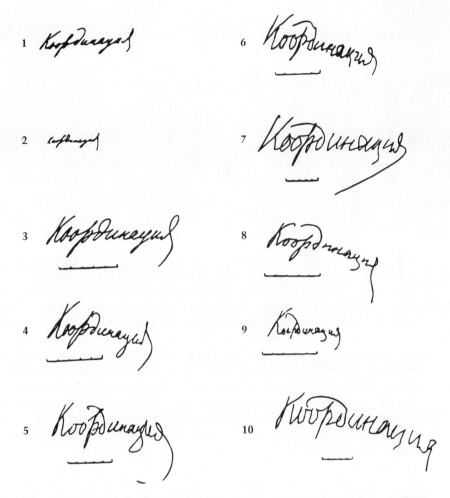

Figure 10.5. You can try this experiment yourself. This example in Russian shows handwriting produced when a pen is held by different effectors. In each case, the writing retains the same overall shape. The words were written with the pen held normally (1, 2), with the hand moving as a unit (3), with the pen attached near the wrist (4), with the pen attached near the elbow (5), with the pen attached to the shoulder (6), with the pen attached to the right shoe (7), with the pen held in the teeth (8), with the pen held by the left hand (9), and with the pen attached to the left shoe (10). The size of the writing has been scaled to fit the figure; the scale for each trial shows centimeters. From "Motor Programs: Concepts and Issues," by S. W. Keele, A. Cohen, and R. Ivry, 1990, in *Attention and Performance 13: Motor Representation and Control*, M. Jeannerod, Ed., Hillsdale, NJ: Erlbaum, p. 89. Figure from Bernstein, N. A. (1947). [On the formation of movement]. Published in Russian by State Medical Literature Publisher (Medgiz).

David Rosenbaum, Sandra Kenny, and Marcia Derr (1983; see also Rosenbaum, Inhoff, & Gordon, 1984) tested this idea by having participants practice some sequences of key presses such as *IiIiMmMm*, where *I* and *i* refer to the index fingers of the right and left hands, respectively, and *M* and *m* refer to the middle fingers of the right and left hands, respectively. Participants

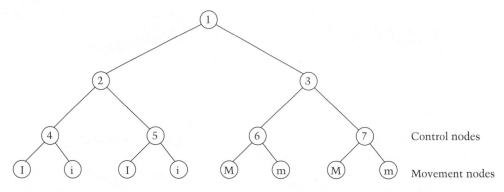

Figure 10.6.   Hypothetical hierarchy that could control movement. The movement nodes control muscles that move fingers. *I*, index finger right hand; *i*, index finger left hand; *M*, middle finger right hand; *m*, middle finger left hand. The control nodes tell the movement nodes what to do.

were asked to produce these responses as quickly as possible. The experimenters were mainly interested in the time between key presses. They started with the simple assumption that nodes on the tree must be traversed to execute a response. For example, the first two key presses (*Ii*) have just one node between them (node 4). But the next key press (*I*) requires traversing three nodes (4, 2, and 5). Making the further assumption that it takes time to traverse nodes, the experimenters could make predictions about the time between key presses. The researchers found that the number of nodes traversed in the hierarchy was an extremely good predictor of the time between key presses, as shown in Figure 10.7. (See Rhodes, Bullock, Verwey, Averbeck, & Page, 2004, for a review.)

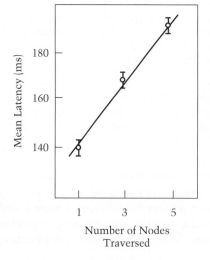

Figure 10.7.   Results from Rosenbaum et al. (1983) supporting the hypothesis that movements are planned hierarchically in a key pressing task. The graph shows that the time between key presses depends on the number of nodes that must be traversed for the next key press (assuming they are organized in a hierarchy). From "Hierarchical Control of Rapid Movement Sequences," by D. A. Rosenbaum, S. B. Kenny, and M. A. Derr, 1983, *Journal of Experimental Psychology: Human Perception and Performance, 9,* Fig. 3, p. 93.

Other evidence supports the idea of levels of a hierarchy, with lower levels controlling motor output and higher levels supporting more abstract representations of desired output. Donald MacKay and Robert Bowman (1969) tested this idea in a clever way with English/German bilingual participants in a speech production task. Participants practiced saying aloud an odd sequence of words, "I have rearranged this bed fourteen times in one morning," and they got faster at saying it with practice. After a short break, participants switched languages and had to say another sentence as quickly as possible in their other language. This transfer sentence was either the same sentence they had just practiced or a new sentence, and participants were faster when it was the same; thus, the benefit of practicing a sequence of words transfers to a new language.

The experimenters argued that the results reveal two levels of control. The bottom level controls the articulators (tongue, lips) that pronounce the words, and participants are so practiced in making these movements that they really can't improve much. A higher, more abstract level controls the words that are to be said, and when creating a novel sentence (especially the odd one used in the experiment) there is a lot of room for improvement. When asked to switch into the other language, the participants were still able to use that abstract representation; they could employ a different set of rules to translate these abstract representations into commands to the articulators.

There appears to be good evidence for motor programs that are abstract in that they can be applied to different effectors. There is also evidence that more complex programs take increasing time to generate. Furthermore, it appears that motor programs are represented as multilevel hierarchies.

Sequencing in the Brain

There is good evidence for these multiple levels of organization in the brain, indicating the secondary motor cortices—the supplementary motor area and premotor cortex—are important for planning, whereas the primary motor cortex is important for execution. Many studies have been conducted using brain imaging techniques and asking participants to plan a movement, but not to execute it—that is, to imagine making the movement. A study by Martin Lotze and his colleagues (1999) is typical. They had participants engage in a 60- to 90-min training period during which they imagined making a fist and opening their hand in time to a metronome. The participants were to work on making the imagery as vivid as possible, but the experimenters also recorded electromyographic activity to ensure the participants were not making any muscle movements. This training is important because when asked to vividly imagine making a movement, people often make small muscle movements without realizing it. After this training period, participants were scanned with fMRI while they either imagined the movements or actually executed the movements. The results showed considerable activity in secondary motor cortex during motor imagery. There was activity in primary motor cortex, but less in the imagery condition than in the execution condition.

Opening and closing one's fist is not much of a sequence, but other brain imaging data show that activity in the secondary motor areas increases as participants must produce increasingly complex motor sequences (e.g., Harrington et al., 2000). These data support earlier findings using single cell recording techniques in monkeys. For example, Jun Tanji and Keisetsu Shima (1994; see Tanji & Hoshi, 2001, for a review) taught monkeys sequences of simple movements. A handle could be pushed, pulled, or turned, and monkeys learned four sequences of these three movements, each cued with a different colored light. The researchers recorded from supplementary motor cortex and found some neurons that responded specifically in preparation for a particular sequence—for example, the neuron was active once the light appeared signaling "push-pull-turn." But the neuron did not fire after the light signaling "push-turn-pull." That means that the neuron was not coding "get ready to push" but was participating in the preparation of one specific sequence. Other neurons fired between two parts of a sequence (e.g., before the "pull" in "turn-pull-push"), but the same neuron wouldn't fire before the "pull" in "push-pull-turn," which again shows that it was specific to a sequence.

In summary, the secondary motor cortices plan hierarchies of sequential movement, and the primary motor cortex is critical for executing these planned movements.

Stand-on-One-Foot Questions

6. What are the key features of a motor program?
7. What evidence is there that motor programs are organized hierarchically?

Questions That Require Two Feet

8. Initially, it was believed that motor programs don't need feedback. Now, we see that that was an overstatement. What negative consequences could you see for programs not using perceptual feedback?
9. One of the advantages of a hierarchical representation of a motor program is generalization, the ability to apply old knowledge to a new situation. Can you see why a hierarchical representation is especially well suited to generalization?

How Is Perceptual Information Integrated Into Ongoing Movements?

Preview

Both vision and proprioception make important contributions to movement. Sighted people sample visual feedback in ongoing movements frequently, although the feedback need only be brief. Proprioception is vitally important, which we know from the study of rare neurological cases. Unfortunately, the role of proprioception is difficult to study in the laboratory.

People sometimes think of perceptual and motor functions as separate, but that is not really accurate. Perception obviously influences motor activity. We gather perceptual information before making an action, as when we judge the distance of an object to determine whether we can reach it, and during an action, as when we use visual feedback in driving a car. In less obvious ways, movement also aids perception. Moving our bodies allows our sense organs to be transported to different places, and moving our eyes and head allows us to maintain a stable image of a moving object on the retina. In this section, we focus on how perceptual information informs the motor system.

Vision

In chapter 3, we discussed the evidence that there are two visual systems: the "what" system and the "how" system. The "what" system is responsible for object recognition and for determining object location, and the "how" system is responsible for determining how objects can be manipulated by the motor system. In this section, we discuss data that reveal how visual information is used by the motor system. Most of these data were collected before the what/how distinction was proposed, so they were not interpreted within that framework. Still, today we would guess that the effects discussed in this section are relevant to the "how" system.

One question of long-standing interest to researchers is the frequency with which visual information is needed. Is a reaching movement completely planned before it is initiated so it doesn't need any visual feedback along the way, or is it only partially planned so ongoing visual feedback is required to complete the movement accurately?

In one experiment, Howard Zelaznik and his colleagues (Zelaznik, Hawkins, & Kisselburgh, 1983) measured the accuracy of participants moving a stylus to a target. The researchers varied whether lights were on or off during the movement and how quickly the movement was to be made. If there is no opportunity to collect perceptual feedback during a movement, it makes no difference whether the lights are on or off. How slow does a movement have

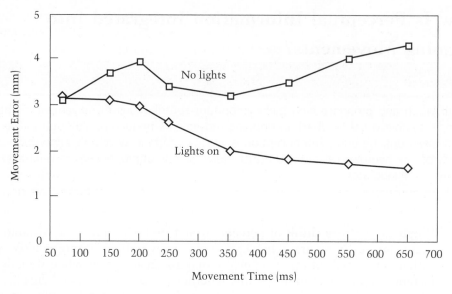

Figure 10.8. Graph showing the results of Zelaznik et al. (1983). Participants who have vision available while making a simple movement can make use of it even when the movement is as fast as 150 ms, and the advantage of having vision available increases as the movement may be made more slowly. There is no advantage for vision at the fastest movement time, which is 70 ms. Adapted from "Rapid Visual Feedback Processing in Single-Aiming Movements," by H. N. Zelaznik, B. Hawkins, and L. Kisselburgh, 1983, *Journal of Motor Behavior, 15,* Fig. 2, p. 229.

to be before having the lights on makes a difference? Figure 10.8 shows that the speed of the movement is irrelevant to accuracy when the lights are off because no perceptual feedback is available. For the fastest movements, having the lights on doesn't help (compared with the no-lights control group), but when movements take 150 ms or longer, perceptual feedback makes them more accurate.

The researchers also tried the experiment another way. They let the participant start the movement but then turned off the lights. At what point in the movement is it irrelevant if the reachers turn out the lights? How close to the target does the participant have to be before turning out the lights has no effect on the movement? The answer using this method was quite close to the other estimate; if the movement was 135 ms (or less) from completion, perceptual feedback didn't matter. (See also Carlton, 1981a, 1981b; Elliott & Allard, 1985; Spijkers & Lochner, 1994.)

The question of how visual feedback is used has also been examined by asking participants to intercept a moving target, typically by catching a ball. In these experiments, visual information is sometimes available and sometimes unavailable, and is meant to mimic real-life situations such as driving through fog or attempting to catch a baseball that is "lost in the lights." The basic finding from such studies is that constant visual information is not needed; periodic visual information can be substituted with little cost to performance (see Bennett, Rioja, Ashford, & Elliott, 2004; Elliott, Zuberec, & Milgram, 1994; Lyons, Fontaine, & Elliott, 1997; and van der Kamp, Savelsbergh, & Smeets, 1997, for this and related work).

For example, Digby Elliott and his colleagues (1994) asked participants to catch tennis balls shot from a ball machine at a distance of 8 to 12 m. The participants wore liquid-crystal spectacles that could either be transparent or opaque, controlled moment to moment by a computer. Across four experiments using a variety of conditions, what seemed to matter was getting frequent glimpses of the ball. Catching was reasonably successful (around 75%) when participants had just an 8-ms glimpse of the ball every 72 ms. But once the time between glimpses got longer than 80 ms, performance dropped quickly, even each glimpse was longer (e.g., 40-ms glimpses separated by 160 ms). It is clear, then, that visual information is used to refine ongoing movements and thus to improve accuracy, but vision is not sampled continuously. The visual system updates the ongoing motor plan periodically, as evidenced by the fact that vision can be interrupted with little cost to motor performance, and there is evidence that the system uses this feedback throughout movements (Saunders & Knill, 2003).

Proprioception

Proprioception is driven by receptors in the muscles and skin, and perhaps the joints. There are two types of receptors in the muscles: **Muscle spindles** in the fleshy part of the muscles are most active when the muscle is stretched, and **golgi tendon organs** located where muscles and tendons are joined are most active when the muscle contracts. **Cutaneous receptors** are located in and under the skin, and some of these (often called mechanoreceptors) respond when the skin is displaced by pressure. Pressure is often caused by motor movements, as when one picks up an object. To appreciate the importance of cutaneous receptors, imagine picking up a glass and being unable to tell how much pressure your grip was exerting. It would be hard to know whether you were about to crush the glass or whether it was going to slip through your fingers. Joint receptors are a type of neuron located in joints. It was initially believed that many of these receptors fired preferentially when a joint was set to a particular angle (Skoglund, 1956), but later experiments cast doubt on this interpretation; it appears that joint receptors may fire mostly in response to extreme joint angles (Clark & Burgess, 1975).

Some important information has come from neurologic patients who experience a selective loss of proprioception. One such patient, known by his first name, Ian, has been described by Cole (1995; see also Cole & Paillard, 1995, for a description of another patient with a similar problem). Ian is unusual because he has lost proprioception from the neck down. It is not rare to lose feeling in one arm or leg, but it is quite rare to lose feeling throughout the body. Ian's problem appears to have been caused by a virus that led his body's defense system to attack the nerve cells that carry proprioceptive information.

By observing Ian's difficulties, we can deduce some of the likely functions of proprioception in motor control.

Most striking is the extent to which the loss of proprioception devastated Ian's ability to move. After Ian lost proprioception, he had no control over his body. Trying to move was, in fact, dangerous as his limbs flailed uncontrollably. Nor could Ian maintain a posture. For example, if a nurse tried to seat him in a chair, he would lean sideways and flop to the floor in a disorganized heap.

Ian eventually relearned how to move by replacing his reliance on proprioception with a reliance on vision. However, this relearning process was far from easy. It took 1 year of practice before Ian could stand. In time, he learned to walk, but his movements would not be mistaken for those of a healthy person. His walking is also easily disrupted. If someone accidentally bumps into him, he will likely fall. To this day, walking requires his complete attention; there seems to have been no development of automaticity despite years of practice.

There are some types of movements for which vision is not a suitable replacement for proprioception, notably, grip strength and fine-motor movements. For example, Ian must maintain full concentration when holding an egg because it is hard for him to modulate his grip strength. If he gets distracted, he will likely crush it. Fine-motor movements refer to movements (usually of the fingers) that require multiple small adjustments, for example, buttoning buttons or writing with a pen. Vision can't replace proprioception for these small movements because the effectors (your fingers) block your view.

Formal studies verify the anecdotes from such case reports. For example, Jerome Sanes and his colleagues (Sanes, Mauritz, Dalakas, & Evarts, 1985) tested seven patients who had lost proprioception (the term for loss of proprioception is *deafferentation*). These deafferented patients had typically lost feeling in their hands or feet, varying in how far toward the trunk the loss went. The experimenters tested the patients' ability to maintain a position of the wrist and to maintain wrist position when force was applied. These tasks were performed either with or without vision of the wrist.

Patients were able to perform the tasks with vision, but without vision they could not maintain posture normally. Figure 10.9 shows the performance of the patients and one control participant when they were asked to maintain the position of the wrist joint. When visual feedback was removed, the wrists of the patients rapidly drifted in random directions.

The patients showed similar deficits in making movements. With visual feedback, their movements were quite accurate. Without the feedback, their movements had abnormal trajectories and endpoints. (See also Cole & Paillard, 1995; Fleury et al., 1995; Ghez, Gordon, Ghilardi, & Sainburg, 1995; Jackson, Jackson, Husain, Harvey, Kramer, & Dow, 2000).

We have discussed vision and proprioception separately, but your mind doesn't treat them separately. It integrates both sources of information to locate objects and parts of the body. So what happens if they suggest different locations in space for objects? Proprioception changes if the body changes (e.g., as you grow), so the brain must change its interpretation of what proprioceptive information means. If the body changes rapidly—for example, during a

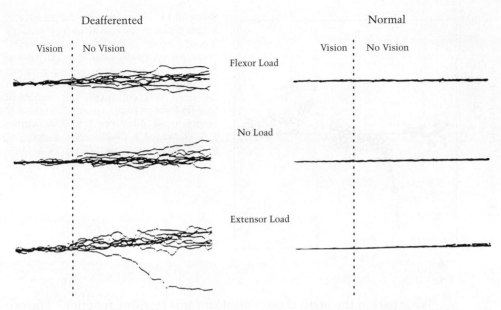

Deafferented   Normal

Vision : No Vision   Vision : No Vision

Flexor Load

No Load

Extensor Load

Figure 10.9. Tracings showing the position of the hand in a deafferented patient (left) and a normal control participant (right). Each line represents hand position on one trial. In the top and bottom tracing there was a load (meaning pressure in one direction or the other); the middle tracing shows no load. Notice that for the control participant, hand position is steady. For the patient, hand position is fairly steady at the left part of each tracing when vision is available. Once vision is not available, the patient cannot maintain a steady hand position, with or without a load. From "Motor Control in Humans with Large-Fiber Sensory Neuropathy," by J. N. Sanes, K.-H. Mauritz, M. C. Dalakas, and E. V. Evarts, 1985, *Human Neurobiology, 4,* Fig. 1, p. 105.

growth spurt in adolescence or if the body is maimed—the brain may not be able to change quickly enough. It is possible to examine such situations experimentally by asking a participant to wear wedge prism spectacles that shift the visual world to the right (or left).

People wearing prism spectacles are indeed quite impaired in throwing objects at targets, but they greatly improve after about 30 trials. Tom Thach and his colleagues (Martin, Keating, Goodkin, Bastian, & Thach, 1996) had participants throw clay balls at a target, and they observed this pattern; participants initially made errors by throwing to the left of the target but rapidly adapted. When participants removed the glasses, they again made errors, this time to the right of the target. This continued compensation for the spectacles (although participants no longer wore them) is called an aftereffect; it dissipates after another 30 trials. These effects are shown in Figure 10.10.

The aftereffect occurs because proprioception has changed. It feels to the participant as though he or she is throwing directly ahead of the body, even though the arm moves to the right. These results show that the nervous system can adjust to changes in perceptual input. The system is biased to assume that vision and proprioception should agree, and if they disagree, proprioception is changed to bring it in line with vision.

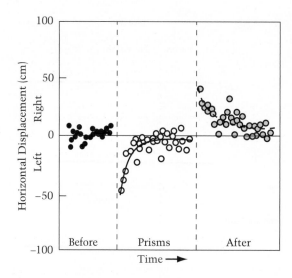

Figure 10.10. Graph showing the accuracy of people throwing clay balls at a target. Accuracy is good "Before" donning the prism spectacles. Errors are systematic when they put on the prisms, but quickly improve. When participants take off the prisms, there is a systematic bias in the other direction. From "Throwing While Looking Through Prisms. I. Focal Olivocerebellar Lesions Impair Adaptation," by T. A. Martin, J. G. Keating, H. P. Goodkin, A. J. Baston, and W. C. Thach, 1996, *Brain, 119*, Fig. 1B, p. 1185.

What part of the brain is responsible for this learning function? The cerebellum has been implicated. The researchers also tested patients with lesions to the cerebellum or lesions to brainstem structures that provide input to or receive output from the cerebellum. These patients typically did not improve their throwing accuracy when the prism spectacles were worn, nor did they show the aftereffect when the spectacles were removed. Other work with monkeys (Baizer, Kralj-Hans, & Glickstein, 1999) indicates that the caudal portion of the cerebellum is critical to this function. This area of the cerebellum receives visual input from the cortex and thus is consistent with the idea that part of the cerebellum is important in the modification of different sources of sensory input if they disagree.

Stand-on-One-Foot Question

10. How would you summarize the ways vision is used in ongoing motor movements?

Questions That Require Two Feet

11. Have you ever had a loss of proprioception?

12. We've emphasized the importance of proprioception to motor behavior. But proprioception has been much less studied than other senses. Can you think of why that might be?

How Are Motor Skills Learned?

Preview

Motor skills have three important properties: They can be generalized to new situations, they are well retained over long delays, and they come to require less attention (i.e., they become automatic). We also discuss two approaches to studying skill acquisition: the generalized motor program perspective and the multiple systems perspective. The former is primarily a cognitive theory, and the latter draws heavily on neuroscientific research.

Motor control refers to planning and executing movements. **Motor skill learning** refers to increasing accuracy of those movements with practice. Acts can become more accurate spatially or temporally. Spatial accuracy means moving the effectors to the correct positions in space, such as when a diver positions his body correctly for a twist. Temporal accuracy means moving the effectors at the right time and with the right speed, such as when a batter learns to time his swing for a change-up pitch.

Three Properties of Motor Skill Learning

Three seemingly obvious properties of motor skill are more subtle than they seem at first. Other properties of skill learning are not at all obvious. Theories of motor skill learning attempt to tie all these properties together.

Perhaps the prototypical example of motor skill acquisition is learning to ride a bicycle. If you endured this rite of childhood you can well appreciate three properties of motor skill learning. First, motor skills generalize. Once you have learned to ride a bicycle, you can ride any bicycle, not just the one on which you trained. The properties of the bicycle may be different—the wheel size, the gear ratios—but your skill will transfer to the new machine. You can also ride in new environments, not just the one in which you trained. Second, retention of motor skills is quite good. The expression "Once you learn how to ride a bicycle, you never forget" has been tested and proved true by more than one creaky 40-something who hasn't been on a bicycle in more than 20 years. Third, motor skills become automatic. Early in training, motor skills demand attention, but with practice attention demands drop significantly. Let's look at each principle more closely.

GENERALIZATION.   Earlier in this chapter, we noted that although people are trained to write on a horizontal surface using small movements of the dominant hand, writing skill generalizes readily, if imperfectly, to other muscle groups (e.g., the entire arm), to other effectors (e.g., the nondominant hand), and with spatial transformations (e.g., when you write on a vertical surface such as a blackboard; Wang & Sainburg, 2003). Similarly, once you have learned to throw a baseball, the skill will transfer to new situations: You can throw different distances, you can throw a tennis ball or softball, and so on.

Although it is true that many skills are generalizable, there are surprising exceptions to this rule. Daniel Lordahl and James Archer (1958) used a laboratory device called the pursuit rotor. In this task, the participant must try to keep the tip of a handheld wand in contact with a target on a rotating platter. The dependent measure is the amount of time during a trial that the stylus is on the target. Participants practiced with the platter turning at either 40, 60, or 80 rotations per minute (rpm). At transfer to the 60-rpm version, participants who had trained at 40 or at 80 rpm performed much worse than those who had trained at 60 rpm (for whom transfer involved no change, obviously). The 40-rpm group scores were 14% those of the 60-rpm group, and the 80-rpm group scores were 31% of the 60-rpm group.

Why was transfer so poor? A long-held idea is that transfer will be good to the extent that the new task is similar to the old task (Thorndike & Woodworth, 1901; see also Holding, 1976). But in the experiment just described, adjusting the speed of the platter doesn't seem like a big change; aren't the tasks still very similar?

It may be that transfer depends not just on overall similarity, but on the representation used in the skill. If the experimenters change something that is irrelevant to the skill, good transfer will be observed; if they change something that is part of the representation of the skill, transfer will be poor (Willingham, 1997b, 1998b). The pursuit rotor data may indicate that timing is a crucial part of what is learned in this skill, so when the timing is changed, performance suffers. Presumably, the experimenters could change other aspects of the task that are not part of the representation, such as the size of the target, with little impact on the skill.

LONG-TERM RETENTION. Remarkable retention has been reported for some motor skills. For example, Edwin Fleishman and James Parker (1962) trained participants on a complex control task meant to simulate an attack run in an airplane guided by radar. Participants saw a randomly drifting target on an oscilloscope and were to maintain contact with it by manipulating stick and rudder controls. Training took place in 17 sessions across 6 weeks. Performance during training is shown on the left side of Figure 10.11. Participants were retested after delays of 9, 12, or 24 months. As shown in the right side of the figure, retention of this skill was complete.

In other experiments, retention is not complete but is still impressive. Eva Neumann and Robert Ammons (1957) used a quite different skill involving 16 switches arranged in two concentric circles of 8 switches. Participants were to turn a switch in the inner circle and then turn the correct switch in the outer circle; a buzzer sounded if the choice was correct. Participants were trained for 63 trials, with 8 attempts in each. Participants were retested between 1 minute and 1 year later. Figure 10.12 shows that there is forgetting of this perceptual–motor skill; participants seem to have forgotten everything

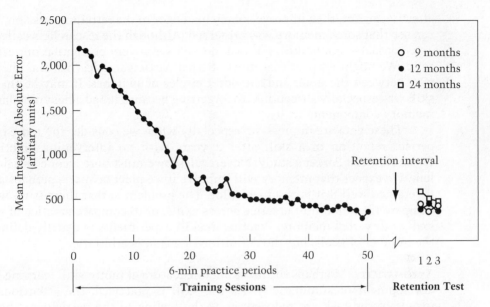

Figure 10.11. Results from Fleishman and Parker (1962). Retention is nearly perfect on this task, despite no practice for 2 years. From *Motor Control and Learning: A Behavioral Emphasis,* by R. A. Schmidt and T. D. Lee, 1999, Champaign, IL: Human Kinetics Press, Fig. 14.3, p. 392. Adapted from "Factors in the Retention and Relearning of Complex Psychomotor Performance and Related Skills," by E. A. Fleishman and J. F. Parker, 1962, *Journal of Experimental Psychology, 64.*

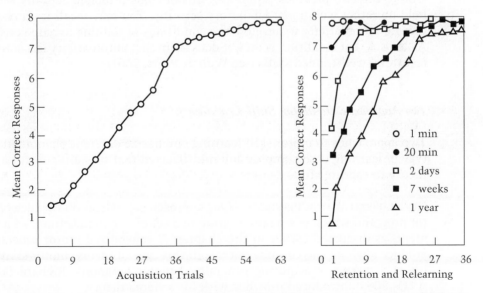

Figure 10.12. Results from Neumann and Ammons (1957). Retention is cut in half 2 days after training and has apparently disappeared after 1 year. But note that the skill is relearned much more quickly in the second training session. From R. A. Schmidt and T. D. Lee, 1999, Fig. 14.4, p. 393. Adapted from "Acquisition and Long-Term Retention of a Simple Serial Perceptual–Motor Skill," by E. Neumann and R. B. Ammons, 1957, *Journal of Experimental Psychology, 53.*

after 1 year. Yet, they improve somewhat faster in the retraining session, so we can see that some memory was preserved. Although the researchers called this a perceptual—motor skill, the task doesn't seem very perceptual or very motoric. We might suspect that most of what participants learned was the mapping between the inner and the outer circles of switches. It may be that this skill was especially susceptible to forgetting because it had a heavy declarative memory component.

These data are impressive, especially when we consider the more or less perfect retention of a skill after 2 years with no intervening practice in Fleishman and Parker's study. Nevertheless, we must note a conceptual problem. We expect that memory will improve if we practice more; perhaps a skill is retained well if it is practiced a lot. The problem is that there is no way to compare the amount of practice across skills, or to compare practice of motor skill with verbal memory. Practice in skill experiments is usually defined by the number of trials, but the definition of a trial is arbitrary.

AUTOMATICITY. Perhaps the most notable feature of motor skill learning is the development of automaticity. As the skill is practiced, the attentional demands of the task are reduced, as is the feeling to the participant that the movements must be consciously directed. For example, when you learned to drive, you likely attended to and consciously directed how hard to press the accelerator and how far to turn the steering wheel. With practice, these components of driving became automatic; you didn't need to attend to them. Unlike the two previous principles, this obvious principle actually seems to hold up rather well under laboratory scrutiny. You may recall from chapter 4 that for automaticity to develop, the conditions of training remain consistent. As long as that condition is met, it does seem that automaticity is a consistent feature of well-trained skills (see Wulf & Prinz, 2001).

Two Approaches to Motor Skill Learning

Two approaches to motor skill learning emphasize different phenomena. This type of learning is so complex and multifaceted that it is difficult for a single theory to capture all its aspects.

GENERALIZED MOTOR PROGRAM. One approach capitalizes on the idea of a motor program, which is a representation of a set of commands to make a movement, as discussed earlier in the chapter. A **generalized motor program** can produce a whole class of movements. In this type of theory, motor skill learning is a matter of acquiring generalized motor programs. Richard Schmidt (1975, 2003) introduced this idea with his schema theory.

By a class of movements, we mean similar movements that might have different endpoints or results with small changes to the program. An example would be a throwing motion: Throwing a baseball 20 yards or throwing a basketball 5 yards are acts that require different patterns of muscle activation, but they obviously have much in common. The generalized motor program produces these different movements when different value for program parameters are used.

Suppose I tell you that I have a catapult, and I offer to let you play around with it. You take it out to a field, and you begin hurling baseballs with it. The catapult arm is marked from 1 to 10, signifying how far back the arm is pulled. You find that with the catapult arm set to position 1, the baseball goes 10 yards. If you set the arm to position 3, the baseball goes 30 yards; position 8, 80 yards. Now suppose you want to hurl a baseball 50 yards—what's your best guess as to where to place the arm? Obviously, position 5 is the best choice.

The relationship can be described by the function *distance = arm position* × 10. Because distance is the outcome you're interested in, and arm position is available for you to control, you can produce any desired distance by plugging in the appropriate arm position, once you know the relationship.

Motor skill learning might work in an analogous way, but instead of varying the arm position of a catapult, you vary the muscle force you apply in a throwing motion. You could learn the relationship between muscle force and the distance a ball goes. Naturally, throwing depends on more than just muscle force; it depends on the trajectory your arm takes, how you move your back and your arm, and so on. Those complications do not change how the theory could work in principle, but the final program will be more complicated.

The generalized motor program, then, can be thought of as a function that relates some input parameters to a pattern of movements that will produce a desired outcome. A great advantage of the schema theory is that it can account for the generalizability of motor behavior. The schema theory posits that practice leads not just to improvement in a particular skill, but also to the development of a generalized motor program. Just as we can learn the relationship between the arm position and the distance a catapult will throw a ball, we can learn how various input parameters of the human body will change the distance a thrown ball will go.

One of the key predictions of schema theory is that your ability to generalize what you've learned should be better if you've had training in a broader variety of situations. To see why, imagine that two groups of people are using identical catapults that have 100 possible arm settings. Each group throws a ball 20 times. One group practices with targets 30 and 35 feet away (see the left panel of Figure 10.13). From the results of that group, you can relate distance and arm position with the following formula:

Distance = Arm position × 1.7 feet

Thus, if the next day I asked one of these participants to produce a distance of 50, they would guess that the proper arm position would be 43.

Now, suppose another group practices throwing at targets 30 and 90 feet away (see the right panel of Figure 10.13). The relationship between arm position and distance is not what we believed it was. Based only on the observations of arm positions around 30, it looked like the relationship between arm position and distance is more or less linear. When you have observations

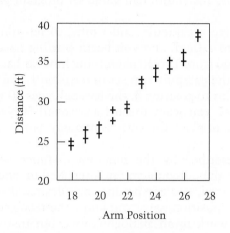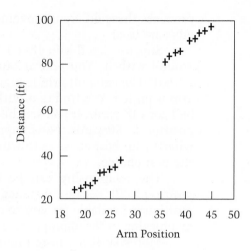

Figure 10.13. Two hypothetical data sets. On the left, a group uses a catapult to shoot a ball at two targets, 30 and 35 feet away. On the right, a group shoots at targets 30 and 90 feet away. The graph on the left makes it look like the relationship between arm position and distance is a straight line—it's only when you see data from a larger variety of arm positions that you know that that is not true. More variability in the parameter that you set (arm position) makes it more likely that you will end up with an accurate idea of the relationship between the parameter that you set (arm position) and the outcome (distance).

across a wider range of arm positions, it is clear that the relationship is not linear. It is in fact best described by this equation:

$$\text{Distance} = 20.01 \,(\text{arm position})^3 + 0.924 \,(\text{arm position})^2$$
$$- 24.9 \,(\text{arm position}) + 233.7$$

If you've tested only arm positions near 30, you end up with the first formula and you predict that to achieve a distance of 50 you should set the arm position to 43. If you've tested arm positions near 25 and arm positions near 90, you will use the second formula and predict that to achieve a distance of 50 you should set the arm position to 30 or 31, not to 43. The underlying properties of the systems are identical, but you see the properties of the system much better with training across a broader range of the parameters.

It is not clear whether the data support this prediction of Schmidt's theory, despite the fact that dozens of studies have addressed the issue (see Shea & Wulf, 2005, for a review). Some researchers (e.g., Newell, 2003) claim that the data do not support the theory, whereas others (Sherwood & Lee, 2003) argue that they do.

MULTIPLE PROCESSES.   When we try to locate the anatomical basis of motor skills, we quickly discover that a great many brain regions contribute to motor skill learning. More recently, researchers have suggested that this multiplicity of areas indicates that motor skill learning may well involve several closely interlinked systems (see Doyon, Penhune, & Ungerleider, 2003;

Hikosaka, Nakamura, Sakai, & Nakahara, 2002; Sanes, 2003; Willingham, 1998a). There is no single process that learns all types of skill; rather, there are several systems, each of which learns a different aspect of skill. Although there is some variation in the particular skills that different researchers discuss, most agree on four different types of motor skill. The distinction between these different types of skill is based on their differing anatomy.

The first type of skill is implicit motor sequence learning, which is perhaps the most extensively studied. **Implicit** in this context means unconscious; it usually refers to learning or the expression of learning of which the participant is unaware. Implicit motor sequencing tasks are usually designed as relatively simple choice tasks. For example, the participant sees four boxes on a screen. When a light appears in a box, the participant pushes one of four corresponding buttons. The participant isn't told that the stimuli appear in a repeating sequence. The sequence might be rather long (say, 12 stimuli) so it may not be that noticeable. The interesting finding is that even though the participant never catches on to the repeating sequence, he or she will learn it. The learning is evident because the response times to the stimuli get faster with practice. Furthermore, we know that the learning is specific to the sequence because if the stimuli begin to appear randomly, response times get slower (Nissen & Bullemer, 1987).

Implicit sequence learning depends on a network of brain areas. We said earlier that the secondary motor cortices are important for the planning of motor sequences. They also participate in the implicit learning of motor sequences, as do the basal ganglia, the parietal cortex, and the prefrontal cortex. This generalization comes from single-cell recording studies in monkeys (e.g., Hikosaka et al., 2002; Lee & Quessy, 2003), from studies of human neurologic patients (Boyd & Winstein, 2001; Gomez-Beldarrain, Grafman, Ruiz de Velasco, Pascual-Leone, & Garcia-Monco, 2002; Willingham & Koroshetz, 1993), and from brain imaging studies (Doyon et al., 2003; Grafton, Hazeltine, & Ivry, 1998; Willingham, Salidis, & Gabrieli, 2002).

Sequencing tasks can also be learned **explicitly**—that is, participants may become aware of the sequence and memorize it using declarative memory, or the experimenter may tell them in the instructions to learn the sequence. This type of learning can also be considered a motor skill because the knowledge can be used to improve motor performance; if you know where the next stimulus will appear, you can prepare your response. In fact, people respond even faster with explicit (conscious) knowledge than when they have implicit (unconscious) knowledge (Curran & Keele, 1993; Willingham, Nissen, & Bullemer, 1989). The parts of the brain that support this learning are close to, but not exactly the same as, those supporting unconscious learning. Prefrontal, parietal, and secondary cortexes contribute, but in slightly different areas (De Weerd et al., 2003; Eliassen, Souza, & Sanes, 2001).

The third type of learning task are **adaptation** tasks, in which you learn new motor responses to a perceptual stimulus. For example, when you first learned how to use a mouse, you had to learn how to get the cursor to move by manipulating the mouse. You can't test how people learn how to use a mouse, however, because just about everyone already knows that, so researchers change how the mouse works—they ask people to move the cursor to targets on the screen, but the relationship of the mouse and cursor is changed, usually so the cursor moves 90 degrees clockwise of the direction the mouse moves. (If you want to try it, just rotate your mouse 90 degrees, and you'll get the idea.) Another paradigm uses the prism spectacles that I described previously. Imaging studies show that posterior parietal cortex is key to supporting this learning (Clower, Hoffman, Votaw, Faber, Woods, & Alexander, 1996; Flament, Ellerman, Kim, Ugurbil, & Ebner, 1996). This result makes sense in light of single-cell recording studies, which show that this area is important for translating visual information into information that the motor system can use directly (e.g., Andersen, Snyder, Bradley, & Xing, 1997).

When you're learning to use a mouse (or a rotated mouse), the relationship between what you see and what you should do is systematic—if you want the cursor to move to the right, you move your hand to the right. If you want it to move left, you move your hand to the left, and so on. Other relationships between stimuli and motor responses are **arbitrary visual-motor associations**, meaning that no rule relates one to the other. For example, there's nothing about a red light that indicates depressing the brake pedal, and nothing about the green light that indicates depressing the accelerator. These associations are arbitrary. The neurophysiology of this type of learning has been studied in much detail in monkeys, and the neural network supporting it has been pretty well worked out. It includes the ventral prefrontal cortex, the posterior parietal cortex, the premotor cortex, and parts of the basal ganglia and medial temporal lobe (see Wise & Murray, 2000, for a review).

The different types of motor skill tasks and the brain structures that support their learning are summarized in Table 10.1. The thing to note about

Table 10.1.   *Types of Motor Skill Learning from the Multiple Systems View*

Skill	Example	Brain areas
Implicit sequence learning	Choice response task with an embedded sequence—participant not told about the sequence	Posterior parietal cortex Supplementary motor area Basal ganglia
Explicit sequence learning	Choice response task with an embedded sequence—participant told about and encouraged to memorize the sequence	Posterior parietal cortex Dorsolateral frontal cortex Premotor cortex
Adaptation	Learning to use a mouse; adapting to prism spectacles	Posterior parietal cortex
Arbitrary visual-motor association	Red means stop, green means go	Ventral prefrontal cortex Posterior parietal cortex Premotor cortex Medial temporal cortex

Table 10.1 is the lack of overlap in the brain areas supporting the different types of skill. The main area of overlap is the posterior parietal cortex, which is no great surprise because that area is concerned with spatial information, and these types of tasks use space. Other than that, the overlap is minimal. Note how different this approach is than the generalized motor program idea, which sought a single explanation for different types of skill. It may not be an accident that these two widely divergent approaches rely on very different types of data—one cognitive and the other neuroscientific. They have yet to be brought together in a single framework, as desirable as that would obviously be.

In this chapter, we have been concerned primarily with behaviors that are planned outside awareness. We seldom think about how to reach for a glass or how to sequence well-learned movements such as tying our shoes. In chapter 11, we consider cognitive processes that are very much the stuff of careful contemplation—how we reason and make decisions.

Stand-on-One-Foot Questions

13. What are the three obvious properties of motor skill that we discussed, and which one applies without qualification across skills?
14. Why should skills that have been practiced under more variable conditions be easier to generalize than skills that were practiced under less variable conditions, according to Schmidt's schema theory?
15. What are the four types of motor skills, according to the multiple processes perspective?

Questions That Require Two Feet

16. If a generalized motor program is behind skilled motor behavior, what parameters of movement do you think would likely be part of the program?
17. Neither the schema theory nor the multiple processes perspective says much about how declarative memory (discussed in chapters 6 and 7) fits into motor skill. Why would that be an important part of a theory?
18. We said that some motor skills can be learned outside awareness (i.e., you're never aware of learning them), but it is not clear whether these skills require attention. If a skill could be learned outside awareness but required attention, what might that mean?

KEY TERMS

adaptation
anticipatory postural
  adjustment
arbitrary visual-motor
  association
control nodes
cutaneous receptors
degrees of freedom
  problem

effector
efficiency theories
explicit
generalized motor
  program
golgi tendon organs
implicit
jerk
joint space

mass spring model
motor control
motor program
motor skill learning
movement nodes
muscle spindles
proprioception
synergy
trajectory

Decision Making and Deductive Reasoning

Do People Consistently Make Optimal Decisions?

- Normative or Rational Models
- Demonstrations of Human Irrationality

What Shortcuts Do People Use to Make Decisions?

- Representativeness
- Availability
- Anchoring and Adjustment
- Information We Ignore
- Probabilities Versus Frequencies
- Summary

Do People Reason Logically?

- Formal Logic
- Human Success and Failure in Reasoning: Conditional Statements
- Human Success and Failure in Reasoning: Syllogisms
- General Models of Reasoning
- Summary

You probably don't even notice the number of decisions you make each day. Take the bus or walk? Say "hello" to the acquaintance or pretend not to see her? Paper or plastic? Similarly, you probably do not notice the frequency with which you reason deductively. I may say to you, "If we buy the milk up the street, we'll save a nickel." If you then go up the street and buy the milk, you obviously expect to save a nickel. This expectation is based on deductive reasoning, although you probably wouldn't notice that you had engaged in reasoning at all. In this chapter, we examine how we make decisions and how we reason.

We consider these two topics in the same chapter because for both types of problems, we can derive answers that are objectively correct. Other questions do not have such clear answers, and we consider those in chapter 12. The first question we address in this chapter is **Do people consistently make optimal decisions?** That is, if there is an objectively correct answer, is that the one people choose? As we'll see, the answer is often "No."

That fact doesn't mean that people never make optimal decisions, but it does indicate that we do not use rules designed for optimality. One reason is that it would often be time consuming and difficult to derive optimal answers to moderately complex questions. We need shortcuts to help us derive good (but not necessarily optimal) solutions. **What shortcuts do people use to make decisions?** As we'll see, the most influential answer to this question is that people use what we might call reasoning shortcuts, procedures that allow us to arrive at an answer quickly and with little effort and that usually produce a correct answer.

In decision making, a choice must be made from among two or more outcomes. In most reasoning problems, we are presented with an argument and asked what conclusion can be made, or we are asked to evaluate the validity of a conclusion that is supplied. For example, I might ask what conclusions (if any) could be drawn from these two premises.

On Thursdays, I eat melon.
Today is not Thursday.

As mentioned earlier, deductive reasoning is similar to decision making in that we can objectively identify correct answers. Deductive reasoning is different, however, in that the problems are often less complex, at least in principle. We might therefore entertain the possibility that people are optimal problem solvers in this domain (i.e., they reason in accordance with the rules of formal logic). **Do people reason logically?** Alas, the answer is "No," as you probably already guessed. If people use shortcuts in decision making, we might guess that they also use shortcuts in reasoning problems. To some extent that's true, but some models of reasoning that don't use such shortcuts seem to do a better job of accounting for people's behavior.

Do People Consistently Make Optimal Decisions?

Preview

Decision making generally entails selecting from two (or occasionally more) options. We can define criteria by which some choices are better than others. One criterion is rationality, which means that choices are internally consistent: Decisions are made in the same way each time. In normative models of decision making, a second criterion dictates which choice is best. For example, a possible criterion would be to maximize financial gain. Evidence shows, however, that people's choices are neither rational (they are not consistent) nor normative (they do not conform to any criterion, such as maximizing financial reward).

In a way, **decision making** can be said to encompass all human behavior. As you read this book, you are making a decision not to find a pair of scissors and cut it into very small pieces, you are making a decision not to hunker on the floor and chatter like a squirrel, and so on. When researchers say that they study decision making, however, they usually mean a situation in which someone must select one path from two or more explicit courses of action offered.

Normative or Rational Models

Most of us want to think of ourselves as sensible, and part of being sensible is making effective choices. There are two ways in which our choices can be effective or ineffective. First, our choices may or may not be **rational**, meaning internally consistent. For example, we might expect choices to show **transitivity**: If some relationship holds between the first and the second of three elements and also between the second and the third elements, then it ought to hold between the first and the third. For example, if I prefer apple pie to Bavarian cream pie and Bavarian cream to chocolate cake, then I should prefer apple pie to chocolate cake. Rational choices must also be consistent; I can't say that I like classical music better than funk and that I also like funk better than classical. Notice that the requirement of rationality has no bearing on the particular choices a person makes. The theory doesn't prescribe that I should like apple pie better than Bavarian cream. Rationality simply means that there is consistency across the choices made.

Other theories, however, are prescriptive, meaning that some choices are considered better than others and usually that one choice is optimal from among the possibilities. These are called **normative theories**. What makes a choice the optimal one varies with the particular theory. In **expected value** theory, the optimal choice is the one that offers the largest financial payoff, taking into account the probability of the payoff. For example, suppose you were offered the following choices:

A. 0.5 chance of winning $50

B. 0.25 chance of winning $110

The expected value of each choice is easy to calculate: It's the probability of winning multiplied by the value of the prize. Thus, the expected value of the first choice is $0.50 \times \$50 = \$25$. The expected value of the second choice is $0.25 \times \$110 = \$27.50$. Hence, if expected value guides our decisions, we will always select the second choice.

In the next section, we discuss in more detail how people's choices violate normative and rational models. People often make choices that are not optimal if expected value is the guide. Anyone who buys a lottery ticket or gambles in a casino is not making choices guided by expected value. Every bet in a casino favors the house, not the player (see Table 11.1); hence, expected value dictates that casino guests should make the choice of not wagering.

Setting casino games aside, it is easy to think of instances where expected value would not guide your choices. For example, suppose that it's late in the afternoon, you skipped lunch, and you're broke. I offer you these choices:

A. 0.85 chance of winning $10

B. 0.25 chance of winning $45

Table 11.1.   Average Return for Casino Games

Game	Bet	Average Return (%)
Roulette	Single number	94.7
Roulette	Red or black	97.2
Blackjack	Varies	~99
Craps	Pass or don't pass	98.6
Slot machine	Nickel	84.8
Slot machine	Quarter	89.8
Baccarat	Banker	98.6
Baccarat	Player	98.2

Average return indicates the percentage of your money you can expect to recoup over an infinitely long session of betting. Odds are from Reber (1999). Roulette odds depend on the wheel, which varies by locale; odds shown are for most U.S. casinos. Odds of blackjack and baccarat depend in part on the skillfulness of choices made by the player and on the rules, which vary slightly by locale. The return of slot machines also varies.

Expected value dictates that you should take Choice B. The expected value of Choice A is $8.50, and for Choice B, it's $11.25. But we've said that you're hungry and you're broke. You may well think to yourself, "I'm quite likely to get the $10, but I'm not very likely to get the $45. Although it would be nice to have the extra $35, I really want to make sure I get some money so that I can go get something to eat." This is an example of maximizing **expected utility**. Utility is the personal value we attach to outcomes rather than to their absolute monetary value. In this case, the extra $35 does not have sufficient utility to justify the risk of not getting the $10. Similarly, I might offer you 1 sandwich for $1 or 100 sandwiches for $50. In terms of expected value, you're better off with 100 sandwiches. But what will you do with 100 sandwiches?

Here's another example of a choice that is probably guided by expected utility, not expected value:

A. 1.0 chance of winning $1
B. 0.00000014 chance of winning $3 million

This problem represents the typical odds of winning the state lottery in Virginia. You can either be certain of keeping your dollar (by not playing in the first place), or you can sacrifice your dollar to try to win $3 million at odds of about 1 in 7 million. The expected value clearly favors keeping your dollar. From the utility perspective, however, the expected utility of losing $1 dollar is low, and the expected utility of $3 million is quite high.

Although the concept of utility (first introduced by von Neumann & Morgenstern, 1944) helps in understanding people's choices, people do not always behave as expected utility theory would predict.

Demonstrations of Human Irrationality

We can point to at least two principles that should be observed if decisions are made rationally: description invariance and procedure invariance. **Description invariance** means that people will consistently make the same choice irrespective of how the problem is described to them as long as the basic structure of the choices is the same. **Procedure invariance** means that people will consistently make the same choice irrespective of how their preference for that choice is measured. You might ask them to choose among several alternatives, make a series of pairwise comparisons, or assign a monetary value to each choice; it shouldn't matter. Experiments have repeatedly shown, however, that neither procedure invariance nor description invariance holds.

Here are two problems that were presented to participants in a study by Amos Tversky and Danny Kahneman (1986). They gave each problem to about 125 participants. The numbers in parentheses indicate the percentage of participants selecting each choice.

Suppose I give you $300, but you must also select one of these two options:

A. 1.0 chance of gaining $100 (72%)
B. 0.5 chance of gaining $200 and a 0.5 chance of gaining nothing (28%)

Suppose I give you $500, but you must also select one of these two options:

A. 1.0 chance of losing $100 (36%)
B. 0.5 chance of losing nothing and a 0.5 chance of losing $200 (64%)

Notice that these two problems are formally similar to one another; the monetary outcomes (factoring in the $300 or $500 with which you started) are the same, so the expected utilities should be the same, but the dominant choice nevertheless reverses. Why? The **problem frame**—the way the problem is described—has changed. The first gives you a choice between gains; the second offers a choice between losses. Although the formal outcome of the two problems is the same, the description (or frame) affects the choice that people make. Thus, description invariance is violated in this problem.

Another aspect of framing, **psychic budgets** (Thaler, 1980), concerns how we mentally categorize money that we have spent or are contemplating spending. For example, you may not buy yourself a coat that you like because you consider it too expensive. You are putting it in the mental category "luxury" and are unwilling to allocate that sum to a luxury. Suppose your spouse suggests buying that coat as a present for you. Now the same coat at the same price is in a different mental category—"gift"—and it doesn't seem to be such a bad deal anymore, even though if you and your spouse share a checking account, the cost to you is the same.

Another related effect involves the **sunk cost**, an investment that is irretrievably spent and therefore should not affect present decision making. The investment need not be of money; it could be time, emotion, and so on. Sunk costs almost always refer to an investment that, in retrospect, was spent unwisely. For example, have you ever sat through a movie you weren't enjoying because you wanted to "get your money's worth"? When you think about it, you really can't get your money's worth. The movie stinks, and nothing will make it worth $10. The $10 is gone—it's a sunk cost. Whether you stay (and suffer through a bad movie) or leave (and do something more pleasurable) does not change the fact that your $10 is gone (see Photo 11.1).

A related concept is **loss aversion**: The unpleasantness of a loss is larger than the pleasure of a similar gain. People may be more motivated to make risky choices because of loss aversion. In a classic study on this phenomenon, Kahneman, Jack Knetsch, and Richard Thaler (1990) showed all the participants in their study a coffee mug, telling half the participants that the mug was theirs to keep. All participants were told to assign a value to the mug and were also told that the real market value of the mug would

Photo 11.1. Two unfinished meals—seared tuna (cost: $26) and hot dog (cost: $2). Suppose each meal is poor. Would you be more tempted to finish the tuna "to get your money's worth?" Why? Your $26 is gone, and no part of it will be recovered by suffering through the rest of a poor meal.

be revealed at the end of the experiment. If the price an individual participant assigned to the mug was higher than the market value, the participant got the mug (e.g., someone who assigned a value of $10 to a mug with a market value of $8 could keep the mug). If the assigned price was lower, the participant got the cash. The interesting finding was that people who were initially told they could keep the mug assigned much higher prices to the mug ($7.12) than people who were merely shown the mug ($3.12). This effect is caused by the way people view the transaction. The people who were shown the mug figured they were going to get a mug or some cash. The people who were told that they owned the mug viewed the transaction as their having to give up their mug (a loss) to get some cash. Because of loss aversion, people don't want to give up "their" mugs, and they demand a high price ($7.12) for doing so.

You'll recall that we initially said that we might test people's decisions for two types of rationality: description invariance (making the same choice irrespective of the problem description) and procedure invariance (making the same choice irrespective of the procedure by which preference is measured). The previous examples show violations of description invariance: People make different choices depending on how the problem is described. What about procedure invariance? Does the way that a preference is measured affect the choice? Research has repeatedly shown that people's choices change depending on how the choice is elicited. For example, suppose you give people a choice between these two outcomes:

A. 8/9 chance to win $4
B. 1/9 chance to win $40

When asked to choose directly, most people (71%) prefer Choice A. Now suppose we elicit choice another way: "What is the minimum price at which you would sell your right to this choice? You know that you have an 8/9 chance to win $4, but I am ready to give you cash so that I now have an 8/9 chance to get the $4. What is the minimum amount of money I would have to give you for you to sell your right to play this game to me? And what price would you assign to Choice B?". When asked to assign prices, 67% of participants assign a higher monetary value to Choice B than to Choice A (Tversky, Slovic, & Kahneman, 1990).

Another example comes from a study by Tversky, Shmuel Sattath, and Paul Slovic (1988). They asked participants to select between two programs that were designed to reduce casualties caused by traffic accidents. Program X cost $55 million, and 500 casualties would be expected in the next year. Program Y cost $12 million, and 570 casualties would be expected next year. When comparing them directly, most participants selected the more expensive program that saves more lives. In another version of the problem, participants were told only the number of casualties, and they were asked to assign a price differential that would make the two programs equivalent choices. Nearly all participants assigned a price difference indicating that $43 million is too much extra to pay to save 70 lives. Again, people's decisions vary depending on how these decisions are elicited.

Thus far, we have shown that people don't make their decisions based on the principles of expected value or expected utility, and indeed that their choices vary depending on how the problem is described or how their preference is elicited. But how optimal is optimal selection? Optimizing means picking the best solution out of all those available. Thus, to optimize, we must either evaluate all possible options or develop a formula that will provide the best solution, even if we don't evaluate all options. Either one of those may require a lot of calculation, especially for moderately complex problems. If you are choosing a car, for example, are you going to test drive every model on the market? Are you going to thoroughly research the safety of each car and bargain with multiple dealers for the best price on every model before making a selection? Wouldn't these steps be necessary if you are to optimize? Getting the optimal solution may not be optimal in terms of the cost to you of computing it.

Herb Simon (1957) suggested that instead of optimizing, people satisfice. **Satisficing** means selecting the first choice that is above some threshold (in other words, that is satisfactory). A classic example of the need to satisfice is in selecting a car. You can't compare every model, evaluate every feature of every model, test drive every model with every possible combination of features, and compare prices on all these models . . . and then do the same thing for all the used models (see Photo 11.2). A more realistic approach is to start generating all possible solutions and select the first satisfactory solution. Even better would be to start by generating solutions that are likely to be satisfactory. We can't generate all the possibilities, so we need a shortcut that will generate a few that are likely to be satisfactory. We want to know what sorts of shortcuts could generate likely solutions.

Photo 11.2.   We can't evaluate all our options when buying a car—we must satisfice.

Stand-on-One-Foot Questions

1. *What is the difference between normative and rational models?*
2. *What is the difference between expected value and expected utility, and how are they similar?*
3. *How do we know that people do not make rational choices?*

Questions That Require Two Feet

4. *Can utility theory explain why people gamble in casinos?*
5. *Suppose I offered you a bet: If you win, you get a nickel, but if you lose, you die. Presumably, I would have to give you pretty steep odds in your favor before you would accept such a bet. In fact, you might even say that you would not accept such a bet regardless of the odds. Try rephrasing the question so more people would accept the bet. Hint: Think of a situation in which people don't necessarily realize that they may be risking their lives.*

What Shortcuts Do People Use to Make Decisions?

Preview

Instead of making detailed calculations to select choices, people appear to use heuristics—simple rules that require little calculation and usually yield an acceptable solution. However, heuristics can lead to nonoptimal choices. We discuss three heuristics in this section: representativeness (an event is judged to be probable if it has properties that are representative of a process or category), availability (an event is judged to be probable if one can think of many examples of the event), and anchoring and adjustment (the judged probability of an event is influenced by an initial estimate of its probability). In addition, we examine the sorts of information people systematically ignore, even though it would be informative in making decisions. We also examine another approach to choice that suggests that people may not use these heuristics. Rather, it appears that they do because the problems psychologists have given people use probabilities (the likelihood that something will occur), and humans are evolutionarily prepared to think about frequencies (how often something occurs).

Most psychologists think that people use **heuristics** as shortcuts when they make decisions. These are simple cognitive rules that are easy to apply because they don't require much calculation. Heuristics usually yield acceptable choices but may lead to disadvantageous or inconsistent decisions. A heuristic can be contrasted with an **algorithm**, a formula that produces consistent outcomes and may, if selected correctly, produce optimal outcomes. Algorithms can be complex and difficult to compute. Expected value, for example, is an algorithm; if you calculate the expected value of two choices, you will always end up making the same decision, regardless of how the problem is described or how preferences are elicited. We've just shown that people don't use expected value or expected utility. It has been proposed that they use heuristics instead of these algorithms.

Representativeness

Representativeness is a heuristic used when people are asked to judge the probability that something belongs to a category. We are likely to place something in a category if it has features strongly associated with that category. For example, consider these two descriptions from a study by Tversky and Kahneman (1983):

> Linda is 31 years old, single, outspoken, and very bright. She majored in philosophy. As a student, she was deeply concerned with issues of discrimination and social justice and also participated in antinuclear demonstrations.
>
> Which of these is more likely?
>
> **A.** Linda is a bank teller.
> **B.** Linda is a bank teller and is active in the feminist movement.

Photo 11.3.   Suppose that I have tossed four coins (top row) and then tossed another four (bottom row). Which combination of heads and tails is more likely, the one depicted in the top row or in the bottom row?

People incorrectly think that the second statement is more likely to be true than the first. There is some probability that Linda is a bank teller, and if she's a bank teller, she may or may not also be a feminist. The odds of a conjunction of probabilities (two simultaneous probabilities) can never be higher than one of the constituent probabilities. But people erroneously select the second statement because the description of Linda evokes that of a stereotypical feminist. The representativeness heuristic dictates that an individual (Linda) with features (deeply concerned with social justice) strongly associated with the category (feminist) is likely to be a member of the category.

Representativeness also can be based on the feature that is strongly associated with a process. For example, suppose I toss four coins two times, as shown in Photo 11.3. Which outcome is more likely? The answer is that both outcomes are equally likely. The second toss seems more random, however, because there is no pattern apparent in the toss. For that reason, the second toss is representative of randomness, and because you know that randomness is the process that produces patterns of coin tosses, you judge it to be more likely than the first toss. This may also be the mechanism behind the **gambler's fallacy**. When an event hasn't occurred for a while in a random game (e.g., an even number in a roulette game), it feels as though an even number is "due."

Availability

To use the **availability** heuristic to judge the probability of events, you simply try to call examples of the event to mind, and if many examples can be called to mind easily, you judge an event to be more probable. Tversky and Kahneman (1973), for example, asked 152 participants whether there are more words in English that have *r* as the first letter or *r* as the third letter. The answer is that there are more with *r* as the third letter of the word, but 69% incorrectly judged that it's the first. Tversky and Kahneman argued that it is easy to think of words with *r* as the first letter but quite difficult to think of words with *r* as the third letter; your mind is not organized in a way that lets you access words according to their third letter.

Here's another problem (Tversky & Kahneman, 1973) in which participants may use availability to make a judgment:

Ten people are to form committees.

How many different committees of *x* members can they form?

They showed 118 people this problem, with *x* equal to some number between 2 and 8. As shown in Figure 11.1, as *x* increased, participants' estimates of the

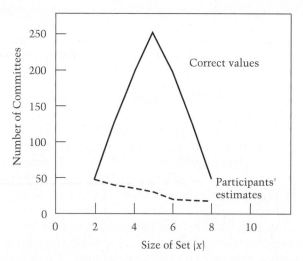

Figure 11.1. People's estimates of the numbers of committees that can be created from a group of 10 people. The experimenters varied the size of the committees. Note that the graph for the correct values is in an inverted U shape because you can create the same number of committees from two values of *x* that add up to 10. In other words, every time you create a 2-person committee, you have also created a de facto 8-person committee (the people you excluded in creating the 2-person committee). Participants' estimates systematically decrease as *x* increases because it is more difficult to generate committees as *x* increases (i.e., they are less available).

number of committees decreased systematically, although the true value increases and then decreases. The experimenters argued that people use the availability heuristic to answer this question. It is easier to mentally generate two-person committees than six-person committees, so people assume there must be more of them.

Anchoring and Adjustment

The **anchoring and adjustment** heuristic is used to estimate probabilities. We start with an initial probability value (the anchor) by doing a partial computation of the problem or using a probability estimate suggested by some statement in the problem. We then adjust this estimate upward or downward on the basis of other information in the problem. For example, Tversky and Kahneman (1973) gave participants 5 s to estimate the answer to this problem: $1 \times 2 \times 3 \times 4 \times 5 \times 6 \times 7 \times 8$. The correct answer is 40,320, but the median estimate was 512. When the order of the factors was reversed to $8 \times 7 \times 6 \times 5 \times 4 \times 3 \times 2 \times 1$, the median estimate was much higher at 2,250. The experimenters hypothesized that participants start this problem by multiplying a few of the first numbers (anchoring) and then adjusting this initial estimate upward. The order of the factors matters because it affects the size of the anchor. Both estimates are too low because adjustments are usually insufficient in any problem in which anchoring and adjustment is applied.

Anchoring and adjustment has been shown to influence many judgments, including preference judgments (Carlson, 1990), judgments of answers to factual questions (Tversky & Kahneman, 1974), estimates of probabilities of events such as nuclear war (Plous, 1989), and estimates of preferences of one's spouse (Davis, Hoch, & Ragsdale, 1986). It certainly is used in marketing. The television pitchman declares "You're not going to pay $1,500 for this rotisserie!" in order to set a very high anchor. You know that $1,500 is a ridiculous price so you mentally adjust downward. Adjustments are usually inadequate, however, so when the pitchman tells you the real price, it seems like a bargain.

In one study, anchoring and adjustment was also shown to be important in some legal settings. Gretchen Chapman and Brian Bornstein (1996) had participants read a one-page description of a personal injury suit in which a woman sued a health maintenance organization, arguing that the birth control pills prescribed for her had caused her ovarian cancer. The experimenters varied the amount of compensation the woman sought: $100, $20,000, $5 million, or $1 billion. Participants awarded greater compensation as the amount of requested compensation increased. The researchers argued that participants used the requested amount of compensation as an anchor and then adjusted their award, depending on their assessment of the facts of the case.

Information We Ignore

Researchers have argued that there are certain types of information that we systematically ignore when we make decisions. Thus, these are not heuristics that are invoked, but these effects nevertheless have important consequences for decision making.

IGNORING SAMPLE SIZE. **Sample size** is the number of things in a group that you are evaluating. For example, suppose you want to know the height of the average student at your college or university. It's unlikely that you will measure the height of each student; instead, you'll pick a group of students to measure. How big of a group should it be? It turns out that whether the sample is large or small has an impact on what you're likely to find in your measurement. When a sample is large, its average value is closer to the average value of the entire group. In other words, suppose that there are 4,000 people at your school, and their average height is 67 inches. If I randomly select 100 people of the 4,000 (sample size = 100), I am more likely to find that the average height of those 100 is close to 67 inches than if my sample size is 10 people.

Sample size is important in calculating such probabilities, but people do not seem to be naturally sensitive to this information. Tversky and Kahneman (1974) gave participants this problem:

> A certain town is served by two hospitals. In the larger hospital, about 45 babies are born each day, and in the small hospital, about 15 babies are born each day. About 50% of all babies are boys. However, the exact percentage varies from day to day. Sometimes it may be higher than 50%, sometimes lower.
>
> For a period of 1 year, each hospital recorded the days on which more than 60% of the babies born were boys. Which hospital do you think recorded more such days?
>
> **A.** The larger hospital (22%)
> **B.** The smaller hospital (22%)
> **C.** About the same (i.e., within 5% of each other) (56%)

The correct answer is B. A large sample is much less likely to deviate from 50% than a small one, but people do not seem to appreciate that fact. Tversky and Kahneman argued that people solve this problem by using the representativeness heuristic: Whether a particular birth is a boy or girl is random at each hospital, and because the process producing the gender is random, it seems that there is an equal chance of deviation from randomness.

IGNORING THE BASE RATE. A classic problem is used to demonstrate this principle:

> In a certain city there are two cab companies, the Blue and the Green. In this city, the Blue company owns 85% of the cabs and the Green owns 15%. A cab is involved in a hit-and-run accident. An eyewitness says she thinks it was a green cab. The eyewitness vision is tested, and it is determined that under the lighting conditions at the time of the accident,

she can correctly identify the color of the cab 80% of the time. What are the odds that the hit-and-run cab was green?

Many participants think that there is an 80% chance that it was green, but in fact there is only a 40% chance that it was a green cab. Why? Think of it this way. If I told you that 80% of the cabs were blue cabs and that there wasn't an eyewitness, what would you say the chances are that it was a blue cab? Assuming the drivers of the two companies are equally safe or reckless, you'd say 80%, right? In the problem described previously, you still have that information (80% are blue), but now you have additional information based on the eyewitness. The eyewitness account does not invalidate the information about the percentage of cabs; that information should still be taken into account. This information is the **base rate**—the frequency of an event (e.g., the number of blue cabs) among a larger pool of events (the total number of cabs).

If this seems difficult to understand, consider another example. Suppose you and I are walking along the Champs-Elysées in Paris one Sunday afternoon and I suddenly say, "Wow! I just saw a penguin in that café. Did you see it? It popped out for a second and then ran back in. At least, I think it was a penguin. I guess I'm around 80% sure." What would you say the odds are that I actually saw a penguin? Even if vision tests showed that I'm 80% accurate in identifying penguins under those conditions, you'd say chances are very small that I actually saw one because with the extremely rare exception of a zoo escapee or perhaps the shooting of a television commercial, there are no penguins in Paris cafés. The base rate is extremely low (see Figure 11.2).

A practical and very important example of the importance of base rate information in medical decision making was illustrated by David Eddy (1982). The diagnostic tests physicians use are usually imperfect. Eddy's example concerned the use of mammography to detect breast cancer. Suppose 10,000 women are given a mammogram, and if a woman has cancer, the probability is 0.92 that the test result will be positive. If she does not have cancer, the probability is 0.88 that the results will be negative. Eddy asked, "If a woman's test result comes back positive, what are the odds that she does indeed have cancer?" The answer is not 0.92; again, it depends on the base rate.

In Table 11.2, the base rate is set at 1 woman out of 100 having cancer. A total of 100 women out of 10,000 have cancer, and of those 100 women, 90 have a positive test (0.9 probability). Of the 9,900 women without cancer, 8,700 have a negative test (0.88 probability). So, a total of 1,290 women have a positive test, but only 90 of those have cancer. With a positive test, the odds of having cancer is about 0.07. Most of the women who show a positive mammogram don't have cancer—the test is a false positive.

How is this possible? The overall low rate of cancer given a positive test comes about because of the low base rate. We assumed a low base rate of 1% because we said that these 10,000 women were selected randomly. Depending on their age, all women are encouraged to get mammograms, so a low base rate

Mourning Warbler *Oporornis philadelphia L 5¼" (13 cm)* Lack of bold white eye ring distinguishes **adult male** from Connecticut Warbler. **Adult female** and especially **immatures** may show a thin, nearly complete eye ring, but compare with Connecticut. Immatures generally have more yellow on throat than MacGillivray's; compare also with female Common Yellowthroat (page 388). Immature males often show a little black on breast. Mourning Warblers hop rather than walk. **Call** is a flat, hollow *chip*. **Song** usually has two parts: a s eries of slurred two-note phrases followed by two or more lower phrases. **Range:** Fairly common in dense undergrowth, thickets, moist woods; nests on theground. Most spring migration is west of the Appalachians.

MacGillivray's Warbler *Oporornis tolmiei L 5¼" (13 cm)* Bold white crescents above and below eye distinguish all plumages from male Mourning and all Connecticut Warblers. Crescents may be very hard to distinguish from the thin, nearly complete eye ring on female and immature Mourning Warblers. **Immature** MacGillivray's Warblers generally have grayer throat than immature Mournings and a fairly distinct breast band above yellow belly. Field identification is often difficult. MacGillivray's hops rather than walks. **Call** is a sharp, harsh *tsik*. **Song** has two parts: a buzzy trill ending in a downslur. **Range:** Fairly common; found in dense undergrowth; nests on the ground.

Figure 11.2.   A section of a bird identification book. Note that the book provides some base rate information—whether the bird is common in a given geographic area. The Mourning warbler and MacGillivray's warbler look quite similar. But if you live in Manitoba, you know you've seen a Mourning warbler, and if you live in California, you know you've seen a MacGillivray's warbler.

among these women may not be unreasonable. The situation would be quite different for a group of women who were getting a mammogram because they had some other symptom indicative of cancer, such as a lump in the breast. Then, we would expect the base rate of the presence of cancer to be quite a bit higher.

Table 11.2.   *Hypothetical Mammogram Outcome for 10,000 Women*

	Women With Cancer	Women Without Cancer	Total
Women with positive test	90	1,200	1,290
Women with negative test	10	8,700	8,710
Total	100	9,900	10,000

Probabilities Versus Frequencies

Some researchers, notably Gerd Gigerenzer and Ulrich Hoffrage, claim that much of the work we discuss in this section has a serious flaw. They have made an evolutionary argument that our minds are designed to keep track of frequencies, not probabilities. They argue that people have a hard time reasoning and making decisions when problems are presented in terms of probabilities because our minds are not set up to deal with probabilities.

The implication is that people should perform much better on choice problems presented in terms of frequencies instead of probabilities. In one study (Hoffrage, Lindsey, Hertwig, & Gigerenzer, 2000; see also Hoffrage, Kurzenhauser, & Gigerenzer, 2005), 96 advanced medical students solved problems that involved using probabilities or frequencies in medical diagnosis.

Probability Format

The probability that a woman at age 40 will get a positive mammography in routine screening is 10.3%. The probability of breast cancer and a positive mammography is 0.8% for a woman at age 40 who participates in routine screening. A woman in this age group had a positive mammography in a routine screening. What is the probability that she actually has breast cancer?

_____%.   10.3%   of   .8%

Frequency Format

One hundred and three of every 1,000 women at age 40 get a positive mammography in routine screening, and 8 of every 1,000 women at age 40 who participate in routine screening have breast cancer and a positive mammography. Here is a new representative sample of women at age 40 who got a positive mammography in routine screening. How many of these women do you expect to actually have breast cancer?

_____ of _____.

Figure 11.3 shows that the students performed much better with frequencies than with probabilities.

Why is base rate neglect apparently greater for probability than for frequency information? Gigerenzer and Hoffrage argued that because our minds

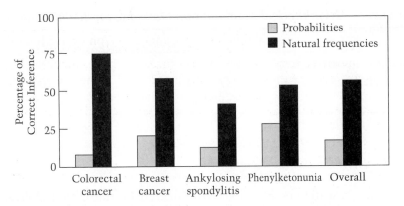

Figure 11.3. Advanced medical students were much better at solving diagnosis problems presented in frequencies rather than as probabilities. From Hoffrage et al., 2000, *Science, 290,* p. 2261 (Fig. 1).

evolved in preliterate societies where information would be remembered in terms of frequencies, we are not designed to think about probabilities. By analogy, numbers can be represented as Roman numerals, but we wouldn't want to do long division that way because the representation is inappropriate for the process. Similarly, it is possible to solve these sorts of problems using probabilities, but because we usually represent this information in frequencies, we're not very good at dealing with probabilities.

Other researchers take issue with Gigerenzer's statement that "the mind is a frequentist." They don't take issue with the data—people perform much better with data presented in some formats than others—but they do take issue with the conclusion that it's frequencies that make the difference. They claim that the frequency version of the problem does not simply change probabilities and frequencies, but rather it changes the *type* of probabilities presented. Other critics claim that important information implicit in the probability version is made explicit in the frequency version; deemed especially important is that some groups are really subsets of other groups, for example, that some people who test positive don't have the disease (Evans, Handley, Perham, Over, & Thompson, 2000; Fiedler, Brinkmann, Betsch, & Wild, 2000; Girotto & Gonzalez, 2001; Johnson-Laird, Legrenzi, Girotto, Legrenzi, & Caverni, 1999; Lewis & Keren, 1999; Macchi, 2000; Mellers & McGraw, 1999; Newell & Shanks, 2004; Oppenheimer, 2003; Sloman, Over, Slovak, & Stibe, 2003). You will not be shocked to learn that Hoffrage and Gigerenzer disagreed with these critics (Gigerenzer, 2001; Gigerenzer & Hoffrage, 1999; Hoffrage, Gigerenzer, Krauss, & Martignon, 2002). This debate is still far from settled. It is obvious that presentation format makes a substantial difference in performance (Broder & Schiffer, 2003), but the reasons are not yet clear.

SUMMARY   There are two main points in the preceding sections. First, people do not behave rationally when they make choices. This irrationality takes two forms: Our choices don't show procedure invariance (making the same choice regardless of how preference is measured) or description invariance (making the same choice regardless of how the choice is described).

Second, people do not always make optimal choices of the type dictated by expected value or expected utility theory. Note that the claim is not that people *never* make an optimal choice. Rather, we're assuming that there is some set of mechanisms that guides people's choices, and if the mechanisms were built to optimize, people would select optimally every time. Because they don't select optimally every time, we assume that a mechanism built on a different principle guides choice. So what is it? The argument presented here is that people use different heuristics, or rules, that are easy to use and that provide rapid answers that are usually effective.

It's important to emphasize that heuristics usually provide good answers. In the examples we've reviewed, heuristics are made to look maladaptive or even foolish. These problems were set up to pit heuristics against expected utility or probability calculations, so the answers based on heuristics are not optimal, but that doesn't mean that heuristics don't lead to good answers most of the time.

Stand-on-One-Foot Questions

6. *What are the three heuristics that people use to estimate probabilities, and how do they work?* Representativeness, Availability, Anchoring & Adjustment

7. *What type of information do people typically ignore when making choices?* - Sample Size/

8. *What is the core of Gigerenzer's argument about why the problems posed to participants in typical choice experiments are unfair and make people look more foolish than they really are?* Base Rate / frequencies vs probabilities

Questions That Require Two Feet

9. *Explain what this sentence means: "You should have no faith in lie detector tests because people who evaluate lie detector tests ignore the base rate of liars."*

10. *You may have noticed that projects often seem to take longer than you expected when you planned them. Can you apply the anchoring and adjustment heuristic to guess why your estimate is often wrong?*

11. *Recall from chapter 7 that you might falsely remember something happening if it is part of a script. For example, you might falsely remember that a waitress offered a customer a menu, even if that didn't happen. Can you relate this idea to base rate?*

Do People Reason Logically?

Preview

We have seen that people don't always make optimal choices. What happens with a problem that is more obviously amenable to logical processes? Two important conclusions about deductive logic as it applies to conditional statements and syllogisms are that people do not use deductive logic to solve these problems and that the content of the problem has a big impact on people's success in solving it. People can best evaluate conditional statements that are thought of as permissions ("If you want to do A, you must do B first to be allowed to do A") or precautions ("If you want to do A, do B first as a precaution"). Broadly speaking, the same conclusions apply to our ability to evaluate syllogisms—people are not logical, and the content of the syllogism matters—but it is harder to say what allows people to solve syllogisms successfully.

Decision making is not the only type of problem with which humans are faced. Indeed, another class of problems also arguably has a single answer. These problems can be analyzed using formal logic, and we start with the same question that began our discussion of decision making: Do people use these formal processes to answer such questions? It is not an exaggeration to say that our ability to reason supports much of what we think makes our lives as humans pleasant and interesting; even the simplest actions we perform are often the end product of reasoning processes (for a broader discussion of the role of reasoning in life, see Calne, 1999). We engage these processes dozens of times each day, usually without even noticing that we are doing so. Suppose you're sitting in your room and you know that you have a class at 11:00. You check the clock and see that it is 10:50. You leave your room to go to class. We could say that that simple act has this structure:

> If it's almost 11:00, I should leave for class.
> It's almost 11:00.
> Therefore, I should leave for class.

This example probably seems so simple as to be uninformative, and in fact people are quite good at reasoning in this sort of situation. As we will see, however, there are many other situations in which people do not reason quite so well.

Formal Logic

We noted that there are optimal or correct answers to many choice problems. That is also true of **deductive reasoning**, in which answers can be derived by formal logic. As was true with choice behavior, people do not always select this objectively correct answer; in fact, there are certain types of problems that people consistently get wrong, and they tend to make the same types of mistakes. These errors indicate that formal logic processes do not drive people's behavior. The mechanisms that do drive reasoning are under debate, and we discuss several proposals.

In a deductive reasoning task, we can apply formal logical processes and derive an objectively correct solution. These problems begin with some number of **premises**, statements of fact that are assumed to be true. Given these premises, deductive reasoning allows us to make further statements of fact— **conclusions**—that must also be true:

Premise	If an election is contentious, many people will turn out to vote.
Premise	This election is contentious.
Conclusion	Many people will turn out to vote.

Because of the structure of the two premises, the conclusion must be true. What's important in deductive reasoning is the form of the argument. We don't use deductive reasoning to ascertain the truth of the conclusion in the real world; we use it to determine whether the conclusion necessarily follows from the premises. For example, consider the following:

Premise	If snow is black, it makes a good hiding place for coal.
Premise	Snow is black.
Conclusion	Snow makes a good hiding place for coal.

In this case, the second premise is false; nevertheless, the argument is deductively valid, meaning that the conclusion must be true if the premises are true. It may seem silly to get excited about (or even mildly interested in) deductive reasoning if it can lead to ridiculous conclusions such as this one, but the point is to let you know what kind of conclusions can be drawn soundly, given the evidence of what you already know. Ascertaining the accuracy of what you already know (e.g., whether snow is black) is up to you.

Inductive reasoning shows that a conclusion is more likely (or less likely) to be true. It does not allow us to say that the conclusion must be true, as deductive reasoning does:

Premise	If I cook cabbage, then the house smells funny.
Premise	The house smells funny.
Conclusion	I cooked cabbage.

This conclusion is not deductively necessary. There could be other reasons the house smells funny: I may have cooked brussels sprouts, I may be cat-sitting for a friend, and so on. Although the conclusion is not deductively necessary, we could still inductively conclude that it is more likely that I cooked cabbage than if the premises were not true. If my house didn't smell funny, it would

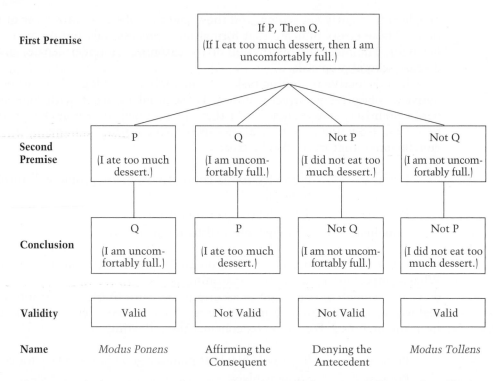

Figure 11.4. The four common conditional statement forms. The first premise states a condition (if P, then Q), and the second premise asserts that either P or Q is not true. Although an infinite number of invalid conclusions might be drawn from the premises, the four conclusions shown here are important enough to be considered in detail in the psychological literature.

certainly be less likely that I had cooked cabbage. Thus, deduction allows you to make conclusions with certainty, whereas induction only allows you to change the probability of a conclusion being true.

How do we know when a deductive argument is valid? Deductive arguments have been studied extensively in two formats: conditional statements and syllogisms. **Conditional statements** actually have three statements. The first is a premise of the form "If P, then Q." P is a condition and Q is a consequence; if condition P is met, then consequence Q follows. The second premise makes a statement about whether P or Q is true or not true. The third premise is a conclusion about P or Q. If you follow the four classic logical forms shown in Figure 11.4, you will understand why some of the conclusions are valid and some are not. The first one (_modus ponens_) is rather obvious: If I ate too much dessert, then I must be uncomfortably full. The next example (affirming the consequent) states that I am uncomfortably full, but it doesn't necessarily follow that I must have eaten too much dessert; I might have eaten too much dinner, for example. In logical problems, the word _if_ does not mean "if and only if." "If P, then Q" means that P causes Q, but it does not preclude other things from causing Q.

Similarly, in the third example (denying the antecedent), I didn't eat too much dessert, but it doesn't necessarily follow that I am not uncomfortably full; I might be full for other reasons. In the final example (*modus tollens*), we are told that I am not uncomfortably full; it must be true, therefore, that I did not eat too much dessert.

The other logical form that has been studied in some detail is the **syllogism**, which, like a conditional statement, has three parts: two premises followed by a conclusion. Conditionals include an "if–then" statement, whereas for syllogisms, all three statements are statements of fact. This is an example of a syllogism:

> All computers are annoyances.
> A Macintosh is a computer.
> Therefore, a Macintosh is an annoyance.

The easiest way to evaluate the truth of a syllogism is using a Venn diagram, as shown in Figure 11.5. It's also important to try to falsify the syllogism. Many syllogisms can be true under some circumstances, but we're

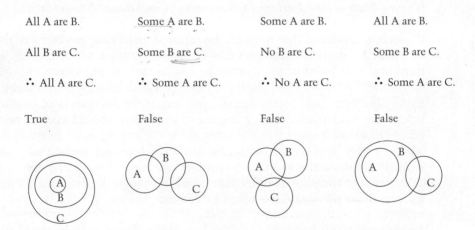

The syllogism must be true under all conditions to be considered true. Thus, a syllogism that we call "false" may be true under certain conditions. Such a syllogism is still considered false.

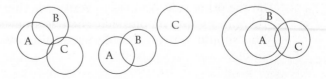

Figure 11.5.   Four sample syllogisms, one true and three false. Note that for a syllogism to be true, it must always be true. The second line of illustrations shows that many syllogisms may be true under some circumstances, but because they are not always true, they are considered false.

interested in logical imperatives: If the first two premises are true, can we conclude that the third statement must be true?

Naturally, you don't need to phrase syllogisms using just letters, as in the figure. For example, consider this problem:

> Some cigarettes are made from tobacco products.
> Some tobacco products are unhealthful.
> Therefore, some cigarettes are unhealthful.

This syllogism sounds like it might be true, but in fact it is false. It has the same logical structure as the second syllogism in Figure 11.5, which is also false. (The "∴" symbol means *therefore*.)

As with conditional statements, the point of syllogisms is to discover how statements can be combined so a logically valid conclusion must follow. Researchers investigating syllogistic reasoning typically ask participants to evaluate a syllogism to determine whether any conclusions can be drawn from the two premises, and if so, what they are.

Human Success and Failure in Reasoning: Conditional Statements

It was long assumed that humans are rational, behaving according to the rules of logic. If a correct deduction can be made, humans will make it, was the thinking. This point of view originated with the ancient Greek philosophers, particularly Aristotle, and continued into the 20th century. Jean Piaget, the famous developmental psychologist, argued that the final stage of cognitive development is characterized by the use of logic. You should keep in mind that people need not be aware of the rules of logic for those rules to guide their behavior; I may speak grammatically, but that does not mean that I can consciously produce the rules of grammar, any more than I can give a precise description of the physics of bicycle riding, although my movements may conform to those physical laws when I ride one.

THE WASON CARD PROBLEM.   In the late 1960s, Peter Wason (1968, 1969) devised a compelling demonstration that humans do not always reason well. He posed this problem:

> The figure shows four cards. Each card has a letter on one side and a digit on the other side. You are to verify whether the following rule is true: If there is a vowel on one side, there is an even number on the other side. You should verify this rule by turning over the minimum number of cards.

Before you continue reading, think over the problem in Figure 11.6. Which cards would you turn over, and why? By the way the cards from left to right give you the following information: P, Q, Not P, and Not Q.

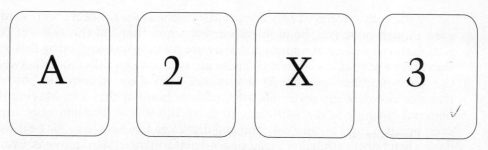

Figure 11.6. The Wason card selection problem embodies a conditional logic problem. The first premise is the rule "If there is a vowel, there is an even number" ("If P, then Q"). Each card is equivalent to a second premise; from left to right, they are P, Q, Not P, and Not Q. By selecting cards to turn over, the participant is deciding which of these second premises can lead to a valid conclusion.

Most college students (and, more generally, most people) do not answer this problem correctly. The correct answer is that you should turn over the A card and the 3 card. Most people realize that you must turn over the A card. The tricky one is that 3 card. For the A card, you can see that because there's a vowel on one side, there ought to be an even number on the other. The 3 card cannot have a vowel on the other side; if it does, it disproves the rule. Across a wide variety of studies, about 15% of college students answer this problem correctly, although the percentage varies a bit from study to study. Even students who have just finished a one-semester course in logic don't do much better (Cheng, Holyoak, Nisbett, & Oliver, 1986). These studies indicate that people do not have a sort of all-purpose system into which they can deposit problems and produce the logical answer. Does that mean that we never act logically?

CONCRETENESS OR FAMILIARITY? Consider this version of the Wason card task administered by Richard Griggs and James Cox (1982), shown in Figure 11.7:

> The cards in front of you have information about four people sitting at a table. On one side of a card is a person's age and on the other side of the card is what the person is drinking. Here is a rule: If a person is drinking beer, then the person must be older than 19 years of age. Select the card or cards that you definitely need to turn over to determine whether they are violating the rule.

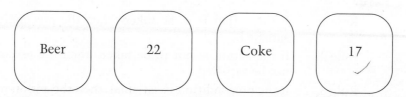

Figure 11.7. This problem is analogous to the one using vowels and digits in Figure 11.6, but people find it much easier. Why?

Participants averaged 72% correct (they turned over the Beer and 17 cards), even though none got the problem correct when they did the abstract version that uses letters and numbers. Why are participants so good at this version and so poor at the abstract? There are two obvious differences between the letters/number and coke/beer versions. They differ in terms of how abstract or concrete the materials are, and how familiar they are. Making the material concrete is not sufficient to make the Wason problem easy, however, because rules about how food and drinks go together (e.g., "If I eat haddock, then I drink gin") don't lead to good performance (Manktelow & Evans, 1979; see also Griggs, 1984; Reich & Ruth, 1982; Valentine, 1985; Yachanin, 1986).

Another possibility is that the beer/coke version of the problem is familiar. Participants have seen this rule enforced, and so they can simply rely on their memory. The familiarity explanation doesn't seem to be complete, however, because unfamiliar versions have been used with participants who solve the problem at high rates. For example, Leda Cosmides (1989) told a story about a foreign culture in which married men had a tattoo on their chests and in which cassava root was an aphrodisiac. When told to check the rule "If a man eats cassava root, then he must have a tattoo on his chest," participants' performance was very high. Thus, familiarity with a rule is not necessary to good performance.

PRAGMATIC REASONING SCHEMAS. Patricia Cheng and Keith Holyoak (1985) suggested that abstract mental structures help us reason. **Pragmatic reasoning schemas** are generalized sets of rules that are defined in relation to goals. They are called *pragmatic* because they lead to inferences that are practical in solving problems. Logical rules, in contrast, can lead to valid inferences that may not be of much help. For example, the rule "If I have a headache, I should take an aspirin" leads to the valid inference "If I need not take an aspirin, then I don't have a headache." This deduction is logically sound but not very practical.

Cheng and Holyoak (1985) suggested that people have abstract reasoning schemas for experiences such as permissions, obligations, and causations. The permission schema (which is most relevant to the problems we've been looking at) describes a situation in which a precondition must be satisfied before some action can be taken, such as "If you want to drink beer, then you must be at least 21 years old." The schema for permissions is composed of four if–then rules:

Rule 1   If the action is to be taken, then the precondition must be satisfied.

Rule 2   If the action is not to be taken, then the precondition need not be satisfied.

Rule 3   If the precondition is satisfied, then the action may be taken.

Rule 4   If the precondition is not satisfied, then the action must not be taken.

The schema becomes active if the problem contains words like *allowed* or *permitted*, or if the problem is described in terms matching one of the rules in the schema ("To use this exercise machine, you must put on a safety harness."). Once the schema is active, the rules serve as a guide to what sort of evidence (if any) is needed to evaluate whether the permission rules are being followed. If you know that people are not taking the action (not drinking beer), then they need not satisfy the precondition (be older than 21) from Rule 2; if they are taking the action, then they had better have fulfilled the condition from Rule 4.

Cheng and Holyoak (1985) demonstrated the importance of the permission schema by varying whether they gave participants a rationale for the rule they were to evaluate in a card selection problem. They gave participants the standard abstract card selection task but phrased it in terms of permission; they said that to take action A, one had to have fulfilled precondition P. The cards said, "Has taken action A," "Has fulfilled precondition P," and so on. They found that 61% of college students they tested answered correctly, whereas only 19% got the right answer when the problem was not framed in terms of permission. Thus, even though the materials were abstract and unfamiliar, participants were much more successful when the permission schema was activated.

THE EVOLUTIONARY PERSPECTIVE.   Leda Cosmides and John Tooby (1992, 2000; Sugiyama, Tooby, & Cosmides, 2002) and Gerd Gigerenzer and his colleagues (Gigerenzer & Hug, 1992; Gigerenzer & Todd, 1999) appealed to evolutionary concerns in reasoning (as they did in choice behavior described earlier). They argued that humans evolved as social animals, meaning that we live in communities and have social ties that we rely on to help us survive. A social network requires that individuals either help or punish other members of the community, depending on their behavior. Cosmides and Tooby argued that this rule is so important that our cognitive systems have evolved to make the rule easy to understand. They argued that we are especially good at detecting cheaters—people who are violating a social contract, such as underage people drinking alcohol.

An interesting prediction of the evolutionary perspective is that the definition of *cheater* varies, depending not on the logical structure of the problem but on the observer's social perspective. Gerd Gigerenzer and Klaus Hug (1992) provided a compelling example of this effect. They used the rule "If an employee works on the weekend, then that person gets a day off during the week." For half the participants, the story surrounding the rule encouraged the participant to take the role of the employer; the other half took the perspective of the worker (see Figure 11.8).

Participants who took the employer's perspective tended to select Q and Not P: They are trying to catch cheaters (people who take a day off during the week without working on the weekend). Participants who took the employee's perspective tended to select P and Not Q. These participants also seem to be trying to catch cheaters, but in this case they are trying to be sure that the

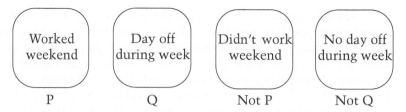

Figure 11.8.   The cards people select in this version of the problem depend on the perspective they are instructed to take—as an employer or a worker.

employers are not cheating. They seek to ensure that if a fellow employee worked during the weekend, he or she got a day off during the week. (See Holyoak & Cheng, 1995, for the pragmatic reasoning schema account of these perspective effects.) Critics have suggested that the versions of the Wason card selection task that seem to fit the evolutionary account actually have properties other than their "fit" to hypothetical modules that cause good performance (e.g., Carlisle & Shafir, 2005; Sperber & Girotto, 2002).

So, in the end, what do we know about how people reason in this paradigm? We know that people are not logic machines who can plug any problem into logic algorithms, with the correct answer popping out. The content of the problem matters. We also know that familiarity with the content (i.e., the problem is about something you know) is neither necessary nor sufficient for successful reasoning. It's not necessary because we know that people can reason well about unfamiliar things (e.g., cassava roots and tattoos), and we know it's not sufficient because in some situations people reason poorly about domains with which they are probably somewhat familiar (e.g., foods and drinks that go together). We do not, as yet, have a complete understanding of the reasoning that goes into this task.

Human Success and Failure in Reasoning: Syllogisms

We would like to understand the critical features of a problem that help people reason well. So far, we have discussed evolutionary theories and pragmatic reasoning schemas as hypotheses about the key features of reasoning. Later, we discuss more general theories of reasoning that encompass conditional statements and other sorts of problems. But first we turn to another type of logic problem: syllogisms.

The first thing to know about our ability to reason with syllogisms is that we're not very good at it. In one study that used many of the possible forms, participants got 52% correct (Dickstein, 1978; see also Evans, Handley, Harper, & Johnson-Laird, 1999, and Johnson-Laird, 1999). Chance performance was 20% because participants were shown five possible conclusions and were asked to select one. Why do people find syllogisms so difficult? It is not the case that people simply cannot deduce the correct implications and then make a guess. Errors on syllogisms are quite systematic (see Dickstein, 1975), which indicates that people aren't guessing; rather, there is some principle guiding their choice of conclusions, but that principle leads to incorrect conclusions. Researchers have proposed several candidates for this faulty process. Note at the outset that all the hypotheses we're about to discuss may account for the performance of people on some problems, but none of them is a complete account.

One type of mistake people make is **conversion error** (Dickstein, 1975, 1976; Revlis, 1975) in which the participant reverses terms that should not be reversed. Some terms, such as *no* and *some*, can be reversed. If I say, "No dogs are plumbers," I can also say, "No plumbers are dogs." Similarly, if I assert, "Some knives are weapons," I can assert, "Some weapons are knives." The terms *all* and *some . . . not* are not convertible, however. If I assert, "All canaries are birds," that does not justify asserting, "All birds are canaries." Stating, "Some mammals are not whales" does not justify saying, "Some whales are not mammals." The conversion error occurs when participants believe that they can safely convert a statement that they should not convert. For example, the syllogism "Some Cs are Bs; all As are Bs" does not have a valid conclusion. But if the person reading it converted the second premise, then he or she could conclude that some Cs are As, and indeed, that conclusion is a typical error that people make, possibly indicating that they convert the second premise (Evans, Newstead, & Byrne, 1993). Although conversion probably leads to some errors, it cannot be a complete account because some participants are aware that some quantifiers cannot be converted (Newstead & Griggs, 1983) and because participants make errors where conversion is not a potential problem.

Another problem is **conversational implicature**. This daunting term refers to the fact that syllogisms are a logical form and thus use the language of logicians, which is not always the same as everyday language, although it is easily confused. For example, when the term *some* is used in a syllogism, it really means "at least one, and possibly all." It is perfectly appropriate to say "Some triangles have three sides," even though all triangles have three sides. In normal usage, people say "some" to mean "more than one, but not all." Thus, when people read "some" in a syllogism they probably think of the term in its conversational sense instead of its logical sense (Begg & Harris, 1982). Although these interpretations occur, analyses of the types of errors people make indicate that conversational implicature accounts for some, but not many, syllogistic reasoning errors (and may apply to other types of deduction; Bonnefon & Hilton, 2002).

Another source of the systematic errors people show in syllogistic reasoning is the **atmosphere** created when the two premises of a syllogism are both either positive or negative or when the quantifiers (e.g., *all* or *none*) of the premises are the same (Simpson & Johnson, 1966; Woodworth & Sells, 1935). For example, consider these syllogisms:

No As are Bs.   Some As are Bs.

No Bs are Cs.   Some Bs are Cs.

No As are Cs.   Some As are Cs.

Both conclusions seem appropriate because they are consistent with the atmosphere created by the premises, either because they are all negative (example on left) or because they all use the same quantifier (example on right). Yet, neither syllogism is true. (See the Venn diagrams in Figure 11.5.)

Atmosphere accounts for about 50% of the erroneous responses in a multiple-choice format (Dickstein, 1978) and nearly that many in an open-ended test where the participant must supply the conclusion (Johnson-Laird & Bara, 1984). Nevertheless, it is not a complete explanation of syllogistic reasoning because it only explains how participants approach a subset of syllogisms.

People may also be influenced by **prior beliefs**. Syllogisms are supposed to be a purely logical exercise in which we evaluate the conclusion only in light of its relationship to the premises. In other words, the premises "All *As* are *Bs*" or "All dogs are cats" should contribute to our evaluation of a syllogism in the same way. In fact, however, people are more likely to reject a syllogism as false if the conclusion is known to be false. John St. B. T. Evans and his colleagues (Evans, Barston, & Pollard, 1983; see also Newstead, Pollard, & Evans, 1992) compared two syllogisms of the same form:

No cigarettes are inexpensive.	No addictive things are inexpensive.
Some addictive things are inexpensive.	Some cigarettes are inexpensive.
Some addictive things are not cigarettes.	Some cigarettes are not addictive.

Both syllogisms are valid, but 81% evaluated the one on the left as valid, whereas only 63% evaluated the one on the right as valid.

In another example, Jane Oakhill, Phillip Johnson-Laird, and Alan Garnham (1989; Oakhill & Johnson-Laird, 1985) presented participants with one of these two syllogisms:

All the Frenchmen in the room are wine drinkers.
Some of the wine drinkers in the room are gourmets.
Some of the Frenchmen in the room are gourmets.

All the Frenchmen in the room are wine drinkers.
Some of the wine drinkers in the room are Italians.
Some of the Frenchmen in the room are Italians.

Note that both have the same form ("Italians" has replaced "gourmets" in the second syllogism). No valid conclusion can be drawn from the first two premises, but the majority of participants incorrectly accepted the conclusion in the first syllogism, whereas almost none did in the second syllogism (see also Cherubini, Garnham, & Oakhill, 1998; Klauer, Musch, & Naumer, 2000).

These four factors—conversion errors, conversational implicature, atmosphere, and prior beliefs—can affect performance on syllogistic reasoning tasks, but it should be emphasized that these effects do not overwhelm whatever other mechanisms might be at work; many participants get the problem right. Even more important is that each effect applies to only selected problems, and thus their explanatory power is limited. We cannot consider the naming of these effects to be a model of reasoning. We turn next to a discussion of more complete models of reasoning that have been proposed.

General Models of Reasoning

In this section, we consider three models of reasoning that seek to account for a wide variety of reasoning situations, not just a single class of problems.

JOHNSON-LAIRD'S MENTAL MODELS THEORY.   Philip Johnson-Laird and his associates (Johnson-Laird, 1999; Johnson-Laird & Byrne, 1991; see Johnson-Laird, 2005, for an overview) proposed that the meaning, or semantics, of a problem is crucial to its solution. In the **mental models theory**, the meaning of the premises remains in a meaning-based format. The premises are used to construct a mental model of the situation that represents a possible configuration of the world; for example, the premise on the left of Figure 11.9 might give rise to the mental images on the right. (Mental models are not the same as mental images. For the sake of simplicity, we won't represent the mental models themselves.)

Mental models don't just represent the world; they can also be used for deduction because we can combine mental models. The fact that more than one mental model can represent a premise (as in Figure 11.10) has important implications for the way the theory works. Figure 11.10 shows two mental models that might be drawn from a pair of premises. In the top example, the conclusion is valid. In the bottom example, the conclusion is invalid. This invalid conclusion is traceable to the image based on the mental model for the first premise. The person may have committed a conversion error, believing that because all shaded figures are triangles it is also true that all triangles are shaded figures.

How can we avoid such errors? We must generate multiple mental models representing all possible situations, given the stated premises. Thus, we

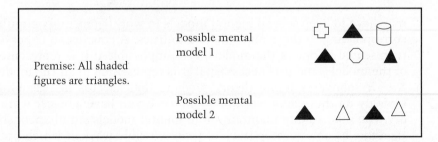

Figure 11.9.   Mental models for the premise "All shaded figures are triangles." The mental models are presented as visual images for simplicity; true mental models are meaning-based structures that might be used to generate mental images but are not images themselves.

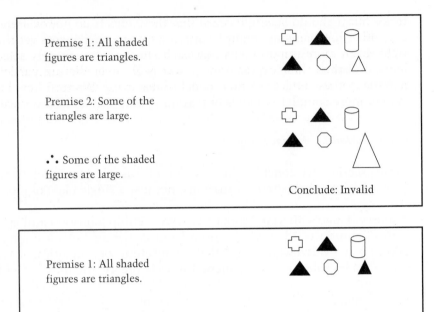

Figure 11.10. This example shows how your mental model might change as new premises are stated and how you would use the mental model to evaluate the validity of a conclusion. Look at the top example. The first mental model is one of several possible models based on this premise. The mental model is changed when the second premise is stated. The conclusion, "Some of the shaded figures are large," is inconsistent with the mental model, so you would conclude that the syllogism is invalid. In the second example, you start with a different mental model of Premise 1. With this mental model, you end up accepting the validity of the conclusion.

may have to keep several mental models in working memory simultaneously, corresponding to these multiple possibilities. A conclusion is possible if it is represented in one of the models; it is impossible if it is represented in none of the models; and it is necessary if it is represented in all the models.

It sounds as if the theory predicts that success in reasoning depends strongly on the size of working memory. If you have a bigger working memory, you'll be able to maintain more mental models simultaneously and will therefore be able to keep track of more possible ways in which premises can be interpreted. That prediction seems to be supported by the data; as syllogisms offer more possible interpretations, participants have a harder time evaluating their truth (Johnson-Laird, Byrne, & Schaeken, 1992).

John St. B. T. Evans and his colleagues (Evans et al., 1999; see also Birney & Halford, 2002) presented participants with 256 syllogisms, in each case asking them to evaluate the conclusion as necessary, possible, or impossible. The mental models theory was quite successful in predicting participants' responses. Of 36 problems whose conclusions are necessary, 18 could be solved with a single mental model and 18 required multiple models, according to a previous analysis by Johnson-Laird and Bara (1984). Evans and his colleagues found that 81% of the single-model problems were evaluated correctly, but only 59% of the multiple-model problems were.

Limitations of working memory seem only to predict that people will fail on problems that are difficult, but the types of errors that people make are systematic, beyond this failing. Johnson-Laird proposes that many errors arise from the **principle of truth**, which states that people tend to construct mental models representing only what is true and not what is false. One reason they do so is to reduce the load on working memory. For example, for the premise "There is a mailbox or a pair of glasses," they would construct three mental models representing (a) the mailbox, (b) the glasses, and (c) both the mailbox and the glasses. They would *not* represent what is missing: That is, in the case where they represent only the mailbox, they would not represent the fact that the glasses are not present. Failing to explicitly represent all possibilities often leaves the reasoner unable to draw a conclusion, or causes him or her to draw the wrong conclusion (Goldvarg & Johnson-Laird, 2000; Johnson-Laird & Savary, 1999).

CHATER AND OAKSFORD'S INFORMATION GAIN MODEL. **Probability models** of reasoning, including Chater and Oaksford's (1999) model, hold that people seldom engage in deductive reasoning in the everyday world. Rather, they make judgments based on probabilities. For example, when you hear "Rover is a dog," you assume that Rover has fur not by deduction ("Dogs have fur; Rover is a dog; therefore, Rover has fur") but because you know there is a high probability that a dog has fur. Thus, when participants apparently "fail" on logical reasoning tasks in the laboratory, it's because they treat them as probability tasks—the same way they treat everyday reasoning tasks.

One implication of this view is that people use probabilities to assess the likelihood that they will find useful information. Consider the version of the Wason card problem in Figure 11.11. Are you really going to snatch the cup from the 4-year-old and inspect it to ensure that she's not drinking beer? Kris Kirby (1994) reported that 65% of participants said they would check the 4-year-old, compared with 86% who said they would check the 19-year-old (the drinking age was 21 when this experiment was conducted). The base rate of 4-year-olds drinking beer is extremely low. Mike Oaksford and Nick Chater (1994, 1996, 1998, 2003) pointed out that most researchers act as though the potential relationships of P and Q are equally probable in the world; that is, that given P (drinking beer), there is an equal likelihood of Q (22 years old) or Not Q (4 years old). In this problem, that is clearly not the case, and participants are sensitive to the difference.

Chater and Oaksford (1999) proposed that people's main motivation in reasoning tasks may be to seek out information that will be maximally informative,

Figure 11.11. Version of the Wason card problem used by Kirby (1994). People are more likely to check the 19-year-old than the 4-year-old, indicating that people are sensitive to the likelihood that they will find useful information.

not necessarily information that will lead to answers that are correct according to formal logic. For the Wason card problem, they used a statistical method that they claim can evaluate the amount of information likely to be obtained when each card is turned over, and they developed a model using the same principles that accounts for syllogistic reasoning (Chater & Oaksford, 1999; for a summary of their work, see Oaksford & Chater, 2001).

DUAL PROCESS MODELS. Several researchers have proposed **dual process models**, which hold that reasoning may be supported by two different processes (Evans, 2003; Evans & Over, 1996; Sloman, 1996; Stanovich, 1999). System 1 is based on evolutionarily older cognitive processes—indeed, it is the process that other animals use—and it uses simple association. The processing in System 1 is not open to consciousness—you are only aware of the decision you make, and you may, in fact, make the decision and initiate action without really having thought about it. System 2 is uniquely human. It is the system that allows abstract reasoning, but it is slow. Unlike System 1, you are aware of each step, because each step takes place in working memory. For that reason, System 2 is limited by your working memory capacity.

This framework has a lot of appeal. It incorporates a basic fact about reasoning. As noted by Cheng and Holyoak (1995), and by Oaksford and Chater (2001), it seems that much of what we do need not be guided by reasoning. Our concerns are much more pragmatic. It's easiest to assume that the world is the way it always is and that we can act as we usually do, and everything will be fine. For example, I needn't engage in reasoning to know that "If I turn the key, the door will unlock." That's what always happens, so a simple association will do. However, sometimes we *do* reason. This point was made forcefully by Keith Stanovich (1999). He pointed out that some people fairly consistently give the normative answer on a wide variety of reasoning problems, and these people also tend to have high scores on the SAT (scholastic aptitude test), which may be taken as a measure of general cognitive ability. We need a theory that can account for the fact that people are often illogical, but sometimes they *are* logical.

Stanovich has also offered some interesting evidence that the same individuals might use one system or the other, depending on how the question is phrased. Stanovich and Richard West (1998) compared people who solved the abstract version of the Wason selection task and people who didn't, and found that the SAT scores of the former were higher than those of the latter. But when they used the drinking age version of the problem, the SAT scores were no different. The interpretation is that when confronted with an unfamiliar problem, participants had to use System 2, which is closely associated with cognitive capacities; therefore, you get the relationship with SAT scores. But when confronted with the drinking age problem, participants relied on System 1 because they have experience with this sort of problem. The performance of System 1 is unrelated to cognitive ability, so no relationship with SAT score was observed in this version of the problem.

Another source of evidence supporting dual system models comes from brain imaging studies. Vinod Goel and his colleagues (Goel, Buchel, Frith, & Dolan, 2000) showed differences in the neural network that supported reasoning about syllogisms that were formally the same, but that differed in content. In the no content condition, syllogisms took the following form:

> All P are B.
> All B are C.
> Therefore, all P are C.

In the content condition, they took the following form:

> All poodles are pets.
> All pets have names.
> Therefore, all poodles have names.

Performance was about the same in the content and no content conditions (79% vs. 77%), but the brain activations differed. The content condition showed much left temporal lobe activity, an area we discussed in chapter 8 as possibly being important for storing semantic memories. The no content version showed a good deal of activation in the left parietal lobe. There were also areas that were common to both versions (basal ganglia and left prefrontal cortex, among others).

SUMMARY   We've reviewed two types of reasoning problems. Conditional reasoning problems ("If P, then Q") can be difficult or easy, depending on the materials used; we examined several theories accounting for these effects, including the evolutionary perspective and pragmatic reasoning schemas. Syllogisms have four features that affect performance, but none of the current theories is a complete theory of reasoning.

We also examined three general theories of reasoning: Johnson-Laird's mental models theory, which emphasizes the semantic content of the premises; Chater and Oaksford's probability model, which emphasizes that people may have nonlogical reasons that motivate their choices in a reasoning problem; and dual process models, which hold that people sometimes use simple associations to solve reasoning problems and at other times use slower processing that is more typical of what we think of as reasoning.

As we noted at the beginning of this chapter, when we say "reasoning," we refer to a situation in which it is obvious that one of a limited set of answers is correct, for example, regardless of whether a syllogism is true or false. Obviously, not all the situations that humans encounter are of this sort. Some are much more open ended, which means that the problem provides much less guidance to the possible answers. In the next chapter, we turn to these problems.

Stand-on-One-Foot Questions

12. *What is the difference between deductive and inductive reasoning?*

13. *Is it true that familiarity is the critical feature that determines whether people will successfully evaluate a conditional statement such as the one embodied in the Wason card selection task?*

14. *What are the three general models of reasoning we discussed?*

Questions That Require Two Feet

15. *Another way we might reason is based solely on memory. You simply remember a similar case and apply what you did last time (assuming that it worked). How often do you think you use this strategy (called case-based reasoning)?*

16. *The probability models seem to argue that people don't actually reason in reasoning problems but rather try to maximize the amount of information they can obtain. Assuming that this result is true, can we say that people don't reason?*

KEY TERMS

algorithm	description invariance	principle of truth
anchoring and	dual process models	prior beliefs
adjustment	expected utility	probability models
atmosphere	expected value	problem frame
availability	gambler's fallacy	procedure invariance
base rate	heuristics	psychic budgets
conclusion	inductive reasoning	rational
conditional statements	loss aversion	representativeness
conversational	mental models theory	sample size
implicature	normative theories	satisficing
conversion error	pragmatic reasoning	sunk cost
decision making	schemas	syllogism
deductive reasoning	premise	transitivity

CURRENT DIRECTIONS IN COGNITIVE SCIENCE

Recommended readings

Mellers, B. A., & McGraw, A. P. (2001). "Anticipated emotions as guides to choice." (pp. 106–113) When you make a decision, you anticipate how you would feel should one outcome or the other be obtained. How will I feel if I win $100? How will I feel if I give up this coffee mug I just got? Mellers and McGraw review research that indicates, contrary to our intuitions, that we don't always know how we are going to feel about different outcomes, and indeed, that the same outcome can lead to different emotions in different settings.

Yaniv, I. (2004). "The benefit of additional opinions." (pp. 114–120) In the decision-making studies that we reviewed, participants were on their own—they decided which choice to make. But in life most of us seek the opinions of others when we have an important decision to make (whether to propose marriage, which college to attend). In this article, Yaniv summarizes what we know about combining opinions, and the conditions under which doing so helps us.

12 *Problem Solving*

How Do People Solve Novel Problems?

- Problem Spaces
- Selecting Operators

How Do People Apply Experience to New Problems?

- Background Knowledge
- Analogy
- Functional Fixedness √

What Makes People Good at Solving Problems?

- How Do Experts Differ From Novices?
- How Do People Become Experts?
- What Makes Nonexperts Good at Solving Problems?

In chapter 11, we discussed decision making and reasoning for closed-ended problems, meaning that there was a limited number of possible answers or that a subset of the possible answers was provided, with the person left to choose between them. A **problem** can be defined very generally as any situation in which a person has a goal that is not yet accomplished. That general definition encompasses what we called decision making in chapter 11. When psychologists talk about problem solving, however, they mean open-ended problems in which the person knows the goal, but nothing in the problem describes how to accomplish the goal.

According to this definition of a problem—you have a goal that you have not accomplished—you are faced with dozens of problems every day. You want a pizza but you don't have one; that's a problem. You want to be outside but you're in a classroom; that's a problem. These problems are uninteresting because you have faced them (and solved them) countless times before. Your response to these problems is so automatic that you don't even think there is a problem to be solved. When you think of a problem, you more likely think of one of those little puzzles made out of two twisted nails that you are supposed to disentangle.

Problems like getting outside and untwisting nails are at opposite ends of a continuum, namely, a continuum of relevant experience. The "getting outside" problem can be solved based on past experience. The twisted nails problem usually cannot. In the nails problem, you don't have much in memory that will help you, so you must recruit processes that will give you some guidance on how to solve the problem. We could imagine that all problems will vary in the extent to which previous experience guides us.

Indeed, the ends of this continuum illustrate two main themes of research on problem solving: Memory (i.e., prior experience) is important, and general problem-solving routines also come into play. Many problems are not at the extremes I've just described; they are neither completely familiar (so you can't solve a problem by remembering how it was solved last time) nor completely unfamiliar (so past experience is no guide). Rather, most problems are solved through using a combination of memories of similar problems that might be applicable to the current problem and general-purpose problem-solving strategies.

To study general problem-solving routines, psychologists have used problems with which most people are unfamiliar to prevent participants from relying on their memories of similar problems. Our first question is **How do people solve novel problems?** As we'll see, people engage general-purpose strategies to deal with problems they have never seen before.

Again, it is not always the case that people have either complete knowledge or absolutely no knowledge of a problem. Often, they have some knowledge that might be applicable to a problem. **How do people apply experience to new problems?** You would think that some experience would be better than no experience, but that's not always true. Although experience with similar problems can help, it is often difficult to recognize that past experience is relevant. Furthermore, prior knowledge can put you in a mental rut; you might approach new problems in the same way you approached old problems, even if that approach is not appropriate.

Finally, we'll consider the question **What makes people good at solving problems?** As you might guess from the foregoing discussion, there are two main sources of skill in problem solving. You might be good at using the general-purpose processes; or you might have many problem solutions in secondary memory that will apply to other problems.

How Do People Solve Novel Problems?

Preview

When people have experience with a problem, they can proceed as they did the last time they faced it. Without relevant experience, people fall back on general strategies. Working forward means to look for ways to get closer to the goal, but it is often ineffective. Working backward means to begin at the goal and try to mentally work back to the beginning of the problem. Means–ends analysis combines working forward and backward on problems, dictating when it is effective to set subgoals that should be completed before the main goal is tackled.

The heart of problem solving is change. When you are presented with a situation that is not satisfactory, you want to change it in some way to meet a goal. There are usually so many ways to make changes that it is unclear how to proceed.

Problem Spaces

Before we get to the particulars of how people solve unfamiliar problems, we need to discuss how psychologists think about and describe problems. Allen Newell and Herb Simon (1972) emphasized the usefulness of thinking in terms of a **problem space** that includes all possible configurations a problem can take. For example, consider the classic puzzle called the Tower of Hanoi depicted in Figure 12.1. The puzzle includes a board with three pegs and three rings of decreasing size. The goal is to move all the rings from the left peg to the right peg. There are three rules describing how you can move the rings:

1. You can move only one ring at a time.
2. You can move only the top ring on a peg.
3. You cannot put a larger ring on top of a smaller ring.

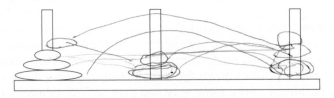

Figure 12.1.   The Tower of Hanoi puzzle.

Figure 12.2. Use this figure to work the Tower of Hanoi puzzle shown in Figure 12.1. Put three coins of decreasing size (a quarter, a nickel, and a penny) on the leftmost dot and try to move the coins to the rightmost dot, following these rules: you can move only one coin at a time, you can move only the top coin on a stack, and you can't put a larger coin on top of a smaller coin. If this puzzle seems too easy, use four coins.

The Tower of Hanoi is used as an example several times in this chapter. You'll get more out of these examples if you work through the problem yourself using coins of different sizes—a quarter, a nickel, and a penny—as described in Figure 12.2.

The problem space for the Tower of Hanoi puzzle can be thought of as all possible configurations of the puzzle board (see Figure 12.3). Each position is called a state of the problem space. More generally, a **problem state** is a particular configuration of the elements of the problem. Notice that links between the different states indicate the possible paths through the problem space. You can't simply jump from one state in the problem space to another; you must move from state to state by way of the links. What determines how

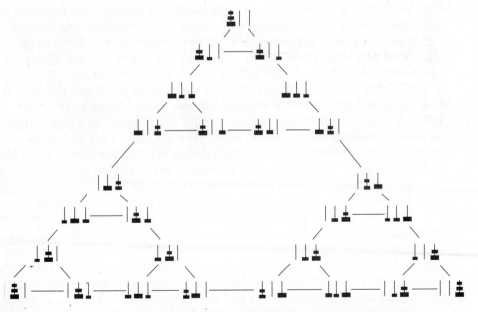

Figure 12.3. Problem space for the Tower of Hanoi puzzle. It's easist to understand the figure by starting at the top and following the choices. You always have the option of moving backward in the space by returning to the position you just occupied.

the states are linked? The links represent **operators**, processes that can be applied to the problem to change its configuration (to change where you are in the problem space). For example, an operator in the Tower of Hanoi problem is to move a disk. Typically, certain conditions must be met before you are allowed to apply an operator. In the Tower of Hanoi, you cannot move a ring that has another ring on top of it, and you cannot place a larger ring on top of a smaller ring.

Selecting Operators

The key to problem solving is selecting the operators that will move you efficiently through the problem space to the goal. Obviously, if you simply move through the problem space randomly, you might accidentally end up at the goal, but you'd like to be certain that you will reach the goal. Furthermore, it would be desirable to reach the goal directly rather than via a circuitous route. How do you select operators to ensure a reasonably direct route to the goal?

You could imagine doing a **brute force search**, examining every possible answer until you find the correct one. For example, suppose you were working a crossword puzzle and saw the letters _alt with the clue "seasoning." You could sequentially substitute each letter of the alphabet (*aalt, balt, calt*) in the blank space until you get to *s* and solve *salt*. The advantage of a brute force search is that it's very simple to apply, but the disadvantage is that it doesn't restrict the part of the problem space through which you must search; you have to try all the possibilities. As the number of possibilities increases modestly, the number of combinations increases rapidly because of a phenomenon called **combinatorial explosion**. For example, suppose the clue was _al_. You could still do a brute force search by putting *a* in the first blank space and trying the letters of the alphabet in the second blank space (*aala, aalb, aalc*, and so on). If that doesn't work, you can try the next letter of the alphabet in the first space and the others in sequence in the second blank space (*bala, balb, balc*). Notice that although we've doubled the number of blank letters, the number of states in the problem space that we must explore has more than doubled. In fact, if there are 26 possible letters to fill in the blanks and 2 blanks to be filled, there are 26^2 possible combinations of letters in the blanks for a total of 676. If we add one more blank, the possibilities increase to 26^3 or 17,576. Thus, it's clear that a brute force search is often impractical.

What strategy do we use instead if a brute force approach is not helpful? It appears that people use heuristics to guide their search for operators that will move them through the problem space. A **heuristic** in problem solving means the same thing that it did in decision making: It's a simple rule that can be applied to a complex problem. Heuristics require minimal computation and often yield an acceptable answer but do not guarantee one.

One problem-solving heuristic is **hill climbing**, which means that you look for an operator that will take you to a state in the problem space that appears to be closer to the goal than where you are now. Imagine the goal of the problem state as the top of a hill. Each step you take is a change in the problem space; to decide where to step, you evaluate whether the step you are contemplating would take you closer to the top of the hill. The hill-climbing heuristic is certainly more effective than brute force—you are at least evaluating moves before you try them—but it is still applicable only to a limited number of problems. Many problems require that you move backward in the problem space to reach your goal. Take the *hill climbing* name literally for a moment and suppose that your goal is to reach the highest point in an area. You take a few steps, the choice of each step guided by whether taking that step leads you upward, and find yourself at the top of a hill. But nearby you see a hill that is still higher than the one you're on. Given your present position, you can't use the hill-climbing strategy to get to the top of this highest hill because you would have to go downhill, away from the goal, to ultimately reach it.

Animals sometimes get caught in a similar bind. Maybe you have seen a dog on a leash straining to reach something that it could easily reach if it went around an obstacle so the leash would no longer be caught. Although we might snicker about the mental superiority of our species, the fact is that humans are not indifferent to moving backward in a problem space. We can do it, obviously, or else many problems would be insoluble, but we are more likely to make errors if we must move backward, and we are slower to make these moves than hill-climbing moves. This phenomenon was demonstrated by John Thomas (1974; see also Greeno, 1974), who examined participants solving the familiar Hobbits and Orcs problem. In this version, the participant is told that there are three Hobbits and three Orcs on one side of a river. They all want to cross the river, but their boat can hold only one or two creatures. Orcs must never outnumber Hobbits on either side of the river—otherwise, the Orcs will devour the Hobbits. How can all the creatures get across the river safely? The problem space for the Hobbits and Orcs problem is depicted in Figure 12.4. The asterisk marks the state from which participants are slow to move and from which they often make errors. At that point, moving forward in the problem space (i.e., toward the goal) requires the participant to make a move that *seems* to be away from the goal, taking some creatures away from the goal side of the river. Although humans can move away from a goal, we are reluctant to do so.

Another heuristic for moving through a problem space is **working backward**. As the name suggests, in this heuristic one begins at the goal state of the problem space and tries to work back to the starting state. This heuristic is useful when the goal state is known but the initial state is not. For example, consider the double-money problem, posed by Wayne Wickelgren (1974):

> Three people play a game in which one person loses and two people win each game. The one who loses must double the amount of money that each of the other two players has at that time. The three players agree to play three games. At the end of the three games, each player has lost

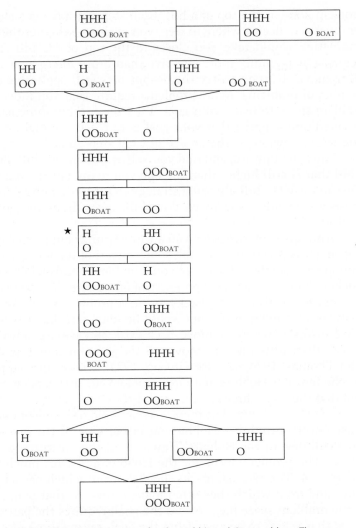

Figure 12.4. Problem space for the Hobbit and Orcs problem. The space is fairly linear (there are few branches) because the boat greatly restricts what you can do at any point. The key is that at one point in the problem (marked by the star) you have to move some creatures away from the goal shore back to the starting shore. People are slow to make that move, indicating that they are influenced by the hill-climbing heuristic.

one game, and each player has $8. What was the original stake of each player?

We could try to solve this problem by selecting some initial state for the stakes of the three players and working forward, evaluating the outcome, and if the correct answer is not obtained, trying to adjust the initial state. However, it is much easier to work backward. If all three players end with $8,

Table 12.1.   **The Double-Money Problem**

Game	Player 1	Player 2	Player 3
Ending stake	8	8	8
Stake before game 3	16*	4	4
Stake before game 2	8	14*	2
Stake before game 1	4	7	13*

*Loser of a game.

after the last game the loser had doubled the money of the two winners; hence, before the last game the winners must have each had $4, and the loser must have had $16. Because we know that each player won exactly once, it is easy to trace back the stakes, as shown in Table 12.1. (In each game, the asterisk indicates the loser.)

As you can see, the problem is easy to solve if we work backward from the goal state to the initial state. Wickelgren (1974) argued that problems are well suited to this heuristic if the goal state is known but there are many possible initial states. If there are many possible initial states, there may not be an intelligent heuristic by which one could select an initial state (and then see whether it leads to the goal state). Working forward on problems like this has been likened to finding a needle in a haystack, but working backward on such problems is more like the needle working its way out of the haystack (Newell, Shaw, & Simon, 1962).

By far, the most thoroughly tested and probably the most broadly applicable heuristic is **means–ends analysis**, which uses a combination of forward- and backward-moving strategies:

1. Compare the current state with the goal state. If there is no difference between them, the problem is solved.
2. If there is a difference between the current state and the goal state, set a goal to solve that difference. If there is more than one difference, set a goal to solve the largest difference.
3. Select an operator that will solve the difference identified in Step 2.
4. If the operator can be applied, apply it. If it cannot, set a new goal to reach a state that would allow the application of the operator.
5. Return to Step 1 with the new goal set in Step 4.

Take as an example the simple act of taking a cat to the vet. Means–ends analysis would solve that problem this way:

Step 1. What is the difference between my current state (at home) and my goal state (at the vet with my cat)? The difference is one of distance.
Step 2. Set a goal to reduce distance.
Step 3. What operator reduces distance? A car reduces distance.

Step 4. A condition of using a car is that it not have an uncaged cat in it.

Step 5. Set a subgoal to make the car suitable to carry cats.

Step 1. What is the difference between my current state (no cat carrier) and my goal state (have a cat carrier)? The difference is one of distance (at pet store).

Step 2. Set a goal to reduce distance.

Step 3. What operator reduces distance? A car reduces distance.

You get the idea. Being able to set a new goal is the key advantage of means–ends analysis. More accurately, the new goal is a subgoal in service of the larger goal of being able to apply the operator of using the car to take the cat to the vet. Setting subgoals is important to allow you to move away from the goal when necessary (unlike the hill-climbing heuristic) in service of achieving another goal that will bring you closer to the goal state. If there is a potentially useful operator that can't be applied, the means–ends analysis heuristic tries to make it applicable. The hill-climbing heuristic abandons an operator that can't be applied immediately and seeks another method (e.g., if you can't take the cat in your car without a pet carrier, you could walk to the vet with the cat in your arms).

Even if problems can be described in ways that sound consistent with means–ends analysis, do people actually use means–ends analysis when they solve problems? Allen Newell and Herb Simon (1972) developed a computer program that solved problems by using means–ends analysis. The program was designed to be general in its applicability to a broad range of problems and so was called the **General Problem Solver**.

Newell, Simon, and their colleagues used verbal protocols to test whether the General Problem Solver provides an accurate description of how humans solve problems. In a **verbal protocol**, the experimenter asks the participant to solve a problem while talking out loud, continuously describing his or her thoughts about solving the problem. The experimenter prompts participants to speak if they fall silent for more than a second or two. The assumption is that the participant has conscious access to at least some of the mental processes that support solving the problem. Although this assumption is controversial (Nisbett & Wilson, 1977), Anders Ericsson and Herb Simon (1993) made an effective case that such data are useful, and indeed, they have proposed a model of how and when information becomes available for verbal report. Newell and Simon (1972) examined the verbal protocols of several participants who worked abstract logic problems and found an impressive degree of correspondence between the steps they reported taking as they solved the problem and the steps that the General Problem Solver took. The important finding was not so much the detailed match between participant and model but the finding that the general character of their approach was similar: Both humans and the model sought to reduce differences between their current state and the goal, and both created subgoals when an operator could not be applied that would reduce a difference. This source of evidence was collected using logical proof problems. Similar methods have been applied using many other problems (Ernst & Newell, 1969).

So far we have discussed a specific type of problem in which the problem solver has no experience that seems relevant. Although such problems arise periodically in real life, it is probably more typical that you have some experience in memory that seems to apply to some aspect of the problem.

Stand-on-One-Foot Questions

1. *Why are heuristics needed for problem solving?*
2. *Name three heuristics for unfamiliar problems.*   brute force
3. *Summarize how means–ends analysis works.*

climb the hill, working backward

Questions That Require Two Feet

4. *We said that the hill-climbing heuristic would not be successful in getting you to the top of the largest hill in an area if you happened to first scale a smaller hill. Could means–ends analysis get you to the top of the largest hill in the area? How would it do so?*
5. *Which has a bigger problem space, chess or checkers? Why? How could you shrink the problem space of either game?*
6. *Which of the methods we've discussed so far do you think the average person would use in trying to open a safe? Which method might a professional safecracker use?*

How Do People Apply Experience to New Problems?

Preview

Problem-solving strategies change if we have relevant background knowledge. Background knowledge may help us classify problems and see their underlying structure. It may also help because sufficient knowledge means that some of the operators may be automatized, leaving attention free for unfamiliar aspects of the problem. Drawing an analogy to a different problem that shares the same underlying structure may help, although people are not very skilled in drawing analogies. Background knowledge can actually hurt performance if people try to apply old knowledge to a new problem when it isn't applicable. Even when people make this mistake, the problem sometimes yields to repeated attempts to solve it.

For problems that are completely unfamiliar to the solver, we don't have to worry about how prior knowledge might affect attempts at a solution. Now we're ready to consider what happens when the solver has some relevant background knowledge. We can assume that some knowledge must be better than no knowledge for solving problems. As we'll see, that is generally true, but in some situations background knowledge hurts problem-solving efforts, and psychologists have been especially interested in exploring those situations.

Background Knowledge

Although we discuss how prior knowledge can negatively affect problem solving, bear in mind that most of the time background knowledge is helpful. The ways in which background knowledge helps are pretty straightforward in the context of the General Problem Solver. First, if you have background knowledge of the domain, you are better able to classify the problem and therefore to understand the problem's critical components. Recall from chapter 4 our discussion of chess masters in William Chase and Herb Simon's (1973) study. They showed that chess masters are able to remember the positions of chess pieces very accurately by chunking pieces into meaningful configurations. They don't perceive 32 chess pieces; they perceive a much smaller number of chunks, each composed of several pieces. The perception of the board in chunks relies on prior experience: If the pieces are arranged randomly, chess masters perceive (and remember) the board no differently than novices. Perception of the board in chunks greatly reduces the search space of problem solving. Domain knowledge allows better perception of the most important part of the problem that should be addressed and thereby restricts the search to the key part of the problem space.

The second way that domain knowledge can help problem solving is by automatizing some of the problem-solving steps so they do not demand attention. One of the first (and most important) steps to automatize is what operators are available and how they move in the problem space. For example, if you are just learning how to play chess, you must think hard about how the knight and the rook move, as well as the oddity that the pawns move ahead one space but can move two spaces from their starting position, take other pieces on the diagonal, and take pieces in passing ("en passant") from their starting position. Until you have thoroughly learned the rules for piece movement, it is difficult to form much strategy.

Here's an example of a problem in which the rules are fairly complex; we might imagine that the problem will be difficult to solve without gaining greater familiarity with the rules:

> In the inns of certain Himalayan villages is practiced a refined tea ceremony. The ceremony involves a host and exactly two guests, neither more nor less. When his guests have arrived and seated themselves at his table, the host performs three services for them. These services are listed in the order of the nobility the Himalayans attribute to them: stoking the fire, fanning the flames, and pouring the tea. During the ceremony, any

of those present may ask another, "Honored Sir, may I perform this oner-
ous task for you?" However, a person may request of another only the
least noble of the tasks which the other is performing. Furthermore, if a
person is performing any tasks, then he may not request a task that is no-
bler than the least noble task he is already performing. Custom requires
that by the time the tea ceremony is over, all the tasks will have been
transferred from the host to the most senior of the guests. How can this
be accomplished?

You probably had to read this problem several times just to understand the
rules. It's hard to even consider how to get to the goal because the operators
are so complicated that they occupy all your working memory capacity.

Contemplating moves through a problem space requires working memory; it becomes difficult to maintain the goal and the operators in working
memory if the operators are not automatized so they take little or no working
memory capacity. Recall the example of taking the cat to the vet. The solution
to this problem relied heavily on background knowledge, especially on knowledge of how subgoals could be achieved. When confronted with a problem of
distance, we know immediately that an automobile is an effective operator to
reduce distance; we don't have to cast about for a solution. If we did not know
that a good solution is to use a car, that subgoal might require a considerable
search that would occupy working memory, which might mean that other
components of the problem would be lost from working memory.

You would think that having some knowledge about a problem is bound
to be better than having no knowledge, and in most cases, familiarity does
help. We think about how the various parts of a problem relate to one another
and draw an analogy between those relationships and the relationships in another familiar problem that we know how to solve. For example, if you are familiar with calculating probabilities in gambling games and are confronted
with a probability question in a statistics class, you may see the similarity of
the statistics question to gambling questions you are familiar with and successfully solve the statistics question.

Another type of familiarity with part of a problem is not so helpful, however. Instead of being familiar with the relationships between parts of a problem, you may be familiar with the isolated components of a problem. In those
situations, people often have a hard time thinking of objects outside their normal use. For example, a rubber dog bone is a toy—that's its attribute—and it
won't seem to be something that could be used as a pencil eraser in a pinch.
In this case, familiarity with the object hurts problem-solving performance.

Analogy

Were you able to solve the problem involving the Himalayan tea ceremony? Did
you notice that an analogy could be drawn between this problem and the Tower
of Hanoi problem that you saw (and perhaps solved) earlier in this chapter?
Figure 12.5 should make this analogy concrete. What can we say about the effect of prior knowledge on problem solving? Here's a situation in which you

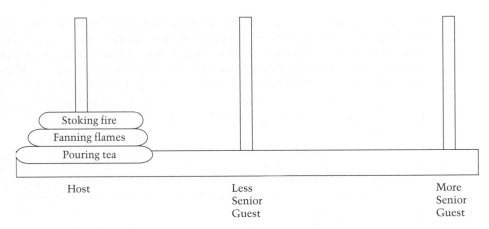

Figure 12.5. The tea ceremony problem is analogous to the Tower of Hanoi problem. Did you see the analogy?

thought about a problem quite recently, and you were given a new problem that is directly analogous to it, yet you didn't use your knowledge of this prior problem to solve this one. How is that possible?

The first thing you should know is that this finding is common. The classic studies on analogy were conducted by Mary Gick and Keith Holyoak (1980, 1983). They used a problem originally devised by Karl Duncker (1945) called the radiation problem that reads as follows:

> Suppose you are a doctor faced with a patient who has a malignant tumor in his stomach. It is impossible to operate on the patient, but unless the tumor is destroyed the patient will die. There is a kind of ray that can be used to destroy the tumor. If the rays reach the tumor all at once at a sufficiently high intensity, the tumor will be destroyed. Unfortunately, at this intensity the healthy tissue that the rays pass through on the way to the tumor will also be destroyed. At lower intensities the rays are harmless to healthy tissue, but they will not affect the tumor either. What type of procedure might be used to destroy the tumor with the rays without destroying the healthy tissue?

Most people find this problem extremely difficult, and even if they work on it for a long time, only about 10% of participants solve it. The answer is that you could use several of the rays at low intensity and point them in such a way that they all meet at the tumor. Thus, only the tumor would be exposed to a high intensity of the rays, and surrounding tissue would not be damaged. (This principle is actually used in cancer treatment.) Again, this is a difficult problem, but suppose that when you took up the radiation problem, you had just finished reading the following story:

> A dictator ruled a small country from a fortress. The fortress was situated in the middle of the country and many roads radiated outward from it, like spokes on a

wheel. A great general vowed to capture the fortress and free the country of the dictator. The general knew that if his entire army could attack the fortress at once it could be captured. But a spy reported that the dictator had planted mines on each of the roads. The mines were set so that small bodies of men could pass over them safely, since the dictator needed to be able to move troops and workers about; however, any large force would detonate the mines. Not only would this blow up the road, but the dictator would destroy many villages in retaliation. A full-scale direct attack on the fortress therefore seemed impossible.

The general, however, was undaunted. He divided his army up into small groups and dispatched each group to the head of a different road. When all was ready he gave the signal, and each group charged down a different road. All of the small groups passed safely over the mines, and the army then attacked the fortress in full strength. In this way, the general was able to capture the fortress.

Gick and Holyoak found that if participants were told that the fortress story they had just read might help them solve the radiation problem, 100% came up with the correct solution. However, if the experimenters did not tell them to use the fortress story, only 35% of the participants solved the radiation problem. Indeed, if the two stories are separated by a delay or presented in different contexts, almost none of the participants use the analogy (Spencer & Weisberg, 1986).

Do people need to be told to use an analogy? That doesn't seem right—surely, we spontaneously use analogy sometimes (Dunbar, 2001). A critical predictor of whether people will use an analogous problem that they've seen before is **surface similarity**, that is, whether the problems use the same elements (e.g., tumors and rays). **Structural similarity** refers to whether the content of the problem that allows you to solve it is the same. For example, the radiation and fortress problems are structurally similar because the solution to both entails dispersing strength and focusing it only at the point to be attacked. People seem to be more sensitive to surface similarity when considering analogy. For example, Mark Keane (1987) found that 88% of his participants used analogy to solve a problem, even if they had read the analogous story several days before, as long as the analogous story was extremely similar—in this case, another surgery story. When the story was changed so it still entailed rays being focused on a target, but now the target was intercontinental missiles, the use of the analogy dropped to 58%. From these studies, we might conclude that surface similarity of problems is the key to whether participants will think of using an analogy. Although results have varied across different experiments and methods, most have supported the greater importance of surface features over structural features (Catrambone, 2002; Chen, 1995; Gentner, Ratterman, & Forbus, 1993; Ross, 1987, 1989), although structural features do seem to also play a role (Clement, Mawby, & Giles, 1994; Holyoak & Koh, 1987).

There may, however, be an effect of how well one knows the target problem. For example, have a look at this problem:

A treasure hunter is going to explore a cave on a hill near a beach. He suspected there might be many paths inside the cave so he was afraid he might get lost. Obviously, he did not have a map of the cave; all that he had with him were some common items such as a flashlight and a bag. What could he do to make sure he did not get lost trying to get out of the cave later?

Did you think of a solution? When Zhe Chen, Lei Mo, and Ryan Honomichl (2004) presented American college students with this problem, about 75% were able to solve it, but only about 25% of Chinese students could do so. The reason, the researchers argued, was that American students are familiar with the story of Hansel and Gretel, which includes the idea of leaving a trail of breadcrumbs or pebbles to find your way back from a mysterious place (see Figure 12.6). Chinese students do not grow up hearing that story. The researchers also presented a story analogous to one that Chinese children often hear when growing up, and the percentage of solvers from each country was reversed. The researchers also asked participants whether they thought of the story when trying to solve the problem. Many did (about 67% Chinese; 37% American), but interestingly, conscious recollection of the problem did not carry the effect. In other words, American students who did not remember the Hansel and Gretel story were still more likely to solve the problem than the Chinese students. (The same was true for the Chinese story.)

These results seem a marked contrast to the other experiments we've discussed. Surface similarity is minimal, but people access the analogous story and successfully apply it, in some cases perhaps accessing it outside awareness. An important difference in this study is that students likely hear a familiar story more than once, perhaps many times. A second experiment showed that surface similarity is still important in drawing analogies to these childhood stories. When the experimenters made one or two elements similar to the original story, participants were more likely to remember the story, more likely to draw the analogy, and more likely to solve the problem.

Thus far, we have talked about analogy in terms of people's success in considering whether to use an analogous problem, and we're assuming (rightly, it seems) that if a participant considers using it, he or she will be successful in doing so. Sometimes, however, you have already thought of using an analogy but still have problems mapping a sample problem to the problem to be solved. For example, for students studying physics, chemistry, or statistics, having a formula to work from is not enough; they need to see sample problems to fully understand how to use the formula. Brian Ross (1987; see also Chen, 1995; Novick & Holyoak, 1991; and Ross, 1989) studied people's success in using sample problems to help them solve novel problems. In all cases, the formulas to solve the problems were available. The upshot of Ross's study was that people are strongly influenced by the surface similarity of sample problems. If the objects play different roles in the problems, people are often confused. That is, if rays are things that do the attacking in one problem but in another problem they are the thing attacked, people will have a much harder time grasping the similarity between the problems. So, at least two processes are needed to make effective use of an analogy. It must occur to the

Grimm's Fairy Tale.
HANSEL AND GRETHEL

Figure 12.6.   A scene from Hansel and Gretel, a story that many Western children
are told.

person that an analogous problem may be helpful, and the person must succeed in drawing a correspondence between the elements of the two problems.

Can we make it easier for people to draw analogies? Some researchers
have suggested that with continued exposure, participants develop an abstract
schema for a particular type of problem (Holyoak & Thagard, 1989; Ross &

Kennedy, 1990). Recall from chapter 6 that a schema is a memory representation that captures the general features of an object or event. In this case, a schema would contain the deep structure of the problem and a solution strategy that would be applicable across a variety of problems with this structure. As we discuss later in this chapter, it is certainly true that experts can readily describe the underlying structure of problems that have different surface structures. It therefore seems logical to infer that when we practice a particular type of problem, such as calculating conservation of energy in physics, we are building a schema that can be applied to a variety of problems in that domain.

There does seem to be evidence that practice with a class of problems promotes development of a schema that is general enough to handle problems of that class. Laura Novick and Keith Holyoak (1991) gave participants problems that illustrated the use of algebraic procedures. Participants then tried to apply these principles to novel problems. The experimenters assessed whether applying the analogous problems to the new problems created a schema; they measured schema quality by asking participants to describe which parts of the solution procedures were common to the two problems. The participants with higher-quality schemas tended to show more transfer from the analogous problem. Other experiments supporting the idea of schema induction have shown that repeated solution of analogous problems makes participants better able to make inferences consistent with the schema (Donnelly & McDaniel, 1993; Robins & Mayer, 1993).

A key theme in this section on analogy is that mapping is important—specifically, the relational mapping between the parts of one entity and another entity. For example, if you're drawing an analogy between the solar system and an atom, then the relationships of the parts of the solar system should be similar to the relationships of the parts of the atom. The attributes of the objects are not so important in mapping the analogy. It doesn't matter that the sun is hot; what matters is how the sun relates to the planets (they orbit around it, just as electrons orbit the nucleus of an atom).

We might ask what happens if you don't have a ready analogy. What happens if you don't focus on the relationships between the parts of the problem and instead focus on the attributes? For example, if you aren't thinking about the planets revolving around the sun, will you focus on the sun's heat? Focusing on the common attributes of objects can cause difficulties in problem solving when these attributes are not the ones that are critical for solving the problem.

Functional Fixedness

We start this section with a sample problem adapted from a classic experiment by Karl Duncker (1945). In Photo 12.1, you see a candle, some matches, and a box of tacks. The goal is to have the lit candle about 5 feet off the ground. You've tried melting some of the wax on the bottom of the candle and sticking it to the wall, but that wasn't effective. How can you get the lit candle to be 5 feet off the ground without your having to hold it there?

Photo 12.1. Elements in Duncker's (1945) classic problem.

Could you solve the problem? The solution is to dump the tacks out of the box and tack the box to the wall, where it can serve as a platform to support the candle.

Here's another simple problem. Dan and Abe played six games of chess. Dan won four, and Abe won four. There were no ties. How is that possible? The answer to that problem is that they were not playing against one another. Both of these are examples of **insight problems** in which it seems to the solver that the solution (assuming that it is solved) comes all at once, in a moment of illumination. It has long been assumed that insight problems differ from other problems in that they do not yield to an analytical approach; for example, the Hobbits and Orcs problem described earlier is usually solved step by step, through an analysis of the requirements and constraints of the problem. The candle problem requires just one thing: understanding that the box can serve as a platform. The lack of analytical procedure and the flashing "Aha!" feeling to the solution go hand in hand. People usually report feeling stumped by an insight problem, as though they've hit a brick wall. Then they get an idea, seemingly out of nowhere, and the problem is solved.

The subjective impression I've just described may ring true to you, but do we really know that it's true? Do people feel as though they can't solve the problem and then suddenly find that they have solved it? In a word, yes. Janet Metcalfe and David Wiebe (1987; see also Metcalfe, 1986a, 1986b) examined this question by administering insight questions or algebra problems to their

Table 12.2.   Insight and Algebra Problems Used in Metcalfe and Wiebe's (1987) Study of Insight

Sample Insight Problems	Sample Algebra Problems
A prisoner was trying to escape from a tower. He found in his cell a rope that was half long enough to permit him to reach the ground safely. He divided the rope in half and tied the two parts together and escaped. How could he have done this?	Factor: $x^2 - 6x + 9$
A landscape gardener is given instructions to plant four special trees so each one is exactly the same distance from each of the others. How is this possible?	$(3x^2 + 2x + 10)(3x)$
Describe how to cut a hole in a 3×5-in. card that is big enough for you to put your head through.	Solve for x: $1/5x + 10 - 25$

participants. Sample problems are shown in Table 12.2. Participants were given 4 min to solve each problem. Every 15 s, they were to rate from 1 to 7 how close they believed they were to a solution (how "warm" they were getting). The pattern of warmth ratings differed between the algebra and insight problems. For the algebra ratings, at the time of solution everyone gave a rating of 7, which makes sense because they had just solved the problem. Fifteen seconds before that, many of the ratings were still at 6 or 7; participants knew they were getting warm. Moving backward in time, the warmth ratings for the algebra problems became more crowded toward the bottom of the scale. The ratings for the insight problems reflected a different pattern. Although participants were confident at the time of solution, just 15 s before then they did not feel very "warm" at all. Indeed, the pattern of ratings was the same at every time interval until solution. Thus there is good evidence that insight is a sudden solution, not incremental, and that people don't know that it's coming.

The other types of solutions we've talked about have all been quite incremental. Means–ends analysis is a systematic working through of a problem space. Applying an analogy also seems incremental: We must find the appropriate analogy, then map the new problem to the old one, then work through the old solution, and so on. How are insight problems solved, given that these incremental solutions don't seem appropriate?

We can characterize insight problems as involving an impasse; something in the description of the problem doesn't fit, and we are tempted to say, "This problem can't be solved." When we hear that two people played six games of chess and each won four, at first it seems that that information can't be right. If we accept that insight problems entail an impasse, we can ask two questions: What causes the impasse, and how is the impasse resolved?

WHAT CAUSES THE IMPASSE IN AN INSIGHT PROBLEM?   Many insight problems reach an impasse because of the way in which a concept is used (e.g., Knoblich, Ohlsson, Haider, & Rhenius, 1999; Knoblich, Ohlsson, & Raney, 2001). For example, in the candle problem, the box is presented as something that can hold tacks, not as a piece of cardboard with a flat surface that could serve as a platform. In the tree-planting problem, people typically do not think of planting a tree on top of a hill, but nothing in the problem precludes that solution, just as nothing precludes finding an alternative use for a box.

Thus, it seems that one cause of an impasse may be that people's interpretation of concepts is biased, based on their prior experience: Boxes serve the function of holding things, trees are planted in flat gardens, and so on. This phenomenon of **functional fixedness**, as the name implies, means that people tend to fixate on an object serving its typical function and fail to think of an alternative use, even though it would be helpful in the problem. James Macgregor, Thomas Ormerod, and Edward Chronicle (2001; Chronicle, MacGregor, & Ormerod, 2004; Ormerod, MacGregor & Chronicle, 2002) suggested that the insight problems actually begin with hill climbing—the participant first tries to minimize the distance between the current state and the goal. It's only when this method does not solve the problem and the participant can't think of anything else to do that the impasse is reached. Thus, in their formulation, the impasse is due to a failed method, rather than to the representation of concepts.

Some data favor the impasse-as-concept idea. If the key object is presented so it is not so obviously typical, problem solving is facilitated. People more often solve the candle problem if the box is depicted as empty, with the tacks next to it (Adamson, 1952). In another example of this effect, Martin Scheerer (1963) presented a problem in which part of the solution required that participants tie two sticks together. People readily noticed and used a piece of string depicted as hanging from a nail in the wall, but if the piece of string was holding up a picture, it seldom occurred to them that they could use it. (For more technical predictions, see Jones, 2003.)

At other times, an impasse is reached not because an object needs to be used in an atypical fashion but because the description of the problem encourages people to represent it in a way that makes its solution very difficult. In the tree-planting problem, for example, people think of a garden as a flat (or perhaps sloped) lawn, which leads them to represent the problem as "Place four points equidistant on a plane," an impossible task. Nothing in the problem says that the four points must be in a plane, but most people's concepts of gardens lead them to represent it that way.

In the cases described so far, people tend to think too narrowly about the functions of the objects in the problem, whether that is because of the mental representation or because they have tried the hill-climbing heuristic and failed. Another type of impasse may occur because we are used to using a particular procedure to solve a problem. The classic case in which participants become fixed in a problem-solving procedure is Luchins's water jar problem (Luchins, 1942). To measure a particular amount of water, the participant is provided with three measuring jars, a water tap, and a drain to pour off excess water. For Problem 1 in Table 12.3, the required amount (20 oz) could be obtained by filling jug A (29 oz) and then pouring off enough to fill jug B (3 oz) three times.

Table 12.3.   Luchins's (1942) Water Jug Problem (capacity in ounces)

Problem	Jug A Capacity	Jug B Capacity	Jug C Capacity	Required Amount
1	29	3		20
2	21	127	33	40
3	14	163	25	99
4	18	43	10	5
5	9	42	6	21
6	20	59	4	31
7	23	49	3	20
8	15	39	3	18
9	28	76	3	25
10	18	48	4	22
11	14	36	8	6

All the problems in Table 12.3, except 1 and 9, can be solved by filling jug B, then subtracting A, then subtracting C twice (desired amount = B − A − 2C). Problems 7 through 11 can also be solved in a simpler way, involving only A and C (either adding or subtracting). The interesting finding is that participants who have solved Problems 2 through 6 continue to use the formula B − A − 2C for these later problems, even though it is unnecessarily complex. Not surprisingly, if you start participants immediately on Problem 7, they solve it the simpler way. Furthermore, Problem 9, which can't be solved with B − A − 2C, proves difficult for participants who have been using that formula for the other problems, even though a much simpler solution is correct. **Set effects** like this occur when a particular problem-solving procedure is applied because of past experience, even if it is not appropriate to the current problem. The extent to which participants are subject to set effects depends on the training procedure. People are less likely to get stuck in a mental rut if they solve a variety of problems during training (Chen & Mo, 2004).

How Is the Impasse Resolved?   We've gone on at some length about how an impasse is created in these problems, but some people solve them, so we must consider how the impasse is resolved. Why does it finally occur to some participants to dump the tacks out and use the box as a platform? Why did that idea occur after several minutes of thinking and not after a few seconds of thinking?

The insight problems we've been discussing were first proposed by Gestalt psychologists, who are best known for their work in perception. A key point they made was that perception of a figure is often determined by the relationship between its components. The Gestaltists emphasized that the same figure may be perceived in more than one way. For example, in the

Figure 12.7. A Necker cube. The perceptual organization of the cube is unstable, so it flips between two interpretations. Simply staring at the figure for several seconds will usually make your perception of the figure change.

well-known Necker cube illusion, perception of the cube's structure flips between two stable organizations (see Figure 12.7). Gestalt psychologists suggested that a similar process called **restructuring** was at work in insight problems (see Kohler, 1929), making participants perceive a whole that had not been seen before. The relationship of the elements of the problem change, just as the relationships of the lines making up the cube change; the lines themselves do not alter, but your interpretation of how they relate to one another changes. In problem solving, suddenly the box is not related to the tacks as a container; it is thought of as something that the tacks can stick on the wall. The processes that support this restructuring were believed to be unconscious.

An interesting finding indicated that the restructuring is actually not so sudden; the feeling of insight might be sudden, but it is preceded by a more gradual cognitive process. Kenneth Bowers and his colleagues (Bowers, Regehr, Balthazard, & Parker, 1990) gave participants a variant of the Remote Association Test in which participants saw two sets of words, such as the following:

Playing	Still
Credit	Pages
Report	Music

For one set, a single unnamed word could make noun phrases of each presented word. In this case, it's the first set, and the word is *card*, yielding *playing card, credit card*, and *report card*. The words in the other set were selected randomly, and there was no single word to unify them. Every 8 s, the participants made a judgment about which was the coherent triad of words. They had to make this judgment even if they hadn't found a solution; they were to simply make a guess based on any hunch that they had, and they were asked to rate their confidence about their judgment. The findings showed that when participants believed they were merely guessing about which was the coherent triad, they did indeed perform at chance. When they started having some confidence in their judgments (even though they still had not solved the triad), they were correct about 60% of the time. In other words, when people had a hunch or an intuition about which was the coherent triad, their intuitions were better than chance predictors.

This study indicates that people have meaningful intuitions before they solve a problem, even though the eventual solution of the problem might feel like a sudden insight. Can it be shown that something like restructuring is happening to support these intuitions? Francis Durso and his colleagues

(Durso, Rea, & Dayton, 1994) found a way to measure restructuring in a rather open-ended problem, and they too found that the change came slowly and started before participants were aware of it. They gave participants this puzzle: "A man walks into a bar and asks for a glass of water. The bartender points a shotgun at the man. The man says 'thank you' and walks out." Participants were asked to figure out what piece of information was missing that would make the story sensible. Participants were allowed to ask the experimenter yes–no questions to help them get to the answer. Half the participants could not solve the puzzle and half solved it. (The solution is that the man wanted the water because he had the hiccups, but the bartender cured him by scaring him with the shotgun.)

The experimenters asked participants to rate the relatedness of pairs of words in the puzzle. Some were relevant to the puzzle (*man, bartender*), some were relevant to the solution (*surprise, remedy*), and some were objects that might be in a bar (*TV, pretzels*). Participants rated 91 combinations of 14 words, and the experimenters used the relatedness ratings to construct graphs of relatedness through a technique called pathfinder scaling. Graphs for people who could and could not solve the puzzle are shown in Figure 12.8. The bold box shows the concept that is the focal point of the graph (i.e., the concept with the shortest distance to other concepts). As you can see, the central concept for solvers was "relieved," whereas for nonsolvers it was "bartender." The people who couldn't solve the puzzle focused on the bartender pulling out the shotgun; those who could solve it focused on what drew the story together, namely the relieving effect of the shotgun.

In a second experiment, the researchers took these same measures as a second group of participants were attempting to solve the puzzle. From Experiment 1, they derived three categories of word pairs, based on the relatedness judgments: Related words were connected in all pathfinder graphs, and unrelated words were not connected in any of the pathfinder graphs. Insight words were connected in the pathfinder graphs for people who solved the problem but not in the graphs for people who didn't solve the problem. The experimenters collected ratings of related, unrelated, and insight word pairs (plus some filler word pairs) as participants worked on the problem. The average similarity of word pairs stayed the same for related and unrelated words, but it increased for the insight word pairs. Even more interesting, these words started to seem related before the participant had solved the puzzle. Thus, restructuring was taking place before the participant successfully solved the problem.

In this section, we have examined what happens when a problem solver has some knowledge that is relevant to a problem, but not extensive knowledge. We have emphasized situations in which partial knowledge is detrimental to problem solving. Again, such situations are rare; psychologists engineer problems to have this characteristic because they help us understand how people solve problems, just as psychologists interested in visual perception design visual illusions.

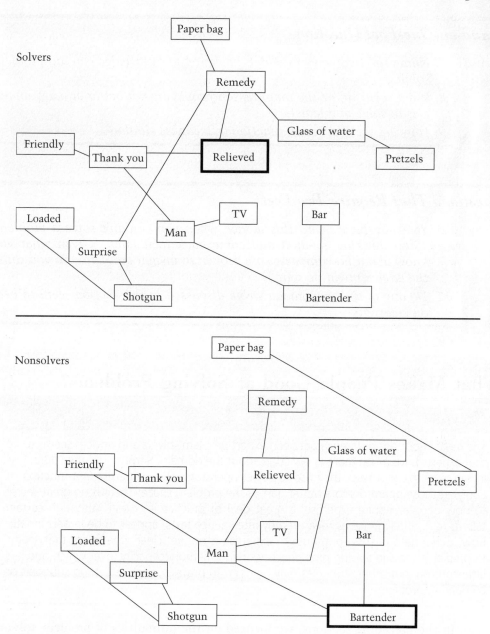

Figure 12.8. Pathfinder graph representing participants' mental representations of concepts in the bartender–shotgun problem used by Durso et al. (1994). Compare the differences in the representation of those who solved the puzzle and those who did not. The boldface box is the representation with the shortest distance to other concepts.

Stand-on-One-Foot Questions

7. *Name the two ways in which background knowledge can aid problem solving.*
8. *What seems to be the main reason people are not better at using analogies to solve problems?*
9. *How are set effects and functional fixedness similar?*

Questions That Require Two Feet

10. *You may have heard this advice when you couldn't solve a problem: "Stop thinking about it and come back to it later." Given what you know about how impasses are broken in insight problems, do you think the advice might be sound?*
11. *Do any of the phenomena we've discussed in this section seem to bear on creativity?*

What Makes People Good at Solving Problems?

Preview

The most important difference between expert problem solvers and novices seems to be that experts have much more knowledge about the domain. Surprisingly, they differ less in terms of the processes they use to select operators. Their expertise is a function of applying those operators to a better part of the problem space. There is no great secret to how people acquire expertise; a great deal of practice is crucial. Although certain talents (e.g., intelligence as measured by intelligence tests) appear to be largely innate, how such innate talents contribute to expertise is not yet clear. One factor that seems to predict success in solving problems is working memory capacity (over which one has little control), but other strategies may be open to practice, such as setting subgoals or comparing problems.

In the preceding sections, we focused on the difficulties of problem solving. What do people do when they lack experience that is relevant to a problem, and how can prior experience lead people astray? In this section, we turn our attention to successful problem solving. By characterizing the differences between expert problem solvers and novices, we hope to better understand why experts are so successful in solving problems. By extrapolating the findings about experts to novices, we may be able to learn how novices can improve their problem solving.

How Do Experts Differ From Novices?

By definition, an expert is someone who is very good at solving problems in a particular domain, such as chess, physics, or baking. Some of the earliest and most influential work on expertise examined chess masters. Chess is an excellent domain in which to study expertise because it has a large number of possible moves (in contrast to, say, tic-tac-toe), allowing high levels of expertise, but at the same time the game is bounded, so comparing performance among players is straightforward (it is not easy to compare the expertise of two bakers). In fact, chess masters are an ideal group to study because their expertise is verified through tournaments that have a standard scoring system by which players can be compared.

On the basis of our previous discussion of problem solving, we might expect two differences between experts and novices: Experts might have more knowledge about the domain, and they might be better at selecting operators to move through the problem space. There is excellent evidence for the first proposal (more knowledge) but mixed evidence for the second (better operators).

William Chase and Herb Simon (1973), following up on classic experiments by Adrianus De Groot (1946/1978), reported that chess masters have extensive knowledge of game positions, as we discussed in chapter 5. Chess masters can remember nearly perfectly all the positions of the pieces after just a brief exposure to the board. However, masters perform about as well as novices if the chess pieces are not in a midgame position but are arranged randomly. The importance of the midgame position indicates that masters rely on their stored memory of previous games in performing this working memory task. Novices and masters both remember the same number of chunks of information from the chess board, but for a novice, a single piece is a chunk of information, whereas for a master a group of chess pieces is a chunk. For example, a master might perceive a rook, king, and three pawns in the corner of the board as a chunk: This is the standard position of these pieces after a player has castled. It is estimated that chess masters may have as many as 50,000 chess patterns stored in secondary memory (Gobet & Simon, 1998; Simon & Gilmartin, 1973). That experts have a large number of patterns stored in secondary memory has been verified in other domains such as bridge, electronic circuit design, and computer programming.

Experts not only have more information stored in secondary memory than novices do, but they also organize the information differently. For example, Micheline Chi and her colleagues (Chi, Feltovich, & Glaser, 1981) asked participants to sort physics problems depicted on cards. Physics novices tended to sort cards on the basis of surface features of the problem, such as the objects used; for example, all the problems that concerned inclined planes might be grouped together. Physics experts classified problems according to the physical law applied; for example, all problems concerning conservation of motion might be classified together. These results have been extended to other domains, such as computer programming, and to objects such as rice bowls and pictures of dinosaurs (Bedard & Chi, 1992).

Experts' secondary memory is more extensively interconnected than that of novices, and it is interconnected in ways that are consistent with their expertise. For example, a study by Frank Hassebrock and his colleagues (Hassebrock, Johnson, Bullemer, Fox, & Moller, 1993) examined the memory of participants at three levels of expertise (novice, trainee, and expert) for information about a medical case. Participants were asked to make a diagnosis and then recall the information presented in the case. Initially, all participants remembered about the same amount. One week later, however, those with more medical expertise remembered less of the case overall.

A more fine-grained analysis of the recall data showed that participants with more expertise remembered a greater proportion of the information that was critical in making a diagnosis. Furthermore, their memory recall was structured similarly to their diagnosis; they remembered information in the same order in which they used it to make the diagnosis. This study shows that new memories within participants' domains of expertise are influenced by the organization of existing memories in that domain (see Figure 12.9).

There is very good evidence that experts have more domain-relevant information stored in memory and that they store this information differently than novices. How about the processes (operators) that move us through a problem space? Do experts engage different problem-solving strategies than

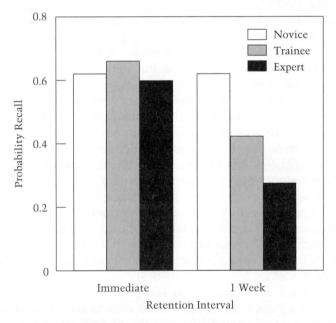

Figure 12.9. Data from Hassebrock et al.'s (1993) study showing that experts remember fewer of the details from a medical case than novices do after a 1-week delay. More detailed analysis showed that the experts remembered the details that were important for diagnosis and little else.

novices? Early research indicated that they do (Larkin, McDermott, Simon, & Simon, 1980; Simon & Simon, 1978). For example, in one study (Larkin et al., 1980) participants were asked to talk aloud about their strategies as they solved physics problems. It appeared that novices most often worked backward: They identified the variable requested in the problem and then tried to think of a formula that would yield that variable. Next, they considered what variables in the formula were unknown and tried to generate other formulas that could give them those values. Experts, however, seemed to examine the problem and then solve it starting at the beginning of that chain of inference, as though they could look ahead and see the entire solution path.

More recent evidence has questioned this distinction in processing between novices and experts (Zajchowski & Martin, 1993, cited in Clarke & Lamberts, 1997). In one study (Priest & Lindsay, 1992), the experimenters sought to test a larger group of participants than had been tested in the typical experiment, and they also sought to use some measure other than verbal protocols to assess whether people were working forward or backward. Therefore, they asked 79 participants to write out all the equations and formulas they used as they solved problems. One measure of reasoning is the order in which formulas appeared in the solution. The results showed that there was no difference between experts and novices in terms of how they worked the problems; both groups used primarily forward reasoning.

Not only is there apparently little difference in the procedures that experts and novices apply to problems, but it has also been suggested that these processes are not very important in expertise. Indeed, in his original studies of chess expertise, De Groot (1946/1978) claimed that top-level masters and expert players search the problem space equally deeply; however, the best players are able to restrict their search to branches of the tree that are much more productive (i.e., that lead to better moves).

The relative unimportance of search processes in chess expertise is supported in a study by Bruce Burns (2004) (see also Gobet & Simon, 1996). Burns compared chess players ability when they played blitz chess (5 min allowed for the entire game) to their ability when playing normal tournament chess. The idea is that recognition memory operates very quickly, but search processes in problem solving are very slow. Thus, if expertise is based mostly on recognition memory, restricting time (as in a blitz tournament) will impair everyone equally. If, however, expertise is based on search, the limited time allowed restricts search so it's the expert players who will really be affected by the time limit.

As mentioned earlier, the skill of all chess players is ranked on a common scale, so Burns (2004) could take the ratings from regular tournaments and predict who should win a game of Blitz chess. Burns analyzed data from 13 tournaments involving 1,177 data points. He found that player's performance in regular tournaments was an excellent predictor of their play in blitz chess. The interpretation is that chess expertise relies mostly on fast processes supported by recognition memory, and much less on slower processes of searching the problem space.

How Do People Become Experts?

We have seen that experts differ from novices chiefly in their amount of knowledge about the domain, but we haven't discussed how to become an expert. The evidence points to two factors that you probably can name: You need to practice a great deal, and to reach great heights of proficiency you probably need some inherent talent as well. Although this chapter is about problem solving, much of the interesting work on expertise comes from other domains (e.g., athletics and music), so this section also cites that literature. As far as we know, generalizations can be made from the development of expertise in those domains to the development of expertise in problem solving.

The importance of deliberate practice has been emphasized by Anders Ericsson (Ericsson, Krampe, & Tesch-Roemer, 1993). Ericsson defines **practice** as having the following characteristics:

- The person must be motivated.
- The task must be at the appropriate level, neither too easy so the person can perform it effortlessly nor too difficult so the person cannot perform it.
- There must be immediate corrective feedback. (For example, high-level chess players study games published in newspapers, try to anticipate the next move of each player, and then check to see whether they have anticipated correctly.)
- It involves the repetition of the same or similar tasks.

These characteristics distinguish practice from play (in which the purpose is to derive pleasure) or performance (in which the purpose is to give pleasure to others).

It takes not only practice, but also extensive practice to become an expert. A number of authors have referred to a **ten-year rule**: About a decade of intense practice is needed to reach the upper levels of expertise. Herb Simon and William Chase (1973) noted that the ten-year rule seemed to apply to chess expertise, and it also seems to apply to a number of other domains, including musical composition (Hayes, 1981), musical performance (Sosniak, 1985), mathematics (Gustin, 1985), tennis (Monsaas, 1985), long-distance running (Wallingford, 1975), livestock evaluation (Phelps & Shanteau, 1978), radiographic diagnosis (Lesgold, 1984), medical diagnosis (Patel & Groen, 1991), and presumably, golf (see Photo 12.2).

All these studies examined people who had already achieved expertise in their respective fields and then determined how long they had been practicing; the figure was always 10 years or more. Another approach to determining the importance of practice is to examine people who are trying to become experts and see whether those who are practicing more now seem to be making better progress toward expertise. That was the approach taken by Ericsson and his colleagues (1993). The experimenters studied violinists at a music academy. Some were studying to be music teachers, so although they were competent

Photo 12.2. Tiger Woods has practiced golf intensely since he could stand. His outstanding skill is certainly consistent with the ten-year rule.

players, they had no aspirations to become professionals. From other students who hoped for professional careers, the professors at the academy nominated a group of 10 violin students who were most likely to succeed as soloists. Ten other violin students were selected who, although very good, were not quite at that level. The experimenters then had the three groups of participants (future music teachers, good violinists, and best violinists) keep diaries of their practice schedules (and other activities) and estimate the number of hours they had practiced at different ages (see Figure 12.10).

As you can see in Figure 12.10, the best violists practiced more than the good violinists, who (not surprisingly) practiced more than the aspiring music teachers. Keep in mind that these are self-reported data, meaning that participants told the experimenters how much they practiced, so these numbers may reflect the amount of practice they aspired to rather than actually executed.

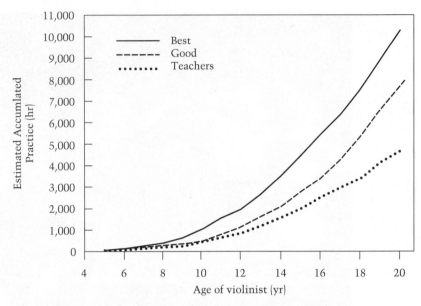

Figure 12.10.   Graph from Ericsson et al. (1996) showing the cumulative amount of practice by two groups of aspiring musical performers (expert violinists and good violinists) and those who planned to teach music.

Still, the results are noteworthy, especially given that one could propose that the best violinists would be the ones with the most innate talent and they would not need to practice as much as the other groups (see also Charness, Tuffiash, Krampe, Reingold, & Vasyukova, 2005; Kramp & Ericsson, 1996).

Thus far, we've emphasized practice, practice, practice. What about talent? Doesn't the raw material with which we start have some impact on success? Interestingly, some researchers argue that talent has little to do with success, and it's practice that really matters. Some aspects of performance are clearly attributable to practice. As we've discussed, chess masters can remember chess positions so well, not because they have superior working memory capacity, but because they have studied chess positions. But what about perfect pitch (the ability to name tones accurately), which professional musicians are more likely to have? Isn't perfect pitch something you're born with? Ericsson (1996) suggested that perfect pitch can be acquired at an early age (Takeuchi & Hulse, 1993) and indeed suggests that other apparently innate factors such as strength and speed are the product of training.

That's probably taking the influence of practice too far. For example, some data show that practice is a poor predictor for certain athletic events, especially sprints (Hodges, Kerr, Starkes, Weir, & Nananidou, 2004). Returning to problem solving for a moment, there is a great deal of evidence that certain types of talent are at least in part innate (i.e., you are born with them). The best known of these is intelligence, at least as measured by standard intelligence tests. How can you tell whether people are smart because they were

Photo 12.3. Twins typically have very similar intelligence, whether they were raised together, as these two supermen were, or raised apart.

born smart or because they have done things that made them smart? Tom Bouchard and Matt McGue (1981) examined identical twins who were raised apart. Because they are identical twins, they have the same genetic inheritance, but because they were raised apart (usually because they were adopted by different families), their life experiences could be quite different. McGue and Bouchard reported that the intelligence test scores of identical twins reared apart were more similar than the scores of fraternal twins (who don't have identical genes) reared apart (see Photo 12.3). A similar technique was more recently applied to examine whether perfect pitch is innate or learned, and it appears that the genetic component is much greater than the environmental component (Drayna, Manichaikul, de Lange, Snieder, & Spector, 2001).

   Another way to answer the question "Which comes first, talent or practice?" is to look at the histories of people who have achieved prominence in their fields. After interviewing experts from a variety of fields, Benjamin Bloom (1985) proposed that there is some consistency in the development of children who later become eminent. In the first stage, the child becomes exposed to the domain under playful conditions. The child shows interest and promise relative to other children. In the second stage, the parents arrange for instruction with a teacher or coach who works well with children. The importance of practice and a regular schedule of practice is emphasized. During this stage, the parents show a great deal of enthusiasm and support for the activity, providing a series of teachers of increasing expertise and increasing the financial commitment (which can be great). In the third stage, usually in the midteens, a decision is made to commit to the activity full time and to seek out the very best teaching and training conditions, which often means that the child must leave home. Nearly all students who eventually achieve greatness have a teacher at this stage who has reached the top level of the field. In the fourth and final stage, the student has absorbed most or all of what the teachers can offer and begins to make innovations in the domain.

From these data, it appears that talent and practice interact. In the second and third stages, the parents clearly set up an environment that is optimal for the practice and development of the skill. But the very first stage is characterized by the student showing talent and promise. Parents often report that the skill seems to "come out of nowhere." Indeed, it is possible that the children who practice the most (including the violin players in the 1993 study by Ericsson and colleagues) are those who have the most talent. As Ellen Winner (2000) points out, most children must be cajoled into practicing violin or working math problems; gifted children must be torn away from these activities.

It seems a safe bet that both talent and practice are crucial to high levels of success. We mostly have data on people who have been identified as gifted, and we have verified that these people were talented and worked hard (see also Lubinski, Webb, Morelock, & Benbow, 2001). What we don't have is much data on other groups of people, such as those who were talented but didn't work hard or those who were not talented but worked very hard. These data are needed to sort out the relative contributions of talent and practice.

What Makes Nonexperts Good at Solving Problems?

In this section, we are discussing what makes people good at solving problems, but thus far we have focused on experts. Suppose you don't want to be an expert—you're not willing to commit the next 10 years to practice—but you'd like to improve your problem-solving skills. What makes people more effective problem solvers? We discuss three factors. First, having a large working memory capacity seems to help problem solving, but of course you can't increase your working memory capacity. Two other strategies that may improve problem solving are setting subgoals and comparing problems.

WORKING MEMORY CAPACITY.   Working memory seems to make an important contribution to problem solving. A prominent role for working memory in problem solving is sensible in light of the framework discussed early in this chapter: using operators to move through a problem space. You must keep several things in working memory simultaneously to use means–ends analysis, for example, the current subgoal, the operator you are trying to apply, and the conditions of that operator. Perhaps more important, you must shuttle information between working memory and secondary memory; as a subgoal is achieved, you must retrieve the next goal, search secondary memory for appropriate operators, and so on.

Kenneth Kotovsky and his colleagues (Kotovsky, Hayes, & Simon, 1985; Kotovsky & Simon, 1990) argued for the importance of working memory in problem solving. They administered different **isomorphs** of the Tower of Hanoi problem to participants. These are problems with a different cover story but with a problem space that is the same size and has the same number of branches and the same minimum solution path. Here is one such isomorph:

Three five-handed extraterrestrial monsters were holding three crystal globes. Because of the quantum mechanical peculiarities of their neighborhood, both monsters and globes come in exactly three sizes with no others permitted: small, medium, and large. The small monster was holding the medium-size globe; the medium-size monster was holding the large globe; and the large monster was holding the small globe. Because this situation offended their keenly developed sense of symmetry, they proceeded to shrink and expand the globes so each monster would have a globe proportionate to its own size. Monster etiquette complicated the solution of the problem because it requires the following:

Only one globe may be changed at a time.

If two globes have the same size, only the globe held by the larger monster may be changed.

A globe may not be changed to the same size as the globe of the larger monster.

By what sequence of changes could the monsters have solved this problem?

You can see that this problem is like the Tower of Hanoi problem discussed earlier. People found this version of the problem extremely difficult, however. Why? Kotovsky and his colleagues (1985; Kotovsky & Simon, 1990) argued that the problem is one of working memory. The rules are complicated. There is no physical realization of the problem (e.g., a board with pegs), so participants have to remember where they are in the problem space (in this case, which monster is holding which globe). Just thinking about the rules and imagining the monsters uses up most people's working memory capacity, so they have nothing left over to work the problem.

Other work has shown that people are less successful in solving syllogisms if the premises are given orally rather than in writing, presumably because maintaining the premises in working memory reduces the capacity to manipulate them to evaluate the syllogism (Gilhooly, Logie, Wetherick, & Wynn, 1993). A somewhat similar approach was taken in a study by Pierre Barrouillet (1996), who examined working memory contributions to transitive inference by varying the amount of irrelevant information that appeared between key statements that could be used to make inferences. He reported that increasing the number of irrelevant statements increased erroneous inferences, presumably because of the difficulty of maintaining the statements for a longer time in working memory.

Table 12.4.   Sample Questions from Kyllonen and Christal's (1990) Study

Test Name	Sample Question
Arithmetic reasoning	Pat put in a total of 16.5 hours on a job during 5 days of the past week. How long is Pat's average workday?
Number sets	Select the set that doesn't fit: 234 567 357 678
Necessary arithmetic operations	Chairs priced at $40 each are being sold in lots of four at 85% of the original price. How much would four chairs cost?
Nonsense syllogisms	All trees are fish. All fish are horses. Therefore, all trees are horses. True or false?
Three-term series	Dick is better than Pete; John is worse than Pete. Who's best: Dick, John, or Pete?

Another method that has been used to examine the relationship between working memory and problem solving is statistical association. In an article provocatively titled "Reasoning Ability Is (Little More Than) Working-Memory Capacity?" Patrick Kyllonen and Raymond Christal (1990) reported that people who have a large working memory capacity also score well on tests of reasoning, whereas those with small working memory capacity score poorly. They reported four studies, each with 400 or more people tested. Reasoning ability was tested with a total of 15 tests across the four experiments. Sample problems are shown in Table 12.4.

The authors found a consistently high correlation (around .8 or .9 across experiments) between their measures of working memory and measures of reasoning ability. Even an article arguing that working memory and intelligence were not as strongly related as everyone thinks still claimed a correlation of .48 (Ackerman, Beier, & Boyle, 2005). This strong relationship is consistent with the idea that effective reasoning and problem solving depend on working memory capacity (see also Carpenter, Just, & Shell, 1990; Engle, Tuholski, Laughlin, & Conway, 1999; Kane, Hambrick, Tuholski, Wilhelm, Payne, & Engle, 2004; Reber & Kotovsky, 1997), as are data showing a relationship between working memory capacity and children's performance in school (Gathercole, Pickering, Knight, & Stegmann, 2004).

Thus far, our discussion of how nonexperts can be better problem solvers has focused on working memory, so the advice really boils down to this: "If you want to be a good problem solver, have a good working memory." But working memory capacity does not feel as if it is under our control. You can increase the amount of information you can keep in working memory by studying a particular domain; for example, you can increase your working memory for chess positions by learning a lot about chess. But that is tantamount to committing yourself to becoming an expert. Is there no simpler way to improve problem-solving skills? Two methods have been pursued: setting subgoals and comparing problems.

SETTING SUBGOALS.   Richard Catrambone (1994, 1995, 1996, 1998; Catrambone & Holyoak, 1990) has investigated the effect of encouraging people to set subgoals. Catrambone noted that people tend to memorize a series of steps that depend on the surface features of the problem (Chi et al., 1981; Larkin et al., 1980; Ross, 1987, 1989). Therefore, if the surface features of the problem change, the memorized solution is of no use because the solution steps were tied to the surface features (Reed, Ackinclose, & Voss, 1990). Catrambone suggested that people should be taught to form subgoals because problems within a domain are likely to share a subgoal even if the steps to achieve it vary. For example, in physics problems of the sort used by Chi and colleagues (1981), people should be taught the subgoal of first determining which of the physical laws is applicable to the problem; that subgoal will always be useful, although achieving it will vary from problem to problem.

Unfortunately, trying to teach people subgoals explicitly is not very effective. For one thing, people like to see examples, not just abstract solution procedures, when they are trying to solve problems (Cheng et al., 1986; LeFevre & Dixon, 1986). Attempts to teach people subgoals directly have not worked well (see Reed & Bolstad, 1991). Catrambone (1996) tried a different method. He showed participants example problems and applied labels to groups of steps, with the idea that people would chunk these steps together into a subgoal. Here is one problem:

> A judge noticed that some of the 219 lawyers at City Hall owned more than one briefcase. She counted the number of briefcases each lawyer owned and found that 180 of the lawyers owned exactly one briefcase, 17 owned two briefcases, 13 owned three briefcases, and 9 owned four briefcases. Use the Poisson distribution to determine the probability of a randomly chosen lawyer at City Hall owning exactly two briefcases.

Catrambone had participants study the solution. In one condition, one of the steps was labeled "Total number of briefcases owned," thereby highlighting that an interim step was to calculate the total number of objects. At transfer, all participants saw a different problem:

> Over the course of the summer, a group of five children used to walk along the beach each day collecting seashells. We know that on Day 1 Joe found four shells, on Day 2 Sue found two shells, on Day 3 Mary found five shells, on Day 4 Roger found three shells, and on Day 5 Bill found six shells. Use the Poisson distribution to determine the probability of a randomly chosen child finding three shells on a particular day.

This is similar to the briefcase problem, but it requires finding total frequency in a different way. Finding the total is actually simpler in the transfer problem, but participants might not know how to solve it if they didn't understand that part of the solution procedure is to find the total number of objects. Catrambone (1995, 1996) found that participants who had seen the subgoal as part of the solution procedure during training were about twice as likely to solve this new problem.

COMPARING PROBLEMS. Gick and Holyoak (1983) proposed that transfer to new problems occurs if there is an abstract schema for the problem and its solution—that is, for the deep structure of the problem. For example, the schema for the radiation problem would include the idea of the dispersal of force and its regathering at the critical point. Gick and Holyoak suggested that participants could be made to induce the deep structure of problems by having them compare problems that have different surface structures but share deep structure. They conducted a study that supported the idea, but a more complete set of studies was presented by Richard Catrambone and Holyoak (1990).

Catrambone and Holyoak had half their participants read two stories with the same deep structure (the fortress problem and another problem in which firefighters encircled a fire and threw buckets of water on it). The other half heard one of these stories and a control story with a different deep structure. Next, half the participants in each group were asked to compare the stories, and half were not. Finally, all participants were given the radiation problem we discussed earlier. As you might expect, reading one analogous story did little to help solve the problem—about 15% of these participants solved it. The group that read two analogous stories and did *not* compare them fared little better—about 25% solved it. But 47% of the participants who read two stories and compared them solved the radiation problem. The interpretation is that the process of comparison induced participants to extract the deep structure of the problem, which they spontaneously applied to the new problem (see also Bassok & Holyoak, 1989; Bernardo, 1994; Gentner, Loewenstein, & Thompson, 2003; Loewenstein & Gentner, 2001).

What these experiments seem to highlight is the difficulty of the problem; when we learn a new solution to a problem, we tend to represent the problem in the concrete terms in which it was presented, and when a new problem comes along, we search memory for problems that are similar in surface structure, not deep structure. Comparison helps presumably because it encourages participants to think about what the examples have in common and thereby highlighting the common thread.

In Chapters 10 and 11, we considered high-level thought, namely, reasoning, decision making, and problem solving. We next consider what is arguably the pinnacle of cognition—language. We begin in chapter 13 by considering the structure of language, which should convince you that language is indeed different than other types of cognition.

Stand-on-One-Foot Questions

12. *How do experts differ from novices?*
13. *What is the definition of practice?*
14. *Other than practice, what makes someone good at solving problems?*

Questions That Require Two Feet

15. *Does practice guarantee expertise?*
16. *Do you think working memory capacity is an important limitation in insight problems?*
17. *Considering everything you've read in this chapter, what is the best advice you would give to, say, a high school student studying geometry who wants to know the best way to learn to solve problems in that domain?*

KEY TERMS

brute force search	isomorph	restructuring
combinatorial explosion	means–ends analysis	set effects
functional fixedness	operators	structural similarity
General Problem Solver	practice	surface similarity
heuristic	problem	ten-year rule
hill climbing	problem space	verbal protocol
insight problems	problem state	working backward

CURRENT DIRECTIONS IN COGNITIVE SCIENCE

Recommended readings

Klahr, D., & Simon, H. A. (2001). "What have psychologists (and others) discovered about the process of scientific discovery?" (pp. 91–98) Many of the experiments described in this chapter can be a little frustrating because the "problems" investigated feel rather trivial. They are relatively simple, they can be solved in minutes, and the stakes for solving them or failing to solve them are low. They feel more like puzzles than problems. In this article, Klahr and Simon examine problems that are long-lasting and complex, namely, scientific problems. They conclude that many of the principles discovered in the laboratory also apply to scientific problem solving.

Siegler, R. S. (2000). "Unconscious insights." (pp. 99–105) To me, one of the more interesting findings in problem-solving research is that "insights" are preceded by cognitive change. I discussed one study in that vein (the bartender/shotgun riddle). In this article, Siegler provides more evidence on this topic, this time using an arithmetic insight in children.

13 *Language Structure*

What Is Language?

- The Definition of Language
- Levels of Language
- Grammar

Is Language Special?

- Is Language Developmentally Special?
- Is Language Particularly Human?
- Is Language Cognitively Special?

410

What Is Language?

Preview

The task of defining language is difficult, but a definition is crucial to letting us know what we are trying to account for. It is useful to think of language structure at four levels: speech sounds (phonemes), words, sentences, and groups of sentences (texts). The structure of our language, or grammar, shows us just how complex language is and lets psychologists know exactly what they are trying to explain.

Before we approach the upper reaches of linguistic usage, we follow the example of grade schools and begin at the beginning, with the definition of language.

The Definition of Language

We've begun several previous chapters by defining terms: attention, working memory, and so on. **Language** proves more difficult to define. Suppose that your dog has different vocalizations (barks, whines, etc.) that it makes when he or she is hungry, wants to go outside, or wants to play, and you know how to interpret your dog's "utterances." Could we say that you and your dog speak a small language?

By standard definitions, the answer would be "no." The following properties are usually deemed critical to language (Clark & Clark, 1977):

- **Communicative:** Languages permit communication between individuals.
- **Arbitrary:** The relationship between the elements in the language and their meaning is arbitrary. There is no special reason the word *chair* must have the referent that it does. It would be perfectly acceptable for the utterance *table* to have the referent that *chair* now does. The word *big* doesn't have to be in some sense "bigger" than the word *minuscule*. Arbitrariness is a key feature of symbols. A sound stands for a meaning, but which sound stands for which meaning is arbitrary.
- **Structured:** Language is structured, meaning that the pattern of symbols is not arbitrary. It makes a difference whether you say, "The boy ran from the angry dog," "The dog ran from the angry boy," or "Boy the from dog ran the angry."
- **Generative:** The basic units of language (words) can be used to build a limitless number of meanings.
- **Dynamic:** Language is not static. It is changing constantly as new words are added and as the rules of grammar (slowly and subtly) change. New languages are created, and some languages die out.

Our example of communication between you and your dog has some of the properties essential to language, but it is missing others. It is communicative—the relationship between utterance and meaning appears arbitrary—and it might be dynamic—new utterances might be added, but there is no structure to the communication; utterances are composed of a single sound, associated with a single meaning. The communication also lacks generativity. Your dog's vocalizations can't be combined to create new meanings.

You might wonder why the definition of language really matters. If you and your dog communicate, can't you call that a language, if you want to? The definition matters because the pieces of the definition tell us what we are trying to account for when we try to understand how people use language. For example, you may recall from chapter 1 that generativity was behind one of the important criticisms Noam Chomsky leveled at B. F. Skinner's behavioristic account of language. Skinner argued that the principles of operant and classical conditioning could account for how children learn language. Chomsky argued that they could not because language is generative; behaviorist principles can account for whether someone is more likely to repeat an action taken previously, but a distinctive property of language is that we almost never say the same thing twice. In essence, Chomsky was saying that Skinner's theory was bound to miss the mark because Skinner failed to appreciate what language is. That is why psychologists are eager to be sure that they understand the properties of language; it's a mistake we don't want to make again.

The example of your linguistic dog highlights the way that the definition is used. Psychologists use the definition to help us classify animal communication—for example, "Is communication between dolphins really a language?" Just as often, however, psychologists use the definition as a reminder of what a theory of language must do. If, for example, you develop a theory of language and the theory makes no provision for how language might change over time, then you have omitted one of the defining properties of language (it's dynamic) and would know that your theory is either incorrect or incomplete. The definition of language is a description of what a complete theory must account for.

Levels of Language

An important part of the description of language is to recognize that there are different levels at which one can describe it. There are individual sounds (called phonemes), which are combined to form words, which are combined to form sentences, which are combined to form complex ideas (called texts). These levels of analysis should be considered separately because each level has different rules governing what is allowable at that level and what is not. Just as the five properties that composed our definition of language help define what a psychological theory of language should do, so too the rules describing how the components of language may combine to help constrain what psychological theories should look like. We take a brief look at the four levels of language, and then return to the question of what we might learn from the rules of what's allowable at each level.

PHONEMES. The lowest level is an analysis of the sounds that comprise words. (Throughout the chapter, we refer to spoken language, with the understanding that similar analyses would apply to languages that use gesture, such as American Sign Language.) Individual speech sounds, called **phonemes**, roughly correspond to letters of the alphabet. Some letters must do double duty: For example, *a* is pronounced differently in *baby* and *back*, and *th* is pronounced differently in *thin* and *then*; these are different phonemes. In all, there are about 46 phonemes in English; the exact count varies among experts. Table 13.1 shows a standard taxonomy of phonemes found in English.

The rules governing this level concern the phonemes that are used in the language. English uses roughly 46 phonemes, but there are about 200 in use worldwide. For example, the phoneme that corresponds to the letter *x* in the South African city name "Ixopo" is articulated as a click. This phoneme is not used in English (it is in Zulu), so English speakers are usually confounded in trying to pronounce it. (I practiced for a couple of weeks in high school, coached by a South African friend. I never got it.)

Other rules concern the potential differentiation of phonemes, for example, whether two closely related sounds are to be considered different phonemes. For example, the *p* sounds in *pill* and in *spill* are slightly different. You can observe this by holding your hand close to your mouth as you pronounce each word. You can feel a puff of air distinctly when you say *pill* but not *spill*. That

Table 13.1. *Standard Taxonomy of Phonemes in English*

Consonants				Vowels		Diphthongs	
p	pill	O	thigh	i	beet	ay	bite
b	bill	oˇ	thy	l	bit	æw	about
m	mill	sˇ	shallow	e	bait	$y	boy
t	till	zˇ	measure	3	bet		
d	dill	cˇ	chip	æ	bat		
n	nil	jˇ	gyp	u	boot		
k	kill	l	lip	*	put		
g	gill	r	rip	8	but		
n	sing	y	yet	o	boat		
f	fill	w	wet	$	bought		
v	vat	W	whet	a	pot		
s	sip	h	hat	E	sofa		
z	zip			i	marry		

Source: Clark & Clark (1977).

puff of air (called aspiration) makes no difference to the identification of the phoneme in English—if you pronounce *spill* with the *p* aspirated, a listener would still say it is properly pronounced. Such close variations of a phoneme are called allophones. In Thai, however, whether the p is aspirated *does* make a difference. It's a different phoneme, not an allophone. Similarly, English distinguishes some sounds as phonemes (e.g., *r* and *l*) that are allophones in other languages (e.g., Japanese). There are also regional variations within a language. My father, like many Southerners, grew up pronouncing the vowel sounds in *pen* and *pin* as allophones, which became a mild nuisance when he moved to the Northeast as an adult, where they are pronounced using different phonemes.

WORDS.   The 46 English phonemes are combined in various ways to produce all of the approximately 600,000 words in the English language. There are interesting rules, however, on how these phonemes may be combined, and where they may appear in a word. For some consonants, sound is created as air is stopped in the vocal tract. These are called stop consonants (e.g., p, b, d). In English, words may begin with one stop consonant (e.g., *pea, dab*) but not two; you could not invent a word "bdat." Other languages permit combinations that are forbidden in English. For example, in my mother's native Slovak, words without phonemes that correspond to vowels are permissable. Mom, with other schoolchildren, learned the vowelless sentence "Strč prst skrz krk" as a curiosity. (It translates to "push your finger through your neck." Right.)

SENTENCES.   It is easy to appreciate that there are rules for the construction of sentences. It is noticeable when these rules are violated, as in word strings such as "Ate I the to went yesterday carnival much and too," or more subtly, "Yesterday I went to the carnival and eat too much." It is also notable that we can create sentences without meaning that nevertheless sound grammatical, for example "Sarah aubly bamped the mingen." What makes word strings grammatical or nongrammatical?

The order of phonemes played a role in the proper construction of words, and we might guess that word order is critical in the construction of grammatical sentences. To some extent, that's true. If we arrange words randomly, they are unlikely to form a sentence ("master suave approached ingénue dance the the"). Our example of a sentence using nonsense words that nevertheless sounds grammatical ("Sarah aubly bamped the mingen") uses a few tell-tale markers ("Sarah," the ending "ly", the word "the") that are in the right order; "bamped Sarah aubly mingen the" doesn't sound grammatical.

But word order is not sufficient. For example, we might note the sentence "The suave dance master approached the ingénue" and conclude that the proper word order dictates that the subject comes first, then the verb, and then the direct object. But this rule for word order would not yield a correct interpretation of "The ingénue was approached by the suave dance master." Much of the psychology of language has been devoted to the level of sentence processing, so we return to this level after we finish our brief tour of the four levels of language processing.

TEXTS.   When psychologists refer to a **text**, they typically mean a group of related sentences forming a paragraph or a group of related paragraphs. Here's a rather mundane example of a text:

> I went to the store to buy a CD, but I didn't see anything I liked. Next I went to the mall to buy a shirt, but I didn't have much cash. Then I bought some lunch, and on the way home I ran into a friend. We talked on the corner for a while, and then I went home.

Now, here's an example of some sentences that don't form a coherent text:

> I went to the store, but I didn't see anything I liked. The wren brought a little spider to her young for them to eat. Jim tiptoed quietly through the halls, snickering to himself, thinking of the milkshakes. I had left over parts after reassembly, so I may have done something wrong.

Obviously, the difference between the first paragraph and the second lies in the connections among the sentences. Let's be more specific about the connections that are important for the good construction of a text. One is that the sentences are about the same thing—in the first paragraph, about me. Another important type of connection is logical connections. The second sentence is logically connected to the first because it continues the idea that I'm shopping and had several items to buy at several different stores. The sentences in the second paragraph cannot be connected logically, nor are they about the same object, so they cannot be assembled into a text. You might note that although the first paragraph has temporal ordering—first one thing happens, then the next, and then the next—temporal ordering alone is not enough to make good text. Just add the words "then" or "next" to the beginning of each sentence in the second paragraph to add the idea that they happen in order and you'll see it doesn't make it seem like a coherent text.

The important point to take away from these two sample paragraphs is that once psychologists have determined how sentences are comprehended, their job is not finished. When people are reading or hearing a story, they build a representation of the story that spans more than a sentence. That representation is a text. It is possible, or even likely, that one's culture affects how texts are constructed. Recall the story "War of the Ghosts" from chapter 8. That story sounds odd to many Westerners because their expectations about how a text is formed are not met (there are missing logical connections between sentences), but it is obviously a coherent text in the Native American culture from which it came.

Grammar

We've briefly discussed four levels of language—phonemes, words, sentences, and texts—and we've said that each level is characterized by rules: rules about which phonemes are permissible, rules about how phonemes can combine to form words, how words can combine to form sentences, and how sentences can combine to form texts. How do these rules help psychologists understand how the mind perceives and produces language? For phonemes and words, the answer seems to be "it doesn't help much." The rules vary across languages, and important consistencies in those rules have not been uncovered. On occasion, knowledge of these rules gives psychologists an edge in discovering how people produce and perceive phonemes and words. We discuss those topics in chapter 14. Knowledge of what makes a text coherent has been somewhat more helpful; as we see in chapter 14, the expectation of logical connectivity is very important in text comprehension because it prompts us to make inferences about missing information.

Sentences are a different story because the structure of grammatical sentences has been the subject of intensive study, and the knowledge accrued from that study has been vital to our understanding of the psychological processes contributing to sentence comprehension and production. As you probably know, different languages have different grammatical rules. What interests psychologists is the possibility that there are rules about how words can be combined into sentences that are applicable to *all* languages—a set of super rules, often called a universal grammar, to which the grammars of all languages must adhere. If such rules could be described (e.g., Nowak, Komarova, & Niyogi, 2001), it would likely be a big help in formulating theories about how the mind comprehends sentences (for an example, see Lidz, Gleitman, & Gleitman, 2003).

If our goal is to describe the set of rules that allows the production of grammatical sentences, we must define what makes a sentence grammatical. We can't use the rules found in a grammar book. We're trying to find out what rules are in people's minds as they produce and perceive sentences, and those need not correspond to the rules of "accepted" grammar that appear in books. When psychologists use the term **grammar**, they mean a set of rules that describes the permissible sentences that can be constructed in a language. We begin with grammar because it tells us what people do when they produce and perceive sentences.

One option might be to follow some people around and note what they say; from what they say, we can divine the rules they used to generate these sentences. That's not a bad idea, but what people say is not a clear window into the rules that produce sentences. Sentences often have stops, starts, and "ums" because people lose their train of thought, forget a word and start the sentence over again, and so on. Thus, a friend might say, "Have you gone to that new . . . uh . . . not the taco place, but it's the one with the, you know, not where John used to work, but across the street from there, with the funny, uh, roof thingie?" Both you and the person who produced this utterance would agree that it is not grammatical, but you probably wouldn't notice that if it were said in the course of casual conversation. (The next time you're in a group of people, take note of how often sentences are ungrammatical.)

For these reasons, Noam Chomsky (1957, 1965) argued persuasively that a distinction should be made between competence and performance. **Competence** is people's knowledge of grammar; **performance** is the way people actually talk. Competence is our pristine, pure knowledge of how we think sentences should be produced. Performance is the way we actually produce them once this knowledge has passed through the vagaries of an imperfect memory, the social pressures of conversation, and the other factors that influence sentence production. How, then, can you know what people's competence is when you can't judge competence from performance? Chomsky suggested having people read a sentence and asking them whether it seems grammatical. Participants typically show good agreement when this method is used. For example, which of following sentences appear grammatical to you?

The dog ate the bone.
Dog ate.
The dog ate.
Ate bone the dog.
The bone ate the dog.
By the dog the bone was.
The dog the bone was eaten.
The bone was eaten by the dog.
The dog ate the bone?

Now we have a method by which to analyze grammar. So, what are the rules by which sentences are generated? Early attempts to describe these rules by behaviorist psychologists treated sentences as chains of associated words we call **word-chain grammars**, which propose that grammatical sentences are constructed word by word, with the speaker selecting the next word based on the associations of the rest of the words in the sentence. If you have the start of a sentence, such as "The boy took his baseball bat and hit the _____," you might well guess on the basis of past associations that the next word is likely to be *ball*. Although there is some evidence that people can anticipate upcoming words (Van Berkum, Brown, Zwitserlood, Kooijman, & Hagoort, 2005), the problem with word-chain grammars is that someone could end that sentence with the word *window, umpire,* or *squid,* and these sentences would still be grammatical. How can we explain the grammaticality of these weird sentences using the concept of associations?

Chomsky (1965) developed the famous sentence "Colorless green ideas sleep furiously" to demonstrate that a sentence composed of words that are very unlikely to follow one another can still be grammatical. This sentence, although odd, certainly passes our test of sounding grammatical, yet how often have we heard something green also described as colorless? How often have ideas been said to sleep? Probably never, yet we effortlessly understand the sentence, so it doesn't seem likely that we need to have previous experience with words as associated to comprehend sentences.

One step that might seem to bring us closer to a correct grammar is to specify only what the next part of speech will be instead of trying to specify the next word. We're still dealing with word-chain grammars, so the next part of speech would be based on associations of the parts of speech of the words that have already appeared in the sentence. For example, we could specify that a noun will have to fill the space in the sentence about the baseball bat. Some researchers did develop such grammars, but they were ineffective. There are two problems with grammars that treat language as parts-of-speech chains. First, there are still too many possible combinations. For example, the sentence "The boy took his baseball bat and hit the _____" could be completed by a noun (*ball*), but the next word could also be an adjective (*smelly ball*). Nevertheless, the fact that we could make a lot of choices in creating sentences does not seem to be an insurmountable problem. It points to a more complicated device to generate the proper chain of words but does not indicate that developing a grammar is impossible.

Chomsky pointed out a second problem that is fatal to word-chain grammars: Languages have dependencies in them that can span many words and can be embedded within one another. Uttering a particular word commits the speaker to uttering another word (or type of word) later in the sentence. For example, once you utter a singular (or plural) subject of a sentence, the verb must agree in number, wherever the verb later appears in the sentence, for example, "The little *dogs*, whose master was the nastiest, most foul-mouthed monster who had ever simultaneously threatened me with litigation and tried to romance me, *were* quite loving to me." Despite all the intervening words (and there is no telling how many or few intervening words there will be), the speaker must be sure that the subject and verb agree in number. There are other word dependencies in English. For example, if you use the word *either*, then later in the sentence you will probably use the word *or*.

Dependencies can be combined and embedded within one another. For example, you can start with "Either Carole or Nicola will go" and then embed another clause, forming "Either Carole or Nicola will go, or Trisha and Karen will go." The options for embedding are endless, and each way in which these dependencies might be embedded requires a different mechanism within a word-chaining device. We could generate an infinite number of such embedded sentences, but an infinitely complex word-chain generator is not an option.

The solution is to abandon linear chains and switch to a grammar that represents sentences as hierarchies. In particular, psychologists have turned to **phrase structure grammars** in which each node of the hierarchy is a phrase (see Figure 13.1).

The advantage of phrase structure grammar is that it specifies a limited number of sentence parts and a limited number of ways in which these

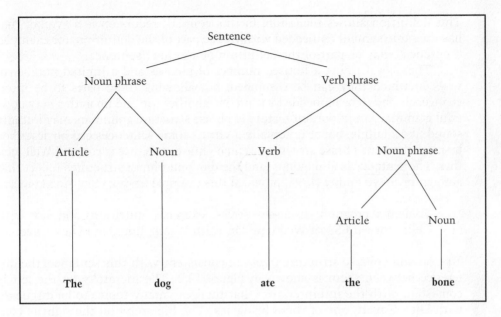

Figure 13.1.   A sample phrase structure.

sentence parts can be combined. Nevertheless, the system offers great flexibility in creating sentences. Here is a partial list of sentence parts:

>Sentence = noun phrase + verb phrase
>Verb phrase = verb + noun phrase
>Noun phrase = noun
>Noun phrase = adjective + noun
>Noun phrase = article + noun
>Verb = auxiliary + verb

Note one way in which we have greatly simplified our grammar: *Noun phrase* has been defined just once, but it appears within other phrases. Thus, a noun phrase is part of a sentence, and it is also part of a verb phrase (as shown in Figure 13.1). A word-chain grammar would have needed to duplicate the machinery of generating noun phrases for the two different functions they serve. In a phrase structure grammar, phrases are treated as interchangeable parts, and phrases can be joined into the hierarchies representing sentences as needed.

Phrase structures can handily account for the embedding problem that arises when forms such as *either . . . or* are used. We can define phrases like this:

>Sentence = noun phrase + verb phrase
>Sentence = *either* sentence *or* sentence
>Sentence = sentence *and* sentence
>Sentence = *if* sentence *then* sentence

This definition allows **recursion**. In this context, recursion is a symbol that has the same symbol embedded within it as part of the definition; for example, "sentence" may be part of the definition of another "sentence."

Thus, by defining a limited number of phrases and a limited number of ways in which they can be combined, but allowing these parts to be interchangeable and to be embedded within one another, we end up with a very powerful grammar. An important feature of phrase-structure grammars may initially sound like a failing, but it is actually a virtue; some sentences can be described by more than one phrase structure. Which phrase structure is correct? Well, neither. The sentence is ambiguous, and the different phrase structures reflect that ambiguity. Steve Pinker (1994) provided this example from a television guide:

> Tonight's program discusses stress, exercise, nutrition, and sex with Celtic forward Scott Wedman, Dr. Ruth Westheimer, and Dick Cavett.

Two possible phrase structure trees are consistent with this sentence; the difference between them is shown in Figure 13.2. The hierarchy on the left is consistent with the interpretation that there are many topics to be discussed with Dick Cavett, one of them being sex. The hierarchy on the right is consistent with the interpretation that one of the topics to be discussed is having sex with Dick Cavett. (Naturally, the ambiguity of such sentences may be resolved by background knowledge, such as the likelihood of various topics being discussed on television.)

As helpful as phrase structure grammars are, Chomsky (1957) pointed out that they cannot give a complete account of how we interpret language. Consider these two sentences:

> The professor is a terrific teacher.
> The professor is a terrible teacher.

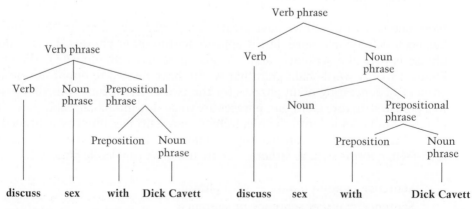

Figure 13.2. Two possible phrase structures corresponding to the same sentence, illustrating one source of ambiguity in sentences.

The phrase structures of these two sentences are the same, so phrase structures are obviously not capturing the important difference between them. Now consider these two sentences:

The professor's antics stunned the class.
The class was stunned by the professor's antics.

The phrase structures of these two sentences are quite different, but they nevertheless communicate the same idea. Chomsky argued that ambiguous sentences such as these constitute evidence for two different levels of representation. One is **deep structure**, which corresponds to the meaning of a sentence. We can take the deep structure of a sentence, apply transformations to it, and obtain a different phrase structure hierarchy called the **surface structure**, which yields the order in which words will be uttered. The idea, then, is that we might start with the deep structure "Dan hit the ball" but then apply a transformation to the deep structure that yields different surface structures: "Dan hit the ball" or "The ball was hit by Dan."

A single deep structure can be transformed in different ways, leading to different surface structures. Similarly, transformations of different deep structures can lead to the same surface structure. That is the account provided for sentences that have only one phrase structure but are nevertheless ambiguous. Thus, we might start with the deep structure corresponding to "Relatives visiting someone can be a nuisance" or the deep structure "To visit relatives can be a nuisance." Although the deep structures are different, when the proper transformations are applied to each, they yield an identical surface structure: "Visiting relatives can be a nuisance."

The distinction between surface and deep structures has changed over the years, particularly in terms of the transformations that change deep structures into surface structures (see Gernsbacher, 1994, for different alternatives). Nevertheless, the differentiation of surface and deep structure is still useful.

This section provides a detailed description of how language is structured. You'll note that we devoted much more time to this definition than we did in other chapters. That's true in part because language is so complex that the definition is bound to be complex. But the effort will prove worth it because understanding the structure of language helps psychologists know for what they are trying to account. For example, we know that for comprehension to occur, a listener must derive the correct phrase structure of a sentence. If we hadn't bothered to carefully consider the structure of language, we wouldn't approach the problem of sentence comprehension that way.

We will not move directly to the question of comprehension, however. We treated language somewhat differently than other topics through our careful consideration of its definition, and we did so because language seems special, compared with other topics in cognitive psychology. We are going to continue this chapter by considering three other ways that language might be special. Does language have a special status during development? Is language an especially human faculty? How does language relate to other cognitive processes?

Stand-on-One-Foot Questions

1. *What is language?*
2. *What's the difference between competence and performance?*
3. *What is wrong with word-chain grammars?*

Questions That Require Two Feet

4. *I've argued here that structure is important in language, but it seems that sometimes structure is not so important. For example, if a child said to you, "You, me, cookie, go now, hurry," you would know what the child meant even though this is not a grammatical utterance. How is that possible?*
5. *If the relationship between sound and meaning is arbitrary (as definitions of language claim), where do words come from? Are they random?*

Is Language Special?

Preview

Language has three properties that seem to make it different than other cognitive processes. It is special because humans seem to be primed to learn language with no explicit instruction, although they must be exposed to the language within a critical period of childhood. Language is also special because humans are the only species with this capability. Careful inspection of the data on efforts to teach language to nonhuman primates shows that they may acquire some rudiments of language, but what they learn misses the key parts of the definition of language set out early in this chapter. Language is also special because it influences other cognitive processes. The particular language that you know makes some concepts easy to express and other concepts difficult to express, and this has a subtle, but real, effect on how you think.

The question posed at the beginning of this section is easily answered: Yes, language is special. But the manner in which it is special is open to debate (e.g., Hauser, Chomsky, & Fitch, 2002; Pinker & Jackendoff, 2005). In this section, we discuss three ways in which language is special. First, it is developmentally special because humans are primed to learn it. Despite the incredible complexity of language, all humans learn language without explicit instruction but merely by exposure. Second, it is uniquely human. We are the only species to use language. Third, the particular language that one knows influences other cognitive processes. People who know different languages think a little bit differently.

Is Language Developmentally Special?

When we say that language is developmentally special, we mean that children learn language differently than they learn other skills, such as how to solve math problems. There is fairly strong evidence that our brains are prepared to learn language, and with relatively little prompting, will do so.

Some of the evidence that supports this point of view is the consistency of language learning around the world. All children go through the same steps of language learning in the same order. The first stage is **cooing**: The baby makes long drawn-out vowel sounds ("oooooooh") or consonant-vowel combinations ("gaaaaah") (see Photo 13.1). Cooing begins at the age of 1 or 2 months. Cooing includes all phones (components of phonemes) but is composed mostly of vowel sounds. During this stage, children can hear the difference between all phonemes, including those that are allophones in the language that they will learn. By the age of 1 year, however, they can no longer discriminate those allophones (Kuhl, 1991; see Jusczyk, 1997, for a review). The second

Photo 13.1. This 3-month-old makes vowel sounds (e.g., "a a a a h") when she interacts with her parents, and when she experiments with her voice.

stage is **babbling**, which begins between 6 and 10 months. Babbling includes more consonant-vowel combinations and repetitions (e.g., "dadadada"). Babbling contains primarily the phonemes of the language that the child hears, but also includes some from the others (Boysson-Bardies, 1999). With continued exposure, babbling increasingly takes the rhythms and intonations of their home language.

The first word usually appears between 10 and 15 months. By 18 months, the child's vocabulary will be about 50 words and will mostly include names of frequently encountered objects. The child will use a single word for many purposes. For example, "juice" may be a request ("I want more juice"), a comment ("There's the juice"), or a lament ("I just spilled all my juice!"). By the end of the second year, the child has begun to use two-word combinations: *more juice, daddy go, no doggie*. Children consistently omit auxiliary verbs, prepositions, and articles. Speech in this phase is often called telegraphic; when sending a telegram, people usually use the fewest possible words that will still convey meaning because longer telegrams cost more. Children's speech in this phase shows that economy.

There is no three-word stage of language production—children go straight from two-word combinations to sentences, but it is not until age 4 or so that sentence structure is really consistent. Children's flexibility and sophistication with syntax continues, adding unusual sentence forms and so on, until about age 10.

It is notable that children worldwide all go through the same stages of language development, which is consistent with the idea that the process of language learning is, in part, innate. Even more impressive is that children tend to make the same sorts of errors in learning language. One such error is **overextension**. Children want to talk about more than their limited vocabulary allows them to express, so they use the words they know for many referents. Any four-legged animal is a *doggie*, any liquid or body of water is *juice*, and any man on the street is called *daddy* (to the consternation of the real daddy). Another error that all children make is **overregularization**, which refers to applying linguistic rules to exception words where the rule should not be applied. Most of the research on overgeneralization has been conducted with English speakers, and in English plurals can usually be formed by adding *-s* to a noun, and the past tense can be formed by adding *-ed* to a verb. There are, however, exceptions. For example, the plural of *foot* is *feet*, and the past of *go* is *went*. The interesting pattern that children show is to initially use the correct irregular form, then to go through a period of overregularization (*foots, goed*) and then to return to using the correct irregular form (see Pinker & Ullman, 2002, for a discussion).

What is even more impressive is the speed with which this learning takes place. Consider that by age 4, the average child has learned the rules of grammar for his or her language. (The knowledge is implicit because the child can use the rules but cannot describe them.) Thousands of professors of linguistics have tried to fully describe the syntactic rules for a language but have not yet achieved it. Not only do children learn this complex system rapidly, but they also do all their learning by observing examples, receiving very little corrective feedback. Parents seldom correct their child's grammatical errors; if the child says "Yesterday we goed to the park", the parent will likely respond as though the error did not exist. One reason is that kids' speech is full of errors, and parents wisely pick their battles—they correct the child when he or she says something that is not true. A second reason parents ignore grammatical errors is that they quickly learn that correction does little good. Consider this exchange between cognitive scientist Martin Braine and his daughter (Braine, 1971, p. 161):

CHILD: Want other one spoon, daddy.
FATHER: You mean, you want the other spoon?
CHILD: Yes, I want the other one spoon, please daddy.
FATHER: Can you say "the other spoon"?
CHILD: Other ... one ... spoon.
FATHER: Say "other."
CHILD: Other.
FATHER: "Spoon."
CHILD: Spoon.
FATHER: "Other spoon."
CHILD: Other ... spoon. Now give me other one spoon?

Vocabulary, like syntax, is learned at a remarkably fast rate. Between the age of 18 months and first grade, children learn about 5 to 10 new words *every day* (Carey, 1978). Also, like syntax, much of this learning occurs through observation, rather than explicit instruction. This principle is illustrated in a classic study by Susan Carey and Elsa Bartlett (1978). During a normal preschool class, the experimenter asked the child to "bring me the chromium tray, not the red one." Although the word *chromium* was novel to all children, they did not protest and ask for a definition. Two trays were in plain view and one was red, so the child made the simple deduction that *chromium* must be the color of the other tray. Furthermore, after this single exposure to the word, 1 week later about half the children were able to pick a *chromium* color chip from several choices.

It may be, however, that this rapid vocabulary learning is not uniquely human. A border collie named Rico (see Photo 13.2) has recently been reported to have a large vocabulary (about 200 words) and to have learned some of these words in the same manner that children do (Kaminsky, Call, & Fischer, 2004). Rico can fetch a named item from another room. In one experiment, the researcher named a novel item. Rico ran into the other room where there were nine familiar items and one unfamiliar item. Seventy percent of the time, Rico successfully inferred that the novel label must go with the unfamiliar item and fetched it. Much more impressive, after that single exposure, Rico remembered the label for the item 50% of the time after a 4-week delay.

Photo 13.2. Rico, in the act of retrieval.

You may wonder why, if learning language is supposed to be such a breeze, it is so hard to learn a second language in school? The answer is that there appears to be a **critical period** for learning language (Lenneberg, 1967). You will recall from chapter 1 that a critical period is a window of opportunity during which something can be learned effortlessly, but if the window is missed it is learned with difficulty, if at all. Jackie Johnson and Elissa Newport (1989) conducted a classic study showing this effect. They administered a test of English grammar to Chinese and Korean immigrants who had come to the United States at different ages between 3 and 39 years. They had lived in the United States for between 3 and 26 years. The interesting finding was that performance on the grammar test was not predicted by how long a participant had lived in this country, but rather was a function of how old they were when they arrived. The younger the participants were when they first started learning English, the better they knew English grammar. This effect, however, stopped at puberty; once people were age 16 or so, their age of arrival did not predict their knowledge of English syntax. The interpretation of these data is that there is a critical period for learning language. Participants who arrived after puberty missed the critical period and were never as fluent as participants who started learning English within the critical period. The more exposure the participant had to English within the critical period, the better his or her proficiency would be.

Other investigations have reported similar outcomes (Birdsong & Molis, 2001; DeKeyser, 2000; but see Hakuta, Bialystok, & Wiley, 2003).

Perhaps the most dramatic evidence of the extent to which humans are primed to use language comes from children who have *invented* languages. There are several reports of congenitally deaf children who were not exposed to a gestural language such as American Sign Language (ASL), but whose caregivers instead created some signs. The children quickly created new signs for objects and had a much larger vocabulary than their caregivers. More important, the children spontaneously imposed some grammatical structure on the signs, whereas the parents did not (Feldman, Goldin-Meadow, & Gleitman, 1978; Goldin-Meadow, Gelman, & Mylander, 2005; Goldin-Meadow, & Mylander, 1998; Singleton & Newport, 2004). Even more remarkable was the case of a large group of deaf Nicaraguan children. A statewide program for the deaf was started in Nicaragua in 1979, at which point hundreds of deaf children were brought together to two schools. Few or none had any exposure to a formal sign language, nor did the teachers have such knowledge. The children rapidly developed their own system of communication, which was relatively crude, and lacked syntactic sophistication. When younger children entered the school, however, they refined the system and added the syntax that had been missing (see Photo 13.3; Senghas & Coppola, 2001; Senghas, Kita, & Özyürek, 2004). What these remarkable studies tell us is that children can go beyond the linguistic input that they receive and create language themselves. But it appears that they must be within the critical period to do so.

Photo 13.3.   Children speaking Nicaraguan sign language, which children there developed on their own.

We have reviewed data indicating several ways in which language appears to be developmentally special: Children all go through the same stages when they learn it; children all make the same types of mistakes when they learn it; children learn language with remarkable speed, if they learn it within the critical period; and children can go beyond the input they receive and produce communication that is more language-like than anything they have experienced, if given the chance within the critical period.

Is Language Particularly Human?

As you undoubtedly know, several human researchers have undertaken to teach language to nonhuman primates (chimps, gorillas, bonobos). Why did they do so? The obvious answer—that it would be cool to talk to apes—is accurate, but it is not sufficient motivation. Most researchers are interested in these language projects because they tell us something interesting about the cognitive capabilities of nonhuman primates. In this chapter, we've discussed some of the complexities of the grammatical structure of language. Are nonhuman primates able to master these complexities?

Notice that this goal is very different from the goal of being able to communicate with a chimp. If you simply want to be able to know what a chimp wants to do (perhaps you want it to be able to make requests) and you want to be able to give it commands, that is a different undertaking from teaching the chimp language. To keep the distinction clear in our minds, we can return to the definition of language that we discussed earlier in the chapter, and we can contrast that with simple communication. We said that language is communicative, arbitrary, structured, generative, and dynamic. Most animal communication systems have only the first of these properties. In the wild, chimps use a series of grunts and howls to communicate specific meanings—danger from a snake, for example—but these communicative signals are not arbitrary. They are fixed in their meaning and seem to be part of the animal's genetic inheritance. The same is true of the communication systems of honeybees (which communicate about food sources), birds (whose song often signals ownership of territory), and other nonhuman animals.

Some researchers of ape language have commented that as some humans discover greater and greater linguistic abilities in primates, other humans scurry off to redefine language, effectively raising the bar to ensure that we are the only species that can *really* use language (see the exchange between Kako, 1999, and Shanker, Savage-Rumbaugh, & Taylor, 1999). Having read this far in the chapter, you can appreciate that the insistence on the use of grammar is not an arbitrary requirement but is essential to a definition of language.

So, just how well can nonhuman primates learn a language? Not all that well. Early attempts to teach language to primates were doomed to fail because the researchers tried to teach chimps vocal speech. The chimp's vocal tract and articulators can't form the sounds properly. Asking chimps to produce vocal speech is like asking humans to flap their arms and fly; our arms aren't suited to make us airborne, and the chimp vocal tract is not suited to allow the clear pronunciation needed for vocal speech.

American Sign Language

In the 1960s, several projects were initiated to solve that problem. Beatrice and Allen Gardner (Gardner & Gardner, 1967a, 1967b, 1975; Gardner, Gardner, & Van Cantfort, 1989) raised a chimp, Washoe, in the manner of a human infant, with exposure to toys, play areas, and activities. More important, the Gardners spoke ASL to Washoe and used only ASL in her presence. Furthermore, the Gardners actively taught ASL to Washoe. They molded her hands into the correct shape for signs and rewarded her for signing correctly. This process of actively teaching the language to the chimp and actively teaching it how to articulate the words of the language was adopted by other researchers. Herb Terrace and his associates (Terrace, Petitto, Sanders, & Bever, 1979) also used ASL to train a chimp that they named Nim Chimpsky (a play on the name of linguist Noam Chomsky). Still another researcher who sought to use ASL is Francine Patterson (1978, 1981), who taught a gorilla, Koko. Koko may be the best-known nonhuman "speaker" because she seems to have been the most widely covered in popular press. There were even references to Koko in two different episodes of the TV show *Seinfeld*. (If that's not making it, I don't know what is.)

David Premack (1971, 1976a, 1976b) took quite a different approach. He trained a chimp, Sarah, to communicate by placing metal-backed chips on a magnetic board. The chips symbolized nouns (*chocolate, dish, Sarah*), verbs (*is, give, insert*), concepts (*same, if–then*), and adjectives (*red, yellow*). The chips were arbitrary in their appearance; for example, the chip corresponding to the concept *chocolate* did not look like a piece of chocolate. Somewhat similar in spirit is the approach taken by Sue Savage-Rumbaugh and her colleagues (Savage-Rumbaugh, Romski, Sevcik, & Pate, 1983; Savage-Rumbaugh, Rumbaugh, & Boysen, 1978; Savage-Rumbaugh, Rumbaugh, Smith, & Lawson, 1980). They taught a chimp named Lana and later a bonobo named Kanzi (Savage-Rumbaugh, Shanker, & Taylor, 1998) a language they called Yerkish, named for the Yerkes primate center where they worked and Lana lived. Lana had 24-hour access to a computer keyboard on which were printed arbitrary symbols, each symbol standing for a concept. Lana could punch the keys to form "sentences." The symbols on the keys she pressed were echoed on a screen, and Yerkish communication from a trainer could appear on the screen. An advantage of having the utterance echoed on a screen was that it reduced the working memory requirements for the speaker; the length of an utterance would not be artificially limited simply because the speaker could not keep a long utterance in mind.

These primates had an opportunity to learn at least two aspects of language that, if they learned them, would represent a remarkable achievement. The first thing they might learn is the symbolic nature of words. They might simply know that they are often given chocolate when they push a key with a particular symbol—that's not very different from what a pigeon can learn. Or they might understand the abstract relationship between the symbol and chocolate. If so, they should be able to use the symbol in many different contexts, not just to obtain the referent. This question concerns the property of language we have called arbitrariness, the notion that a word is a symbol.

A second question we can ask about primate language is whether primates understand how to use syntax. As we've discussed, humans are very sensitive to syntax, even to simple aspects of word order. For example, *water bird* is a bird that lives on or near water, whereas *bird water* refers to a particular type of water that is for birds. Can primates appreciate the difference between the two?

The claims made for the learning of primates in these studies ranges from modest to modestly spectacular. Patterson claims that the gorilla, Koko, has obtained the largest vocabulary among the primate speakers, well-formed syntax, spontaneous signing (not simply signing in response to a request to sign), and, most amazingly, puns, jokes, and cunning lies. The problem is that Patterson has not published data in scientific journals for a number of years, so her claims would have to be taken at her word. No scientist expects to be believed without a critical review of his or her work by knowledgeable peers. Unfortunately, these interesting claims about primate language cannot be verified.

Many of the other claims fall in a second and considerably less grand group. Washoe acquired 132 signs, Nim acquired 125, and estimates from other groups are in this range. There are some problems with these data, however. The researchers on the Washoe project may well have been too optimistic (or generous) in how they coded signs. Chimps have a limited repertoire of signs that they perform in the wild, without ever being taught. One is a reaching gesture with palm up, which indicates that they want something. Another is shaking the hand, which indicates hurrying. The lion's share of the two-word combinations recorded on the Wahsoe project involved the words *hurry, please, come,* and *more.* Thus, about half the two-word combinations arguably involved signs that were not taught to Washoe. Jane Goodall, upon visiting the Nim Chimpsky project, remarked that she recognized all Nim's "signs" as gestures that chimps perform in the wild (Pinker, 1994). These data bear on our assessment of whether the ape's language has the characteristic of arbitrariness. This appears to be less of a problem in studies using truly arbitrary symbols for communication instead of hand gestures.

How can we be sure that any of the primates are really using words as symbols? When a primate is trained to execute a gesture and receives a food reward or praise for doing so, how does that differ from the bar-pressing rat? In one experiment, Savage-Rumbaugh and her colleagues (1978) had two chimps engage in a "conversation." The first observed a trainer hide a food item in a container and then pressed the key on a keyboard with the symbol for the food item, thereby telling the second chimp (who never saw the food) what item was hidden. The second chimp was then to request that specific food item, and if it did so correctly, the two split the food.

This result sounds impressive as an example of two chimps communicating, but does it show that chimps are using words as symbols? Robert Epstein and his colleagues didn't think so (Epstein, Lanza, & Skinner, 1980). They got the same behavior from pigeons, named Jack and Jill, housed in adjoining cages with a transparent wall between them. Jack pecked a key labeled "What color?" That was a cue for Jill to look behind a curtain where there were three lights—red, green, and yellow—that were not visible to Jack. After ascertaining which light was illuminated, Jill pecked one of three keys—*R, G,* or *Y*—that Jack could see. Jack then pecked a key labeled "Thank you," whereupon Jill was given a food reward. Jack then pecked one of three keys indicating which light was illuminated and received his own reward. Thus, we can conclude either that pigeons can use symbolic language or that we need more stringent tests of the symbolic use of language.

What would be a satisfactory demonstration of the use of words as symbols? The key property to look for is transfer to a novel testing situation. If you try a new ice cream flavor, *cassis*, you can use the word cassis in all sorts of situations: You can request cassis ice cream, describe cassis, and comment on cassis. If, instead, you've learned something in a rote manner, as an operantly conditioned response, the behavior is inflexible or is generalizable in predictable and limited ways. Primates in these language studies receive many practice trials and are drilled in the use of these signs, and nevertheless speak about a fairly limited range of topics, most of which are requests for things. That said, it's true that at least in some cases they combine signs in ways that they have not been taught to do (Terrace et al., 1979), indicating at least some rudimentary use of words that they have learned as symbols.

There are a few celebrated examples of seeming spontaneity in ape language. One was an instance in which Washoe was near a swan on a pond and the trainer asked, "What that?" Washoe responded, "Water bird," thus appearing to coin a new term for an as yet unnamed object. However, Washoe might have simply been commenting that water was visible, and so was a bird.

What about grammar? Recall that a defining characteristic of language is that it is structured. Also recall that ignoring the importance of grammar in language is a serious mistake; grammar is at the very heart of what makes language language. The truth about primate grammar is that they just don't get it, except in the most rudimentary form. The best analysis of chimp grammar comes from Terrace and his colleagues' analysis of Nim's "sentences." They found that he did seem to understand some basic ideas about word order; for example, he put *more* before another word (*chocolate, tickle*) far more often than by chance. However, analysis of videotapes indicated that Nim's sentences often were full or partial imitations of something his trainer had just finished saying. Finally, we must consider the mind-cracking sameness of primate utterances. Here are the top 10 (in order) four-word "sentences" uttered by Nim:

Eat drink, eat drink.
Eat Nim eat Nim.
Banana Nim banana Nim.
Drink Nim drink Nim.
Banana eat me Nim.
Banana me eat banana.
Banana me Nim me.
Grape eat Nim eat.
Nim eat Nim eat.
Play me Nim play.

Nim's longest utterance, at 16 words, was "Give orange me give eat orange me eat orange give me eat orange give me you."

Bonobos likely have greater linguistic competence than chimps (Brakke & Savage-Rumbaugh, 1995, 1996), and at least one has achieved a vocabulary of several hundred words (Savage-Rumbaugh, 1986). Perhaps the most important difference is that bonobos seem to be more ready to spontaneously learn something about language. Sue Savage-Rumbaugh (1986) notes that her star pupil, Kanzi (see Photo 13.4), initially learned by watching his mother training, not by receiving training himself. Further work has shown that bonobos can learn new words through observation (Lyn & Savage-Rumbaugh, 2000). This is important because it undercuts that argument that primates don't learn much about language but really learn what to do to be rewarded. Nevertheless, the learning is rather slow, taking between 6 and 86 exposures to comprehend a word. The average first-grader knows between 8,000 and 14,000 words (Carey, 1978).

The final word on nonhuman primate language is this: It's not close to the language humans use, a conclusion that is likely obvious to you, having read the previous section about how humans acquire language. We began this section by noting that the question of whether nonhuman primates can use language would be interesting because it would tell us something about their mental capabilities. It seems likely that there is some use of words as symbols in the speech of primates and probably some nonrandom ordering of the symbols, showing some primitive understanding of grammar. But the main question posed has been answered: Apes cannot learn language or much of anything like language.

Photo 13.4.   Kanzi.

Ironically, the opposite conclusion seems to have taken hold in the public imagination. People seem to be under the impression that some apes have been taught to speak to us in a Dr. Doolittle scenario. This "fact" is most often trotted out to humble us, the human species, for being so arrogant as to think that we are special, when in fact other animals have the capability of language, thus proving that we are not that different. Some of the researchers on these projects have reached conclusions in this vein.

As Steve Pinker (1994) eloquently pointed out, the very comparison shows remarkable human arrogance. Why pick language as the metric by which we evaluate whether we are the same as other species? That's a contest humans can't lose. Why not compare chimps with humans in terms of the ability to climb? Why not compare our memories with those of seed-caching birds such as corvids, which can remember thousands of locations in which they've hidden seeds? Why not compare our perceptual abilities with that of honeybees, which can perceive ultraviolet light? The point is that humans are unique, but so are all other species. Each species has abilities and failings. The claim that we should compare our linguistic abilities with those of apes to evaluate their worth is scientifically empty. (For a readable and thought-provoking article on these points, see Povinelli & Bering, 2002.)

Is Language Cognitively Special?

To this point, we have focused on language as an independent system. We have treated language as though it were disconnected from the other topics in this book: memory, problem solving, reasoning, and so on. In one way—a trivial way—we know that language influences thought because different words that you might utter lead to different thoughts in my mind. We can also safely draw the trivial conclusion that entertaining different thoughts leads me to utter different words. The deeper question is whether there is a more intimate relationship between language and thought. For example, are certain types of thought dependent on having the words to express them? Can we use linguistic abilities as a measure of people's abilities to think in particular ways?

There is little doubt that how and what we think affects what we say and that what we say affects how we think. But is there a deeper relationship between language and thought? It is not the case that each language has the same set of words representing the same concepts and that languages differ only in the sound of these words. Instead, languages differ in the concepts for which words exist, and in some languages, particular aspects of a concept are highlighted by grammar. Do such differences mean that the speakers of these different languages actually think differently?

The idea that language molds thoughts and molds our perception of reality was advanced by linguist Edward Sapir (1956):

> We see and hear and otherwise experience very largely as we do because the language habits of our community predispose certain choices of interpretation.

This perspective was carried on by one of Sapir's students, a businessman and amateur linguist, Benjamin Whorf (1956). Their position became known as the **Sapir–Whorf hypothesis** or sometimes simply the **Whorfian hypothesis**. The strongest version of the Whorfian hypothesis is that thought is so intimately tied to language that thoughts generated in one language may be impossible to express in another language. This strong position has few adherents. It is generally accepted that all languages are flexible enough and powerful enough to express the ideas of other languages. The difference may be one of convenience. For example, in the Kiriwina language of New Guinea, the word *mokita* means "truth that everyone knows but no one speaks about." Americans surely are familiar with this concept and can express it, but it is simpler to express in Kiriwina (Hunt & Agnoli, 1991).

The weak version of the Whorfian hypothesis has received more careful investigation. It states that every language favors some thought processes over others; it's not that your language makes some thoughts impossible, but rather that the language you speak biases you to think in certain ways. This weak version was initially studied in color perception and memory and in counterfactual thinking. In both cases, the data indicated that there was little influence of language on cognition. It turns out, however, that we *can* identify influences of language on cognition; the early conclusions were premature.

EARLY DATA FROM COLOR NAMING AND COUNTERFACTUALS.   One myth about the Whorfian hypothesis should be laid to rest: It is not true that Eskimo (i.e., Innuit) languages have a large number of ways to refer to the concept *snow*. Whorf mentions this possible example and claims that there are three words for snow in "Eskimo." The example has been picked up in popular culture and exaggerated to mythic status (Martin, 1986). English has a fair number of words for snow—*snow, slush, sleet, powder*—and may not have any fewer than Inuit languages (Pinker, 1994).

Much of the early systematic work on the Whorfian hypothesis was conducted on color naming. In one of the original studies, Roger Brown and Eric Lenneberg (1954) selected color naming because colors have properties that are objectively describable (wavelength), but different languages divide the color spectrum into different numbers of hues. In their experiment, Brown and Lenneberg showed one group of participants a set of colors. Some were agreed on as readily namable, and these colors were considered codable (i.e., linguistically codable). Other participants were then asked to view colors (both codable and not) and were later given a recognition test. Memory was somewhat better for codable colors than noncodable ones, providing weak evidence for the Whorfian hypothesis; the way that participants named colors seemed to affect their memory for them.

Later research on color memory painted a different picture, however. Eleanor Rosch (then E. R. Heider, 1972), whose categorization research we discussed in chapter 8, examined the color memory of people who speak different languages. Most notably, she went to New Guinea and tested speakers of

Dani, a language that has but two color terms: *mola* for lighter colors such as white, yellow, and orange and *mili* for darker colors such as black, purple, and blue. Rosch administered a recognition memory task for colors. There were two key findings. First, the Whorfian hypothesis might lead us to expect that the Dani would easily confuse all *mola* colors, but that's not what happened. Although their scores were lower overall than English speakers, the Dani made the same sorts of mistakes English speakers did, and their performance was best on the same chips on which English speakers excelled (the "reddest" red, for example). The second finding came from a follow-up experiment by Rosch and Donald Oliver (Heider & Oliver, 1972). They administered a recognition test to both Dani and English speakers in which participants were to remember a color chip and then select it from two choices. The crucial comparison was whether the two choices crossed a color line. Sometimes the two chips were similar, but one would be called green by most English speakers and the other blue. Other times the two choices were equally similar (the same difference in wavelength), but both would be called blue. Participants performed equally well when the two choices were on the same side or different sides of the color line, and that was true for both Dani and English speakers. These influential results were widely cited as demonstrating that language has little, if any, influence on thought, although some researchers pointed out that there were some problems in the way the experiments were designed (Lucy & Shweder, 1979).

More recent data, however, is in accord with the original Brown and Lenneberg (1954) studies, indicating that there *are* influences of language on color memory. Ian Davies and his colleagues (Roberson, Davies, & Davidoff, 2000) set out to reproduce as closely as possible the results reported by Heider. They tested English speakers and participants from Papua, New Guinea, who speak Berinmo, which has five basic color terms. They found that memory performance matched naming performance; in other words, the sorts of mistakes people made *did* match how they named colors. They also found (unlike Heider) that recognition was easier if the two choices crossed the color line compared with when they did not. Finally, they found that everyone's memory was best for focal colors (the "reddest" red) as Heider reported, but they noted that that was because everyone was biased to pick focal colors when they couldn't remember the color and were just guessing.

Davies and colleagues have examined color memory in a different set of languages: Himba, which is spoken in Namibia; English, Russian, and Setswana, which is spoken in Botswana (Davies, Sowden, Jerrett, Jerrett, & Corbett, 1998; Roberson, Davidoff, Davies, & Shapiro, 2005). The researchers asked participants to sort color chips into groups, and they dictated to participants the number of categories they should create (between 2 and 12). They predicted that there would be greater agreement among Setswana speakers when they were sorting into a small number of groups, because Setswana has only 6 color names, and greater agreement among the English and Russian speakers when he dictated a large number of groups, because those languages have 11 or 12 color names, respectively. As Davies et al. put it, "The most striking

Photo 13.5. A Himba woman (right) taking a color test as researcher Anna Androvlaki (left) looks on.

feature of the results was the marked similarity of the [color] groups chosen across the three language groups" (p. 433). However, there were small, reliable differences in expected direction predicted by the Whorfian hypothesis (see Photo 13.5).

Thus, the conclusion from the literature on color naming and memory is that there probably *is* an effect of language on thought in this domain. It might not be huge, but it seems to be real.

Another early attempt to test the Whorfian hypothesis concerned counterfactual reasoning in speakers of Mandarin Chinese (henceforth, we'll simply call it Chinese). Counterfactual reasoning refers to considering what would happen if something were true that is not true. English speakers use the subjunctive tense: "If we had been on time, we could have made the plane." Chinese does not have a subjunctive tense. If the supposition is obviously false, a Chinese speaker constructs counterfactuals using a normal "if–then" sentence: "If I am a member of the Rolling Stones, I will retire before I embarrass myself." The listener understands that I am not a member of the Rolling Stones and am instead offering advice about what the Stones should do. If the listener cannot be expected to know that the supposition is false, the speaker must explicitly state that fact: "Mrs. Wong not know English. If Mrs. Wong know English, she then can read the *New York Times*" (Au, 1983, p. 157).

Alfred Bloom (1981) presented data indicating that Chinese speakers could not understand a simple story that entailed counterfactual reasoning. Terry Au (1983, 1984) showed in a series of studies that this conclusion was wrong. She attributed Bloom's results to poor translations of the Chinese. Au provided better translations of the stories and reported that her Chinese participants showed normal understanding of counterfactuals, just as English speakers did.

These two early attempts to test the Whorfian hypothesis were plagued by problems, but they are presented here to give a sense of why very little of this work was done until the 1990s. It looked like language didn't influence thought very much; the few attempts to find such influences had failed. (Today, we know that language *does* influence color memory to some extent.) Furthermore, these experiments are difficult and expensive to conduct; researchers have to find native speakers of two languages that differ in an interesting way, the materials must be translated properly, and so on.

RECENT DATA: LANGUAGE INFLUENCES THOUGHT.   More recent work has used better measures to test the Whorfian hypothesis, more often testing whether language influences thought rather than whether language makes thought possible or likely. Much of this work examines the memory representation for objects and how it is used. Some recent work has shown dramatic effects in the role of language and the understanding of number.

John Lucy (1992, 1997; Lucy & Shweder, 1979) examined the influence of language on memory representations in English and Yucatec Maya. English counting terms serve as a modifier for the noun (as in *one candle*). Yucatec Maya uses classifiers that describe the material of the object counted (e.g., *one long thin wax*). We might speculate, therefore, that speakers of this language would be especially sensitive to the materials from which objects are made. In one experiment, Lucy presented participants with three objects (e.g., a candle, a stick, and some wax) and asked them to say which two went together. Yucatec speakers tended to classify by material (candle with wax) whereas English speakers tended to classify by shape (candle with stick). There is also evidence that language not only influences how we think about materials, but also how we think about space (Majid, Bowerman, Kita, Haun, & Levinson, 2004).

Other studies have examined the effect of grammatical gender systems. English codes gender only in some nouns (e.g., *girl, boy*) and some pronouns (e.g., *he, she*). Spanish marks nouns, pronouns, adjectives, and determiners. The Spanish word for *telescope* (*telescopio*) is masculine, and articles and adjectives follow the noun's gender; hence, to refer to *a telescope* we must use a masculine article (*un telescopio*). Other languages have different grammatical gender systems. German, for example, marks only pronouns and determiners, and it has three categories of gender (masculine, feminine, and neuter). A good deal of work has been devoted to examining whether people think of nouns as following their grammatical gender classification. Most of these studies report support for the Whorfian hypothesis in languages such as Arabic (Clarke, Losoff, McCracken, & Rood, 1984), Hebrew (Guiora, Beit-Halachmi, Fried, & Yoder, 1983), Italian (Ervin, 1962), and Spanish (Sera, Reittinger, & del Castillo Pintado, 1991). For example, in one study (Sera, Elieff, Forbes, Burch, Rodriguez, & Dubois, 2002), participants were shown line drawings of objects. They were told that a movie would be made in which objects would come to life, and their job was to say whether they believed a particular object should have a male or female voice. French and Spanish speakers tended to assign voices that matched grammatical gender (although German speakers did not, a finding of some interest that would take us far afield on this subject).

The strongest effects in keeping with the Whorfian hypothesis come from studies of number. Two studies have examined the ability to use number concepts among speakers of languages that have limited words for number: members of the Pirahã tribe (Gordon, 2004) who have specific words for "one" and "two" and refer to larger quantities as "many," and speakers of Mundurukú (Pica, Lemer, Izard, & Dehaene, 2004) who use number words for one through five and "many" for larger numbers. The researchers administered a variety of tests that included different types of quantity matching, simple addition and subtraction with small numbers, and comparison for quantity of larger groups of objects. Speakers of languages that do use counting terms are believed to have two representations of numerosity: one verbal and one nonverbal. To put it informally, you can either count and compute, or you can estimate. For example, if I show you two large groups of dots (as in Figure 13.3) and ask which has more, you can count or you can judge by how the groups look.

Speakers of Pirahã and Mundurukú have the same nonverbal system that you do. They can estimate quantity about as well as you can when you use your nonverbal system, and it performs well and poorly in the same situations that yours does. For example, you are faster and more reliable in using this system when the differences are proportionally large (comparing 20 to 10 dots, or 100 to 50) than when they are proportionally small (comparing 20 to 18 dots, or 100 to 90). What these speakers cannot do is perform tasks that require the use of precise numbers. For example, speakers of Mundurukú were asked

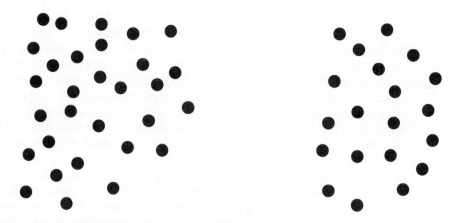

Figure 13.3. If asked to judge which group has more dots, you could either count the number in each group or you could judge by the look of the group.

to perform a subtraction task where the result could be named (i.e., the result was 5 or less) but the operands might be larger (e.g., 6 − 4). Participants performed well if the initial operand was 5 or less, but dropped to near-chance levels when it was 6 or larger. These data indicate that speakers of languages that do not explicitly enumerate quantities above 5 (or above 2) have difficulty using these concepts. In contrast, these data also show that a lack of verbal counting has no bearing on the nonverbal representation of number.

There is reasonable support for a modest version of the Whorfian hypothesis. It is clear that any language spoken by a community will be flexible enough to express almost any idea; the one exception discovered thus far is the use of explicit counting. Different languages do make such expression easier or more difficult. The Whorfian effects that we might expect to see relatively frequently, therefore, will not be the dramatic loss of an ability, as in the Pirahã and Mundurukú studies, but modest pluses or minuses in processing speed. Research in the last five or ten years has uncovered such costs and benefits. The next step should be some attempt to systematize these costs and benefits into a theory that integrates language and thought.

In this chapter, we've focused on what makes language special. We've discussed its structure, and then discussed developmental evidence, cross-species evidence, and evidence from within human cognition that language is special. In chapter 14, we'll discuss how human language actually works.

Stand-on-One-Foot Questions

6. What is the evidence that humans are primed to learn language?

7. What key features of language would you want to evaluate if you were investigating the use of language by apes? In the final analysis, can apes use language, based on these criteria?

8. Is some version of the Whorfian hypothesis likely to be correct?

Questions That Require Two Feet

9. If the strong version of the Whorfian hypothesis were correct, what would that imply about people who speak more than one language?

10. If there is a critical period for language, what might this fact imply about learning languages in school? What might it imply about bilingual education?

KEY TERMS

babbling	overextension	recursion
competence	overregularization	Sapir–Whorf hypothesis
cooing	performance	(Whorfian Hypothesis)
critical period	phonemes	surface structure
deep structure	phrase structure	text
grammar	grammars	word-chain grammars
language		

CURRENT DIRECTIONS IN COGNITIVE SCIENCE
Recommended readings

Saffran, J. R. (2003). "Statistical language learning: Mechanisms and constraints." (pp. 123–130) One of the more exciting findings in language research during the last decade has been the discovery by Saffran and her coworkers that infants are sensitive to the statistical properties of language. This sensitivity suggests a way that infants might solve the problem of finding word boundaries. In this chapter, Saffran offers a readable review of what can be a technically challenging subject.

Landauer, T. K. (1998). "Learning and representing verbal meaning: The latent semantic analysis theory." (pp. 131–137) In this chapter, I noted that children learn vocabulary at an incredible rate, but I didn't say anything about how that happens. This process has stumped philosophers and psychologists for centuries. One of the really puzzling aspects of this problem is that people simply don't have that much exposure to a wide variety of words. Most of the words you hear in conversation are from a relatively small set, and the words you encounter in print don't seem to be processed often enough to enter into memory. Landauer offers a theory of how this learning can take place.

Povinelli, D. J., & Bering, J. M. (2002). "The mentality of apes revisited." (pp. 169–176) In commenting on the ape language literature, I said that too often the interpretation of this literature is marred by an attempt to compare humans and other animals on some yardstick, instead of appreciating the marvelous (and wildly different) cognitive abilities of different species. Povinelli and Bering make this argument more eloquently and incisively than I could.

Language Processing

What Makes Language Processing Difficult?

- Phonemes
- Words
- Sentences
- Texts

How are Ambiguities Resolved?

- Phonemes
- Words
- Sentences
- Texts

Dixon was alive again. Consciousness was upon him before he could get out of the way; not for him the slow gracious wandering from the halls of sleep, but a summary, forcible ejection. He lay sprawled, too wicked to move, spewed up like a broken spider crab on the tarry shingle of the morning. The light did him harm, but not as much as looking at things did; he resolved, having done it once, never to move his eyeballs again. A dusty thudding in his head made the scene before him beat like a pulse. His mouth had been used as a latrine by some small creature of the night, and then as its mausoleum. During the night, too, he'd somehow been on a cross-country run and then been expertly beaten up by secret police. He felt bad.

—Kingsley Amis, *Lucky Jim*

In this chapter, we discuss in some detail why we should be amazed by our ability to understand this paragraph from *Lucky Jim*, and we try to unravel some of the processes that make the feat possible.

First, note what your experience is when you read a paragraph or listen to someone speak. You feel that you read or hear words, not individual letters or sounds. Of course, it must be the case that you do read individual letters—how else could you differentiate *dead* and *bead*?—but you must do so with such speed that the process is not open to awareness. As we'll see, the process of differentiating individual speech sounds—phonemes—is even more difficult than identifying letters during reading.

Identifying letters to form words seems difficult enough, but the problem is still more complicated. For example, did you stumble over the word *light* in the paragraph? Presumably, you did not pause to wonder whether it referred to brightness, lack of weight, or a joyous mood. It seems difficult enough to find the right word in memory amid the clutter of the approximately 60,000 words we know; what do you do when the word you need to find in memory has more than one meaning?

We can also note that even if the mind successfully retrieved the meanings of all the words, there is still great ambiguity in a simple string of words. Take the simplest sentence of the paragraph, "He felt bad." Interpreting those three words depends critically on word order, the importance of which becomes obvious if we change the word order. "He bad felt" might mean he is likened to a piece of felt cloth of poor quality. "Felt he bad" gives the same sense of someone enduring negative sensations, but it has an interrogative note and sounds as though it were uttered by Yoda. How do you know that "He felt bad" was not an imprecation of the manner in which Dixon feels things? Sure, he feels, but he's not very good at it.

Finally, we might consider the larger context of the paragraph. Even if you understand an individual sentence, the meaning of that sentence is often lost if it is not put in the context of the surrounding sentences. Does Amis really want you to know that Dixon has a bad taste in his mouth and that it hurts to move his eyes? Yes, but the author wants you to know those things as a way of communicating that Dixon is waking up with a historic hangover.

Amis's purpose probably was achieved—you likely made this inference—although a hangover is never mentioned. How did you know it? There must be some process by which successive sentences are put together into broader ideas and themes, and indeed this process is so successful that you can draw new inferences from these ideas.

Our goals in this chapter are straightforward. **What makes language processing difficult?** Our analysis of the Amis paragraph gives you a sense of the kinds of problems the mind faces in trying to decode language. Language appears to be full of ambiguities—words have multiple meanings, sentences can be interpreted in more than one way—so why is it that other people's speech and the text we read rarely seem ambiguous? In the second part of the chapter, we ask **How are ambiguities resolved?** As we'll see, a key idea is the use of multiple sources of information at the same time. A word may be ambiguous in isolation, but if we recruit other sources of information—such as the sentence the word is in or the conversational context—that usually helps resolve ambiguity.

What Makes Language Processing Difficult?

Preview

We discussed four levels of language: phonemes, words, sentences, and texts. It turns out that there are ambiguities at each level that make language perception difficult. Phoenemes are pronounced differently, depending on the speaker and context. Words are difficult to discern because there is no break between them. Sentences are difficult to understand because even small changes in word order can have a big impact on meaning, and some sentences (e.g., *time flies like an arrow*) are inherently ambiguous. The challenge in understanding texts is that they are usually underspecified, meaning that the speaker leaves much unsaid, assuming that the listener will make the correct inferences. We must therefore understand how people know which inferences to make.

In chapter 13, we discussed the structure of language in some detail, emphasizing the idea that language has a hierarchical structure: Speech is composed of phonemes, which are combined into words, which are combined into sentences, which are combined into texts. In this chapter, we focus on how phonemes, words, sentences, and texts are processed. As we have done in other areas of cognition, we begin by considering what makes the problem difficult, and then move to the mind's solutions.

Phonemes

Why is the perception of phonemes difficult? After all, there are only 46 sounds to be perceived and categorized in English. In visual perception, you might have to identify anything out in the world, but if someone utters the word *boot*, you simply perceive the three phonemes that compose that word (*b, u, t*), string them together, and thereby hear the word. Even though people can perceive phonemes quite rapidly in accelerated speech—perhaps as many as 50 phonemes per second (Foulke & Sticht, 1969)—the problem doesn't seem like it should be that tough because there are only 46 possible things to hear.

The first difficulty is that individual speakers produce phonemes quite differently. Differences between speakers from different regions of the United States can be quite large. For example, New Englanders are famous for dropping *r*, except at the beginning of a word (when I lived in Boston the standard sentence to parody a New England accent was "Pahk the cah in Hahvahd Yahd," meaning "Park the car in Harvard Yard"). Variation in phoneme pronunciation becomes still more extreme among nonnative speakers of English, who may have learned a different set of phonemes than the 46 used in English. Despite substantial variations in how speakers produce phonemes, listeners are able to understand their speech; you have doubtless heard English spoken by native speakers of Russian, Chinese, Arabic, and so on. Nevertheless, it is true that native speakers of English make more errors in perceiving speech generated by nonnative speakers of English, and the extent to which they make errors depends on the strength of the speaker's accent (Schmid & Yeni-Komshian, 1999).

Another difficulty of phoneme perception is that phoneme production varies not only between speakers, but also for an individual speaker. If you had a stockpile of phonemes that you could string together like beads to form words, a phoneme would sound the same regardless of the word in which it appeared, but individual phonemes are affected by the surrounding phonemes. For example, if you say the word *tulip* slowly, you'll notice that you round your lips before the *t* sound. Why? Because your lips need to be rounded to properly say the upcoming *u* sound. Rounding your lips early doesn't affect the *t* sound, so you may as well round them early. This phenomenon of making one movement in a way that anticipates future movements or is influenced by a past movement is called **coarticulation**. When you say the word *tulip*, you don't simply utter each phoneme in the order it appears. Because of these anticipatory movements, phoneme production is somewhat sloppy, irregular, and variable from word to word. Why is it, then, that we don't hear other people's pronunciation as sounding sloppy and irregular? We discuss the answer in the next section.

Words

When you hear someone speaking, your perception is that the person utters discrete words: It seems that there are small pauses between words, small bits of dead air. That turns out not to be true, as shown in the sound spectrogram in Figure 14.1. When people speak, they produce a continuous stream of

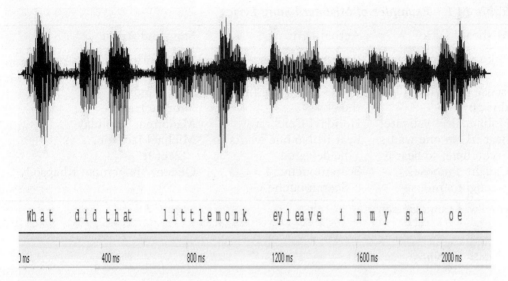

Figure 14.1. A sound spectrogram represents sound on a graph. Time is on the X axis and Frequency (low to high) is on the Y axis. The intensity of the sound at any point in the graph is represented by the darkness of the spectrogram. The important thing to notice is that there is not silence between words.

phonemes. To convince yourself that this is true, recall the last time you heard someone speak a language you do not understand. It is impossible to tell where the breaks are between words. For this reason, researchers sometimes call speech a **speech stream** to emphasize its continuous nature.

The continuous nature of speech would seem to pose a special problem for infants learning to talk. For example, suppose a mother says to her daughter "Okay cutie, it's time to get out of that orange bassinet." What the infant actually hears is more akin to "Okaycutieitstimetogetoutofthatorangebassinet." An adult at least has knowledge of what words *could* be making up a sentence. But how could an infant know that "orange" and "bassinet" are units? For all the infant knows, the speech stream should be segmented into three units: "or," "angebass," and "inet." Later, the potential for ambiguity in word boundaries becomes fun for kids, as in sayings like "I scream; you scream: We all scream for ice cream."

Even for adults, the segmentation of phonemes into words is subject to error. A rich source of such errors is misheard song lyrics. Most of us have had the humiliating experience of singing along with the radio, only to have a friend squint and say "What did you just sing?" and learn that we had been mishearing the lyric all along. Some examples appear in Table 14.1. How are we able to segment phonemes into words? Why do we seldom mishear spoken words but make more errors when words are sung?

A final problem to consider for word perception. Even if you hear the word correctly, many words have multiple meanings. If I say "I really like hot dogs," do I mean that I like frankfurters or that I like athletes who show off? How do you access the correct meaning?

Table 14.1. Examples of Misheard Song Lyrics

Misheard Lyric	Actual Lyric	Song and Artist
Take a bike ride, sir	Paperback writer	The Beatles, "Paperback Writer"
'scuse me, while I kiss this guy	'scuse me, while I kiss the sky	Jimi Hendrix, "Purple Haze"
Hollandaise! Salivate!	Holiday! Celebrate!	Madonna, "Holiday"
Beat it! No one wants you here, so beat it	Beat it! No one wants to be defeated	Michael Jackson, "Beat It"
Caught a moose, caught a moose	Scaramouche, Scaramouche	Queen, "Bohemian Rhapsody"

From www.amiright.com.

Sentences

Suppose that all the problems we've discussed so far have been resolved, and perceiving words (and their constituent phonemes) is effortless. Can we therefore understand all sentences? Unfortunately, the problems are just beginning, as you might guess from our discussion of grammars in chapter 13.

It seems clear enough that the order in which the words are perceived is a crucial determinant of the meaning of the sentence; drawing words from a sack would yield meaningless word strings, not sentences ("Wish John he jumped had higher"). Even small changes in word order can dramatically change the meaning of sentences. Compare "John wished he had jumped higher" to "He wished John had jumped higher." The reversal of two words completely changes the meaning. We would guess that word order is one determinant of how a phrase structure (discussed in chapter 13) is assigned to a sentence.

We'll see that word order is indeed important to deriving meaning from sentences, but it's not the whole story. Consider the sentence "Time flies like an arrow." The meaning seems unambiguous, yet there are at least five grammatically correct interpretations from this single order of words, one of which is depicted in Figure 14.2. Note that in interpretations 2 to 5, *flies* refers to a type of insect:

1. Time moves quickly, as an arrow does.
2. Assess the pace of flies as you would assess the pace of an arrow.
3. Assess the pace of flies in the same way that an arrow would assess the pace of flies.
4. A particular variety of flies (time flies) adores arrows.
5. Assess the pace of flies, but only those that resemble an arrow.

Figure 14.2. One interpretation of the sentence "Time flies like an arrow."

Despite the fact that there are five possible interpretations of the sentence, few people perceive the ambiguity, and most perceive the intended meaning (interpretation 1).

What is the process by which the mind assesses word order so we appreciate the difference between "Hit John with the big bat" and "John hit with the big bat", and so we choose one among many interpretations of an ambiguous sentence such as "Time flies like an arrow"?

Texts

One of the most notable (and most frequently studied) phenomena of text comprehension is that people make inferences when they read a text. This brief text appeared in chapter 13. Sadly, it's back. Have another look at it:

> I went to the store to buy a CD, but I didn't see anything I liked. Next I went to the mall to buy a shirt, but I didn't have much cash. Then I bought some lunch, and on the way home I ran into a friend. We talked on the corner for a while, and then I went home.

Did I bring anything home? Your answer probably is "no," but the paragraph never states explicitly whether I did. I could have bought a CD as a gift for a friend even if I didn't care for the music. I could have purchased the shirt with a credit card (or shoplifted it). I might have brought my lunch home with me; the paragraph never said where I ate the lunch. These objections seem silly, but their very silliness drives home an important point: Most people reading this text probably would make the same inferences you made. Nevertheless, the reason we make these inferences is far from obvious. What is it about a text that leads you to make an inference? You probably didn't infer that I wept when I found I didn't have the money for the shirt. Why not? That's not stated in the text, but neither is the fact that I came home without the shirt, and you probably were happy to make that inference. What inferences are important enough that our cognitive system makes them (often outside awareness), and what aspects of a text lead us to make inferences?

This section highlights the complexity of language perception. In the next section, we discuss how the mind unravels this complexity to arrive at meaning.

Stand-on-One-Foot Questions

1. *Name again the four levels at which we are analyzing language.*
2. *For each level, name at least one ambiguity that makes perception difficult.*
3. *At which level is grammar, as discussed in chapter 13, relevant?*

Questions That Require Two Feet

4. *Can you guess why song lyrics, in particular, are easily misheard? Hint: Look at the actual lyrics in Table 14.1, and imagine a friend saying them to you during a conversation.*
5. *Can you guess why "Time flies like an arrow" is seldom interpreted in any sense but the common one?*

How are Ambiguities Resolved?

Preview

We have discussed ambiguities in language at four levels of analysis. Our cognitive system uses various strategies to resolve these ambiguities. Ambiguous phonemes are identified through the use of higher-level context and through mechanisms that are somewhat forgiving of slight mispronunciations. Words can be read in either of two ways: through a process that directly matches spelling to the word in memory or through a process that translates the spelling into a sound pattern, which is then matched to the word's sound in memory. Sentences are also disambiguated through higher-level contextual information, and a similar mechanism may be at work that helps make inferences in longer texts.

We have identified some of the problems in perceiving language. In this section, we discuss how our minds are able to resolve these ambiguities.

Phonemes

We said that the perception of phonemes is difficult because there is so much variability in how they are produced, both across different speakers (e.g., because of accents) and even by the same speaker because of coarticulation. However, other factors help listeners makes sense of this noisy input. First, the surrounding context helps disambiguate phonemes that are pronounced sloppily. Richard Warren (1970) showed that listeners can not only adjust for phonemes that are poorly pronounced, but can also adjust when phonemes are missing altogether. In one experiment, participants heard this sentence: "The state governors met with their respective leg*slatures convening in the capital city." Participants heard this sentence on tape, with a cough spliced into the sentence where you see the * replacing the phoneme corresponding to the letter *i*. Remarkably, not only did everyone understand the sentence, but almost none of the participants perceived that any part of the sentence was missing. In another experiment (Warren & Warren, 1970; see also Warren & Sherman, 1974), participants heard several sentences:

> It was found that the *eel was on the axle.
> It was found that the *eel was on the shoe.
> It was found that the *eel was on the orange.
> It was found that the *eel was on the table.

Once again, the * indicates the location in which a phoneme was replaced by a cough spliced into the tape. Participants heard different phonemes depending on the context. In the first sentence, they heard *wheel*, in the second they heard *heel*, in the third *peel,* and in the fourth *meal.* People were not consciously contemplating what sound was missing and then making a guess as to what they should have heard; they believed that they heard the complete word. This demonstration is all the more remarkable because the information that clarified the missing phoneme occurred four words later. This phenomenon is called the **phoneme restoration effect**: A missing phoneme is restored by the context and is never consciously identified as missing (see Samuel, 1996, for a review). If you think about your own experience, it seems believable that participants didn't notice that one phoneme was replaced by a cough; someone might cough while you are sitting in a lecture hall listening to a speaker, and it doesn't disrupt your perception of the talk.

A second source of disambiguating information comes from vision. You may have noticed that if you are listening to someone whose speech is difficult to understand (e.g., because of a thick accent or because he or she speaks softly), you find yourself watching the person's mouth carefully as he or she talks. When I was in college I had an English professor who was very shy, and his lecturing style was to look toward the floor and mumble. Although the class was small and the auditorium was large, we all sat in the front row and stared at his mouth, straining to catch his words.

The use of vision in the perception of speech is at the root of the **McGurk effect**, named for one of its discoverers (MacDonald & McGurk, 1978; McGurk & MacDonald, 1976). To demonstrate this effect, researchers show a videotape of someone pronouncing "pa pa pa" repeatedly. However, the soundtrack has been dubbed with someone pronouncing "na na na" repeatedly. Participants perceive the person on the videotape to be saying "ma ma ma." (Other sets of phonemes yield similar effects.) Participants fuse the two differing sources of information into a sound that best fits that auditory and visual pattern. The effect holds when the visual information is degraded (MacDonald, Andersen, & Bachmann, 2000), when participants try to ignore the visual information (Kerzel & Bekkering, 2000), and even for one's own speech, viewed in a mirror (Sams, Mottonen, & Sihvonen, 2005). Importantly, vision doesn't just change auditory perception into something else, as in the McGurk effect; it's been shown that your auditory perception is better when you have supporting visual information (Schwartz, Berthommier, & Savariaux, 2004).

Still another factor that aids in our perception of phonemes is **categorical perception**, which refers to the fact that we do not perceive slight differences in phonemes; phonemes can vary along certain dimensions with no cost in their perceivability. The phonemes p and b are produced in a similar way; the lips are initially closed and then opened, releasing air. When b is pronounced, the vocal cords vibrate simultaneously with the expulsion of air, whereas when p is pronounced there is a short delay between the expulsion of air and when the vocal cords begin to vibrate. That delay (called voice onset time) is the only difference between b and p, so listeners must be alert for the length of the voice onset time. We would imagine that when voice onset time is very short the phoneme will sound like p, when it is long it will sound like b, and when it is of medium length it will sound like something between p and b. That's not what happens, however. The utterances are categorized as b or p; we never hear something as a mushy, between-p-and-b sound.

Alvin Liberman and his associates (Liberman, Harris, Hoffman, & Griffith, 1957) conducted the landmark study on this phenomenon. They programmed a computer to synthesize speech and could therefore precisely separate in time the sound simulating the rush of air from the sound simulating voicing. They varied voice onset time between −150 ms (voicing starting before the rush of air) and +150 ms. Their results were systematic. Up to a value of about 10 ms participants agreed the sound was b, and above a value of 40 ms participants agreed it was p. If the voice onset time was between 10 and 40 ms, people might hear the sound as b or p (the likelihood varied between people), but the interesting finding was that if it sounded like b with a 20-ms voice onset time, that b sounded perfectly well formed, just as good as a b with a −10-ms voice onset time. The point is that the auditory system seems to place each speech stimulus into a category, and once the stimulus is categorized, it becomes a perfectly good example of the category. The advantage for speech perception is obvious. It doesn't matter if a phoneme is produced somewhat sloppily as long as it is closer to the target phoneme than to another phoneme (see Diehl, Lotto, & Holt, 2004 for a review).

One oddity, however, is that categorical perception occurs for both speech and nonspeech sounds such as chirps and bleats (Pastore, Li, & Layer, 1990). Furthermore, categorical perception occurs not only in humans, but also in other animals, including chinchillas, quail, and chimpanzees, whose perceptual abilities can be tested in operant conditioning paradigms (Kuhl, 1989; Moody, Stebbins, & May, 1990), and crickets show categorical perception of pure tones (Wyttenbach, May, & Hoy, 1996). Thus, categorical perception may not be an adaptation that is specific to human linguistic abilities but rather may be an accidental property of the way our (and other species') auditory system is designed. Or, it may be that language evolved in humans to take advantage of this property of our auditory system that was already present (Kuhl, 1986).

We've listed three ways in which the auditory system can disambiguate phonemes. What have researchers said about how these sources of information are put together? Can we be more specific about the mechanism by which phonemes are perceived?

Liberman and his colleagues (Liberman, 1996; Liberman, Cooper, & Shankweiler, 1967; Liberman & Mattingly, 1985) proposed a **motor theory of speech perception** (for an alternative motor theory, see Fowler, 1986). The core of this theory is that speech perception shares processes with speech production or relies on knowledge about how speech is produced. For example, the phonemes at the start of the word *put* and at the end of the word *top* are produced differently because of the phonemic context—that is, because of coarticulation—but they don't sound different to the listener. Liberman would argue that the speaker does not intend for these sounds to be different, and the listener knows that. The speech perception processes are closely tied to speech production mechanisms, making it easy to infer what the speaker wanted to produce and thereby undoing the effects of coarticulation. The speech perception processes can account for coarticulatory effects and therefore perceive what the speaker intended to produce (well-formed *p*s), rather than the sloppy phonemes that were actually produced.

Neuroscientific research provides compelling evidence for the involvement of motor areas of the brain in speech perception. In a straightforward study, Stephen Wilson and his associates (Wilson, Saygin, Sereno, & Iacoboni, 2004) imaged participants in fMRI while they listened to monosyllabic sounds (e.g., "pa") or pronounced them. As shown in Photo 14.1, an area of ventral premotor cortex was active during both passive listening and active production of speech sounds, lending support to the hypothesis that speech perception uses some of the same mechanisms as speech production (see also Skipper, Nusbaum, & Small, 2005).

Other neuroscientific research on this topic uses a different approach. Transcranial magnetic stimulation is a technique that applies a brief magnetic pulse through the skull to stimulate the brain in a localized area. Stimulating

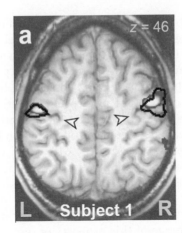

Photo 14.1. This is a horizontal view—as if the top of the head had been cut off, and you were looking down at the person's brain. The front of the head is at the top of the figure. The white that the arrows point to is very high levels of activity as people listen to meaningless syllables. The black outline represents where the activity is in motor and premotor cortex when these same people *produce* these meaningless syllables. The point is that there is a lot of activity in motor areas when people *perceive* speech.

the part of the motor cortex that controls the right index finger, for example, makes the person move that finger. A mild magnetic pulse might not elicit a finger movement unless the person was thinking of moving his or her finger anyway; in that case, the pulse might push the movement over the threshold.

Luciano Fadiga and his associates (Fadiga, Craighero, Buccino, & Rizzolatti, 2002) took advantage of this property to test the motor theory of speech perception. They stimulated the area of the motor cortex that controls the tongue, using a weak pulse, and at the same time had participants listen to phonemes over headphones. The weak magnetic stimulation caused tongue movements only if participants were listening to a phoneme that called for a lot of tongue movement when pronounced; when they listened to other phonemes, stimulation did not produce any tongue movement. This experiment provides fairly direct evidence that a brain area known to be involved in the production of speech is influenced by (and possibly participates in) speech perception.

Although the motor theory of speech perception is well known and has considerable support, there are other approaches that emphasize more general perceptual processes in our understanding of speech (e.g., Diehl & Kluender, 1989; Lotto, 2000).

Words

We have said that there are mechanisms that help our perceptual system make sense of poorly pronounced phonemes: The context of a sentence helps us infer what missing phoneme would be appropriate, and categorical perception lets us hear a phoneme correctly as long as it's close to the intended phoneme. Does that mean that recognizing words is a snap? No.

Let's start by considering the problem that babies initially face—the speech stream is continuous, and it's not clear how they could know when one word ends and another begins. It appears that babies solve this problem by sensitivity to the statistical regularities of language. Suppose a mother says "Pretty baby!" The child could segment this utterance as "Pre tybay be" or "Pre ty bay be." But consider this. Whenever a mother says "pretty" the sound "pre" was followed by "ty." How often was "pre" followed by some other sound? Probably not that often. The sound "ty," however, might be followed by lots of other sounds, as the child might hear "pretty roses" or "pretty cake" or "pretty fine golf swing." Sounds in the middle of words are likely to be followed by a limited set of sounds, but sounds at the end of words have a wider range of sounds that might come next.

Jenny Saffran and her colleagues (Saffran, Aslin, & Newport, 1996) showed that babies are sensitive to these statistical regularities. In a fascinating experiment, they had infants listen to just 2 min of synthesized speech, composed of four pseudowords, randomly ordered: *tibudo, pabiku, golatu,* and *daropi.* The speech was continuous with syllables evenly spaced, so it would sound like tibudopabikugolatudaropigolatutibudogolatu and so on. Note that, just as in the "pretty baby" example previously, sounds at the beginning or in the middle of words (e.g., "bu") can only be followed by one other sound ("do"), whereas sounds at the end of a word (e.g., "do") can be followed by any of the three sounds that starts a different word ("pa," "go," or "da"). After the babies were exposed to this speech, the researchers played several isolated sounds, half of which were one of the pseudowords (e.g., "tibudo") and half of which were sounds that crossed word boundaries (e.g., "dopabi"). Infants showed a preference for the latter, which indicates that these sounds were novel for the infants (hence the preference) because they had detected the boundaries of the pseudowords during exposure (Saffran et al., 1996; see also Aslin, Saffran, & Newport, 1998; Saffran, 2001, 2002; Saffran & Thiessen, 2003; for a review, see Kuhl, 2004). It also appears that highly familiar words (e.g., the baby's own name) may play a special role in helping babies figure out word segmentation boundaries (Bortfeld, Morgan, Golinkoff, & Rathbun, 2005).

What about the perception of words in adults, who have memory representations for words? Most researchers believe that people recognize words through a matching process in which a spoken word is compared with a mental dictionary called a **lexicon** that contains representations of all the words they know—not the meaning, but the pronunciation, spelling, and part of speech for each word. The lexical entry has a pointer to another place where the meaning is stored. A sample lexical entry is as follows:

Pronunciation: blæk
Spelling: black
Part of speech: adjective
Meaning pointer: → (This directs the system to another location where the meaning is stored.)

When someone is speaking and pronounces a string of phonemes, the phoneme string is compared with the pronunciations of the words in the lexicon. If the phoneme string matches an entry, the word has been identified, and the cognitive system has access to the other properties of the word, including the spelling, part of speech, and meaning. Of course, the matching process must be incredibly rapid to keep up with naturally occurring speech.

One question is how that matching process occurs. Most models of this process (Dell, Schwartz, Marting, Saffran, & Gagnon, 1997; Gaskell & Marslen-Wilson, 2001; Marslen-Wilson & Welsh, 1978; McClelland & Elman, 1986) propose that the first few phonemes that are perceived cause words that are consistent with that input to become active. As more phonemes are perceived, some words become inconsistent with the activation and drop out. The word representations also compete with one another, and so as one representation is "winning," others are necessarily "losing."

One such model is the TRACE connectionist network model of James McClelland and Jeffrey Elman (1986; for another example, see Dell et al., 1997), of a type we introduced in chapter 8. The model has nodes that may become active; they are connected by links that can pass activation to other nodes or inhibit the activity of other nodes. As shown in Figure 14.3, there are three layers of nodes. The bottom layer represents acoustic features that are the building blocks of phonemes. The next layer represents phonemes. A particular pattern of active acoustic features is connected to an individual phoneme, so if all those features are active, the node for the phoneme becomes quite active; if one or two features are missing, the phoneme is active, but less so. The third layer of nodes represents words. A particular pattern of phoneme nodes is connected to an individual word node, so if the right phonemes are active they pass their activation to the word node, making the word active. Notice, too, that there are connections not only from the lower-level layers going up, but also going in the other direction. Suppose you heard the phonemes *swi* (corresponding to the letters *swee*). The activation of those phonemes would propagate activation upward to the word level, activating words that start with that sound, such as *sweet* and *sweep*. The activation of those words would in turn propagate activity downward in the model, leading to activity of the phonemes *t* and *p*. Thus, the TRACE model includes processes that could compensate for poorly pronounced or missing phonemes, as in the phoneme restoration effect.

Marslen-Wilson (1987) described interesting evidence for the idea that when you hear the beginning of a word, multiple candidate words in the lexicon are active—candidates that the beginning of the word might turn out to be. For example, suppose you heard the phonemes corresponding to the letters "capt." Both the words *captive* and *captain* ought to be activated in the lexicon. But if you heard "captain", then clearly only the lexical entry *captain* should be active. To test this possibility, Marslen-Wilson had participants listen to words and simultaneously perform a lexical decision task. In a **lexical decision** task (introduced in chapter 8) a letter string appears on a computer

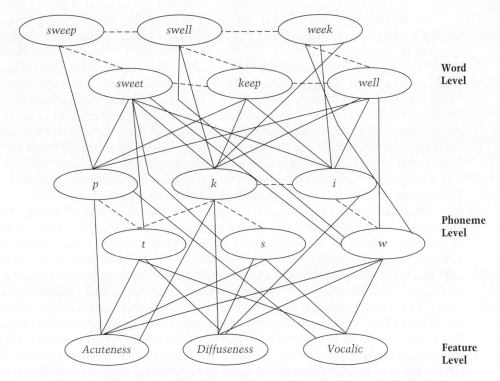

Figure 14.3. A simplified version of McClelland and Elman's (1986) TRACE model. The lines indicate links between nodes; to keep the figure simple, only some of the links are shown. The solid lines are excitatory connections, and the dotted lines are inhibitory. Note that the links within a level are inhibitory (again, not all links are shown) because more than one word is not pronounced; if the word is more likely to be *sweep*, then it is less likely to be *sweet*, and *sweet* should be inhibited. The links between levels are excitatory, and they are bidirectional. If the phonemes *s, w,* and *i* are active, that will activate the words that are consistent with those phonemes (such as *sweet* and *sweep*); the word activations will activate phonemes that are consistent with those words (*p* and *t*).

screen, and the participant must say whether it is a word. Lexical decision tasks are open to **semantic priming** (also discussed in chapter 8). If you have recently been thinking about a related word, then the lexical decision is made more quickly. Thus, if you've just heard the word "captain" you would be a little faster in making the lexical decision to the printed word SHIP than to a word unrelated to "captain," such as SHELL. Now, here's the prediction, which is a little tricky. Suppose a word for the lexical decision task appears in the middle of the spoken word, so that all you've heard so far is "capt." The prediction is that both *captain* and *captive* would be active in the lexicon, so you should be fast in responding on the lexical decision task to words related to either one (e.g., SHIP and GUARD). But if the lexical decision task comes just a little later, after the whole word is spoken, you'll only be fast on the lexical decision task to words related to whatever word was spoken. Those results were exactly what was observed.

All findings we have discussed thus far have concerned the comprehension of spoken words. What about reading written words? **Dual route models of reading** contend that there are two mechanisms for reading (Baron & Strawson, 1976; Behrmann & Bub, 1992; Coltheart, Curtis, Atkins, & Haller, 1993; Coltheart & Rastle, 1994; Forster & Chambers, 1973; Paap & Noel, 1991; for an approach to reading that is not dual route, see Seidenberg & McClelland, 1989). One route uses a direct lexicon lookup procedure based on the word's spelling; this route simply matches the written word to the spelling entries in the lexicon. The second route uses a translation procedure that converts the written letters to a sound and then matches the sound to the auditory entry in the lexicon; after the written input has been converted to sound, recognizing the written word is similar to recognizing a spoken word.

This dual route model neatly accounts for several findings that are otherwise difficult to accommodate. When you see words like *slint* or *papperine*, you can read them aloud, if you so desire. How? These aren't real words, so you have no lexical entry for them. This ability seems to require postulating that readers know a set of rules that convert letters and groups of letters into phonemes—call them letter-to-phoneme rules. This set of rules cannot completely account for reading, however, because readers also successfully read so-called exception words such as *colonel* and *pint* whose pronunciation is not in line with the letter-to-phoneme rules. The dual route model proposes that these words are not handled by the letter-to-phoneme translation processes. If they were, you would pronounce *colonel* as *kahlownell* and *pint* would rhyme with *hint*. Instead, you use the spelling of these words to establish that they are in the lexicon. The spelling also lets you gain access to the lexical entry for the word and then its pronunciation.

Thus, the dual route model can easily account for our ability to read nonwords such as *slint*, which uses the letter-to-phoneme route; irregular words such as *pint*, which uses the spelling-lookup route; and regular words such as *cake*, which might use either route. But do we really need two routes? Can we find more compelling evidence that these routes are truly separate?

One form of evidence comes from different types of dyslexia. You are probably aware that dyslexia is a problem in reading. **Acquired dyslexia** is a reading problem in an adult that is caused by brain damage (as from a stroke or removal of a brain tumor) in people who were normal readers before the injury. There are two types of acquired dyslexia. In **surface dyslexia** the reading of nonwords (and regular words) is preserved, but the patient has difficulty reading irregular words. Hence, the patient could read *nurse* or *glebe* but might read *glove* as rhyming with *cove* and *flood* as rhyming with *mood* (Marshall & Newcombe, 1973). An extreme case of this disorder, patient K.T. (McCarthy & Warrington, 1986), could read irregular words correctly only about 47% of the time, even if they were quite common, but could read regular words accurately 100% of the time. The clear interpretation within the dual route model is that the letter-to-phoneme rules are intact in this patient, but there is selective damage to the spelling-lookup route.

An altogether different type of dyslexia is observed in other patients who have selective difficulty in reading nonwords. They can correctly read irregular words such as *yacht* and regular words such as *cup*, but they cannot read nonwords. This pattern of reading abilities is called **phonological dyslexia** (Beauvois & Derouesne, 1979). One extremely impaired patient could read regular words correctly with 90% accuracy even when they were long (e.g., *satirical*), but he could not read even simple nonwords such as *nust* aloud. Even more incredibly, the patient could name individual letters successfully, but he could not say which sound they made, although he could repeat the sound if it were given to him (Funnell, 1983).

The dual route model is also consistent with brain imaging data. A meta-analysis of 35 brain imagining studies showed that there are indeed two separate pathways associated with reading. The letter-to-sound translation route was associated with activation of the left hemisphere structure in the superior temporal lobe, which is closely associated with processing sound. The direct lookup route was associated with activation at the junction of the occipital and temporal lobes in the left hemisphere (sometimes referred to as the visual word form area) and with areas associated with meaning, such as the lateral part of the temporal lobe (Jobard, Crivello, & Tzourio-Mazoyer, 2003; see also Price & Mechelli, 2005).

The dual route model also accounts for some patterns of data in normal adult readers. For example, suppose I gave you a lexical decision task in which you must say whether a letter string forms a word; for example, you might see *wolt* or *beep*. Now suppose you saw the word *koat* or *phocks*. Both have pronunciations that match real words (*coat* and *fox*), but they are not words. What should the dual route model predict? Response times to these nonwords should be slower than to nonwords whose pronunciation does not match real words because the two routes will conflict as to the correct answer. The letters-to-phonemes route identifies the sound pattern as matching a word in the lexicon, whereas the spelling-lookup route does not identify a word in the lexicon with this spelling. This expected pattern of response times has been verified (Rubenstein, Lewis, & Rubenstein, 1971).

The dual route model also predicts that normal readers, when reading aloud, should be slower with exception words such as *yacht* than regular words such as *round*. Exception words lead to two conflicting readings of *yacht*: the correct pronunciation derived from the lexicon (which was accessed via the spelling-lookup route) and an incorrect pronunciation derived from the letter-to-phoneme rules that would sound something like *yatcht*, rhyming with *patched*. There is no conflict for regular words such as *round*, however, because both routes produce the same sound. The data are more or less consistent with the prediction (Paap & Noel, 1991; Seidenberg, Waters, Barnes, & Tanenhaus, 1984; Taraban & McClelland, 1987), but the effect seems small or nonexistent when researchers examine irregular words that are very common in the language and that participants therefore are likely to have a great deal of experience reading.

We might also wonder whether access to the lexicon is biased by the context of the sentence. For example, consider these three sentences, each ending with the word *spring:*

This has been a cold and rainy spring.
This is a broken and rusty old spring.
This really is not a very good spring.

The word *spring* is ambiguous, but the first two sentences provide a biasing context for which meaning is appropriate. If you read or heard these sentences you would likely be aware of only the appropriate meaning. Does that mean that only that meaning is accessed from the lexicon? Are both meanings accessed in the third sentence, where the meaning of *spring* remains ambiguous?

Greg Simpson and Merilee Krueger (1991; see also Tabossi & Zardon, 1993; Vu, Kellas, Petersen, & Metcalf, 2003) had participants read sentences like these aloud. As they read the last word, another appeared on the screen, and they were to read it aloud as quickly as possible. The final word could be related to one meaning (e.g., *season*) or the other (e.g., *coil*), or it could be unrelated (e.g., *cow*). It would be easier to read a word if a semantically related meaning was active in the lexicon. The unrelated word therefore provides a baseline for how quickly each participant can read words. If the biasing context affects lexical access, then people should be faster at reading words related to the meaning of *spring* that the sentence biases. That's what the results showed; context affects lexical access.

When the biasing context matched the final word, participants were faster in reading it (compared with their time in reading the completely unrelated word). If the biasing context did not match the final word, there was no advantage in reading time and therefore presumably no lexical access for that meaning of the word. The delay between the end of the sentence (when the lexicon would be accessed for the homophone) and the presentation of the word had no effect on the pattern of results (see Figure 14.4).

The models we've been talking about here seem very dependent on the specific word forms for reading. How do they square with your ability to read the following paragraph?

Aoccdrnig to a rscheearch at Cmabrigde Uinervtisy, it deosn't mttaer in waht oredr the ltteers in a wrod are, the olny iprmoetnt tihng is taht the frist and lsat ltteer be at the rghit pclae. The rset can be a toatl mses and you can sitll raed it wouthit porbelm. Tihs is bcuseae the huamn mnid deos not raed ervey lteter by istlef, but the wrod as a wlohe.

It turns out that this work was not done at Cambridge University, and seems to have been traced to a letter published in the *New Scientist* in 1999. Regardless, the phenomenon is certainly surprising. But the purported reason—that we read words as a whole—is inaccurate. For example, this sentence

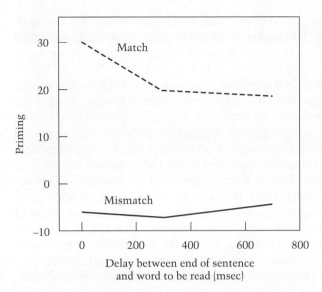

Figure 14.4. Results of the experiment by Simpson and Krueger (1991). When the biasing context matched the final word, priming was observed, but no priming was observed when it did not. Priming is shown as a difference score; it's the degree to which people could read the last word faster than a control word. Note that the delay between the end of the sentence and the occurrence of the to-be-read word had no impact on the amount of priming. These results indicate that lexical access is biased by context.

"A ldnat-innsogg goal of huamn eiqnruy is to uerndnatsd oeuvlress" is probably somewhat harder to read. (It's the first sentence from the preface of this book—"A long-standing goal of human enquiry is to understand ourselves.") The paragraph is easy to read for a few reasons. First, words of two or three letters aren't changed at all, and these short words tend to be function words like "of," "for" "be," "and," and "the," which provide clues to parts of speech and grammatical structure. In the original paragraph, many of the words are inact or have just two letters transposed. Also, some of the words have the same sound when scrambled (e.g., huamn), so the reading route that depends on sound could decode them. Matt Davis (who is actually at Cambridge University) has posted an interesting analysis of this phenomenon on the web (www.mrc-cbu.cam.ac.uk/~mattd/Cmabrigde/); see also Grainger & Whitney, 2004).

Sentences

Suppose that the perception of phonemes and words has proceeded apace, and we are attempting to understand how these words combine to form a sentence. As we mentioned earlier, it is obviously not sufficient to simply perceive words; the sentence "I'd rather die than swim" has very different meaning from "I'd rather swim than die," and the difference between these sentences is clearly not a difference of words but a difference in the arrangement of words. We said earlier that sentences are represented in terms of phrase structures. Thus, much of the debate centers on how listeners take the word-by-word input of speech and build the appropriate hierarchical phrase structure representation for each sentence. For example, consider this sentence: "The horse raced past the barn fell."

Even after rereading it, you still may not understand what the sentence means. Here's a rephrasing that makes it clearer: "The horse that was raced past the barn is the one that fell." Even if you understood the meaning without the rephrasing, you probably felt jarred when you came to the word *fell*. A sentence like this is a **garden path sentence**, one in which your cognitive system builds a phrase structure, but later it becomes clear that something must be wrong with the phrase structure as built. The cognitive system is led down the garden path, so to say, by a pattern of words that indicates one structure but actually requires another structure. Let us call the psychological mechanism that derives phrase structures from sentences the sentence parser. The sentence parser assumes that *raced* is the main verb of the sentence. This assumption need not be true; why, then, doesn't the sentence parser wait until all the evidence is in? For whatever reason, the parser takes gambles. Most of the time the gambles are good ones, and sentence processing proceeds smoothly. Occasionally, the parser makes a mistake and needs to tear apart the phrase structure representation it had been building and start over again.

This simple example points the way to some of the important dimensions on which models of sentence processing differ. First, we might ask what cues the sentence parser uses to derive an interpretation. Second, we might ask when the parser commits to an interpretation. Clearly, it had committed itself to a particular interpretation of the ongoing sentence before it reached the last word (*fell*). Does it have to assign a place to each word coming in? Does it have a buffer of three or four words so it can suspend judgment on a particular word until it gets more information? Third, we might ask whether the parser is influenced by surrounding context. Suppose you saw this pair of sentences:

> ANNA: Did the horse standing by the pond fall, or was it the one that Rebecca raced past the barn?
> WARREN: The horse raced past the barn fell.

Perhaps the parser is sensitive to the semantics of the words that it is parsing. For example, suppose the sentence had been, "The horse led past the barn fell." *Led* typically is not an active verb for horses. Horses are led; they don't lead others. Would that make any difference in how people interpret the sentence, perhaps making them less likely to traipse down the garden path? Let's look at some of the cues the parser uses to build phrase structures.

Key words provide an important cue to the correct phrase structure organization. For example, the word *a* indicates that a noun phrase follows; *who*, *which*, and *that* indicate a relative clause. One source of support for their importance comes from studies in which the key words are omitted. Jerry Fodor and Merrill Garrett (1967) presented participants with one of two variants of a sentence; one had the key words, and the other did not.

> The car that the man whom the dog bit drove crashed.
> The car the man the dog bit drove crashed.

Both sentences contain relative clauses, but in the second sentence the relative pronouns have been removed. Participants were to listen to one of these sentences and paraphrase it to show that they understood it; they were faster and more accurate in paraphrasing the sentence that contained the relative pronouns. Presumably, the relative pronouns are cues that there is a relative clause in the sentence (see also Hakes & Cairns, 1970; Hakes & Foss, 1970).

Another cue the parser uses is word order; more specifically, the parser assumes that sentences will be active. People are faster in determining the meaning of a sentence in the active voice ("Bill hit Mary") than in the passive voice ("Mary was hit by Bill") (Slobin, 1966).

There are many sentences in which word order and key words are not enough to go on, however. When a new word is perceived, it's not clear how it should be parsed. Lyn Frazier (1978, cited in McKoon & Ratcliff, 1998) proposed a rule that the parser might use in such cases: the **principle of minimal attachment**. The idea is that the parser is biased to add new words and phrases to a node that already exists on the hierarchy rather than creating a new node. In a classic study examining this proposal, Keith Rayner and his associates (Rayner, Carlson, & Frazier, 1983) showed participants two similar sentences that differed in their phrase structures:

The spy saw the cop with binoculars, but the cop didn't see him.

The spy saw the cop with a revolver, but the cop didn't see him.

The relevant part of the phrase structure for each sentence is shown in Figure 14.5. Note that in the sentence on the left, *binoculars* is part of the verb phrase started by *saw*, whereas in the sentence on the right, *revolver* requires that a new node be generated to represent the noun phrase. Rayner and his associates

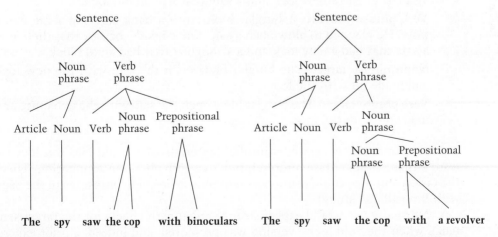

Figure 14.5. Phrase structures for the key parts of the sentences in the experiment by Rayner et al. (1983). Note that the hierarchical structure is more complex for the phrase on the right.

recorded participants' eye movements while they read these (and similar) sentences and found that reading times were longer when minimal attachment was violated, and the increased time resulted from locations of the violation; participants' eyes dwelled on those locations longer (see Frazier & Clifton, 1996, for a review of supportive evidence).

Other researchers have suggested that other syntactic cues help guide parsing. For example, some researchers have indicated that the most important cue is recency, meaning that people try to attach a new word to the words most recently encountered (Phillips & Gibson, 1997). This prediction often overlaps with the principle of minimal attachment, but not always. Still other researchers emphasize the role of working memory in parsing. There is much evidence that the size of working memory is correlated with how quickly and accurately a person can parse complex sentences (King & Just, 1991) and with how many interpretations of an ambiguous sentence he or she can maintain simultaneously (Gibson, 1998; MacDonald, Just, & Carpenter, 1992; Miyake, Carpenter, & Just, 1994).

Until the mid-1990s, most researchers believed that the types of cues we've been discussing—key words, minimal attachment, word order, working memory—accounted for how sentences were parsed. Note that all these cues are syntactic cues; the semantics or meaning of the sentence plays no role in parsing it.

More recent work shows that semantics does matter (Altmann, Garnham, & Dennis, 1992; Altmann, Garnham, & Henstra, 1994; Britt, 1994; Britt, Perfetti, Garrod, & Rayner, 1992; Grodner, Gibson, & Watson, 2005). For example, Gerry Altmann and Mark Steedman (1988) provided participants with a strong semantic context to bias the interpretation of the key phrase:

Noun phrase context: A burglar broke into a bank carrying some dynamite. He planned to blow open a safe. Once inside, he saw that there was a safe that had a new lock and a safe that had an old lock.

Verb phrase context: A burglar broke into a bank carrying some dynamite. He planned to blow open a safe. Once inside, he saw that there was a safe that had a new lock and a strongbox that had an old lock.

Noun phrase target: The burglar blew open the safe with the new lock and made off with the loot.

Verb phrase target: The burglar blew open the safe with the dynamite and made off with the loot.

The experimenters generated stimulus materials that could bias a reader toward either a noun phrase interpretation or a verb phrase interpretation. Then, the target sentence could contain a noun phrase or a verb phrase (as in the "spy with binoculars" study).

Normally, we would expect strong garden path effects for the target sentence when the "old lock" version was presented, and indeed, a prior experiment with a neutral context showed that such effects were obtained. In this experiment, however, the effects were moderated by the biasing context: People read the critical phrase more quickly when the context had biased them to expect it.

So what, finally, can we say about parsing? We've discussed a number of candidates that might guide parsing, including syntactic factors (key words, minimal attachment, recency), frequency, and semantics (i.e., meaning). Which of these possibilities are correct? More recent models combine syntax and semantics (see Boland & Blodgett, 2001; Gibson & Pearlmutter, 1998; McRae, Spivey-Knowlton, & Tanenhaus, 1998), although they vary a good deal in how they combine the information and in the time course for doing so.

Texts

A text is a group of connected sentences forming a paragraph or paragraphs. We started our discussion of sentences by noting that a sentence is much more than a group of words. Likewise, a text is more than a group of sentences. We discuss two key aspects of text comprehension: making inferences about texts and seeking coherence within texts.

Much of what we understand to be true in a text is never explicitly stated but rather is inferred. Here's an example:

Billy walked slowly to the front of the room. The teacher waited for him.

How old is Billy? Is he a student? Why is he walking slowly? In a text that is just two sentences long, you probably infer that Billy is young and that he's walking slowly because he's reluctant to face the teacher, and in turn, you've inferred that he's reluctant to face the teacher because he's done something wrong. You know these facts although they are never stated because you apply background knowledge to your understanding of the text.

People exert effort to make texts coherent. We do not passively record the meanings of the sentences given; we tie them together so they make sense. Sometimes we struggle to integrate sentences so they make sense together. Imagine your reaction if I presented this text:

Billy walked slowly to the front of the room. The teacher waited for him. The crowd roared as the Americans won the gold.

The final sentence seems out of place, as though it belongs in some other story. Our response to a sentence that doesn't make sense is to search long-term memory for information that might make the text sensible. Suppose that earlier in the story you had been told that Billy's father is on the Olympic hockey team and that Billy had been caught listening to the game on a contraband radio, despite his teacher's stern warning not to do so. If you search long-term memory and find that information, the final sentence becomes comprehensible.

When do we make inferences? When do we recruit background knowledge to help us make sense of a text? To address these questions, we need to first consider how texts are represented. Most researchers (see Fletcher & Chrysler, 1990; Glenberg & Langston, 1992; Schmalhofer & Glavanov, 1986) agree that there are three levels of representation in text processing, as first suggested by Teun van Dijk and Walter Kintsch (1983): a surface code, a textbase, and a situation model. The **surface code** represents the exact wording and syntax of the sentences. The **textbase** represents the ideas of the text in a format called propositions, but it does not preserve the particular wording and syntax. If you make inferences as you read the text, those inferences are stored in the textbase as well. The **situation model** refers to still deeper knowledge, corresponding to an integration of the knowledge provided by the text and prior knowledge (Zwaan & Radvansky, 1998). Figure 14.6 shows the textbase and situation model representations corresponding to a text.

We have already discussed the components of the surface code—wording and syntax—but the components of the textbase and situation model take a different form. The basic unit of textbases and situation models is the **proposition**, which we have defined as the most basic unit of meaning that has a truth value. We discussed propositions in the context of visual imagery, when we compared visual images with verbal representations (propositions). Propositions have the syntax *relation(argument)*. A relational term can be a verb, an adjective, or a conjunction, and the arguments are nouns. For example, the proposition *red(car)* represents the idea that a particular car is red. The proposition *gave(boy, girl, ball)* represents the idea that the boy gave the ball to the girl.

Textbase:

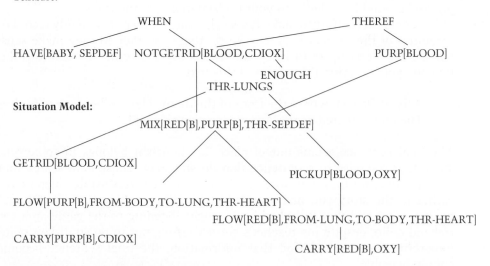

Situation Model:

Figure 14.6. Contraint Satisfaction network.

How do we know that the surface code, textbase, and situation model are separate in the mind? A commonly used technique is to have participants read a text and then take a recognition test for different types of sentences. For example, participants might read this text (adapted from Reder, 1982, who used only a subset of the probe questions described here):

> The heir to a large hamburger chain was in trouble. He had married a lovely young woman who had seemed to love him. Now he worried that she had been after his money after all. He sensed that she was not attracted to him. Perhaps he consumed too much beer and french fries. No, he couldn't give up the fries. Not only were they delicious, he got them for free.

Later, participants could be asked whether the following sentences were part of the story:

> He had married a lovely young woman who had seemed to love him. (verbatim sentence)
> The heir had the feeling that the woman did not find him good looking. (paraphrase)
> The heir got his french fries from his family's hamburger chain. (plausible inference based on the situation model)
> The heir was careful to eat only healthful food. (false statement)

Participants are to say whether the sentences presented appeared in the story. We can estimate the contributions of different representations to performance on the recognition test. For example, to the extent that people are accurate in rejecting paraphrases and accepting verbatim sentences, they must be using a memory of the surface code. If they accept paraphrases but reject inferences, this is a measure of their reliance on the textbase representation, and if they accept inferences but reject false statements, this indicates a reliance on the situation model.

Most studies show that participants' reliance on different representations changes over time. If they are tested soon after reading the text, participants rely on the surface code (i.e., they remember what they have read almost word for word). However, if there is a delay, participants come to rely more on the textbase (they remember the meaning of what they read, but they are not very accurate in remembering the exact words used to convey the information), as shown in Figure 14.7.

Factors besides time contribute to the detail of the surface code, the textbase, and the situational model. Rolf Zwaan (1994) examined whether the genre of the writing influences how people read text. He provided a short text for participants to read and told them that it was either a passage from a novel or a clipping from a newspaper story.

Participants' memory for the text varied, depending on the genre they believed the text was from. If they believed they were reading a newspaper story,

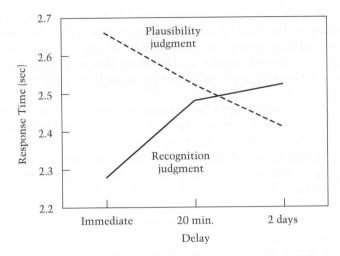

Figure 14.7. Data from Reder (1982). The data show response times to make recognition judgments (this sentence appeared in the story) and plausibility judgments (this sentence describes something plausible, given the story). Shown here are data from plausible sentences. Note that plausible judgments initially are slower, but the pattern reverses as time passes, indicating that participants initially rely on the surface code to make judgments but later rely on the textbase.

participants didn't remember specific words and phrases used in the story (the surface code) and instead remembered the broadest outline of the story (situation model). The reverse was true if they believed they were reading part of a novel. This finding is sensible: When you read a novel you expect the style to be important, whereas for a newspaper story you're concerned mostly with the facts. Other work indicates that people remember different aspects of a text, depending on the perspective they are encouraged to take (Baillet & Keenan, 1986; Lee-Sammons & Whitney, 1991) or their goals in reading it (Aaronson & Ferres, 1986; Noordman, Vonk, & Kempff, 1992).

These differences in memory that appear with changes in time or perspective of the reader are taken as evidence that the surface code, textbase, and situation model are separate. How and when are the textbase and situation model constructed? According to the most influential models of reading (Just & Carpenter, 1992; Kintsch, 1988), the textbase and situation models are built in parallel as people comprehend the surface code. If that's true, that means that people make inferences as they read. Again, remember that these inferences are automatically generated, not consciously considered and weighed.

There has been debate about the type of inferences people draw. Most researchers agree that inferences are drawn when information is missing from the text. If the text says, "Jennifer drove the nail," no information is provided about what she used to drive it. Our background knowledge about nails would lead to the inference that Jennifer used a hammer. In Kintsch's (1988) model, the inference is made this way. A word or set of words from the text would enter working memory and then activate related concepts in long-term memory. This activation would cycle between working memory and long-term memory several times in such a way that concepts with strong activations become more active and those with weak activations become less active. After this process, concepts from long-term memory that are strongly related to concepts in the text become strongly activated; that is, reading about someone driving a nail results in the concept *hammer* becoming active because it is so closely related to *nail* and *drive*.

The number of inferences that could be generated from even a brief, simple text is almost unlimited. One can make inferences about the characters' motivations, why they did what they did, things they might have done that were not in the text, things they didn't do, and so on. The cognitive resources to generate inferences are assumed to be limited, so a limited number of inferences must be drawn. What sorts of inferences might be drawn? Most researchers believe that we are motivated to make inferences about the goals of the characters (e.g., Trabasso & Wiley, 2005) or when some information is missing from what we read. We try to use knowledge from long-term memory to make the text sensible. The evaluation of whether information is contradictory or missing is based on the situation model (Albrecht & O'Brien, 1993; Graesser, Singer, & Trabasso, 1994; Hess, Foss, & Carroll, 1995; Singer, Graesser, & Trabasso, 1994).

Here's an example of an experiment in this vein. Edward O'Brien and Jason Albrecht (1992) measured reading times as participants read a paragraph. A sentence in the paragraph was made to be either consistent or inconsistent with an earlier sentence. Here is an example of the sort of paragraph they used:

> As Kim stood (inside/outside) the health club she felt a little sluggish. [Workouts always made her feel better. Today she was particularly looking forward to the exercise class because it had been a long, hard day at work. Her boss had just been fired and she had to fill in for him on top of her own work.] *She decided to go outside and stretch her legs a little.* She was getting anxious to start and was glad when she saw the instructor go in the door of the club. Kim really liked her instructor. Her enthusiasm and energy were contagious.

In the first sentence, half the participants read that Kim was inside the club and half that she was outside. The critical sentence is in italics, and you can see that this sentence describes her as going outside. This sentence makes sense if Kim was described in the first sentence as being inside, but not if she was described as being outside. The experimenters also manipulated how far apart this potentially conflicting information was in the story. In the sample paragraph, there are three sentences between the two conflicting sentences. Those three intervening sentences were omitted for some participants. Thus, there were two independent variables in this experiment: whether the initial information conflicted with the crucial sentence and whether this initial

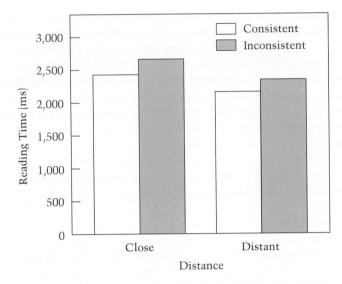

Figure 14.8. Results from O'Brien and Albrecht's (1992) study indicating that participants compare information in new sentences with information from prior sentences. Participants were slower to read a sentence that was inconsistent with an old sentence, even if the conflicting sentence was distant from the one they were reading.

information appeared one sentence before the crucial sentence or three sentences before the crucial sentence. Figure 14.8 shows reading times for the crucial sentence. Participants are always faster in reading the crucial sentence when it is consistent with the information presented earlier. It is presumed that reading times are longer because participants are struggling to make sense of the conflicting information. It is also important that the advantage for the consistent version is maintained even when three sentences separate the initial and the test sentence.

O'Brien and Albrecht (1992) argued that participants maintain a situation model as they read and that new information is integrated in the model as it comes in, and there seems to be good evidence for this idea of consistent updating (e.g., Zwaan & Madden, 2004). If the reader has been told that Kim is outside and later is told that she *goes* outside (implying that she is not already outside), the inconsistency is detected and is reflected in a slower reading time as the participant tries to make sense of the conflicting information.

It is possible that the longevity of inferences may vary: Some inferences are made and discarded, whereas others are maintained (see Millis & Just, 1994). It is also likely that making inferences depends on working memory, so there may be substantial individual differences in the number of inferences made, depending on the reader's working memory capacity (Radvansky & Copeland, 2004; Whitney, Ritchie, & Clark, 1991; for a review of the literature on inferences, see Graesser, Millis, & Zwaan, 1997).

Stand-on-One-Foot Questions

6. *What factors help in the perception of phonemes?*
7. *What are the two routes to the lexicon in reading, according to dual route theories?*
8. *What are garden path sentences, and why are they important?*
9. *What causes people to draw inferences from texts?*

Questions That Require Two Feet

10. *Given what you know about lexical access, describe what happens when someone relates a pun.*
11. *What do you think would happen to a text if the writer ensured that you did not have to draw any inferences? Would the text seem especially well written and clear?*
12. *Suppose you and I are planning a hike. I look out the window, where I see it is pouring rain. I turn to you and say, "This is ideal weather." What does this example tell you about sentence processing?*

KEY TERMS

acquired dyslexia	McGurk effect	proposition
categorical perception	motor theory of speech	semantic priming
coarticulation	perception	situation model
dual route models of	phoneme restoration	speech stream
reading	effect	surface code
garden path sentence	phonological dyslexia	surface dyslexia
lexical decision	principle of minimal	textbase
lexicon	attachment	

CURRENT DIRECTIONS IN COGNITIVE SCIENCE

Recommended readings

Ferreira, F., Bailey, K. G. D., & Ferraro, V. (2002). "Good-enough representations in language comprehension." (pp. 138–145) We described sentence processing as though it were rather formulaic—there are cues in the environment to which processes are applied, and the outcome is an interpretation of a sentence. Further, our discussion made it seem that the interpretation was almost always right. When something goes wrong (as in a garden-path sentence) we go back and try again until we get the interpretation right. Ferreira, Bailey, and Ferraro, offer a different point of view. They suggest that language comprehension is a little sloppy, and that, as we do in problem-solving, humans might satisfice; we stop processing once we come up with an interpretation that seems good enough, rather than one that is perfect.

Zwaan, R. A. (1999). "Situation models: The mental leap into imagined worlds." (pp. 146–152) In our discussion of situation models, we mostly focused on the fact that they are constructed. Zwaan summarizes recent research that probes what drives a situation model. In other words, there are many organizing principles around which one could develop a situation model—Zwaan describes the work indicating that situation models are organized around space, time, and people and their goals.

Afterward

I began this book by asking whether you have ever wondered how we see or how we remember things, and by then answering my own question with "probably not." I said then that simple questions such as "How do we see?" are pitched at the wrong level of analysis, and we must develop more specific questions for the answer to be informative. If you have read to this point, it is hoped that you are now convinced that posing such questions and seeking the answers is both informative and interesting. I close the book with two more questions, often asked by my students at the end of the course: "How do the subfields described in each chapter relate to one another?" and "What is going to happen next in cognitive psychology?"

After taking an introductory cognition course, students are often frustrated by what they perceive to be the splintered nature of the discipline. I raised this issue in chapter 1. Cognitive psychologists have found it useful to treat processes in relative isolation from one another, and it's true that they don't spend as much time as they might trying to connect the pieces. It's also true that most cognitive psychologists do develop a mental model of how the pieces fit together, even if they don't formalize those ideas into a theory. I well remember my first few years of graduate school, during which I felt that I was a fact collector. I read articles and attended talks, and I had a mental sack of facts that grew larger and larger. And then, some time during my fourth or fifth year of study, the facts coalesced into a framework of how I thought the mind worked. When I learned new things, I didn't just drop them into my mental sack, I was able to relate them to other things that I already knew. I mention my experience because I've asked other cognitive psychologists about it, and their experience was the same. It's not surprising because it follows the principles of expertise that we discussed in chapter 12. One of the hallmarks of expertise is deeper knowledge that is better organized.

So, how *do* the subfields in cognitive psychology relate to each other? My answer is not all that satisfying. In fact, we don't have very well-developed theories of how the parts fit together, but if you study the parts for 5 years or so, you will think you know how they fit together. It's a bad answer, and it's a depressing one because it admits such ignorance. But while we're berating the field for what we don't know, let's also bear in mind that there is a great deal that we do know.

You might think that my answer to the second question ("What is going to happen next in cognitive psychology?") will build on my answer to the first. Namely, that the field is moving toward integrating the topics covered in this book into larger-scale theories. I don't think so. Rather, the field seems poised to re-examine three assumptions it made when the field began in the 1950s.

The first assumption concerns the role of emotion. Cognitive psychologists have tended to believe that emotion would be difficult to study. Many held the silent assumption that emotion probably didn't change cognition much anyway. That assumption is clearly wrong, and in the last few years, cognitive psychologists have found a number of ingenious ways to study emotion. (We mentioned some in chapter 6.) Just as the study of mental imagery began with researchers studying the effect of imagery on other cognitive processes and then progressed to studying imagery in its own right, so, too, I expect that the study of emotion will begin with researchers examining its effect on other cognitive processes (as they already do for memory and decision making) and will later advance to studying emotion itself from a cognitive perspective.

A second assumption in the field has been that culture probably has little impact on cognition. (Note that we discussed the impact of language on cognition in chapter 13, but we didn't discuss culture.) The assumption has been that the basic architecture of the mind is the same throughout the world, and although the culture in which you grew up would influence what ended up in your memory, it wouldn't fundamentally change the way you think. That assumption is increasingly under assault and has been shown to be wrong at least some of the time.

A third assumption is rooted in the response of cognitive psychologists to behaviorism. You will recall that behaviorists would not use a construct such as "consciousness" because it was not observable. Once cognitive psychologists decided that it was acceptable to use abstract constructs in their theories, consciousness came back into play, for example, in distinguishing procedural from declarative memory, as described in chapter 8. Researchers failed, however, to do much to define consciousness or to specify how they believed it worked. You'll recall from chapter 2 that doing so is the key to developing meaningful theories that use abstract constructs. Serious study of consciousness has greatly increased in the last few years, and I expect that trend will continue.

I started by emphasizing that the questions we ask are crucial, as are the assumptions that drive these questions. In closing the book on that same theme, I also encourage you to continue your study of cognition. I leave you with two suggestions from the *Current Directions in Cognitive Science* reader that relate to the forward-looking themes I've mentioned.

Recommended readings

Norenzayan, A., & Nisbett, R. E. (2000). "Culture and causal cognition." **(pp. 81–87).** Although we did not discuss how people understand causality, this chapter provides an excellent introduction to how culture can influence cognition.

Roser, M., & Gazzaniga, M. S. (2004). "Automatic brains, interpretive minds." (pp. 162–168). This is an enormously ambitious chapter, and the result is fascinating. The authors seek to explain how the various processes that are distributed throughout the brain are knit together into a unitary conscious experience. They propose that this knitting together includes interpretation, not just integration, and they close with speculation on how this process, at its most advanced stages, becomes the personal narrative that each person tells him- or herself.

Appendix

Signal Detection Theory

In some areas of cognitive psychology, we conduct experiments in which participants are asked to detect faint signals in spite of background noise. For example, participants might be asked to watch a computer monitor on which a faint light occasionally appears. Such tasks occur in some professions as well. Radar and sonar operators try to detect signals indicative of ships or planes, doctors listen for the sound of a heart murmur, and radiologists search for abnormalities on X-ray images.

How can we evaluate whether someone is effective or ineffective at detecting such signals? Take the simple example of detecting a faint visual signal. On each trial of such an experiment, the participant must either say "Yes" or "No," meaning the signal was or was not present. (Sometimes, the signal really wasn't there.) It's therefore easy to evaluate the participant's accuracy. Actual signals of possible outcomes on each trial are shown in Table A.1. Obviously, hits and correct rejections represent accurate decisions, and misses and false alarms represent inaccurate decisions.

There are really two factors that go into this decision. One is sensitivity—just how good the participant is at detecting signals—and the other is bias. Bias represents the criterion for saying that a signal is present. If the researcher says, "Whatever you do, don't miss any signals!", participants are likely to be very liberal in saying that they see a signal. If the researcher says, "Whatever you do, don't say that you see a signal when there is not really one there!", participants will be much more conservative. Note that being conservative or liberal in judging whether a signal is present has nothing to do with absolute sensitivity in seeing a signal.

Signal detection theory allows researchers to separate sensitivity and bias. The easiest way to understand how it works is to examine Figure A.1. Suppose that the horizontal axis represents the intensity of the signal. You can

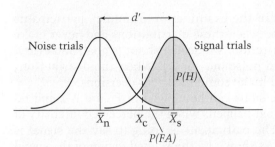

think of it as the amount of activity in your visual cortex, if you like. The vertical axis is the frequency of a particular type of trial (high means very frequent, low means very infrequent). There are two distributions, labeled "Noise trials" and "Signal trials." "Noise" means background noise—the flicker of the computer monitor, for example. "Signal" really represents the signal and the background noise; thus, for most signal trials, there is more signal intensity than for most noise trials. The distributions overlap in this example because the perceived intensity of the signal or the background noise can vary from trial to trial, so sometimes it happens that a noise trial is perceived as more intense than a (signal + noise) trial. Although the distributions overlap, their averages (or means, labeled $\overline{X}$) are separate, in the center of the distributions. The distance between the averages is labeled d' ("d-prime"). This is a measure of the participants' sensitivity, their absolute ability to differentiate between the noise and the signal + noise. Here's another way to think about it. Suppose that the task were to detect the sound of someone shouting "Hey!" (signal) amid the background noise of a classroom during a final examination. In that case the intensity of the noise would be very low, and the intensity of the signal would be very high. The noise distribution would be far to the left, and the signal + noise distribution would be far to the right, so the distance between them (d') would be large. If the signal were the sound of someone talking and the background noise a loud rock concert, the two distributions would be very close together, and d' would be small.

Participants will also set a criterion for how intense a signal must be before they will decide that it must contain the signal. That criterion is shown in Figure A.1 as X_c. Any stimulus of greater intensity than that will be called signal, and any stimulus of lesser intensity will be called no signal. When the

Table A.1. *Trials types, based on participant's decision regarding presence or absence of signal*

Participant's Decision	Signal Present	Signal Absent
Present	Hit	False alarm
Absent	Miss	Correct rejection

two distributions are far apart (as in the examination example), participants could put the criterion anywhere between these distributions and never make a mistake; everything above the criterion is indeed a shout (signal) and everything below the criterion is indeed noise (no shout). When the distributions overlap, however, participants will make some incorrect decisions.

The correct and incorrect decisions can be viewed in Figure A.2 and related to Table A.1. Consider first what happens when the perceived intensity of the signal is above the criterion. The participant is going to say the signal is present. That will usually be true: As shown by the shaded region of the signal distribution, in most of the trials where the participants say "Yes," the signal is present. Note, however, that one trial of the noise distribution is above the criterion, so there is some chance that a trial above the intensity criterion will actually be a noise trial. That's a false alarm, where the participant says there is a signal but only noise was present.

We can analyze the other decision the same way. When the participant says there is no signal (i.e., there is only noise), most of the time that decision is correct; it's a correct rejection. But some signal trials have so little intensity that they fall below the criterion. When that happens, the trial is a miss. The participant calls it a "no signal" trial because the intensity was below criterion, but the signal was actually present.

Note that the proportion of hits, misses, false alarms, and correct rejections will change as the criterion moves to the right or left if the participant changes his or her estimates of how important it is to gain certain accurate judgments or to avoid certain inaccurate ones.

The graph shows you the two values the experimenter really wants to know: the d' or absolute accuracy the participant brings to the task, and the participant's criterion in making the judgments. Again, the participant's sensitivity and criterion shape the number of hits, misses, false alarms, and correct rejections. The technique in signal detection analysis is basically to work backward from the way we've described it. The experimenter takes the participant's performance (hits, misses, false alarms, correct rejections) as shown in Table A.1 and uses those values to infer the sensitivity and bias. We won't go into the mathematical procedures of how that's done. Thus, researchers

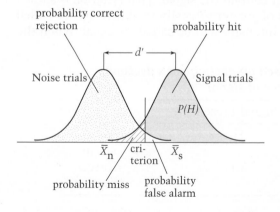

Figure A.2.

can take the participant's performance and tease apart the two factors that contribute to their decision: the sensitivity and the criterion brought to the detection task.

Statistical Significance

What if I tell you that I have a trick coin that comes up heads every time it's tossed. You inspect it, and it looks like a normal coin. You toss it, and it comes up heads. Are you convinced that it's a trick coin? Probably not, or at least, you shouldn't be. After all, a regular coin comes up heads half the time. Maybe the coin came up heads by chance. What would you do to get a better test of the coin? How many heads in a row would you need to see before you were willing to accept that this was a trick coin? Three? Ten?

There are three steps to note about our thinking here. First, the expected outcome (heads) can occur by chance; therefore, we want to see an outcome that is unlikely to come up by chance—the coin comes up heads three times in a row, for example—before we are convinced. That is the core idea of statistical significance: We look for an outcome that is so improbable, we figure it could not have occurred by chance.

Second, we need to know how rare an event would have to be before we are willing to accept it as improbable. Table A.2 shows the odds of tossing a fair coin a given number of times and having it come up heads each time.

In psychology, the standard cutoff is a probability of .05. If you know the odds of something occurring by chance and you observe a deviation that would occur with a probability of .05, then you conclude that there are forces other than chance at work; in other words, this must be a trick coin. Thus, in the coin example we'd want to see five heads in a row, to take us to a probability smaller than .05, before we'd be convinced that the coin is unfair.

Table A.2.   *Probability of outcomes of a series of tosses with a fair coin*

Number of Tosses	Probability of All-Heads (approx.)
1	.5
2	.25
3	.125
4	.063
5	.031
6	.016
7	.008
8	.004
9	.002
10	.001

Third, we need to know the odds of the event occurring by chance. To evaluate whether the coin is unfair, we need to know what happens with a fair coin. In the case of the coin, that's easy because it should be heads half the time. For other questions, it's not quite as obvious. For example, suppose we develop a tonic that is supposed to make people feel more energetic. How could we evaluate whether it works? We could give the tonic to someone each day and see whether the person feels energetic. But giving it to just one person is rather like tossing the coin only one time; it's too easy for the one person to feel energetic by chance. We could give the tonic to 10 people and see how many of them feel energetic. But what are the odds of feeling energetic by chance, without the tonic? In the case of the coin, we know what should happen by chance. In the case of the tonic, we can't predict what happens by chance, so we need to measure the energy level of a second group of people who don't get the tonic. Then, we can compare the self-rated energy levels of people who do and do not get the tonic and ask, "Are the energy ratings of the tonic drinkers higher than the ratings of the people who don't take the tonic?"

Suppose that we find that the tonic drinkers' energy ratings are indeed higher. Isn't it possible that they are a little higher just due to chance? Absolutely. In the case of the coin, we demanded that it come up heads many times before we were willing to accept it as a trick coin: There needed to be an extreme difference between what we observed (runs of all-heads) and what would be expected by chance (half heads). The same principle applies to the tonic example. Not just any difference between the groups will do. The difference between the groups needs to be so extreme that it is very unlikely to have occurred by chance. It's easy to calculate the relevant odds for the coin. It's more complicated for the tonic example, but the principle is the same. Statistical significance refers to observing a difference between two groups that is so large that we conclude it is very unlikely to have occurred by chance.

Correlation

In psychology, we care deeply about variables. (*Variable* refers to any property that an object can take: Hair color is a variable, as is age, drug dose, alertness, political affiliation, and so on.) Specifically, we frequently want to know if one variable affects another: For example, does age affect alertness? We examine this by measuring a number of people for two variables—age and alertness. We can pose our question in terms of statistical significance: Does age affect alertness or doesn't it? (Statistical significance is discussed in the previous section.) Statistical significance is critical because it tells us *whether* one thing affects the other. If there is not a statistically significant effect of one variable on the other, then we can't say that age affects alertness.

But even if we know that one variable does affect another, we don't know *how much* of an effect it has. A correlation coefficient is a way of describing this relationship. A correlation coefficient varies between +1.0 and −1.0. A correlation of +1.0 is a perfect positive relationship, which means that increases in one variable are perfectly predictable from increases in the other. For example, suppose I weigh 10 people in pounds, then weigh them all again in kilograms. Now I have two variables—weight in pounds for each person and weight in kilograms for each person. These two variables will show a perfect positive correlation of +1.0. You virtually never see two variables that are perfectly correlated; it usually happens when you do something silly like correlate the same variable with itself (as we did by measuring weight in two different ways).

A correlation near 0 means that the two variables are not related. For example, we might guess that a person's shoe size is unrelated to his or her memory ability. A negative correlation (approaching −1.0) means that as the value of one variable gets bigger, the value of the other value gets smaller. For example, we might expect that ratings of job satisfaction and absenteeism are negatively correlated: The happier you are in your job, the fewer days that you are absent from your job.

For the purposes of this book, there are three things you should know about correlations.

1. **Relationship of correlation and statistical significance.** Statistical significance tells you whether two variables are related, and a correlation characterizes that relationship (e.g., are increases in one variable associated with increases or decreases in the other variable?). Statistical significance is actually a function of the size of the correlation and the number of observations made. Thus, a correlation of +.42 might be statistically significant or it might not, depending on how many observations went into the calculation. For example, in a small group of people, you might observe only a few small-footed people who are not alert and a few hyperactive bigfoots, so you might think that shoe size is related to alertness.

2. **Size of the correlation.** A correlation near zero—say, .03—could nevertheless be statistically significant. As a rule of thumb, researchers usually think of correlations of around +.2 as moderate and +.4 as sizable.

3. **Correlation and causation.** A correlation tells you that two variables are associated—as one gets bigger, the other gets smaller (or bigger)—but it tells you *nothing* about whether one variable is causing the change in the other. For example, suppose that you observed a positive correlation between attendance at religious services and family income. One person might say, "God takes care of His own. People who go to religious services prosper." But then someone else might say, "No, going to church doesn't cause wealth. Rather, people who are wealthy have more time, and they have greater opportunity to go to church." Thus, the first variable may influence the second, or the second might influence the first.

It's also possible that a third variable could drive a correlation. Suppose there is a significant positive correlation between the number of ice cream cones sold in a city and the number of crimes committed. We could imagine public demonstrations demanding that ice cream not be sold anymore—clearly, more ice cream means more crime. Perhaps people get overexcited from the sugar rush. Or perhaps the cause moves in the other direction—people commit crimes, including robberies, so they will have more money, and they blow their ill-gotten gains on ice cream cones. Neither of these hypotheses make much sense, but you could explain the correlation by appealing to a third factor—heat. When the weather is hot, people buy more ice cream cones and also commit more crimes than they do when it's cool. Thus, the correlation between crime and ice cream is really caused by a third variable—heat—that we initially hadn't even considered. The final word is that knowing that two variables are associated means that we know they are associated *and nothing else.* We cannot make any statements about how changes in one variable causes changes in the other.

Replication

To replicate an experiment means to do it again. The motivation for performing an experiment again is to see whether the results are similar the second time the experiment is performed. If so, researchers will say that the results have been replicated. Researchers are more convinced that the results of an experiment are valid if they have been replicated. There are two reasons that's true.

First, there is always some chance that an experimental result was a fluke. For example, suppose I test whether eating raw seafood improves fertility. I take 200 couples and have 100 of the couples eat raw oysters every day, and at the end of 6 months I compare how many oyster-eating couples and how many nonoyster-eating couples have conceived. I find that more oyster eaters have conceived. That result could just be a fluke—one group or the other had to be higher (except for the unlikely event of a tie), so how do we know that eating oysters really promotes fertility?

Evaluating the results for statistical significance is supposed to protect against that; the whole point of statistical significance is that it determines whether the difference between two experimental conditions is so great that it is unlikely to have occurred by chance. The logic is this: If eating oysters *didn't* promote fertility, what are the odds there would have been such a big difference between the oyster eaters and the nonoyster-eating group? The usual cutoff is .05, meaning that if the difference you observed in the experiment would only happen 5% of the time by chance, there was really no difference between the two groups. (If this isn't making sense, see the "Statistical Significance" section.)

What you have to remember is that *there is a 5% chance that when you get a statistically significant difference, it's a fluke.* That's what the 5% criterion means—you're saying there's just a 5% chance that this result is a fluke. So, 95% of the time your result is right, but the other 5% of the time your result is wrong.

If you replicate a result, you are that much more confident that the result is not a fluke. Now the odds are $0.05 \times 0.05 = 0.0025$, or 0.25%, that the results are a fluke. So, if an experiment replicates, you are more confident that the results are reliable.

Replication brings a second advantage. Suppose that I conducted the oyster study. You might be more convinced of the result if someone else did the study over again. The fact is that research is hard to do well. Mistakes are easy to make. If I made a mistake that influenced the results of the experiment the first time I did it, if I replicate the experiment, won't I also replicate the mistake? That's another reason people are more confident about the results of an experiment when they see it replicated, especially by a different set of researchers.

Another type of replication is a conceptual replication. Here, you don't set out to do an experiment exactly the same way; rather, I want to replicate the basic idea of the experiment. For example, the original hypothesis of the oyster experiment was that eating raw shellfish would help fertility. A conceptual replication might entail eating raw clams instead of oysters.

Studying for Exams

There are some obvious things that you should do to prepare for a test. You should find out what you can from the instructor: What material will be covered and what won't? What is the format (multiple choice, short answer, essay)? You should study the material as you go along during the semester. Don't leave it all for the last day or two before the final exam. You are surely familiar with this advice.

Here are some other pointers that may (or may not) help you get ready for exams:

1. **Recognize the structure of the material.** Class lectures, like textbooks, are organized hierarchically. (Hierarchical representations of the chapters in this textbook are available at www.prenhall.com/willingham.) Most instructors make between three and seven main points during a lecture. Obviously, you should know these points, but they are so basic to the topic (e.g., deep processing helps memory) that you're unlikely to be tested on them. The next levels down consist of material that supports the main points—usually experiments—and then one level down from that are the details of the experiments (Figure A.3).

   A common mistake in studying is to begin at the bottom level. Students simply start rereading their notes or copying them over. A much better strategy is to think in terms of the lecture organization. What were the main conclusions of the lecture? What supporting evidence was provided for each conclusion? A good study strategy would be to actually create your own outline for each class—that will force you to think about what the main conclusions were and what material supported each

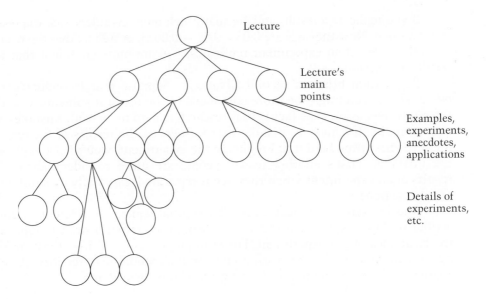

Lecture

Lecture's
main
points

Examples,
experiments,
anecdotes,
applications

Details of
experiments,
etc.

Figure A.3.

conclusion. (The usefulness of alternative representations was emphasized when I took an introductory cognitive psychology course in college with Ruth Day, and it's a topic on which she's written; see Day, 1988).

Instructors frequently test you on the relationships between levels: Why does a particular study support a conclusion? Why was a particular stimulus crucial to use in an experiment? To answer such questions, you need to consider the relationship between levels of the hierarchy; perhaps you will describe an experiment to support one of the conclusions.

2. **Don't just look over your notes.** This study strategy is the one I hear most often, and it is the worst. By looking over your notes, you get a feeling of familiarity for the material—but you're not going to be tested for familiarity. During the test you will not have access to your notes, so you need to study in a way that is as similar as possible to the test conditions. As noted in chapters 6 and 7, retrieval works best when it is as similar as possible to encoding.

3. **Create an outline; then test yourself.** As described previously, making an outline is helpful. Once you believe you understand the structure of the material, create flashcards and test yourself. This practice is useful because you will be testing yourself under conditions that are closer to the real test, that is, conditions in which you can't see the answer.

4. **Find a study partner.** After you've already done a fair amount of studying, you are ready to quiz a partner. The advantages of this strategy are that when you're quizzing your partner, you're forced to think of questions that might be on the test, and when your partner is quizzing you, you of

course get more practice in answering questions. Even better, your partner may well have noticed the importance of some material that you missed.

Taking an Exam

What should you do when you take a test? I hear three common reasons students don't do as well as they expected on an exam (I should note that I give only multiple-choice exams):

1. **I could narrow it down to two choices, but then I had to guess.** A common reason this happens is that students add assumptions or extra information to a question. People are smart and inventive, and we are good at formulating special conditions under which a wrong answer *could* be correct (e.g., if there were no gravity and time moved backward). If you find yourself thinking, "But if thus and so were the case, then D could be right," then D is not right. Answer only the question; don't add anything. Also, be sure that you are *answering* the question. Answer D may be a true statement, but it may not answer the question. Pick the choice that answers the question, and not simply the one that states something you know to be true.

2. **There was material on the test that I didn't expect.** Clearly, in this case, you've studied the wrong material. You need to think more carefully about what is important in the lectures and book and what isn't.

3. **I thought I did well, and I still don't understand why I got a low grade.** When this happens, it is often simply a matter of studying 20% harder than you did. What has likely happened is that you confidently picked distractors (wrong answers) that were close to the right answers. The distractors are, of course, written to be difficult. As much as it would be fun to take a test with questions like these:

   Biederman's geon theory is

   a. a feature theory using 3D features
   b. a chapter of *Paradise Lost*
   c. the poorest selling CD by the Beatles
   d. a new burger at McDonald's

   Such questions wouldn't provide much information to your professor about how much cognitive psychology you know. Hence, you can expect the distractors to be closely related to the correct answer, and distinguishing them will require detailed knowledge. If you are confidently selecting wrong answers, the reason is most often that you simply didn't know the material well enough.

Answers

Chapter 1

1. The first assumption is about what questions should be addressed first. The second type of assumption is something you believe, which may or may not be true, that colors your view of a cognitive process even before you start to study it.

2. For much of the 20th century, many psychologists (especially Americans) assumed that any theory of the mind could describe only the environment and people's behaviors. These psychologists were called behaviorists. They assumed that because observation is a critical part of the scientific method and researchers can't observe thought directly, thought cannot be part of a scientific theory. This assumption seems quite solid, but it overlooks the possibility that we can propose ways in which thoughts lead to behaviors. In other words, we can make thoughts indirectly observable if we specify what sort of thoughts lead to what sort of behaviors. That is the approach that cognitive psychologists have used.

3. People believed it probably wouldn't work because that would mean that human behavior was deterministic, which they could not believe was true.

4. They were interested primarily in the origin of knowledge: Was knowledge largely innate, or was it acquired through experience? Other psychological questions were addressed during the Renaissance (e.g., learning and perception), but they were usually in service of the larger question of the origin of knowledge.

5. Initially, psychologists sought to explain the contents of consciousness. Behaviorism changed the goal of the discipline to explaining behavior.

6. I would say most people don't hold it, given the belief in extrasensory perception (ESP), astrology, and the like. ESP and astrology are exactly the sort of explanations we're talking about; they are unobservable explanations for worldly events. You could gather evidence for or against these phenomena (and there is a great deal of evidence indicating that they are not real), but true believers always have an answer, such as "If you try to gather evidence about it, the ESP goes away" or "Astrology works, but not perfectly every time—it describes only general tendencies of what will occur." Thus, in the end you really *can't* gather evidence that would disprove the existence of these phenomena—whatever occurs, there is an explanation—yet, many people accept such explanations for things that occur.

7. I think they should, but not in the sense in which introspectionists use them. A great deal of work in cognitive and social psychology has shown that people's introspections on how and why they do things are not always accurate (Nisbett & Wilson, 1977), but there are times when people's descriptions of how they solve problems can be informative. Most important, introspections should be part of the data that are to be explained (Marr, 1982). If you are developing a theory of vision, for example, it should explain why a hill over there looks steep even if it isn't. Our introspective experience is part of mental life, and it is worthy of explanation.

8. New data indicated that behaviorism was not completely successful in accounting for animal behavior (e.g., fixed action patterns, critical periods) and for some aspects of human behavior (language, apparent strategies in memory retrieval).

9. The heart of the information processing paradigm is the comparison of the brain to a computer. Both process information, in that both take in information, represent it symbolically, manipulate the symbols with different processes, refer to memory, and produce an output. Another important part of the information processing paradigm is that information processing occurs in discrete stages, as shown in the "What is your hometown?" example.

10. Partly by reference to other disciplines. They argued that neuroscience and artificial intelligence researchers used abstract representations in their work with no apparent loss of rigor. They were also successful in arguing that certain problems, such as accounting for human ability in language, seemed to require such representations for an adequate explanation.

11. The answer is very likely to be "Yes." On the one hand, you could point to the fact that children seem to reach developmental milestones at around the same time: rolling over, crawling, first steps, first words, and so on. On the other hand, the critical period idea suggests that if those crucial time windows are missed, it will be difficult to learn the skill later, and the fact that most children learn them at around the same age doesn't speak to that issue. There are only a few examples of children who, because of severe deprivation, seemed not to have the chance to learn to speak, for example, and these cases seem to support the idea of a critical period for language (Itard, 1962).

Other data based on larger numbers of children support the idea of a critical period for language. Children appear to be "programmed" to learn language, learning vocabulary at the unbelievable rate of an average of about nine words per day between the ages of 2 and 9. You may know someone who was

raised bilingually. Children can learn two languages almost as quickly as one (research confirms this observation). However, this is true only when they are quite young. Once a child is older (e.g., and taking a foreign language in school) it is much harder to learn another language. We return to this issue in chapter 13.

12. To be honest, I don't even have a very good guess as to the ratio of failures to successes, but I'm confident that the ratio is very low. I pose this question simply to emphasize that your mind is constantly performing remarkable cognitive feats of which you are unaware. That's part of the point of the "What is your hometown?" analysis: to show that even cognitive processes that appear very simple actually are quite complex when you consider them in information processing terms. One of the ways cognitive psychologists think about this point is to consider what it would take to get a computer to perform the same function. Viewed in that light, it becomes clear that cognitive processes that seem easy to us—recognizing objects, reaching for things—are extremely complex.

13. Yes, absolutely. That is how cognitive psychologists often approach these problems. As I mentioned in that discussion, cognitive psychologists typically work on just one problem (e.g., memory) rather than trying to figure out how the entire cognitive system works because just one component of the system is dauntingly complicated. If you're trying to figure out how memory works, you could approach it the same way we did in the "What is your hometown?" example. You could figure that memory starts with some information coming in from the environment (someone says "I just saw a quincunx"), and the end product of the memory search is that you conclude that you are unfamiliar with a quincunx. How do you determine that you don't know that? Do you check every single part of your memory, or do you check for a while, and then quit? Wait a minute—what does it mean to "check" memory? How might memories be organized such that you can "check" them? And off you go . . . .

Chapter 2

1. Empiricism (a commitment to test ideas experimentally), public verifiability (a willingness to make our hypotheses and experiments available to others to critique), and solvable problems (recognition that science can solve some problems, but not others).

2. Develop alternate theories; derive signature predictions for each theory; obtain data to compare the theories.

3. Descriptive (describes the world as it is), relational (describes relationships among variables), and experimental (describes relationships among variables and how they are caused).

4. The problem is that most of the techniques that are crucial to well-conducted science are so technical that the average newspaper reader (or reporter for that matter) cannot be an informed critic. Seeking publicity before publication draws criticism because no one who could really spot problems in the way the research was done has had a chance to point out those problems.

5. We choose one theory as better than another by deriving signature predictions for each theory, conducting an experiment, and determining which theory made the right prediction. We cannot derive signature predictions for Freud's psychoanalytic theory because it predicted everything. Knowing that someone had a very strict father, for example, did not allow one to predict whether he would grow up to be shy or outgoing.

6. True experiments? No. Experimental work requires that the experimenter manipulate the independent variable—in this case, the gender of the subject. You can't randomly make someone a man or a woman for the purpose of an experiment, so any research on gender will be relational, not experimental. That's why gender differences are so controversial. It's known that fewer women go into upper level science and math courses in high school and college; is that because they are female, is it due to being treated as though they will not be competent in math because they are female, or is it some other variable? Because these

variables are all associated, it is very difficult to determine.

7. We need to know where the brain is damaged or where the brain is active, and we need to know which cognitive function is engaged during a task. We need this information because the logic of localization is that if a brain area supports a cognitive function, then damage to that area will lead to impairment of the function or engagement of the function will lead to activation of the area.

8. Because each technique of localization has drawbacks. The logic of localization is not perfect. For example, a deficit following a brain lesion may not be due to the part of the brain that is lesioned, but rather due to a severing of fibers that connect two distant areas. If many different techniques all lead to a similar conclusion, then we can worry much less about the drawbacks of each technique.

9. There does seem to be something magical about brain imaging in the public imagination. As noted in the chapter, brain imaging data don't make a phenomenon any more special or "real." The pictures, however, are very alluring because they do represent something about what the brain is doing as a person thinks. We know that thought is rooted in the brain, but thought seems so immaterial that seeing a material representation of it holds a natural fascination. It is also probably relevant that the color-coded pictures are easy to understand. An electroencephalogram (EEG) allows researchers to peek at what the brain is doing while a person thinks, and EEG data have been available for years, but waveforms are difficult to understand.

10. You might think that a lesion that is the consequence of *surgery*, rather than an accident or a stroke, might yield a study that is an experiment, but that won't do either. Keep in mind that people who need surgery (for the treatment of epilepsy or the removal of a tumor) do not have brains like everyone else. So comparing the brains of people who have had surgery to the brains of people who have not is problematic—are they different because of the surgery, or were they different even before the surgery? A true experiment can be conducted when a lesion is randomly made or not made to each participant, and this can be done when the participants are nonhuman primates. Although performing such surgery in the name of science is controversial, it is undeniable that we have learned a great deal about the brain from such studies.

Chapter 3

1. Size and distance; shape and orientation; and light source, reflectance, and shadow.

2. You would think that the answer would relate to familiar size. You would assume that the car will be the normal size for a car, so if it looks small it's probably a regular-size car but far away. To a point, that's true. As we see in the next section, however, familiar size helps only a little bit in disambiguating size and distance.

3. No. The earth is much bigger than the moon, so you'd have to move farther away from the earth than the surface of the moon for it to work, or you'd have to move your thumb closer to your eye.

4. Surfaces are uniformly colored, light sources are above the visual scene, and surface lightness is interpreted depending on the ratios of lightness of areas that are next to one another in the same plane.

5. In top-down processing, conceptual knowledge influences the lower-level processing. In bottom-up processing, raw and unprocessed information gives rise to conceptual knowledge.

6. The most important difference concerns what we assume is in the environment and what we think is in the mind. The computational point of view assumes that the visual cues in the environment are basically lines; the environment is viewed as an impoverished source of visual information, so a fair amount of computation is necessary for this impoverished input to be made into something sensible. According to the ecological point of view, in contrast, the environment is a wonderfully rich source of information. The psychologist's first job is to discover what these sources of

information are and which ones humans use in vision. Ecological psychologists argue that once we do a good job of describing the environment, the job of describing how the mind uses this information will be much easier.

7. Close your textbook and rotate it 45 degrees; it doesn't look like the title is skewed. Why? Because you still see the title relative to the frame of reference of the book cover; relative to the book cover, the title is not skewed—it's still in the same position. Relative to gravity, it is skewed, but vision dominates as a frame of reference in this.

8. Because the day was brilliantly clear, there was no atmospheric perspective. With that cue to distance gone, the city looked oddly like a model.

9. Get low. Strangers may seem scary to toddlers not only because they are strange, but also because they appear so big. People (including toddlers) focus on faces, so get your face down to the eyeheight of the toddler.

10. One set of theories says the representation is object centered, meaning that the parts of the objects are located relative to one another. The other set of theories holds that they are viewer centered, meaning that there would be several representations for each object, one for each point of view.

11. Object representations may be localized (e.g., all faces in the same part of the cortex), visual processing may be localized (e.g., visual expertise in one part of the brain), or object representations may be distributed.

12. There is evidence in both monkeys and humans that different parts of the brain support tasks demanding "what" knowledge and "how" knowledge, namely the temporal lobe for "what" and the parietal lobe for "how." The second type of evidence comes from humans with intact brains. On occasion, the "what" and "how" systems evaluate visual objects differently, such as the steepness of hills.

13. Researchers in this area emphasize that our conscious perception matches not only the absolute angle of the hill (obviously), but also the difficulty we would have in climbing a particular hill. A difference of a few degrees makes a large difference in terms of the energy it would take to climb the hill. Furthermore, once a hill is much steeper than 45 degrees it is more or less impossible to climb without equipment, so all hills this steep or steeper look like cliffs.

14. Faces come to mind as an object that we almost always see right side up, and faces are notoriously difficult to recognize when they are inverted, as described in the chapter.

15. Even though Hal sees Rosemary as thin (what system), his motor system makes the correct moves to hug her based on her actual size (how system).

Chapter 4

1. It *seems* that people can, but it is actually difficult to be certain because it is always possible that people switch attention rapidly between tasks rather than truly dividing attention.

2. There must be consistency in the task, especially in the responses required for stimuli. For example, in the Shiffrin and Schneider experiments, it had to be the case that a particular letter was either a target or a distractor. It couldn't be a target on one trial and then a distractor on the next trial.

3. A multiple resource theory claims that there are multiple pools of attention, perhaps divided by modality (one pool for vision, one for audition, and so on). Although the idea has some appeal, it has proved difficult to be very specific about how these different pools are set up and when they are called on.

4. It could be that music with words takes more attention to listen to, but I think another explanation is more likely. It may be that these people cannot help but process the words semantically. Semantic processing of spoken (or sung) words may be automatic. Processing the meaning of the sung words interferes with processing the words that are read. Thus, it's not that music with words takes more attention to listen to; rather, the words are processed regardless of whether you want them to be, and this interferes with reading.

5. A multiple resources model. The comedian apparently believed that there should be no interference between vision (looking for the house number) and audition (listening to the music). The fact is that we do find the music distracting. As described in the text, even though there is certainly less interference when different modalities are used, there is still some common demand, so people try to minimize the interference.

6. You might guess that because driving is automatic, it doesn't make much difference whether you're talking on a cellular phone; there should be attention to spare while driving. In fact, heavy use of cellular phones (more than 50 min per month) is a risk factor for accidents (Violanti & Marshall, 1996). But you would expect that the expertise of the driver would be a factor, and this seems to be true. Using cellular phones while driving is a greater risk for less experienced drivers, apparently because they are more likely to glance away from the road (usually to dial) for long periods of time and at risky moments when attention to the road is crucial (Wikman, Nieminen, & Summala, 1998). Still other data show that there is a cost to driving—you miss traffic signals and you're slower to react—even using a hands-free phone. Exactly why is not known, but the authors (Strayer & Johnston, 2001) suggest it's because you are imaging a context (the person on the other end of the line) other than the one in which you're driving.

7. The evidence indicates that it's early. A number of studies indicated that the filter might be late, but in those cases it appears that participants might not have been attending solely to the material to which they were told to attend; they seem to have been occasionally "sampling" the other channel. Some proposed that the filter is "movable," but this probably means that there is a fixed filter (which is early) and that you can choose to allocate more or less attention to other sources. For example, you can listen closely to your friend at a party and try to ignore other conversations, or you can listen to your friend and simultaneously try to monitor the party around you to see whether anyone is talking about anything interesting.

8. It selects objects for further processing, not locations in space.

9. In a disjunctive search, the target differs from the distractors on just one feature (e.g., color), and the search is easy; in fact, it occurs automatically, meaning that all the elements in the field are evaluated simultaneously and that the participant experiences pop-out. In a conjunctive search, the target is defined by the conjunction of two features (e.g., color and shape), and visual search is difficult; the search progresses serially, not in parallel.

10. At the start of the chapter, we noted that it is crucial to be able to monitor the environment for things that are not currently attended to determine whether attention should be refocused. The heroine apparently is not processing unattended sounds very carefully. Again, it seems as if the filter is early, so to detect the scuffling sound as threatening (e.g., and not caused by a tree limb scraping the house), she might need to be focusing attention away from her shower periodically, but the situation she thinks she's in (showering at home) does not warrant frequent sampling of the environment for threatening sounds. You may have noticed the same phenomenon. If you are talking to a friend in your living room at noon, you may not notice the scratching noise of a squirrel on the roof because you have chosen not to allocate much attention to your surroundings. However, a very similar noise may enter awareness if you are talking to your friend while walking down a dark and deserted street at night in a strange New York City neighborhood because you have allocated more attention to monitoring your surroundings.

11. Any situation in which two objects are intertwined (i.e., they spatially overlap) and you successfully attend to just one indicates that you are directing attention to an object, not a location. Another example would be looking at your reflection in the glass of a picture frame and successfully ignoring the picture.

12. Inhibition of return will make it harder to select a recently selected object for attention; ironic processes of mental control will make you select something for attention that you don't want to select; and attending to certain types of stimuli for more than 30 min leads to decreased sensitivity in detecting important features of the stimuli (we discussed this as a problem of vigilance).

13. The psychological refractory period and the attentional blink both entail apparent failures of attention, but the tasks are so simple that it seems unlikely that they are due to inadequate attentional resources. Rather, they are likely structural effects, meaning that the decrement in performance is due to competition for cognitive structures other than attention.

14. As you know from reading this chapter, trying not to think about something is ineffective, *if* your cognitive resources are low (as they often are after a breakup). The best strategy would be to tell your friend to go ahead and think about his girlfriend all he wants, perhaps even to the point of forcing himself to think about her. It's hard to predict when thoughts of the girlfriend will subside, but they will likely do so faster if he uses this technique than if he tries not to think about her.

15. Car alarms have a terrible bias: They go off not only for robbers, but for people nudging the car as they walk by, cats jumping on the hood, and sometimes a bystander taking a deep breath nearby. They are like a radar operator who constantly says, "I see a ship!" Car alarms are completely ineffective because they rely on the idea that people will go running to investigate when they hear a car alarm. No one does because alarms go off all the time, just as you would ignore the radar operator who kept claiming to see ships all the time.

16. This is a vigilance task at its worst. These people must watch screens for weapons that virtually never appear, yet if they miss a weapon, the results could be catastrophic. I mentioned in this chapter that a warning signal of possible danger is very helpful, but the signal must be reliable. The software to enable such signals does not seem to be available for this task. The only option open to us is to make the shifts of these workers as short as possible because sensitivity in vigilance tasks declines rapidly.

Chapter 5

1. The partial report procedure allows a more accurate estimate than the whole report procedure of how much information people can apprehend with a brief exposure. In the partial report, participants are exposed to stimuli and immediately thereafter are given a cue as to which stimuli to report. Because the cue is given after the stimuli have disappeared, the participant cannot know which stimuli he or she will be asked to report, so the percentage of stimuli successfully reported may be taken as a fair estimate of all the stimuli that are reportable. The whole report procedure underestimates the span of apprehension because participants forget some of the stimuli apprehended, even as they are reporting others; the partial report procedure avoids that problem.

2. Visual or iconic memory has a large capacity (as many as 15 items or more, depending on conditions), it fades quickly (anywhere from 0.25 to 2 s, depending on conditions), and it can be masked, meaning you can knock the contents of sensory memory out by presenting new stimuli. Echoic memory has similar characteristics, although it is shorter lived (0.25 s).

3. Films typically are shot at 24 frames per second, meaning that each frame of the film would appear for about 42 ms. The shutter of a typical film projector is not open continuously: It is closed more than it is open, so when you watch a film you are looking at a black screen more than you are looking at the movie. Iconic memory carries you over these intervals and makes the visual experience continuous even though the visual stimulation is not.

You may come up with your own examples, but I can tell you about one time I actually used iconic memory. In my old apartment, I didn't have a phone by the bed. If it rang in the middle of the night I had to walk out to the kitchen to answer it. I didn't feel like turning on the light because it was too bright, but I didn't want to crash into furniture on the way to the phone either. I used iconic memory by flipping the lights on for just a moment. That gave me a tachistoscopic flash of the room, and I could read iconic memory to avoid the furniture on the way to the phone.

4. No, retinal afterimages are not the same as iconic memory. Their mechanism is different (they are caused by bleaching of the retinal cells), but your experience wouldn't tell you that. Two differences that you might notice from your experience are that afterimages have the color opposite to the stimulus (in you stare at something green, the afterimage is red). We said that iconic memory can be cued by color, so it's clearly not an afterimage—if it were you'd pick the wrong color. The other way that afterimages differ is that they move when your eyes move (try it). Iconic memory does not move with your eyes.

5. Material may be coded acoustically (in terms of sound), semantically (in terms of meaning), or visuospatially (in terms of visual appearance).

6. Forgetting occurs because of proactive interference, retroactive interference, and decay. Proactive interference is the forgetting of new material caused by having learned material earlier. Retroactive interference is the forgetting of previously learned material caused by learning new material. Decay is the spontaneous loss of previously learned material.

7. Not really. That is people's performance on the digit span task, it's true, but it is more accurate to say that the capacity of primary memory depends on how the participant codes the material. The code is important because an acoustic code has a capacity of about 2 s of material. The capacity in visuospatial code is about four objects. The capacity in the semantic code depends on the participant's ability to chunk the material.

8. You can't rule out the possibility of proactive interference from processing just before the experiment. You have no way of knowing what people were doing before they began the experiment, so if some percentage of the participants had just finished studying or thinking about materials similar to those used in the experiment right before they walked in. This objection is probably impossible to overcome, making it very difficult to develop a primary memory task that is not susceptible to proactive interference.

9. The best plan is to space your studying so there are breaks between study sessions. If you can't do that, at least try to study dissimilar subjects back to back because interference is greater when the subjects are similar.

10. Yes, you would expect that to be true because digit span tasks are coded auditorily, and the auditory code depends on time. Thus, if digits take longer, on average, to say in one language than another, the average digit span in that language should be smaller. There is evidence supporting that conjecture from bilingual speakers of English and Welsh (Ellis & Hennelly, 1980; Murray & Jones, 2002) and from Arabic, which has two ways of pronouncing each digit (Shebani, van de Vijver, & Poortinga, 2005).

11. *Primary memory* is a generic term that is not tied to any particular theory. *Short-term memory* is a term from a particular theory, the modal model. (Short-term memory was proposed to code material exclusively acoustically, to lose material exclusively through decay, and so on.) *Working memory* is also a term from a particular theory, Baddeley's working memory model. In popular culture, *short-term memory* has taken on the generic meaning. Among psychologists, *short-term memory* usually has the more specific meaning tied to the modal model. However, psychologists do use the term *long-term memory* in the generic sense.

12. The phonological loop is composed of the phonological store, which is the site where 2 s of acoustic material can be stored, and the articulatory control process, which allows us to write acoustic information to the phonological loop through subvocal rehearsal.

13. This irrelevant verbiage gains obligatory access to the phonological loop, which is where I'm trying to keep the instructions she just gave me. A nod and a smile would be better.

14. Such patients exist, and their long-term memory is surprisingly good. Remember, the phonological loop is not the only pathway to long-term memory, as evidenced by the fact that people can still encode and rehearse

things under articulatory suppression. Vocabulary in their native language doesn't seem impaired in these patients, probably because they have had a lot of practice, but they are impaired in learning vocabulary words in a new language, where the main thing to be learned is the sound of the unfamiliar word (Baddeley, Papagno, & Vallar, 1988).

Chapter 6

1. Emotion has an impact, but naturally we remember many things that are not emotional, so it seems likely that this factor affects memory in a limited number of circumstances. Depth of processing—the extent to which material is considered in terms of its meaning—has a profound impact on encoding.

2. Not by itself. But encoding something deeply more times (rather than fewer times) does help.

3. Depth of processing predicts that the extent to which a memory is encoded depends solely on the depth of processing during encoding. It turns out that the match between encoding and retrieval processes is also important. The other problem concerns the theory of levels of processing. The theory is not detailed enough to differentiate two different tasks that are shallow.

4. Clearly, the best advice you can offer is to process the material deeply. That means that you have to think about what the material means, and the best way to do that is to generate questions with which to test yourself. Thinking of your own questions has the added advantage of getting you to imagine what your instructor is likely to ask. Regarding remembering names at a party, the advice is more or less the same. If you want to remember names, you have to actually think about the person's name. Most people who don't remember names (including me—I'm horrible) simply don't pay much attention when they first hear the name.

5. Before you give an explanation, verify that this is true. When someone tells me they remember little of their wedding day, I have to curb the desire to cock my head and narrow my eyes in a mask of police-inquisitor suspicion. "Oh really. You don't remember getting dressed that morning? You don't remember the kiss-the-bride part?" One of the first things you learn as a psychologist is that your own experiences and intuitions (and those of your wedding-amnesic friends) can be a terrific source of hypotheses about the human mind, but you shouldn't believe something based on subjective experience alone. Psychology books are full of examples of things that many people believe, yet they are false. (For starters, most people believe in ESP.)

To my knowledge, no one has examined in a rigorous experimental situation whether high emotion can lead to a failure of memory. Let's suppose for a moment that it were true. It might be that emotionality has what is called an inverted U effect on memory. That means that when emotional levels are low, a bit more emotion improves memory, but that when emotion levels are high, more emotion harms memory. This inverted U relationship is found in certain types of physical performance tasks, so it might be observed for memory, but this is speculation.

6. I think advertisements that are well remembered, such as jingles, are processed more deeply. It may be that advertisements that are repeated often may become more memorable. You can think of each repetition of a commercial as another opportunity for you to encode the material deeply. Even if you ignore the ad the first 20 times you see it, perhaps on the next viewing you'll see that the advertised car really does have more leg room, by golly.

7. It reduces what you have to remember by allowing you to chunk, it guides your interpretation of details through the activation of schemas, and it makes unusual things stand out.

8. It ought to be. You can test this hypothesis easily enough. If you're a baseball fan (for example), watch a game (or part of a game) with a nonfan and later see who remembers more of the game.

9. It's easy to guess at what the schemas for these "types" of people would be. Librarians are typically women, they are spinsters, they have glasses and wear their hair in buns, and they are not a lot of fun. Engineers are male, they have little sense of humor and mediocre interpersonal skills, and they wear out-of-date clothes and pocket protectors. It is a sobering thought that our minds may be designed in such a way that we automatically categorize objects (including people) and abstract out schemas (stereotypes) to fit the categories. Naturally, the fact that we know these stereotypes does not mean that we have to act in accordance with them.

10. Here's one way you could do it. There are three main effects of prior knowledge on encoding: It reduces what you have to remember, it guides your interpretation of details, and it makes unusual things stand out. You could chunk those three main points into one image. Take a tour *guide* (complete with map, camera, and foreign phrase translation book) and *reduce* him in size. Then, put him with a tour group of regular-size people who are sitting so he *stands* out. Silly, yes, but bizarre images are effective for memory.

11. It would make deep processing easier. Recall that deep processing involves connecting new information to information that you already know. If you have more prior knowledge, it will be easier to connect the new information to things you already know.

12. It was "Hey! What did that little monkey leave in my shoe?" This sentence does not fit the schema for a textbook well, and it is therefore likely to be well remembered.

Chapter 7

1. Free recall, cued recall, recognition, and savings in relearning are the four measures. They differ in sensitivity in that one measure of memory may indicate that some information has been forgotten, but another measure may show that some part of the memory remains in the storehouse.

2. The most important factor at retrieval is the cues that are provided. Cues that more closely match how the material was encoded are more likely to lead to successful retrieval. Thus, if the measure provides more cues, one of the cues is likely to be helpful.

3. The cues are more important, as shown by the recognition failure of recallable words effect.

4. Prior knowledge tells us what usually happens in similar situations. We can use that in two ways. First, we may try harder to retrieve a bit of information because we know from prior knowledge that the event must have happened (as when we struggle to remember the type of cake served at a child's birthday party because we know from prior knowledge that cake must have been served). Second, we may mistake knowledge from prior experience for retrieval of a particular event. For example, we may mistakenly believe that cake was served at a particular child's birthday party because the serving of cake is so consistent with our prior experience of children's birthday parties.

5. Overuse of prior knowledge and source confusion.

6. He or she might come up with something, but it would be mostly a reconstruction. The delay of 19 months was not picked arbitrarily. In February 1987, Ronald Reagan challenged reporters at a press conference to remember what they were doing August 8, 1985. The reporters were silent. Reagan was trying to make the point that it is hard to remember the events of a specific day 19 months ago, and in a way he was right. Your memory is not designed to answer questions of this sort because it is not indexed according to date. It is indexed by events. If I went to the Metropolitan Museum of Art that day, I may (or may not) be able to recover that fact, but if I did, it would require lots of reasoning about where I was on August 8. However, if you simply ask, "Have you ever been to the Metropolitan Museum of Art?", my answer would be immediate and confident. Cues to the same event can be either very effective or very ineffective in leading you to remember the event.

7. This seems like a straightforward case of recognition failure of a recallable stimulus. Suppose that you are walking down the street in your hometown. If someone stopped you and said, "Can you tell me what Peter, that guy in the room down the hall, looks like?" You'd say, "Sure," and you would be able to generate a mental image of Peter and describe him—in short, you recall his face. But when you're walking down the street, you fail to recognize his face. His face is in a context different from the one in which you learned it, just as the word *chair* alone is in a different context from the one in which you learned it if you saw it in the presence of the word *glue.*

8. Forgetting can occur when you don't have the right cue for retrieval because the association between the cue and the target memory is compromised in some way or because the target memory itself is lost.

9. This proposal is impossible to disprove, but it is viewed as quite unlikely by memory researchers. The standard observations in support of the idea (hypnosis, Penfield's stimulation studies) are more likely to be reconstructions than real memories.

10. Probably, but it seems to happen very infrequently. It's difficult to obtain convincing evidence of repression because it is always possible that the memory is inaccurate; that the person did not truly forget the event, although he or she may think it forgotten; or that the loss of the memory was caused by a normal forgetting process, not repression.

11. Interference is the big enemy in trying to learn new material. As we've seen, interference can be proactive or retroactive, so long bouts of studying pay diminishing returns. The more you try to learn in a single session, the more difficult learning becomes because of proactive interference, and the more likely you are to forget the material studied earlier because of retroactive interference. Therefore, short, frequent study sessions, broken up by other activities, are the most efficient.

12. The big difference between the ironic processes and the controlled retrieval case is the availability of attention. In the ironic processes experiments, participants get the intrusive "white bear" thoughts *when they are distracted by something else*, or when they are tired, intoxicated, or in some other way impaired. Anderson's participants were not in that state. Thus, people get different effects of trying not to think about something, depending on what else they are doing at the time.

Chapter 8

1. The classical view proposes that people categorize an object by comparing it to a list of necessary and sufficient properties that an object must have to fit a category. Hence, the description of an uncle is "brother of a parent." If a man is the brother of a parent, he is an uncle because he meets the necessary and sufficient conditions for that category. The data indicating that the classical view is either wrong or incomplete concerned participants' ratings of typicality of category exemplars (and other typicality effects). No exemplar of a category should seem more or less typical if we use a list of necessary and sufficient conditions to put items into that category. Either an object meets the category requirements or it doesn't, and an object is therefore either a member of the category or not. Because this seems not to be the case (at least for some categories some of the time), the classical view must be either incorrect or incomplete.

2. Prototype theory and exemplar theory both propose that new exemplars are categorized by evaluating the similarity of the exemplar to memory representations; if it is similar, it is deemed to be a member of the category. The difference is that the exemplar theory proposes that each exemplar of a category is stored in memory, whereas the prototype theory proposes that a prototype is abstracted from many exemplars and then stored.

3. It appears that both types of categorization occur. Recent models include both mechanisms. An important job is to specify when one or the other mechanism will do the learning.

4. This theory seems to require an endlessly large memory store. How big would memory have to be for me to store every instance of a car I look at as a new car? And every dog, and every chair, and so on? This problem has not been overlooked by categorization researchers. One easy solution that some models have taken is to set a criterion for similarity for an individual exemplar to be stored. If the exemplar that you're looking at is similar to an exemplar already in memory, there is no need to store it again (although the fact that you've seen this exemplar again may be stored). This saves you from having 10 million exemplars of your mother stored in memory.

5. The newspapers use the word *grandma* for shock value. Why is it shocking? It's the tension between the classical, rule-driven meaning of *grandma* and the prototypical grandmother. Anyone who is female and the parent of a parent is a grandma. That's the classical categorization definition. The prototypical features of a grandma include much more, such as being sweet, baking cookies, knitting, and sitting quietly at home. Therefore, it's exciting when a grandma does something vigorous or outrageous.

6. First, your memory shows an excellent addressing system in that it can retrieve material very quickly, despite the great volume of material it potentially has available. Second, if the desired information is not in memory, the system makes available information that is either close in meaning or relevant so that you can make an inference that allows you to answer the question.

7. Advantages: It allows the retrieval of object properties, it allows content-addressable storage, typicality is a natural outgrowth of the model, the model creates defaults, and it's resistant to faulty input.

8. The chief difference is one of representation. In a model with a local representation, a concept is represented by the activity of a single node. In a model with a distributed representation, a concept is represented by the pattern of activation across multiple nodes.

9. You may recall that early empiricist philosophers placed a great deal of emphasis on associations; the building of associations was at the heart of intelligent behavior. Spreading activation models have association at their heart. The links between nodes are nothing more than associations. These models represent an advance over earlier associationist ideas, however, because they are more precise in their predictions. Regarding consciousness, the associationist nature of the model leads to a natural prediction about consciousness. Because activity passes between the nodes in the model, something is always active in the network. We could say that whatever is active is what is in consciousness, so the ebb and flow of activity in the model represents the flow of consciousness.

10. This question is a bit unfair because my hunch is that you would probably say "distributed," and I think the real answer is that neither is very realistic in any important way. On the surface, the distributed models look more like networks of neurons. Psychologists are fairly confident that a concept is not represented in a single neuron, and the local representation appears to claim just that, if you take a single node in the network to be a single neuron. But models using the distributed representation still only use hundreds or thousands of "neurons" to represent processes that surely require millions of neurons in the brain. Thus, neither model is especially realistic in terms of biological plausibility; both are useful as models of cognitive processes. Other researchers have worked hard to develop models that take neuroanatomy and neurophysiology quite seriously (e.g., Granger, Wiebe, Taketani, & Lynch, 1996; Levy, 1996), but we haven't discussed those models here.

11. There are a great many of these unbalanced association pairs, in which a strong association (*salt–pepper*) doesn't go the other way (*pepper–salt*). Some researchers have argued that this means each node should be connected by two links, one for each direction. The link from *salt* to *pepper* would be strong, but the link from *pepper* to *salt* would be weak.

12. Most cognitive psychologists agree that the critical feature is different processes and representations that operate on them. Most of the evidence thus far indicates that hypothetical memory systems are separate in terms of the brain structures that support them. Many researchers are willing to bet that anatomic separability goes hand in hand with cognitive differences, but it has been difficult to prove that these anatomically separate systems are also cognitively separate.

13. The proposal that memory systems are separate grew out of the attempt to explain why amnesic patients are able to learn some tasks normally. Initially researchers proposed that some memory process was damaged in amnesia but that certain tasks didn't require that process—those were the tasks that amnesic patients could learn. No one could figure out what that process might be, however, so researchers began to consider the idea that some types of memory were intact in amnesia because they were supported by a separate memory system.

14. At least five: systems supporting declarative memory, repetition priming, motor skill learning, classical conditioning, and emotional conditioning.

15. It seems likely that these various memory systems all affect behavior simultaneously. For example, when you're learning a new sport, you often acquire information through declarative memory, and motor skill processes also contribute. Suppose you are an experienced tennis player and you want to start playing squash. A squash coach might tell you that your stroke looks too much like a tennis stroke: You keep your wrist locked instead of whipping it, as a squash player would. In this case, the motor skill system is producing behavior consistent with its experience (squash movement), and the declarative system is trying to influence the movement based on the coach's instruction (a declarative memory). Most researchers would agree that these systems may well influence one another directly and that more than one may influence behavior (as in the tennis and squash example), but how this works has not been examined in any detail.

16. Emotional conditioning. A conditioned stimulus (smell of alcohol in the hospital) was consistently paired with an unconditioned stimulus (painful needle), which leads to an unconditioned response (fear). With enough pairings, the conditioned stimulus leads to a conditioned response (uneasiness, a milder version of fear).

17. The tennis and squash example from question 15 is a good one. I think another example can be found whenever you are afraid of something but try to control your fear. Suppose I am afraid of snakes but I want to overcome my fear, so I hold a small python (also hoping to impress the friends I'm with). The emotional conditioning system might be telling me to drop the snake and run, whereas the declarative system would be calling up memories that show that this small snake poses no real threat and that I should hang on to it.

Chapter 9

1. The key results were that concrete word pairs were better remembered than abstract word pairs and that people reported using imagery with the concrete words. Paivio accounted for these data with the dual coding hypothesis, arguing that concrete words are better remembered because they can be coded two ways (verbally or as images), whereas abstract words can only be coded one way (verbally).

2. The two key results were that mentally rotating an object a greater distance took more time and that mentally rotating an object in depth was not harder than rotating it in the picture plane. This result was important because it was the first study that offered a clear way to study how images are transformed. It was also important because the data were very orderly, implying that a single (perhaps simple) process underlies mental rotation.

3. This question has been studied frequently, and researchers have found that bizarreness helps memory (Campos, Perez, & Gonzalez, 1997; McDaniel, Einstein, DeLosh, May, & Brady, 1995; Sharpe & Markham, 1992; Worthen, 1997, but see Ironsmith & Lutz, 1996; Wollen, Weber, & Lowry, 1972). Why

bizarreness helps is not really known. It is always possible that a bit more effort must be put into bizarre images or that they are more distinctive (but see McDaniel et al., 1995). The bizarreness effect was mentioned by the Greeks, but the precise reasons for the memory advantage of bizarre images is still unknown.

4. It depends on the event and on what you're doing, but when you listen to a sporting event, you are likely to engage mental imagery to understand what is happening in the game. For example, if you hear the announcer at a baseball game say, "It's a line drive straight up center field, but the runner at first is going anyway. The ball is caught, and the centerfielder is throwing it back to first to try to tag him up. It's going to be close, but now the runner at third is trying for home." If you're a fan, you're very likely to generate a visual image of this action. We've reviewed data showing that imagery interferes with visual tasks. Thus, listening to a sporting event that encourages you to visualize the action may not be a great idea if you are performing a task that is visually demanding, such as driving a car or using power tools.

5. Images might be an epiphenomenon, the results of experiments consistent with the idea that people use images may result from demand characteristics, and the results of imagery experiments can be explained by models of cognition that use propositions alone.

6. Propositions are relational; images do not describe a particular relationship. Propositions have syntax; images do not. Propositions have a truth value; images do not. Propositions are abstract; images are specific. Propositions are not spatial; images are inherently spatial.

7. They showed that demand characteristics are not a factor in imagery experiments. They proposed more specific imagery theories so more specific predictions could be tested. Most important, they collected data in a variety of paradigms that were easy to account for with an imagery theory but were increasingly difficult to account for with a theory that used only propositions.

8. Here's one way to account for this effect. You need to make two assumptions: Details are embedded in larger features, and you can have only a limited number of features active in working memory at one time. For example, suppose you are imaging a rabbit. Now suppose you are asked whether a rabbit has a pink nose. You need more information about the head. This information is embedded in the "head" representation, so you unpack the "head" representation to get more details about it. All the information about the head (including the information about the pink nose) cannot be included when one initially images a rabbit because of working memory limitations. When the question about the nose is asked, the representation is abandoned, and another is generated that includes more details about the head. The creation of this new representation leads to the epiphenomenal feeling of zooming in.

9. Psychologists distrust participants' introspections because in other areas of psychology participants' introspections are wrong at least as often as they are right. First, for many cognitive processes participants have no introspections at all; no one knows how their perceptual processes or motor control processes work. So what reason is there to think that for this particular cognitive function (answering certain types of questions about rabbits' noses and the like) you have reliable introspections? Second, people's introspections often are wrong. For example, participants who are comparing different brands of a product show a bias to select the product on the far right if they are arranged in a line. When asked whether such a factor might have influenced their behavior, however, almost all participants denied it, "usually with a worried glance at the interviewer suggesting that they were dealing with a madman" (Nisbett & Wilson, 1977, p. 244). People's introspections are fine as sources for hypotheses, but they are not trustworthy as data about mechanisms.

10. Images must be generated and maintained; then, they can be inspected and transformed.

11. Visual imagery concerns what objects look like (e.g., their color, their basic shape).

Spatial imagery concerns objects' locations (e.g., where objects are in a scene) and spatial transformations of objects in imagery (e.g., mental rotation). Visual imagery is in the ventral visual pathway (the temporal lobe), and spatial imagery is in the dorsal visual pathway (the parietal lobe).

12. The key result was discovered as follows. Participants were asked to image multipart objects on a visible grid. Xs appeared in the grids, and the response time to say whether the Xs would be on the imaged objects depended on the location of the Xs, such that if the Xs were on parts of the object that would be imaged first, response times were short. If the Xs were on parts of the object that would be imaged later, response times were longer. This result was interpreted as showing that participants created the image part by part, and as soon as they imaged the part where the X was, they could answer the question as to whether the X covered the part.

13. Imagery seems to have many properties in common with Baddeley's visuospatial sketchpad. Imagery is limited in how much it can contain, its capacity can be increased through chunking, and it seems to have dissociable visual and spatial aspects.

14. We've briefly mentioned that imagery might aid perception. If you're imaging an object, it is easier to perceive an object that matches your image, but that situation may be rare in the real world. Imagery may play an important role in certain types of problem solving. For example, a Nobel Prize-winning physicist has said that he often thought of physics problems not in terms of formal proofs but in terms of imaginary physical models of the systems (Feynman & Leighton, 1985). For a brief review of other reports of the importance of imagery in scientific problem solving, see Shepard and Cooper (1986). For a more detailed discussion of the uses of imagery in creativity, see Finke (1996).

15. I have to admit that I believe I don't have much ability to imagine odors. But there are data indicating that people can. In one experiment (Djordjevic, Zatorre, Petrides, & Jones-Gotman, 2004a; see also Djordjevic, Zatorre,

Petrides, & Jones-Gotman, 2004b), people were to try to detect very faint smalls while they either imagined an odor that matched the odor or did not match. People will more accurate when the imagined odor matched the faint odor that they were trying to detect. To ensure that the effect wasn't due to just *thinking* about the object, in another condition subjects did visual imagery of the matching object or a different object; in that case, there was no effect. As we've discussed in some detail, it's easy to determine the function of visual imagery. But the possible function of imagery for odors is lost on me. It may be that it doesn't serve much of a function, and our ability to do it is rather accidental to the way that the mind evolved. If you can think of a function, e-mail me.

Chapter 10

1. The three approaches are efficiency theories, which propose setting a criterion of efficiency and selecting the most efficient movement; synergy theories, which propose that because most movements are constrained by synergies of the body, the degrees of freedom problem is not as bad as it first seems; and the mass spring theory, which proposes that because only the endpoints of movements are planned, not the trajectories, the degrees of freedom problem is not as difficult as it first appears.

2. Straight paths in Cartesian space, minimum distance of joint movement, minimum muscle torque, minimum muscle stiffness, minimum jerk of the moving effector.

3. Yes, it's possible. Synergies are biases in which joints or muscles work together. They are not strict rules dictating that joints or muscles must always work together in a particular way.

4. The heart of the degrees of freedom problem is that we can make any movement in more than one way. If there were only one way to move your body to reach a goal (a unique solution) then the degrees of freedom problem wouldn't exist. But the ability to

make each movement in more than one way is not a liability. It is what gives you flexibility in making movements so you can make effective movements even if the effector is partly disabled (e.g., if you have a cast on your wrist).

5. This is a problem, but it can be solved by proposing that in such situations you actually choose more than one endpoint. The first endpoint might be to the side of the obstacle, and the second endpoint would be the target object. In that way, you could reach around obstacles.

6. It contains a full set of commands for a movement sequence. The commands can be executed without the need for peripheral feedback. The program can be applied to more than one set of muscles.

7. In a key-pressing task, the time between key presses is well predicted by the number of nodes that need to be traversed in a hierarchical representation of the sequence.

8. The purpose of feedback is to detect error and thereby enable the correction of error. No matter how many times you've practiced a movement, there can always be some error in its execution; perhaps the environment is slightly different than it has been in the past, or perhaps there is always some slight variability in the way the muscles execute commands. Whatever the source, it is sensible to monitor the movement outcome so it can be corrected, if necessary.

9. You should be able to duplicate a piece of the hierarchy and plug it into a new hierarchy with very little change; you simply need to change one control node so it now includes the imported piece of hierarchy.

10. On the one hand, vision is quite helpful to improving the accuracy of ongoing movements; movements are definitely more accurate with vision than without it. On the other hand, you don't need all that much visual information during an ongoing movement. The exact amount depends on the duration of each visual "snapshot" and on the amount of time these snapshots are separated, but movements can still be quite accurate, even if participants have visual information during only 30% of the movement.

11. Almost all of us have this sensation after sleeping on an arm—we wake up and find that we cannot feel that arm. Indeed, if you try to move it, the arm flops about much as Ian described his limbs working when his problem first developed.

12. A big problem is that proprioception is difficult to manipulate. Unlike the case for vision or hearing, in which the experimenter can create stimuli for the participant, proprioceptive inputs are difficult to control. It used to be believed that if you apply a blood pressure cuff to a person's arm for a while that proprioceptive input would be cut off, but even that rather crude manipulation doesn't seem to work.

13. Generalization, long-term retention, and automaticity. Automaticity seems to occur for all skills (in the neurologically intact person).

14. These conditions are more effective training because the greater variability gives you a more accurate picture of the relationship between the movement parameters that you control and the outcome of the movement.

15. Implicit motor sequencing, explicit motor sequencing, adaptation, and arbitrary visual-motor association.

16. Because a program is, by definition, applicable to multiple effectors, it must represent where to move in space (it's not representing the muscle movements to get there). We might guess that some parameters would be the *distance* between the targets (you can make the movements large or small); the *force* of the movements (you can make the movements hard or soft); and the *speed* of the movements (you can move fast or slow). There has been a good deal of experimentation directed at the generalizability of skills, and it confirms what your intuition would tell you; many skills can be generalized along these dimensions.

17. It is important because it captures a common practice in the real world. Coaches give verbal instructions to athletes. What athletes remember is in declarative memory; the coach tells a diver that she's arching her back too much as she enters the water, for example. She remembers that information in declarative memory as she's on the board, preparing for her next dive. Then, this memory influences the next dive—she doesn't arch her back as much. How did this declarative memory influence motor skill? The present theories have little to say about this phenomenon.

18. It would be some indication that attention and awareness are separable. Normally, we think that if we are attending to something, then we are aware of it. The results of these studies have been controversial, but the basic story is that some researchers report that if participants are distracted with a secondary task, learning of the unconscious skill is disrupted, whereas other researchers hold that the learning is not much affected by the secondary task. As of this writing, the issue awaits clarification.

Chapter 11

1. Rational models are those in which decisions are internally consistent, that is, in which decisions don't conflict with one another. Normative models of decision making propose a criterion by which choices can be compared and a best choice can be selected.

2. They are similar because they are both criteria that could be used in normative theories of decision making. They differ in that expected value is based solely on the financial return that can be expected from a particular choice, whereas expected utility considers the value a person places on the return and the likelihood that the return will be obtained.

3. Their choices do not show transitivity, and their choices change, depending on the problem frame.

4. I doubt it. Utility theory might help in explaining why people play lotteries because the utility of the huge prize is so much greater than the utility of the small amount needed to play. (Although the expected value of a lottery is so abysmally bad, it's still difficult to understand why people play.) That is not true of typical casino games, where the amount bet and the payoff are not very different. Why, then, do people gamble at casinos? As you would guess, the reasons are many and complex, but a large part of the reason probably results from people believing that they have special knowledge that gives them an edge over the house, if not consistently, than at least at particular moments of play. If you want to see a cornucopia of these (useless) methods, there are many for sale via the World Wide Web.

5. You're walking down the street in Washington, DC, and you want to by a soda. You see a sign on a pushcart ahead indicating that sodas cost $.75, but you see a pushcart across the street where they cost $.70. Would you cross the street to save a nickel?" It's safe to say that some people who would refuse the bet would nevertheless cross the street (incurring a very small risk of being killed) to save a nickel.

6. *Representativeness*: An event is judged to be more likely to belong to a category if it has the features of the category that are deemed important. *Availability*: The likelihood of an event is assumed to be proportional to the ease with which examples of the event can be brought to mind. *Anchoring and adjustment*: The person starts with some initial probability value (anchor) by doing a partial calculation of the problem or by using a probability statement in the problem, then adjusts that initial estimate upward or downward on the basis of other information in the problem.

7. Sample size information, which is important in judging the consistency or stability of a probability. People ignore base rate information (information about the frequency or likelihood of an event in a population) if they get any other information that helps them evaluate a particular event.

8. Gigerenzer argues that people's cognitive systems are biased to use frequencies of events, not probabilities of events. By giving participants problems that describe probabilities, we give them information that is in a format that their cognitive systems cannot readily use.

9. Suppose that people who read lie detector test results are 80% accurate in detecting liars. (I don't think that they are, but let's ignore

that for the moment.) Suppose now that I am an employer; some of my employees are stealing from the company, and I want to determine who. I want all my employees to submit to a lie detector test. Employee 1 walks in and claims not to have stolen, but the operator of the lie detector equipment says that Employee 1 is lying. What are the chances that Employee 1 has stolen from the company? The fact is that we don't know the chances. To figure that out, we would need some base rate information. If 95% of the people in the company aren't stealing, then the chances that this person is stealing are only 40%. When you're administering a lie detector test, you almost never know the base rate of lying, and because the lie detector test is imperfect, base rate information is essential to tell you the chances that any one person is lying.

10. When planning a project, people consider the different components of the project and estimate the time it will take to perform each one. These estimates might be accurate, but people seldom take into account the odds that something will go wrong. The probability of any one thing going wrong is quite low, but there are so many potential things that could go wrong, in aggregate the odds of a problem may be fairly high. People use the total time and fail to adjust adequately.

11. Your memory system is wisely *using* baserate information, instead of ignoring it, as is often done in decision making. When the script "going to a restaurant" is being played out, the server usually offers a menu—the base rate for that occurrence is very high. So, when you're recalling a particular instance, if you are not sure that it *didn't* happen, it's reasonable to go with the baserate and assume that it did.

12. Deductive reasoning allows us to state that a conclusion must be true, given the premises. Inductive reasoning allows us to say only that a conclusion is more or less likely, given the premises.

13. No, familiarity does not seem to be the critical feature. Keep in mind that people can perform well on the problem, even if it concerns unfamiliar material (e.g., tattoos and cassava), and they sometimes don't perform well, even if it concerns familiar material (e.g., what sort of food and drink go together well). The ideas of permission and precaution schemas seem to better describe participants' performance in these tasks.

14. Johnson-Laird's mental models theory, which emphasizes meaning; Oaksford & Chater's probability model, which emphasizes the practical uses of reasoning and ways of gaining more information; and the dual process models, which emphasize that each person may be capable of both simple associative reasoning and of more complex formal reasoning.

15. Case-based reasoning seems somewhat less interesting than other forms of reasoning, perhaps because it seems as if it is hardly reasoning at all. Nevertheless, it seems likely that we often remember courses of action we pursued in the past if they worked out well. When you see that the time is 10:50 and you know that you have a class in 10 min, is it really necessary to reason about your next course of action, or can you rely on your memory of similar situations to guide you? This question is not settled, but my money is on memory.

16. No. To draw such a conclusion would actually be a to commit a logical fallacy.

> People don't reason on the Wason card selection task.
>
> The Wason card selection task is a reasoning task.
>
> Therefore, people don't reason on all reasoning tasks.

Chapter 12

1. Heuristics are needed to select operators; most problem spaces are too large for a brute force search, and if the problem is unfamiliar, we need some way to reduce the search space.

2. Hill climbing, working backward, and means–ends analysis.

3. First, identify the difference between your current state and the goal state. Second, search for an operator that addresses the largest difference between your current state and goal state. Third, if you cannot apply that operator, set a subgoal to reach a state where you can apply that operator. Continue until there is no difference between your current state and the goal state.

4. Yes, means–ends analysis would work. Your initial goal is to reach the highest hill. You would first set an operator of moving toward the top of the hill. If you hit an obstacle to moving toward the top of the highest hill (e.g., you were at the top of a small hill, or you faced a wall), you would set a subgoal to get to a state in which you would again be able to move toward the top of the hill (e.g., going downhill briefly).

5. Chess has the larger problem space because it has more pieces and each piece can move in more ways. You could reduce the problem space of chess or checkers by reducing the number of pieces or restricting the options for how the pieces move.

6. It seems clear that working backward won't help because you don't know the goal state. Hill climbing can't work for the same reason: If you don't know the goal, you don't know what constitutes moving toward the goal. The average person might try a brute force search but would probably give up quickly. Means–ends analysis might work if you could set subgoals that would get you closer to the goal. One possible subgoal might be determining that you have the first number right by feeling a bearing fall in the lock, for example.

7. Background knowledge can help you see the deep structure of the problem, not just the surface features. Background knowledge may also yield automatization of some of the operators, which frees working memory to work on higher-level strategies to address the problem.

8. The key problem appears to be in noticing that an analogy is appropriate in the first place. When people know that an analogy is available, they can usually (but not always) map from the familiar problem to the new problem. Unfortunately, people are too easily distracted by the surface features of a problem rather than the deep features, so they often fail to use analogies.

9. In both cases, you inappropriately apply past knowledge to a new problem. In functional fixedness, you use an object in a way that you have used it in the past; in a set effect, you apply a problem-solving procedure that you have used in the past.

10. This technique is called incubation, and although it sounds plausible, the evidence that it works is far from overwhelming (Goldman, Wolters, & Winograd, 1992; Smith & Blankenship, 1991), although one more recent study claimed that sleep, not just time, would help problem solving (Wagner, Gais, Haider, Verleger, & Born, 2004). It seems plausible because the impasse may be caused by functional fixedness or set effects: You keep retrieving the same nonworkable ideas. If you leave the problem, it seems possible that you would represent the problem differently on your return, avoiding the impasse.

11. Creativity, although a topic of great intrinsic interest, has been notoriously difficult for psychologists to study. A big part of the problem is that it is hard to study; you can't simply say to someone, "Okay, I've got my equipment all set, the video camera is on, go ahead and be creative NOW!" Nevertheless, we can look at creative behaviors retrospectively and see that they have some of the characteristics of insight problems: Creativity involves reformulating components that we are familiar with and making new, greater wholes from the components. The brilliance of a concept such as Ebay is in both its familiarity (a garage sale is an opportunity to find treasure in someone else's junk) and its exploitation of new technology (you can search through the junk at computer speed). Creativity can also be manifest by seeing underlying similarities where others had not. The operating system of the Macintosh computer was a creative product because it created an analogy to a desktop, a concept that noncomputer users were familiar with and that was readily applicable to computer use. The analogy was so compelling that it became the standard in the personal computer industry.

12. Experts have more domain knowledge than novices, and their knowledge is better organized; *better* in this case means that it is organized according to deep structure, which makes the knowledge more readily applicable to new problems. Experts may well use different procedures in solving problems, but there is no strong evidence supporting that conjecture yet.

13. Practice is not merely engaging in the activity. Deliberate practice implies engaging in the activity to improve proficiency, which means that the person must be motivated, the task must be at the correct level to encourage improvement, there must be immediate corrective feedback, and there must be repetition.

14. A large working memory capacity will make someone a good problem solver. Proficiency in setting subgoals may also be a helpful problem-solving strategy.

15. On the face of it, we almost never see an expert who has not engaged in a lot of practice. The caveat is that all the data are correlational; the person who did all that practicing did so because he or she wanted to practice a lot. So, perhaps people who practice a lot are destined to become experts, but if you just took a person at random and made him or her practice the violin 6 hours a day for 10 years, you'd end up with a good violinist but not an expert. In other words, the correlational nature of the evidence may lead us to conclude that practice is a necessary condition for expertise, but it may not be a sufficient condition.

16. I don't think it is. In most insight problems (e.g., the candle and radiation problems), we are not struggling to juggle in mind all the different elements of the problem. Rather, the difficulty is restructuring the problem space, and that is not especially demanding of working memory.

17. The first and best advice is simply to practice. The next best advice is to look for the deep structure of problems. Try to avoid simply applying formulas as a series of steps, as though for a recipe. Instead, try to understand what those steps are doing—in other words, try to understand the subgoals that each step or group of steps is achieving. One way to do that may be to compare problems to see how they are similar or different.

Chapter 13

1. Definitions of language differ, but most of them include these characteristics: Language is communicative; the relationship between elements in the language and their meaning is arbitrary; the pattern of elements is structured; language is generative, meaning that the basic elements can be combined in an infinite number of ways; and language is dynamic, meaning it is always evolving.

2. Competence is people's knowledge of grammar (the rules they use to produce sentences). Performance refers to the sentences people actually produce. Competence is not the same as performance because the sentences people actually produce (performance) are influenced not only by their knowledge of grammar (competence), but also by other cognitive factors, such as working memory limitations, or social factors, such as the desire to stop talking when interrupted.

3. They can't capture certain key properties of the way we produce sentences. For example, they cannot explain why we accept as grammatical sentences with words that we never hear together, such as "Color green ideas sleep furiously." Also, the machinery of word-chain grammars cannot produce sentences with remote dependencies (either . . . or) with other grammatical structures embedded within them.

4. It's possible because the context and your background knowledge limit the number of interpretations you will entertain as being possible. Because of your past experience with children, you know that the child is saying (roughly), "Let's go get a cookie now" and is unlikely to be saying, "You, me, and the cookie should all leave now." Imagine now that the child says, "Abe, Sarah kick now." You don't know whether Abe kicked Sarah or Sarah kicked Abe because background knowledge doesn't help.

5. Sequences of sounds are not completely random—consonants and vowels tend to alternate—and this is doubtless because such combinations are easier to pronounce, given the musculature of the tongue, lips, and so on. Some researchers (MacNeilage & Davis, 2000) have argued that they have uncovered four sequential sound patterns that are very easy to produce, given these factors. In addition, they claim that these patterns are (a) commonly found in infant babbling, (b) commonly found in languages worldwide, and (c) found in proto-towords—that is, hypothetical words from extinct languages that would have given rise to words in today's languages.

6. Children worldwide go through the same stages of language development and make the same sorts of errors. Children also learn language incredibly rapidly, and this rapidity is subject to a sensitive period. Most impressive, children who are exposed to impoverished language will actually go beyond this input, and end up producing more language-like speech than what they were exposed to. One feature you'd want to evaluate is the extent to which they seem to use words as abstract symbols and not simply as part of a stimulus–response pair. Roughly speaking, that's the difference between knowing that *apple* has the referent of the piece of fruit and being able to use the term *apple* in many different contexts and knowing that if you make a particular hand motion, you often get a piece of apple in return. The second thing you'd want to know is whether they have any appreciation of grammar. As described earlier in the chapter, grammar is central to language because it gives language its flexibility and power.

7. Using words outside the context in which they were learned (which would be evidence for understanding and using words as symbols) and a sensitivity to word order (which would be evidence for syntax). It's hard to draw a firm line for which the near side definitely is language and the far side definitely is not. Apes can do some of the things that characterize language, and they do them in a rudimentary way. To most psychologists, that's not really language.

8. Language probably has some influence on thought in terms of the likelihood that you will think in a particular way or the speed with which you can think a particular way. These effects are likely to be small, in most instances, however. The exception may be the use of number terms in the (probably few) languages that do not have number terms. Culture, not language, may have a bigger impact on cognition.

9. They should be smarter, on average, than people who speak one language. If certain types of cognition are easier in one language than another, then bilinguals have more types of cognition at their disposal than people who speak just one language. At this point, there is no conclusive evidence that being bilingual makes people any smarter than being monolingual (Hakuta, 1986; Okoh, 1980).

10. Answers to these sorts of questions are seldom straightforward, but based solely on the critical period, it would seem that introducing a foreign language as early as possible (instead of waiting until the upper grades, as at most schools) would make sense. It would also indicate that kids who do not speak English might be able to pick it up fairly effectively if they were immersed in it, and teaching them in their native language might come at the cost of missing the critical period, during which they might learn English relatively easily.

Chapter 14

1. Phonemes, words, sentences, texts.

2. Phonemes are produced differently by different speakers and differently by the same speaker in different contexts. There is no break in the speech stream, making it hard to discern where one word ends and another begins. For sentences, the right assignment of phrase structure must be made to groups of words, and sometimes sentences are actually ambiguous in terms of the number of interpretations that are possible, even though they don't seem ambiguous when we hear them. For texts, speakers can't tell us absolutely everything so we must make inferences or assumptions to fill in the gaps, but it's not obvious how we know which assumptions to make.

3. Grammars are relevant to the level of the sentence.

4. One reason song lyrics are difficult to understand is that they are often quite odd ("'Scuse me, while I kiss the sky"). There is simply no telling what the words are going to be. People do use information about what is likely to have been said to understand speech. At the same time, predictability clearly is not the only source of information because we are perfectly able to understand the strangest string of words when they are uttered slowly and clearly. But if other cues are degraded—perhaps the phonemes are slurred and they are uttered as many instruments play—the cues of what the words are likely to mean may be all the more important.

5. The other meanings sort of make sense, but they are decidedly odd. No one has ever heard of a variety of flies called "time flies," and there is seldom a reason to assess the pace of flies. But the first interpretation of the words "time flies" is a metaphor for time moving quickly, as in the familiar saying "time flies when you're having fun." These observations give us a hint that meaning, or semantics, will play a role in the processes that assign phrase structures for sentence interpretation.

6. We can use high-level meaning information to fill in phonemes that are severely degraded (phoneme restoration effect); we perceive phonemes that are slightly degraded as being normal phonemes (categorical perception); and we use visual information to supplement auditory information (McGurk effect).

7. One route is a direct matching process between the spelling of the word and the lexical entry spelling. The other route translates the spelling of the word into a sound and matches this sound to the sound entries in the lexicon.

8. A garden path sentence is one that seems to make no sense toward the end of the sentence because the grammar seems wrong. This occurs because the listener was parsing a sentence and toward the end of the sentence a word was perceived that made it clear that the ongoing parsing scheme was incorrect. Garden path sentences are important because errors in parsing are helpful in determining how parsing is performed and because they show us that the mind parses sentences as words are perceived; we do not wait for the sentence to be completed before we start parsing.

9. People appear to draw inferences when the text they are reading has some information that is missing or inconsistent. The chief debate is over how the cognitive system recognizes that information is missing. Most researchers think that texts are compared with information from long-term memory and with the text itself to find inconsistencies (in one of my favorite examples, Madame Bovary's eyes change color during the course of the novel) or missing information (e.g., simple inferences from long-term memory such as that nails are usually driven by hammers).

10. Under normal circumstances, the context of a sentence biases lexical access so only the appropriate meaning of an ambiguous word becomes active. In the case of a pun, both meanings become active and enter awareness. Note that a simple dual interpretation is not enough for humor ("This is not a very good spring" is not funny). There must be something about the context that makes both meanings potentially applicable, as when a waitress told my table that the only dessert left was pudding, whereupon an acquaintance countered, "You're pudding me on." (The rest of us hid behind our menus.)

11. The text would be criminally boring. The text "Billy walked slowly to the front of the room. The teacher waited for him" would turn into the following:

> Billy—he's a student in the class—was walking toward the front of the room. By "front" of the room, I mean the place where the blackboard is and the way all the students face when they're sitting. Anyway, he was walking on the floor; I mean, he wasn't walking on top of the desks or anything. And he was walking slowly—not very slowly, to the point that it might take him an hour to reach the front of the room, but just an average sort of slow. I think he was walking slowly because he was afraid. I can't be sure of that, because he didn't say so . . . .

This sort of demonstration indicates that not only can we draw inferences as we read texts, but also doing so is a normal part of reading and saves a good deal of time.

12. This example indicates that sentence processing is sensitive to higher-level concerns. In this case, you would decode the meaning of the sentence, recognize that it was inappropriate given the context, and interpret it as sarcastic.

Glossary

Abstract construct A theoretical set of processes and representations that you think are useful in explaining some data. An example would be the articulatory loop of working memory.

Abstract word One that does not refer to a physical object.

Accommodation A cue to distance in visual perception. It depends on sensing how much the lens of the eye has changed shape in order to focus the image on the retina; the shape change varies with the distance of the object.

Acoustic confusion effect Errors in primary memory based on sound (e.g., thinking one heard *g* instead of *d*). The presence of such errors indicates that participants use an acoustic code in primary memory on the task.

Acquired dyslexia A reading problem caused by brain damage in adults who were normal readers before the injury.

Activation The level of energy or excitement of a node, indicating that the concept the node represents is more accessible for use by the cognitive system.

Adaptation A type of motor skill learning in which a new motor response is learned to a visual stimulus (e.g., learning to use a computer mouse). The way that the stimulus and response go together is systematic, which contrasts with arbitrary visual-motor associations.

Addressing system Scheme to organize memories in which each memory is given a unique address that can be used to look it up.

Algorithm A formula that can be applied to choice situations. It has the advantage of producing consistent outcomes, but algorithms may be complex and difficult to compute. Algorithms often are compared with heuristics.

Amygdala A collection of nuclei believed to be especially important for processing emotion.

Analog Representation that has important properties of pictures (e.g., that it occurs in a spatial medium) but is not itself a picture. Mental images are usually referred to as analog representations.

Anatomic dissociation Evidence that two different tasks are supported by different parts of the brain.

Anchoring and adjustment A heuristic used to estimate probabilities in which the person starts with some initial probability value (anchor) by doing a partial calculation of the problem or by using a probability statement in the problem, and then adjusting that initial estimate upward or downward based on other information in the problem.

Anterior Toward the front of the head (synonym of "rostral").

Anticipatory postural adjustment Muscle contractions that counteract changes in the center of gravity that occur due to other movements (e.g., reaching movements).

Arbitrary visual-motor association An association that must be learned between a visual stimulus and a motor response. The relation between the two is arbitrary (e.g., a red light signifying that one should depress the brake pedal of the car). There is nothing inherent in redness that signifies this action. Arbitrary visual-motor associations can be contrasted with adaptation tasks, in which the visual stimulus and motor response go together in some systematic way.

Articulatory control process The process that allows one to enter information into the phonological store; it is literally the process of talking to yourself.

Articulatory suppression Refers to demanding that participants keep the articulatory system busy with nonsense during encoding (usually by saying "thethethethe" or something similar), thereby ensuring that they will not code stimuli in the phonological store.

Associationism The belief that knowledge begins with sensory information and that sensations may combine to form more complex ideas.

Atmosphere A situation in which two premises of a syllogism are both either positive or negative or use the same quantifier. People are biased to accept as valid a conclusion that maintains the atmosphere.

Atmospheric perspective A cue to depth. Objects in the distance look less distinct because they are viewed through more dust and water particles in the air that scatter light.

Attention The mechanism for continued cognitive processing. All sensory information receives some cognitive processing; attention ensures continued cognitive processing.

Attentional blink In a rapid serial visual presentation, observers have trouble identifying the second target if it appears anywhere between 100 to 600 ms after the first target.

Automatic A process that takes few or no attentional resources and that happens without intention, given the right set of stimuli in the environment.

Availability A heuristic in which the likelihood of an event is evaluated by the ease with which examples of the event can be called to mind.

Babbling The second stage of language development. It includes more consonant-vowel combinations than cooing does, and repetitions (e.g., "dadadada").

Base rate The frequency of an event in the general population. When judging the likelihood that an event occurred, people tend to ignore the base rate if they are given any other information about the event.

Behaviorism An approach to psychology that claims that the appropriate subject matter of psychology is behavior, not mental processes. It also emphasizes that psychologists should focus on that which is observable (i.e., stimuli in the environment and people's overt behaviors).

Bias In signal detection theory, a measure of the participant's bias to either report or not report the presence of a signal. Bias is measured independently of the participant's actual ability to detect signals.

Bottom-up processing Processing that starts with unprocessed sensory information and builds toward more conceptual representations.

Broca's area An area in the left frontal lobe that is important for language.

Brute force search A problem-solving strategy in which all possible answers are examined until the correct solution is found.

Case study A type of scientific research in which a single individual is observed on a number of occasions. Case studies are usually used only when there is a rather unusual individual to be studied.

Categorical perception Refers to the fact that people do not perceive slight variations in how phonemes are pronounced. Phonemes can vary along certain dimensions with no cost in their perceivability.

Category A group of objects that have something in common.

Caudal Toward the back of the head (synonym of "posterior").

Caudate Subcortical structure closely related to the putamen that is important in movement and likely in some cognitive functions.

Central executive The cognitive supervisor and scheduler, which integrates information from different sources and decides on strategies to be used in tasks and allocates attention.

Cerebellum A very large structure at the back and toward the bottom of the brain, it contributes to movement, and some higher forms of cognition.

Chunk A unit of knowledge that can be decomposed into smaller units of knowledge. Similarly, smaller units of knowledge can be combined ("chunked") into a single unit of knowledge (e.g., chunking the numbers 1, 9, 0, and 0 into a unit to represent the year 1900).

Cingulate gyrus A gyrus in the medial part of the brain. It's function is not clear, but it may contribute to attention and working memory.

Classical conditioning A training procedure that produces a conditioned reflex.

Classical view of categorization The view that concepts are represented as lists of necessary and sufficient properties.

Coarticulation Making a movement in a way that anticipates future movements.

Cognitive economy The principle of designing a cognitive system in a way that conserves resources (e.g., memory storage space).

College sophomore problem The concern that findings from cognitive psychology may not generalize well because most experiments are conducted on college sophomores.

Combinatorial explosion The phenomenon in which the number of states in the problem space increases very rapidly, even with modest increases in the number of attributes of the problem that might be changed. For example, if one tries to look four moves ahead in a chess game instead of two moves ahead, the number of states in the problem much more than doubles.

Competence People's knowledge of grammar, that is, the rules that they use to construct sentences. Competence is contrasted with performance, which refers to the way that people actually talk. Performance is influenced not only by the rules of grammar, but also by lapses of memory and other factors that make the sentences people utter less grammatical than their competence indicates.

Computational approach The dominant approach discussed throughout the book, it assumes that the information provided by the environment is impoverished and that the

cognitive system must do a lot of computation to derive the richness of environment.

Computed tomography A technique using X-ray technology for showing the three-dimensional structure of the brain, important for lesion studies. It does not show activation.

Concept The mental representation that allows one to generalize about objects in a category.

Conclusion A statement of fact derived by logical processes. One may confidently propose that a conclusion is true or false within a problem based on its logical relation to the premises. Whether the conclusion is true in the real world depends on the truth or falseness of the premises.

Concrete word Concrete words refer to real objects in the word (e.g., pencil, train).

Conditional statements A logical form composed of three statements. The first premise states, "If condition p is met, then q follows." The second premise states whether p or q is true. The third is a conclusion about p or q.

Conditioned reflex A reflex that is learned (i.e., that is the product of experience).

Conditioned response In classical conditioning, the response elicited by a conditioned stimulus after training. It is usually similar but not identical to the unconditioned stimulus.

Conditioned stimulus In classical conditioning, a stimulus that before training does not elicit a consistent response. During training, its presentation is paired with the unconditioned stimulus.

Conjunctive search In a visual search task, a search in which the target differs from the distractors on two features, for example, the target is large and red and although some of the distractors are large and some are red, none of the distractors are both large and red. It requires a conjunction of two features (largeness and redness) to identify the target.

Construction Similar to the idea of reconstruction. Reconstruction is the process by which memories are recalled. Construction is a particular memory that feels to the participant like a real memory but has no basis in fact.

Content-addressable storage Scheme by which to organize memories in which the content of the memory itself serves as the storage address.

Context Information about the time and place in which a memory was encoded.

Context effect The idea that memory will be better if the physical environment at encoding matches the physical environment at retrieval.

Continuous task A task in which there is no obvious beginning and ending to each trial; there is a continuous stream of stimuli and responses (e.g., a pursuit tracking task). Compare with Discrete task.

Control nodes In a hierarchical sequencing representation, the control nodes tell the movement nodes what to do.

Controlled retrieval When a person actively tries not to retrieve a declarative memory.

Convergence A cue to distance. As an object gets closer, an observer crosses his or her eyes more to keep the image of the object on the center of the fovea of each eye. The extent to which the eyes are crossed can be used as a cue to distance.

Converging operations The strategy of using multiple techniques to address a single question, to make up for the fact that each technique has some flaws.

Conversational implicature The tendency for people to treat the language of logic as though it has the same meaning as everyday language.

Conversion error An error in dealing with a syllogism in which a person reverses one of the premises. For example, the premise reads "All As are Bs," and the participant believes that it is also true that "All Bs are As."

Cooing The first stage of language in which the baby makes long drawn-out vowel sounds ("oooooooh") or consonant-vowel combinations ("gaaaaah").

Critical features Features of objects that don't change as the object undergoes various transformations (e.g., gets larger or rotates in space).

Critical period A window of opportunity during which a particular type of learning will be easy for the organism. If the critical period is missed, however, the learning will be difficult or even impossible.

CT See Computed tomography.

Cue Some information from the environment (or that the participant is able to generate) as a starting point for retrieval.

Cued recall A way of testing memory in which the experimenter provides the participant the time and place in which the memory was encoded, as well as some hint about the content of the to-be-remembered material (e.g., "Tell me the words I read to you an hour ago. One of them was something to eat.").

Cutaneous receptors Receptors in and under the skin. Some of these respond when the skin is displaced by pressure. This is important in detecting the pressure exerted by muscle contraction, as when you grip a glass.

Decay Refers to the hypothesis that forgetting results (at least in part) from the spontaneous decomposition of memories over time.

Decision making A situation in which a person is presented with two or more explicit courses of action, with the requirement that he or she select just one.

Declarative memory Memory for facts and events, often contrasted with procedural memory.

Deductive reasoning Problems to which one can apply formal logic and derive an objectively correct solution.

Deep processing Thinking about the meaning of stimulus materials at encoding.

Deep structure In language, the deep structure is the representation of a sentence constructed according to a basic set of phrase structure rules, without any transformations applied to the resulting representation. If transformations are applied, the sentence might be turned into a question or be phrased in the passive voice, for example.

Default value A characteristic that is a part of a schema that is assumed to be true in the absence of other information. For example, unless one is told otherwise, one assumes that a dog is furry; furriness is a default characteristic for dogs.

Degrees of freedom problem The problem of how the mind selects which way to execute a movement, given that there are many ways to make any given movement.

Demand characteristics Anything about the way the experiment is conducted that signals to the participant what the desired, appropriate, or expected behavior is.

Dependent variable In an experiment, the dependent variable is the one that the experimenter measures with the expectation that its value will depend on changes in the independent variable. Only experimental research uses dependent variables.

Depth of processing A description of how one thinks about material at encoding. Depth refers to the degree of semantic involvement (i.e., the word's meaning).

Description invariance A requirement of rational decision making, it is the idea that people will consistently make the same choice irrespective of how the problem is described to them as long as the basic structure of the choices is the same. In fact, description invariance is not met.

Descriptive research A type of scientific research in which one seeks only to describe the world as it is, not to describe relationships among different entities in the world. It can be contrasted with relational research and with experimental research.

Deterministic The view that all acts (including human acts) have antecedent causes in the physical world.

Dichotic listening Task in which participants listen to material on headphones, and each earpiece plays a different message. Participants are to attend to just one message and must shadow that message to show that they are doing so. The dichotic listening task is often used to study how much the unattended material is processed.

Digit span task Participants hear a list of digits read to them, one digit per second, and must immediately recite the list in the correct order. This task has been used to measure primary memory capacity since the turn of the 20th century.

Discrete task A task in which each trial has a discrete beginning and ending (e.g., a simple response time task). Compare with Continuous task.

Disjunctive search In a visual search task, a search in which the target differs from the distractors on just one feature (e.g., the target is larger than the distractors or the target is the only stimulus that has a horizontal line in it).

Distractor Items that appear on a visual search experiment trial that are not the target item that the participant is to find. Also used in recognition memory experiments to denote incorrect responses. Synonyms of distractor in memory experiments are *foil* and *lure*.

Distributed representation A representational scheme in which a concept is distributed across multiple units.

Dorsal Toward the top of the head.

Dual coding hypothesis Paivio's proposal that concepts can be encoded verbally, in terms of mental images, or both.

Dual process models Models of reasoning that propose that reasoning is supported by a fast, unconscious, associative process, and by a slower, sequential process associated with consciousness.

Dual route models of reading Models that posit two mechanisms for reading. One route uses a direct matchup of the spelling and entries in the lexicon, and the other translates the letters into sounds and then matches the sound to the auditory entry in the lexicon.

Dual task paradigm A paradigm requiring participants to perform two tasks simultaneously. It is used to study the limits of attention.

Early filter A theory proposing that attention acts as a filter early in the processing stream. Implies that all sensory stimuli are analyzed for their physical characteristics, but only those that are attended to are analyzed for their semantic characteristics.

Echoic memory Name given to the auditory variety of sensory memory.

Ecological approach Emphasizes that the environment has rich sources of information in it and that the computations the visual system needs to perform are probably not that extensive.

Ecological validity The extent to which an experiment represents "the real world." High

Glossary **511**

ecological validity means that the conditions of the experiment seem similar to the ones that would be encountered in everyday life.

EEG   See Electroencephalogram.

Effector   Part of the body that you use to have an effect on the environment (e.g., the hand, the foot).

Efficiency theory   A solution to the degrees of freedom problem in motor control, which claims that movements are evaluated for their efficiency, and the most efficient movement is selected.

Electroencephalogram   A technique for recording electrical activity of the brain, in which electrodes are placed outside the scalp. It is used to localize brain activity and is especially useful for its temporal accuracy.

Emotional conditioning   Classical conditioning in which the unconditioned response is an emotion.

Empiricism   One of the three principles of the scientific method. It means that one is dedicated to learning about the world through conducting experiments.

Empiricist   The view that most human knowledge is acquired over one's lifetime through experience.

Epiphenomenon   A phenomenon that is not related to the function of a system. Some researchers argued that images are an epiphenomenon; the sensation of "seeing" an image is real, but that doesn't mean that the sensation has anything to do with the actual cognitive task being performed.

Episodic buffer   A component of the working memory model of primary memory. It stores information in a multimodal code; that is, the code can represent visual, auditory, or semantic information.

Episodic memory   Memory that is associated with a particular time and place, with a this-happened-to-me feeling.

ERPs   See Event-related potentials.

Event-related potentials   A method of averaging EEG waves from tens or hundreds of trials to eliminate random variation from trial to trial.

Exemplar   An instance of a category.

Exemplar model   Model of categorization that maintains that all exemplars are stored in memory, and categorization judgments are made by judging the similarity of the new exemplar to all the old exemplars of a category.

Expected utility   A normative theory of choice in which the best choice is the one that offers the reward with the greatest personal value to the individual, not necessarily the greatest financial reward. The theory allows that in some situations, it may be more valuable to an individual to be very likely to get a modest reward rather than to have a small probability to get a large reward.

Expected value   A normative theory of choice in which the best choice is the one that offers the largest financial payoff.

Experimental research   A type of scientific research in which the value of one variable (e.g., self-esteem) is changed to observe its affect on another variable (e.g., memory ability). Experimental research allows one to draw conclusions about causality, that is, that changes in one variable cause changes in another.

Explicit   A type of memory retrieval that is conscious, usually measured by verbal report. Explicit retrieval would typically be supported by declarative memory; "declarative" refers to the memory system, and "explicit" refers to the type of memory test.

Eyeheight   The height of the observer's eyes from the ground. Can be used as a cue to object size.

False memory   A memory of an event that never occurred that the participant nevertheless believes did occur.

Familiar size   Using one's knowledge of the typical size of an object as a cue to the likely size and distance of an object. For example, if a child appears larger than an adult, it is likely that the child is closer to the observer.

Feature-matching theory   A theory of visual object identification proposing a memory representation of an object's list of features.

Fixed-action patterns   Complex behaviors in which an animal engages, despite very limited opportunities for practice or reward. Usually taken as evidence for innate or inborn learning.

Flashbulb memories A very rich, very detailed memory that is encoded when something that is emotionally intense happens.

fMRI See Functional magnetic resonance imaging.

Foil See Distractor.

Fovea The part of the retina that is most accurate in discerning fine details. The fovea is near the center of the retina.

Frame of reference In visual perception, the position or orientation of an object is always located relative to another object. This is called the frame of reference in which the target object is located.

Free recall A way of testing memory in which the experimenter provides no cues other than the time and place in which the memory was encoded (e.g., "Tell me the words I read to you an hour ago.").

Functional fixedness In problem solving, one is fixated on an object serving its typical function, and one fails to think of an alternative use of the object, even though it would be quite useful in the problem.

Functional magnetic resonance imaging A technique to localize human brain activity during a cognitive task. It depends on the fact that the magnetic properties of blood changes, depending on whether it carries oxygen.

Functionalism A school of psychology in the late 19th century that held that the functions of mental processes were paramount and that psychologists should therefore focus on describing the function of thought processes.

Fusiform gyrus A gyrus on the bottom of the temporal lobe that is especially important for object recognition.

Galvanic skin response An indirect measure of nervousness that measures how much moisture (perspiration) is on the participant's palms.

Gambler's fallacy When an event hasn't occurred in a while, believing that it is more likely to occur soon, even if the process generating events is random. For example, if three even numbers come up on a roulette wheel, the belief that an odd number is more likely to come up next would be an instance of the gambler's fallacy.

Garden path sentence A sentence in which the cognitive system initially builds one phrase structure as the sentence is perceived, but later in the sentence it becomes clear that this in-progress phrase structure is incorrect.

General Problem Solver An artificial intelligence program that uses the means–ends analysis heuristic. The General Problem Solver has been successful in solving a variety of problems.

Generalize Usually applied to categories, it means to use information gathered from one exemplar to a different exemplar of the same category. For example, if you learn that a specific dog likes to have its stomach rubbed, you may generalize that knowledge to other dogs and assume that they too like to have their stomachs rubbed.

Generalized motor program A motor program that can produce not just a specific movement, but a whole class of movements.

Generative A property of systems that can produce new, novel output. Language is generative, meaning you can produce and understand completely novel utterances. Generativity seemed difficult to achieve with behaviorist accounts of language, which seemed successful in predicting the likelihood that one would repeat an action, not in describing how a novel action could be generated.

Golgi tendon organs Receptors located where the muscles and tendons join that are active when muscles stretch. They are important for proprioception.

Graceful degradation A property of a model (of memory or of another cognitive process), whereby if the model is partially damaged it is able to continue functioning, although not as accurately. The human brain often shows graceful degradation; if it is damaged, cognitive processes are often compromised but can still partially function.

Grammar A set of rules that describes the legal sentences that can be constructed in a language.

GSR See Galvanic skin response.

Gyrus (plural: gyri) In the wrinkled appearance of the brain, a valley is a gyrus.

Hemispatial neglect A deficit of attention caused by brain damage in which a patient ignores the half of the visual world opposite the brain damage.

Heuristics Simple cognitive rules that are easy to apply and that usually yield acceptable decisions but can lead to errors.

Hierarchical theory Theory of memory organization in which concepts are organized in a taxonomic hierarchy (e.g., animal is above bird, which is above canary) and characteristic properties are stored at each level.

Hill climbing A heuristic in which one searches for an operator that will take you to a state in the problem space that appears to be closer to the goal than you are now.

Hippocampus Subcortical structure that is important for memory storage.

Homunculus A small person inside the head who performs cognitive functions such as looking at images on a screen. Proposing a homunculus explains nothing, and no one would ever do it on purpose; accusing someone of having a homunculus in his or her model is a scathing criticism.

Iconic memory Name given to the visual variety of sensory memory.

Image inspection Processes engaged to better know the visual characteristics of an image.

Implicit A type of memory retrieval that is unconscious and is measured not by verbal report, but via some performance measure. The experimenter can tell that the participant has learned by how the participant performs some task.

Incidental memory test A memory test in which the participants are not expressly told that their memory will be tested later.

Independent variable In an experiment, the independent variable is the one that the experimenter manipulates. Only experimental research uses independent variables.

Inductive reasoning Reasoning that allows one to say that a conclusion is more or less likely to be true but does not allow one to say that a conclusion must be true.

Information processing An approach to studying the human mind. It assumes that humans are processors of information, and that representations and processing operating on them underlie cognition. It also assumes that information is processed in stages.

Inhibition A mechanism that suppresses unwanted memories that are triggered by a cue. This suppression occurs to keep these competitors from being retrieved instead of the target memory.

Inhibition of return A phenomenon of attention. If attention focuses on an object and then moves to another object, it is difficult to return attention to that object for several seconds.

Insight problem A problem in which the solver believes that the answer comes all at once, in an "Aha!" moment of illumination.

Intentional memory test A memory test in which the participants are told that their memory will be tested later.

Introspectionism A method of studying the mind that became nearly synonymous with structuralism. The method entails observing one's thought processes, but it was deemed important that a more experienced introspectionist train a novice in the method. Researchers using introspection were almost always structuralists, seeking to use introspection to describe the basic components of consciousness.

Intrusion On a memory test, material that is appropriate to another context is inappropriately produced as a response in the wrong context.

Inverse projection problem The problem of recovering three-dimensional shape from a two-dimensional projection, such as the projection on the retina.

Isomorph A problem with a different surface story that has a problem space of the same size, number of branches, and minimum solution path as a target problem.

Jerk Rate of acceleration. Used as a measure of efficiency in one theory addressing the degrees of freedom problem.

Joint space In motor control, a representation for planning movements that uses joint angles.

Language Although definitions vary, key properties of language are often considered to be communicative, arbitrary, structured, generative, and dynamic.

Late filter A theory proposing that attention acts as a filter late in the processing stream. Implies that all sensory stimuli are analyzed for their physical characteristics and their meaning, but only those that are attended to enter awareness.

Lateral Toward the side of the head.

Levels of processing framework A framework for understanding memory that proposes that the most important factor determining whether something will be remembered is the depth of processing.

Lexical decision Task in which the participant sees a letter string on a screen and must decide as quickly as possible whether the letter string forms a word.

Lexicon The mental dictionary, which has information stored about all the words a person knows. The lexicon stores the pronunciation, spelling, and part of speech of each word and has a pointer to another location in which the meaning is stored.

Light source, reflectance, and shadow indeterminacy Refers to the fact that the amount of light hitting the retina from an object depends on the light source, the reflectance of the object, and whether the object is in shadow.

Likelihood principle Suggestion that among the many ways of interpreting an ambiguous visual stimulus, the visual system will interpret it as the stimulus that is most likely to occur in the world.

Limited Continued cognitive processing cannot occur for all available sensory stimuli; simply put, you can't pay attention to everything simultaneously.

Linear perspective A cue to depth. Parallel lines converge in the distance, so the closer they are to converging, the farther away the location.

Links Representation of the relationship between concepts. In the hierarchical model, the links are labeled (e.g., "has this property"), whereas in spreading activation models the links simply pass activation from one node to another.

Local contrast Dependence of the perceived surface lightness on the ratios of lightness of areas that are next to one another and are in the same plane.

Local representation A representational scheme in which a concept has a single location (e.g., it is represented in one node in a semantic network).

Localization Finding a location in the brain that supports a cognitive process.

Loss aversion The unpleasantness of a loss is larger than the pleasantness of a similar-size gain.

Luminance The amount of light your eye receives.

Lure See Distractor.

Magnetic resonance imaging A technique that uses magnetic properties of hydrogen for showing the three-dimensional structure of the brain. It is important for lesion studies but does not show activation.

Mask An array of tiny random black and white squares or a stimulus of randomly oriented squiggles and lines. A mask is used to knock another stimulus out of iconic memory. Mask can also be used as a verb (e.g., "The second stimulus masked the first.").

Mass spring model A model addressing the degrees of freedom problem that capitalizes on a biomechanical property of the way our muscles and limbs are designed. It proposes that endpoints are selected for movements, but trajectories are not planned.

McGurk effect An effect showing that both visual and auditory information are used in phoneme perception.

Means–ends analysis A problem-solving heuristic that uses a set of rules about when to work forward or backward and when and how to set subgoals.

Medial Toward the center of the head.

Mental models theory A semantic representation corresponding to a possible configuration of the world. Mental models are the heart of Johnson-Laird's mental models theory of deductive reasoning.

Modal model A model composed of the most common features of models of short-term memory in the early 1970s. The modal model turned out to be incorrect in many details.

Monitoring process   In Wegner's model of mental control, the monitoring process searches for mental contents that are inconsistent with desired thoughts. The purpose is to serve as a warning system that mental control is failing. This process does not require attentional resources.

Motor control   Our ability to plan and execute movements.

Motor program   A representation supporting movement that has three key features: It contains a set of commands for movement, peripheral feedback is not needed, and the commands can be applied to different effectors.

Motor skill learning   Increasing accuracy (either spatial or temporal accuracy) of motor acts that occur as a result of practice.

Motor theory of speech perception   A theory positing that speech perception shares processes with or relies on knowledge about how speech is produced.

Movement nodes   In a hierarchical sequencing representation, the movement nodes control muscles.

MRI   See Magnetic resonance imaging.

Multiple resources   A theory of attention in which attention is believed to be composed of a number of pools of attention, each dedicated to a different type of task.

Muscle spindles   Receptors in the fleshy part of muscles that detect muscle stretch. They are important for proprioception.

Nativist   The view that much of human knowledge is innate.

Naturalistic observation   A method of collecting scientific data wherein the researcher observes behavior in its natural setting, for example, an ethologist observing a bird in the wild.

Neurons   The cells in the brain that support cognition.

Nodes   Representation of concepts in hierarchical and spreading activation theories.

Nondeterministic   The view that at least some acts have antecedent causes outside the physical world.

Normative theories   A theory of choice that describes a set of rules by which some choices are better than others and one choice can be said to be optimal.

Object-centered representation   A mental representation of what an object looks like relative to the object itself. The representation can support recognition of the object when it is viewed from any perspective.

Obligatory access   Refers to the fact that verbal information (but not all sounds) appears to be entered into the phonological loop by its mere presence, even if the participant does not want it to enter.

Occam's razor   The principle that parsimony is important in evaluating scientific theories. Specifically, if two theories account for data equally well, the simpler theory is to be preferred.

Occlusion—in memory   A source of forgetting. There is a stronger link from a cue to some undesired memory than to the target, and the cue therefore always calls up the undesired memory.

Occlusion—in perception   A cue to depth. An object that occludes another is closer.

Operant conditioning   Learning whereby the animal (or person) makes a response that has consequences (e.g., reward or punishment). These consequences change the probability that the response will be made again.

Operating process   In Wegner's model of mental control, the operating process seeks mental contents that are consistent with desired thoughts. For example, if one is trying not to think of a white bear, the operating process seeks distractions from that thought. This process requires attentional resources.

Operator   A process one can apply to a problem to change to a different state in the problem space.

Optic ataxia   A neurologic syndrome characterized by a deficit in visually controlled reaching, but not in identifying objects.

Overextension   The tendency for children to use a word they know in place of other words they do not know (e.g., calling any four-legged animal "doggie").

Overregularization   Applying linguistic rules to exception words where the rule should not be applied (e.g., adding "ed" to make the past tense of irregular verbs, yielding "We goed to the park yesterday").

Parahippocampal gyrus   A gyrus on the bottom of the temporal lobe that is especially important for memory.

Parallel distributed processing   A model using a distributed representation with nodes and links. The model learns as weights are modified.

Parallel search   A visual search in which all the stimuli in a field are evaluated simultaneously. One can tell that a search is parallel if adding extra distractors to the search does not increase the participant's response time. Participants usually experience pop-out with parallel searches.

Parsimonious   A theory is parsimonious if it is the simplest theory possible that accounts for all the data. The noun is parsimony.

Parsing paradox   For some ambiguous figures, it seems impossible to identify the figure without knowing its parts, but its parts cannot be identified unless one knows the figure.

Partial report procedure   Developed by Sperling to examine iconic memory, it's a procedure whereby participants are shown an array of stimuli (usually letters or numbers) very briefly and then are given a cue telling them which subset of the stimuli to report. This method showed that participants perceive most of the stimuli in a complex array.

Participant   Any human who provides data for a psychological study.

PDP   See Parallel distributed processing.

Performance   The grammaticality of the sentences that people utter. Performance is influenced not only by the grammatical rules people know (competence), but also by other factors such as lapses of memory and social considerations such as interruptions.

Permastore   A hypothetical state of memory from which memories are not forgotten.

PET   See Positron emission tomography.

Phoneme restoration effect   Phonemes that are poorly produced are "restored" by higher-level processes so the perceiver believes that the missing phoneme actually was present. The system can infer what the missing phoneme should have been based on the context.

Phonemes   Individual speech sounds.

Phonological dyslexia   A pattern of reading difficulty in which the person has difficulty reading nonwords (e.g., slint) but can read irregular words (e.g., yacht).

Phonological loop   The part of the working memory model in which auditory information is stored.

Phonological store   The part of the phonological loop that can store about 2 s of auditory information.

Phrase structure grammars   A grammar that represents sentences hierarchically, with each node of the hierarchy corresponding to a phrase structure.

Pictorial cues   Cues to distance that can be used in two-dimensional pictures.

Picture theory of imagery   The experience of visual imagery is created by activating a memory representation. This memory representation was created by viewing objects in the real world.

Positron emission tomography   A technique using the decay of a radioactive tracer to localize human brain activity during a cognitive task.

Posterior   Toward the back of the head (synonym of "caudal").

Practice   In developing expertise, practice is defined as activity designed to improve skill (as opposed to play or performance) and therefore must include corrective feedback and repetition and must be at the appropriate level of difficulty.

Pragmatic reasoning schemas   Sets of rules defined in relation to goals that can be used to evaluate situations such as permissions or obligations. A key aspect of pragmatic reasoning schemas is that they encourage conclusions that are practical in the real world, as opposed to formal logic, which can lead to conclusions that are technically correct but not useful.

Preattentively   Refers to processing that occurs regardless of whether attention is applied to the stimulus.

Premise A statement of fact taken to be true for the purposes of a logical problem.

Primary memory Hypothetical buffer in which information may be held briefly. Contrast with Secondary memory.

Principle of minimal attachment The principle that as the cognitive system parses sentences, it is biased to build phrase structures in such a way that it adds new words to existing nodes in the phrase structure hierarchy rather than creating new nodes.

Principle of truth Proposal in Johnson-Laird's model of deductive reasoning that people tend to construct models representing only what is true, not what is false.

Prior beliefs Real-world knowledge that can influence people's evaluation of a syllogism. They are more likely to accept as true a syllogism with a conclusion that they know is true and to reject a syllogism with a conclusion that they know is false.

Proactive interference Earlier learning interferes with new learning.

Probabilistic view of categorization Category membership is proposed to be a matter of probability. Prototype and exemplar models fall within the probabilistic view.

Probability model An approach to studying reasoning, based on the idea that when presented with what experimenters think of as reasoning problems, participants actually treat them as probability problems.

Problem In the study of problem solving, a problem is any situation in which a person has a goal and that goal is not yet accomplished.

Problem frame The particular way a problem is described. Several problems may offer the same core set of payoffs and probabilities of payoffs, but the problems could vary in terms of how they are described.

Problem space All possible configurations that a problem can take.

Problem state A particular configuration of the elements of the problem.

Procedural memory Type of memory that changes the way you respond to or do things; it encompasses motor skill learning, classical and emotional conditioning, and priming. It's often contrasted with declarative memory.

Procedure invariance A requirement of rational decision making, it is the idea that people will consistently make the same choice irrespective of how their preference for that choice is measured. In fact, procedure invariance is violated.

Process A process manipulates representations in some way. For example, a computer might have a process for addition to add numbers. The mind might have a process that maintains the activity of a representation in primary memory, thus keeping it in consciousness.

Property inheritance A characteristic of some models of categorization; concepts inherit properties from the concepts that are higher in the hierarchy.

Proposition A verbal representation of knowledge. It is the most basic unit of meaning that has a truth value.

Proprioception A sense of the body's location generated by any of a number of special receptors in the joints, skin, and muscles.

Prosopagnosia A neurologic syndrome characterized by a difficulty in recognizing faces via visual input.

Prototype A prototype has all the features that are characteristic of a category.

Psychic budget How we mentally categorize money we have spent or are considering spending.

Psychological refractory period A period of time after one response is executed during which a second response cannot be selected.

Public verifiability One of the three principles of the scientific method. It means that one will make one's hypotheses and experimental data available to everyone to examine and to critique.

Putamen Subcortical structure closely related to the caudate that is important in movement and likely in some cognitive functions.

Rational In the context of decision making, rational choices are ones that are internally consistent (e.g., that show transitivity).

Recognition test Method of testing memory in which the experimenter presents the participants with the to-be-remembered material, along with other material that was not initially encoded (distractors). The participant must select the to-be-remembered items from among these other items.

Recognition failure of recallable words The effect in which words that were not recognized are nevertheless recalled successfully on a later test.

Reconstruction The idea that memories are not simply pulled out of the storehouse; rather, they are interpreted in terms of prior knowledge to reconstruct what probably occurred.

Recursion A process can be recursive if it calls on itself to get its job done. A definition of something is recursive if the definition contains the thing defined. For example, one definition of a sentence is "two sentences joined by the word 'and.'"

Reflex An automatic action by the body that occurs when a particular stimulus is perceived in the environment.

Rehearse To practice material in an effort to memorize it.

Relational research A type of scientific research in which one seeks to describe the relationship of two variables (e.g., income and intelligence) without specifying whether changes in one causes changes in the other.

Relative height A cue to depth. Objects that are higher in the picture plane are farther away.

Release from proactive interference Refers to the effect in which proactive interference dissipates if one changes the stimulus materials.

Repetition priming Effect in which performance of a task is biased by one's having seen the same words or pictures sometime earlier.

Representation A symbol for an entity or concept in the real world. For example, a computer might use a binary code 011 to represent the concept 8.

Representativeness A heuristic that leads you to judge the probability of an event as more likely to belong to a category if it has the features of the category that you deem important.

Repression The active forgetting of an episode that would be too painful or threatening to the self to be remembered.

Response selection A hypothetical stage of processing in which a response to a stimulus is selected (e.g., to push a button), but the actual preparation of the motor act (e.g., finger movement) is not yet complete.

Response to stimulus interval The time after the participant has responded but before the next stimulus has appeared.

Restructuring A process emphasized by Gestalt psychologists, applied to a problem whereby one perceives a whole that had not been seen before.

Retina The layer of light-sensitive cells on the back of the eye.

Retinal disparity The disparity in retinal location of the same image for the two eyes.

Retrieval-induced forgetting The phenomenon whereby retrieving some memories makes you forget other, related memories.

Retroactive interference Later learning interferes with earlier learning.

Rostral Toward the front of the head (synonym of "anterior").

Sample size The number of things in a group that you are evaluating. People mistakenly ignore sample size in judging the reliability or consistency of a measure.

Sapir–Whorf hypothesis Synonymous with Whorfian hypothesis.

Satisficing Selecting the first choice that is satisfactory (i.e., above some threshold), rather than evaluating every choice and selecting the best of those. Psychologists believe that people must satisfice most of the time because there are usually too many choices to allow evaluation of all of them.

Savings in relearning A way of testing memory in which the participant learns some material (e.g., a list of words) to a criterion (e.g., can recite the list twice without error). After a delay, the participant must relearn the list to criterion again. If the participant can reach criterion in fewer trials the second time, he or she has shown savings in relearning.

Schema   A memory representation containing general information about an object or an event. It contains information representative of a type of event rather than of a single event.

Script   A type of schema that describes a series of events.

Secondary memory   Repository for memories. Contrast with Primary memory.

Selective   The assumption that one is able to disburse the limited resource of attention as desired.

Semantic memory   Memories that are not associated with a particular time and place or with a feeling that the memory happened to you. Semantic memories cover world knowledge (e.g., "frogs are green").

Semantic network   Name given to all the nodes and links in a spreading activation model.

Semantic priming   Effect in which performance of a task is biased by having seen semantically related words or pictures viewed earlier.

Sensitivity   In signal detection theory, a measure of the participant's absolute ability to detect a signal. Sensitivity is measured independently of any bias the participant might have to report or not report signals. Also, the ability of a test to detect memories that are in the storehouse.

Sensory memory   General term referring to sensory buffers that can hold much information, but only for a second or so.

Serial search   A visual search in which each stimulus in a field is evaluated one at a time. One can tell that a search is serial if adding extra distractors to the search increases the participant's response time. Participants do not experience pop-out with serial searches.

Set effects   In problem solving, a set effect occurs when a particular problem-solving procedure is applied because it has been effective in the past, even if it is not appropriate to the current problem.

Shadow   In a dichotic listening task, participants listen to material on headphones, and each earpiece plays a different message. Participants are to attend to just one message and must shadow that message to show that they are doing so. Shadowing means repeating the to-be-attended message aloud as they hear it.

Shallow processing   Thinking about the surface characteristics of stimulus materials (i.e., what they look like, sound like, and so on).

Shape and orientation indeterminacy   Refers to the fact that shape and orientation are indeterminate from a two-dimensional projection (e.g., a coin that looks like an ellipse if it is turned).

Short-term memory   A particular theory of primary memory. Short-term memory is usually accorded a duration of 30 s (if the material is not rehearsed) and a capacity of about five chunks of information.

Signal detection theory   A method of analyzing data that provides separate measures of sensitivity and bias.

Single-cell recording   A technique in which a very fine probe is inserted in the brain that can record the activity of a single neuron or a small group of neurons.

Situation model   A level of representation in text processing. The situation model refers to deep knowledge of a text that represents an integration of information from the text and knowledge the reader had before reading the text.

Size and distance indeterminacy   Refers to the fact that the size of an object on the retina is determined by the actual size of the object and by the distance of the object from the observer.

Solvable problems   One of the three principles of the scientific method. It is an acknowledgment that the scientific method is useful for addressing some problems but is not useful for addressing others.

Source   The source of a memory refers to where and when it was encoded, whether someone told you the information or whether you experienced it directly or just thought about it.

Source confusion   An error in a source memory. For example, you mistake your own thought for an event that actually happened (or vice versa). Another type of source confusion is mixing up the time and location information of two real memories. For example, you might read the *New York Times* and the *National Enquirer* on the same morning and think you read an article in one paper, whereas it was actually in the other.

Span of apprehension   The amount of information that can enter consciousness at once.

Spatial imagery   Imagery that emphasizes where objects or parts of objects are located. Spatial imagery can be contrasted with visual imagery, which emphasizes how things look.

Speech stream   A term used to refer to spoken speech that emphasizes its continuous nature. Although we perceive speech to be composed of individual words (and therefore to have short breaks between the words), speech sounds are produced fairly continuously.

Spinal cord   The long column of neurons in the vertebral column that collects somatosensory information and sends motor information to the muscles.

Spontaneous recovery   The sudden uncovering of a memory that was believed to be forgotten.

Spreading activation model   A model in which memory is conceived of as a network of nodes connected by links, and activation spreads from node to node via the links.

Stereopsis   A cue to distance that depends on the fact that our two eyes get slightly different views of objects.

Strength view of memory   The idea that memories vary in how strongly they are represented, and more strongly represented memories are easier to retrieve.

Structural explanation   An explanation for the limitation of performing multiple cognitive tasks simultaneously that emphasizes limitations in cognitive structures (e.g., working memory) rather than attentional resources.

Structural similarity   Refers to whether two problems share content that allows them to be solved by the same strategy (e.g., if problems can both be solved by Newton's second law, they share structural similarity, even if one

involves a falling body and the other an inclined plane).

Structuralism   A school of psychology in the late 19th century, the goal of which was to describe the structures that comprise thought. Researchers often used the introspective method.

Sulcus (plural: sulci)   In the wrinkled appearance of the brain, a hill is a sulcus.

Sunk cost   An investment (e.g., of money, time, emotion) that is irretrievably spent and should not affect current decisions about spending but nevertheless often does.

Surface code   A level of representation in text processing. The surface code refers to the exact wording and syntax of sentences.

Surface dyslexia   A pattern of reading difficulty in which the person has difficulty reading irregular words (e.g., yacht) but can read nonwords (e.g., slint).

Surface similarity   Refers to whether two problems share similar elements (e.g., if both problems entail inclined planes, the problems have surface similarity even if very different strategies are necessary to solve them).

Surface structure   In language, the order in which words are uttered in a sentence. The surface structure is the product of the deep structure plus any transformations that are applied to the deep structure.

Syllogism   A logical form composed of three statements of fact: two premises and a conclusion.

Synergy   A bias for a set of joints or muscle groups to work together in a particular way.

Tacit knowledge   In the imagery debate, tacit knowledge is a participant's knowledge of how objects in the real world move. It was suggested by some that participants used this tacit knowledge to simulate real-world movement and thereby produce results in imagery experiments that match real-world phenomena.

Target   Term used in visual search experiments for the item that the participant is expected to find. Also used in recognition memory experiments to denote the to-be-remembered material at test.

Template A viewer-centered representation. A simple template matching theory of object recognition says that you compare what you see to templates stored in memory.

Ten-year rule The phenomenon that experts in almost all fields are seldom able to compete at the very highest levels with less than a decade of intense practice.

Text A group of related sentences forming a paragraph or a group of related paragraphs.

Textbase A level of representation in text processing. The textbase represents the ideas of the text but does not preserve the particular wording and syntax.

Texture gradient A cue to depth. A field is assumed to have a uniform texture gradient, so if more detail is visible in part of the field, it is assumed to be closer.

Thalamus A collection of nuclei in the center of the brain; it is often thought of as a relay station for sensory and motor information.

Tip-of-the-tongue phenomenon An effect in which you are certain you know a concept but cannot think of the proper term for it.

Top-down processing Processing in which conceptual knowledge influences the processing or interpretation of lower-level perceptual processes.

Trajectory The path of a movement.

Transfer appropriate processing The idea that memory will be better to the extent that the cognitive processes used at encoding match the cognitive processes used at retrieval.

Transitivity If a relationship holds between the first and second of three elements and it holds between the second and third, it should hold between the first and third. If choices were rational, there would be transitivity of preference between choices. However, transitivity does not always hold.

Typicality The fact that some members of a category are viewed as better (i.e., more typical) exemplars than others (e.g., a golden retriever is a typical dog, whereas a Chihuahua is not).

Unconditioned response In classical conditioning, the response to an unconditioned stimulus (e.g., salivation).

Unconditioned stimulus In classical conditioning, a stimulus that leads to a consistent response from the animal before any training begins (e.g., food).

Unlearning A source of forgetting. Practicing a new association between a cue and a target memory weakens the associative link between the cue and another memory.

Ventral Toward the bottom of the head.

Verbal protocol A method of gathering data in problem-solving (or other) experiments. The participant is asked to solve a problem and to simultaneously describe his or her thoughts. These descriptions are assumed to bear some relationship to the cognitive processes that actually support solving the problem and so can be used as a window into these processes.

Viewer-centered representation A mental representation of what an object looks like relative to the observer.

Vigilance The ability to maintain attention to a task in which stimuli appear infrequently.

Visual agnosia A neurologic syndrome characterized by a difficulty in identifying objects using visual input.

Visual imagery Sometimes visual imagery refers to any imagery in the visual modality. It also has a more specialized meaning, referring to imagery tasks that emphasize what things look like. Visual imagery can be contrasted with spatial imagery, which emphasizes where things are located.

Visuospatial sketchpad A buffer on which visual or spatial information can be manipulated and briefly stored. It is believed to be similar to and perhaps synonymous with visual imagery.

Wernike's area An area in the superior part of the left temporal lobe that is important for language.

What/how hypothesis Alternative to the what/where hypothesis, this proposal holds that the visual system segregates analysis of what objects are (object recognition and location) and how to manipulate them (visual information dedicated to the motor system).

What/where hypothesis   Hypothesis that the visual system segregates analysis of what objects are (object recognition) and where they are (spatial location).

Whorfian hypothesis   The idea that language influences thought. The strong version of the hypothesis holds that certain thoughts are impossible to entertain in certain languages. The weaker version holds that it may be easier to entertain certain thoughts in certain languages.

Word-chain grammars   A proposal that people construct sentences by chaining one word after another, according to a set of rules about what words would be admissible next in the chain or what words are highly associated with words already in the sentence.

Word length effect   The finding that participants can remember more words if the words can be said quickly.

Working backward   A problem-solving heuristic in which one begins at the goal state of the problem and tries to work back to the starting state.

Working memory   Specific theory of primary memory proposed by Baddeley and Hitch (1974), it has three parts: a phonological loop, a visuospatial sketchpad, and a central executive. Working memory is proposed to be a workspace for cognitive processes, not simply a short-term storage device.

References

Aaronson, D., & Ferres, S. (1986). Reading strategies for children and adults: A quantitative model. *Psychological Review, 93,* 89–112.

Ackerman, P. L., Beier, M. E., & Boyle, M. O. (2005). Working memory and intelligence: The same or different constructs? *Psychological Bulletin, 131,* 30–60.

Adamson, R. E. (1952). Functional fixedness as related to problem solving: A repetition of three experiments. *Journal of Experimental Psychology, 44,* 288–291.

Adelson, E. H. (1998). *Illusions and demos.* Retrieved October 13, 2005, from http://web.mit.edu/persci/people/adelson/checkershadow_illusion. html.

Admiraal, M. A., Kusters, M., & Gielen, S. (2004). Modeling kinematics and dynamics of human arm movements. *Motor Control, 8,* 312–338.

Aguirre G. K., & D'Esposito, M. (1997). Environmental knowledge is subserved by separable dorsal/ventral neural areas. *Journal of Neuroscience, 17,* 2512–2518.

Albrecht, J. E., & O'Brien, E. J. (1993). Updating a mental model: Maintaining both local and global coherence. *Journal of Experimental Psychology: Learning, Memory, and Cognition, 19*(5), 1061–1070.

Alivisatos, B., & Petrides, M. (1997). Functional activation of the human brain during mental rotation. *Neuropsychologia, 35*(2), 111–118.

Allard, F., & Starkes, J. L. (1991). Motor-skill experts in sports, dance, and other domains. In K. A. Ericsson & J. Smith (Eds.), *Toward a general theory of expertise: Prospects and limits* (pp. 126–152). New York: Cambridge University Press.

Allen, S. W., & Brooks, L. R. (1991). Specializing the operation of an explicit rule. *Journal of Experimental Psychology: General, 120,* 3–19.

Allport, A. (1989). Visual attention. In M. I. Posner (Ed.), *Foundations of cognitive science* (pp. 631–682). Cambridge, MA: MIT Press.

Alpert, J. L., Brown, L. S., Ceci, S. J., Courtois, C. A., Loftus, E. G., & Ornstein, P. A. (1996). *Working group on investigation of memories of childhood abuse: Final report.* Washington, DC: American Psychological Association.

Altmann, E. M., & Gray, W. D. (2002). Forgetting to remember: The functional relationship of decay and interference. *Psychological Science, 13,* 27–33.

Altmann, G., & Steedman, M. (1988). Interaction with context during human sentence processing. *Cognition, 30*(3), 191–238.

Altmann, G. T., Garnham, A., & Dennis, Y. (1992). Avoiding the garden path: Eye movements in context. *Journal of Memory & Language, 31*(5), 685–712.

Altmann, G. T. M., Garnham, A., & Henstra, J.-A. (1994). Effects of syntax in human sentence parsing: Evidence against a structure-based proposal mechanism. *Journal of Experimental Psychology: Learning, Memory, and Cognition, 20*(1), 209–216.

Alvarez, G. A., & Cavanagh, P. (2004). The capacity of visual short term memory is set both by visual information load and by number of objects. *Psychological Science, 15,* 106–111.

Andersen, R. A., Snyder, L. H., Bradley, D. C., & Xing, J. (1997). Multimodal representation of space in the posterior parietal cortex and its use in planning movements. *Annual Review of Neuroscience, 20,* 303–330.

Anderson, F. C., & Pandy, M. G. (2001). Dynamic optimization of human walking. *Journal of Biomechanical Engineering, 123,* 381–390.

Anderson, J. R. (1993). *Rules of the mind.* Mahwah, NJ: Erlbaum.

Anderson, M. C. (2003). Rethinking interference theory: Executive control and the mechanisms of forgetting. *Journal of Memory & Language, 49,* 415–445.

Anderson, M. C., Bjork, R. A., & Bjork, E. L. (1994). Remembering can cause forgetting: Retrieval dynamics in long-term memory. *Journal of Experimental Psychology: Learning, Memory, and Cognition, 20,* 1063–1081.

Anderson, M. C., & Green, C. (2001). Suppressing unwanted memories by executive control. *Nature, 410,* 366–369.

Anderson, M. C., & Levy, B. (2002). Repression can (and should) be studied empirically. *Trends in Cognitive Sciences, 6,* 502–503.

Anderson, M. C., & Spellman, B. A. (1995). On the status of inhibitory mechanisms in cognition: Memory retrieval as a model case. *Psychological Review, 102*(1), 68–100.

Anderson, R. C., & Pichert, J. W. (1978). Recall of previously unrecallable information following a shift in perspective. *Journal of Verbal Learning & Verbal Behavior, 17*(1), 1–12.

Arlemalm, T. (1996). Recognition failure: The influence of semantic cue-target integration: A short note. *European Journal of Cognitive Psychology, 8,* 205–214.

Arnell, K. M., & Duncan, J. (2002). Separate and shared sources of dual-task cost in stimulus identification and response selection. *Cognitive Psychology, 44,* 105–147.

Arnell, K. M., & Jolicoeur, P. (1999). The attentional blink across stimulus modalities: Evidence for central processing limitations. *Journal of Experimental Psychology: Human Perception and Performance, 25,* 630–648.

Ashby, F. G., & Maddox, W. T. (2005). Human category learning. *Annual Review of Psychology, 56,* 149–178.

Ashby, F. G., & O'Brien, J. B. (2005). Category learning and multiple memory systems. *Trends in Cognitive Sciences, 9,* 83–89.

Ashby, F. G., Alfonso-Reese, L. A., Turken, A. U., & Waldron, E. M. (1998). A neuropsychological theory of multiple systems in category learning. *Psychological Review, 105,* 442–481.

Aslin, R. N., Saffran, J. R., & Newport, E. L. (1998). Computation of conditional probability statistics by 8-month-old infants. *Psychological Science, 9,* 321–324.

Atkinson, R. C., & Shiffrin, R. M. (1968). Human memory: A proposed system and its control processes. In K. W. Spence & J. T. Spence (Eds.), *The psychology of learning and motivation* (Vol. 2). New York: Academic Press.

Attneave, F., & Curlee, T. E. (1983). Locational representation in imagery: A moving spot task. *Journal of Experimental Psychology: Human Perception and Performance, 9*(1), 20–30.

Au, T. K. (1983). Chinese and English counterfactuals: The Sapir–Whorf hypothesis revisited. *Cognition, 15*(1–3), 155–187.

Au, T. K. (1984). Counterfactuals: In reply to Alfred Bloom. *Cognition, 17*(3), 289–302.

Averbach, E., & Sperling, G. (1961). Short term storage of information in vision. In C. Cherry (Ed.), *Information theory.* London: Butterworths.

Awh, E., & Pashler, H. (2000). Evidence for split attentional foci. *Journal of Experimental Psychology: Human Perception and Performance, 26,* 834–846.

Awh, E., Serences, J., Laurey, P., Dhaliwal, H., van der Jagt, T., & Dassonvile, P. (2004). Evidence against a central bottleneck during the attentional blink: Multiple channels for configural and featural processing. *Cognitive Psychology, 48,* 95–126.

Baddeley, A. (1986). *Working memory.* Oxford: Clarendon Press/Oxford University Press.

Baddeley, A. (1996). Exploring the central executive. *Quarterly Journal of Experimental Psychology: Human Experimental Psychology, 49A,* 5–28.

Baddeley, A. (2000). The episodic buffer: A new component of working memory? *Trends in Cognitive Sciences, 4,* 417–423.

Baddeley, A. (2001). Is working memory still working? *American Psychologist, 56,* 849–864.

Baddeley, A. (2003). Working memory: Looking back and looking forward. *Nature Reviews Neuroscience, 4,* 829–839.

Baddeley, A., Gathercole, S., & Papagno, C. (1998). The phonological loop as a language learning device. *Psychological Review, 105*(1), 158–173.

Baddeley, A., & Lieberman, K. (1980). Spatial working memory. In R. Nickerson (Ed.), *Attention and performance VIII* (pp. 521–539). Mahwah, NJ: Erlbaum.

Baddeley, A. D. (1966). Short-term memory for word sequences as a function of acoustic, semantic, and formal similarity. *Quarterly Journal of Experimental Psychology, 18,* 362–365.

Baddeley, A. D., Grant, W., Wight, E., & Thomson, N. (1975). Imagery and visual working memory. In P. M. A. Rabbitt & S. Dornic (Eds.), *Attention and performance V* (pp. 205–217). London: Academic Press.

Baddeley, A. D., & Hitch, G. J. (1974). Working memory. In G. Bower (Ed.), *The psychology of learning and motivation* (Vol. 8). New York: Academic Press.

Baddeley, A. D., Lewis, V., & Vallar, G. (1984). Exploring the articulatory loop. *Quarterly Journal of Experimental Psychology: Human Experimental Psychology, 36A*(2), 233–252.

Baddeley, A. D., Papagno, C., & Vallar, G. (1988). When long-term learning depends on short-term storage. *Journal of Memory & Language, 27,* 586–595.

Baddeley, A. D., Thomson, N., & Buchanan, M. (1975). Word length and the structure of short-term memory. *Journal of Verbal Learning & Verbal Behavior, 14*(6), 575–589.

Bahrick, H. P. (1984). Semantic memory content in permastore: Fifty years of memory for Spanish learned in school. *Journal of Experimental Psychology: General, 113*(1), 1–29.

Bahrick, H. P. (2000). Long-term maintenance of knowledge. In E. Tulving & F. I. M. Craik (Eds.), *The Oxford handbook of memory* (pp. 347–362). London: Oxford University Press.

Baillet, S. D., & Keenan, J. M. (1986). The role of encoding and retrieval processes in the recall of text. *Discourse Processes, 9*(3), 247–268.

Baizer, J. S., Kralj-Hans, I., & Glickstein, M. (1999). Cerebellar lesions and prism adaptation in Macaque monkeys. *Journal of Neurophysiology, 81,* 1960–1965.

Barclay, J. R., Bransford, J. D., Franks, J. J., McCarrel, N. S., & Nitsch, K. (1974). Comprehension and semantic flexibility. *Journal of Verbal Learning & Verbal Behavior, 13*(4), 471–481.

Baron, J., & Strawson, C. (1976). Use of orthographic and word-specific knowledge in reading words aloud. *Journal of Experimental Psychology: Human Perception and Performance, 2*(3), 386–393.

Barrouillet, P. (1996). Transitive inferences from set-inclusion relations and working memory. *Journal of Experimental Psychology: Learning, Memory, and Cognition, 22*(6), 1408–1422.

Bartlett, F. C. (1932). *Remembering: A study in experimental and social psychology.* Cambridge: Cambridge University Press.

Bassok, M., & Holyoak, K. J. (1989). Interdomain transfer between isomorphic topics in algebra and physics. *Journal of Experimental Psychology: Learning, Memory, and Cognition, 15,* 153–166.

Battig, W. F., & Montague, W. E. (1969). Category norms of verbal items in 56 categories: A replication and extension of the Connecticut category norms.

Journal of Experimental Psychology, 80(3, Pt. 2), 1–46.

Baumeister, R. F., Campbell, J. D., Krueger, J. I., & Vohs, K. D. (2003). Does high self-esteem cause better performance, interpersonal success, happiness, or healthier lifestyles? *Psychological Science in the Public Interest, 4,* 1–44.

Baylis, G. C., & Driver, J. (1993). Visual attention and objects: Evidence for hierarchical coding of location. *Journal of Experimental Psychology: Human Perception and Performance, 19*(3), 451–470.

Beauvois, M. F., & Derouesne, J. (1979). Phonological alexia: Three dissociations. *Journal of Neurology, Neurosurgery, and Psychiatry, 42,* 1115–1124.

Becker, M. W., Pashler, H., & Anstis, S. M. (2000). The role of iconic memory in change-detection tasks. *Perception, 29,* 273–286.

Bedard, J., & Chi, M. T. (1992). Expertise. *Current Directions in Psychological Science, 1*(4), 135–139.

Begg, I., & Harris, G. (1982). On the interpretation of syllogisms. *Journal of Verbal Learning & Verbal Behavior, 21*(5), 595–620.

Behrmann, M., & Bub, D. (1992). Surface dyslexia and dysgraphia: Dual routes, single lexicon. *Cognitive Neuropsychology, 9*(3), 209–251.

Bennett, S., Rioja, N., Ashford, D., & Elliott, D. (2004). Intermittent vision and one-handed catching: The effect of general and specific task experience. *Journal of Motor Behavior, 36,* 442–449.

Berardi, N., Pizzorusso, T., & Maffei, L. (2000). Critical periods during sensory development. *Current Opinion in Neurobiology, 10,* 138–145.

Bergerbest, D., Ghahremani, D. G., & Gabrieli, J. D. E. (2004). Neural correlates of auditory repetition priming: Reduced fMRI activation in the auditory cortex. *Journal of Cognitive Neuroscience, 16,* 966–977.

Berkeley, G. (1709/1948–1957). *The works of George Berkeley.* (A. A. Luce & T. E. Jessop, Eds.). London: Thomas Nelson and Sons.

Bernardo, A. B. (1994). Problem-specific information and development of problem-type schemata. *Journal of Experimental Psychology: Learning, Memory, and Cognition, 20,* 379–395.

Biederman, I. (1981). On the semantics of a glance at a scene. In M. Kubovy & J. Pomerantz (Eds.), *Perceptual organization.* Mahwah, NJ: Erlbaum.

Biederman, I. (1987). Recognition-by-components: A theory of human image understanding. *Psychological Review, 94*(2), 115–117.

Biederman, I., & Gerhardstein, P. C. (1993). Recognizing depth rotated objects: Evidence and conditions for 3D viewpoint invariance. *Journal of Experimental Psychology: Human Perception and Performance, 19,* 1162–1182.

Birdsong, D., & Molis, M. (2001). On the evidence for maturational constraints in second-language acquisition. *Journal of Memory and Language, 44,* 235–249.

Biriukov, P. (1906/1996). *Leo Tolstoy, his life and work: Autobiographical memoirs, letters and biographical material.* Charlottesville: University of Virginia Library. Retrieved October 13, 2005, from http://etext.lib.virginia.edu/toc/modeng/public/BirLeoT.html.

Birney, D. P., & Halford, G. S. (2002). Cognitive complexity of suppositional reasoning: An application of the relational complexity metric to the knight-knave task. *Thinking & Reasoning, 8,* 109–134.

Bisiach, E., & Luzzatti, C. (1978). Unilateral neglect of representational space. *Cortex, 14,* 129–133.

Blaxton, T. A., Zeffiro, T. A., Gabrieli, J. D. E., Bookheimer, S. Y., Carrillo M.C., Theodore W.T., et al. (1996). Functional mapping of human learning: A positron emission tomography activation study of eyeblink conditioning. *Journal of Neuroscience, 16,* 4032–4040.

Bloom, A. H. (1981). *The linguistic shaping of thought: A study in the impact of language on thinking in China and the West.* Mahwah, NJ: Erlbaum.

Bloom, B. S. (1985). Generalizations about talent development. In B. S. Bloom (Ed.), *Developing talent in young people* (pp. 507–549). New York: Ballantine.

Boland, J. E., & Blodgett, A. (2001). Understanding the constraints on syntactic generation: Lexical bias and discourse congruency effects on eye movements. *Journal of Memory & Language, 45,* 391–411.

Bolhuis, J. J., & Honey, R. C. (1998). Imprinting, learning and development: From behaviour to brain and back. *Trends in Neurosciences, 21*(7), 306–311.

Bonnefon, J.-F., & Hilton, D. J. (2002). The suppression of Modus Ponens as a case of pragmatic preconditional reasoning. *Thinking & Reasoning, 8,* 21–40.

Booth, M. C. A., & Rolls, E. T. (1998). View-invariant representations of familiar objects by neurons in the inferior temporal visual cortex. *Cerebral Cortex, 8,* 510–523.

Bortfeld, H., Morgan, J. L., Golinkoff, R. M., & Rathbun, K. (2005). Mommy and me: Familiar names help launch babies into speech-stream segmentation. *Psychological Science, 16,* 298–304.

Bouchard, T. J., & McGue, M. (1981). Familial studies of intelligence: A review. *Science, 212*(4498), 1055–1059.

Bousfield, W. A. (1953). The occurrence of clustering in the recall of randomly arranged associates. *Journal of General Psychology, 49,* 229–240.

Bower, G. H. (1972). Mental imagery and associative learning. In L. Gregg (Ed.), *Cognition in learning and memory.* New York: Wiley.

Bower, G. H., Black, J. B., & Turner, T. J. (1979). Scripts in memory for text. *Cognitive Psychology, 11*(2), 177–220.

Bower, G. H., & Springston, F. (1970). Pauses as recoding points in letter series. *Journal of Experimental Psychology, 83,* 421–430.

Bowers, K. S., Regehr, G., Balthazard, C., & Parker, K. (1990). Intuition in the context of discovery. *Cognitive Psychology, 22*(1), 72–110.

Boyd, L. A., & Winstein, C. J. (2001). Implicit motor-sequence learning in humans following unilateral stroke: The impact of practice and explicit knowledge. *Neuroscience Letters, 298,* 65–69.

Boysson-Bardies, B. de (1999). How language comes to children: From birth to two years. (M. DeBrevoise, Trans.). Cambridge, MA: MIT Press.

Braine, M. D. S. (1971). The acquisition of language in infant and child. In C. Reed (Ed.), *The learning of language* (pp. 7–95). New York: Appleton-Century-Crofts.

Brakke, K. E., & Savage-Rumbaugh, E. S. (1995). The development of language skills in *pan*: I. Comprehension. *Language & Communication, 15,* 121–148.

Brakke, K. E., & Savage-Rumbaugh, E. S. (1996). The development of language skills in *pan*: II. Production. *Language & Communication 17,* 361–380.

Bransford, J. D., & Johnson, M. K. (1972). Contextual prerequisites for understanding: Some investigations for comprehension and recall. *Journal of Verbal Learning and Verbal Behavior, 11,* 717–726.

Breitmeyer, B. G., & Ganz, L. (1976). Implications of sustained and transient channels for theories of visual pattern masking, saccadic suppression, and information processing. *Psychological Review, 83*(1), 1–36.

Brewer, J. B., Zhao, Z., Desmond, J. E., Glover, G. H., & Gabrieli, J. D. E. (1998). Making memories: Brain activity that predicts how well visual experience will be remembered. *Science, 281*(5380), 1185–1187.

Britt, M. A. (1994). The interaction of referential ambiguity and argument structure in the parsing of prepositional phrases. *Journal of Memory & Language, 33*(2), 251–283.

Britt, M. A., Perfetti, C. A., Garrod, S., & Rayner, K. (1992). Parsing in discourse: Context effects and their limits. *Journal of Memory & Language, 31*(3), 293–314.

Broadbent, D. E. (1958). *Perception and communication.* Oxford: Oxford University Press.

Broadbent, D. E. (1982). Task combination and selective intake of information. *Acta Psychologica, 50*(3), 253–290.

Broadbent, D. E., & Broadbent, M. H. (1987). From detection to identification: Response to multiple targets in rapid serial visual presentation. *Perception & Psychophysics, 42*, 105–113.

Broder, A., & Schiffer, S. (2003). Take the best versus simultaneous feature matching: Probabilistic inferences from memory and effects of representation format. *Journal of Experimental Psychology: General, 132*, 277–293.

Brooks, L. R. (1968). Spatial and verbal components of the act of recall. *Canadian Journal of Psychology, 22*, 349–368.

Brown, J. (1958). Some tests of the decay theory of immediate memory. *Quarterly Journal of Experimental Psychology, 10*, 12–21.

Brown, R. (1958). *Words and things.* Glencoe, IL: Free Press.

Brown, R., & Kulik, J. (1977). Flashbulb memories. *Cognition, 5*(1), 73–99.

Brown, R., & McNeill, D. (1966). The "tip of the tongue" phenomenon. *Journal of Verbal Learning & Verbal Behavior, 5*(4), 325–337.

Brown, R. G., & Marsden, C. D. (1988). Internal versus external cues and the control of attention in Parkinson's disease. *Brain, 111*, 323–345.

Brown, R. W., & Lenneberg, E. H. (1954). A study in language and cognition. *Journal of Abnormal & Social Psychology, 49*, 454–462.

Bruner, J. S., Goodnow, J. J., & Austin, G. A. (1956). *A study of thinking.* New York: Wiley.

Bryan, W. L., & Harter, N. (1897). Studies in the physiology and psychology of the telegraphic language. *Psychological Review, 4*(1), 27–53.

Bryant, D. J. (1991). Exceptions to recognition failure as a function of the encoded association between cue and target. *Memory & Cognition, 19*, 210–219.

Buckner, R. L., & Koutstaal, W. (1998). Functional neuroimaging studies of encoding, priming, and explicit memory retrieval. *Proceedings of the National Academy of Sciences, 95*, 891–898.

Buckner, R. L., & Petersen, S. E. (1996). What does neuroimaging tell us about the role of prefrontal cortex in memory retrieval? *Seminars in the Neurosciences, 8*, 47–55.

Buckner, R. L., Petersen, S. E., Ojemann, J. G., Miezin, F. M., Squire, L. R., & Raichle, M. E. (1995). Functional anatomical studies of explicit and implicit memory retrieval tasks. *Journal of Neuroscience, 15*, 12–29.

Bundesen, C., & Larsen, A. (1975). Visual transformation of size. *Journal of Experimental Psychology: Human Perception and Performance, 1*(3), 214–220.

Bunzeck, N., Wuestenberg, T., Lutz, K., Heinze, H.-J., & Jancke, L. (2005). Scanning silence: Mental imagery of complex sounds. *Neuroimage, 26*, 1119–1127.

Burgund, E. D., & Marsolek, C. J. (2000). Viewpoint-invariant and viewpoint-dependent object recognition in dissociable neural subsystems. *Psychonomic Bulletin & Review, 7*, 480–489.

Burke, A., Heuer, F., & Reisberg, D. (1992). Remembering emotional events. *Memory & Cognition, 20*, 277–290.

Burke, D. M., MacKay, D. G., Worthley, J. S., & Wade, E. (1991). On the tip of the tongue: What causes word finding failures in young and older adults? *Journal of Memory & Language, 30*, 542–579.

Burns, B. D. (2004). The effects of speed on skilled chess performance. *Psychological Science, 15*, 442–447.

Cabeza, R., & Nyberg, L. (2000). Imaging cognition. II. An empirical review of 275 PET and fMRI studies. *Journal of Cognitive Neuroscience, 12*, 1–47.

Cahill, L., Babinsky, R., Markowitsch, H. J., & McGaugh, J. L. (1995). The amygdala and emotional memory. *Nature, 377*, 295–296.

Cahill, L., & McGaugh, J. L. (1995). A novel demonstration of enhanced memory associated with emotional arousal. *Consciousness & Cognition: An International Journal, 4*(4), 410–421.

Calne, D. B. (1999). *Within reason: Rationality and human behavior.* New York: Pantheon.

Campos, A., Perez, M. J., & Gonzalez, M. A. (1997). The interactiveness of paired images is affected by bizarreness and image vividness. *Imagination, Cognition & Personality, 16*(3), 301–307.

Carey, S. (1978). The child as a word learner. In M. Halle, J. Bresnan, & G. A. Miller (Eds.), *Linguistic theory and psychological reality* (pp. 264–293). Cambridge, MA: MIT Press.

Carey, S., & Bartlett, E. (1978). Acquiring a single new word. *Papers and Reports on Child Language Development, 15*, 17–29.

Carlesimo, G. A., Perri, R., Turriziani, P., Tomaiuolo, F., & Caltagirone, C. (2001). Remembering what but not where: Independence of spatial and visual working memory in the human brain. *Cortex, 36,* 519–534.

Carlisle, E., & Shafir, E. (2005). Questioning the cheater-detection hypothesis: New studies with the selection task. *Thinking & Reasoning, 11,* 97–122.

Carlson, B. W. (1990). Anchoring and adjustment in judgments under risk. *Journal of Experimental Psychology: Learning, Memory, and Cognition, 16*(4), 665–676.

Carlton, L. G. (1981a). Processing visual feedback information for movement control. *Journal of Experimental Psychology: Human Perception and Performance, 7,* 1019–1030.

Carlton, L. G. (1981b). Visual information: The control of aiming movements. *Quarterly Journal of Experimental Psychology: Human Experimental Psychology, 33A,* 87–93.

Carpenter, P. A., Just, M. A., & Shell, P. (1990). What one intelligence test measures: A theoretical account of the processing in the Raven Progressive Matrices Test. *Psychological Review, 97*(3), 404–431.

Casati, R. (2004). The shadow knows: A primer on the informational structure of cast shadows. *Perception, 33,* 1385–1396.

Castiello, U., & Stelmach, G. E. (1993). Generalized representation of handwriting: Evidence of effector independence. *Acta Psychologica, 82,* 53–68.

Catrambone, R. (1994). Improving examples to improve transfer to novel problems. *Memory & Cognition, 22*(5), 606–615.

Catrambone, R. (1995). Aiding subgoal learning: Effects on transfer. *Journal of Educational Psychology, 87*(1), 5–17.

Catrambone, R. (1996). Generalizing solution procedures learned from examples. *Journal of Experimental Psychology: Learning, Memory, and Cognition, 22*(4), 1020–1031.

Catrambone, R. (1998). The subgoal learning model: Creating better examples so that students can solve novel problems. *Journal of Experimental Psychology: General, 127*(4), 355–376.

Catrambone, R. (2002). The effects of surface and structural feature matches on the access of story analogs. *Journal of Experimental Psychology: Learning, Memory, and Cognition, 28,* 318–334.

Catrambone, R., & Holyoak, K. J. (1990). Learning subgoals and methods for solving probability problems. *Memory & Cognition, 18*(6), 593–603.

Cermak, L. S., & Butters, N. (1972). The role of interference and encoding in the short-term memory deficits of Korsakoff patients. *Neuropsychologia, 10,* 89–96.

Chao, L. L., Martin, A., & Haxby, J. V. (1999). Are face-responsive regions selective only for faces? *Neuroreport, 10,* 2945–2950.

Chapman, G. B., & Bornstein, B. H. (1996). The more you ask for, the more you get: Anchoring in personal injury verdicts. *Applied Cognitive Psychology, 10*(6), 519–540.

Charlot, V., Tzourio, N., Zilbovicius, M., Mazoyer, B. M., & Denis, M. (1992). Different mental imagery abilities result in different regional cerebral blood flow activation patterns during cognitive tasks. *Neuropsychologia, 30*(6), 565–580.

Charness, N., Tuffiash, M., Krampe, R., Reingold, E., & Vasyukova, E. (2005). The role of deliberate practice in chess expertise. *Applied Cognitive Psychology, 19,* 151–165.

Chase, W. G., & Simon, H. A. (1973). Perception in chess. *Cognitive Psychology, 4*(1), 55–81.

Chater, N. (1996). Reconciling simplicity and likelihood principles in perceptual organization. *Psychological Review, 103*(3), 566–581.

Chater, N., & Oaksford, M. (1999). The probability heuristics model of syllogistic reasoning. *Cognitive Psychology, 38,* 191–258.

Chen, W., Kato, T., Zhu, X. H., Ogawa, S., Tank, D. W., & Ugurbil, K. (1998). Human primary visual cortex and lateral geniculate nucleus activation during visual imagery. *Neuroreport, 9,* 3669–3674.

Chen, Z. (1995). Analogical transfer: From schematic pictures to problem solving. *Memory & Cognition, 23*(2), 255–269.

Chen, Z., & Mo, L. (2004). Schema induction in problem solving: A multidimensional analysis. *Journal of Experimental Psychology: Learning, Memory, and Cognition, 30,* 583–600.

Chen, Z., Mo., L., & Honomichl, R. (2004). Having the memory of an elephant: Long-term retrieval and the use of analogues in problem solving. *Journal of Experimental Psychology: General, 133,* 415–433.

Cheng, P. W., & Holyoak, K. J. (1985). Pragmatic reasoning schemas. *Cognitive Psychology, 17*(4), 391–416.

Cheng, P. W., Holyoak, K. J., Nisbett, R. E., & Oliver, L. M. (1986). Pragmatic versus syntactic approaches to training deductive reasoning. *Cognitive Psychology, 18*(3), 293–328.

Cherry, E. C. (1953). Some experiments on the recognition of speech, with one and with two ears. *Journal of the Acoustical Society of America, 25,* 975–979.

Cherubini, P., Garnham, A., & Oakhill, J. (1998). Can any ostrich fly? Some new data on belief bias in syllogistic reasoning. *Cognition, 69*(2), 179–218.

Chi, M. T. H., Feltovich, P., & Glaser, R. (1981). Categorization and representation of physics problems by experts and novices. *Cognitive Science, 5*, 121–152.

Chincotta, D., Underwood, G., Ghani, K., Papadopoulou, E., & Wresinksi, M. (1999). Memory span for Arabic numerals and digit words: Evidence for a limited-capacity visuo-spatial storage system. *Quarterly Journal of Experimental Psychology, 2A*, 325–351.

Chomsky, N. (1957). *Syntactic structures.* The Hague: Mouton.

Chomsky, N. (1959). A review of B. F. Skinner's verbal behavior. *Language, 35*, 26–58.

Chomsky, N. (1965). *Aspects of the theory of syntax.* Cambridge, MA: MIT Press.

Christianson, S.-A. (1989). Flashbulb memories: Special, but not so special. *Memory & Cognition, 17*, 443.

Chronicle, E. P., MacGregor, J. N., & Ormerod, T. C. (2004). What makes an insight problem? The roles of heuristics, goal conception, and solution recoding in knowledge-lean problems. *Journal of Experimental Psychology: Learning, Memory, and Cognition, 30*, 14–27.

Chun, M. M., & Potter, M. C. (1995). A two-stage model for multiple target detection in rapid serial visual presentation. *Journal of Experimental Psychology: Human Perception and Performance, 21*, 109–127.

Clark, F. J., & Burgess, P. R. (1975). Slowly adapting receptors in cat knee joint: Can they signal joint angle? *Journal of Neurophysiology, 38*, 1448–1463.

Clark, H. H., & Clark, E. V. (1977). *Psychology and language: An introduction to psycholinguistics.* New York: Harcourt, Brace, Jovanovich.

Clarke, M., Losoff, A., McCracken, M., & Rood, D. (1984). Linguistic relativity and sex/gender studies: Epistemological and methodological considerations. *Language Learning, 34*, 47–67.

Clarke, S., Adriani, M., & Tardif, E. (2005). "What" and "where" in human audition: Evidence from anatomical, activation, and lesion studies. In R. Konig, P. Heil, E. Budinger, & H. Scheich (Eds.), *The auditory cortex: A synthesis of human and animal research* (pp. 77–94). Mahwah, NJ: Erlbaum.

Clarke, V. J., & Lamberts, K. (1997). Strategy shifts and expertise in solving transformation rule problems. *Thinking & Reasoning, 3*(4), 271–290.

Cleary, A. M., Langley, M. M., & Seiler, K. R. (2004). Recognition without picture identification: Geons as components of the pictorial memory trace. *Psychonomic Bulletin & Review, 11*, 903–908.

Clement, C. A., Mawby, R., & Giles, D. E. (1994). The effects of manifest relational similarity on analog retrieval. *Journal of Memory and Language, 33*, 396–420.

Clower, D. M., Hoffman, J. M., Votaw, J. R., Faber, T. L., Woods, R. P., & Alexander, G. E. (1996). Role of posterior parietal cortex in the recalibration of visually guided reaching. *Nature, 383*, 618–621.

Cohen, J. D., Perlstein, W. M., Braver, T. S., Nystrom, L. E., Noll, D. C., Jonides, J., et al. (1997). Temporal dynamics of brain activation during a working memory task. *Nature, 386*, 604–608.

Cohen, M. S., Kosslyn, S. M., Breiter, H. C. DiGirolamo, G. J., Thompson, W. L., Anderson, A. K., Cohen, N. J., & Squire, L. R. (1980). Preserved learning and pattern-analyzing skill in amnesia: Dissociation of knowing how and knowing what. *Science, 210*, 207–210.

Cole, J. (1995). *Pride and a daily marathon.* Cambridge, MA: MIT Press.

Cole, J., & Paillard, J. (1995). Living without touch and peripheral information about body position and movement: Studies with deafferented subjects. In J. L. M. A. J. Bermudez (Ed.), *The body and the self* (pp. 245–266). Cambridge, MA: MIT Press.

Colle, H. A., & Welsh, A. (1976). Acoustic masking in primary memory. *Journal of Verbal Learning & Verbal Behavior, 15*(1), 17–31.

Collins, A. M., & Loftus, E. F. (1975). A spreading-activation theory of semantic processing. *Psychological Review, 82*(6), 407–428.

Collins, A. M., & Quillian, M. R. (1969). Retrieval time from semantic memory. *Journal of Verbal Learning & Verbal Behavior, 8*(2), 240–247.

Collins, A. M., & Quillian, M. R. (1972). How to make a language user. In E. Tulving & W. Donaldson (Eds.), *Organization of memory* (pp. 309–351). New York: Academic Press.

Coltheart, M., Curtis, B., Atkins, P., & Haller, M. (1993). Models of reading aloud: Dual-route and parallel distributed-processing approaches. *Psychological Review, 100*(4), 589–608.

Coltheart, M., & Rastle, K. (1994). Serial processing in reading aloud: Evidence for dual-route models of reading. *Journal of Experimental Psychology: Human Perception and Performance, 20*, 1197–1211.

Conrad, C. (1972). Cognitive economy in semantic memory. *Journal of Experimental Psychology, 92*(2), 149–154.

Conrad, R. (1964). Acoustic confusions in immediate memory. *British Journal of Psychology, 55*(1), 75–84.

Conway, M. (2002). *Levels of processing 30 years on.* London: Taylor & Francis.

Cooper, L. A. (1975). Mental rotation of random two-dimensional shapes. *Cognitive Psychology, 7*(1), 20–43.

Cooper, L. A., Schacter, D. L., Ballesteros, S., & Moore, C. (1992). Priming and recognition of transformed three-dimensional objects: Effects of size and reflection. *Journal of Experimental Psychology: Learning, Memory, and Cognition, 18*, 43–57.

Cooper, L. A., & Shepard, R. N. (1975). Mental transformation in the identification of left and right hands. *Journal of Experimental Psychology: Human Perception and Performance, 1*(1), 48–56.

Corkin, S. (1968). Acquisition of motor skill after bilateral medial temporal lobe excision. *Neuropsychologia, 6*, 255–265.

Corkin S. (2002). What's new with the amnesic patient H.M.? *Nature Reviews Neuroscience, 3*, 153–160.

Cornoldi, C., Cortesi, A., & Preti, D. (1991). Individual differences in the capacity limitations of visuospatial short-term memory: Research on sighted and totally congenitally blind people. *Memory & Cognition, 19*(5), 459–468.

Corteen, R. S., & Wood, B. (1972). Autonomic responses to shock-associated words in an unattended channel. *Journal of Experimental Psychology, 94*(3), 308–313.

Cosmides, L. (1989). The logic of social exchange: Has natural selection shaped how humans reason? Studies with the Wason selection task. *Cognition, 31*(3), 187–276.

Cosmides, L., & Tooby, J. (1992). Cognitive adaptations for social exchange. In J. Barkow, L. Cosmides, & J. Tooby (Eds.), *The adapted mind: Evolutionary psychology and the generation of culture* (pp. 163–228). New York: Oxford University Press.

Cosmides, L., & Tooby, J. (2000). The cognitive neuroscience of social reasoning. In M. Gazzaniga (Ed.), *The cognitive neurosciences* (2nd ed., pp. 1259–1270). Cambridge, MA: MIT Press.

Courtney, S. M., Ungerleider, L. G., Keil, K., & Haxby, J. V. (1996). Object and spatial visual working memory activate separate neural systems in human cortex. *Cerebral Cortex, 6*, 39–49.

Cowan, N. (1987). Auditory sensory storage in relation to the growth of sensation and acoustic information extraction. *Journal of Experimental Psychology: Human Perception and Performance, 13*(2), 204–215.

Craik, F. I., & Lockhart, R. S. (1972). Levels of processing: A framework for memory research. *Journal of Verbal Learning and Verbal Behavior, 11*, 671–684.

Craik, F. I., & Tulving, E. (1975). Depth of processing and the retention of words in episodic memory. *Journal of Experimental Psychology: General, 104*, 268–294.

Craik, F. I., & Watkins, M. J. (1973). The role of rehearsal in short-term memory. *Journal of Verbal Learning & Verbal Behavior, 12*, 599–607.

Craver-Lemley, C., & Reeves, A. (1992). How visual imagery interferes with vision. *Psychological Review, 99*(4), 633–649.

Curran, T., & Keele, S. W. (1993). Attentional and nonattentional forms of sequence learning. *Journal of Experimental Psychology: Learning, Memory, and Cognition, 19*, 189–202.

Daneman, M., & Carpenter, P. A. (1980). Individual differences in working memory and reading. *Journal of Verbal Learning & Verbal Behavior, 19*(4), 450–466.

Daugman, J. (1990). Brain metaphor and brain theory. In E. Schwartz (Ed.), *Computational neuroscience*. Cambridge, MA: MIT Press.

d'Avella, A., & Bizzi, E. (2005). Shared and specific muscle synergies in natural motor behaviors. *Proceedings of the National Academy of Sciences, 102*, 3076–3081.

d'Avella, A., Saltiel, P., & Bizzi, E. (2004). Combinations of muscle synergies in the construction of a natural motor behavior. *Nature Neuroscience, 6*, 300–308.

Davies, I. R. L., Sowden, P. T., Jerrett, D. T., Jerrett, T., & Corbett, G. G. (1998). A cross-cultural study of English and Setswana speakers on a colour triads task: A test of the Sapir–Whorf hypothesis. *British Journal of Psychology, 89*(1), 1–15.

Davis, H. L., Hoch, S. J., & Ragsdale, E. E. (1986). An anchoring and adjustment model of spousal predictions. *Journal of Consumer Research, 13*, 25–37.

Davis, G., & Holmes, A. (2005). The capacity of visual short-term memory is not a fixed number of objects. *Memory & Cognition, 33*, 185–195.

Dawson, M. E., & Schell, A. M. (1982). Electrodermal responses to attended and nonattended significant stimuli during dichotic listening. *Journal of Experimental Psychology: Human Perception and Performance, 8*, 315–324.

Day, R. S. (1988). Alternative representations. In G. H. Bower (Ed.), *The psychology of learning and motivation* (Vol. 22, pp. 261–305). San Diego: Academic Press.

De Groot, A. D. (1946/1978). *Thought and choice in chess*. The Hague: Mouton.

De Weerd, P., Reinke, K., Ryan, L., McIsaac, T., Perschler, P., Schnyer, D., et al. (2003). Cortical mechanisms for acquisition and performance of bimanual motor sequences. *Neuroimage, 19*, 1405–1416.

Deese, J. (1959). On the prediction of occurrence of particular verbal intrusions in immediate recall. *Journal of Experimental Psychology, 58*, 17–22.

DeKeyser, R. M. (2000). The robustness of critical period effects in second language acquisition. *Studies in Second Language Acquisition, 22*, 499–533.

Dell, G. S., Schwartz, M. F., Marting, N., Saffran, E. M., & Gagnon, D. A. (1997). Lexical access in aphasic and nonaphasic speakers. *Psychological Review, 104*, 801–838.

Demb, J. B., Desmond, J. E., Wagner, A. D., Vaidya, C. J., Glover, G. H., & Gabrieli, J. D. E. (1995). Semantic encoding and retrieval in the left inferior prefrontal cortex: A functional MRI study of task difficulty and process specificity. *Journal of Neuroscience, 15*, 5870–5878.

Denis, M., & Carfantan, M. (1985). People's knowledge about images. *Cognition, 20*(1), 49–60.

Descartes, R. (1664/1972). *Traite de L'homme [Treatise on man]*. (T. Hall, Trans.). Cambridge, MA: Harvard University Press.

D'Esposito, M., & Postle, B. R. (1999). The dependence of span and delayed-response performance on prefrontal cortex. *Neuropsychologia, 37*, 1303–1315.

D'Esposito, M., Postle, B. R., Ballard, D., & Lease, J. (1999). Maintenance versus manipulation of information held in working memory: An event-related fMRI study. *Brain & Cognition, 41*, 66–86.

Deutsch, J. A., & Deutsch, D. (1963). Attention: Some theoretical considerations. *Psychological Review, 70*, 51–61.

Di Lollo, V. (1980). Temporal integration in visual memory. *Journal of Experimental Psychology: General, 109*, 75–97.

Dickstein, L. S. (1975). Effects of instructions and premise order on errors in syllogistic reasoning. *Journal of Experimental Psychology: Human Learning and Memory, 1*(4), 376–384.

Dickstein, L. S. (1976). Differential difficulty of categorical syllogisms. *Bulletin of the Psychonomic Society, 8*(4), 330–332.

Dickstein, L. S. (1978). The effect of figure on syllogistic reasoning. *Memory & Cognition, 6*(1), 76–83.

Diehl, R. L., & Kluender, K. R. (1989). On the objects of speech perception. *Ecological Psychology, 2*, 121–144.

Diehl, R. L., Lotto, A. J., & Holt, L. L. (2004). Speech perception. *Annual Review of Psychology, 55*, 149–179.

Dinges, D. F., Whitehouse, W. G., Orne, E. C., Powell, J. W., Orne, M. T., & Erdelyi, M. H. (1992). Evaluating hypnotic memory enhancement (hypermnesia and reminiscence) using multitrial forced recall. *Journal of Experimental Psychology: Learning, Memory, and Cognition, 18*, 1139–1147.

Djordjevic, J., Zatorre, R. J., Petrides, M., & Jones-Gotman, M. (2004a). The mind's nose effects of odor and visual imagery on odor detection. *Psychological Science, 15*, 143–148.

Djordjevic, J., Zatorre, R. J., Petrides, M., & Jones-Gotman, M. (2004b). Effects of perceived and imagined odors on taste detection. *Chemical Senses, 29*, 199–208.

Domjan, M. (2005). Pavlovian conditioning: A functional perspective. *Annual Review of Psychology, 56*, 179–206.

Donnelly, C. M., & McDaniel, M. A. (1993). Use of analogy in learning scientific concepts. *Journal of Experimental Psychology: Learning, Memory, and Cognition, 19*(4), 975–987.

Dooling, D. J., & Christiaansen, R. E. (1977). Episodic and semantic aspects of memory for prose. *Journal of Experimental Psychology: Human Learning and Memory, 3*, 428–436.

Doyon, J., Penhune, V., & Ungerleider, L. G. (2003). Distinct contribution of the cortico-striatal and cortico-cerebellar systems to motor skill learning. *Neuropsychologia, 41*, 252–262.

Drayna, D., Manichaikul, A., de Lange, M., Snieder, H., & Spector, T. (2001). Genetic correlates of musical pitch recognition in humans. *Science, 291*, 1969–1972.

Driver, J., & Spence, C. J. (1994). Spatial synergies between auditory and visual attention. In C. M. M. Umilta (Ed.), *Attention and performance 15: Conscious and nonconscious information processing* (pp. 311–331). Cambridge, MA: MIT Press.

Dudai, Y. (2004). The neurobiology of consolidations, or, how stable is the engram? *Annual Review of Psychology, 55*, 51–86.

Dunbar, K. (2001). The analogical paradox: Why analogy is so easy in naturalistic settings yet so difficult in the psychological laboratory. In D. Gentner, K. J. Holyoak, & B. Kokinov (Eds.), *Analogy: Perspectives from cognitive science* (pp. 313–334). Cambridge, MA: MIT Press.

Duncker, K. (1945). On problem-solving. *Psychological Monographs, 5*, 113.

Dupoux, E., Kouider, S., & Mehler, J. (2003). Lexical access without attention? Explorations using dichotic priming. *Journal of Experimental Psychology: Human Perception and Performance. 29*, 172–184.

Durso, F. T., Rea, C. B., & Dayton, T. (1994). Graph-theoretic confirmation of restructuring during insight. *Psychological Science, 5*(2), 94–98.

Easterbrook, J. A. (1959). The effect of emotion on cue utilization and the organization of behavior. *Psychological Review, 66*, 183–201.

Eddy, D. M. (1982). Probabilistic reasoning in clinical medicine: Problems and opportunities. In D. Kahneman, P. Slovic, & A. Tversky (Eds.), *Judgment under uncertainty: Heuristics and biases*. Cambridge: Cambridge University Press.

Eich, E., & Macaulay, D. (2000). Are real moods required to reveal mood-congruent and mood-dependent memory? *Psychological Science, 11*, 244–248.

Eliassen, J. C., Souza, T., & Sanes, J. N. (2001). Human brain activation accompanying explicitly directed movement sequence learning. *Experimental Brain Research, 141*, 269–280.

Elliott, D., & Allard, F. (1985). The utilization of visual feedback information during rapid pointing movements. *Quarterly Journal of Experimental Psychology: A, Human Experimental Psychology, 37A*, 407–425.

Elliott, D., Zuberec, S., & Milgram, P. (1994). The effects of periodic visual occlusion on ball catching. *Journal of Motor Behavior, 26*, 113–122.

Ellis, N. C., & Hennelly, R. A. (1980). A bilingual word-length effect: Implications for intelligence testing and the relative ease of mental calculation in Welsh and English. *British Journal of Psychology, 71*, 43–51.

Engle, R. W., & Bukstel, L. (1978). Memory processes among bridge players of differing expertise. *American Journal of Psychology, 91*, 673–689.

Engle, R. W., Tuholski, S. W., Laughlin, J. E., & Conway, A. R. A. (1999). Working memory, short-term memory, and general fluid intelligence: A latent-variable approach. *Journal of Experimental Psychology: General, 128*(3), 309–331.

Epstein, R., Graham, K. S., & Downing, P. E. (2003). Viewpoint-specific scene representations in human parahippocampal cortex. *Neuron, 37*, 865–876.

Epstein, R., Lanza, R. P., & Skinner, B. F. (1980). Symbolic communication between two pigeons (Columba livia domestica). *Science, 207*(4430), 543–545.

Epstein, W. (1965). Nonrelational judgments of size and distance. *American Journal of Psychology, 78*, 120–123.

Erdelyi, M. H. (1994). Hypnotic hypermnesia: The empty set of hypermnesia. *International Journal of Clinical and Experimental Hypnosis, 42*, 379–390.

Erickson, M. A., & Kruschke, J. K. (1998). Rules and exemplars in category learning. *Journal of Experimental Psychology: General, 127*, 107–140.

Ericsson, K. A. (1996). The acquisition of expert performance: An introduction to some of the issues. In K. A. Ericsson (Ed.), *The road to excellence: The acquisition of expert performance in the arts and sciences, sports, and games* (pp. 1–50). Mahwah, NJ: Erlbaum.

Ericsson, K. A., Krampe, R. T., & Tesch-Roemer, C. (1993). The role of deliberate practice in the acquisition of expert performance. *Psychological Review, 100*(3), 363–406.

Ericsson, K. A., & Simon, H. A. (1993). *Protocol analysis: Verbal reports as data* (Rev. ed.). Cambridge, MA: MIT Press.

Ernst, G. W., & Newell, A. (1969). *GPS: A case study in the generality of problem solving*. New York: Academic Press.

Ervin, S. M. (1962). The connotations of gender. *Word, 18*, 249–261.

Estes, W. K. (1994). *Classification and cognition*. New York: Oxford University Press.

Evans, J. St.-B. T. (2003). In two minds: Dual-process accounts of reasoning. *Trends in Cognitive Sciences, 7*, 454–459.

Evans, J. St.-B. T., Barston, J. L., & Pollard, P. (1983). On the conflict between logic and belief in syllogistic reasoning. *Memory & Cognition, 11*(3), 295–306.

Evans, J. St.-B. T., Handley, S. J., Harper, C. N. J., & Johnson-Laird, P. N. (1999). Reasoning about necessity and possibility: A test of the mental model theory of deduction. *Journal of Experimental Psychology, 25*, 1495–1513.

Evans, J. St.-B. T., Handley, S. J., Perham, N., Over, D. E., & Thompson, V. A. (2000). Frequency versus probability formats in statistical word problems. *Cognition, 77*, 197–213.

Evans, J. St.-B. T., Newstead, S. E., & Byrne, R. M. J. (1993). *Human reasoning: The psychology of deduction*. Mahwah, NJ: Erlbaum.

Evans, J. St.-B. T., & Over, D. E. (1996). Rationality in the selection task: Epistemic utility versus uncertainty reduction. *Psychological Review, 103*, 356–363.

Fadiga, L., Craighero, L., Buccino, G., & Rizzolatti, G. (2002). Speech listening specifically modulates the excitability of tongue muscles: A TMS study. *European Journal of Neuroscience, 15*, 399–402.

Faillenot, I., Toni, I., Decety, J., Gregorie, M. C., & Jeannerod, M. (1997). Visual pathways for object-oriented action and object recognition: Functional anatomy with PET. *Cerebral Cortex, 7*, 77–85.

Fang, F., & He, S. (2005). Viewer-centered object representation in the human visual system revealed by viewpoint aftereffects. *Neuron, 45*, 793–800.

Fanselow, M. S., & Poulos, A. M. (2005). The neuroscience of mammalian associative learning. *Annual Review of Psychology, 56*, 207–234.

Farah, M. J. (1984). The neurological basis of mental imagery: A componential analysis. *Cognition, 18*, 245–272.

Farah, M. J. (1990). *Visual agnosia: Disorders of object recognition and what they tell us about normal vision.* Cambridge, MA: MIT Press.

Feldman, A. G. (1986). Once more on the equilibrium-point hypothesis (1 model) for motor control. *Journal of Motor Behavior, 18*, 17–54.

Feldman, H., Goldin-Meadow, S., & Gleitman, L. R. (1978). Beyond Herodotus: The creation of language by linguistically deprieved deaf children. In A. Locke (Ed.), *Action, gesture, and symbol: The emergence of language* (pp. 351–414). London: Academic Press.

Fellows, L. K., Heberlein, A. S., Morales, D. A., Shivde, G., Waller, S., & Wu, D. H. (2005). Method matters: An empirical study of impact in cognitive neuroscience. *Journal of Cognitive Neuroscience, 17*, 850–858.

Fernberger, S. W. (1921). A preliminary study of the range of visual apprehension. *American Journal of Psychology, 32*, 121–133.

Feynman, R. P., & Leighton, R. (1985). *"Surely you're joking, Mr. Feynman!": Adventures of a curious character.* New York: Bantam.

Fiedler, K., Brinkmann, B., Betsch, T., & Wild, B. (2000). A sampling approach to biases in conditional probability judgments: Beyond base rate neglect and statistical format. *Journal of Experimental Psychology: General, 129*, 399–418.

Finke, R. A. (1980). Levels of equivalence in imagery and perception. *Psychological Review, 87*(2), 113–132.

Finke, R. A. (1996). Imagery, creativity, and emergent structure. *Consciousness & Cognition: An International Journal, 5*(3), 381–393.

Finke, R. A., Pinker, S., & Farah, M. J. (1989). Reinterpreting visual patterns in mental imagery. *Cognitive Science, 13*, 51–78.

Finke, R. A., & Shepard, R. N. (1986). Visual functions of mental imagery. In K. R. Boff & L. Kaufman (Eds.), *Handbook of perception and human performance* (Vol. 2, pp. 1–55). New York: Wiley.

Finkenauer, C., Luminet, O., Gisle, L., El-Ahmadi, A., Van der Linden, M., & Philippot, P. (1998). Flashbulb memories and the underlying mechanisms of their formation: Toward an emotional-integrative model. *Memory & Cognition, 26*, 516–531.

Flament, D., Ellermann, J. M., Kim, S.-G., Ugurbil, K., & Ebner, T. J. (1996). Functional magnetic resonance imaging of cerebellar activation during the learning of a visuomotor dissociation task. *Human Brain Mapping, 4*, 210–226.

Flash, T., & Gurevich I. (1997). Models of motor adaptation and impedance control in human arm movements. In P. Morasso & V. Sanguineti (Eds.), *Self-organization, computational maps, and motor control* (pp. 423–481). Amsterdam: Elsevier Science.

Flash, T., & Hogan, N. (1985). The coordination of arm movements: An experimentally confirmed mathematical model. *The Journal of Neuroscience, 5*, 1688–1703.

Fleishman, E. A., & Parker, J. F. (1962). Factors in the retention and relearning of perceptual motor skill. *Journal of Experimental Psychology, 64*, 215–226.

Fletcher, C. R., & Chrysler, S. T. (1990). Surface forms, textbases, and situation models: Recognition memory for three types of textual information. *Discourse Processes, 13*(2), 175–190.

Fletcher, P. C., Frith, C. D., Baker, S. C., Shallice, T., Frackowiak, R. S., & Dolan, R. J. (1995). The mind's eye: Precuneus activation in memory-related imagery. *Neuroimage, 2*, 195–200.

Fleury, M., Bard, C., Teasdale, N., Paillard, J., Cole, J., Lujoie, Y., et al. (1995). Weight judgment: The discrimination capacity of a deafferented subject. *Brain, 118*, 1149–1156.

Fodor, J. A., & Garrett, M. (1967). Some syntactic determinants of sentential complexity. *Perception & Psychophysics, 2*(7), 289–296.

Fodor, J. D. (1995). Comprehending sentence structure. In L. R. Gleitman & M. Liberman (Eds.), *An invitation to cognitive science* (Vol. 1, pp. 209–246). Cambridge, MA: MIT Press.

Folstein, J. R., & Van Petten, C. (2004). Multidimensional rule, unidimensional rule, and similarity strategies in categorization: Event-related brain potential correlates. *Journal of Experimental Psychology: Learning, Memory, and Cognition, 30*, 1026–1044.

Forster, K. I., & Chambers, S. M. (1973). Lexical access and naming time. *Journal of Verbal Learning & Verbal Behavior, 12*(6), 627–635.

Foster, D. H., & Gilson, S. J. (2002). Recognizing novel three-dimensional objects by summing signals from parts and views. *Proceedings of the Royal Society, London: B, Biological Sciences, 269,* 1939–1947.

Foulke, E., & Sticht, T. G. (1969). Review of research on the intelligibility and comprehension of accelerated speech. *Psychological Bulletin, 72*(1), 50–62.

Fowler, C. A. (1986). An event approach to the study of speech perception from a direct realist perspective. *Journal of Phonology, 14,* 3–28.

Franconeri, S. L., Hollingworth, A., & Simons, D. J. (2005). Do new objects capture attention? *Psychological Science, 16,* 275–281.

Frazier, L., & Clifton, C., Jr. (1996). *Construal.* Cambridge, MA: MIT Press.

Freyd, J. J. (1987). Dynamic mental representation. *Psychological Review, 94,* 427–438.

Freyd, J. J., & Finke, R. A. (1984). Representational momentum. *Journal of Experimental Psychology: Learning, Memory, and Cognition, 10*(1), 126–132.

Funnell, E. (1983). Phonological processes in reading: New evidence from acquired dyslexia. *British Journal of Psychology, 74*(2), 159–180.

Gabrieli, J. D. E. (1998). Cognitive neuroscience of human memory. *Annual Review of Psychology, 49,* 87–115.

Gabrieli, J. D. E., Fleischman, D. A., Keane, M. M., Reminger, S. L., & Morrell, F. (1995). Double dissociation between memory systems underlying explicit and implicit memory in the human brain. *Psychological Science, 6,* 76–82.

Gallo D. A., Roberts M. J., & Seamon, J. G. (1997). Remembering words not presented in lists: Can we avoid creating false memories? *Psychonomic Bulletin & Review, 4,* 271–276.

Gardner, B. T., & Gardner, R. A. (1967a). Teaching sign language to a chimpanzee: II. Demonstrations. *Psychonomic Bulletin, 1*(2), 36.

Gardner, B. T., & Gardner, R. A. (1975). Evidence for sentence constitutents in the early utterances of child and chimpanzee. *Journal of Experimental Psychology: General, 104*(3), 244–267.

Gardner, H. (1985). *The mind's new science: A history of the cognitive revolution.* New York: Basic Books.

Gardner, R. A., & Gardner, B. T. (1967b). Teaching sign language to a chimpanzee: I. Methodology and preliminary results. *Psychonomic Bulletin, 1*(2), 36.

Gardner, R. A., Gardner, B. T., & Van Cantfort, T. E. (Eds.). (1989). *Teaching sign language to chimpanzees.* Albany: State University of New York Press.

Garry, M., Manning, C. G., Loftus, E. F., & Sherman, S. J. (1996). Imagination inflation: Imagining a childhood event inflates confidence that it occurred. *Psychonomic Bulletin & Review, 3,* 208–214.

Gaskel, M., & Marslen-Wilson, W. D. (2001). Simulating parallel activation in spoken word recognition. In M. H. Christiansen & N. Chater (Eds.), *Connectionist psycholinguistics* (pp. 76–105). Westport, CT: Ablex.

Gathercole, S. E., Pickering, S. J., Knight, C., & Stegmann, Z. (2004). Working memory skills and educational attainment: Evidence from national curriculum assessments at 7 and 14 years of age. *Applied Cognitive Psychology, 18,* 1–16.

Gauthier, I., Curran, T., Curby, K. M., & Collins, D. (2003). Perceptual interference supports a nonmodular account of face processing. *Nature Neuroscience, 6,* 428–432.

Gauthier, I., Skudlarski, P., Gore, J. C., & Anderson, A. W. (2000). Expertise for cars and birds recruits brain areas involved in face recognition. *Nature Neuroscience, 3,* 191–197.

Gentner, D., Loewenstein, J., & Thompson, L. (2003). Learning and transfer: A general role for analogical reasoning. *Journal of Educational Psychology, 95,* 393–408.

Gentner, D., Rattermann, M. J., & Forbus, K. D. (1993). The roles of similarity in transfer: Separating retrievability from inferential soundness. *Cognitive Psychology, 25,* 431–467.

Gernsbacher, M. A. (Ed.). (1994). *Handbook of psycholinguistics.* San Diego: Academic Press.

Gerwig, M., Hajjar, K., Dimitrova, A., Maschke, M., Kolb, F. P., Frings, M., et al. (2005). Timing of conditioned eyeblink responses is impaired in cerebellar patients. *Journal of Neuroscience, 25,* 3919–3931.

Ghez, C., Gordon, J., Ghilardi, M. F., & Sainburg, R. (1995). Contributions of vision and proprioception to accuracy in limb movements. In M. S. Gazzaniga (Ed.), *The cognitive neurosciences* (pp. 549–564). Cambridge, MA: MIT Press.

Gibson, E. (1998). Linguistic complexity: Locality of syntactic dependencies. *Cognition, 68,* 1–76.

Gibson, E., & Pearlmutter, N. J. (1998). Constraints on sentence comprehension. *Trends in Cognitive Sciences, 2,* 262–268.

Gibson, J. J. (1979). *The ecological approach to visual perception.* Boston: Houghton Mifflin.

Gick, M. L., & Holyoak, K. J. (1980). Analogical problem solving. *Cognitive Psychology, 12*(3), 306–355.

Gick, M. L., & Holyoak, K. J. (1983). Schema induction and analogical transfer. *Cognitive Psychology, 15*(1), 1–38.

Gigerenzer, G. (2001). Content-blind norms, no norms, or good norms? A reply to Vranas. *Cognition, 81,* 93–103.

Gigerenzer, G., & Hoffrage, U. (1999). Overcoming difficulties in Bayesian reasoning: A reply to Lewis and Keren (1999) and Mellers and McGraw (1999). *Psychological Review, 106,* 425–430.

Gigerenzer, G., & Hug, K. (1992). Domain-specific reasoning: Social contracts, cheating, and perspective change. *Cognition, 43*(2), 127–171.

Gigerenzer, G., & Todd, P. M. (1999). Fast and frugal heuristics: The adaptive toolbox. In G. Gigerenzer, P. Todd, & the ABC Research Group (Eds.), *Simple heuristics that make us smart. Evolution and cognition* (pp. 3–34). New York: Oxford University Press.

Gilhooly, K. J., Logie, R. H., Wetherick, N. E., & Wynn, V. (1993). Working memory and strategies in syllogistic-reasoning tasks. *Memory & Cognition, 21*(1), 115–124.

Gilhooly, K. J., Wood, M., Kinnear, P. R., & Green, C. (1988). Skill in map reading and memory for maps. *Quarterly Journal of Experimental Psychology: Human Experimental Psychology, 40,* 87–107.

Girotto, V., & Gonzalez, M. (2001). Solving probabilistic and statistical problems: A matter of information structure and question form. *Cognition, 78,* 247–276.

Glanville, A. D., & Dallenbach, K. M. (1929). The range of attention. *American Journal of Psychology, 41,* 207–236.

Glenberg, A. M. (1997). What memory is for. *Behavioural and Brain Sciences, 20,* 1–55.

Glenberg, A. M., & Langston, W. E. (1992). Comprehension of illustrated text: Pictures help to build mental models. *Journal of Memory & Language, 31*(2), 129–151.

Gobet, F., Lane, P. C. R., Croker, S., Cheng, P. C.-H., Jones, G., Oliver, I., et al. (2001). Chunking mechanisms in human learning. *Trends in Cognitive Sciences, 5,* 236–243.

Gobet, F., & Simon, H. A. (1996). The roles of recognition processes and look-ahead search in time-constrained expert problem solving: Evidence from grand-master–level chess. *Psychological Science, 7*(1), 52–55.

Gobet, F., & Simon, H. A. (1998). Expert chess memory: Revisiting the chunking hypothesis. *Memory, 6*(3), 225–255.

Godden, D. R., & Baddeley, A. D. (1975). Context-dependent memory in two natural environments: On land and underwater. *British Journal of Psychology, 66*(3), 325–331.

Goel, V., Buchel, C., Frith, C., & Dolan, R. J. (2000). Dissociation of mechanisms underlying syllogistic reasoning. *Neuroimage, 12,* 504–514.

Goldin-Meadow, S., Gelman, S. A., & Mylander, C. (2005). Expressing generic concepts with and without a language model. *Cognition, 96,* 109–126.

Goldin-Meadow, S., & Mylander, C. (1998). Spontaneous sign systems created by deaf children in two cultures. *Nature, 391,* 279–281.

Goldman, W. P., Wolters, N. C., & Winograd, E. (1992). A demonstration of incubation in anagram problem solving. *Bulletin of the Psychonomic Society, 30*(1), 36–38.

Goldvarg, Y., & Johnson-Laird, P. N. (2000). Illusions in modal reasoning. *Memory & Cognition, 28,* 282–294.

Gomez-Beldarrain, M., Grafman, J., Ruiz de Velasco, I., Pascual-Leone, A., & Garcia-Monco, C. (2002). Prefrontal lesions impair the implicit and explicit learning of sequences on visuomotor tasks. *Experimental Brain Research, 142,* 529–538.

Gomi, H., & Kawato, M. (1996). Equilibrium-point control hypothesis examined by measured arm stiffness during multijoint movement. *Science, 272,* 117–120.

Gonsalves, B., Reber, P. J., Gitelman, D. R., Parrish, T. B., Mesulam, M. M., & Paller, K. A. (2004). Neural evidence that vivid imagining can lead to false remembering. *Psychological Science, 15,* 655–660.

Goodale, M. A., & Milner, A. D. (1992). Separate pathways for vision and action. *Trends in Neurosciences, 15,* 20–25.

Goodale, M. A., & Milner, A. D. (2004). *Sight unseen: An exploration of conscious and unconscious vision.* Oxford: Oxford University Press.

Goodale, M. A., & Westwood, D. A. (2004). An evolving view of duplex vision: Separate but interacting cortical pathways for perception and action. *Current Opinion in Neurobiology, 14,* 203–211.

Gopher, D., Brickner, M., & Navon, D. (1982). Different difficulty manipulations interact differently with task emphasis: Evidence for multiple resources. *Journal of Experimental Psychology: Human Perception and Performance, 8*(1), 146–157.

Gordon, P. (2004). Numerical cognition without words: Evidence from Amazonia. *Science, 306,* 496–499.

Graesser, A. C., Millis, K. K., & Zwaan, R. A. (1997). Discourse comprehension. *Annual Review of Psychology, 48,* 163–189.

Graesser, A. C., Singer, M., & Trabasso, T. (1994). Constructing inferences during narrative text comprehension. *Psychological Review, 101*(3), 371–395.

Graf, P., Shimamura, A. P., & Squire, L. R. (1985). Priming across modalities and priming across category levels: Extending the domain of preserved function in amnesia. *Journal of Experimental Psychology: Learning, Memory, and Cognition, 11*, 386–396.

Grafton, S. T., Hazeltine, E., & Ivry, R. B. (1998). Abstract and effector-specific representations of motor sequences identified with PET. *Journal of Neuroscience, 18*, 9420–9428.

Grainger, J., & Whitney, C. (2004). Does the huamn mnid raed wrods as a wlohe? *Trends in Cognitive Sciences, 8*, 58–59.

Granger, R., Wiebe, S. P., Taketani, M., & Lynch, G. (1996). Distinct memory circuits composing the hippocampal region. *Hippocampus, 6*, 567–578.

Graziano, M. S. A., Taylor, C. S. R., & Moore, T. (2002). Complex movements evoked by microstimulation of precentral cortex. *Neuron, 34*, 841–851.

Greenberg, D. L. (2004). President Bush's false "flashbulb" memory of 9/11/01. *Applied Cognitive Psychology, 18*, 363–370.

Greeno, J. G. (1974). Hobbits and orcs: Acquisition of a sequential concept. *Cognitive Psychology, 6*(2), 270–292.

Griggs, R. A. (1984). Memory cueing and instructional effects on Wason's selection task. *Current Psychological Research & Reviews, 3*(4), 3–10.

Griggs, R. A., & Cox, J. R. (1982). The elusive thematic-materials effect in Wason's selection task. *British Journal of Psychology, 73*(3), 407–420.

Grill-Spector, K., Knouf, N., & Kanwisher, N. (2004). The fusiform face area subserves face perception, not generic within-category identification. *Nature Neuroscience, 7*, 555–562.

Grill-Spector, K., & Malach, R. (2001). fMR-adaptation: A tool for studying the functional properties of human cortical neurons. *Acta Psychologica, 107*, 293–321.

Grodner, D., Gibson, E., & Watson, D. (2005). The influence of contrast on syntactic processing: Evidence for strong-interaction in sentence comprehension. *Cognition, 95*, 275–296.

Guiora, A., Beit-Halachmi, B., Fried, R., & Yoder, C. (1983). Language environment and gender identity attainment. *Language Learning, 32*, 289–304.

Gustin, W. C. (1985). The development of exceptional research mathematicians. In B. S. Bloom (Ed.), *Developing talent in young people* (pp. 270–331). New York: Ballantine.

Hakes, D. T., & Cairns, H. S. (1970). Sentence comprehension and relative pronouns. *Perception & Psychophysics, 8*(1), 5–8.

Hakes, D. T., & Foss, D. J. (1970). Decision processes during sentence comprehension: Effects of surface structure reconsidered. *Perception & Psychophysics, 8*, 413–416.

Hakuta, K. (1986). *Mirror of language.* New York: Basic Books.

Hakuta, K., Bialystok, E., & Wiley, E. (2003). A test of the critical-period hypothesis for second-language acquisition. *Psychological Science, 14*, 31–37.

Hamann, S. B., Ely, T. D., Grafton, S. T., & Kilts, C. D. (1999). Amygdala activity related to enhanced memory for pleasant and aversive stimuli. *Nature Neuroscience, 2*, 289–293.

Hambrick, D. Z., & Engle, R. W. (2002). Effects of domain knowledge, working memory capacity, and age on cognitive performance: An investigation of the knowledge-is-power hypothesis. *Cognitive Psychology, 44*, 339–387.

Harrington, D. L., Rao, S. M., Haaland, K. Y., Bobholz, J. A., Mayer, A. R., Binderx, J. R., et al. (2000). Specialized neural systems underlying representations of sequential movements. *Journal of Cognitive Neuroscience, 12*, 56–77.

Harris, C. R., Pashler, H. E., & Coburn, N. (2004). Moray revisited: High-priority affective stimuli and visual search. *Quarterly Journal of Experimental Psychology: Human Experimental Psychology, 57A*, 1–31.

Harris, J. A., Miniussi, C., Harris, I. M., & Diamond, M. E. (2002). Transient storage of a tactile memory trace in primary somatosensory cortex. *Journal of Neuroscience, 22*, 8720–8725.

Hart, J. T. (1965). Memory and the feeling-of-knowing experience. *Journal of Educational Psychology, 56*, 208–216.

Hart, J. T. (1967). Second-try recall, recognition, and the memory-monitoring process. *Journal of Educational Psychology, 58*, 193–197.

Hasan, Z. (1986). Optimized movement trajectories and joint stiffness in unperturbed, inertially loaded movements. *Biological Cybernetics, 53*, 373–382.

Hassebrock, F., Johnson, P. E., Bullemer, P., Fox, P. W., & Moller, J. H. (1993). When less is more: Representation and selective memory in expert problem solving. *American Journal of Psychology, 106*(2), 155–189.

Hauser, M. D., Chomsky, N., & Fitch, W. T. (2002). The faculty of language: What is it, who has it, and how did it evolve? *Science, 298*, 1569–1579.

Haxby, J. V., Gobbini, M. I., Furey, M. L., Ishai, A., Schouten, J. L., & Pietrini, P. (2001). Distributed and overlapping representations of faces and objects in ventral temporal cortex. *Science, 293*, 2425–2430.

Haxby, J. V., Gobbini, M. I., & Montgomery, K. (2004). Spatial and temporal distribution of face and object representations in the human brain. In M. S. Gazzaniga (Ed.), *The cognitive neurosciences* (3rd ed., pp. 889–904). Cambridge, MA: MIT Press.

Hayes, J. R. (1981). *The complete problem solver.* Philadelphia: Franklin Institute Press.

Hayman, C. A., Macdonald, C. A., & Tulving, E. (1993). The role of repetition and associative interference in new semantic learning in amnesia: A case experiment. *Journal of Cognitive Neuroscience, 5*(4), 375–389.

Heath, W. P., & Erickson, J. R. (1998). Memory for central and peripheral actions and props after varied post-event presentation. *Legal and Criminal Psychology, 3*, 321–346.

Hebb, D. O. (1949). *The organization of behavior.* New York: Wiley.

Hebb, D. O. (1968). Concerning imagery. *Psychological Review, 75*, 466–477.

Hécaen, H., & Angelergues, R. (1962). Agnosia for faces. *Archives of Neurology, 7*, 92–100.

Heider, E. R. (1972). Universals in color naming and memory. *Journal of Experimental Psychology, 93*, 10–20.

Heider, E. R., & Oliver, D. C. (1972). The structure of the color space in naming and memory for two languages. *Cognitive Psychology, 3*(2), 337–354.

Heit, E. (2000). Properties of inductive reasoning, *Psychonomic Bulletin & Review, 7*, 569–592.

Henry, F. M., & Rogers, D. E. (1960). Increased response latency for complicated movements and a "memory drum" theory of neuromotor reaction. *Research Quarterly of the American Association for Health, Physical Education, & Recreation, 31*, 448–458.

Hess, D. J., Foss, D. J., & Carroll, P. (1995). Effects of global and local context on lexical processing during language comprehension. *Journal of Experimental Psychology: General, 124*(1), 62–82.

Hess, E. H. (1958). "Imprinting" in animals. *Scientific American, 198*, 81–90.

Higham, P. A. (1998). Believing details known to have been suggested. *British Journal of Psychology, 89*, 265–283.

Hikosaka, O., Nakamura, K., Sakai, K., & Nakahara, H. (2002). Central mechanisms of motor skill learning. *Current Opinion in Neurobiology, 12*, 217–222.

Himmelbach, M., & Karnath, H. O. (2005). Dorsal and ventral stream interaction: Contributions from optic ataxia. *Journal of Cognitive Neuroscience, 17*, 632–640.

Hintzman, D. L. (1992). Mathematical constraints and the Tulving–Wiseman law. *Psychological Review, 99*(3), 536–542.

Hitchcock, E. M., Warm, J. S., Matthews, G., Dember, W. N., Shear, P. K., Tripp, L. D., et al. (2003). Automation cueing modulates cerebral blood flow and vigilance in a simulated air traffic control task. *Theoretical Issues in Ergonomics Science, 4*, 89–112.

Hodges, N. J., Kerr, T., Starkes, J. L., Weir, P. L., & Nananidou, A. (2004). Predicting performance times from deliberate practice hours for triathletes and swimmers: What, when, and where is practice important? *Journal of Experimental Psychology: Applied, 10*, 219–237.

Hoffrage, U., Gigerenzer, G., Krauss, S., & Martignon, L. (2002). Representation facilitates reasoning: What natural frequencies are and what they are not. *Cognition, 84*, 343–352.

Hoffrage, U., Kurzenhauser, S., & Gigerenzer, G. (2005). Understanding the results of medical tests: Why the representation of statistical information matters. In R. Bibace & J. D. Laird (Eds.), *Science and medicine in dialogue* (pp. 83–98). Westport, CT: Praeger.

Hoffrage, U., Lindsey, S., Hertwig, R., & Gigerenzer, G. (2000). Communicating statistical information. *Science, 290*, 2261–2262.

Holding, D. H. (1976). An approximate transfer surface. *Journal of Motor Behavior, 8*, 1–9.

Holyoak, K. J., & Cheng, P. W. (1995). Pragmatic reasoning about human voluntary action: Evidence from Wason's selection task. In S. E. Newstead & J. St.-B. T. Evans (Eds.), *Perspectives on thinking and reasoning* (pp. 67–89). Hillsdale, NJ: Erlbaum.

Holyoak, K. J., & Koh, K. (1987). Surface and structural similarity in analogical transfer. *Memory & Cognition, 15*(4), 332–340.

Holyoak, K. J., & Thagard, P. R. (1989). A computational model of analogical problem solving. In S. O. A. Vosniadou (Ed.), *Similarity and analogical reasoning* (pp. 242–266). New York: Cambridge University Press.

Hubel, D. H., & Wiesel, T. N. (1979). Brain mechanisms of vision. *Scientific American, 241*(3), 150–162.

Hunt, E., & Agnoli, F. (1991). The Whorfian hypothesis: A cognitive psychology perspective. *Psychological Review, 98*(3), 377–389.

Hyde, T. S., & Jenkins, J. J. (1973). Recall for words as a function of semantic, graphic, and syntactic orienting tasks. *Journal of Verbal Learning & Verbal Behavior, 12,* 471–480.

Imamizu, H., Miyauchi, S., Tamada, T., Sasaki, Y., Takino, R., Putz, B., et al. (2000). Human cerebellar activity reflecting an acquired internal model of a new tool. *Nature, 403,* 192–195.

Ironsmith, M., & Lutz, J. (1996). The effects of bizarreness and self-generation on mnemonic imagery. *Journal of Mental Imagery, 20*(3–4), 113–126.

Ishai, A., Haxby, J. V., & Ungerleider, L. G. (2002). Visual imagery of famous faces: Effects of memory and attention revealed by fMRI. *Neuroimage, 17,* 1729–1741.

Ishai, A., Ungerleider, L. G., & Haxby, J. V. (2000). Distributed neural systems for the generation of visual images. *Neuron, 28,* 979–990.

Itard, J.-M. G. (1962). *The wild boy of Aveyron.* New York: Appleton-Century-Crofts.

Jackson, G. M., Jackson, S. R., Husain, M., Harvey, M., Kramer, T., & Dow L. (2000). The coordination of bimanual prehension movements in a centrally deafferented patient. *Brain, 123,* 380–393.

James, W. (1890). *Principles of psychology.* New York: Holt.

Janiszewski, C., & Meyvis, T. (2001). Effects of brand logo complexity, repetition, and spacing on processing fluency and judgment. *Journal of Consumer Research, 28,* 18–32.

Jevons, W. S. (1871). The power of numerical discrimination. *Nature, 3,* 281–282.

Jobard, G., Crivello, F., & Tzourio-Mazoyer, N. (2003). Evaluation of the dual route theory of reading: A meta-analysis of 35 neuroimaging studies. *Neuroimage, 20,* 693–712.

Johnson, J. S., & Newport, E. L. (1989). Critical period effects in second language learning: The influence of maturational state on the acquisition of English as a second language. *Cognitive Psychology, 21,* 60–99.

Johnson, M. K., & Hasher, L. (1987). Human learning and memory. *Annual Review of Psychology, 38,* 631–668.

Johnson, M. K., Hashtroudi, S., & Lindsay, D. S. (1993). Source monitoring. *Psychological Bulletin, 114,* 3–28.

Johnson, M. K., & Raye, C. L. (1981). Reality monitoring. *Psychological Review, 88,* 67–85.

Johnson-Laird, P. N. (1999). Deductive reasoning. *Annual Review of Psychology, 50,* 109–135.

Johnson-Laird, P. N. (2005). Mental models and thought. In K. J. Holyoak & R. G. Morrison (Eds.), *Cambridge handbook of thinking and reasoning* (pp. 185–208). Cambridge: Cambridge University Press.

Johnson-Laird, P. N., & Bara, B. G. (1984). Syllogistic inference. *Cognition, 16*(1), 1–61.

Johnson-Laird, P. N., & Byrne, R. M. (1991). *Deduction.* Mahwah, NJ: Erlbaum.

Johnson-Laird, P. N., Byrne, R. M., & Schaeken, W. (1992). Propositional reasoning by model. *Psychological Review, 99*(3), 418–439.

Johnson-Laird, P. N., Legrenzi, P., Girotto, V., Legrenzi, M. S., & Caverni, J.-P. (1999). Naive probability: A mental model theory of extensional reasoning. *Psychological Review, 106,* 62–88.

Johnson-Laird, P. N., & Savary, F. (1999). Illusory inferences: A novel class of erroneous deductions. *Cognition, 71,* 191–229.

Johnston, W. A., & Heinz, S. P. (1978). Flexibility and capacity demands of attention. *Journal of Experimental Psychology: General, 107*(4), 420–435.

Jolicoeur, P. (1990). Identification of disoriented objects: A dual systems theory. *Mind and Language, 5,* 387–410.

Jolicoeur, P. (1999). Concurrent response-selection demands modulate the attentional blink. *Journal of Experimental Psychology: Human Perception and Performance, 25,* 1097–1113.

Jolicoeur, P., & Kosslyn, S. M. (1985). Is time to scan visual image due to demand characteristics? *Memory & Cognition, 13,* 320–332.

Jones, G. (2003). Testing two cognitive theories of insight. *Journal of Experimental Psychology: Learning, Memory, and Cognition, 29,* 1017–1027.

Jonides, J., Lacey, S. C., & Nee, D. E. (2005). Processes of working memory in mind and brain. *Current Directions in Psychological Science, 14,* 2–5.

Jordan, K., Heinze, H. J., Lutz, K., Kanowski, M., & Jancke, L. (2001). Cortical activations during the mental rotation of different visual objects. *Neuroimage, 13,* 143–152.

Joseph, J. S., Chun, M. M., & Nakayama, K. (1997). Attentional requirements in a "preattentive" feature search task. *Nature, 387,* 805–807.

Jusczyk, P. W. (1997). *The discovery of spoken language.* Cambridge, MA: MIT Press.

Just, M. A., & Carpenter, P. A. (1980). A theory of reading: From eye fixations to comprehension. *Psychological Review, 87,* 329–354.

Just, M. A., & Carpenter, P. A. (1992). A capacity theory of comprehension: Individual differences in working memory. *Psychological Review, 99*(1), 122–149.

Kaernbach, C. (2004). Auditory sensory memory and short-term memory. In C. Kaernbach, E. Schröger, &

H. Müller (Eds.), *Psychophysics beyond sensation: Laws and invariants of human cognition* (pp. 331–348). Mahwah, NJ: Erlbaum.

Kahneman, D. (1973). *Attention and effort.* New York: Prentice Hall.

Kahneman, D., Knetsch, J. L., & Thaler, R. (1990). Experimental tests of the endowment effect and the Coase theorem. *Journal of Political Economy, 98,* 1325–1348.

Kako, E. (1999). Elements of syntax in the systems of three language-trained animals. *Animal Learning and Behavior, 27,* 1–14.

Kaminsky, J., Call, J., & Fischer, J. (2004). Word learning in a domestic dog: Evidence for "fast mapping". *Science, 304,* 1682–1683.

Kane, M. J., Hambrick, D. Z., Tuholski, S. W., Wilhelm, O., Payne, T. W., & Engle, R. W. (2004). The generality of working memory capacity: A latent-variable approach to verbal and visuospatial memory span and reasoning. *Journal of Experimental Psychology: General, 133,* 189–217.

Kanwisher, N., McDermott, J., & Chun, M., M. (1997). The fusiform face area: A module in human extrastriate cortex specialized for face perception. *Journal of Neuroscience, 17,* 4302–4311.

Kayser, C., Körding, K. P., & König, P. (2004). Processing of complex stimuli and natural scenes in the visual cortex. *Current Opinion in Neurobiology, 14,* 468–473.

Keane, M. (1987). On retrieving analogues when solving problems. *Quarterly Journal of Experimental Psychology: Human Experimental Psychology, 39*(1-A), 29–41.

Keele, S. W. (1981). Behavioral analysis of movement. In J. M. Brookhart, V. B. Mountcastle, & V. B. Brooks (Eds.), *Handbook of physiology* (Vol. II, Motor Control, pp. 1391–1414). Bethesda, MD: American Physiological Society.

Keele, S. W., Cohen, A., & Ivry, R. (1990). Motor programs: Concepts and issues. In M. Jeannerod (Ed.), *Attention and performance XIII* (pp. 77–110). Hillsdale, NJ: Erlbaum.

Keele, S. W., Jennings, P., Jones, S., Caulton, D., & Cohen, A. (1995). On the modularity of sequence representation. *Journal of Motor Behavior, 27,* 17–30.

Keele, S. W., & Posner, M. I. (1968). Processing visual feedback in rapid movement. *Journal of Experimental Psychology, 77,* 155–178.

Keppel, G., & Underwood, B. J. (1962). Proactive inhibition in short-term retention of single items. *Journal of Verbal Learning & Verbal Behavior, 1,* 153–161.

Kéri, S. (2003). The cognitive neuroscience of category learning. *Brain Research Reviews, 43,* 85–109.

Kerr, N. H. (1987). Locational representation in imagery: The third dimension. *Memory & Cognition, 15*(6), 521–530.

Kerzel, D., & Bekkering, H. (2000). Motor activation from visible speech: Evidence from stimulus response compatibility. *Journal of Experimental Psychology: Human Perception and Performance, 26,* 634–647.

Kerzel, D., & Ziegler, N. E. (2005). Visual short-term memory during smooth pursuit eye movements. *Journal of Experimental Psychology: Human Perception and Performance, 31,* 354–372.

King, J., & Just, M. A. (1991). Individual differences in syntactic processing: The role of working memory. *Journal of Memory & Language, 30*(5), 580–602.

Kintsch, W. (1988). The role of knowledge in discourse comprehension: A construction integration model. *Psychological Review, 95,* 163–182.

Kirby, K. N. (1994). Probabilities and utilities of fictional outcomes in Wason's four-card selection task. *Cognition, 51,* 1–28.

Klapp, S. T., Anderson, W. G., & Berrian, R. W. (1973). Implicit speech in reading: Reconsidered. *Journal of Experimental Psychology, 100,* 368–374.

Klauer, K. C., & Zhao, Z. (2004). Double dissociations in visual and spatial short-term memory. *Journal of Experimental Psychology: General, 133,* 355–381.

Klauer, K. C., Musch, J., & Naumer, B. (2000). On belief bias in syllogistic reasoning. *Psychological Review, 107,* 852–884.

Klein, I., Dubois, J., Mangin, J.-F., Kherif, F., Flandin, G., Poline, J.-B., et al. (2004). Retinotopic organization of visual mental images as revealed by functional magnetic imaging. *Cognitive Brain Research, 22,* 26–31.

Klein, R. (1988). Inhibitory tagging system facilitates visual search. *Nature, 334,* 430–431.

Klein, R. (2004). Orienting and inhibition of return. In M. S. Gazzaniga (Ed.), *The cognitive neurosciences* (3rd ed., pp. 545–559). Cambridge, MA: MIT Press.

Knight, D. C., Nguyen, H. T., & Bandettini, P. A. (2005). The role of the human amygdala in the production of conditioned fear responses. *Neuroimage, 26,* 1193–1200.

Knoblich, G., Ohlsson, S., Haider, H., & Rhenius, D. (1999). Constraint relaxation and chunk decomposition in insight problem solving. *Journal of Experimental Psychology: Learning, Memory, and Cognition, 25,* 1534–1555.

Knoblich, G., Ohlsson, S., & Raney, G. E. (2001). An eye movement study of insight problem solving. *Memory & Cognition, 29,* 1000–1009

Koelega, H. S., Brinkman, J.-A., Hendriks, L., & Verbaten, M. N. (1989). Processing demands, effort, and individual differences in four different vigilance tasks. *Human Factors, 31*(1), 45–62.

Koelsch, S., Schröger, E., & Tervaniemi, M. (1999). Superior pre-attentive auditory processing in musicians. *Neuroreport, 10,* 1309–1313.

Kohler, S., Kapur, S., Moscovitch, M., Winocur, G., & Houle, S. (1995). Dissociation of pathways for object and spatial vision: A PET study in humans. *Neuroreport, 6,* 1865–1868.

Kohler, W. (1929). *Gestalt psychology.* New York: Liveright.

Konishi, S., Karwazu, M., Uchida, I., Kikyo, H., Asakura, I., & Miyashita, Y. (1999). Contribution of working memory to transient activation in human inferior prefrontal cortex during performance of the Wisconsin Card Sorting Test. *Cerebral Cortex 9,* 745–773.

Kopferman, H. (1930). Psychologishe Untersuchungen uber die Wirkung Zwei-dimensionaler korperlicher Gibilde. *Psychologicshe Forschung, 13,* 293–364.

Koshino, H., Carpenter, P. A., Keller, T. A., & Just, M. A. (2005). Interactions between the dorsal and ventral pathways in mental rotation: An fMRI study. *Cognitive, Affective & Behavioral Neuroscience, 5,* 54–66.

Kosslyn, S. M. (1973). Scanning visual images: Some structural implications. *Perception & Psychophysics, 14*(1), 90–94.

Kosslyn, S. M. (1975). Information representation in visual images. *Cognitive Psychology, 7*(3), 341–370.

Kosslyn, S. M. (1976). Using imagery to retrieve semantic information: A developmental study. *Child Development, 47*(2), 434–444.

Kosslyn, S. M. (1980). *Image and mind.* Cambridge, MA: Harvard University Press.

Kosslyn, S. M. (1995). Mental imagery. In S. M. Kosslyn (Ed.), *Visual cognition: An invitation to cognitive science* (Vol. 2, pp. 267–296). Cambridge, MA: MIT Press.

Kosslyn, S. M., Ball, T. M., & Reiser, B. J. (1978). Visual images preserve metric spatial information: Evidence from studies of image scanning. *Journal of Experimental Psychology: Human Perception and Performance, 4*(1), 47–60.

Kosslyn, S. M., Cave, C. B., Provost, D. A., & von Gierke, S. M. (1988). Sequential processes in image generation. *Cognitive Psychology, 20*(3), 319–343.

Kosslyn, S. M., & Thompson, W. L. (2003). When is early visual cortex activated during visual mental imagery? *Psychological Bulletin, 129,* 723–746.

Kosslyn, S. M., Thompson, W. L., & Albert, N. M. (1997). Neural systems shared by visual imagery and visual perception: A positron emission tomography study. *Neuroimage, 6,* 320–334.

Kotovsky, K., Hayes, J. R., & Simon, H. A. (1985). Why are some problems hard? Evidence from Tower of Hanoi. *Cognitive Psychology, 17*(2), 248–294.

Kotovsky, K., & Simon, H. A. (1990). What makes some problems really hard: Explorations in the problem space of difficulty. *Cognitive Psychology, 22*(2), 143–183.

Kourtzi, Z., Erb, M., Grodd, W., & Bulthoff, H. H. (2003). Representation of the perceived 3-D object shape in the human lateral occipital complex. *Cerebral Cortex, 13,* 911–920.

Kramer, A. F., & Hahn, S. (1995). Splitting the beam: Distribution of attention over noncontiguous regions of the visual field. *Psychological Science, 6,* 381–386.

Krampe, R., & Ericsson, K. A. (1996). Maintaining excellence: Deliberate practice and elite performance in young and older pianists. *Journal of Experimental Psychology: General, 125,* 331–359.

Krishnamoorthy, V., Latash, M. L., Scholz, J. P., & Zatsiorsky, V. M. (2003). Muscle synergies during shifts of the center of pressure by standing persons. *Experimental Brain Research, 152,* 281–292.

Kubovy, M. (1983). Mental imagery majestically transforming cognitive psychology. *Contemporary Psychology, 28,* 661–664.

Kuhl, P. K. (1986). Theoretical contributions of tests on animals to the special-mechanisms debate in speech. *Experimental Biology, 45,* 233–265.

Kuhl, P. K. (1989). On babies, birds, modules, and mechanisms: A comparative approach to the acquisition of vocal communication. In R. Dooling & S. H. Hulse (Eds.), *The comparative psychology of audition: Perceiving complex sounds* (pp. 379–419). Mahwah, NJ: Erlbaum.

Kuhl, P. K. (1991). Human adults and human infants show a "perceptual magnet effect" for the prototypes of speech categories, monkeys do not. *Perception & Psychophysics, 50,* 93–107.

Kuhl, P. K. (2004). Early language acquisition: Cracking the speech code. *Nature Reviews Neuroscience, 5,* 831–843.

Kwak, H.-W., Dagenbach, D., & Egeth, H. (1991). Further evidence for a time-independent shift of the focus of attention. *Perception & Psychophysics, 49*(5), 473–480.

Kyllonen, P. C., & Christal, R. E. (1990). Reasoning ability is (little more than) working-memory capacity? *Intelligence, 14*(4), 389–433.

Lachter, J., Forster, K. I., & Ruthruff, E. (2004). Forty-five years after broadbent (1958): Still no identification without attention. *Psychological Review, 111*, 880–913.

Laney, C., Campbell, H. V., Heuer, F., & Reisberg, D. (2004). Memory for thematically arousing events. *Memory & Cognition, 32*, 1149–1159.

Laney, C., Heuer, F., & Reisberg, D. (2003). Thematically-induced arousal in naturally-occurring emotional memories. *Applied Cognitive Psychology, 17*, 995–1004.

Larkin, J., McDermott, J., Simon, D. P., & Simon, H. A. (1980). Expert and novice performance in solving physics problems. *Science, 208*(4450), 1335–1342.

Le Bihan, D., Turner, R., Zeffiro, T. A., Cuenod, C. A., Jezzard, P., & Bonnerot, V. (1993). Activation of human primary visual cortex during visual recall: A magnetic resonance imaging study. *Proceedings of the National Academy of Sciences of the United States of America, 90*, 11802–11805.

LeDoux, J. E. (2000). Emotion circuits in the brain. *Annual Review of Neuroscience, 23*, 155–184.

Lee, D., & Chun, M. M. (2001). What are the units of visual short-term memory, objects or spatial locations? *Perception & Psychophysics, 63*, 253–257.

Lee, D., & Quessy, S. (2003). Activity in supplementary motor area related to learning and performance during a sequential visuomotor task. *Journal of Neurophysiology, 89*, 1039–1056.

Lee-Sammons, W. H., & Whitney, P. (1991). Reading perspectives and memory for text: An individual differences analysis. *Journal of Experimental Psychology: Learning, Memory, and Cognition, 17*(6), 1074–1081.

LeFevre, J.-A., & Dixon, P. (1986). Do written instructions need examples? *Cognition & Instruction, 3*(1), 1–30.

Lenneberg, E. (1967). *Biological foundations of language.* New York: Wiley.

Leopold, R. L., & Dillon, H. (1963). Psycho-anatomy of a disaster: A long term study of post-traumatic neuroses in survivors of a marine explosion. *American Journal of Psychiatry, 119*, 913–921.

Lesgold, A. M. (1984). Acquiring expertise. In J. R. Anderson & S. M. Kosslyn (Eds.), *Tutorials in learning and memory: Essays in honor of Gordon Bower.* New York: Freeman.

Levine, D. N., Warach, J., & Farah, M. (1985). Two visual systems in mental imagery: Dissociation of "what" and "where" in imagery disorders due to bilateral posterior cerebral lesions. *Neurology, 35*, 1010–1018.

Levy, W. B. (1996). A sequence predicting CA3 is a flexible associator that learns and uses context to solve hippocampal-like tasks. *Hippocampus, 6*, 579–590.

Lewis, C., & Keren, G. (1999). On the difficulties underlying Bayesian reasoning: A comment on Gigerenzer and Hoffrage. *Psychological Review, 106*, 411–416.

Liberman, A. M. (1996). *Speech: A special code.* Cambridge, MA: MIT Press.

Liberman, A. M., Cooper, F. S., & Shankweiler, D. P. (1967). *Human performance in low signal tasks.* Ann Arbor: University of Michigan Press.

Liberman, A. M., Harris, K. S., Hoffman, H. S., & Griffith, B. (1957). The discrimination of speech sounds within and across phoneme boundaries. *Journal of Experimental Psychology, 54*, 358–368.

Liberman, A. M., & Mattingly, I. G. (1985). The motor theory of speech perception revised. *Cognition, 21*(1), 1–36.

Lidz, J., Gleitman, H., & Gleitman, L. (2003). Understanding how input matters: Verb learning and the footprint of universal grammar. *Cognition, 87*, 151–178.

Light, L. L., & Carter-Sobell, L. (1970). Effects of changed semantic context on recognition memory. *Journal of Verbal Learning and Verbal Behavior, 9*, 1–11.

Lindsay, D. S., & Johnson, M. K. (1989). The eyewitness suggestibility effect and memory for source. *Memory & Cognition, 17*, 349–358.

Lipshits, M., & McIntyre, J. (1999). Gravity affects the preferred vertical and horizontal in visual perception of orientation. *Neuroreport, 10*, 1085–1089.

Loewenstein, J., & Gentner, D. (2001). Spatial mapping in preschoolers: Close comparisons facilitate far mappings. *Journal of Cognition & Development, 2*, 189–219.

Loftus, E. F., & Loftus, G. R. (1980). On the permanence of stored information in the human brain. *American Psychologist, 35*(5), 409–420.

Loftus, E. F., Miller, D. G., & Burns, H. J. (1978). Semantic integration of verbal information into a visual memory. *Journal of Experimental Psychology: Human Learning and Memory, 4*, 19–31.

Loftus, E. F., & Palmer, J. C. (1974). Reconstruction of automobile destruction: An example of the interaction between language and memory. *Journal of Verbal Learning and Verbal Behavior, 13*, 585–589.

Logan, G. D. (1988). Toward an instance theory of automatization. *Psychological Review, 95*(4), 492–527.

Logan, G. D. (2002). An instance theory of attention and memory. *Psychological Review, 109*, 376–400.

Logie, R. H., & Marchetti, C. (1991). Visuo-spatial working memory: Visual, spatial or central executive? In C. Cornoldi & M. A. McDaniels (Eds.), *Mental images in human cognition* (pp. 72–102). New York: Springer.

Logothetis, N. K., Pauls, J., & Poggio, T. (1995). Shape representation in the inferior temporal cortex of monkeys. *Current Biology, 5*, 552–563.

López, A., Atran, S., Coley, J. D., Medin, D. L., & Smith, E. E. (1997). The tree of life: Universal and cultural features of folkbiological taxonomies and inductions. *Cognitive Psychology, 32*, 251–295.

Lordahl, D. S., & Archer, E. J. (1958). Transfer effects on a rotary pursuit task as a function of first-task difficulty. *Journal of Experimental Psychology, 56*, 421–426.

Lotto, A. J. (2000). Language acquisition as complex category formation. *Phonetica, 57*, 189–196.

Lotze, M., Montoya, P., Erb, M., Huelsmann, E., Flor, H., Klose, U., et al. (1999). Activation of cortical and cerebellar motor areas during executed and imagined hand movements: An fMRI study. *Journal of Cognitive Neuroscience, 11*(5), 491–501.

Lubinski, D., Webb, R. M., Morelock, M. J., & Benbow, C. P. (2001). Top 1 in 10,000: A 10-year follow-up of the profoundely gifted. *Journal of Applied Psychology, 86*, 718–729.

Luchins, A. S. (1942). Mechanization in problem solving: The effect of Einstellung. *Psychological Monographs, 54*(6), 95.

Luck, S. J., & Vecera, S. P. (2002). Attention. In S. Yantis (Ed.), *Steven's handbook of experimental psychology. Vol. 1, sensation and perception* (3rd ed., pp. 235–286). New York: Wiley.

Luck, S. J., & Vogel, E. K. (1997). The capacity of visual working memory for features and conjunctions. *Nature, 390*, 279–281.

Lucy, J. A. (1992). *Grammatical categories and cognition: A case study of the linguistic relativity hypothesis*. Cambridge: Cambridge University Press.

Lucy, J. A. (1997). Linguistic relativity. *Annual Review of Anthropology, 26*, 291–312.

Lucy, J. A., & Shweder, R. A. (1979). Whorf and his critics: Linguistic and nonlinguistic influences on color memory. *American Anthropologist, 81*, 581–605.

Lyn, H., & Savage-Rumbaugh, E. S. (2000). Observational word learning in two bonobos (Pan paniscus): Ostensive and non-ostensive contexts. *Language & Communication, 20*, 255–273.

Lyons, J., Fontaine, R., & Elliott, D. (1997). I lost it in the lights: The effects of predictable and variable intermittent vision on unimanual catching. *Journal of Motor Behavior, 29*, 113–118.

Lytle, R. A., & Lundy, R. M. (1988). Hypnosis and the recall of visually presented material: A failure to replicate Stager and Lundy. *International Journal of Clinical and Experimental Hypnosis, 36*, 327–335.

Macchi, L. (2000). Partitive formulation of information in probabilistic problems: Beyond heuristics and frequency format explanations. *Organizational Behavior & Human Decision Processes, 82*, 217–236.

MacDonald, J., Andersen, S., & Bachmann, T. (2000). Hearing by eye: How much spatial degradation can be tolerated? *Perception, 29*, 1155–1168.

MacDonald, J., & McGurk, H. (1978). Visual influences on speech perception processes. *Perception & Psychophysics, 24*(3), 253–257.

MacDonald, M. C., Just, M. A., & Carpenter, P. A. (1992). Working memory constraints on the processing of syntactic ambiguity. *Cognitive Psychology, 24*, 56–98.

MacGregor, J. N., Ormerod, T. C., & Chronicle, E. P. (2001). Information processing and insight: A process model of performance on the nine-dot and related problems. *Journal of Experimental Psychology: Learning, Memory, and Cognition, 27*, 176–201.

Mack, A. (2003). Inattentional blindness: Looking without seeing. *Current Directions in Psychological Science, 12*, 180–184.

MacKay, D. G., & Bowman, R. W. (1969). On producing the meaning in sentences. *American Journal of Psychology, 82*, 23–39.

MacNeilage, P. F., & Davis, B. L. (2000). On the origin of internal structure of word forms. *Science, 288*, 527–531.

Maddox, W. T., Ashby, F. G., Ing, A. D., & Pickering, A. D. (2004). Disrupting feedback processing interferes with rule-based but not information-integration category learning. *Memory & Cognition, 32*, 582–591.

Majid, A., Bowerman, M., Kita, S., Haun, D. B. M., & Levinson, S. C. (2004). Can language restructure cognition? The case for space. *Trends in Cognitive Sciences, 8*, 108–114.

Manktelow, K. I., & Evans, J. S. (1979). Facilitation of reasoning by realism: Effect or non-effect? *British Journal of Psychology, 70*(4), 477–488.

Mark, L. S. (1987). Eyeheight-scaled information about affordances: A study of sitting and stair climbing.

Journal of Experimental Psychology: Human Perception and Performance, 13(3), 361–370.

Markman, A. B., & Dietrich, E. (2000). In defense of representation. *Cognitive Psychology, 40*, 138–171.

Marmie, W. R., & Healy, A. F. (2004). Memory for common objects: Brief intentional study is sufficient to overcome poor recall of US coin features. *Applied Cognitive Psychology, 18*, 445–453.

Marois, R., Yi, D.-J., & Chun, M. M. (2004). The neural fate of consciously perceived and missed events in the attentional blink. *Neuron, 41*, 465–472.

Marotta, J. J., & Goodale, M. A. (2001). The role of familiar size in the control of grasping. *Journal of Cognitive Neuroscience, 13*, 8–17.

Marr, D. (1982). *Vision.* San Francisco: W. H. Freeman.

Marshall, J. C., & Newcombe, F. (1973). Patterns of paralexia: A psycholinguistic approach. *Journal of Psycholinguistic Research, 2*(3), 175–199.

Marslen-Wilson, W. D. (1987). Functional parallelism in spoken word-recognition. *Cognition, 25*(1–2), 71–102.

Marslen-Wilson, W. D., & Welsh, A. (1978). Processing interactions and lexical access during word recognition in continuous speech. *Cognitive Psychology, 10*, 29–63.

Martin, A., & Chao, L. L. (2001). Semantic memory and the brain: Structure and processes. *Current Opinion in Neurobiology, 11*, 194–201.

Martin, L. (1986). "Eskimo words for snow": A case study in the genesis and decay of an anthropological example. *American Anthropologist, 88*(2), 418–423.

Martin, T. A., Keating, J. G., Goodkin, H. P., Bastian, A. J., & Thach, W. T. (1996). Throwing while looking through prisms. I. Focal olivocerebellar lesions impair adaptation. *Brain, 119*, 1183–1198.

Massaro, D. W. (1970). Preperceptual auditory images. *Journal of Experimental Psychology, 85*, 411–417.

Mayes, A. R., & Montaldi, D. (2001). Exploring the neural bases of episodic and semantic memory: The role of structural and functional neuroimaging. *Neuroscience and Biobehavioral Reviews, 25*, 555–573.

Mazard, A., Tzourio-Mazoyer, N., Crivello, F., Mazoyer, B., & Mellet, E. (2004). A PET meta-analysis of object and spatial mental imagery. *European Journal of Cognitive Psychology, 16*, 673–695.

McBeath, M. K., Shaffer, D. M., & Kaiser, M. K. (1995). How baseball outfielders determine where to run to catch fly balls. *Science, 268*, 569–573.

McCarthy, R. A., & Warrington, E. K. (1986). Phonological reading: Phenomena and paradoxes. *Cortex, 22*, 359–380.

McClelland, J. L. (1981). *Retrieving general and specific knowledge from stored knowledge of specifics.* Paper presented at the third annual conference of the Cognitive Science Society, Berkeley, CA.

McClelland, J. L., & Elman, J. L. (1986). The TRACE model of speech perception. *Cognitive Psychology, 18*, 1–86.

McCloskey, M. (1991). Networks and theories: The place of connectionism in cognitive science. *Psychological Science, 2*, 387–395.

McCloskey, M., Wible, C. G., & Cohen, N. J. (1988). Is there a special flashbulb-memory mechanism? *Journal of Experimental Psychology: General, 117*, 171–181.

McDaniel, M. A., Einstein, G. O., DeLosh, E. L., May, C. P., & Brady, P. (1995). The bizarreness effect: It's not surprising, it's complex. *Journal of Experimental Psychology: Learning, Memory, and Cognition, 21*, 422–435.

McDermott, K. B. (1996). The persistence of false memories in list recall. *Journal of Memory and Language, 35*, 212–230.

McGaugh, J. L. (2004). The amygdala modulates the consolidation of memories of emotionally arousing experiences. *Annual Review of Neuroscience, 27*, 1–28.

McGeoch, J. A. (1932). Forgetting and the law of disuse. *Psychological Review, 39*, 352–370.

McGurk, H., & MacDonald, J. (1976). Hearing lips and seeing voices. *Nature, 264*, 746–748.

McKoon, G., & Ratcliff, R. (1998). Memory-based language processing: Psycholinguistic research in the 1990s. *Annual Review of Psychology, 49*, 25–42.

McKoon, G., Ratcliff, R., & Dell, G. S. (1986). A critical evaluation of the semantic–episodic distinction. *Journal of Experimental Psychology: Learning, Memory, and Cognition, 12*(2), 295–306.

McMains, S. A., & Somers, D. C. (2004). Multiple spotlights of attentional selection of human visual cortex. *Neuron, 42*, 677–686.

McNeil, J. E., & Warrington, E. K. (1993). Prosopagnosia: A face-specific disorder. *Quarterly Journal of Experimental Psychology: Human Experimental Psychology, 46A*(1), 1–10.

McRae, K., Spivey-Knowlton, M. J., & Tanenhaus, M. K. (1998). Modeling the influence of thematic fit (and other constraints) in on-line sentence comprehension. *Journal of Memory & Language, 38*, 283–312.

Mechelli, A., Price, C. J., Friston, K. J., & Ishai, A. (2004). Where bottom-up meets top-down: Neuronal interactions during perception and imagery. *Cerebral Cortex, 14*, 1256–1265.

Medin, D. L., & Schaffer, M. M. (1978). Context theory of classification learning. *Psychological Review, 85*, 207–238.

Meinz, E. J., & Salthouse, T. A. (1998). The effects of age and experience on memory for visually presented music. *Journal of Gerontology: Psychological Sciences, 53B*, P60–P69.

Mellers, B. A., & McGraw, A. P. (1999). How to improve Bayesian reasoning: Comment on Gigerenzer and Hoffrage (1995). *Psychological Review, 106*, 417–424.

Mellet, E., Tzourio, N., Denis, M., & Mazoyer, B. (1995). A positron emission tomography study of visual and mental spatial exploration. *Journal of Cognitive Neuroscience 7*, 433–445.

Melton, A. W., & Irwin, J. M. (1940). The influence of degree of interpolated learning on retroactive inhibition and the overt transfer of specific responses. *American Journal of Psychology, 53*, 173–203.

Metcalfe, J. (1986a). Feeling of knowing in memory and problem solving. *Journal of Experimental Psychology: Learning, Memory, and Cognition, 12*(2), 288–294.

Metcalfe, J. (1986b). Premonitions of insight predict impending error. *Journal of Experimental Psychology: Learning, Memory, and Cognition, 12*(4), 623–634.

Metcalfe, J., & Wiebe, D. (1987). Intuition in insight and noninsight problem solving. *Memory & Cognition, 15*(3), 238–246.

Meyer, D. E., & Schvaneveldt, R. W. (1971). Facilitation in recognizing pairs of words: Evidence of a dependence between retrieval operations. *Journal of Experimental Psychology, 90*(2), 227–234.

Miller, G. A. (1956). The magical number seven, plus or minus two: Some limits on our capacity for processing information. *Psychological Review, 63*, 81–97.

Millis, K. K., & Just, M. A. (1994). The influence of connectives on sentence comprehension. *Journal of Memory & Language, 33*(1), 128–147.

Milner, A. D., & Goodale, M. A. (1995). *The visual brain in action.* Oxford: Oxford University Press.

Milner, B. (1966). Amnesia following operation on the temporal lobes. In C. W. M. Whitty & O. L. Zangwill (Eds.), *Amnesia.* London: Butterworth.

Minda, J. P., & Smith, J. D. (2001). Prototypes in category learning: The effects of category size, category structure, and stimulus complexity. *Journal of Experimental Psychology: Learning, Memory, and Cognition, 27*, 775–799.

Miyake, A., Carpenter, P. A., & Just, M. A. (1994). A capacity approach to syntactic comprehension disorders: Making normal adults perform like aphasic patients. *Cognitive Neuropsychology, 11*(6), 671–717.

Monsaas, J. A. (1985). Learning to be a world-class tennis player. In B. S. Bloom (Ed.), *Developing talent in young people* (pp. 211–269). New York: Ballantine.

Moody, D. B., Stebbins, W. C., & May, B. J. (1990). Auditory perception of communication signals by Japanese monkeys. In W. C. Stebbins & M. A. Berkley (Eds.), *Comparative perception* (Vol. 2, pp. 311–343). New York: Wiley.

Moray, N. (1959). Attention in dichotic listening: Affective cues and the influence of instructions. *Quarterly Journal of Experimental Psychology, 11*, 56–60.

Moray, N. (1967). Where is capacity limited? A survey and a model. *Acta Psychologica, 27*, 84–92.

Morris, C. D., Bransford, J. D., & Franks, J. J. (1977). Levels of processing versus transfer appropriate processing. *Journal of Verbal Learning & Verbal Behavior, 16*(5), 519–533.

Morton, S. M., & Bastian, A. J. (2004). Prism adaptation during walking generalizes to reaching and requires the cerebellum. *Journal of Neurophysiology, 92*, 2497–2509.

Mozer, M. C., & Smolensky, P. (1989). Using relevance to reduce network size automatically. *Connection Science, 1*, 3–16.

Mueller, S. T., Seymour, T. L., Kieras, D. E., & Meyer, D. E. (2003). Theoretical implications of articulatory duration, phonological similarity, and phonological complexity in verbal working memory. *Journal of Experimental Psychology: Learning, Memory, and Cognition, 29*, 1353–1380.

Munger, M. P., Solberg, J. L., & Horrocks, K. K. (1999). The relation between mental rotation and representational momentum. *Journal of Experimental Psychology: Learning, Memory, and Cognition, 25*, 1557–1568.

Murdock, B. B. (1974). *Human memory: Theory and data.* Mahwah, NJ: Erlbaum.

Murphy, G. L., & Ross, B. H. (2005). The two faces of typicality in category-based induction. *Cognition, 95*, 175–200.

Murray, A., & Jones, D. M. (2002). Articulatory complexity at item boundaries in serial recall: The case of Welsh and English digit span. *Journal of Experimental Psychology: Learning, Memory, and Cognition, 28*, 594–598.

Nairne, J. S. (2002). Remembering over the short-term: The case against the standard model. *Annual Review of Psychology, 53*, 53–81.

Nakano, E., Imamizu, H., Osu, R., Uno, Y., Gomi, H., Yoshioka, T., et al. (1999). Quantitative examinations of internal representations for arm trajectory planning: Minimum commanded torque change model. *Journal of Neurophysiology, 81,* 2140–2155.

Nashner, L. M., Woollacott, M., & Tuma, G. (1979). Organization of rapid responses to postural and locomotor-like perturbations of standing man. *Experimental Brain Research, 36,* 463–476.

Navon, D., & Gopher, D. (1979). On the economy of the human-processing system. *Psychological Review, 86*(3), 214–255.

Neisser, U. (1967). *Cognitive psychology.* New York: Appleton-Century-Crofts.

Neisser, U. (1972). Changing conceptions of imagery. In P. W. Sheehan (Ed.), *The function and nature of imagery.* New York: Academic Press.

Neisser, U. (1984). Interpreting Harry Bahrick's discovery: What confers immunity against forgetting? *Journal of Experimental Psychology: General, 113*(1), 32–35.

Neisser, U., & Becklen, R. (1975). Selective looking: Attending to visually specified events. *Cognitive Psychology, 7*(4), 480–494.

Nelson, K. (1974). Concept, word, and sentence: Interrelations in acquisition and development. *Psychological Review, 81*(4), 267–285.

Neumann, E., & Ammons, R. B. (1957). Acquisition and long-term retention of a simple serial perceptual-motor skill. *Journal of Experimental Psychology, 53,* 159–161.

Newell, A., Shaw, J. C., & Simon, H. A. (1962). The process of creative thinking. In H. E. Gruber, G. Terell, & M. Wertheimer (Eds.), *Contemporary approaches to creative thinking.* New York: Atherton.

Newell, A., & Simon, H. A. (1956). The logic theory machine: A complex information processing system. *IRE Transactions on Information Theory,* IT-2, 61–79.

Newell, A., & Simon, H. A. (1972). *Human problem solving.* Upper Saddle River, NJ: Prentice Hall.

Newell, A. M., & Rosenbloom, P. S. (1981). Mechanisms of skill acquisition and the law of practice. In J. R. Anderson (Ed.), *Cognitive skills and their acquisition* (pp. 1–55). Mahwah, NJ: Erlbaum.

Newell, B. R., & Shanks, D. R. (2004). On the role of recognition in decision making. *Journal of Experimental Psychology: Learning, Memory, and Cognition, 30,* 923–935.

Newell, K. M. (2003). Schema theory: Then and now. *Research Quarterly for Exercise and Sport, 74,* 383–388.

Newman, S. D., Klatzky, R. L., Lederman, S. J., & Just, M. A. (2005). Imagining material versus geometric properties of objects: An fMRI study. *Cognitive Brain Research, 23,* 235–246.

Newstead, S. E., & Griggs, R. A. (1983). Drawing inferences from quantified statements: A study of the square of opposition. *Journal of Verbal Learning & Verbal Behavior, 22*(5), 535–546.

Newstead, S. E., Pollard, P., & Evans, J. S. (1992). The source of belief bias effects in syllogistic reasoning. *Cognition, 45*(3), 257–284.

Nickerson, R. S., & Adams, M. J. (1979). Long-term memory for a common object. *Cognitive Psychology, 11*(3), 287–307.

Nielson, K. A., Yee, D., & Erickson, K. I. (2005). Memory enhancement by a semantically unrelated emotional arousal source induced after learning. *Neurobiology of Learning and Memory, 84,* 49–56.

Nisbett, R. E., & Norenzayan, A. (2002). Culture and cognition. In H. Pashler & D. Medin (Eds.), *Steven's handbook of experimental psychology. Vol. 2: Memory and cognitive processes* (3rd ed., pp. 561–597). New York: Wiley.

Nisbett, R. E., & Wilson, T. D. (1977). Telling more than we can know: Verbal reports on mental processes. *Psychological Review, 84*(3), 231–259.

Nissen, M. J., & Bullemer, P. (1987). Attentional requirements of learning: Evidence from performance measures. *Cognitive Psychology, 19,* 1–32.

Noordman, L. G., Vonk, W., & Kempff, H. J. (1992). Causal inferences during the reading of expository texts. *Journal of Memory & Language, 31*(5), 573–590.

Norman, D. A. (1968). Toward a theory of memory and attention. *Psychological Review, 75*(6), 522–536.

Norman, D. A., & Bobrow, D. G. (1975). On data-limited and resource-limited processes. *Cognitive Psychology, 7,* 44–64.

Nosofsky, R. M., & Palmeri, T. J. (1998). A rule-plus-exception model for classifying objects in continuous-dimension spaces. *Psychonomic Bulletin & Review, 5,* 345–369.

Nosofsky, R. M., Palmeri, T. J., & McKinley, S. C. (1994). Rule-plus-exception model of classification learning. *Psychological Review, 101,* 53–79.

Nosofsky, R. M., & Zaki, S. R. (2002). Exemplar and prototype models revisited: Response strategies, selective attention, and stimulus generalization. *Journal of Experimental Psychology: Learning, Memory, and Cognition, 28,* 924–940.

Novick, L. R., & Holyoak, K. J. (1991). Mathematical problem solving by analogy. *Journal of Experimental*

Psychology: Learning, Memory, and Cognition, 17, 398–415.

Nowak, M. A., Komarova, N. L., Niyogi, P. (2001). Evolution of universal grammar. *Science, 291*, 114–118.

Nozaki, D., Nakazawa, K., & Akai, M. (2005). Muscle activity determined by cosine tuning with a nontrivial preferred direction during isometric force exertion by lower limb. *Journal of Neurophysiology, 93*, 2614–2624.

Oakhill, J. V., & Johnson-Laird, P. N. (1985). The effects of belief on the spontaneous production of syllogistic conclusions. *Quarterly Journal of Experimental Psychology: Human Experimental Psychology, 37A*, 553–569.

Oakhill, J., Johnson-Laird, P. N., & Garnham, A. (1989). Believability and syllogistic reasoning. *Cognition, 31*, 117–140.

Oaksford, M., & Chater, N. (1994). A rational analysis of the selection task as optimal data selection. *Psychological Review, 101*, 608–631.

Oaksford, M., & Chater, N. (1996). Rational explanation of the selection task. *Psychological Review, 103*, 381–391.

Oaksford, M., & Chater, N. (1998). A revised rational analysis of the selection task: Exceptions and sequential sampling. In M. Oaksford & N. Chater (Eds.), *Rational models of cognition* (pp. 372–398). Oxford: Oxford University Press.

Oaksford, M., & Chater, N. (2001). The probabilistic approach to human reasoning. *Trends in Cognitive Science, 5*, 349–357.

Oaksford, M., & Chater, N. (2003). Optimal data selection: Revision, review, and reevaluation. *Psychonomic Bulletin & Review, 10*, 289–318.

Oberly, H. S. (1924). The range for visual attention, cognition and apprehension. *American Journal of Psychology, 35*, 332–352.

O'Brien, E. J., & Albrecht, J. E. (1992). Comprehension strategies in the development of a mental model. *Journal of Experimental Psychology: Learning, Memory, and Cognition, 18*, 777–784.

O'Connor, D. H., Fukui, M. M., Pinsk, M. A., & Kastner, S. (2002). Attention modulates responses in the human lateral geniculate nucleus. *Nature Neuroscience, 5*, 1203–1209.

O'Craven, K. M., Downing, P. E., & Kanwisher, N. (1999). fMRI evidence for objects as the units of attentional selection. *Nature, 401*, 584–587.

O'Craven, K. M., & Kanwisher, N. (2000). Mental imagery of faces and places activates corresponding stimulus-specific brain regions. *Journal of Cognitive Neuroscience, 12*, 1013–1023.

O'Keefe, J., & Nadel, L. (1978). *The hippocampus and the cognitive map.* Oxford: Oxford University Press.

Okoh, N. (1980). Bilingualism and divergent thinking among Nigerian and Welsh school children. *Journal of Social Psychology, 110*, 163–170.

Olsson, H., Wennerholm, P., & Lyxzen, U. (2004). Exemplars, prototypes, and the flexibility of classification models. *Journal of Experimental Psychology: Learning, Memory, and Cognition, 30*, 936–941.

Oppenheimer, D. M. (2003). Not so fast! (and not so frugal!): Rethinking the recognition heuristic. *Cognition, 90*, B1–B9.

Ormerod, T. C., MacGregor, J. N., & Chronicle, E. P. (2002). Dynamics and constraints in insight problem solving. *Journal of Experimental Psychology: Learning, Memory, and Cognition, 28*, 791–799.

Osman, A., & Moore, C. M. (1993). The locus of dual-task interference: Psychological refractory effects on movement-related brain potentials. *Journal of Experimental Psychology: Human Perception and Performance, 19*, 1292–1312.

O'Toole, A. J., Jiang, F., Abdi, H., & Haxby, J. V. (2005). Partially distributed representations of objects and faces in ventral temporal cortex. *Journal of Cognitive Neuroscience, 17*, 580–590.

Owen, A. M., Stern, C. E., Look, R. B., Tracey, I., Rosen, B. R., & Petrides, M. (1998). Functional organization of spatial and nonspatial working memory processing within the human lateral frontal cortex. *Proceedings of the National Academy of Sciences of the United States of America, 95*, 7721–7726.

Paap, K. R., & Noel, R. W. (1991). Dual-route models of print to sound: Still a good horse race. *Psychological Research, 53*(1), 13–24.

Paivio, A. (1963). Learning of adjective–noun paired associates as a function of adjective–noun word order and noun abstractness. *Canadian Journal of Psychology, 17*(4), 370–379.

Paivio, A. (1965). Abstractness, imagery, and meaningfulness in paired-associate learning. *Journal of Verbal Learning & Verbal Behavior, 4*(1), 32–38.

Paivio, A. (1971). *Imagery and verbal processes.* New York: Holt, Rinehart, & Winston.

Paivio, A. (1986). *Mental representations.* Oxford: Oxford University Press.

Paivio, A. (1991). *Images in mind: The evolution of a theory.* London: Harvester Wheatsheaf.

Paivio, A., & Foth, D. (1970). Imaginal and verbal mediators and noun concreteness in paired-associate learning: The elusive interaction. *Journal of Verbal Learning & Verbal Behavior, 9*(4), 384–390.

Palmer, S. E. (1975). The effects of contextual scenes on the identification of objects. *Memory & Cognition, 3*, 519–526.

Palmer, S. E., Simone, E., & Kube, P. (1988). Reference frame effects on shape perception in two versus three dimensions. *Perception, 17*, 147–163.

Parasuraman, R., & Davies, D. R. (1977). A taxonomic analysis of vigilance perfromance. In R. R. Mackie (Ed.), *Vigilance: Theory, operational performance, and physiological correlates* (pp. 559–574). New York: Plenum.

Parsons, L. M. (1987). Imagined spatial transformations of one's hands and feet. *Cognitive Psychology, 19*, 178–241.

Pashler, H. E. (1998). *The psychology of attention.* Cambridge, MA: MIT Press.

Pashler, H., Carrier, M., & Hoffman, J. (1993). Saccadic eye movements and dual-task interference. *Quarterly Journal of Experimental Psychology: Human Experimental Psychology, 46A*(1), 51–82.

Pastore, R. E., Li, X.-F., & Layer, J. K. (1990). Categorical perception of nonspeech chirps and bleats. *Perception & Psychophysics, 48*(2), 151–156.

Patalano, A. L., Smith, E. E., Jonides, J., & Koeppe, R. A. (2001). PET evidence for multiple strategies of categorization. *Cognitive, Affective & Behavioral Neuroscience, 1*, 360–370.

Patel, V. L., & Groen, G. J. (1991). The general and specific nature of medical expertise: A critical look. In K. A. Ericsson & J. Smith (Eds.), *Toward a general theory of expertise* (pp. 93–125). Cambridge: Cambridge University Press.

Patterson, F. G. (1978). The gesture of a gorilla: Language acquisition in another pongid. *Brain & Language, 5*(1), 72–97.

Patterson, F. G. (1981). Can an ape create a sentence? Some affirmative evidence. *Science, 211*, 86–87.

Paulesu, E., Frith, C. D., & Frackowiak, R. S. (1993). The neural correlates of the verbal component of working memory. *Nature, 362*(6418), 342–345.

Peace, K. A., & Porter, S. (2004). A longitudinal investigation of the reliability of memories for trauma and other emotional experiences. *Applied Cognitive Psychology, 18*, 1143–1159.

Penfield, W. (1959). *Speech and brain mechanisms.* Princeton, NJ: Princeton University Press.

Perenin, M. T., & Vighetto, A. (1988). Optic ataxia: A specific disruption in visuomotor mechanisms. *Brain, 111*, 643–674.

Peterson, L., & Peterson, M. J. (1959). Short-term retention of individual verbal items. *Journal of Experimental Psychology, 58*, 193–198.

Phelps, E. (2004). Human emotion and memory: Interactions of the amygdala and hippocampal complex. *Current Opinion in Neurobiology, 14*, 198–202.

Phelps, R. M., & Shanteau, J. (1978). Livestock judges: How much information can an expert use? *Organizational Behavior and Human Performance, 21*, 209–219.

Phillips, C., & Gibson, E. (1997). On the strength of the local attachment preference. *Journal of Psycholinguistic Research, 26*, 323–346.

Pica, P., Lemer, C., Izard, V., & Dehaene, S. (2004). Exact and approximate arithmetic in an Amaxonian indigene group. *Science, 306*, 499–503.

Pillemer, D. B. (1984). Flashbulb memories of the assassination attempt on President Reagan. *Cognition, 16*, 63–80.

Pillemer, D. B, Goldsmith, L. R., Panter, A. T., & White, S. H. (1988). Very long-term memories of the first year in college. *Journal of Experimental Psychology: Learning, Memory, and Cognition, 14*, 709–715.

Pinker, S. (1994). *The language instinct.* New York: William Morrow.

Pinker, S., & Jackendoff, R. (2005). The faculty of language: What's special about it? *Cognition, 95*, 201–236.

Pinker, S., & Ullman, M. T. (2002). The past and future of the past tense debate. *Trends in Cognitive Science, 6*, 456–463.

Plous, S. (1989). Thinking the unthinkable: The effects of anchoring on likelihood estimates of nuclear war. *Journal of Applied Social Psychology, 19*(1), 67–91.

Podgorny, P., & Shepard, R. N. (1978). Functional representations common to visual perception and imagination. *Journal of Experimental Psychology: Human Perception and Performance, 4*(1), 21–35.

Poldrack, R. A., & Willingham, D. T. (2006). Skill learning. In R. Cabeza & A. Kingstone (Eds.), *Handbook of functional neuroimaging of human cognition* (2nd ed.). Cambridge, MA: MIT Press.

Polit, A., & Bizzi, E. (1978). Processes controlling arm movements in monkeys. *Science, 201*, 1235–1237.

Pomerantz, J. R., & Kubovy, M. (1986). Theoretical approaches to perceptual organization: Simplicity and likelihood principles. In K. R. Boff & L. Kaufman (Eds.), *Handbook of perception and human performance* (Vol. 2, pp. 1–46). New York: Wiley.

Posner, M. I. (1978). *Chronometric explorations of mind.* Hillsdale, NJ: Erlbaum.

Posner, M. I., & Cohen, Y. A. (1984). Components of visual orienting. In H. Bouma & D. G. Bouwhuis

(Eds.), *Attention & Performance X* (pp. 531–556). Hillsdale, NJ: Erlbaum.

Posner, M. I., Snyder, C. R., & Davidson, B. J. (1980). Attention and the detection of signals. *Journal of Experimental Psychology: General, 109,* 160–174.

Posner, M. I., & Keele, S. W. (1968). On the genesis of abstract ideas. *Journal of Experimental Psychology, 77*(3, Pt. 1), 353–363.

Posner, M. I., & Keele, S. W. (1970). Retention of abstract ideas. *Journal of Experimental Psychology, 83*(2, Pt. 1), 304–308.

Posner, M. I., & Snyder, C. R. (1975). Attention and cognitive control. In R. L. Solso (Ed.), *Information processing and cognition: The Loyola symposium.* Mahwah, NJ: Erlbaum.

Postle, B. R., Jonides, J., Smith, E. E., Corkin, S., & Growdon, J. H. (1997). Spatial, but not object, delayed response is impaired in early Parkinson's disease. *Neuropsychology, 11,* 171–179.

Povinelli, D. J., & Bering, J. M. (2002). The mentality of apes revisited. *Current Directions in Psychological Science, 11,* 115–119.

Premack, D. (1971). Language in chimpanzee? *Science, 172*(3985), 808–822.

Premack, D. (1976a). *Intelligence in ape and man.* Mahwah, NJ: Erlbaum.

Premack, D. (1976b). Language and intelligence in ape and man. *American Scientist, 64*(6), 674–683.

Price, C. J., & Mechelli, A. (2005). Reading and reading disturbance. *Current Opinion in Neurobiology, 15,* 231–238.

Priest, A. G., & Lindsay, R. O. (1992). New light on novice–expert differences in physics problem solving. *British Journal of Psychology, 83*(3), 389–405.

Proffitt, D. R., Bhalla, M., Gossweiler, R., & Midgett, J. (1995). Perceiving geographical slant. *Psychonomic Bulletin & Review, 2*(4), 409–428.

Proffitt, J. B., Coley, J. D., & Medin, D. L. (2000). Expertise and category-based induction. *Journal of Experimental Psychology: Learning, Memory, and Cognition, 26,* 811–828.

Pylyshyn, Z. (2003). Return of the mental image: Are there really pictures in the brain? *Trends in Cognitive Sciences, 7,* 113–118.

Pylyshyn, Z. W. (1973). What the mind's eye tells the mind's brain: A critique of mental imagery. *Psychological Bulletin, 80*(1), 1–24.

Pylyshyn, Z. W. (1981). The imagery debate: Analogue media versus tacit knowledge. *Psychological Review, 88*(1), 16–45.

Pylyshyn, Z. W. (2002). Mental imagery: In search of a theory. *Behavioral & Brain Sciences, 25,* 157–238.

Pynoos, R. S., & Nader, K. (1989). Children's memories and proximity to violence. *Journal of the American Academy of Child and Adolescent Psychiatry, 28,* 236–241.

Quinlan, P. T. (2003). Visual feature integration theory: Past, present, and future. *Psychological Bulletin, 129,* 643–673.

Quinn, J. G., & McConnell, J. (1996). Irrelevant pictures in visual working memory. *Quarterly Journal of Experimental Psychology, 49A,* 200–215.

Quiroga, R. Q., Reddy, L., Kreiman, G., Koch, C., & Fried, I. (2005). Invariant visual representation by single neurons in the human brain. *Nature, 435,* 1102–1107.

Radvansky, G. A., & Copeland, D. E. (2004). Working memory span and situation model processing. *American Journal of Psychology, 117,* 191–213.

Rajah, M. N., & McIntosh, A. R. (2005). Overlap in the functional neural systems involved in semantic and episodic memory retrieval. *Journal of Cognitive Neuroscience, 17,* 470–482.

Ranganath, C., & D'Esposito, M. (2005). Directing the mind's eye: Prefrontal, inferior and medial temporal mechanisms for visual working memory. *Current Opinion in Neurobiology, 15,* 175–182.

Rasmussen, J., Damsgaard, M., & Voigt, M. K. (2001). Muscle recruitment by the min/max criterion—A comparative numerical study. *Journal of Biomechanics, 34,* 409–415.

Rauschecker, J. P., & Shannon, R. V. (2002). Sending sound to the brain. *Science, 295,* 1025–1029.

Rayner, K., Carlson, M., & Frazier, L. (1983). The interaction of syntax and semantics during sentence processing: Eye movements in the analysis of semantically biased sentences. *Journal of Verbal Learning & Verbal Behavior, 22*(3), 358–374.

Reber, A. S. (1999). *The new gambler's bible.* New York: Crown.

Reber, P. J., & Kotovsky, K. (1997). Implicit learning in problem solving: The role of working memory capacity. *Journal of Experimental Psychology: General, 126*(2), 178–203.

Reder, L. M. (1982). Plausibility judgments versus fact retrieval: Alternative strategies for sentence verification. *Psychological Review, 89*(3), 250–280.

Reed, C. L., Klatzky, R. L., & Halgren, E. (2005). What versus where in touch: An fMRI study. *Neuroimage, 25,* 718–726.

Reed, S. K., Ackinclose, C. C., & Voss, A. A. (1990). Selecting analogous problems: Similarity versus inclusiveness. *Memory & Cognition, 18*(1), 83–98.

Reed, S. K., & Bolstad, C. A. (1991). Use of examples and procedures in problem solving. *Journal of*

Experimental Psychology: Learning, Memory, and Cognition, 17(4), 753–766.

Register, P. A., & Kihlstrom, J. F. (1987). Hypnotic effects on hypermnesia. *International Journal of Clinical and Experimental Hypnosis, 35,* 155–170.

Reich, S. S., & Ruth, P. (1982). Wason's selection task: Verification, falsification and matching. *British Journal of Psychology, 73*(3), 395–405.

Reitman, J. S. (1971). Mechanisms of forgetting in short-term memory. *Cognitive Psychology, 2*(2), 185–195.

Revlis, R. (1975). Two models of syllogistic reasoning: Feature selection and conversion. *Journal of Verbal Learning & Verbal Behavior, 14*(2), 180–195.

Rhodes, B. J., Bullock, D., Verwey, W. B., Averbeck, B. B., & Page, M. P. A. (2004). Learning and production of movement sequences: Behavioral, neurophysiological, and modeling perspectives. *Human Movement Science, 23,* 699–746.

Rhodes, G., Byatt, G., Michie, P. T., & Puce, A. (2004). Is the fusiform face area specialized for faces, individuation, or expert individuation? *Journal of Cognitive Neuroscience, 16,* 189–203.

Richardson, M. P., Strange, B., & Dolan, R. J. (2004). Encoding of emotional memories depends on the amygdala and hippocampus and their interactions. *Nature Neuroscience, 7,* 278–285.

Richardson-Klavehn, A., & Bjork, R. A. (1988). Measures of memory. *Annual Review of Psychology, 39,* 475–543.

Riddoch, M. J., & Humphreys, G. W. (1987). A case of integrative visual agnorisa. *Brain, 110,* 1431–1462.

Rips, L. J. (1975). Inductive judgments about natural categories. *Journal of Verbal Learning & Verbal Behavior, 14*(6), 665–681.

Rips, L. J. (1989). Similarity, typicality, and categorization. In S. O. A. Vosniadou (Ed.), *Similarity and analogical reasoning* (pp. 21–59). New York: Cambridge University Press.

Roberson, D., Davidoff, J., Davies, I. R. L., & Shapiro, L. R. (2005). Color categories: Evidence for the cultural relativity hypothesis. *Cognitive Psychology, 50,* 378–411.

Roberson, D., Davies, I., & Davidoff, J. (2000). Color categories are not universal: Replications and new evidence from a stone-age culture. *Journal of Experimental Psychology: General, 129,* 369–398.

Robins, S., & Mayer, R. E. (1993). Schema training in analogical reasoning. *Journal of Educational Psychology, 85*(3), 529–538.

Roediger, H. L. III, & McDermott, K. B. (1995). Creating false memories: Remembering words not presented in lists. *Journal of Experimental Psychology: Learning, Memory, and Cognition, 21,* 803–814.

Roediger, H. L. III, Watson, J. M., McDermott, K. B., & Gallo, D. A. (2001). Factors that determine false recall: A multiple regression analysis. *Psychonomic Bulletin & Review, 8,* 385–407.

Roediger, H. L. III, Wheeler, M. A., & Rajaram, S. (1993). Remembering, knowing, and reconstructing the past. In D. L. Medin (Ed.), *The psychology of learning and motivation: Advances in research and theory* (Vol. 30, pp. 97–134).

Rogers, S. (1996). The horizon-ratio relation as information for relative size in pictures. *Perception & Psychophysics, 58*(1), 142–152.

Romo, R., & Salinas, E. (2003). Flutter discrimination: Neural codes, perception, memory and decision making. *Nature Reviews: Neuroscience, 4,* 203–218.

Rosch, E. H. (1973). On the internal structure of perceptual and semantic categories. In T. E. Moore (Ed.), *Cognitive development and the acquisition of language* (pp. 111–144). New York: Academic Press.

Rosenbaum, D. A., Inhoff, A. W., & Gordon, A. M. (1984). Choosing between movement sequences: A hierarchical editor model. *Journal of Experimental Psychology: General, 113,* 372–393.

Rosenbaum, D. A., Kenny, S., & Derr, M. A. (1983). Hierarchical control of rapid movement sequences. *Journal of Experimental Psychology: Human Perception and Performance, 9,* 86–102.

Rosenbaum, D. A., Vaughan, J., Barnes, H. J., & Jorgensen, M. J. (1992). Time course of movement planning: Selection of handgrips for object manipulation. *Journal of Experimental Psychology: Learning, Memory, and Cognition, 18,* 1058–1073.

Rosenbaum, R. S., Köhler, S., Schacter, D. L., Moscovitch, M., Westmacott, R., Black, S. E., et al. (2005). The case of KC: Contributions of a memory-impaired person to memory theory. *Neuropsychologia, 43,* 989–1021.

Rosner, S. R., & Hayes, D. S. (1977). A developmental study of category item production. *Child Development, 48*(3), 1062–1065.

Ross, B. H. (1987). This is like that: The use of earlier problems and the separation of similarity effects. *Journal of Experimental Psychology: Learning, Memory, and Cognition, 13*(4), 629–639.

Ross, B. H. (1989). Distinguishing types of superficial similarities: Different effects on the access and use of earlier problems. *Journal of Experimental Psychology: Learning, Memory, and Cognition, 15*(3), 456–468.

Ross, B. H., & Kennedy, P. T. (1990). Generalizing from the use of earlier examples in problem solving. *Journal of Experimental Psychology: Learning, Memory, and Cognition, 16*(1), 42–55.

Ross, N. E., & Jolicoeur, P. (1999). Attentional blink for color. *Journal of Experimental Psychology: Human Perception and Performance, 25*, 1483–1494.

Rothwell, J. C., Traub, M. M., Day, B. L., Obeso, J. A., Thomas, P. K., & Marsden, C, D. (1982). Manual motor performance in a deafferented man. *Brain, 105*, 515–542.

Rouder, J. N., & Ratcliff, R. (2004). Comparing categorization models. *Journal of Experimental Psychology: General, 133*, 63–82.

Rubenstein, H., Lewis, S. S., & Rubenstein, M. A. (1971). Evidence for phonemic recoding in visual word recognition. *Journal of Verbal Learning & Verbal Behavior, 10*(6), 645–657.

Rubin, D. C., & Kozin, M. (1984). Vivid memories. *Cognition, 16*(1), 81–95.

Rumelhart, D. E., Hinton, G. E., & McClelland, J. L. (1986). A general framework for parallel distributed processing. In D. E. Rumelhart, J. L. McClelland, & the PDP Research Group (Eds.), *Parallel distributed processing, Volume 1: Foundations* (pp. 45–76). Cambridge, MA: MIT Press.

Ruthruff, E., Pashler, H. E., & Hazeltine, E. (2003). Dual-task interference with equal task emphasis: Graded capacity sharing or central postponement? *Perception & Psychophysics, 65*, 801–816.

Sadoski, M., & Paivio, A. (2001). *Imagery and text: A dual coding theory of reading and writing.* Hillsdale, NJ: Erlbaum.

Saffran, J. R. (2001). Words in a sea of sounds: The output of statistical learning. *Cognition, 81*, 149–169.

Saffran, J. R. (2002). Constraints on statistical language learning. *Journal of Memory & Language, 47*, 172–196.

Saffran, J. R., Aslin, R. N., & Newport, E. L. (1996). Statistical learning by 8-month old infants. *Science, 274*, 1926–1928.

Saffran, J. R., & Thiessen, E. D. (2003). Pattern induction by infant language learners. *Developmental Psychology, 39*, 484–494.

Sagi, D., & Julesz, B. (1985). Fast noninertial shifts of attention. *Spatial Vision, 2*, 141–149.

Sala, J. B., Rama, P., & Courtney, S. M. (2003). Functional topography of a distributed neural system for spatial and nonspatial information maintenance in working memory. *Neuropsychologia, 41*, 341–356.

Salthouse, T. A. (1984). The skill of typing. *Scientific American, 250*(2), 128–135.

Sams, M., Mottonen, R., & Sihvonen, T. (2005). Seeing and hearing others and oneself talk. *Cognitive Brain Research, 23*, 429–435.

Samuel, A. (1996). Phoneme restoration. *Language & Cognitive Processes, 11*, 647–653.

Sanes, J. N. (2003). Neocortical mechanisms in motor learning. *Current Opinion in Neurobiology, 13*, 225–231.

Sanes, J. N., Mauritz, K.-H., Dalakas, M. C., & Evarts, E. V. (1985). Motor control in humans with large-fiber sensory neuropathy. *Human Neurobiology, 4*, 101–114.

Santello, M., Flanders, M., & Soechting, J. F. (1998). Postural hand synergies for tool use. *Journal of Neuroscience, 18*, 10105–10115.

Sapir, E. (1956). *Culture, language and personality.* Los Angeles: University of California Press.

Saunders, J. A., & Knill, D. C. (2003). Humans use continuous visual feedback from the hand to control fast reaching movements. *Experimental Brain Research, 152*, 341–352.

Savage-Rumbaugh, E. S. (1986). *Ape language: From conditioned response to symbol.* New York: Columbia University Press.

Savage-Rumbaugh, E. S., Romski, M. A., Sevcik, R., & Pate, J. L. (1983). Assessing symbol usage versus symbol competency. *Journal of Experimental Psychology: General, 112*(4), 508–512.

Savage-Rumbaugh, E. S., Rumbaugh, D. M., & Boysen, S. (1978). Symbolic communication between two chimpanzees (Pan troglodytes). *Science, 201*(4356), 641–644.

Savage-Rumbaugh, E. S., Rumbaugh, D. M., Smith, S. T., & Lawson, J. (1980). Reference: The linguistic essential. *Science, 210*, 922–925.

Savage-Rumbaugh, S., Shanker, S. G., & Taylor, T. J. (1998). *Apes, language, and the human mind.* New York: Oxford University Press.

Schacter, D. L. (1996). *Searching for memory.* New York: Basic Books.

Schacter, D. L. (2001). *Seven sins of memory.* New York: Basic Books.

Schacter, D. L., & Buckner, R. L. (1998). Priming and the brain. *Neuron 20*, 185–195.

Schacter, D. L., Chiu, C.-Y. P., & Ochsner, K. N. (1993). Implicit memory: A selective review. *Annual Review of Neuroscience, 16*, 159–182.

Schacter, D. L., & Church, B. A. (1992). Auditory priming: Implicit and explicit memory for words and voices. *Journal of Experimental Psychology: Learning, Memory, and Cognition, 18*, 915–930.

Schacter, D. L., & Slotnick, S. D. (2004). The cognitive neuroscience of memory distortion. *Neuron, 44,* 149–160.

Schacter, D. L., & Tulving, E. (1994). What are the memory systems of 1994? In D. L. Schacter & E. Tulving (Eds.), *Memory systems 1994* (pp. 1–38). Cambridge, MA: MIT Press.

Schank, R. C., & Abelson, R. P. (1977). *Scripts, plans, goals, and understanding.* Mahwah, NJ: Erlbaum.

Scheerer, M. (1963). Problem-solving. *Scientific American, 208*(4), 118–128.

Schellenberg, E. G., Iverson, P., & McKinnon, M. C. (1999). Name that tune: Identifying popular recordings from brief excerpts. *Psychonomic Bulletin & Review, 6,* 641–646.

Schmalhofer, F., & Glavanov, D. (1986). Three components of understanding a programmer's manual: Verbatim, propositional, and situational representations. *Journal of Memory & Language, 25*(3), 279–294.

Schmid, P. M., & Yeni-Komshian, G. H. (1999). The effects of speaker accent and target predictability on perception of mispronunciations. *Journal of Speech Language & Hearing Research, 42*(1), 56–64.

Schmidt, R. A. (1975). A schema theory of discrete motor skill learning. *Psychological Review, 82,* 225–260.

Schmidt, R. A. (2003). Motor schema theory after 27 years: Reflections and implications for a new theory. *Research Quarterly for Exercise and Sport, 74,* 366–375.

Schmolck, H., Buffalo, E. A., & Squire, L. R. (2000). Memory distortions develop over time: Recollections of the O. J. Simpson trial verdict after 15 and 32 months. *Psychological Science, 11,* 39–45.

Schooler, J. W. (2001). Discovering memories of abuse in the light of meta-awareness. *Journal of Aggression, Maltreatment & Trauma, 4,* 105–136.

Schooler, J. W., Bendiksen, M., & Ambadar, Z. (1997). Taking the middle line: Can we accommodate both fabricated and recovered memories of sexual abuse? In M. A. Conway (Ed.), *Recovered memories and false memories. Debates in psychology* (pp. 251–292). Oxford: Oxford University Press.

Schumacher, E., H., Seymour, T. L., & Glass, J. M. (2001). Virtually perfect time sharing in dual-task performance: Uncorking the central cognitive bottleneck. *Psychological Science, 12,* 101–108.

Schwan, S., & Garsoffky, B. (2004). The cognitive representation of filmic event summaries. *Applied Cognitive Psychology, 18,* 37–55.

Schwartz, J.-L., Berthommier, F., & Savariaux, C. (2004). Seeing to hear better: Evidence for early audio-visual interactions in speech identification. *Cognition, 93,* B69–B78.

See, J. E., Howe, S. R., & Warm, J. S. (1995). Meta-analysis of the sensitivity decrement in vigilance. *Psychological Bulletin, 117,* 230–249.

Sekuler, R., & Nash, D. (1972). Speed of size scaling in human vision. *Psychonomic Science, 27,* 93–94.

Seidenberg, M. S., & McClelland, J. L. (1989). A distributed, developmental model of word recognition and naming. *Psychological Review, 96*(4), 523–568.

Seidenberg, M. S., Waters, G. S., Barnes, M. A., & Tanenhaus, M. K. (1984). When does irregular spelling or pronunciation influence word recognition? *Journal of Verbal Learning & Verbal Behavior, 23,* 383–404.

Selfridge, O. G., & Neisser, U. (1960). Pattern recognition by machine. *Scientific American, 203,* 60–68.

Senghas, A., & Coppola, M. (2001). Children creating language: How Nicaraguan sign language acquired a spatial grammar. *Psychological Science, 12,* 323–328.

Senghas, A., Kita, S., & Özyürek, A. (2004). Children creating core properties of language: Evidence from an emerging sign language in Nicaragua. *Science, 305,* 1779–1782.

Sera, M. D., Elieff, C., Forbes, J., Burch, M. C., Rodriguez, W., & Dubois, D. P. (2002). When language affects cognition and when it does not: An analysis of grammatical gender and classification. *Journal of Experimental Psychology: General, 131,* 377–397.

Sera, M. D., Reittinger, E., & del Castillo Pintado, J. (1991). Developing definitions of objects and events in English and Spanish speakers. *Cognitive Development, 6,* 119–142.

Shaffer, D. M., Krauchunas, S. M., Eddy, M., & McBeath, M. K. (2004). How dogs navigate to catch frisbees. *Psychological Science, 15,* 437–441.

Shaffer, L. H. (1975). Control processes in typing. *Quarterly Journal of Experimental Psychology, 27,* 419–432.

Shanker, S. G., Savage-Rumbaugh, E. S., & Taylor, T. J. (1999). Kanzi: A new beginning. *Animal Learning and Behavior, 27,* 24–25.

Shapiro, K. L., Raymond, J. E., & Arnell, K. M. (1994). Attention to visual pattern information produces the attentional blink in rapid serial visual presentation. *Journal of Experimental Psychology: Human Perception and Performance, 20,* 357–371.

Sharpe, L., & Markham, R. (1992). The effect of the distinctiveness of bizarre imagery on immediate and delayed recall. *Journal of Mental Imagery, 16,* 211–220.

Shea, C. H., & Wulf, G. (2005). Schema theory: A critical appraisal and reevaluation. *Journal of Motor Behavior, 37,* 85–101.

Shebani, M. F. A., van de Vijver, F. J. R., & Poortinga, Y. H. (2005). A strict test of the phonological loop hypothesis with Libyan data. *Memory & Cognition, 33,* 196–202.

Shepard, R. N., & Chipman, S. (1970). Second-order isomorphism of internal representations: Shapes of states. *Cognitive Psychology, 1,* 1–17.

Shepard, R. N., & Cooper, L. A. (1986). *Mental images and their transformations.* Cambridge, MA: MIT Press.

Shepard, R. N., & Feng, C. (1972). A chronometric study of mental paper folding. *Cognitive Psychology, 3*(2), 228–243.

Shepard, R. N., & Metzler, J. (1971). Mental rotation of three-dimensional objects. *Science, 171*(3972), 701–703.

Sherry, D. F., & Schacter, D. L. (1987). The evolution of multiple memory systems. *Psychological Review, 94,* 439–454.

Sherwood, D. E., & Lee, T. D. (2003). Cognitive effort and schema theory: Implications for a new theory of motor learning. *Research Quarterly for Exercise and Sport, 74,* 376–382.

Shiffrin, R. M., & Schneider, W. (1977). Controlled and automatic human information processing: II. Perceptual learning, automatic attending and a general theory. *Psychological Review, 84*(2), 127–190.

Shimamura, A. P., Janowsky, J. S., & Squire, L. R. (1991). What is the role of frontal lobe damage in memory disorders? In H. S. Levin, H. M. Eisenberg, & A. L. Benton (Eds.), *Frontal lobe function and dysfunction* (pp. 173–195). New York: Oxford University Press.

Simon, D. P., & Simon, H. A. (1978). Individual differences in solving physics problems. In R. Siegler (Ed.), *Children's thinking: What develops?* Mahwah, NJ: Erlbaum.

Simon, H. A. (1957). *Models of man: Social and rational.* New York: Wiley.

Simon, H. A. (1974). How big is a chunk? *Science, 183,* 482–488.

Simon, H. A., & Chase, W. G. (1973). Skill in chess. *American Scientist, 61*(4), 394–403.

Simon, H. A., & Gilmartin, K. (1973). A simulation of memory for chess positions. *Cognitive Psychology, 5*(1), 29–46.

Simons, D. J., & Chabris, C. F. (1999). Gorillas in our midst: Sustained inattentional blindness for dynamic events. *Perception, 28,* 1059–1074.

Simons, J. S., & Spiers, H. J. (2003). Prefrontal and medial temporal lobe interactions in long-term memory. *Nature Reviews Neuroscience, 4,* 637–648.

Simpson, G. B., & Krueger, M. A. (1991). Selective access of homograph meanings in sentence context. *Journal of Memory & Language, 30,* 627–643.

Simpson, M. E., & Johnson, D. M. (1966). Atmosphere and conversion errors in syllogistic reasoning. *Journal of Experimental Psychology, 72,* 197–200.

Singer, M., Graesser, A. C., & Trabasso, T. (1994). Minimal or global inference during reading. *Journal of Memory & Language, 33*(4), 421–441.

Singleton, J. L., & Newport, E. L. (2004). When learners surpass their models: The acquisition of American Sign Language from inconsistent input. *Cognitive Psychology, 49,* 370–407.

Skinner, B. F. (1938). *The behavior of organisms: An experimental analysis.* New York: Appleton-Century-Crofts.

Skinner, B. F. (1957). *Verbal behavior.* New York: Appleton-Century-Crofts.

Skinner, B. F. (1984). *The shaping of a behaviorist.* New York: New York University Press.

Skipper, J. I., Nusbaum, H. C., & Small, S. L. (2005). Listening to talking faces: Motor cortical activation during speech perception. *Neuroimage, 25,* 76–89.

Skoglund, S. (1956). Anatomical and physiological studies of knee joint innervation in the cat. *Acta Physiologica Scandinavica, 36* (Suppl. 124), 1–101.

Slobin, D. I. (1966). Grammatical transformations and sentence comprehension in childhood and adulthood. *Journal of Verbal Learning & Verbal Behavior, 5*(3), 219–227.

Sloman, S. A. (1996). The empirical base for two systems of reasoning. *Psychological Bulletin, 119,* 3–22.

Sloman, S. A. (1998). Categorical inference is not a tree: The myth of inheritance hierarchies. *Cognitive Psychology, 35,* 1–33.

Sloman, S. A., Over, D., Slovak, L., & Stibel, J. M. (2003). Frequency illusions and other fallacies. *Organizational Behavior & Human Decision Processes, 91,* 296–309.

Smeets, J. B. J., & Brenner, E. (1999). A new view on grasping. *Motor Control, 3,* 237–271.

Smit, A. S., Eling, P. A. T. M., & Coenen, A. M. L. (2004). Mental effort causes vigilance decrease due to resource depletion. *Acta Psychologica, 115,* 35–42.

Smith, E. E., & Medin, D. L. (1981). *Categories and concepts.* Cambridge, MA: Harvard University Press.

Smith, E. E., Shoben, E. J., & Rips, L. J. (1974). Structure and process in semantic memory: A featural model for semantic decisions. *Psychological Review, 81*(3), 214–241.

Smith, J. D. (2005). Wanted: A new psychology of exemplars. *Canadian Journal of Experimental Psychology, 59,* 47–53.

Smith, J. D., & Minda, J. P. (2000). Thirty categorization results in search of a model. *Journal of Experimental Psychology: Learning, Memory, and Cognition, 26,* 3–27.

Smith, S. M. (1988). Environmental context-dependent memory. In G. M. Davies & D. M. Thomson (Eds.), *Memory in context: Context in memory* (pp. 13–44). New York: Wiley.

Smith, S. M., & Blankenship, S. E. (1991). Incubation and the persistence of fixation in problem solving. *American Journal of Psychology, 104*(1), 61–87.

Smith, S. M., Glenberg, A., & Bjork, R. A. (1978). Environmental context and human memory. *Memory & Cognition, 6*(4), 342–353.

Sosniak, L. A. (1985). Learning to be a concert pianist. In B. S. Bloom (Ed.), *Developing talent in young people* (pp. 19–67). New York: Ballantine.

Spencer, R. M., & Weisberg, R. W. (1986). Context-dependent effects on analogical transfer. *Memory & Cognition, 14,* 442–449.

Sperber, D., & Girotto, V. (2002). Use or misuse of the selection task?: Rejoinder to Fiddick, Cosmides, and Tooby. *Cognition, 85,* 277–290.

Sperling, G. (1960). The information available in brief visual presentation. *Psychological Monographs, 74*(11, Whole no. 498).

Sperling, G., & Melchner, M. J. (1978). The attention operating characteristic: Example from visual search. *Science, 202,* 315–318.

Spijkers, W. A. C., & Lochner, P. (1994). Partial visual feedback and spatial end-point accuracy of discrete aiming movements. *Journal of Motor Behavior, 26,* 283–295.

Squire, L. R. (1992). Memory and the hippocampus: A synthesis from findings with rats, monkeys, and humans. *Psychological Review, 99,* 195–231.

Squire, L. R., Stark, C. E. L., & Clark, R. E. (2004). The medial temporal lobe. *Annual Review of Neuroscience, 27,* 279–304.

Staddon, J. E. R., & Cerutti, D. T. (2003). Operant conditioning. *Annual Review of Psychology, 54,* 115–144.

Stanovich, K. E. (1999). *Who is rational?: Studies of individual differences in reasoning.* Mahwah, NJ: Erlbaum.

Stanovich, K. E., & West, R. F. (1998). Cognitive ability and variation in selection task performance. *Thinking & Reasoning, 4,* 193–230.

Sternberg, S. (1966). High-speed scanning in human memory, *Science, 153,* 652–654.

Sternberg, S., Monsell, S., Knoll, R. L., & Wright, C. E. (1978). The latency and duration of rapid movement sequences: Comparisons of speech and typewriting. In G. E. Stelmach (Ed.), *Information processing in motor control and learning* (pp. 117–152). New York: Academic Press.

Stone, J. V., Hunkin, N. M., & Hornby, A. (2001). Predicting spontaneous recovery of memory. *Nature, 414,* 167–168.

Strayer, D. L., & Johnston, W. A. (2001). Driven to distraction: Dual-task studies of simulated driving and conversing on a cellular telephone. *Psychological Science, 12,* 462–466.

Sugiyama, L. S., Tooby, J., & Cosmides, L. (2002). Cross-cultural evidence of cognitive adaptations for social exchange among the Shiwiar of Ecuadorian Amazonia. *Proceedings of the National Academy of Sciences, 99,* 11537–11542.

Tabossi, P., & Zardon, F. (1993). Processing ambiguous words in context. *Journal of Memory and Language, 32,* 359–372.

Takeuchi, A. H., & Hulse, S. H. (1993). Absolute pitch. *Psychological Bulletin, 113*(2), 345–361.

Talarico, J. M., & Rubin, D. C. (2003). Confidence, not consistency, characterizes flashbulb memories. *Psychological Science, 14,* 455–461.

Talarico, J. M., LaBar, K. S., & Rubin, D. C. (2004). Emotional intensity predicts autobiographical memory experience. *Memory & Cognition, 32,* 1118–1132.

Talwar, S. K., Xu, S., Hawley, E. S., Weiss, S. A., Moxon, K. A., & Chapin, J. K. (2002). Rat navigation guided by remote control. *Nature, 417,* 37–38.

Tanji, J., & Hoshi E. (2001). Behavioral planning in the prefrontal cortex. *Current Opinion in Neurobiology, 11,* 164–170.

Tanji, J., & Shima, K. (1994). Role for supplementary motor area cells in planning several movements ahead. *Nature, 371,* 413–416.

Taraban, R., & McClelland, J. L. (1987). Conspiracy effects in word pronunciation. *Journal of Memory & Language, 26*(6), 608–631.

Tarr, M. J. (1995). Rotating objects to recognize them: A case study on the role of viewpoint dependency in the recognition of three-dimensional objects. *Psychonomic Bulletin & Review, 2*(1), 55–82.

Tarr, M. J., & Cheng, Y. D. (2003). Learning to see faces and objects. *Trends in Cognitive Sciences, 7*, 23–30.

Tarr M. J., & Gauthier, I. (2000). FFA: A flexible fusiform area for subordinate-level visual processing automatized by expertise. *Nature Neuroscience, 3*, 764–769.

Tarr, M. J., & Pinker, S. (1990). When does human object recognition use a viewer-centered reference frame? *Psychological Science, 1*, 253–256.

Tassinari, G., & Berlucchi, G. (1995). Covert orienting to non-informative cues: Reaction time studies. *Behavioural Brain Research, 71*, 101–112.

Taub, E., & Berman, A. J. (1968). Movement and learning in the absence of sensory feedback. In S. J. Freeman (Ed.), *The neuropsychology of spatially ordered behavior* (pp. 173–192). Homewood, IL: Dorsey.

Terrace, H. S., Petitto, L. A., Sanders, R. J., & Bever, T. G. (1979). Can an ape create a sentence? *Science, 206*(4421), 891–902.

Thaler, R. (1980). Toward a positive theory of consumer choice. *Journal of Economic Behavior and Organization, 1*, 39–60.

Thomas, J. C. (1974). An analysis of behavior in the hobbits–orcs problem. *Cognitive Psychology, 6*(2), 257–269.

Thompson, R. F. (2005). In search of memory traces. *Annual Review of Psychology, 56*, 1–23.

Thompson-Schill, S. L., Bedny, M., & Goldberg, R. F. (2005). The frontal lobes and the regulation of mental activity. *Current Opinion in Neurobiology, 15*, 219–224.

Thompson-Schill, S. L., Kurtz, K. J., & Gabrieli, J. D. E. (1998). Effects of semantic and associative relatedness on automatic priming. *Journal of Memory & Language, 38*, 440–458.

Thorndike, E. L. (1911). *Animal intelligence* (Vol. 2). New York: Macmillan.

Thorndike, E. L., & Woodworth, R. S. (1901). The influence of improvement in one mental function upon the efficiency of other functions. *Psychological Review, 8*, 247–261.

Tinbergen, N. (1952). The curious behavior of the stickleback. *Scientific American, 182*, 22–26.

Ting, L. H., & Macpherson, J. M. (2005). A limited set of muscle synergies for force control during a postural task. *Journal of Neurophysiology, 93*, 609–613.

Todorov, E. (2004). Optimality principles in sensorimotor control. *Nature Neuroscience, 7*, 907–915.

Todorov, E., & Jordan, M. I. (1998). Smoothness maximization along a predefined path accurately predicts the speed profiles of complex arm movements. *Journal of Neurophysiology, 80*, 696–714.

Toth, J. P., & Hunt, R. R. (1999). Not one versus many, but zero versus any: Structure and function in the context of the multiple-memory systems debate. In J. K. Foster & M. Jelicic (Eds.), *Memory: Structure, function, or process?* (pp. 232–272). London: Oxford University Press.

Trabasso, T., & Wiley, J. (2005). Goal plans of action and inferences during comprehension of narratives. *Discourse Processes, 39*, 129–164.

Treisman, A. M., & Gelade, G. (1980). A feature-integration theory of attention. *Cognitive Psychology, 12*, 97–136.

Tulving, E. (1967). The effects of presentation and recall of material in free-recall learning. *Journal of Verbal Learning & Verbal Behavior, 6*(2), 175–184.

Tulving, E. (1972). Episodic and semantic memory. In E. Tulving & W. Donaldson (Eds.), *Organization and memory*. New York: Academic Press.

Tulving, E. (1983). *Elements of episodic memory*. Oxford: Oxford University Press.

Tulving, E. (2002). Episodic memory: From mind to brain. *Annual Review of Psychology, 53*, 1–25.

Tulving, E., & Pearlstone, Z. (1966). Availability versus accessibility of information in memory for words. *Journal of Verbal Learning & Verbal Behavior, 5*, 381–391.

Tulving, E., Schacter, D. L., McLachlan, D. R., & Moscovitch, M. (1988). Priming of semantic autobiographical knowledge: A case study of retrograde amnesia. *Brain & Cognition, 8*, 3–20.

Tulving, E., Schacter, D. L., & Stark, H. A. (1982). Priming effects in word-fragment completion are independent of recognition memory. *Journal of Experimental Psychology: Learning, Memory, and Cognition, 8*, 336–342.

Tulving, E., & Thomson, D. M. (1973). Encoding specificity and retrieval processes in episodic memory. *Psychological Review, 80*, 359–380.

Turvey, M. T. (1973). On peripheral and central processes in vision: Inferences from an information-processing analysis of masking with patterned stimuli. *Psychological Review, 80*(1), 1–52.

Tversky, A., & Kahneman, D. (1973). Availability: A heuristic for judging frequency and probability. *Cognitive Psychology, 5*(2), 207–232.

Tversky, A., & Kahneman, D. (1974). Judgment under uncertainty: Heuristics and biases. *Science, 185*(4157), 1124–1131.

Tversky, A., & Kahneman, D. (1983). Extensional versus intuitive reasoning: The conjunction fallacy in probability judgment. *Psychological Review,* 90(4), 293–315.

Tversky, A., & Kahneman, D. (1986). Judgment under uncertainty: Heuristics and biases. In H. R. Arkes & K. R. Hammond (Eds.), *Judgment and decision making: An interdisciplinary reader* (pp. 38–55). Cambridge: Cambridge University Press.

Tversky, A., Sattath, S., & Slovic, P. (1988). Contingent weighting in judgment and choice. *Psychological Review, 95*(3), 371–384.

Tversky, A., Slovic, P., & Kahneman, D. (1990). The causes of preference reversal. *American Economic Review, 80*, 204–217.

Ullman, S., & Basri, R. (1991). Recognition by linear combinations of models. *IEEE Transactions on Pattern Analysis and Machine Intelligence, 13*, 992–1006.

Ungerleider, L. G., Doyon, J., & Karni, A. (2002). Imaging brain plasticity during motor skill learning. *Neurobiology of Learning & Memory, 78*, 553–564.

Ungerleider, L., & Mishkin, M. (1982). Two cortical visual systems. In D. J. Ingle, M. A. Goodale, & R. J. W. Mansfield (Eds.), *Analysis of visual behavior* (pp. 549–586). Cambridge, MA: MIT Press.

Ungerleider, L. G., & Haxby, J. V. (1994). "What" and "where" in the human brain. *Current Opinion in Neurobiology, 4*, 157–165.

Uno, Y., Kawato, M., & Suzuki, R. (1989). Formation and control of optimal trajectory in human multijoint arm movement: Minimum torque-change model. *Biological Cybernetics, 61*, 89–101.

Valentine, E. R. (1985). The effect of instructions on performance in the Wason selection task. *Current Psychological Research & Reviews, 4*(3), 214–223.

Vallar, G., & Baddeley, A. D. (1984). Phonological short-term store, phonological processing and sentence comprehension: A neuropsychological case study. *Cognitive Neuropsychology, 1*, 121–141.

Vallar, G., & Papagno. C. (2002). Neuropsychological impairments of verbal short-term memory. In A. D. Baddeley, M. D. Kopelman, & B. A. Wilson (Eds.), *Handbook of memory disorders,* (2nd ed., pp. 249–270). New York: Wiley.

Van Berkum, J. J. A., Brown, C. M., Zwitserlood, P., Kooijman, V., & Hagoort, P. (2005). Anticipating upcoming words in discourse: Evidence from ERPs and reading times. *Journal of Experimental Psychology: Learning, Memory & Cognition, 31*, 443–467.

van der Helm, P. A. (2000). Simplicity versus likelihood in visual perception: From surprisals to precisals. *Psychological Bulletin, 126*, 770–800.

van der Kamp, J., Savelsbergh, G., & Smeets, J. (1997). Multiple information sources in interceptive timing. *Human Movement Science, 16*(6), 787–821.

van Dijk, T., & Kintsch, W. (1983). *Strategies of discourse comprehension.* San Diego: Academic Press.

Van Overschelde, J. P., Rawson, K. A., & Dunlosky, J. (2004). Category norms: An updated and expanded version of the Battig and Montague (1969) norms. *Journal of Memory & Language, 50*, 289–335.

Verwey, W. B. (1999). Evidence for a multi-stage model of practice in a sequential movement task. *Journal of Experimental Psychology: Human Perception and Performance, 25*, 1693–1708.

Violanti, J. M., & Marshall, J. R. (1996). Cellular phones and traffic accidents: An epidemiological approach. *Accident Analysis & Prevention, 28*, 265–270.

Vogel, E. K., Woodman, G. F., & Luck, S. J. (2001). Storage of features, conjunctions, and objects in visual working memory. *Journal of Experimental Psychology: Human Perception and Performance, 27*, 92–114.

von Helmholtz, H. (1910/1964). *Treatise on physiological optics* (J. P. Southall, Trans., Vol. 3). New York: Dover.

von Neumann, J., & Morgenstern, O. (1944). *Theory of games and economic behavior.* Princeton, NJ: Princeton University Press.

Von Wright, J. M. (1968). Selection in visual immediate memory. *Quarterly Journal of Experimental Psychology, 20*, 62–68.

Vu, H., Kellas, G., Petersen, E., & Metcalf, K. (2003). Situation-evoking stimuli, domain of reference, and the incremental interpretation of lexical ambiguity. *Memory & Cognition, 31*, 1302–1315.

Wager, T. D., & Smith, E. E. (2003). Neuroimaging studies of working memory: A meta-analysis. *Cognitive, Affective, & Behavioral Neuroscience, 3*, 255–274.

Wagner, A. D. (2002). Cognitive control and episodic memory: Contributions from prefrontal cortex. In L. R. Squire & D. L. Schacter (Eds.), *Neuropsychology of memory* (3rd ed., pp. 174–192). New York: Guilford.

Wagner, A. D., Schacter, D. L., Rotte, M., Koutstaal, W., Maril, A., Dale, A. M., et al. (1998). Building memories: Remembering and forgetting of verbal experiences as predicted by brain activity. *Science, 281*(5380), 1188–1191.

Wagner, U., Gais, S., Haider, H., Verleger, R., & Born, J. (2004). Sleep inspires insight. *Nature, 427*, 352–355.

Walker, W. R., Vogl, R. J., & Thompson, C. P. (1997). Autobiographical memory: Unpleasantness fades faster than pleasantness over time. *Applied Cognitive Psychology, 11,* 399–413.

Wallingford, R. (1975). Long distance running. In A. W. Tayler & F. Landry (Eds.), *The scientific aspects of sports training* (pp. 118–130). Springfield, IL: Charles C Thomas.

Wang, J., & Sainburg, R. L. (2003). Mechanisms underlying interlimb transfer of visuomotor rotations. *Experimental Brain Research, 149,* 520–526.

Warren, R. M. (1970). Perceptual restoration of missing speech sounds. *Science, 167*(3917), 392–393.

Warren, R. M., & Sherman, G. L. (1974). Phonemic restorations based on subsequent context. *Perception & Psychophysics, 16*(1), 150–156.

Warren, R. M., & Warren, R. P. (1970). Auditory illusions and confusions. *Scientific American, 223*(6), 30–36.

Warren, W. H. (1984). Perceiving affordances: Visual guidance of stair climbing. *Journal of Experimental Psychology: Human Perception and Performance, 10*(5), 683–703.

Warrington, E. K., & Weiskrantz, L. (1968). A study of learning and retention in amnesic patients. *Neuropsychologia, 6,* 283–291.

Warrington, E. K., & Weiskrantz, L. (1970). Amnesic syndrome: Consolidation or retrieval? *Nature, 228,* 628–630.

Warrington, E. K., & Weiskrantz, L. (1979). Conditioning in amnesic patients. *Neuropsychologia, 20,* 233–248.

Wason, P. C. (1968). Reasoning about a rule. *Quarterly Journal of Experimental Psychology, 20*(3), 273–281.

Wason, P. C. (1969). Regression in reasoning? *British Journal of Psychology, 60*(4), 471–480.

Watkins, M. J., & Schiano, D. J. (1982). Chromatic imaging: An effect of mental colouring on recognition memory. *Canadian Journal of Psychology, 36,* 291–299.

Watson, J. B. (1913). Psychology as the behaviorist views it. *Psychological Review, 20,* 158–177.

Waugh, N. C., & Norman, D. A. (1965). Primary memory. *Psychological Review, 72*(2), 89–104.

Wegner, D. M. (1994). Ironic processes of mental control. *Psychological Review, 101,* 34–52.

Wegner, D. M., Schneider, D. J., Carter, S. R., & White, T. L. (1987). Paradoxical effects of thought suppression. *Journal of Personality & Social Psychology, 53,* 5–13.

Weldon, M. S. (1999). The memory chop shop: Issues in the search for memory systems. In J. K. Foster & M. Jelicic (Eds.), *Memory: Structure,* *function, or process?* (pp. 162–204). London: Oxford University Press.

Welford, A. T. (1952). The "psychological refractory period" and the timing of high-speed performance: A review and a theory. *British Journal of Psychology, 43,* 2–19.

Welford, A. T. (1980). The single-channel hypothesis. In A. T. Welford (Ed.), *Reaction time* (pp. 215–252). New York: Academic Press.

Wessel, I., & Merckelbach, H. (1997). The impact of anxiety on memory for details in spider phobics. *Applied Cognitive Psychology, 11,* 223–231.

Wheeler, M. A., & McMillan, C. T. (2001). Focal retrograde amnesia and the episodic-semantic distinction. *Cognitive, Affective, and Behavioral Neuroscience, 1,* 22–37.

Whitney, P., Ritchie, B. G., & Clark, M. B. (1991). Working-memory capacity and the use of elaborative inferences in text comprehension. *Discourse Processes, 14*(2), 133–145.

Whorf, B. L. (1956). *Language, thought, and reality: Selected writings.* Cambridge, MA: Technology Press of MIT.

Wickelgren, W. (1974). *How to solve problems.* San Francisco: W. H. Freeman.

Wickens, C. D. (1984). Processing resources in attention, dual task performance, and workload assessment. In R. Parasuraman & R. Davies (Eds.), *Varieties of attention* (pp. 63–102). New York: Academic Press.

Wickens, C. D. (1992). *Engineering psychology and human performance* (2nd ed.). New York: HarperCollins.

Wickens, D., Dalezman, R., Eggemeier, E., & Thomas, F. (1976). Multiple encoding of word attributes in memory. *Memory & Cognition, 4,* 307–310.

Wikman, A.-S., Nieminen, T., & Summala, H. (1998). Driving experience and time-sharing during in-car tasks on roads of different width. *Ergonomics, 41*(3), 358–372.

Willingham, D. B. (1997a). Systems of memory in the human brain. *Neuron, 18,* 5–8.

Willingham, D. B. (1997b). Implicit and explicit memory do not differ in flexibility: Comment on Dienes & Berry, 1997. *Psychonomic Bulletin and Review, 4,* 587–591.

Willingham, D. B. (1998a). A neuropsychological theory of motor skill learning. *Psychological Review, 105,* 558–584.

Willingham, D. B. (1998b). What differentiates declarative and procedural Memories: Reply to Cohen, Poldrack, and Eichenbaum (1997). *Memory, 6,* 689–699.

Willingham, D. B., & Koroshetz, W. J. (1993). Evidence for dissociable motor skills in Huntington's disease patients. *Psychobiology, 21*, 173–182.

Willingham, D. B., Nissen, M. J., & Bullemer, P. (1989). On the development of procedural knowledge. *Journal of Experimental Psychology: Learning, Memory, and Cognition, 15*, 1047–1060.

Willingham, D. B., Salidis, J., & Gabrieli, J. D. (2002). Direct comparison of neural systems mediating conscious and unconscious skill learning. *Journal of Neurophysiology, 88*, 1451–1460.

Wilson, S. M., Saygin, A. P., Sereno, M. I., & Iacoboni, M. (2004). Listening to speech activates motor areas involved in speech production. *Nature Neuroscience, 7*, 701–702.

Winer, G. A., Cottrell, J. E., Gregg, V., Fournier, J. S., & Bica, L. A. (2002). Fundamentally misunderstanding visual perception: Adults' belief in visual emissions. *American Psychologist, 57*, 417–424.

Wing, A. M. (2000). Motor control: Mechanisms of motor equivalence in handwriting. *Current Biology, 10*, R245–R248.

Winner, E. (2000). Giftedness: Current theory and research. *Current Directions in Psychological Science, 9*, 153–156.

Wise, S. P., & Murray, E. A. (2000). Arbitrary associations between antecedents and actions. *Trends in Neurosciences, 23*, 271–276.

Wittgenstein, L. (1953). *Philosophical investigations.* Oxford: Blackwell.

Woldorff, M. G., & Hillyard, S. A. (1991). Modulation of early auditory processing during selective listening to rapidly presented tones. *Electroencephalography & Clinical Neurophysiology, 79*, 170–191.

Wolfe, J. M., Horowitz, T. S., & Kenner, N. M. (2005). Rare items often missed in visual searches. *Nature, 435*, 439–440.

Wollen, K. A., Weber, A., & Lowry, D. H. (1972). Bizarreness versus interaction of mental images as determinants of learning. *Cognitive Psychology, 3*(3), 518–523.

Wood, N., & Cowan, N. (1995). The cocktail party phenomenon revisited: How frequent are attention shifts to one's name in an irrelevant auditory channel? *Journal of Experimental Psychology: Learning, Memory, and Cognition, 21*(1), 255–260.

Woodruff-Pak, D. S., Goldenberg, G., Downey-Lamb, M. M., Boyko, O. B., & Lemieux, S. K. (2000). Cerebellar volume in humans related to magnitude of classical conditioning. *Neuroreport, 11*, 609–615.

Woodworth, R. (1938). *Experimental psychology.* New York: Holt.

Woodworth, R. S., & Schlossberg, H. (1954). *Experimental psychology* (Rev. ed.). New York: Holt.

Woodworth, R. S., & Sells, S. B. (1935). An atmosphere effect in formal syllogistic reasoning. *Journal of Experimental Psychology, 18*, 451–460.

Worthen, J. B. (1997). Resiliency of bizarreness effects under varying conditions of verbal and imaginal elaboration and list composition. *Journal of Mental Imagery, 21*(1–2), 167–194.

Wraga, M. J. (1999a). The role of eye height in perceiving affordances and object dimensions. *Perception & Psychophysics, 61*, 490–507.

Wraga, M. J. (1999b). Using eye height in different postures to scale the heights of objects. *Journal of Experimental Psychology: Human Perception and Performance, 25*, 518–530.

Wright, C. E. (1990). Generalized motor programs: Reexamining claims of effector independence in writing. In M. Jeannerod (Ed.), *Attention and performance XIII: Motor representation and control* (pp. 294–320). Mahwah, NJ: Erlbaum.

Wulf, G., & Prinz, W. (2001). Directing attention to movement effects enhances learning: A review. *Psychonomic Bulletin & Review, 8*, 648–660.

Wundt, W. (1894). *Lectures on human and animal psychology* (S. E. Creigton & E. B. Tichener, Trans.). New York: Macmillan.

Wyttenbach, R. A., May, M. L., & Hoy, R. R. (1996). Categorical perception of sound frequency by crickets. *Science, 273*, 1542–1544.

Yachanin, S. A. (1986). Facilitation in Wason's selection task: Content and instructions. *Current Psychological Research & Reviews, 5*(1), 20–29.

Yantis, S., Schwarzbach, J., Serences, J. T., Carlson, R. L., Steinmetz, M. A., Pekar, J. J., et al. (2002). Transient neural activity in human parietal cortex during spatial attention shifts. *Nature Neuroscience, 5*, 995–1002.

Yin, R. K. (1969). Looking at upside-down faces. *Journal of Experimental Psychology, 81*, 141–145.

Yovel, G., & Kanwisher, N. (2004). Face perception: Domain specific, not process specific. *Neuron, 44*, 889–898.

Zacks, J. M., Tversky, B., & Iyer, G. (2001). Perceiving, remembering, and communicating structure in events. *Journal of Experimental Psychology: General, 130*, 29–58.

Zacks, R. T., Hasher, L., & Li, K. Z. H. (2000). Human memory. In F. I. M. Craik & T. A. Salthouse (Eds.), *The handbook of aging and cognition* (2nd ed., pp. 293–357). Mahwah, NJ: Erlbaum.

Zajchowski, R., & Martin, J. (1993). Differences in the problem solving of stronger and weaker novices in physics: Knowledge, strategies, or knowledge structure? *Journal of Research in Science Teaching, 30*, 459–470.

Zaki, S. R. (2004). Is categorization performance really intact in amnesia? A meta-analysis. *Psychonomic Bulletin & Review, 11*, 1048–1054.

Zaragoza, M. S., & Mitchell, K. J. (1996). Repeated exposure to suggestion and the creation of false memories. *Psychological Science, 7*, 294–300.

Zelaznik, H. N., Hawkins, B., & Kisselburgh, L. (1983). Rapid visual feedback processing in single-aiming movements. *Journal of Motor Behavior, 15*, 217–236.

Zwaan, R. A. (1994). Effect of genre expectations on text comprehension. *Journal of Experimental Psychology: Learning, Memory, and Cognition, 20*(4), 920–933.

Zwaan, R. A., & Madden, C. J. (2004). Updating situation models. *Journal of Experimental Psychology: Learning, Memory, and Cognition, 30*, 283–288.

Zwaan, R. A., & Radvansky, G. A. (1998). Situation models in language comprehension and memory. *Psychological Bulletin, 123*, 162–185.

Credits

Figure 1.9 From p. 31 in THE HUMAN CENTRAL NERVOUS SYSTEM 3rd edition by R. Nieuwenhuys, J. Voogd, and C. Van Huijzen. Copyright ©1988 by Springer-Verlag. Reprinted by permission.

Figure 2.5 from Biological Psychology by Stephen Klein. Published by Prentice Hall. Copyright © 2000.

Figure 2.6 From COGNITIVE NEUROSCIENCE: THE BIOLOGY OF THE MIND by Michael S. Gazzaniga, Richard Ivry, and George R. Mangun. Copyright © 1998 by W. W. Norton & Company, Inc. Used by permission of W. W. Norton & Company, Inc.

Figure 2.10 From Neil R. Carlson Foundations Of Physiological Psychology, 4/e. Published by Allyn and Bacon, Boston, MA. Copyright © 1999 by Pearson Education. Reprinted by permission of the publisher.

Figure 3.6 "Vision: Space and Movement" by Atkinson et al, from STEVEN'S HANDBOOK OF EXPERIMENTAL PSYCHOLOGY 2nd Edition. Copyright © 1988 by John Wiley & Sons, Inc. Reprinted with permission of John Wiley & Sons, Inc.

Figure 3.13 From Human Information Process- ing 2nd edition by LINDSAY. © 1977. Re-printed with permission of Wadsworth, a division of Thomson Learning: www.thomsonrights. com. Fax 800 730-2215

Figure 3.14 PSYCHOLOGICAL REVIEW, 94 (2), by I. Biederman, from article RECOGNITION-BY-COM-PONENETS: A THEORY OF HUMAN IMAGE UN-DERSTANDING. Copyright © 1987. With per mission from Elsevier.

Figure 5.7 "Theoretic Confirmation of Restruc- turing during Insight" by F. T. Durson, C. B. Rea and T. Dayton, from PSYCHOLOGICAL SCIENCE. Copyright © 1994 by Blackwell Publishing. Reprinted by permission.

Figure 6.2 CONSCIOUSNESS AND COGNITION: AN INTERNATIONAL JOURNAL, 4 (4), by L. Cahill and J. L. McGaugh, from article A NOVEL DEMONSTRATION OF ENHANCED MOMERY ASSOCIATED WITH EMOTIONAL AROUSAL. Copyright © 1996. With permission from Elsevier.

Figure 6.4 JOURNAL OF VERBAL LEARNING AND VERBAL BEHAVIOR, 12 (5), by T. S. Hyde & J. J. Jenkins, from article RECALL FOR WORDS AS A FUNCTION OF SEMANTIC, GRAPH AND SYN-TACTIC ORIENTING TASKS. Copyright © 1973. With permis- sion from Elsevier.

Figure 6.5 COGNITIVE PSYCHOLOGY, 11, by R. S. Nickerson and M. J. Adams, from article LONG-TERM MEMORY FOR A COMMON OBJECT. Copyright © 1979. With permission from Elsevier.

Figure 6.6 JOURNAL OF VERBAL LEARNING AND VERBAL BEHAVIOR, 16 (5), by C. D. Morris, J. D. Brandford and J. J. Franks, from article LEVELS OF PROCESSING VERSUS TRANSFER APPROPRIATE PROCESSING. Copyright © 1977. With permission from Elsevier.

Figure 6.7 JOURNAL OF VERBAL LEARNING AND VERBAL BEHAVIOR, 16 (5), by C. D. Morris, J. D. Brandford and J. J. Franks, from article LEVELS OF PROCESSING VERSUS TRANSFER APPROPRI-ATE PROCESSING. Copyright © 1977. With per-mission from Elsevier.

Figure 7.2 JOURNAL OF MEMORY AND LAN-GUAGE, 9, by L. L. Light & L. Carter-Sobell, from article EFFECTS OF CHANGED SEMANTIC CON-TEXT ON RECOGNITION MEMORY. Copyright © 1970. With permission from Elsevier.

Figure 7.5 From AMERICAN JOURNAL OF PSY-CHOLOGY. Copyright © 1940 by the Board of Trustees of the University of Illinois. Used with per-mission of the University of Illinois Press.

Figure 7.6 TRENDS IN COGNITIVE SCIENCES, 6, by B. J. Levy and M. C. Anderson, from article INHIBITORY PROCESSES AND THE CONTROL OF MEMORY RETRIEVAL. Copyright © 2002. With permission from Elsevier.

Figure 7.7 Reprinted by permission from Macmillan Publishers Ltd: from NATURE SUPPRESSING UNWANTED MEMORIES BY EXECUTIVE CONTROL by M. C. Anderson and C. Green, Copyright © 2001.

Figure 9.10 COGNITIVE PSYCHOLOGY, 7 (1), by L. A. Cooper, from article MENTAL ROTATION OF RANDOM TWO-DIMENSIONAL SHAPES. Copyright © 1975. With permission from Elsevier.

Figure 10.4 CHARACTERISTICS OF MOTOR PROGRAMS UNDERLYING ARM MOVEMENTS IN MONKEYS, from article JOURNAL OF NEUROPHYSIOLOGY, 42, by A. Polit and E. Bizzi.

Copyright © 1979 by The American Physiological Society. Used with Permission.

Figure 12.8 "Forgetting to Remember: The Functional Relationship of decay and Interference" by E. M. Atlman & W. D. Gray, from PSYCHOLOGICAL SCIENCE. Copyright © 2002 by Blackwell Publishing. Reprinted by permission.

Figure 12.9 From AMERICAN JOURNAL OF PSYCHOLOGY. Copyright © 1993 by the Board of Trustees of the University of Illinois. Used with permission of the University of Illinois Press.

Figure 14.5 JOURNAL OF MEMORY AND LANGUAGE, 22 (3), by K. Rayner, M. Carlson & L. Frazier, from article THE INTERACTION OF SYNTAX AND SEMANTICS DURING SENTENCE PROCESSING: EYE MOVEMENTS IN THE ANALYSIS OF SEMANTICALLY BIASED SENTENCES. Copyright © 1983. With permission from Elsevier.

Photo Credits

Chapter 1: Page 12, CORBIS-NY; Page 14, Corbis/Bettman; Page 23, Nina Leen/Time Life Pictures/Getty Images; Page 27, © CORBIS/All Rights Reserved; Page 30, Photo Courtesy of The Computer History Museum; Page 32, Courtesy of Suzanne H. Corkin/© 1997 Journal of Neuroscience.

Chapter 2: Page 42, Saul Sternberg/American Scientist.

Chapter 3: Page 76, U.S. Army Photo; Page 87, Picture Desk, Inc./Kobal Collection; Page 97(a), Getty Images, Inc.; Page 97 (b) Getty Images Inc./Stone Allstock.

Chapter 4: Terry Andrewartha/Nature Picture Library.

Chapter 5: Page 169, Reprinted from Klauer & Zhao (2004), Jep: General, 133, 351-381.

Chapter 6: Jennifer Talarico; Page 183, Getty Images, Inc.

Chapter 7: Page 217, Alamy Images; Page 228, Princeton University Press.

Chapter 8: Page 244, Dr. Scott W. Allen, Specializing the operation of an explicit rule, Journal of Experimental Psychology: General, 120, 3-19, 1991,

APA, reprinted with permission; Page 236, (a) Landov LLC; Page 236 (b) Getty Images, Inc.

Chapter 9: Page 296, Cortex Publishing/Bisiach, E. & Luzzati, © (1978) "Unilateral neglect of representational space"/Cortex 14, 129-133; Page 299, Lawrence M. Parsons, Ph.D.

Chapter 11: Page 350, Reprinted by arrangement from the book "Field Guide to Birds of North America", Fourth Edition. Copyright 1983, 1987, 1999, 2002 National Geographic Society.

Chapter 12: Page 387, Hulton Archive/Getty Images; Page 401, Getty Images, Inc.

Chapter 13: Page 426, © CORBIS/All Rights Reserved; Page 432, AP Wide World Photos.

Chapter 14: Page 452, UCLA Ahmanson/-Lovelace Brian Mapping Center/Reprinted by permission from MacMillian Publishers Ltd. Nature Neuroscience, © 2004.

Author Index

A

Aaronson, D., 466
Abdi, H., 98
Abelson, R. P., 196–97
Ackerman, P. L., 406
Ackinclose, C. C., 407
Adams, M. J., 185, 186
Adamson, R.E., 391
Adelson, E. H., 77
Admiraal, M. A., 306
Adriani, M., 101
Agnoli, F., 434
Aguirre, G. K., 102
Akai, M., 306
Albert, N. M., 287
Albrecht, J. E., 467, 468
Alexander, G. E., 332
Alfonso-Reese, L. A., 245
Alivisatos, B., 291
Allard, F., 193, 320
Allen, S. W., 244
Allport, A., 114
Alpert, J. L., 226
Altmann, E. M., 155, 222
Altmann, G., 462
Alvarez, G. A., 161
Ambadar, Z., 225–26
Ammons, R. B., 326
Andersen, R. A., 332
Andersen, S., 450
Anderson, A. W., 99
Anderson, F. C., 306
Anderson, J. R., 118

Anderson, M. C., 222, 223, 224
Anderson, R. C., 196
Anderson, W. G., 313
Angelergues, R., 98
Anstis, S. M., 151
Archer, E. J., 326
Aristotle, 9, 13
Arlemalm, T., 208
Arnell, K. M., 140, 141
Asakura, I., 245
Ashby, F. G., 245
Ashford, D., 321
Aslin, R. N., 453
Atkins, P., 456
Atkinson, R. C., 163
Atran, S., 238
Attneave, F., 292
Au, T. K., 436–37
Austin, G. A., 235
Averbach, E., 149
Averbeck, B. B., 99, 316
Awh, E., 116, 141

B

Babinsky, R., 180
Bachmann, T., 450
Baddeley, A., 166, 167, 169–70
Baddeley, A. D., 156, 157, 159, 160, 163, 164, 165, 168, 208–9

Bahrick, H. P., 229
Baillet, S. D., 466
Baizer, J. S., 324
Baker, S. C., 287
Ball, T. M., 283
Ballard, D., 168
Ballesteros, S., 97
Balthazard, C., 393
Bandettini, P. A., 266
Bara, B. G., 364, 367
Barclay, J. R., 206–7
Barnes, H. J., 44
Barnes, M. A., 457
Baron, J., 456
Barrouillet, P., 404
Barston, J. L., 364
Bartlett, E., 425
Bartlett, F. C., 194, 211
Basri, R., 95
Bassok, M., 408
Bastian, A. J., 266, 323
Battig, W. F., 238
Baumeister, R. F., 45
Baylis, G. C., 130
Beauvois, M. E., 457
Becker, M. W., 151
Becklen, R., 128–29
Bedard, J., 397
Bedny, S. L., 169
Begg, I., 363
Behrmann, M., 456
Beier, M. E., 406
Beit-Halachmi, B., 437
Bekkering, H., 450

561

Subject Index

A

Abstract construct
  in artificial intelligence,
    29–31
  behaviorist response,
    28–29
  in neuroscience, 31–33
Abstract words, 274
Accommodation, 78
Acoustic codes, 156–57, 159
Acoustic confusion
  effect, 157
Activation, brain, 52–57
Adaptation, motor skill
  learning and, 331–32
Addressing system, 247
Aftereffect, 323
Agnosia, visual, 101
Algorithm, 344
Allophone, 414
Ambiguities
  language, 443–68
  visual, 72–87
Amnesia, 261–62, 263,
    264–65. *See also*
    Forgetting
Amygdala, 65, 180, 266
Analog, 280
Analog representation, versus
  propositional
  representation, 279–85
Analogy, problem solving
  and, 383–88

Anatomic dissociation, 261
Anchoring and adjustment
  heuristic, 347
Anterior, 61
Anticipatory postural
  adjustments, 309
Arbitrary visual-motor
  association, 332
Articulatory control process,
  164–65
Articulatory suppression
  studies, 165
Artificial intelligence, 29–31
Associationism, 13
Assumptions, 3–5
Ataxia, optic, 101–2
Atmosphere, syllogistic
  reasoning errors and,
  363–64
Atmospheric perspective, 81
Attention, 108–41
  allocation, 115–16
  automaticity and, 117–19
  consistent requirements,
    112–14
  definition, 108
  early filter theories,
    122–24
  emotional memory and,
    179
  fate of stimuli not
    selected, 120–32
  inhibition of return,
    133–34

  interaction with other
    cognitive processes,
    137–41
  ironic process of mental
    control, 134–35
  late filter theories, 124–26
  limited, 109–20, 138–41
  maintenance, 136–37
  movable filter model,
    126–28
  multiple resource theories,
    112–14
  parallel performance,
    110–12
  preattention and, 132
  properties, 108–9, 133–37
  psychological refractory
    period, 138–39
  reduction in demands
    with practice, 116–19
  selection failures, 133–34
  selective visual, 128–30
  vigilance and, 136–37
  visual search paradigms,
    131–32
Attentional blink, 139–41
Auditory system, echoic
  memory, 151
Automaticity
  attention, 117–19
  motor skill learning, 328
  problem solving, 382
Availability heuristic,
  346–47